KW-481-371

MEASURING, MODELLING AND EVALUATING COMPUTER SYSTEMS

MEASURING, MODELLING AND EVALUATING COMPUTER SYSTEMS

001.61

Proceedings of the Third International Symposium
sponsored by

IRIA-LABORIA,

IFIP Working Group 7.3

THE COMMISSION OF THE EUROPEAN COMMUNITIES
Joint Research Centre, ISPRA Establishment

and organised by

GMD
Gesellschaft für Mathematik und Datenverarbeitung mbH
Bonn-Bad Godesberg, Western Germany
October 3 - 5, 1977

edited by
H. Beilner
and
E. Gelenbe

WATERFORD REGIONAL
LIBRARY
TECHNICAL COLLEGE

NORTH-HOLLAND PUBLISHING COMPANY - AMSTERDAM • NEW YORK • OXFORD

© North-Holland Publishing Company, Amsterdam and ECSC, EEC EAEC, Brussels and Luxembourg, (1977)

All rights reserved. No part of this publication may be reproduced, stored in a retrieval system, or transmitted, in any form or by any means, electronic, mechanical, photocopying, recording or otherwise, without the prior permission of the copyright owner.

ISBN: 0444 85058 9

First edition 1977
Second printing 1980

PUBLISHERS:
NORTH-HOLLAND PUBLISHING COMPANY
AMSTERDAM, NEW YORK, OXFORD

for

The Commission of the European Communities,
Directorate-General Scientific and Technical
Information and Information Management, Luxembourg

LEGAL NOTICE

Neither the Commission of the European Communities nor any person acting on behalf of the Commission is responsible for the use which might be made of the following information.

PRINTED IN THE NETHERLANDS

CONTENTS

---

* see Errata

* see Errata

Program Chairman's Preface

Computing systems are artificial systems: designed by humans to meet the computional needs of the eventual user community. Their design process is governed by various objectives, amongst them correctness, safety, security, performance (as measured in terms of speed, throughput, utilisation etc), to name but some of the more important ones. With performance amidst the major design objectives, it strikes us as almost contradictory that computing system performance should have to be measured and evaluated at all, other than for purposes of reassuring the designer. Yet, until rather recently the unsatisfactory approach of first building computers and then measuring their performance was prevalent due to the lack of reliable methods and tools to predict, during computer system development, all but the grossest performance characteristics. The consequent search for realistic and effective computer system models, mapping system load onto system performance, has been largely successful in the last years: Standardisation of simulation modelling and, even more importantly, significant progress in the field of analytical (exact and approximate) modelling have drastically improved the postition of conscious system designers and installation managers. We can presently observe the benefits of these advancements of system modelling methodology in various real-life applications. However, performance prediction and forecasting via system models can only be as realistic as the description of system load presented to the models. In my opinion, our understanding of system load, i.e. of user and program behaviour, is still somewhat lagging behind, and I should personally like to see more work done on load and load evolution modelling, in the near future.

The volume in hand includes all papers accepted for presentation at the "Third International Symposium on Modelling and Performance Evaluation of Computer Systems", one in a series of European conferences devoted to important aspects of the state of the art in the area of measuring, modelling and evaluating computing systems. This symposium was structured in sessions as follows:

Session 1: Keynote by C.A. Petri

Session 2: Performance evaluation and modelling of total systems; papers by Vasseur/Guillon, Roehr, Mertens, Asztalos and

Bucci/Streeter.

Session 3: Simulation packages, dynamic resource allocation under deadlock and cost restraints; papers by Baer/Jensen, Sifakis, Winter, Cellary and Booth/Whitby/Strevens.

Session 4: Exact and approximate solutions for queueing networks; papers by Grillo, Denning/Buzen, Marie/Stewart, Gelenbe/Pujolle and Shum/Buzen.

Session 5: Program behaviour and memory management, I/O modelling, control; papers by Batson/Blatt/Kearns, Potier, Krzesinski/Teunissen, Coffman/Hofri and Romoeuf.

Session 6: Measurement and control problems, queueing theory, fault-tolerant computing; papers by Arato, Boulaye/Decouty/Michel/Rolin/Wagner, Walke, Becker/Fortet and Browaeys/Muron.

On behalf of the programme committee, I am very pleased to acknowledge the extensive support of the organiser of the symposium, the Gesellschaft für Mathematik und Datenverarbeitung (GMD), Bonn, and of the co-sponsors, the Institut de Recherche d'Informatique et d'Automatique (IRIA-LABORIA), Rocquencourt, the IFIP Working Group 7.3 (computer system modelling) and the Joint Research Center of the European Communities, Ispra. Sincere thanks are also due to the anonymous referees and to my colleagues on the committee who jointly helped compile a programme of considerable quality.

Dortmund, January, 1978 Heinz Beilner

Foreword

In 1976, IRIA and the Joint Research Centre (JRC) of the Commission of the European Communities, the Ispra Establishment, was invited to host the Second International Workshop on Modelling and Performance Evaluation of Computer Systems in Stresa in October 1976.

This time the Third International Symposium was organised by the Gesellschaft für Mathematik und Datenverarbeitung (GMD) in Bonn-Bad Godesberg in October 1977. This Symposium has a close correlation to the work of GMD in this field.

By this Symposium GMD wants to stimulate the development of fruitful ideas and to support international contacts and cooperation. The Symposium was sponsored by IRIA-Laboria, IFIP Working Group 7.3 and JRC (ISPRA Establishment).

The programme was arranged in a highly qualified way by a Scientific Programme Committee composed of:

SCIENTIFIC PROGRAMME COMMITTEE

H. Beilner	Universität Dortmund, Germany (Chairman)
D.P. Bovet	Universita di Pisa, Italy
E. Gelenbe	Université de Paris-Sud, France
M.M. Lehman	Imperial College, United Kingdom
P.J. Courtois	Laboratoire M.B.L.E., Bruxelles, Belgium
D. Ferrari	Politecnico di Milano, Italy
U. Herzog	Universität Erlangen, Germany
J. Labetoulle	I.R.I.A.-Laboria, France
J. Entfant	Université de Rennes, France
I. Mitrani	University of Newcastle, United Kingdom
G. Regenspurg	GMD, Bonn, Germany

The organisational arrangements were made by Dr. Heyderhoff (GMD), Dr. Zimmermann (GMD) and their staff.

The results of this Symposium are presented for a wider public in this volume.

F. Krückeberg
General Chairman

Measuring, Modelling and Evaluating Computer Systems,
H. Beilner and E. Gelenbe, (eds.)
© North-Holland Publishing Company (1977)

A PRAGMATIC APPROACH TO A QUANTITATIVE PERFORMANCE EVALUATION

B. Mertens
Zentralinstitut für Angewandte Mathematik
Kernforschungsanlage Jülich GmbH
D 5170 Jülich, Germany

Benchmark measurements were performed to determine the most efficient of five different computer configurations (IBM/370-168) and to compare two different operating systems (MVS and TSS) under two different workloads (pure timesharing and mixed timesharing/batch). The usual qualitative performance comparisons on the basis of response times and transaction rates were made, although most of the different measurement were not directly comparable.

Therefore a pragmatic approach was tried to find a consistent measure of performance which allowed a quantitative comparison of the different hardware/software configurations under the different workloads. The so gained results confirmed most of the qualitative conclusions; in addition, all the different systems could be compared on the same scale and the relative performance of other configurations not being measured could be estimated.

1. INTRODUCTION

In 1975/76 the Kernforschungsanlage (KFA) Jülich planned to exchange a system IBM/370-158 used for timesharing and online data processing by a system IBM/370-168. Therefore benchmark measurements were performed to determine the most efficient of five different 168-configurations under the two operating systems MVS and TSS using two types of workload, namely, pure timesharing and mixed timesharing/batch. The evaluation of the measurements was done using the usual procedure of comparing the different response times and transaction rates.

However, most of the measurements were not directly comparable due to the different mix of timesharing transactions and the different batch degradation values observed for the different measurements.

Therefore an approach was tried to find a consistent measure of performance which allowed a quantitative comparison of the different hardware/software configurations under the different workloads.

In this paper the scope and the lay-out of the measurements are presented together with the usual performance analysis based on response times and transaction rates. In addition a pragmatic definition of performance is given and the measurement results are interpreted in terms of this definition.

2. THE MEASUREMENTS

The lay-out of the measurements, namely the hardware configurations being investigated, the operating systems used, the benchmark scripts and the experimental procedure, were governed by restrictions imposed by the data processing environment of the KFA. Therefore a few words are necessary about the computing facilities in the KFA.

In 1975/76 the KFA ran two large scale computers: a /370-168 with four MBytes of main storage and a /370-158 with two MBytes. The '168 did pure batch processing under OS/MVT with HASP (under MVS later on) while the '158 served for timesharing and online data processing under TSS/370. Both machines were coupled by a CTCA and installation written software. One of the main reasons of having TSS instead of an IBM main-line operating system is the fact, that in the beginning of timesharing data processing in the KFA (1971) no other IBM system had the necessary functions to support the JOKER network. JOKER couples approximately 30 minicomputers used for experiment and process control with the central timesharing computer.

The batch machine processed an average of 1200 jobs per day and was CPU bound all the time. The '158 processed an average of 450 timesharing tasks per day with up to 50 tasks running concurrently during the daily peak periods. During those times the '158-CPU was the systems' bottleneck.

Due to the increasing demand of computing power and functions, an upgrading of hardware was considered. The main idea was to exchange the '158-CPU by a '168-CPU with a moderate reconfiguration of channels and auxiliary storage.

To prepare this, benchmark measurements were performed in cooperation with IBM using the TP-driver facility of IBM's World Trade Systems Center in Poughkeepsie, USA. Due to the arguments pointed out above the following requirements governed the lay-out of the measurements:

a) The measurements should identify the best of some '168-configurations within a certain rental value.

b) Both operating systems, TSS and MVS, had to be taken into consideration.

c) The behaviour with respect to pure timesharing as well as mixed batch/timesharing should be investigated.

Due to the limited availability of the TP-driver facility only the following five '168-configurations were measured:

(1) a '168 with three MByte of main storage, one drum (2305-2) at its own BMPX channel and a string of disk drives (3330) at its own BMPX channel.

(2) configuration (1) with an additional drum at the same BMPX

(3) configuration (1) with an additional string of disk drives at its own channel

(4) configuration (1) with an additional MBytes of main storage (4MByte totally)

(5) configuration (1) with an additional drum at the same BMPX but with 2 MByte of main storage only.

Each measurement was performed under the operating systems MVS Release 3.0 and TSS/370 Release 2.0 using two types of benchmark script: "TS ONLY", a pure timesharing script simulating 80 active timesharing users and "MIXED", a mixed script simulating 40 active timesharing users with an additional batch job stream. Thus in total 20 measurements were run.

The timesharing script and the batch job stream reflected the workload profile observed in the KFA (1).

A single measurement was performed in the following way:

1. All the timesharing tasks were started.

2. 15 minutes after the first task started, the batch jobs were initiated (if it was a "mixed" run) and data acquisition began. This ensured that all the housekeeping sections were executed which preceeded all timesharing scripts and guaranteed equal starting conditions for every run.

3. After 15 minutes or the end of the last batch job data aquisition was stopped.

This measurement procedure was chosen because it comes as close to a real timesharing production as possible. Strict limitations of the available machine time caused comparatively low run times for the individual measurements.

More details about the measurements are published elsewhere (1), (2).

3. THE RESULTS

The results of the measurements consisted of: the minimum, maximum, and mean response time for each type of timesharing command, the command count, and the batch elapsed time for the mixed benchmark.

For a comparison of the different measurements the following restrictions have to be regarded:

a) The mix of commands is different for the different measurements. This has two reasons: Firstly, the timesharing scripts for MVS and TSS were not identical although they performed exactly the same timesharing functions. This is due to differences of the command language of the two operating systems. Secondly, because of the different performance of the ten hardware/software configurations, the measurements were started and stopped at quite different locations in the scripts. In fig. 1 the observed frequency of timesharing commands is shown. For ease of comparison the commands are grouped in three groups: trivial commands (having no explicit data set reference), non-trivial commands (having explicit data set reference), and execute commands (which comprise FORTRAN compilation and execution of a user program). As may be seen in fig. 1 the frequency of trivial, non-trivial and execute commands is different in the benchmark scripts (horizontal bars) and different in the measurements (points). Because the amount of computing work varies for the individual timesharing commands the total amount of work processed during the runs is also different.

b) For the mixed timesharing/batch runs the (elapsed) time taken to process the batch job stream varied from 750 to 1300 seconds. Thus a quite different amount of resources was left for the timesharing part of the scripts. This has also to be taken into account when comparing the different measurements.

The usual performance criteria for a timesharing system are response time and transaction rate. In fig. 2 and 3 these two variables are plotted against each other for the trivial (fig. 2) and the non-trivial commands (fig. 3). The execute commands are not presented here because they do not give any new insight. Each point in the plots represents a measurement characterized by a certain hardware configuration (1 to 5), the operating system (MVS or TSS) and the benchmark used (MIXED or TS ONLY).

The following conclusions may be drawn from these plots:

- Trivial commands.

  The best performance (that means short response time connected with high transaction rate) with respect to trivial commands is observed in the following cases:

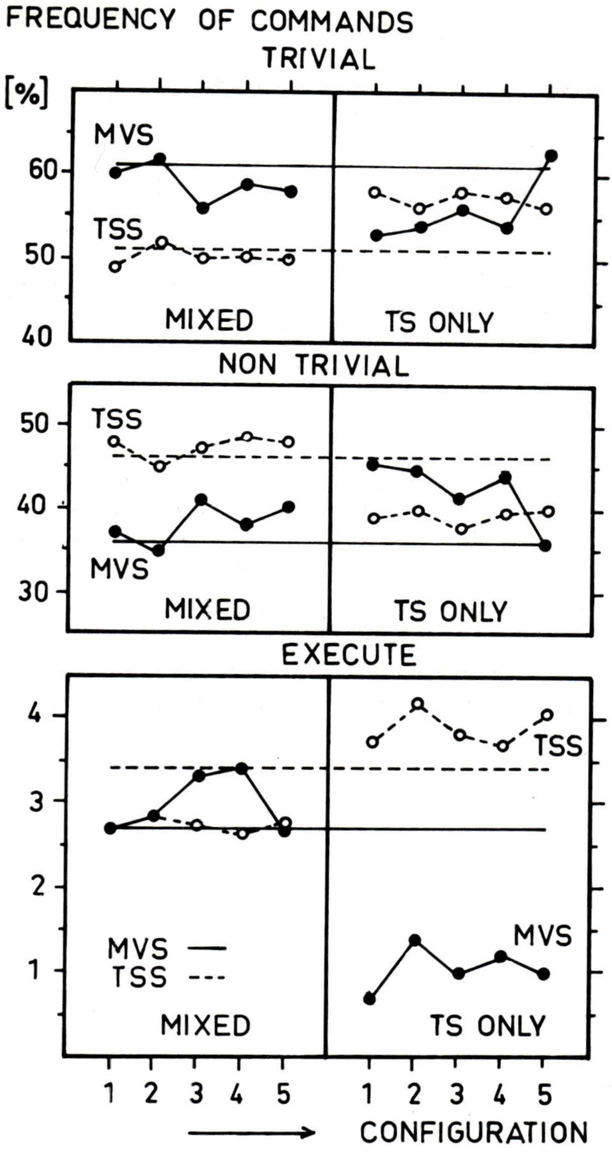

Fig. 1 Frequency of the different types of timesharing commands in percent as observed during the measurements (points). The horizontal bars give the percentage of commands with respect to the benchmark scripts.

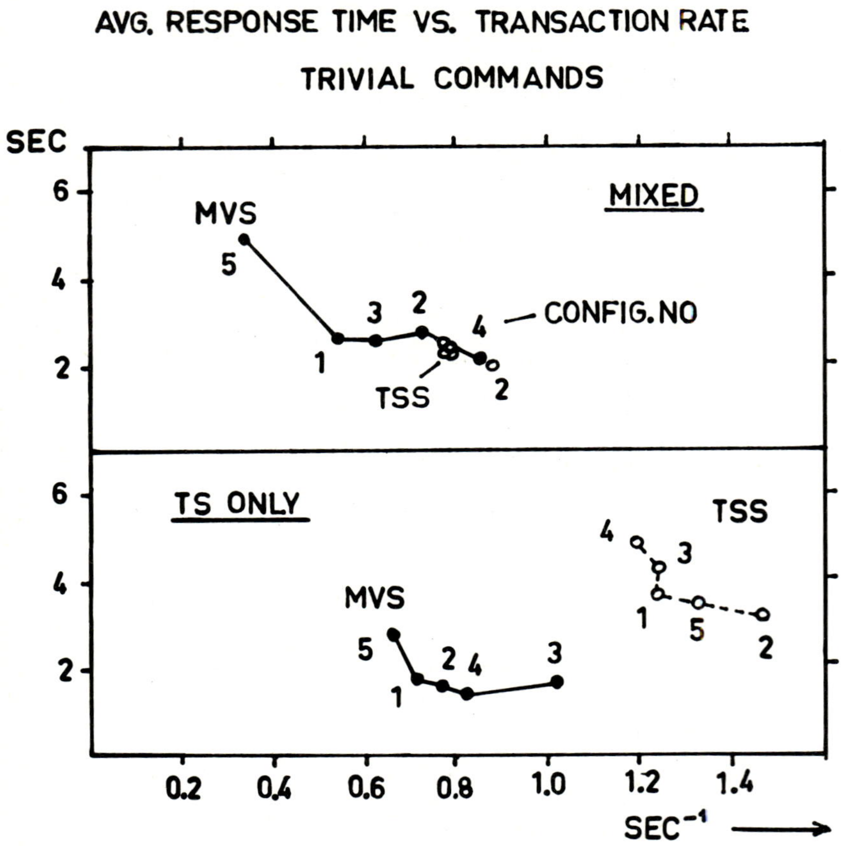

Fig. 2 Response times and transaction rates observed for trivial commands

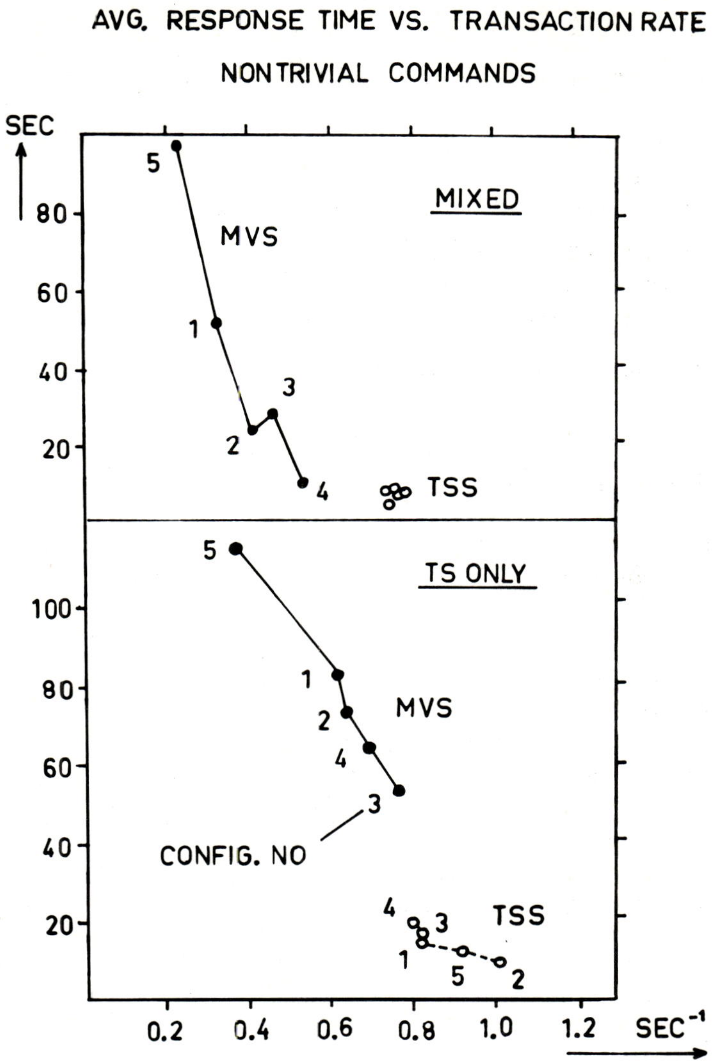

Fig. 3 Response times and transaction rates observed for non-trivial commands

MVS, MIXED benchmark, configuration 4;
MVS, TS ONLY benchmark, configuration 3;
TSS, MIXED and TS ONLY benchmark, configuration 2.

In the TS ONLY case MVS shows the shorter response times than TSS, although TSS has the higher transaction rates.

- Non-trivial commands:
  The best performance is seen in the following measurements:

  MVS, MIXED benchmark, configuration 4;
  MVS, TS ONLY benchmark, configuration 3;
  TSS, MIXED and TS ONLY, configuration 2.

In all the cases TSS shows superior performance compared to MVS.

4. CONSISTENCY CHECK

The response time averaged over all types of commands and the total transaction rate observed in each measurement are not independent from each other. Thus a simple check of consistency may be performed.

If N is the total number of transactions observed during the measurement period T then N/T is the transaction rate r.
If n is the number of timesharing terminals, then on the average N/n transactions are performed by one terminal (or task). For every transaction the time $t_r + t_{del}$ is consumed where t_r is the response time and t_{del} is a delay time which is the sum of input, output and a thinktime of 5 sec (see fig. 4).

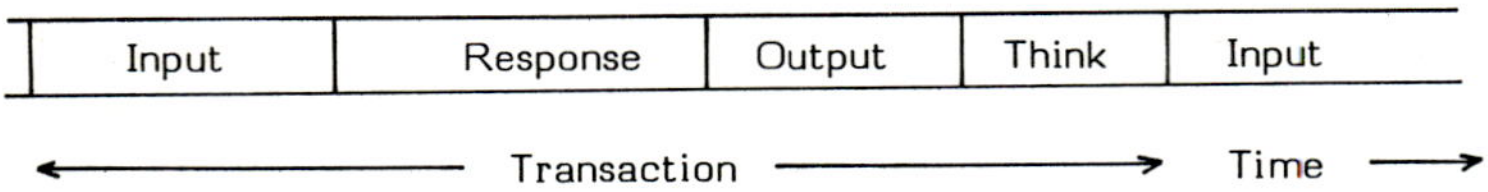

Fig. 4 Course of a single timesharing transaction

If only the average values are considered the following relation is true:

$$T = \frac{N}{n} \quad (t_r + t_{del})$$

or

$$t_r = \frac{n}{r} - t_{del}$$

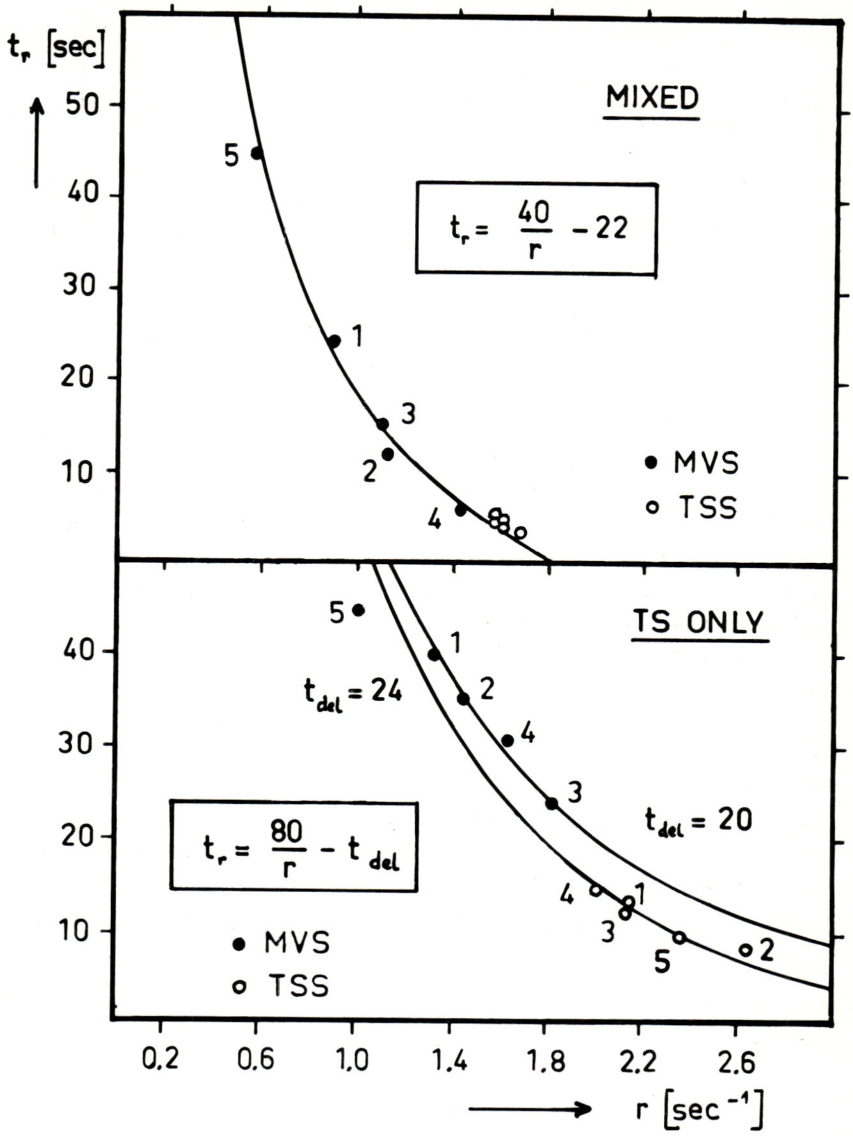

Fig. 5 Average response time t_r as a function of transaction rate r for all the timesharing transactions. The experimental data (points) are given together with the calculated curves.

In the case of the measurements n is fixed (40 for the MIXED, 80 for the TS ONLY benchmark) t_{del} being the only unknown parameter.

Fig. 5 gives the measured points together with the "theoretical" curves. In the MIXED case the experimental values for both, MVS and TSS are satisfactorily fitted by a single hyperbola with t_{del} = 22 sec. Thus for all ten measurements the average delay time is a constant which means that the sum of input and output time is on average independent of the different performance of the various systems and independent of the slightly different mix of transactions.

This is not true for the TS ONLY benchmark. The experimental points for MVS (except configuration 5) and TSS are located on two different hyperbolas with delay times of 20 and 24 seconds. This is due to the fact that the mix of transactions is noticeably different for the TS ONLY runs. TSS processed considerably more execute transactions (see fig. 1) which are characterized by an unusually large output time (this was a bug in the benchmark script). Thus a significantly larger average delay time was obtained indicating that an additional workload was processed under TSS which was not present under MVS. This has to be taken into account when the TSS data is compared with MVS.

From a performance point of view a system is better when it is placed more to the right of the hyperbola. Using this criterion conclusions may be drawn about the performance of the various configurations and operating systems. They essentially confirm the statements given in chapter 3.

5. QUANTITATIVE PERFORMANCE CONSIDERATIONS

All the previous discussions had the disadvantage that the different measurements could not be compared directly due to the different batch degradation and to the different mix of timesharing commands being executed. If the performance of MVS and TSS and of the different hardware configurations is to be compared directly, a quantitative measure of performance is necessary. Therefore an attempt is made to find a quantitative definition of performance and to apply it to the results of the measurements.

To achieve this a theoretical definition of computing work is given. To express this definition in terms of observable quantities three approximations are made.

Work is clearly an additive quantity. Thus, in our case it is the sum over all the N transactions executed during the measurement period T:

(1) $$W = \sum_{k=1}^{N} w_k$$

w_k is the work performed by transaction k. By definition w_k is the "useful" work only which means that this amount of work is necessary to perform that transaction. Thus w_k is a value characteristic of transaction k and therefore independent of the hardware configuration and the operating system on which it may be executed. Therefore the following definition is made:

(2) $$w_k = P_o\, t_k^{min}$$

t_k^{min} is defined by the following consideration: Let C be the set of all possible hardware/software configurations i and t_k^i the execution time for transaction k running alone on configuration i then

(3) $$t_k^{min} = \text{Min}\left\{t_k^i,\ \ i \in C\right\}$$

In plain words: t_k^{min} is the execution time on a "super computer" being best suited for transaction k. Thus t_k^{min} is a property of transaction k and independent of i.

P_o is a constant factor and by definition independent of k and i.

This definition of computing work reflects the fact that for a computer system it is never distinguished between "simple" and "difficult" work but between "short" and "long" work.

The performance P of a computing system may be defined as the work performed per unit of time:

(4) $$P = \frac{Po}{T} \sum_{k=1}^{N} t_k^{min}$$

If during the time T some of the transactions are of the same type we may rewrite the equation:

(5) $$P = \frac{Po}{T} \sum_{j=1}^{M} n_j\, t_j^{min}$$

where j = 1, ... M denotes the M different types of transactions and $n_1 \ldots n_M$ their frequency.

In a real computing system (denoted by "*", $* \in C$) certainly

(6) $$t_j^{min} \leq t_j^{*}$$

where t_j^{*} is the minimum execution time ("response" time in terms of fig. 4) of transaction j running alone on this computing system. Now the following assumption is made:

(7) $$t_j^{min} \approx a\, t_j^* \quad a \leq 1, \quad \text{for all transactions } j$$

a is a constant factor which is by definition independent of the transaction type but (among others) strongly dependent on the processor speed of that real computing system. This assumption means, that a real computer is just a slow "super computer", which is certainly not true, because the "super computer" is specialized on transaction type j. In this sense (7) is a crude approximation only and the performance (5) can be expressed as:

(8) $$P = aPo \sum_{j=1}^{M} \frac{n_j}{T} t_j^* = aPo \sum_{j=1}^{M} r_j t_j^*$$

where $r_j = n_j/T$ is the transaction rate of transaction type j. In this approximation the performance is proportional to the sum of transaction rates (r_j) weighted with factors (t_j^*) which reflect the amount of work per transaction.

Another interpretation of the performance definition (5) is the following:

$$T^* = \sum_{j=1}^{M} n_j t_j^*$$

is approximately the time which is consumed, when all the transactions are executed one after the other on that real computing system. Therefore the expression

$$MPL_{eff} \approx \frac{T^*}{T} = \frac{1}{T} \sum_{j=1}^{M} n_j t_j^*$$

is approximately equal to the effective (observed) multiprogramming level MPL_{eff} and

$$P \approx a\, P_o\, MPL_{eff}$$

Therefore the performance of a computing system is approximately proportional to its effective multiprogramming level. Since the MPL_{eff} is a measure of parallelism within a computer system, definition (4) leads to the conclusion that performance is proportional to the degree of parallelism.

To evaluate the performance of MVS and TSS using the data of the 20 measurements, approximation (7) is used with slightly different meaning of t_j^*. Here it is not the minimum execution time with respect to one computing system, but the minimum observed response time of transaction j for all the 20 measurements. This neglects of course the work which is performed during the delay time t_{del} (i.e. input and output) but this is probably a small, constant number and not significant in this context. Also t_j^* will have a slightly larger value when determined this way, since it is not determined on an empty machine. However, approximation (7) will be improved if more than just one computer system is regarded in this way.

Another way to look at this approximation is to go back to definition (3). If the set of hardware/software configurations C is reduced to the set of systems investigated in the measurements then t_k^{min} is approximated by the corresponding minimal response time observed during the benchmark runs.

In this approximation formula (8) contains (apart from a constant factor) measurable quantities only: the transaction rates r_j and the minimal response time t_j^* observed for transaction j during the 20 measurement runs. Thus the "performance" may be calculated for the five configurations under MVS and TSS. Fig. 6 depicts the results.

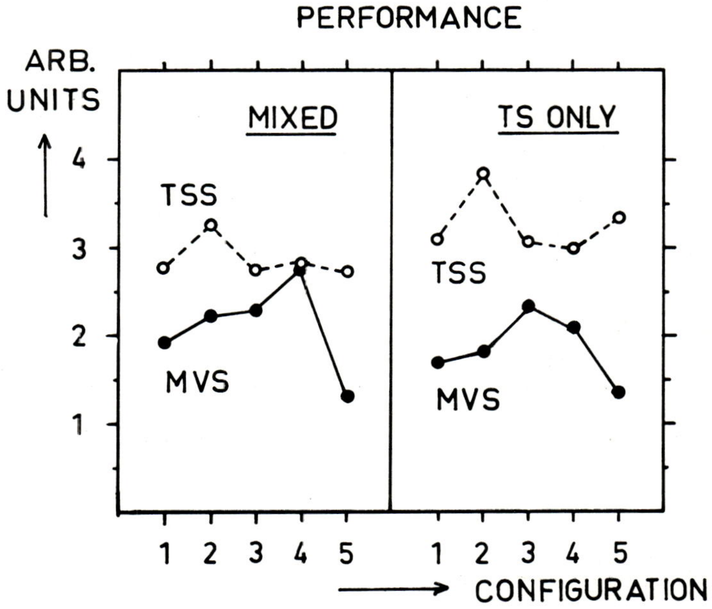

Fig. 6 Performance of the different configurations as observed during the different benchmark runs. The performance (given in arbitrary units) was determined according to formula (8)*).

---

*) Note: For the batch job stream the product $r_j\, t_j^* = (1/t_{el})t_{el}^*$, where t_{el} is the observed batch elapsed time and t_{el}^* is the elapsed time for the job stream running alone with one initiator i.e. without being multiprogrammed.

The following conclusions may be drawn from this figure:

- The best configuration for MVS is no. 4 for the MIXED benchmark and no. 3 for the TS ONLY benchmark. Configuration no. 2 is the best for TSS.
- TSS performs better than MVS on all the configurations and for both types of benchmark. The performance ratio TSS to MVS (best configuration each) is 1.20 (MIXED) and 1.66 (TS ONLY).

Almost all the qualitative statements about performance are confirmed by these considerations. But due to the fact, that the batch work load is included and the different mix of timesharing transactions is taken into account, quantitative comparisons with respect to configuration changes can be made. Not all of these can be discussed here. As an example the following numbers are given (tab. 1):

	MVS		TSS	
	MIXED	TS ONLY	MIXED	TS ONLY
	%	%	%	%
configuration 1	0	0	0	0
+ 2.nd drum	16	7	18	25
+ 2.nd disk ch.	18	37	-2	-1
+ 4.th MByte	42	23	1	-3

Tab. 1 Performance changes with respect to changes in the hardware configuration. The values are relative to configuration 1.

The occurrence of small negative numbers for TSS has two reasons:

- Because of limitations in the measurement time no tuning was done for TSS. Therefore the additional resources were not utilized in an appropriate manner. MVS - on the other hand - had been tuned for every hardware configuration, although an optimally tuned system was not obtained in every case. However, additional recources resulted in an increased performance.
- The accuracy of approximation (8) is limited. Because at least a small positive performance gain is expected when a resource is added, the error of this approximation is at least a few percent.

Besides the advantage of comparing different hardware configurations and operating systems quantitatively the method used here allows an estimation of hardware configurations not being measured. This was of some importance, since the vendor complained about an "unfair" choice of configurations with respect to MVS. The assertion was that MVS would have beaten TSS on configurations with more disk channels and a larger main storage.

To verify that, the following consideration was made:

Firstly, it was assumed that the drum channel in configuration 3 could be exchanged by a disk channel without a gain of performance. (It was argued that no drum was necessary for MVS.) Thus a "new" configuration 3 with three disk channels was supposed to have the same performance as the "old" one.
Secondly, it was assumed that an additional resource (disk channel, main storage) would not increase performance more than it was observed in the measurements. So, if a fourth disk channel was added, performance would not increase more than it was noted for the addition of the third channel.

Doing so, the upper limit of performance could be estimated for the following "MVS-Configurations":

A: a '168 with four MByte of main storage and three DA channels

B: a '168 with three MByte of main storage and four DA channels

C: a '168 with four MByte of main storage and four DA channels

Further, the price (in percent of configuration 1) is calculated for all the configurations. The results, performance versus price, are plotted in fig. 7.

Obviously the configurations A - C are remarkably more expensive than those being measured. Even for these configurations MVS does not come up to the performance of TSS running on configuration 2 (except for configuration C, MIXED benchmark).

Fig. 7 depicts the fact that the current MVS needs a costly hardware to achieve a performance comparable to TSS.

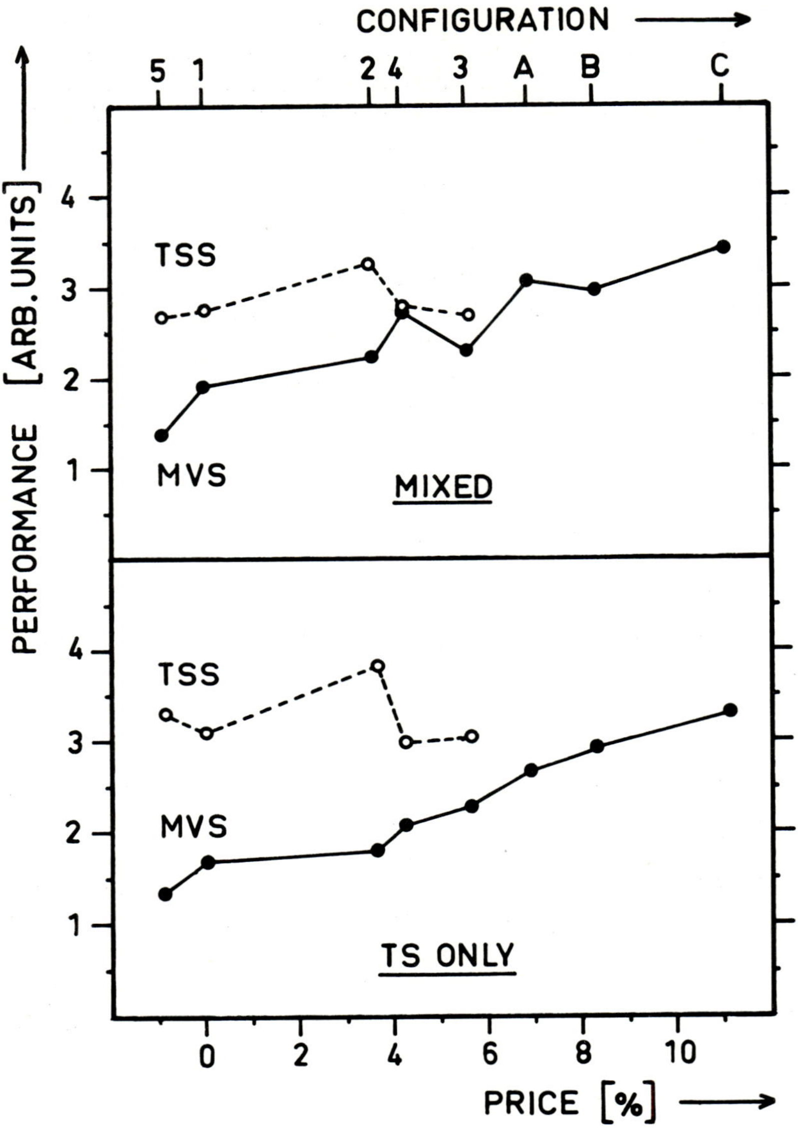

Fig. 7 Performance versus price for the measured (1 - 5) and the calculated (A - C) configurations. The price is given in percent of configuration 1. The performance values given for configuration A - C are estimated upper limits.

6. CONCLUSIONS

The disadvantages of a phenomenological, qualitative performance comparison is removed by having a consistent quantitative measure of performance. Consistent in this context means that the influence of processing different workloads in the different benchmark measurements (which cannot always be avoided) is largely eliminated.

Almost all of the qualitative results obtained from the data are confirmed by the quantitative evaluation. In addition, all the different hardware configurations under the different operating systems could be compared on the same scale. The relative performance of other configurations not being measured could be estimated.

References:

(1) B. Mertens and R. Alexander,
Performance comparisons between the Operating Systems MVS and TSS,
KFA Jülich, Jül-Report 1397, February 1977

(2) R. Alexander, B. Mertens, and R.D. Rumler,
A Timesharing Benchmark on an IBM/370-168,
KFA Jülich, Jül-Report 1280, March 1976

Measuring, Modelling and Evaluating Computer Systems,
H. Beilner and E. Gelenbe, (eds.)
© North-Holland Publishing Company (1977)

Performance Evaluation of the Multijob Supervisor

Asztalos D.

Computer Centre of Hungarian Planning Office

Budapest, Hungary

The purpose of the paper is to draw a picture of the resource requirements by the Supervisor of the Multijob operating system running on an ICL System 4/70 computer. The main concern was to analyse the CPU time distribution among the routines of the kernel, the resident, non-interruptible part of the Supervisor. Two parts of the kernel are discussed in more detail:
1. the realization of the semaphore operations;
2. the WAIT I/O routine.
Some suggestions are made to improve the efficiency of the Supervisor in both cases.

Introduction

The theory and logical design of operating systems have developed significantly in the recent years [3,8]. Some of the theoretical results have been applied to the design of commercial operating systems. The main task which an operating system has to deal with is the sharing of resources involving the control of the synchronized execution of parallel processes. The tools used in operating systems to realize the synchronized execution of processes are the synchronizing primitives. In practice, the primitives are realized as routines of the kernel, the resident, non-interruptible part of the Supervisor. Beyond their special status in the system, the primitives are characterized by their high rate of activation. The CPU time consumed by the execution of the synchronizing primitives forms a very large part of the system overhead in a present-day time sharing system. It is regrettable that only very few data are available on system overhead in the literature [1,4,7,9] and only in [4] one can find a relatively detailed description of the CPU requirements of the Supervisor.
The author believes it is worth-while to examine the performance characteristics of a Supervisor in more detail both for tuning on existing system and for designing a new one.

Description of the system

Multijob runs on the ICL System 4/70 computer. The configuration which was measured consists of 704 Kbytes of main store, 11 disc drives, each with 60 Mbytes of capacity, 6 disc drives, each with 7 Mbytes of capacity, 10 tape drives, the usual slow peripherals, 26 conversational terminals and 2 remote data terminals.
The contents of the main store are: Read-Only-Memory 4 Kbytes, Supervisor kernel 19 Kbytes, interruptible resident processes of the Supervisor 75 Kbytes, Dynamic Buffer Area /transient processes of the Supervisor, system tables and work areas/ 128 Kbytes, round-robin store 60 Kbytes, batch-store 418 Kbytes.

Multijob Supervisor

The ICL System 4/70 computer has four different states and each of them has its own register set. These are P1, P2, P3, P4 states. The user programs are executed in P1 state, whereas the Supervisor runs in the P2 and P3 privileged states. Control is given to P4 state only if a serious hardware error occurs. Some of the Supervisor routines are core resident while others are loaded into the core only on demand. The P3-code has higher priority, is resident and noninterruptible, but not all the resident code is P3. We will refer to P3-code as the kernel.

The kernel is entered on each interrupt caused by the following events:

a/ I/O transfer termination from peripheral units and terminals
b/ execution of a Supervisor Call /SVC/ instruction
c/ timer interrupt /one in each 0.5 sec/
d/ hardware error
e/ program error

The interrupts of type d/ and e/ occur so rarely that their effect can be ignored. The interrupts of type c/ can also be excluded from the analysis because of their regular character.

The main routines of the kernel are:

a/ interrupt analysis
b/ process control routines /create, destroy, suspend, activate/
c/ process dispatcher
d/ semaphores /or monitors/ [5,6]
e/ I/O initiation and termination
f/ check I/O termination (WAIT I/O)

The exit from the kernel is always caused by the process dispatcher allocating the CPU to the process with the highest priority in the CPU queue. If there is no process in the CPU queue the processor executes a looping "idle" process in P2 state till the next interrupt occurs.

The place of the kernel in the system is shown on Figure 1.

The priorities of processes are the following in decreasing order:

a/ P2 resident processes
b/ P2 transient processes
c/ user processes

The priorities of P2 resident processes are fixed while those of P2 transient processes are determined by the order of their calls. The priorities of user programs can be determined by users, but their relative order at the time of execution may be changed only by an operator command.

The core store for transient processes is allocated from a buffer pool, the so called Dynamic Buffer Area. The response time of the system greatly depends on the size of this buffer pool.

The most important P2 processes are the following:

a/ Dynamic Buffer control
b/ Catalogued file handling processes
c/ Communication processes
d/ Round-robin store handling
e/ Interpretation of operator commands

Measurements

The measurement tool used was a software monitor described in detail in [2] . The monitors used in the following measurements are interrupt driven. The checkpoints where the control is given to the measurement routines are shown on Fig.1. At the checkpoint A which is put in the interrupt analysis routine the control is given to the

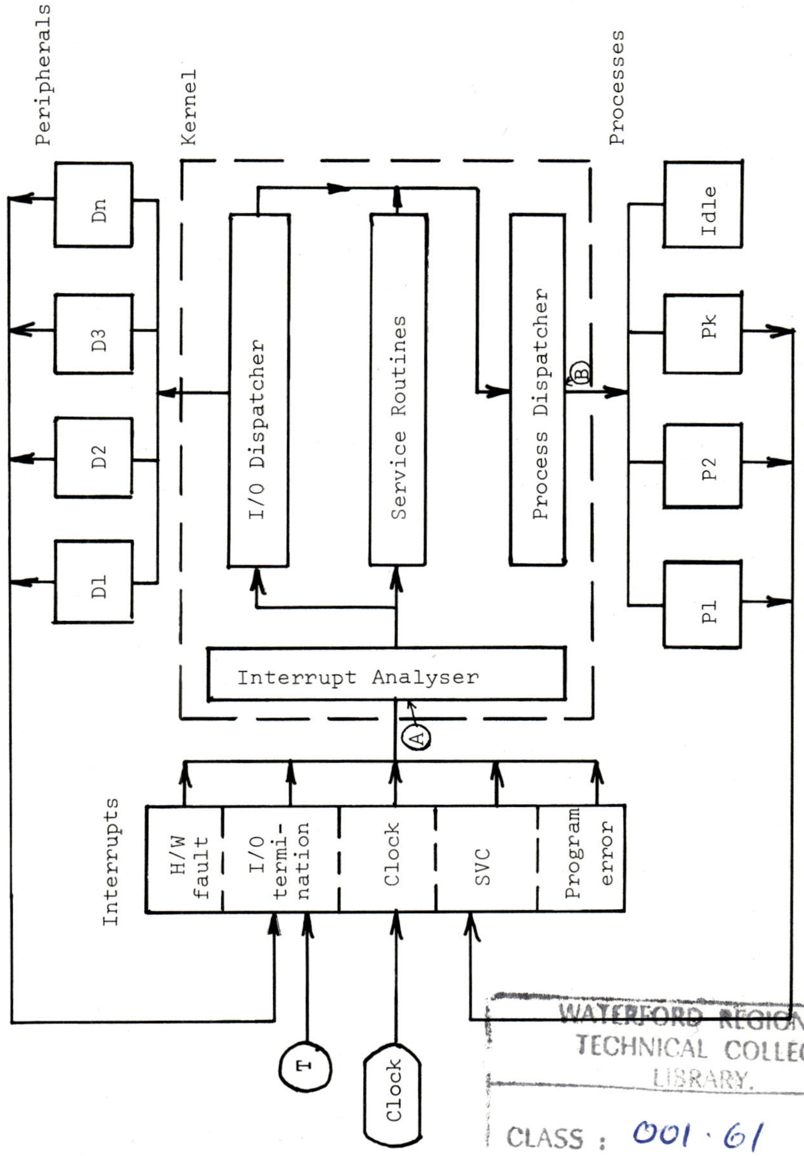

WATERFORD REGIONAL TECHNICAL COLLEGE LIBRARY.
CLASS : 001·61
ACC. No.: 144568

T - terminals
A,B - checkpoints

Figure 1. The place of kernel in the system

pre-kernel measurement routine. The checkpoint B is put in the exit path of the process dispatcher and so the post-kernel measurement routine is executed on each exit from the kernel. A special flag is set on exit indicating which type of processes was entered (P1, P2 active, P2 idle). The monitor is loaded into the system as a usual P1 program. It has an initialization phase which is responsible for the realization of the interface between the checkpoints in the resident Supervisor and the corresponding measurement routines. The latter ones must be non-interruptible and they are executed in the same computer state as the code of Supervisor where the checkpoints are put in (P3 or P2). The I/O activity of the monitor (if there is any) is executed in P1 state. In this case a special signalling mechanism is set up between the measurement routines and the P1 service code of the monitor.

In the experiment described in this paper two monitors (MON-1 and MON-2) were used; each of them occupied 4 Kbytes of core store (the minimum amount of store which can be allocated to a user program) and used 63 μsec of CPU time at each interrupt. This accounts for at most 3 % of the whole CPU load.

The main purpose of the experiment was to draw a picture about the distribution of CPU time among different states of the computer with a particular emphasis on the kernel of the Supervisor. The experiment was executed in two phases. The MON-1 monitor was used in the first phase to measure the distribution of CPU time among the states of the computer. This is shown in Table 1 which containes the results of five measurement periods with total duration of 12729 seconds. The average CPU load in the five measurements was 81.8 %. It can be seen from the Table 1. that the Supervisor has a large CPU consumption, particularly in state P3. An interesting result of the first monitor is that the average CPU time needed by the Supervisor to service one interrupt is about 1 msec. This value is independent of the size of configuration and the type of workload, so it can be used to estimate the CPU requirement of the Supervisor if only the interrupt rate is measured. Of course, in each case when the logical structure of the Supervisor is modified the above value must be redefined experimentally.

Table 1. MON-1 summary results

Total measurement time		12729 sec	100 %
CPU requirements of the	Supervisor	5885	46.23 %
	kernel	4354	34.20 %
	P2 processes	1530	12.02 %
	P1 processes	4271	33.55 %
	monitor	262	2.06 %
Total CPU time		10417	81.83 %
Number of interrupts		5933228	
Rate of interrupts		466/sec	
Average CPU-time needed by the Supervisor to service one interrupt		0.992 msec	

It can be seen from the Table 1. that the kernel requires almost three times more CPU time as the P2 processes do. This was the reason to develop a second monitor which gives a more detailed picture about the kernel activity.

The only way to enter the kernel is if at least one bit of the interrupt flag register is set. Table 2 contains data about the rate of interrupts by their source. The service of SVC instructions requires the largest part of CPU time. The distribution of SVC interrupts by their types is shown in Table 3. The administration of transfer requests (transfer initiation and termination) consumes 48.13 % of

Table 2. Summary results of MON-2. Part I.

Type of interrupt	Rate of interrupts (n/sec)	Percentages of kernel CPU-time	Average CPU time to service 1 interrupt (ms)
I/O termination			
disc	42.8	13.56	1.110
magnetic tape	14.7	4.52	1.078
multiplexor	50.8	9.45	0.652
Supervisor Call instruction	350	72.02	0.721
Timer	2.1	0.43	0.653

Total measurement time	23580 sec
CPU time of kernel	8270 sec
Rate of interrupts	460/sec

Table 3. Summary results of MON-2. Part II.

Distribution of SVC interrupts by their types

Type of SVC interrupt	Rate of interrupts (n/sec)	Percentages of kernel CPU time	Average CPU time to service 1 interrupt (ms)
Transfer initiation	53.2	20.60	1.300
Process control			
create	56.4	6.62	0.408
suspend/activate	21.7	6.14	0.988
destroy	101	20.34	0.675
Semaphores (V & P operations)	89.7	10.02	0.391
Check transfer termination (WAIT I/O)	26.7	8.05	1.058
Total	348.7	71.77	

Total measurement time	23580 seconds
CPU time of the kernel	8270 seconds

the kernel CPU time. Each transfer request has one parameter, the address of the file definition table (FDT). The kernel checks the correctness of the parameter (alignment, address of FDT belongs to the program area), maps the logical address of the data into a physical one, maintains the device queues with the options of off-line seek and of head optimization for discs.

The communication transfers are initiated by a particular P2 process (Communication Control Process). This is one of the reasons why the initiation rate is less than the rate of terminations. The second reason is the use of the off-line seek option when one initiation request may cause two termination interrupts, one for the seek and one for the data transfer. The effectivness of the off-line seek and head optimization options will be discussed in a separate paper.

The process control routines consume the 33.10 per cent of CPU time in kernel state. The create routine is executed when one process calls another one. The destroy routine is executed when a P2 process exits. The suspend and activate routines may be called by the P2 processes for synchronizing purposes. The suspend request stops the execution of the calling process and puts the given wait code in the process descriptor entry (PDE) of the process. The activation request issued by a P2 process is used to reactivate all the suspended processes with a given wait code. The kernel itself may create P2 processes without an SVC instruction having been issued. This is the case with the termination of communication transfers when the control is immediately given to the Communication Control Process. However, the above routines consume the larger part of the CPU time, the author paid most of his attention to the following two routines of the kernel: the routine realizing the semaphore operations (VOP/POP) and the check transfer termination routine (WAIT I/O). The reason of this is that these routines are simpler than the above ones and thus it was possible to introduce an experimental modification into the system with a low level of cost. On the other hand, the examination of these two routines gives a good illustration of our methodlogical approch to the use of measurement techniques in the performance analysis of operating systems.

Semaphore operations

The semaphore operations are incorporated in the VOP/POP routine of the kernel which is responsible for the handling of exclusive software resources. This routine is activated by an SVC instruction issued by a P2 process. The parameters of the call indicate the type of operation (V-entry to a critical section, P-exit from a critical section) and the resource which cannot be shared. There are fourteen different exclusive resources in the Multijob system (e.g., File Catalogue, Job Queue, File of Free Logical Tracks). The best way to describe the activity of VOP/POP routine is to use Hoare's monitor concept [6]. In the following example we show the monitor for the Job Queue File:

```
jobqueue: monitor
sem: integer
nonbusy: condition
procedure vop
begin sem=sem+1
if sem > 1 then  nonbusy.wait
end,
procedure pop
begin
if sem > 0 then sem=sem-1
if sem > 0 then nonbusy.signal
end;
sem=0
end jobqueue
```

The call of the VOP/POP routine may be written as:

```
jobqueue.vop
jobqueue.pop
```

If the value of variable sem is greater than zero at the time of call of the vop procedure then the calling process must be suspended as the required resource has already been allocated to another process. The nonbusy.wait statement in the above example is the symbolical notation for the suspension. If the value of variable sem is greater than one when the pop procedure is called then the table of PDE's must be searched for a process with the highest priority waiting for the released resource. If the entry is found the corresponding process must be reactivated. The symbolical notation of the reactivation is the nonbusy.signal statement in the example. The mutually exclusive execution of the vop and pop procedures is obtained by their realization in P3-code as a part of the kernel. The disatvantage of realizing them in P3 code is that the interrupt analysis routine and the process dispatcher are executed at each call (see Figure 1), in spite of the fact that the latter is needed only in cases when either the wait or the signal statements are executed changing the status of processes. If the resource is free when the vop procedure was called, then the CPU will be allocated to the calling process again. The same is true for the call of pop procedure if the value of sem is equal to one at the time of the call. The figures in Table 4 indicate that less than two per cent of the vop and pop calls involve the execution of wait or signal statements. As to the problem - whether and how the CPU time spent in interrupt

Table 4. Frequency of semaphore operations

Measurement	I.	II.	III.	IV.	V.	VI.
Duration in seconds	2136	1548	5354	2523	1738	6300
Number of semaphore operations (NVP)	258692	106031	343412	254912	121016	504566
Number of semaphore operations with suspension or activation (NSA)	4922	584	3854	3982	1316	7226
NSA/NVP (%)	1.90	0.51	1.12	1.56	1.08	1.43

analysis and process dispatching for 98 % of the calls can be saved, a possible solution would be to implement mutual exclusion some other way. Just this is the case on the SYSTEM 4/70 computer. Any P2 process can temporarily get into an uninterruptible state of execution if the Load Scratchpad privileged instruction and the Interrupt Mask Register belonging to P2 state are used. An interrupt must be generated only in those cases when either a process must be suspended or reactivated.

It requires a large effort to modify the kernel and all the P2 processes using the semaphore operations corresponding to the above suggestions. Thus, at the present time we can only estimate the value of CPU time which would be possible to save. The average CPU time needed to service one vop or pop call is 0.391 msec including the time for interrupt analysis and process dispatching. The same value excluding the latter administrations is 87 μsec when there is no suspension or reactivation (calculated on the base of the code). The difference is 0.304 msec. Taking into account the frequency of semaphore operations the value of the saved CPU time would be

$$0.304 \times 89.7 \times 0.98 = 26.72 \text{ msec}$$

in each second of the elapsed time. This value accounts for 7.81 % of the CPU time spent in P3 state.

WAIT I/O routine

The computation of a process is usually suspended while its transfer requests are being serviced. But in many systems there is an option for processes to activate a transfer and continue the processing as well. The process using this option must issue a signal to the Supervisor before using any of the information to be transfered to make sure that the transfer has been completed. This facility is usually available at the assembly language level, though there are a few high-level languages having statements which allow the programmer to specify this type of option (e.g. PL/1).

The efficiency of the above facility may be measured by two indices:

a/ the number of suspensions in consequence of signalling (number of activations of the WAIT I/O routine)

b/ the average CPU time used by a process between the initiation of the transfer and the time of signalling (t_{OVL}).

In the experiments described in this paper only the first of these indices was measured because of the difficulties to keep a trace of many parallel events in the case of the second index. From Table 3 can be seen that the average CPU time required to execute the WAIT I/O routine (t_{CPU}) is 1.058 msec. The application of this type of processing is only efficient if $t_{OVL} \gg t_{CPU}$ holds. Because it is difficult to measure the second index our aim was to find the places in the system where the value of t_{OVL} would be practically zero at the time of execution. This takes place in each case if there is no code in a process to be executed between the initiation of the transfer request without wait option and the issueing of the signal. We have found after a thorough analysis of the Supervisor code that in each case when a transfer is issued without wait option the value of t_{OVL} is zero. A small amount of code (8 instructions) was introduced into the kernel to suspend any P2 process issueing a non-communication transfer request. The process will be reactivated when the corresponding termination interrupt occurs. It can be seen from Table 5 that after the modification of the system the relative rate of WAIT I/O interrupts has decreased from 0.8536 to 0.7026 (a decrease of 17.68 %).

Table 5. Frequency of WAIT I/O calls

	Without modification	With modification
Total measurement time	13019	17497
Number of transfer requests Without the wait option (N)	371595	652132
Number of WAIT I/O calls (W)	317230	458188
Relative frequency of WAIT I/O calls (W/N)	0.8536	0.7026

Summary

The main purpose of the paper was to demonstrate the power of measurement techniques in the improvement of our knowledge of operating systems and in helping the users to tune the logically correct but inefficient parts of their systems.

References

[1] Adams, J.C., Millard, G.E., Performance Measurement on the Edinburgh Multi-Access System, Proc. of International Computing Symposium, Ed. E. Gelenbe and D. Potier North-Holland, 1975. 105-112

[2] Asztalos D., Performance measurement of operating Systems. OTSzK Közlemények 2, 1974 . (In Hungarian)

[3] Brinch-Hansen, P., Operating System Principles, Prentice-Hall, Englewood Cliffs, New Yersey, 1973

[4] Chiu, W., Dumont, D., Wood, R., Performance Analysis of a Multiprogrammed Computer System. IBM Journal of R&D , Vol.19 No.3. May 1975. 263-271

[5] Dijkstra, E.W., Hierarchical ordering of sequential processes. Acta Informatica 1,2,pp. 115-38. 1971.

[6] Hoare, C.A.R., Monitors: An Operating System Structuring Concept, CACM V17,N10, October 1974. 549-557

[7] Jalics, P.J., Lynch, W.C., Selected Measurements of the PDP-10 TOPS-10 Timesharing Operating System IFIP 74. Software Vol. 242-246.

[8] Shaw, A.C., The Logical Design of Operating Systems. Prentice-Hall, Englewood Cliffs, New Yersey, 1974

[9] Shelness, N.H.,Stephens, P.D., Whitfield, H., The Edinburgh Multi-Access System Scheduling and Allocation Procedures in the Resident Supervisor.in: Operating Systems, Proc. of an International Symposium, Ed. E. Gelenbe and C. Kaiser Springer Verlag, 1974. 293-310

Measuring, Modelling and Evaluating Computer Systems,
H. Beilner and E. Gelenbe, (eds.)
© North-Holland Publishing Company (1977)

A USER-ORIENTED APPROACH TO THE DESIGN OF DISTRIBUTED INFORMATION SYSTEMS

Giacomo Bucci *
Istituto di Elettronica and CIOC,
University of Bologna, Bologna, Italy

Donald N. Streeter
IBM Thomas J. Watson Research Center,
Yorktown Heights, New York, 10598, U.S.A.

INTRODUCTION

The ultimate objective of a computer system designer is to provide a system configuration which meets the user requirements at the least overall cost. However, as systems and usage become more complex, it becomes increasingly difficult for the designer to relate the effects of his choices and decisions to this ultimate objective.

In this paper we describe a macro-model of a computer system "in use", which is intended to provide the designer with a broader perspective in a constructive way. By constructive, we mean that the model provides practical guidance to the designer in making some of his decisions and tradeoffs, and that this guidance is consistent with the objectives of the user. The model describes the dynamics of the interdependency between system and interactive users in a way that permits assignment fo costs to the users' time as well as to the system rental and operation. Optimization of system configuration is then equated to the minimization of overall costs.

One advantage of our approach is that service levels and operating points (such as mean system response time or utilization factor), which are often specified more or less arbitrarily, are determined as outputs from our cost-minimization procedures.

In this paper our user-oriented approach is illustrated via application to the design of an interactive transaction processing system, focusing our attention on the class of systems in which a data base is used in responding one-line to queries from user terminals. IMS, CICS, IDS and TOTAL are well-known examples of systems providing this type of service. This application was chosen because of its

---

* This work has been done while G. Bucci was visiting IBM Thomas J. Watson Research Center

importance, and because of the richness of choices it presents to the system designer. In the process of searching for the optimal system configuration we explicitly evaluate whether or not gains can be achieved by distributing data and computer power throughout regional areas in which user terminals are located. We assume that the system is operated by an organization having branch offices scattered through a wide territorial area.

The assumption underlying this work is that people and organizations will generally prefer the system that helps them do their work for the least cost. Although we have tried to capture more of the relevant costs in this model than is usually done, we do not claim completeness. In any particular case therefore other, unquantified, factors must be considered in the decision-making process.

STATEMENT OF THE DESIGN PROBLEM

The design problem to which we shall apply our method is concerned with the location of data bases within a multi-location organization. Fundamentally, the motivating and forcing question behind our approach is whether a file should be located in one or more local computers instead of, or in addition to, a large centrally-located computer. Although the question is simply stated, many complex factors must be weighed in reaching a decision. They include:

- Communications costs.
- Economies of scale.
- Cost of replicated effort, staff or equipment in the case of multiple systems.
- Overhead costs of supervising large centralized systems.
- Economies of specialization.
- Congestion characteristics of various size system - effects on user waiting time.
- Probability and cost of service interruptions.
- Locality of data requirements. (Probability that local data base contains the data required to process any particular transaction.)
- Costs and delays of accessing, collating and processing data from multiple data bases in cases when some relevant data is not available locally.
- Cost and lead-time for user problem diagnosis, program modification or program developement.
- Flexibility to accommodate unanticipated future information requirements.

Now we will discuss some of these factors very briefly, giving references to more extensive publications:

1) Communications Costs. Costs of data communications obviously can be reduced if adequate processing capability is placed at each location, provided the data is also available locally, without duplication. References |1|, |2|, |3| describe and give cost data for various types and capacities of data transmission services. If multiple copies of data are maintained, communications costs may increase with decentralization due to file updating costs. References |4| and |5| address this problem.

2) Economies of Scale. Computing hardware systems have characteristically exhibited economies of large scale production |6|, |7|. Simply stated, this means that total costs increase less tha proportionately as capacity increases, over some range of capacities. Some more recent tests based on benchmarks report a reduction

in the magnitude of hardware scale benefits as computer technology matures |8|.

3) Cost of Replicated Effort, Staff or Equipment. As computer cost/performance improves, personnel costs (for operations and software support) assume a larger portion of the costs of providing computer services. It has been observed that there are pronounced "economies of scale" for computer personnel |9| that really result from the elimination of replicated effort or replicated competence. In a similar fashion, certain components such as disk storage units must be replicated to store the multiple copies of certain data. When organizations determine the total costs of computer services, including these replication effects along with a "true" economies of scale, they usually conclude that consolidation can provide savings for at least some part of the computing workload |10|, |11|, |12|.

4) Overhead Costs. The complexity of a computing installation is a function both of size, and diversity of applications and services. As the complexity increases, two kinds of overhead costs appear. One is the cost of special personnel and tools required to manage the more complex center. The other kind of overhead is the cost of machine time expended in housework and management of greater complexity.

5) Economies of Specialization. One means of coping with complexity and the resulting overheads is to partition the workload and the data base, and to provide services form smaller, functionally specialized systems. In many cases, the "economies of specialization" more than compensate for any diseconomies of scale |7|, |13|. Minicomputers |14|, intelligent terminals |15|, specialized application subsystems |16| are some of the means of realizing this specialization.

6) Congestion Effects. If transactions arrive at the computer non-uniformly in time, as is usually the case, a degradation in performance (response time) results from subdividing a certain amount of computing capacity into smaller computing units. This scaling effect is described in references |18| and |19|. If a delay cost is associated with the waiting time of the users, then aggregation of computing capacity provides a "statistical economy of scale".

7) Probability and Cost of Service Interruptions. If all of the computing resources of an organization are centralized, remote locations may suffer too great a cost from communication line or central site service interruptions. Delay cost functions can be determined for certain types of computer-dependent functions |20|. In many cases, enough computing capacity is retained at each remote site to perform essential functions when network access is interrupted |12|, |16|. Such hybrid organization tend to complicate problems of data location.

Several attempts have been made to deal with this problem by developing a means of trade-off analysis between the various factors |5|, |19|, |21|, |26|. This paper is another such attempt, dealing broadly, and approximately, with many of the factors involved.

DESCRIPTION OF THE BASIC MODEL

The analysis of this paper starts with a model of an interactive transaction processing system. The model is used to show that, for a given system capacity and for a given application, there is an optimal level of loading and level of concurrent usage that keeps the cost per transaction at minimum. The search for the optimal solution is then extended to cover a range of variation of computer power. The problem of data base partitioning is then considered.

As mentioned earlier we shall consider only systems for interactive processing that allow the user to carry out his own work by engaging a man-machine conversation, based on message exchange, in which a data base is queried and/or updated. We shall call a transaction the operations that are triggered by a user message and satisfied by the corresponding computer response.

Multiprogramming is a common practive in these transaction processing systems. Application programs are stored on a storage device. Each type of input message uniquely identifies the application program(s) that must be loaded into main memory and executed to yield the proper response. Usually, application programs reduce to a sequence of calls to specific subroutines of the data management facility, which is a software package provided with the system to handle items belonging to the data base. Processing an input message implies searching and sometimes updating the data base. Since only a very small portion of the data base can be contained in main memory, each transaction gives rise to a certain number of Input/Output operations.

Because our objective is to study an entire class of systems, we must choose a model general enough to fit any system belonging to it, that is, we need a gross model. As a result the model will at best only approximate the behavior of a particular system. The model we shall make use in the following is, with minor variation, that described in reference |22|. As the authors Boyse and Warn state in that paper, the accuracy of the model in a given situation depends on how the modeled system matches model assumptions and on the validity of input parameters. This is actually true for <u>any</u> model. In their particular case, there is indeed a close match between model prediction and system performance. Besides its generality, the model is understandable and easy to use. It should be noted that, in our context, the model is not intended to represent any specific system. Moreover, because of extensions we introduce, it captures certain aspects of time-shared systems.

A picture of the extended model is shown in Figure 1. We suppose that a population of N active users interacts with the system through terminals. A transaction is divided into two phases. The first phase refers to the time the user spends to prepare and to input his message; the second to the time spent waiting for and receiving service from the system. These intervals are called think-time and response time respectively. The average think-time is designated by Z, the average response time is designated by R.

In order to process an input message the related programs must be loaded into main memory. We assume that once a program has been loaded, it will be held in main memory as long as the processing of the input message is not completely terminated. Furthermore, we assume a fixed level of multiprogramming M, so that the dashed box of Figure 1 always contains M programs, circulating between CPU and I/O processors and competing for the use of these resources. During its life time, a transaction requires an average number P of I/O operations. In other words, a program relinquishes the CPU P times in order to acquire (sometimes to write) data from (into) auxiliary storage. We make the usual assumption that the number of instructions executed by the processor for transaction processing between two con-

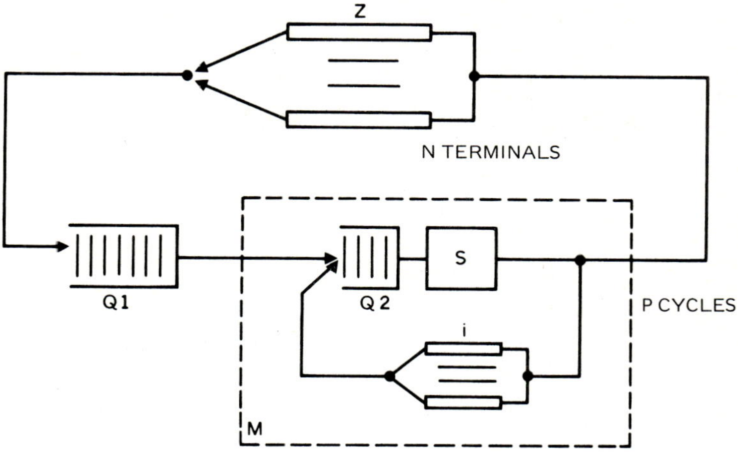

Figure 1

secutive I/O operations has an exponential distribution with mean value $1/\mu o$. It is assumed that no queue occurs at the I/O devices and that the mean service time for an I/O request is i, again assuming an exponential distribution. Thus, inside the dashed box of Figure 1, only queue Q2 exists. From the preceding discussion it is clear that the queue Q1 holds the input messages whose programs are waiting to be entered into main memory.

We extended the model to include the effect of overhead by assuming that, when task switching occurs, a certain amount of CPU time is expended in operations which cannot be considered useful work on behalf of transaction processing.

The total overhead time per task-switch is computed as the sum of two terms. The first term is a time "to" that is assumed to be constant no matter how fast the machine is. Its value depends on the complexity and level of technology to which the machine belongs. The rationale for this statement is that hardware and software complexity have tended to increase in the same way the computer power increases. The second term is the overhead time due to multiprogramming. It is quantified by assuming that, for each task switch, the processor has to perform a number of instructions proportional to M. Figure 2 is a schematization of the preceding concepts in terms of elapsed time. Computer speed is indicated by S, thus $(v1*M)/S$ is the overhead time spent for multiprogramming. As a result, the total CPU time spent in each cycle is given by the following expression

$$c = 1/(\mu o*S) + (v1*M)/S + to \qquad (1)$$

It is convenient to designate with $co = 1/(\mu o*S)$ the time spent in each cycle in processing the input message and to rewrite (1) as

$$c = co*(1 + m1*M + mo*S) \qquad (2)$$

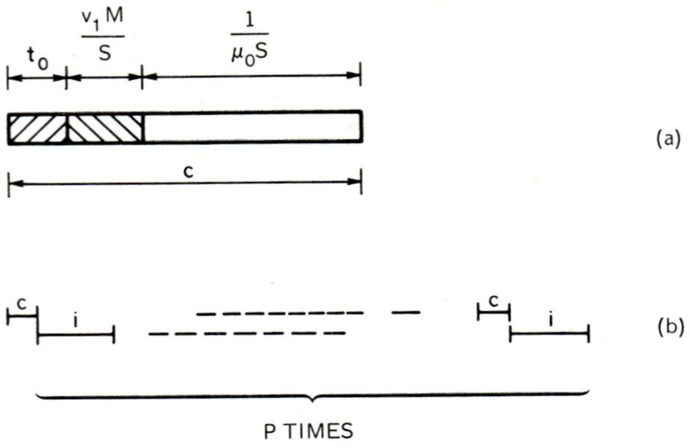

Figure 2

which shows more esplicitly the effect of overhead factors. The time c is still assumed to be exponentially distributed. The meaning of the two coefficients ml and mo is evident. The total average CPU time per transaction is then C = c*P.

If we focus our attention to the closed loop inside the dashed box of Figure 1, we recognize that the cyclic queueing system therein corresponds to the repairman model |23|. The meaning of M, c and i is obvious and we can easily compute the CPU utilization (that, for reasons to follow, we denote Umax), using the following formula:

$$U_{max} = 1 - \frac{1}{\sum_{k=0}^{M} \frac{M!}{(M-k)!} \left(\frac{c}{i}\right)^k} \tag{3}$$

If we are in a situation in which the queue Q1 never empties, we can use the computed value of Umax to determine system throughput and system response time in the way followed in reference |22|.

Since we are going to study the system behavior as a function of the number of terminals, we have to consider also the effect of queue Q1. To this end, we simplify the model by observing that, because of the internal congestion, the system can be thought of as a single server with mean service time C' = C/Umax, operating on the stream of input messages. Thus we replace the model of Figure 1 with the "equivalent" model of Figure 3, which again is the repairman model.

We now compute the utilization of this system as

$$U' = 1 - \frac{1}{\sum_{k=0}^{N} \frac{N!}{(N-k)!} \left(\frac{C}{Z}\right)^k} \tag{4}$$

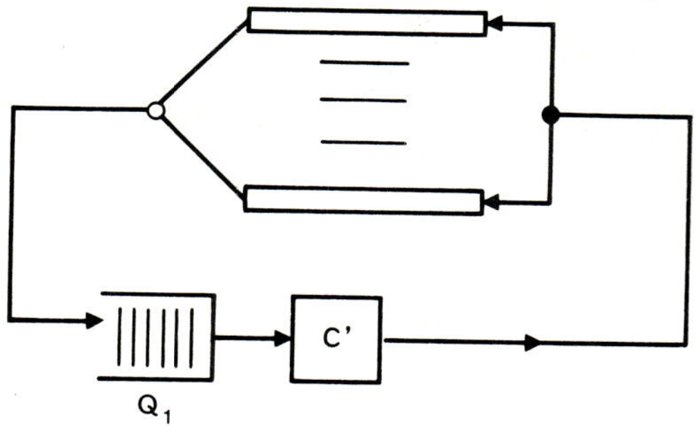

Figure 3

Thus the response time is

$$R = C'*N/U' - Z = C*N/U - Z \tag{5}$$

where U = U'*Umax.

The system throughput, i.e., the number of transactions processed per second, is then given by

$$THRU = C'/C' = U/C \tag{6}$$

whereas the number of messages in the system is

$$L = N - Z*U'/C' = N - Z*U/C$$

It shoulded be noted that, in using the simplified model of Figure 3, we introduce an error for the following reason: Recall that Umax was calculated in (3) based on the assumption that the queue Q1 never empties. Therefore additional messages are always available to maintain the multiprogramming level at M. When we proceed to determine in Equation (4) the performace of the overall system loaded by a finite number of terminals, the utilization is further reduced-precisely because Q1 sometimes does empty. The magnitude of the error introduced by this inconsistency is small provided the $P \gg 1$ and Probability $[L > M] \approx 1$, as shown in reference |24|. These conditions are satisfied in many problems of practical interest.

USE OF THE BASIC MODEL

We now use the model described above in a case study to find the number of terminals that minimizes the cost per transaction.

To begin we imagine an application in which the average transaction is characterized by the following parameters.

$1/\mu o$ = 10,000 instructions/cycle;
P = 10 cycles/transaction.

The mean user think-time is Z = 15 seconds.

The application is implemented on a machine having a speed S = 1,000,000 Instr/Sec (i.e., S = 1 MIP). The degree of multiprogramming is M = 3. We further assume that overhead factors have the following values

$$m1 = .2$$
$$m0 = .2 \times 10^{-6}$$

Thus we have:

$$c = .018 \text{ sec.}$$

The average time required for an I/O operation is assumed to be i = .030 sec.

Computation of Umax gives Umax = .84, thus

$$C' = C/Umax = .18/.84 = .214 \text{ sec.}$$

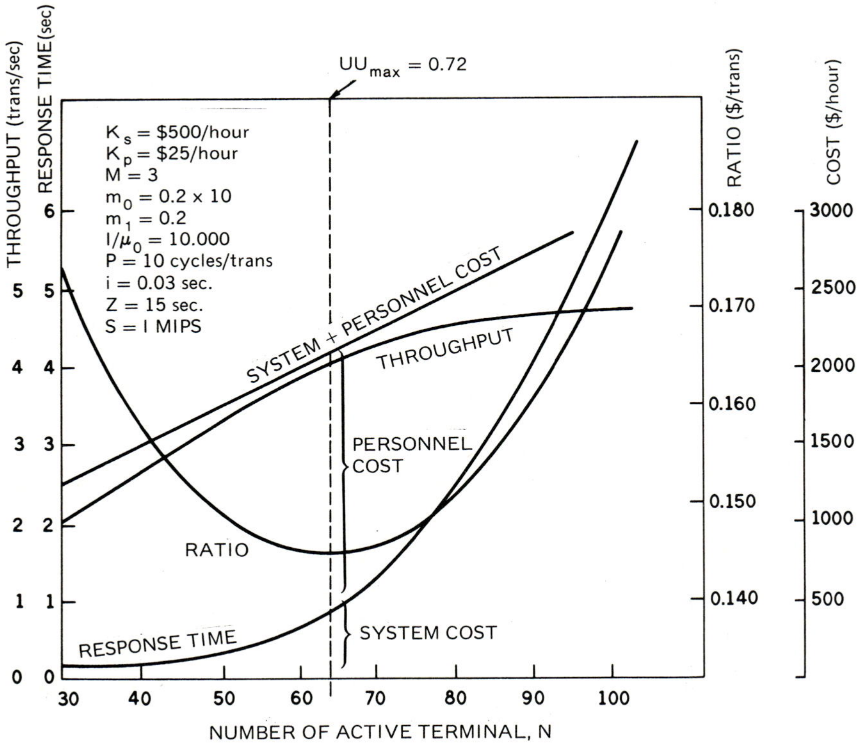

Figure 4

The next step is to introduce the economic aspects of the problem. The following considerations are in order. The total expenditure for employing the system can be divided into two parts. The first is the cost of the system. It includes not only hardware and software costs, but also the cost of personnel running the installation and all other administrative costs. For the purposes of this study we shall assume this cost to be Ks = $500/hour.

The second part includes the cost of interactive terminals and the cost of personnel working of them. This personnel is assumed to carry out clerical work and its unit cost is assumed to be as much as Kp = $25/hour/active terminal. For N active terminals, the total expenditure rate is then simply given by:

Total Cost/ Hour = Ks + KpN

The problem of finding the optimal number of terminals is then the problem of the optimal balance of system and user resources in the process.

By using Equations (3) through (6), it is now possible to determine the system behaviour and the cost per transaction for different loading conditions, that is, for different numbers of active terminals connected to the system. In Figure 4, curves are plotted as a function of N for: (1) system response time, (2) system throughput, (3) total cost per hour and (4) RATIO between the total cost and the system throughput, expressed in dollars per transaction.

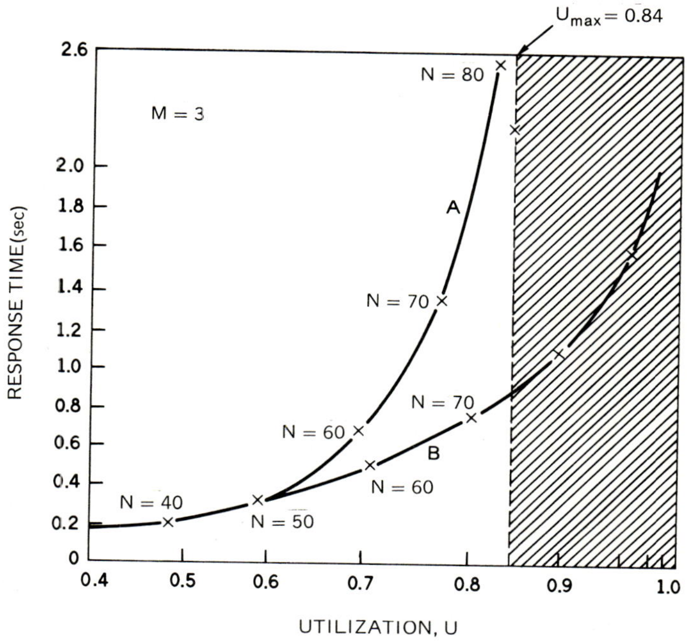

Figure 5

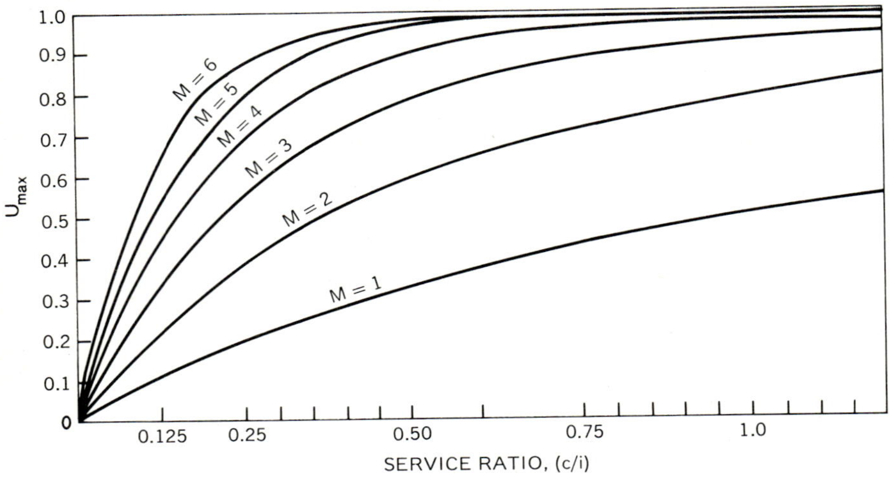

Figure 6

It can be observed that RATIO has a pronounced minimum. In other words, a value exists for N which optimizes the allocation of the resources involved in using the computer system. In this case study, this value of N is approximately 64. The related processor utilization is U = .72.

Before concluding this discussion it may be worthwhile to summarize how these results have been obtained through the use of the model. We started by using the model of Figure 1 to compute the effect of I/O contention on CPU utilization. In this way we established an upper bound for CPU utilization. Then we used this bound to set the service time of the equivalent server of Figure 3 to find system throughput. Figure 5 explains the effect of internal congestion on response time. Curve A has been drawn by plotting the response time of Figure 4 against CPU utilization and marking some points on the curve with the corresponding values of N. It can be seen that, as the number of active terminals increases, the curve approaches the vertical line corresponding to U = Umax. Curve B is the response time for a system like that of Figure 3, but with a mean service time C instead of C' = C/Umax. The shaded zone of Figure 5 represents the range of CPU utilization that can never be achieved, that is, the portion of CPU power which is lost because of I/O service requirements. Figure 6 shows the dependency of Umax on c/i and M. The model of Figure 3 has received much attention in the past. In particular, as shows in |18|, when the system is lightly loaded there is little mutual interference among terminals; whereas, after the saturation point has been reached each additional terminal added to the system completely interferes with the other users. As a result the throughput curve has the shape shown in Figure 4, which in turn determines a minimum for RATIO.

THE EXTENDED MODEL

The foregoing discussion dealt with the miminization of the cost per transaction for a system of a given capacity. We now extend the search for the optimal solution to a wide range of possible speed values, by computing for each S the value if minimal RATIO. In this way we can find whether or not a system capacity exists that allows the implementation of a given application at maximum cost-effectiveness. In this process we implicitly assume that machines are directly comparable. In other woerds, we imagine an idealized series of computers, in which all machines have the same instruction set and only differ in processor speed. This is quite an abstraction of market reality and has been approximately verified only within a series like IBM/370. However, techniques exist to compare effectiveness of different systems |25|. We further assume the machine speed is a continuous variable within the range of our interest.

Traditionally |6|, the cost-effectiveness relationship between members of a family of computing systems has been expressed in the form:

$$\text{Cost} = \text{Constant} \times (\text{Capacity})^{\alpha}.$$

When the cost-capacity exponent, α, take on the value 0.5, the relationship is often referred to as Grosch's law, after Herbert R. Grosch who first asserted its validity in the 1940's.

In terms of the parameters of our model, the expression takes the form:

$$\text{Cost} = Ks(S)^{\alpha}.$$

Where Ks is the total cost of a system having a capacity of 1 MIP. In our usage this cost includes everything but the cost of communication lines, terminals and personnel using the terminals. Included costs cover: hardware, operations and support personnel, floor space, supplies and utilities. Costs are measured in \$/hour. The value of α is still an object of debate in the current literature. In the following we shall assume that it lies between .5 and 1. The lower bound corresponding to the economies of scale as observed in (6), the upper bound corresponding to the lack of economies of scale as observed in (8) for the hardware costs of commercial computation.

To carry out this part of the study an APL program has been implemented which iterates, for a given range of S, the process of optimization described in the preceding paragraph.

Figure 7 shows results for α = .8 and for values of the other parameters (except M) as before. The curve MINRATIO is the locus of minimal RATIO's. This curve is the evenlope of all curves that can be drawn for RATIO in the range .1 MIPS - 3.5 MIPS.

The values of M and N are an outcome of the optimization process. It can be seen that for (approximately) the interval .9 MIPS - 1.6 MIPS, the optimal level of multiprogramming is M = 4. Outside this interval, the values of minimal RATIO that are obtained for M = 4 are higher than those that are obtained for M = 3 on the left for M = 5 on the right. This explains why the RATIO curve shows cusp-like

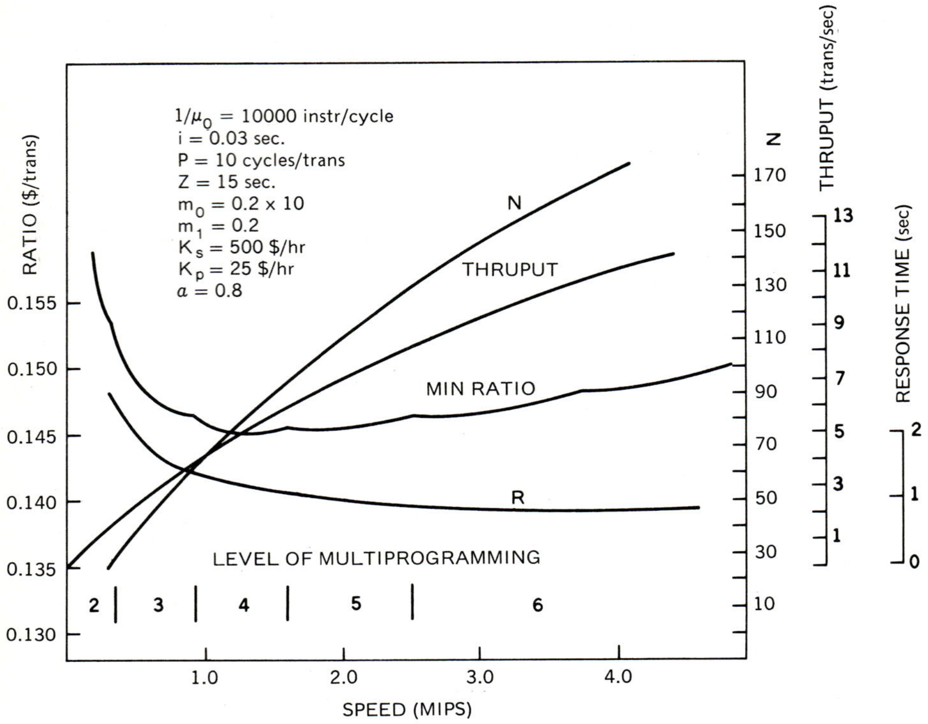

Figure 7

irregularities, which occur at values of S limiting ranges of optimal multiprogramming levels.

Figure 7 shows that MINRATIO has a minimum around S = 1.3 MIPS. This means that the system capacity S = 1.3 MIPS determines the most cost-effective implementation of the given application. Indeed systems with higher or lower capacities can not be configured to perform that well. The system throughput obtained with such machine speed is approximately 5 transactions per second.

In Figure 7 note that the cost per transaction remains within a few percent of the absolute minimum over a wide range of system speed, under the assumed conditions. Within this range |13|, the modest economies of scale are approximately balanced by the overhead factors.

Curves of Figure 7 permit an immediate solution to the basic design problem, i.e., the choice of computer capacity that allows the system to produce a certain throughput volume while keeping the cost at minimum. Indeed, if for a given application a throughput T is required the value of optimal system capacity is directly read on horizontal axis, whereas the curve N gives the number of active terminals to be connected to the system in order to produce T. The cost per transaction is then read on MINRATIO and the optimal multiprogramming levels are identified. Notice that this method makes system throughput the basic design constraint. This is in perfect accord with our desire to provide usage-related performance figures to allow intelligent system choices. As a result, the response time is an outcome of this optimum design process. Later on we shall use this method to explore the feasibility of a distributed system.

MODEL SENSITIVITY

We now turn our attention to explore the dependency of preceding results on various secondary parameters.

In Figure 8, a family of MINRATIO curves is drawn for α = .5, .7, .8 and 1. The remaining parameters are as before. It can be seen that the value of Grosch's exponent has a strong influence in determining the speed for which the minimum occurs. Pronounced economies of scale determine a lower minimum and call for employment of large capacity systems. With α = 1 the minimum is for S = .6 MIPS, while

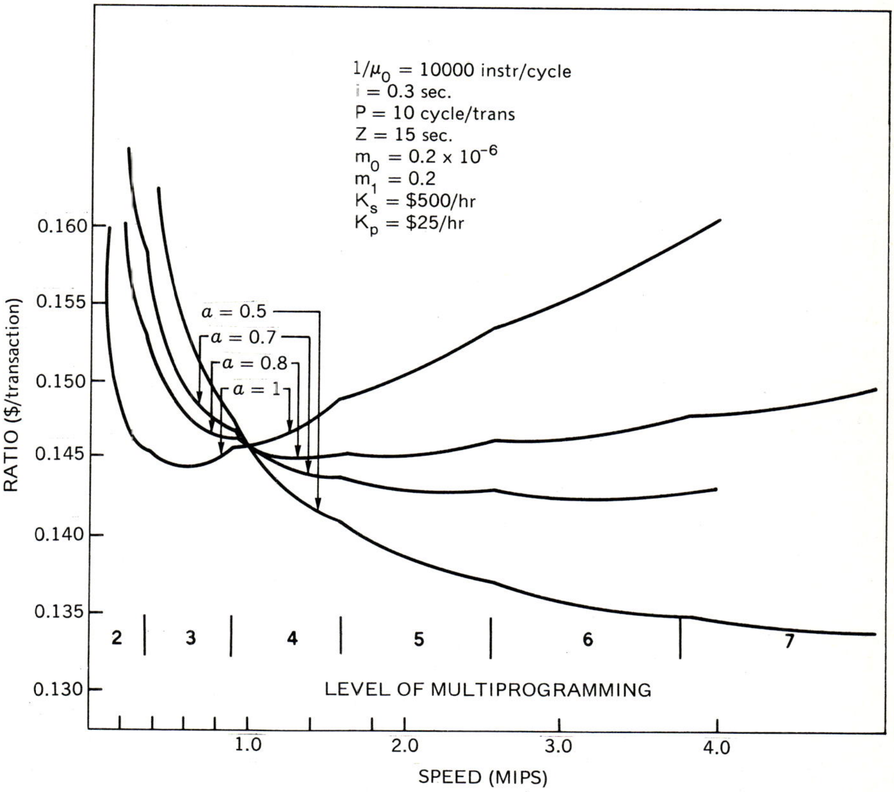

Figure 8

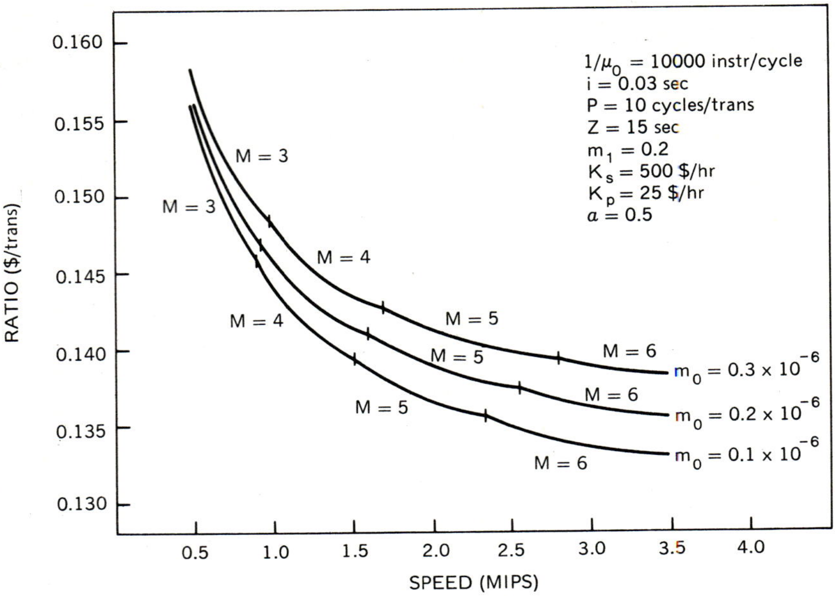

Figure 9

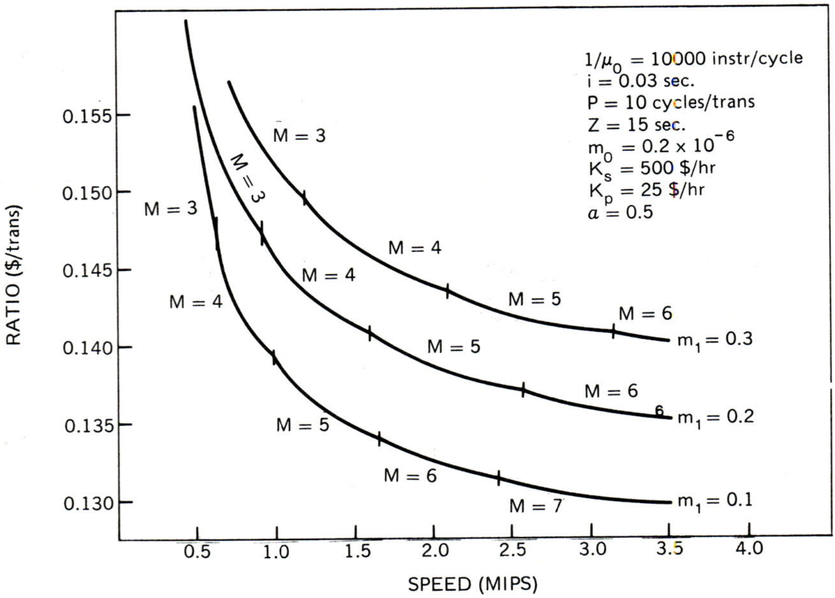

Figure 10

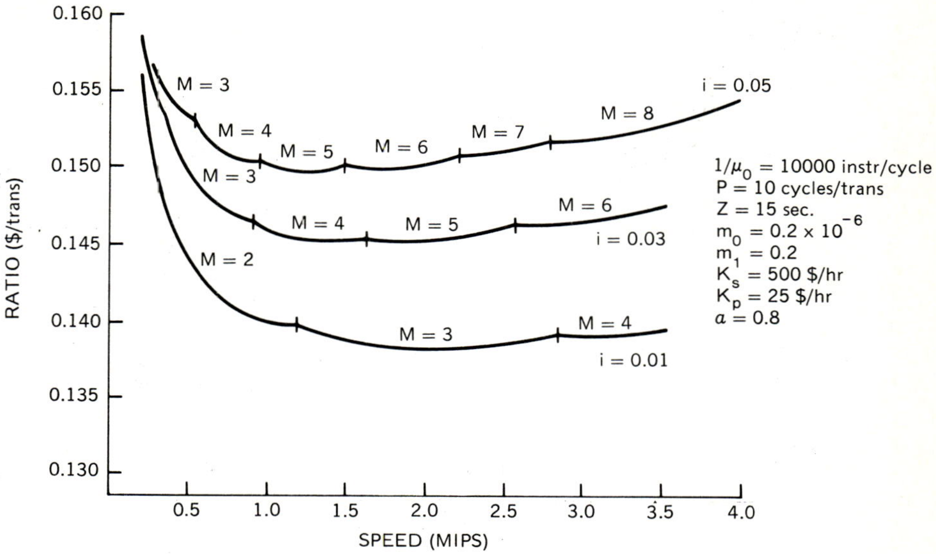

Figure 11

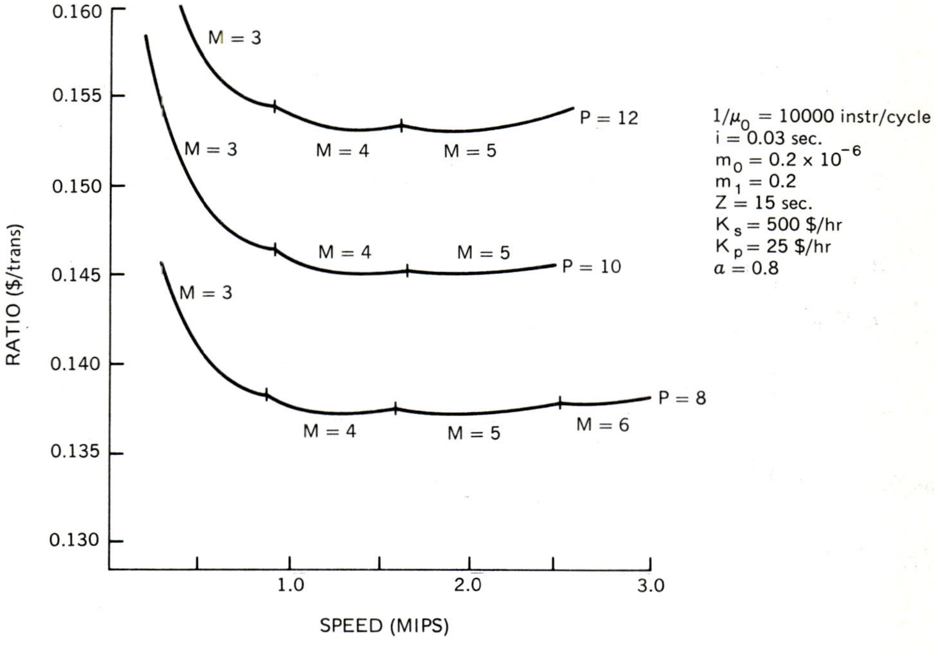

Figure 12(a)

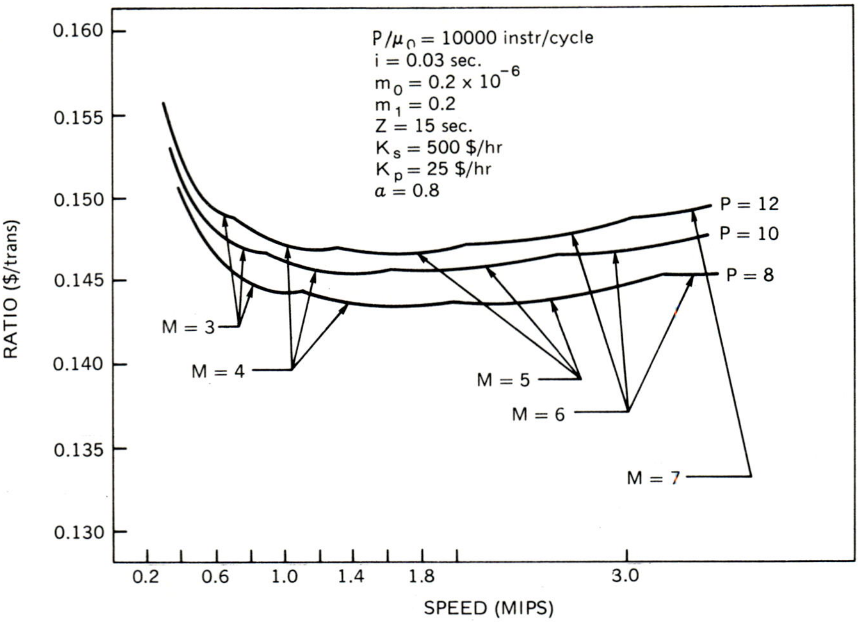

Figure 12(b)

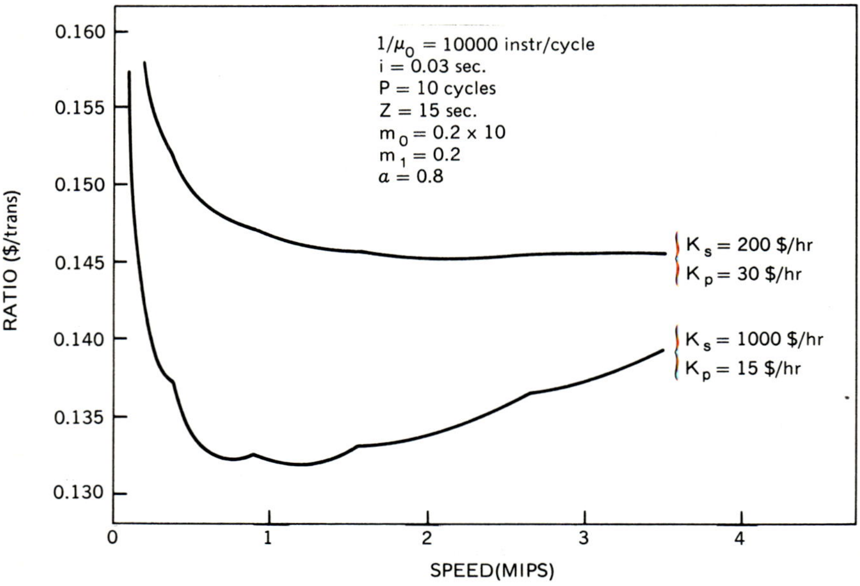

Figure 13

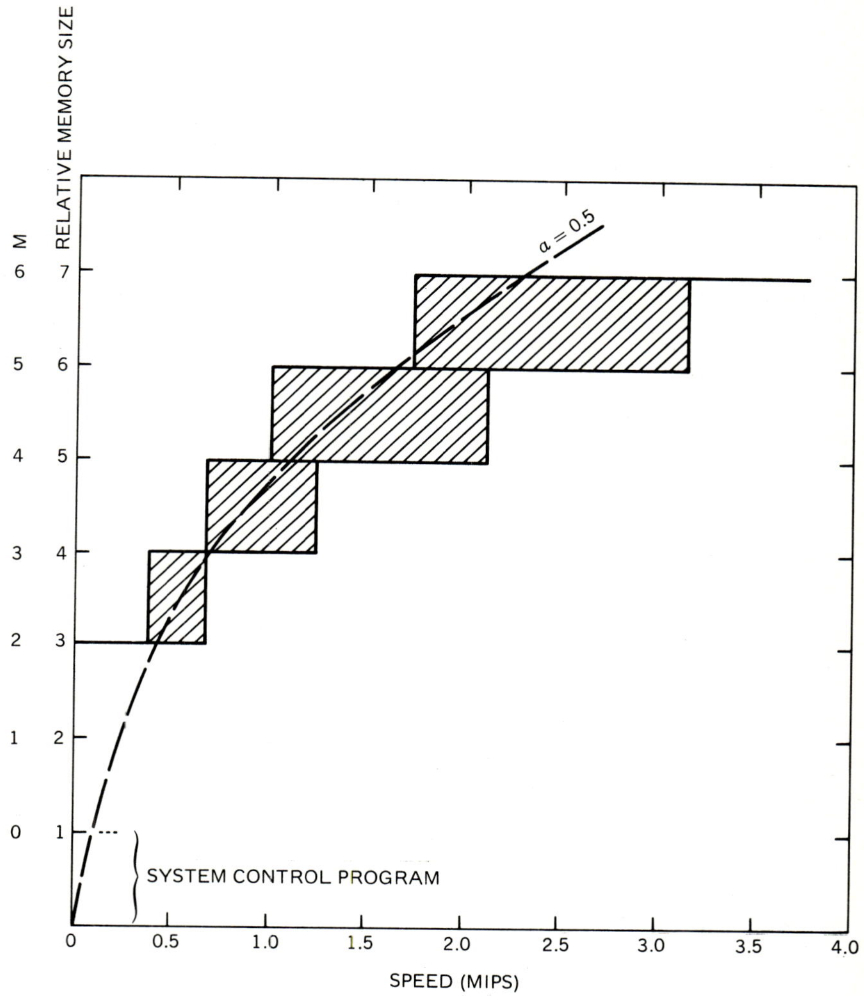

Figure 14

with α = .5 the minimum is for about S = 10 MIPS. This latter speed is higher than is generally available presently; nevertheless, the value of this analysis is not diminished, since it shows that there is an upper bound for cost effectiveness, whatever are economies of scale, provided our assumptions about the nature of overhead are correct.

Figure 9 and 10 show the effect of overhead factors. The influence of I/O time is given by Figure 11. Notice that the curves have essentially the same shape. This suggests that, although a faster I/O device increases system cost-effectiveness, preceding results are still qualitatively valid, no matter how fast the device is.

Figure 12 shows the effect of the number of cycles (i.e., I/O accesses) per transaction, a parameter which basically depends on data base organization. The results of Figure 12a are calculated assuming the number of instructions per cycle remains constant, whereas the results of Figure 12b assume that instructions per transaction remain constant.

The influence of cost coefficients is given by Figure 13. It is easy to prove that the minimum value for MINRATIO is approximately proportional to Kp, whereas, the flatness of the curve depends on the ratio Ks/Kp. The lower Ks/Kp, the flatter the curve and the more the minimum moves to right side, favouring large capacities.

Finally, in Figure 14 is shows an outcome of the preceding analysis. The step function here depicted represents the dimension of required memory, under the assumption that each application program and the control program as well occupy a partition of the same size. The curve can be fitted with an exponential function with exponent close to 0.5. Shaded regions indicate the range of variation produced in this step function by the parameter variations just described. In fact, as pointed out by Figure 11 and Figure 12, the optimal degree of multiprogramming is much influenced by P and i.

A CASE STUDY OF DISTRIBUTION VERSUS CENTRALIZATION

So far, in studying the economics of a single computer installation, we have been able to determine the processor capacity that keeps the cost per transaction at the lowest attainable level, while providing the required system throughput. We now attack the problem of deciding the conditions under which a distributed system can be more cost-effective than a centralized one.

We assume that the interactive transaction processing system to be designed must serve a territorial area in which clusters of terminals can be located, corresponding to branch offices or groups of branch offices. If the system is implemented as a centralized one, the entire data base is stored at the central location to which all communication lines converge. Thus we assume that in the centralized case a communication cost δ is associated with the execution of a transaction. The case of distributed system is more complex, since data items referred in a transaction may or may not be found on the subsystem to which the terminal originating the transaction is connected. Again, we need a certain degree of simplification. Hence, we assume that the data base is partitioned in the following way: (1) data items referred by a particular transaction are all allocated to the same partition and (2) if a transaction refers to data items which are not stored at the subsystem to which the terminal belongs, then the partition contains sufficient information to establish the identity of the subsystem at which these data are stored. We further assume (3) that the communication cost associated to a transaction which is processed on a local computer is zero, whereas, if the transaction must be routed to a remote sybsystem, then, because of hypothesis (1) and (2), the communication cost is δ. Finally, in the distributed case, we assume (4) that the processing necessary to service a transaction is equally divided between the subsystems involved.

Let us now call p the probability that a typical user terminal finds its data at its local subsystem. Then 1 - p is the probability that the transaction must be routed to another subsystem. Hence the communication cost per transaction in the

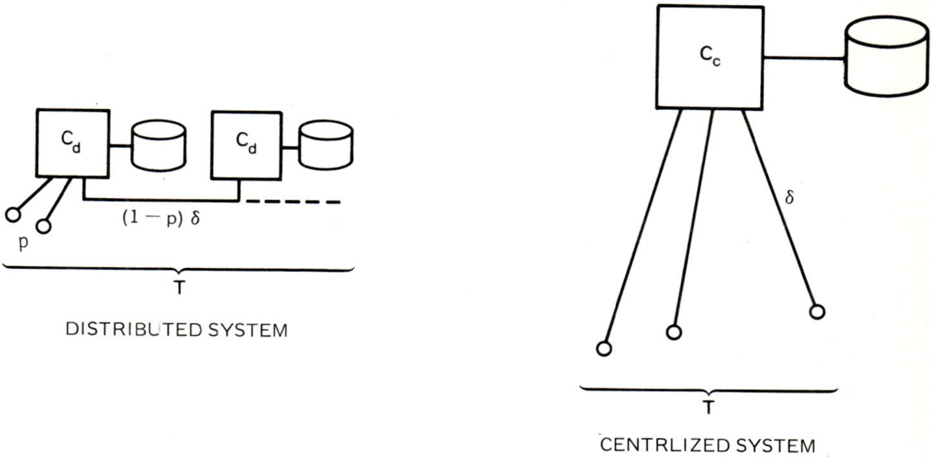

Figure 15

distributed solution is (1 - p)δ. We now compare the centralized so-ution to the distributed one under the constraint that both must provide the same throughput T (in transactions per unit time) and with the assumption that the workload is e-qually divided among n subsystems. Figure 15 is a schematization of preceding as-sumptions. Each subsystem must then provide the throughput

$$T/n + (1 - p)T/n$$

that is

$$(2 - p)T/n.$$

The effective throughput of the distributed system is then

$$(2 - p)T.$$

Now, let us call Cc the cost of processing a transaction in a centralized system that provides a throughput T. Similarly, Cd is the cost of processing a transac-tion in a subsystem that provides a throughput (2 - p)T/n. The value of Cc and Cd can be obtained from the RATIO curves of Figures 7, 8, ff. Notice that it is not required that the same curves are used in determining Cd and Cc. In fact, seconda-ry parameters can be different because of the different level of complexity of a subsystem respect to the centralized one.

In a centralized system the total cost per transaction is then

$$Cc + \delta.$$

In the distributed system the cost per transaction is given by

$$pCd + (1 - p)(2Cd + \delta)$$
$$= (2 - p)Cd + (1 - p)\delta.$$

The relative cost of distributed solution versus the centralized one is finally given by:

$$\text{RELCOST}\left(\frac{\text{DISTRIBUTED}}{\text{CENTRALIZED}}\right) = \frac{(2 - p)Cd + (1 - p)\delta}{Cc + \delta}$$

This relative cost is plotted in Figure 16 as a function of the probability of local "hit" and for different values of Cd, Cc and δ.

The above example assumed that all the data required to respond to a particular transaction would be completely contained within one of the data bases. There is another class of transactions that requires summary data drawn from each of a number of data bases. If, in this case, data must be drawn from each of J data bases

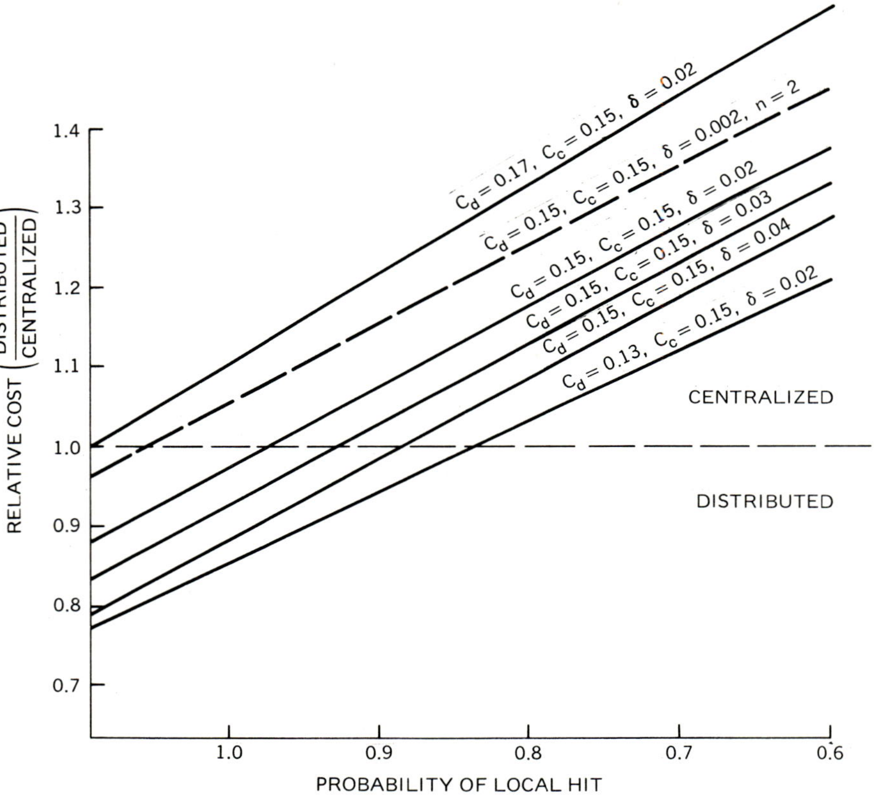

Figure 16

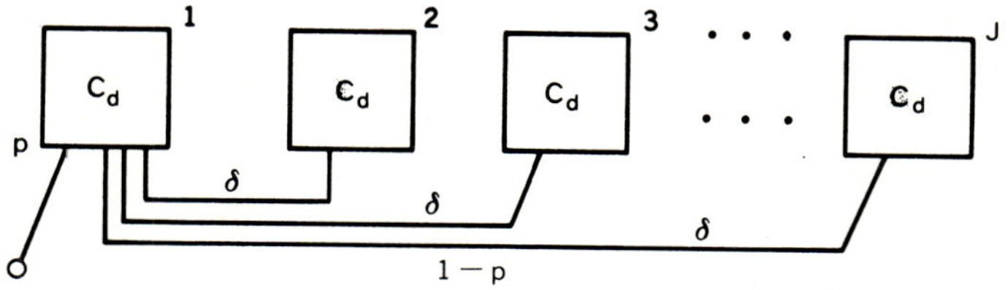

Figure 17(a)

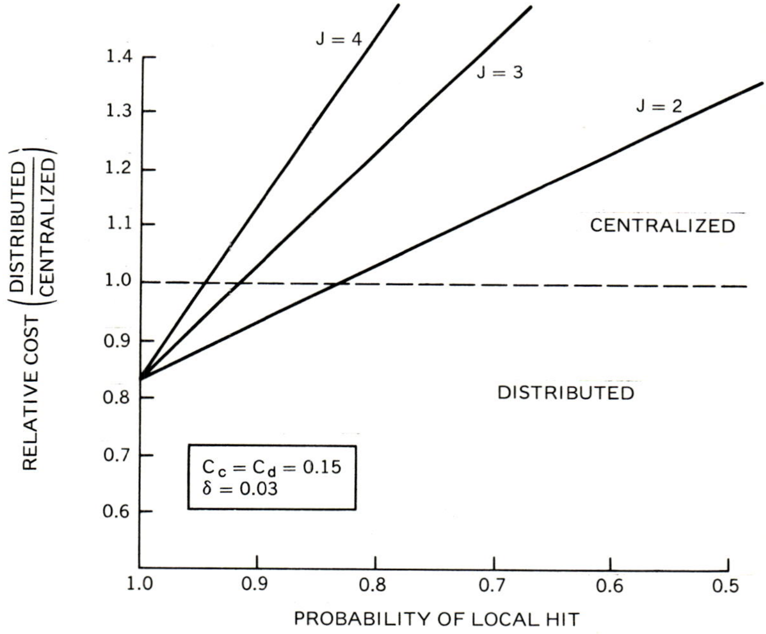

Figure 17(b)

in (1 - p) of the transactions, (as shows schematically in Figure 17a), then the relative transaction processing cost of the centralized distribution configurations is given by:

$$\text{REL. COST}\left(\frac{\text{DISTRIBUTED}}{\text{CENTRALIZED}}\right)$$

$$= \frac{C_d}{C_c + \delta}\,[J - p(J - 1)] + \frac{\delta}{C_c + \delta}\,(J - 1)\,(1 - p)$$

Some results of evaluating this expression are shown in Figure 17b.

Another arrangement of the data bases is as shown in Figure 18a. Using this hierarchic organization, we assume that the data base at the central site contains copies of the local data bases resident at each of the local sites. In this case, a transaction unable to find necessary data locally would be referred to the central site, rather than to one or more of the other local systems. The schematic of this arrangement is shown in Figure 18a. The corresponding relative cost relationship is given by

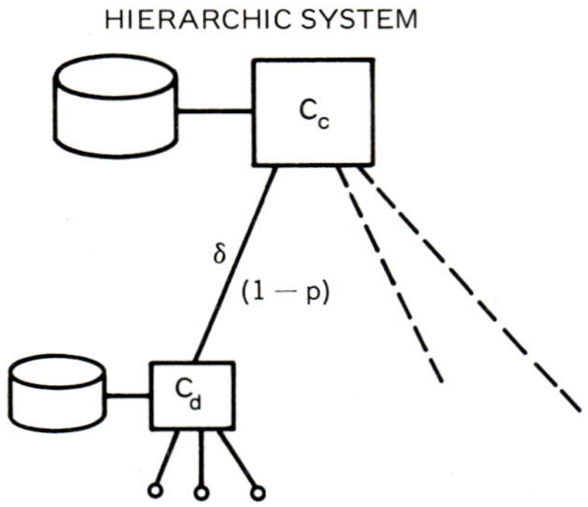

Figure 18(a)

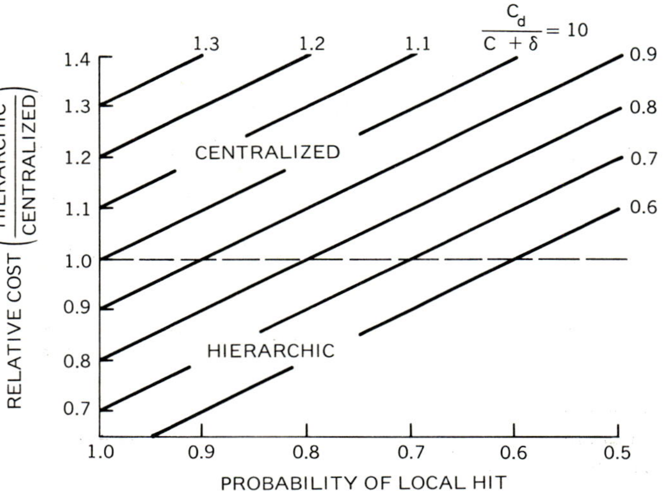

Figure 18(b)

$$\text{REL. COST}\left(\frac{\text{HIERARCHIC}}{\text{CENTRALIZED}}\right) = \frac{\delta}{C_C + \delta} + (1 - p).$$

The results of evaluating this relation are displayed in Figure 18b.

CONCLUSIONS, CAUTIONS AND FUTURE WORK

We have described an approach to the design of complex information systems. Our approach conceives of a computer system as a server having a theoretical capacity which is only partially available for use, due to internal congestion as well as randomness and finiteness of loading. We decompose this compound degradation problem, treating first the limitation imposed by internal congestion and then determining the additional degradation due to workload limitation. If we assign cost rates to system operation and user time, and account for the system utilization consumed by supervisory tasks, we can then find the cost-minimizing levels of loading and multiprogramming and the corresponding response time and throughput.

Newt, assuming the relative cost/performance of the members of a family of systems to be describable by a scale parameter α, (such that overall system costs are proportional to capacity raised to the power α), we can apply our cost-minimization across the family of systems. This analysis permits the determination of "basic transaction processing costs" as executed by various size systems within a family.

To study the additional costs deriving from the degree of partitioning and geographic distribution of data, communications costs and costs of accessing multiple data bases are considered in conjunction with the basic processing costs.

The relative overall cost of centralized or distributed transaction processing is then the resultant of all the above system and usage parameters and costs. The relative advantage is shown to be critically dependent on the locality of required data; that is, on the practical partitionability of the data base.

The model described in this paper, being based on many particularizing and simplifying assumptions represents a gross simplification of a real system. We believe, however, that such models, judiciously used, can be helpful in the process of designing complex systems. Some of the limitations of our model, in its present state are as follows:

— A particular structure of the overhead is used arbitrarily, for the sake of exposition. The actual structure would have to be substituted for any real system.
— Only very simple cases of data distribution and searching have been considered. The assignment of communications and processing costs has been idealized for purposes of exposition, and would have to be complicated in many cases to provide sufficient accuracy.
— The cost/time effects of service interruptions and of program development or modification have not been included in this paper.

References

|1| M. Schwartz, et. al.: Terminal-Oriented Computer-Communication Networks, Proc. IEEE (Nov. 1972), 1408-1423.

|2| A. D. Hall, Ed.: Economies of Scale in Communications Systems, 5 papers in IEEE Transactions on Systems, Man and Cybernetics, Vol. SMC-5, No. 1, (Jan. 1975).

|3| N. Abramson and F. F. Kuo, Eds.: Computer-Communication Networks, Prentice--Hall, Englewood Cliffs, N.Y. (1973).

|4| R. G. Casey: The Optimal Allocation of Files in a Network, SJCC (1972).

|5| H. R. Howson, L. R. Amey and W. D. Thorp: Research and Development of Parametric Cost Models to Evaluate Strategies in the Design of a National Data Bank Network, McGill U. Working Paper (1975). (Available from McGill U. Faculty of Management, Montreal, Que., Canada.)

|6| W. F. Sharpe: The Economics of Computers, Columbia University Press, (1969), 314-362.

|7| K. Roger Moore: Economics of the Network Marketplace, EASTCON 1974 Record (October 1974), 294-302.

|8| R. J. Littrell: Economies of Scale in the IBM 360 and 370, Datamation (March 1974), 83-88.

|9| M. B. Solomon: Economies of Scale and Computer Personnel, Datamation (March 1970), 107-110.

|10| E. Giesa: Planning for the Corporate Data Processing Consodilation Venture, Proc. of the 2nd Annual ACM SIGCOSIM Symposium, Gaithersburg, Maryland (Oct. 1971).

|11| E. Seals and S. M. Drezner: A Computer Centralization Cost Model for Conceptual Design, Rand Report R-1268-PR, Santa Monica, Ca. 90406 (Sept. 1973).

|12| P. E. Zara: An ADP Manager's View of the Confluence of Data Processing and Telecommunications, 1974 Nationale Telecommunications Record (Dec. 1974), IEEE Pub. 74 CHO 902-7 CSCB, 468-475.

|13| E. Stefferud: Economics of Network Delivery of Computer Services, 2nd USA--JAPAN Computer Conference, Tokyo, Japan (Aug. 1975), 523-531.

|14| E. M. Aupperle, Ed.: Special Issue on Minicomputers, Proceedings of the IEEE (Nov. 1973).

|15| R. V. Dickenson. Ed.: Distributed Intelligence in Terminal Systems, 3 articles in IEEE Computer (Nov./Dec. 1971), 17.

|16| Special Issue on Supermarket and Retail Store Systems Journal, Vol. 14, No. 1 (1975).

|17| D. N. Streeter: The Scientific Process and the Computer, John Wiley, New York, N.Y. (1974), 366-373.

|18| L. Kleinrock: Certain Analytic Results for Time-Shared Processors, Proceedings of the IFIPS 1968 Congress (Aug. 1968), 838-845.

|19| D. N. Streeter: Centralization or Dispersion of Computing Facilities, IBM Systems Journal, Vol. 12, No. 3 (1973).

|20| D. N. Streeter: Productivity of Computer-Dependent Workers, IBM Systems Journal, Vol. 14, No. 3, (1975).

|21| M. Kochen and K. W. Deutsch: Decentralization by Function and Location, Management Science, Vol. 18, No. 8 (Apr. 1973).

|22| J. W. Boyse and D. R. Warn: A Straightforward Model for Computer Performance Prediction, ACM Computing Surveys, Vol. 7, N. 2 (June 1975), 73-93.

|23| P. M. Morse: Queues, Inventories and Maintenance, John Wiley, New York (1958).

|24| W. M. Chow: A Queuing Analysis of Multiprogramming Computer Systems, IBM Research Report RC4945 (July 1974), Yorktown Heights, New York.

|25| H. Hellerman and T. F. Conroy: Computer System Performance, McGraw-Hill, New York (1975).

|26| T. C. Chen: Distributed Intelligence for User-oriented Computing, FJCC (1972), 1049-1056.

Measuring, Modelling and Evaluating Computer Systems,
H. Beilner and E. Gelenbe, (eds.)
© North-Holland Publishing Company (1977)

SIMULATION OF LARGE PARALLEL SYSTEMS: MODELING OF TASKS[1]

J.-L. Baer
University of Washington
Seattle, Washington

and

J. Jensen
Texas Tech University
Lubbock, Texas

In the first part of this paper a brief review of the UCLA graph model of computations (GMC) will be given. Its evolution, its place within the hierarchy of graph models, and the type of applications for which it has been used will be summarized.

The second part of the paper is concerned with some recent extensions to the GMC, namely the introduction of replication vertices and modules. Their use for simulation purposes will be outlined and we will show how they impact some formal properties of the model such as proper termination.

In the third and final section, we discuss simulation experiments conducted with this representation of tasks on a general model of a shared resource multi-processor. The influence of the new constructs and the interpretation of the model with respect to attributes such as time, memory requirements and loop replication factors will lead us to some conclusions relative to:

- The design of hardware/software schedulers when priorities are dependent on expected time and memory requirements of individual tasks.

- The methodology, i.e. the use of a full-fledge extended GMC compared with a more simplistic approach like an acyclic bilogic graph.

I. Introduction

The mini, and now micro, revolutions have brought personal computing close to a reality. But there remains a variety of applications for which raw computing power is a necessity. Weather prediction, large scale matrix manipulations and solutions of linear systems of equations, air traffic control, and simulation of large ecological systems are common examples. Tight multiprocessing systems are generally advocated for solving these time-consuming problems. Simultaneously, decreases in hardware cost have fostered an immense interest in distributed function architectures. Additional software and organizational difficulties have appeared with this new system concept of loosely connected processors as e.g. the modes and protocols for interconnections, deadlock prevention, and resource scheduling. In order to assess or to predict the performance of these systems where parallelism plays an important role, we need models either analytical or simulation oriented, or both, which will represent the machines under study and the tasks which will be performed, as well as the executions of these tasks by the

[1] This work was supported in part by NSF Grant MCS-76-09839.

machines. In this paper, we deal mainly with the task representation and more precisely with some extensions to the UCLA Graph Model of Computations (GMC).

The GMC is now the product of fifteen years of research and development. Since its inception it has been modified extensively, it has been applied to several different aspects of the computer system modeling process, it has generated or influenced a number of derivatives, and not surprisingly it has been found to be equivalent (in senses to be defined precisely) to other graph models developed independently during the same time period.

In the first part of this paper, we review briefly the GMC's history. Then we shall discuss our extensions to the model, their rationale and their power. In the next section, we summarize some simulation experiments performed with our model and compare them with what was obtained through previous methodologies.

II. History and Evolution of the GMC

The basis of the model is a directed graph G(W,U) where W is a finite set of nodes representing computations and U a set of arcs showing the flow of control.

Historically, the first UCLA graph model, not yet known as the GMC, was meant to give a representation of programs to be run on a variable structure computer [ESTR 63A][2], [TURN 63]. It was a simple extension of flowcharts with parallelism being introduced by the use of logic conditions. Under the direction of Gerald Estrin, several of his students refined the model. Martin [MART 66] restricted the use of logic conditions so that the nodes of W could be mapped into a pair $L = (L^-, L^+)$ where $L = (+,*) \times (+,*)$ (L^- is the input and L^+ the output logic). Thus, with each node w_i is associated one of the ordered pairs (*,+) , (+,*) , (*,+) , (*,*). If $L^- = *$, w_i is said to be of AND-input logic (respectively EOR if $L^- = +$) and similarly if $L^+ = *$ w_i is said to be of AND-output logic (respectively EOR or branching node). A simulation on the graph model then proceeds as follows (a unique entry node w_1 and a unique exit node w_n are assumed):

- w_1 is initiated.
- At termination of an EOR-output logic node, one and only one of the arcs incident out is enabled (cf. IF statement in a procedural language).
- At termination of an AND-output logic node, all arcs incident out are enabled (cf. FORK statement like in [CONW 63]).
- To be initiated, an EOR-input logic vertex must have one and only one of the arcs incident in enabled.
- To be initiated, an AND-input logic vertex must have all the arcs incident in enabled (cf. JOIN statement).

Martin's main goal was to predict the performance of multiprocessor systems through simulation. The control flows of the tasks were represented by the graph models as defined above. In order to keep the time spent in simulation within reasonable bounds (his procedure was iterative [MART 67B]) a cyclic-acyclic transformation was performed [MART 67A] based on the probabilities of executing nodes [MART 67] and path length approximations [MART 69]. The study of these bilogic graphs was continued by Baer and Bovet. A more formal approach to the definition of the model and procedures to test the legality of an acyclic graph and to obtain node probabilities in a more efficient manner were introduced [BAER 70, BOVE 69]. Refinements on the cyclic-acyclic transformation, bounds on the number

---

2 References prior to 1972 can be found in [2] and will not be repeated here.

of processors needed to achieve maximum parallelism, and a better simulation approach were given in [BAER 68A], [BAER 69]. At the same time, the memory constraints never used in previous simulations were investigated in [BOVE 70].

Because the model was still simple in the means used to express parallelism, it was felt that an automatic detection of parallelism on debugged high-level language programs (more precisely written in FORTRAN) could be attempted. The resulting product would be a parallel program representable by the graph model. Russell and Volansky [RUSS 69], [VOLA 70] conducted such studies.

However, there remained a number of weaknesses in the model, principally its inadequacy to represent (in an uninterpreted fashion) those synchronization problems which had been shown to be of extreme importance by Dijkstra and others [DIJK 68]. While Holt, Dennis and their associates investigated Petri nets [PETR 62], [HOLT 68], [DENN 70] and related models, while Karp and Miller's models were also going through some evolutions [KARP 67], [KARP 69], Gostelow and Cerf at UCLA [GOST 71], [CERF 72] were modifying the bilogic graphs and defined what is now known as the GMC.

In order to introduce the GMC, we need some preliminary definitions: A (complex) digraph G (W,U) is a digraph where W is a set of nodes and U is a set of multiarcs, that is an arc belonging to U is a pair (W_i , W_j) with $W_i \subseteq W$, $W_j \subseteq W$ being (possibly empty) subsets of W. There is a unique entry arc S with $W_i = \emptyset$.

A bigraph B = (G,L,Q) is a triple with G being a digraph as above, L being the logic conditions as defined previously with the difference that $L_i^- = +$ will indicate in the simulation that w_i can be initiated if one of its input arcs is enabled (instead of one and only one), and Q = (Q^-,Q^+) are the (input, output) token value specifications which map WxU into the positive integers (see later for the reason for their introduction). Figure 1 is an example of a bigraph.

Now a GMC C = (B,M,D) is a triple where B is a bigraph, M is an ordered set of memory cells, and D = (D^-,D^+) are data set mappings from W into subsets of M. M and D provide an interpretation for the GMC while B shows the flow of control.

The state of the execution of the GMC is recorded through tokens. When placed on a node w_i they indicate the initiation of the computation modeled by w_i, while on arcs they show the values of the precedence conditions Q existing between nodes in the initial and terminal sets of the arcs. The flow of control is represented by sequences of states.

The simulation on the model includes a "virtual device" called the token machine. It interprets the bigraph and its initial token state to produce a (in general non-unique) computation sequence in which nodes may be initiated and terminated by the computation associated with the GMC. The initiation of w_i can proceed when $L_i^- = *$(respectively $L_i^- = +$) only if for each (respectively at least one) incident arc a there is at least Q (w_i,a) tokens on it. At termination tokens are placed on arcs incident out in a similar manner. Figure 1 illustrates the concept.

It has been found by Gostelow [GOST 71] and later under somewhat different assumptions in [9, 11] that GMC and Petri Nets computation sequences were in the same theoretical class of formal models. While the main impetus behind Petri Nets was to show liveness because they tend to represent non-terminating processes (like in operating systems), the trend for the GMC studies was to show that the graphs were terminating properly, i.e. that they represent correct and terminating programs from the flow of control viewpoint.

Figure 1. A bigraph and two possible states.

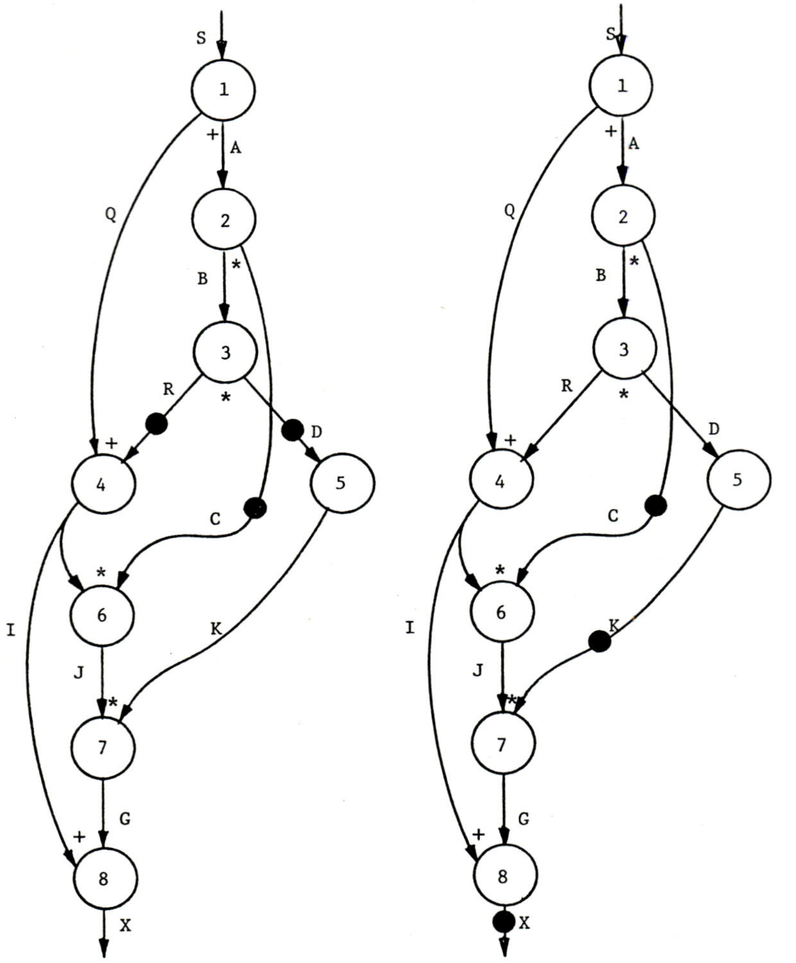

a) Possible Token State After Firing of 1, 2, 3

b) Terminal State in the Sequence Begun by Firing 1, 2, 3

<u>Proper termination</u> (PT) is a property of the control graph which is independent of the interpretation given to the GMC. A bigraph is PT if given an initial marking (or state), generally a token on arc S, only a finite number of tokens are required from the token machine to reach a terminal state defined as a unique token on X. Applications of this concept which come immediately to the surface are the determination of the completion of the process, its reusability as a module in other computations, and the checking for the absence of deadlocks. For example with an initial token on S, the graph of Figure 1a is not PT as shown in Figure 1b.

In order to reduce the checking of all possible computational sequences, a finite number by definition of PT but a number which grows exponentially with the size of the graph, Gostelow et al give a procedure which allows the collapsing of nodes and arcs. More specifically, the GMC can be seen as a transition system [5,8] with the initiation and termination of a node's execution being lumped into a transformation equation (TE). For example, the graph of Figure 2 is shown with its TE's. The reduction procedure can be grossly summarized as the combination of several TE's into 1, as e.g. for the graph of Figure 2

Figure 2. A Completely Reducible Bigraph.

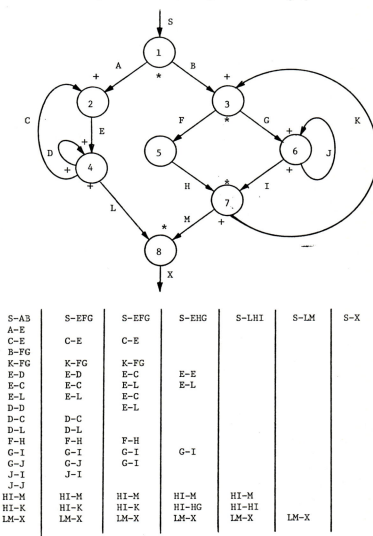

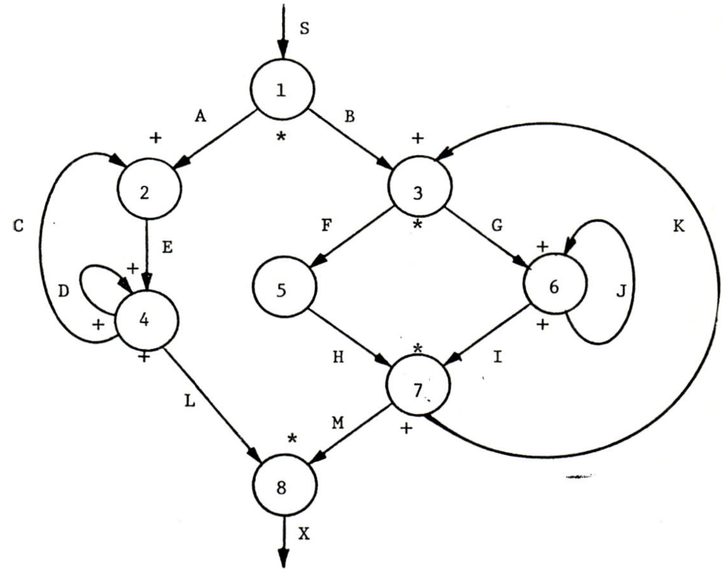

S-AB	S-EFG	S-EFG	S-EHG	S-LHI	S-LM	S-X
A-E						
C-E	C-E	C-E				
B-FG						
K-FG	K-FG	K-FG				
E-D	E-D	E-C	E-E			
E-C	E-C	E-L	E-L			
E-L	E-L	E-C				
D-D		E-L				
D-C	D-C					
D-L	D-L					
F-H	F-H	F-H				
G-I	G-I	G-I	G-I			
G-J	G-J	G-I				
J-I	J-I					
J-J						
HI-M	HI-M	HI-M	HI-M	HI-M		
HI-K	HI-K	HI-K	HI-HG	HI-HI		
LM-X	LM-X	LM-X	LM-X	LM-X	LM-X	

S → AB)
=> S → BE)
A → E)

since there is no A remaining as a left-hand node of a TE. It can be proven that a sufficient (but not a necessary) condition for a graph to be PT is that it is completely reducible i.e. that the only remaining TE after the reduction procedure is

S → X (as e.g. in Figure 2)

We shall see in the next section how the GMC can model constructs found in (parallel) programming languages and systems. Applications of the GMC can be found in [GOST 71] for deadlock detection, [CERF 72] for the study of synchronization primitives, and in [12] for the study of computer network protocols. In this latter reference, Postel has tried to give rules for the modularization of GMC's.

Recently two new slants have been followed in the study of the GMC. The first one is to use the GMC as one module of a design methodology including structural, functional and behavioral components [4]. The other is to introduce more interpretation in the bigraph itself and this approach is expanded in the remaining of this paper. More details can be found in [6].

Finally, to close this "historical" review, one should emphasize the influence of the GMC (and ancestors) over the field of graph models of computations. Typical examples are the E-nets [10] and the extended Petri Nets [3] developed at the University of Washington which combine features of the GMC and of Petri Nets.

III. Representative Power of the Model: Colored Tokens and Replication Modules

A bilogic graph without multiarcs is powerful enough to model the constructs found in procedural programming languages and to express parallelism of the FORK-JOIN or parbegin-parend form [2]. In the GMC example of Figure 2 the output logic of node 3 corresponds to a forking process and the associated join is modeled by the input logic at node 7. The subgraph composed of nodes {3,5,6,7} and arcs {F,G,H,I,J,K} could be a model for the segment of program:

```
Repeat
node 3   parbegin
         begin  action at node 5 end
         begin  for loop at node 6 end
         parend
until    condition at node 7;
```

An equivalent Petri Net model for the same segment is shown in Figure 3. As can be seen there is some analogy between places in the net and nodes in the GMC, and between transition and arcs. A formal comparison can be found in [GOST 71].

Even if we had allowed self-loops in the Petri Net, that is the deletions of place 6' and of transition J_2, the representation would have been more cumbersome. Furthermore, the continuity of interpretation given by the input and output logics in the GMC is lost in the Petri Net where predicates are modeled by places (cf. places 6 and 7) while other events correspond to the firing of transitions.

This simplicity of representation in the GMC disappears when semaphores and critical sections are modeled. The multiarc scheme (cf. e.g. [CERF 72]) is not as elegant as the Petri Net representation. This is exemplified in Figure 4 where nodes 3 and 6 are to be mutually exclusive and where M plays the role of a semaphore. (A more complex example would be more convincing).

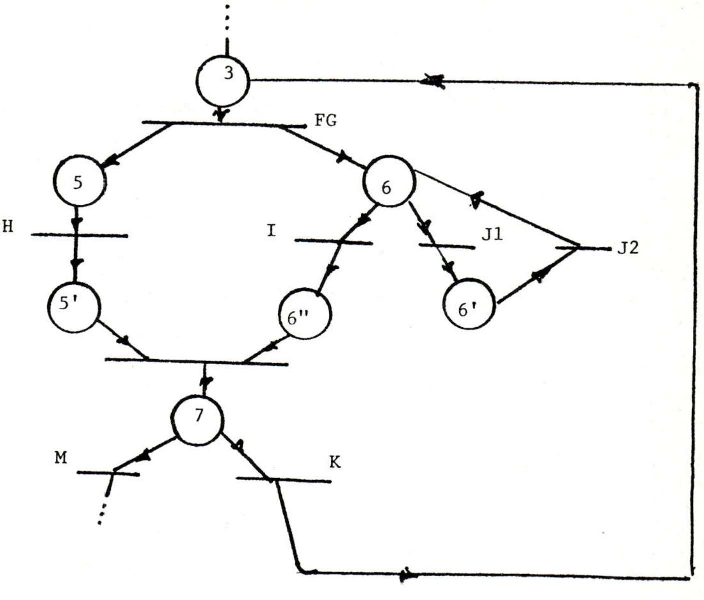

Figure 3. A Petri Net Modelling

As in Petri Nets, the inability of testing for the absence of a token on a given arc limits the descriptive power of the GMC. In order to remedy this situation, one can impose a true EOR condition as an input logic like in the original bi-logic graph. In Petri Nets one can impose an EOR logic [3] or a NOT logic [1]. The cost of this modification is that all properties such as proper termination or liveness become undecidable since the modified model will have the power of a Turing machine [1].

In this study we chose to use GMC's rather than Petri Nets since our goal is to represent application tasks which are meant to terminate rather than cyclic processes which should be live. Although there is no theoretical advantage to use one model rather than the other we have found that in the context of this particular project that we were more comfortable with GMC's. As an aside it is also worthwhile to note that the reduction procedure could be applied to vector addition systems reachability tree construction [KARP 69] if we were not interested in all the states represented as nodes in the tree. In the sequel of this paper, we keep the GMC terminology and a rather informal discourse.

From a pragmatic viewpoint, a requirement for the model is to be easily decomposable into modules. The first reason for modularization is that it exists in the subjects to be modeled (e.g. subroutines). The second is that since properties such as proper termination are checked by exponential algorithms, modularization will decrease (exponentially) the vector space of states. However modularization is not easily obtained if one wants to keep formal properties such as PT.

Consider first the modeling of a subroutine M that we shall assume to be pure code. It can be represented by a GMC in its own right and we can impose

Figure 4a - Example Showing Mutual Exclusion

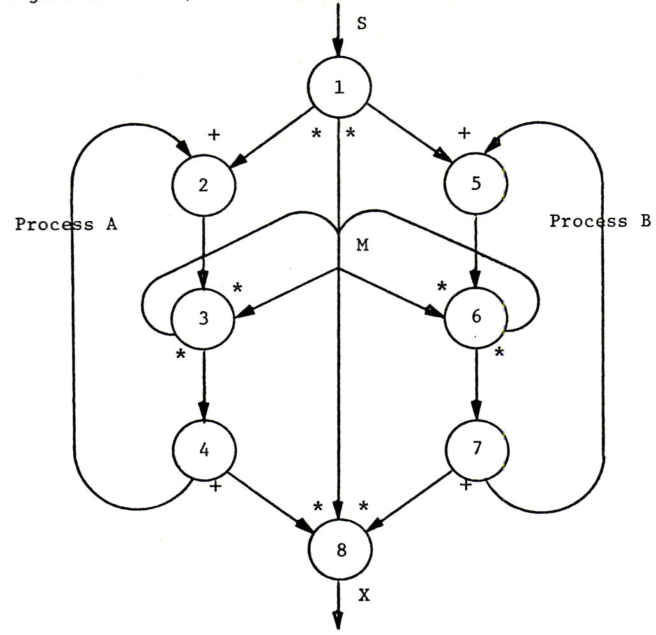

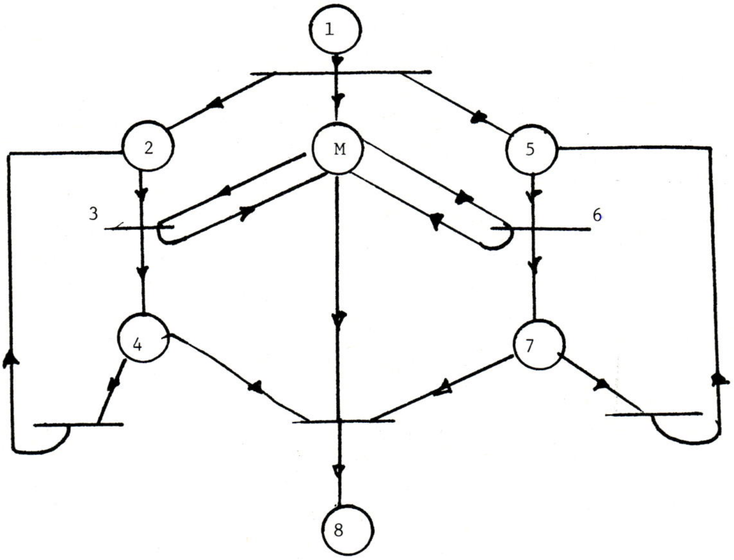

Figure 4b Petri Net Modeling of Mutually Exclusive Processes.

that this module be PT when a single token is placed on its input arc (this property will be denoted PT(1)). A call from some node 1 and return to node 2 is shown in Figure 5a, with the subroutine being the node labelled M. Now if M is called at various places, the modeling looks like Figure 5b. If in this latter figure nodes 1 and 3 can be activated concurrently, then two tokens might be placed on the multiarc ({1,3},{M}) resulting in 2 activations of M. But PT(1) is not carried over to PT(k), i.e. a PT GMC with a single token on its input arc is not necessarily PT when k tokens are now placed on the input arc.

Figure 5. Modeling Subroutines.

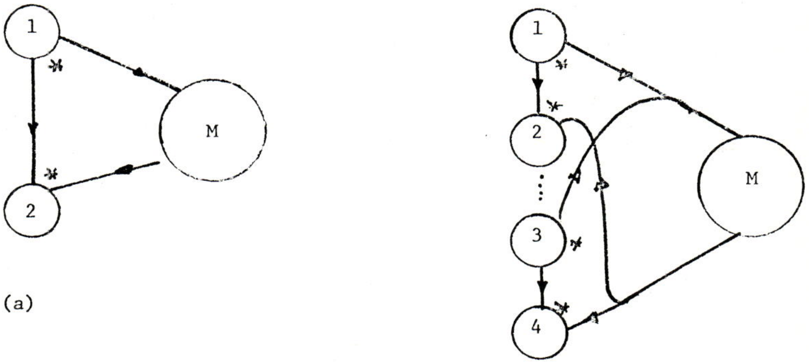

(a) (b)

That PT(1) does not imply PT(k) can easily be shown with an example where the initialization with k tokens, k > 1, lead to the application of a TE which could have never fired with k = 1 (cf. Figure 6). Even if we restrict ourselves to consider a restricted class of GMC's where all TE's are firable with an initial input of a single token, we can find graphs which are PT(1) and not PT(k). It suffices to have TE's which have non-identical but common elements in their left-hand sides to build a counter example. If we restrict further the GMC's to prohibit this overlap then we can conjecture that those restricted GMC's which are PT(1) are also PT(k) (e.g. PT(1) graphs without multiarcs are PT(k)).

But the PT(k) notion is not sufficient to model adequately tasks sharing modules. In terms of the model, the tokens might have to carry some attributes indicating their owner so that some nodes can be initiated only when all tokens at its input have the same owner. Therefore we extend the GMC model so that now tokens are <u>colored</u>.

Each of the k tokens initially placed on S is taken to be of a different color, and the token machine is restricted so as to require all tokens used in the same "move" to be of the <u>same</u> color.

With this addition we can now clear some potential ambiguity. For example, consider the GMC of Figure 7a. If two undistinguishable tokens are put on arc S, we can reach the state ABCD (cf. Figure 7b), and there we do not know which of these tokens go in pairs. However if the initial tokens are given the colors L and R, the state diagram is that of Figure 7c and we see that states AB | CD and AD | CB are now different. The use of tokens distinguished in this way not only corrects the behavior of this example, but relieves the requirement for the PT(k) property as well.

Figure 6. A Graph which is PT(1) and not PT(2).

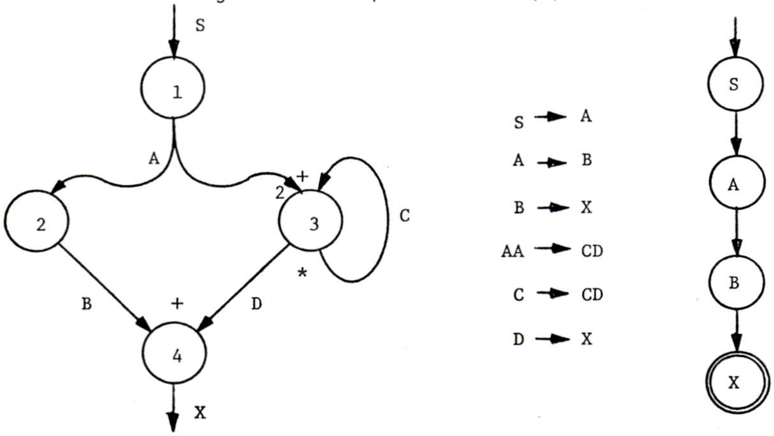

(a)

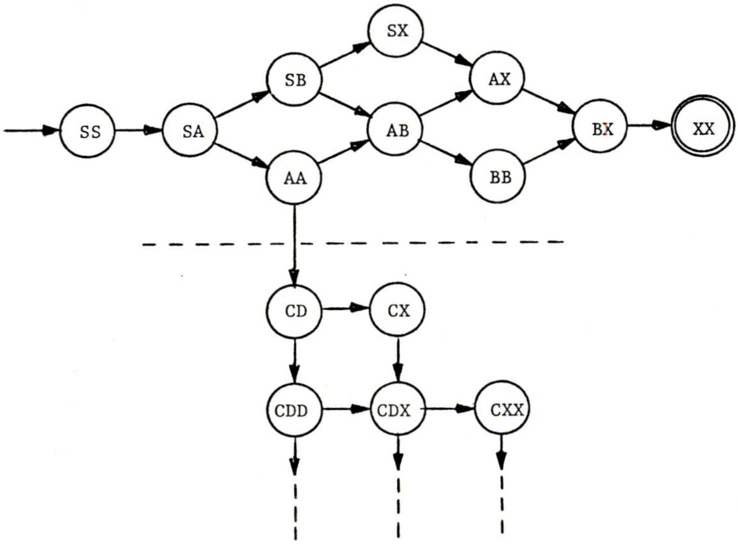

Figure 7. States with and without colored tokens.

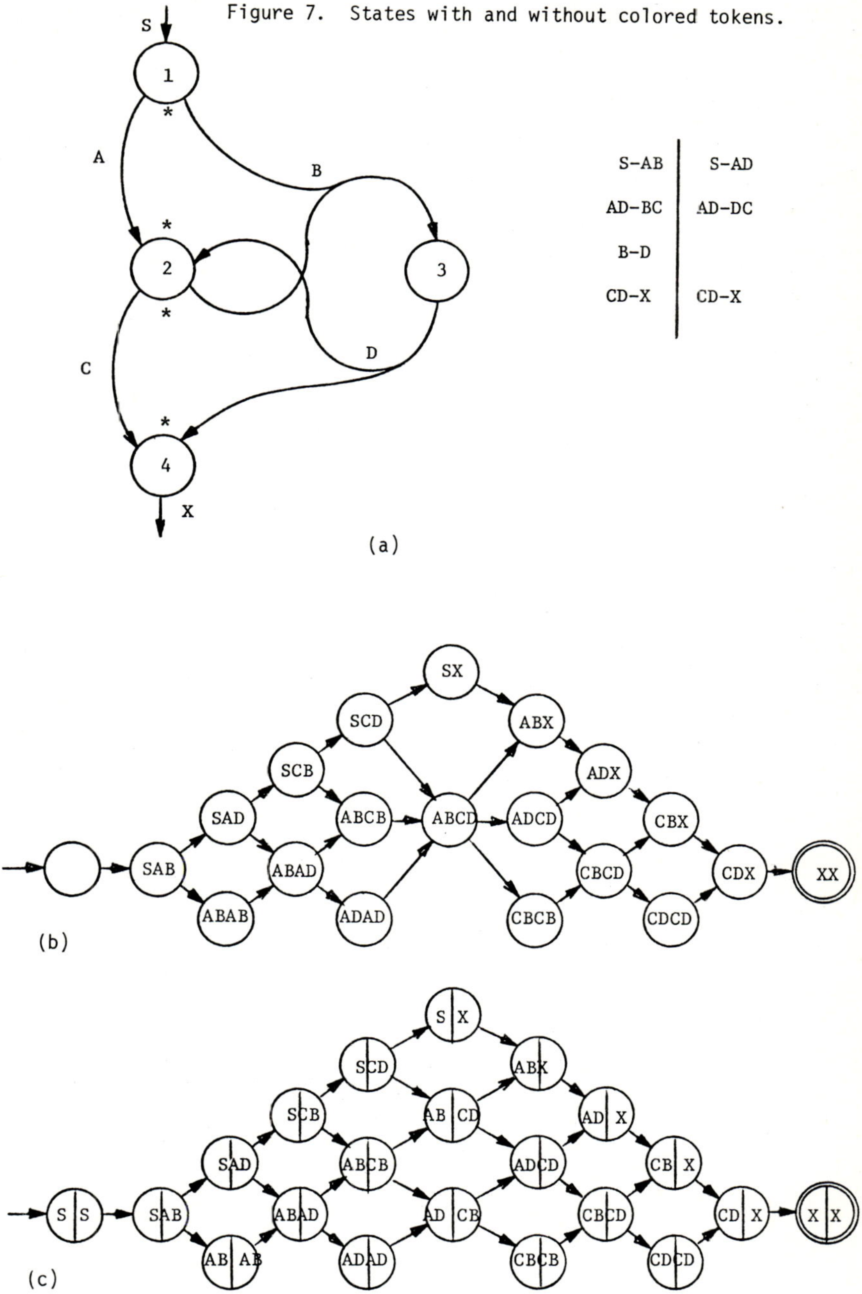

With colored tokens and the PT property we can model shared procedures with several concurrent activations. The second problem associated with modularization is the detection of connected modules within a GMC.

The first idea is to define this sub-GMC module M as a PT subgraph (or PT(k) with colored tokens) with a single simple entry arc, a single simple exit arc and all other arcs in the sub-GMC having all members of their initial and terminal node sets within M. Evidently since M is PT, it can be replaced by another PT module M^1 having the same topological requirements.

In [12] other forms of subgraphs are considered. The number of entry and exit nodes and arcs are not restricted. The notions of completely reducible and PT can be generalized as completely reducible modules being subgraphs whose TE set may be reduced such that every arc in a left hand side is an input arc (i.e. an arc with at least one tail within the module) and every arc in a right hand side is an output arc (i.e. an arc with at least one head within the module). Similarly, a proper module is a subgraph such that if a state diagram is generated beginning with every possible subset of the input arcs, every terminal state will be composed entirely of input and output arcs. A further restriction in both cases is that no local arc (i.e. an arc with at least one tail and one head within the module) may also be an output arc.

One of the primary motivations for this extension was to allow modules to interface with semaphores. But for example the mutual exclusion GMC of Figure 4a cannot be so modularized because the common semaphore is a local arc. Because of this fact, the comparative simplicity in analyzing only PT(k) subgraphs, and our orientation toward user task modeling, we shall restrict ourselves to the single entry, single exit case.

One contribution which we make to the model is the capability of representing various forms of node or subgraph replication within a GMC. We consider first the finite, simultaneous replication of loop constructs as might be denoted by a "DO PARALLEL" statement in some programming language. In this instance, the same portion of code is to be executed several times in parallel (the number may be an input variable to the program) with a single index discriminating the parallel paths. This case is modeled simply by a PT(k) graph module, where k is the repeat-factor of the loop. Since the tokens can be colored with their respective value of k, a replicated loop can be modeled by a PT module.

The second case which could be considered is when a portion of code is to be reused in a serial fashion because of data dependencies precluding simultaneous replication. Here we do not really need colored tokens but decided on using them for simplicity and homogeneity in the implementation. Again the color models the value of k. Our concern now is not on how many colored tokens to put on the initial arc of the module but how many colors are to be and have been used.

To model loops we introduce a new node type named replication node (Figure 8) which has all the properties of the other nodes with some additions. Each replication node v has two new arcs (S and X of the sub-GMC) which link to the PT module it controls and an attribute K(v) taken to be the maximum color-count for the sub-GMC controlled by v. A formal definition of K(v) and of its protection from being overwritten by members of the module controlled by v is given in [6]. If v is of the replicator type upon initiation it deposits k tokens of different colors and terminates when the k tokens reappear on X. When of the serial type one token is deposited on S only and v awaits for it to reappear on X. Then the process is repeated k-1 times before the token can leave v.

To implement nested loops, each token carries a stack of colors. A new color is added at each level of looping and matching of tokens is done by complete stack identity.

Figure 8 - The Replication Vertex

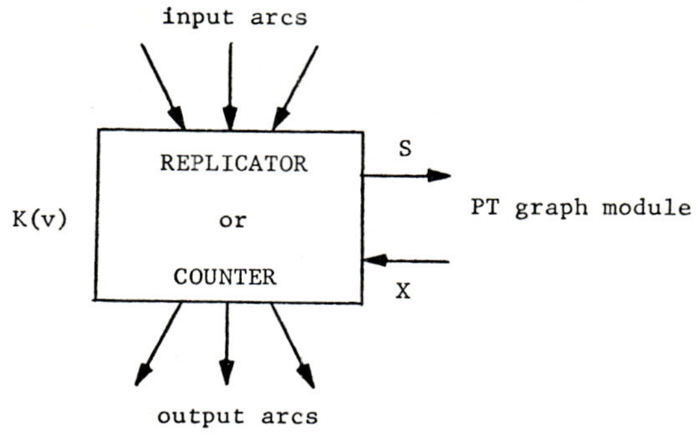

The nesting of replication modules produces another problem in modeling mutual exclusion. Suppose that the graph in Figure 4, showing two processes cycling in parallel with corresponding nodes 3 and 6 mutually excluded, is the PT module associated with a replicator node. Further, let nodes 3 and 6 represent accesses to a shared resource, such as allocation of a unit of disk space. Processes A and B will each be replicated k times in parallel, but which nodes will be mutually excluded? The intended choice in this case was to mutually exclude all k instances of node 3 and all k instances of node 6. However this will not occur with the model we have described. The semaphore M will have a total of k different-colored tokens placed upon it, one from each termination of node 1, causing only the k pairs of corresponding instances of nodes 3 and 6 to be mutually excluded. This example, to be modeled correctly, requires the semaphore to be initiated outside the replicated module, thus violating the requirement that modules be single-entry and single-exit. Examples such as this place limits on the modeling capability of the GMC.

Despite these few limitations the modeling power of the GMC is enhanced by the addition of replication modules and colored tokens. Provided that care is taken to avoid the misuse of semaphores within graph modules (as in the example just described), there are very few program structures which cannot be modeled. At worst, the unfortunate locations of semaphores can make modularization of programs difficult, due to the single-entry/single-exit restriction. Clearly the model we have described has sufficient capabilities to represent the various tasks to be executed in a large multiprocessing system, in a more succinct and more powerful fashion than its predecessor.

IV. Simulation Models and Experiments

Our goal in extending the GMC was to facilitate the description of tasks to be run on a multiprocessor system, and to ease the simulation of the execution of these tasks. It was felt that the extended GMC could be representative, or at least its control component, of the type of information produced by a compiler and passed on to a hardware/software scheduler. Therefore we designed some simulation experiments which were to test the adequacy of the extended GMC, and the effectiveness of various scheduling algorithms when the system being simulated was a large shared resource multiprocessor.

The simulation model then is a composite of the activation of several submodels:

- A machine model; in our case we chose a shared resource multiprocessor, i.e. rings of phased skeletal CPU's, with caches, sharing a common memory and a set of functional units.
- An extended partially interpreted extended GMC, with the partial interpretation (node attributes) to be explained below, as model of tasks.
- A scheduling model, i.e. a set of various scheduling algorithms combining a priori information such as the task's GMC and dynamic information provided either by polling or interrupt mechanisms.
- A load model, i.e. how many tasks and of what mix (I/O bound, CPU bound, etc.).
- A contention model [7] for the system's shared resources. This was deemed necessary because contention arises at the instruction level (e.g. two simultaneous requests for a multiply unit) while the tasks are representative of larger modules such as blocks of statements.

In this paper we restrict ourselves to some observations regarding the task modeling and scheduling experiments, i.e. the outcomes of the simulations.

In order to evaluate the appropriateness of our extensions, we decided to model anew the graphs that had been used in previous simulations [MART 67B], [BAER 68A]. With each node we associated a time attribute, or weight, which we chose in such a way that they could be a reasonable output from some compiler analysis. Some memory attributes were also given indicating how much main memory was needed for the activation of the task. Arcs incident out of branching nodes were assigned probabilities. Transformations were also made on the original graphs so that they would be PT. Finally, we introduced graph modules and replication nodes as defined in the previous section. This last change was particularly rewarding since it cut significantly in the number of nodes in the graph while giving a better picture of the flow of control and the symmetry of some computations. For example, Figure 9a shows one of the original graphs and its transformation appears in Figure 9b.

In previous simulations a cyclic-acyclic transformation was performed and then the acyclic graph was simulated. This gave the opportunity of performing more simulation runs but it is potentially inaccurate and at the least invalidated. Our first experiments were therefore to check the validity of the cyclic-acyclic transformation by performing simulations on the acyclic graph and the extended GMC and comparing the results. The simulations were run on a Xerox Sigma 5 using a FORTRAN and assembly language system implementing some of the SIMULA 67 class concept.

First of all, by fixing some parameters such as branching probabilities, we were able to compare the results of the two types of simulation in terms of total completion time and hence be reasonably certain of the correctness of the cyclic simulation. Second as could be expected, the simulation time was much greater in the cyclic case (about 5 times for the graphs of Figure 9) since many more (21.7 times) node initiations and terminations had to be simulated. Also because of the higher frequencies of the calls to the scheduler included in the cyclic simulation, that is polling of the processors to see if they can be scheduled or responses to interrupts, the total elapsed time was larger in this latter case (a little over 20%). In a sense this measures the scheduling overhead that one would encounter in a real system. The tasks execution times, i.e. the amount of time the processors spent computing, was not significantly different. This was due to the fact that tasks time attributes had small variances,

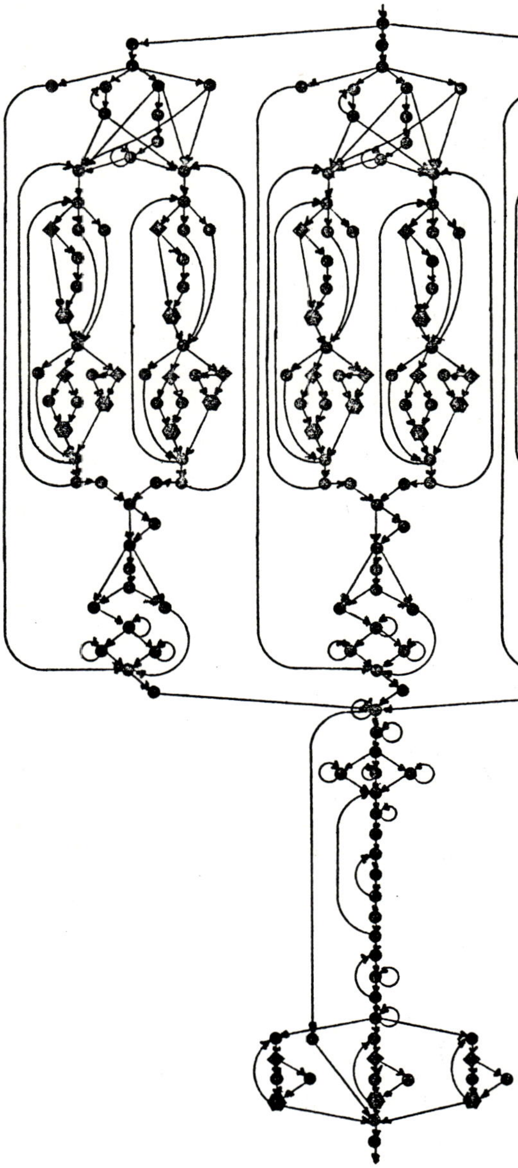

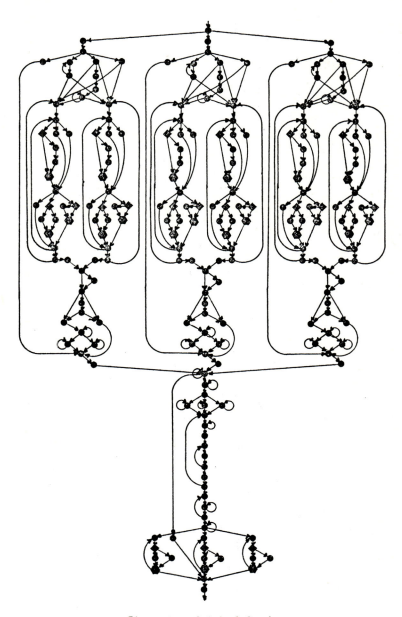

Figure 9a. Original Graph

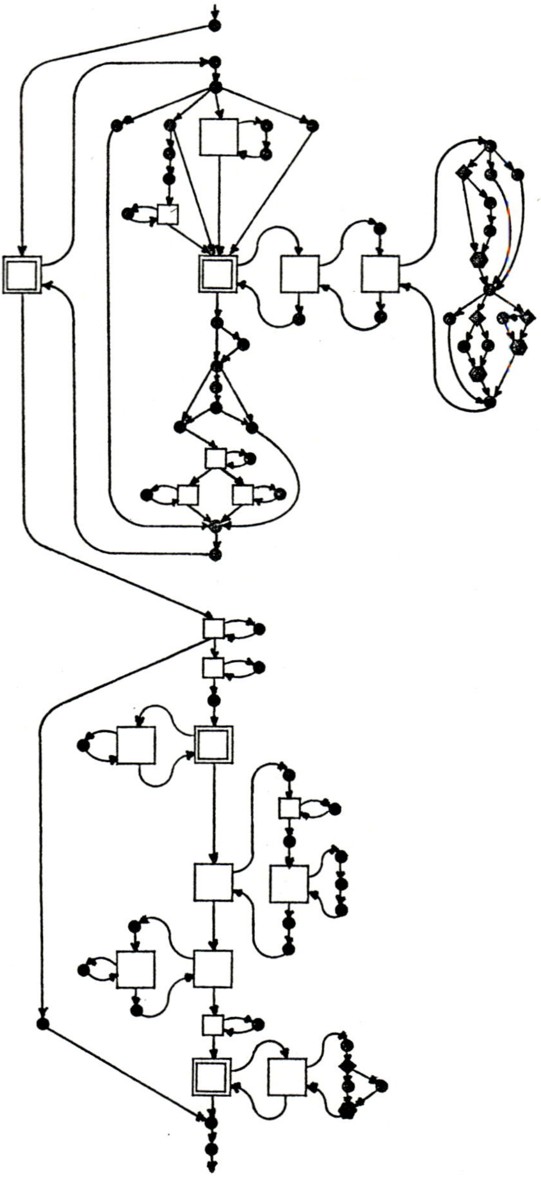

Figure 9b. Transformed Graph

hence making the cyclic-acyclic transformation more accurate. Therefore, one can conclude that while the cyclic representation may be considerably more faithful in representing the flow of control in the actual program, the penalty in simulation time is severe. However, if one wants to get a more accurate measure of the scheduling overhead, the cyclic simulation is mandatory. On the other hand, if one is looking for a larger-scale view of the system, then an acyclic simulation is reasonable provided that task times are of the same order of magnitude and with small variances.

Although the cyclic-acyclic transformation appeared validated, we carried on several more experiments on the cyclic version in order to see if conclusions which had been reached in the area of scheduling algorithms on the acyclic version were still valid. First we considered only the time attributes. The scheduling strategies were divided into 3 groups:

- Yardstick, that is random selection (RAND), and F.I.F.O. (or dynamic).
- Local, i.e. those in which a priori task priorities are calculated from the parameter of the task alone, as for example LTF (longest time first), STF (shortest time first), MISF (most immediate successors first).
- Global, i.e. those in which knowledge of the whole GMC and other tasks priorities are needed, as e.g. HLF (highest level first), HWLF (highest weighted level first), MSF (most total successors), LPF (longest expected path length first) and LWPF (longest weighted path length first).

Our experiments confirmed previous results, namely that local priorities are no better than FIFO and that among the global ones, a simple priority scheme such as HLF is best mostly if the system is heavily loaded (between 15 and 20% less idle time can be incurred cf. Figure 10).

One of the goals of these experiments was to try and find a local strategy that would perform near to the global strategies or to determine which of the global strategies would perform best. It was hoped that when memory becomes a critical resource that an LMF algorithm (largest memory first) might out-perform the other heuristic approaches. Therefore we tested this strategy by placing a limit on the total memory occupancy at a given time in the system, causing the scheduler to pass over some tasks with large memory requirements for smaller ones if they do not fit in the available memory. (Contiguity of memory is ignored here.) It was expected that as memory became restricted, all of the non-memory-oriented strategies would degrade rapidly in their performance to the point where a simple memory strategy like LMF may succeed.

For this reason an investigation was made into the memory capacity limit. The LMF algorithm was tested for a few processor values over a wide selection of memory limits. This resulted into the selection of memory limits equal to the largest task occupancy, 3/2 and twice this value as an appropriate test range for systems with 3 to 6 processors.

In the next simulation series, the global strategies were run under varying memory capacities in order to see how they measured against the LMF algorithm as memory becomes a critical resource. HLF was chosen as being representative for the comparisons with RAND, FIFO and LMF. Figure 11 shows the effect of the memory constraint on each algorithm's performance. The performance of LMF is considerably disappointing. The path length or global algorithms are again clearly better than the others, although the margin of improvement dwindles rapidly when memory becomes critical.

Figure 10. Comparison of Scheduling Algorithms

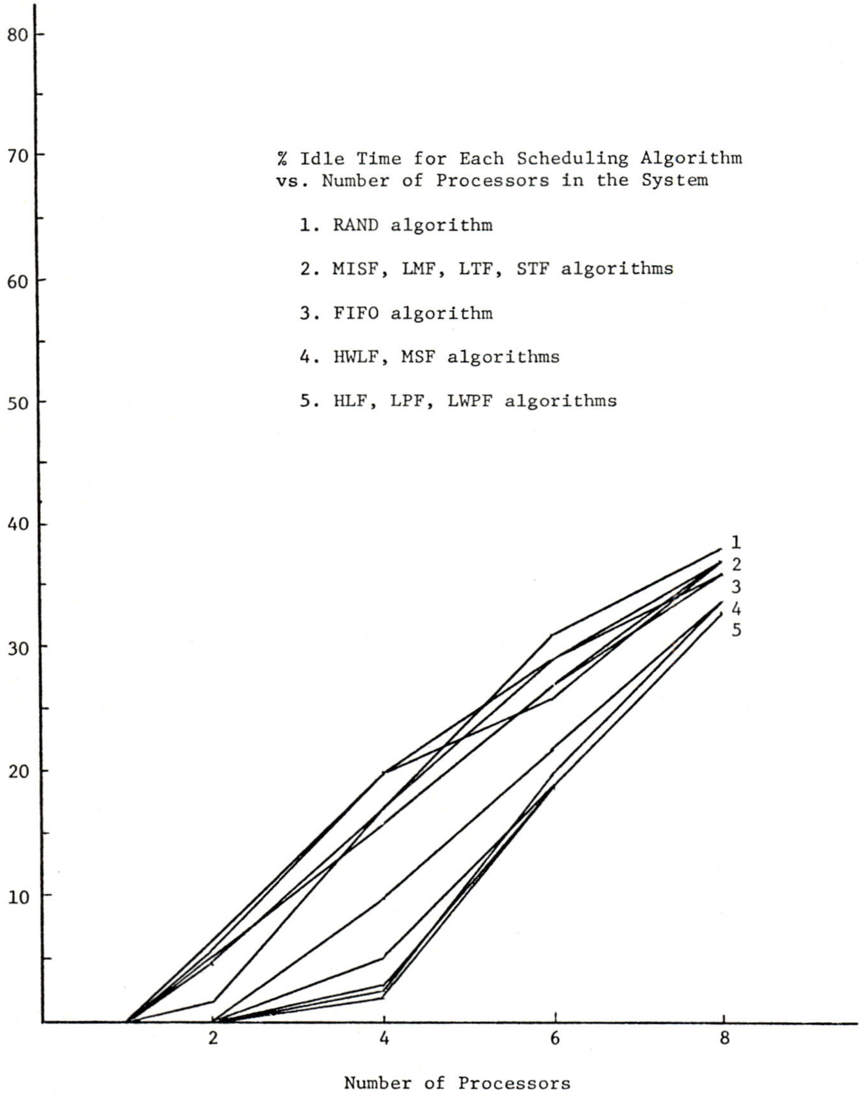

Figure 11. Scheduling Algorithms under Memory Constraints

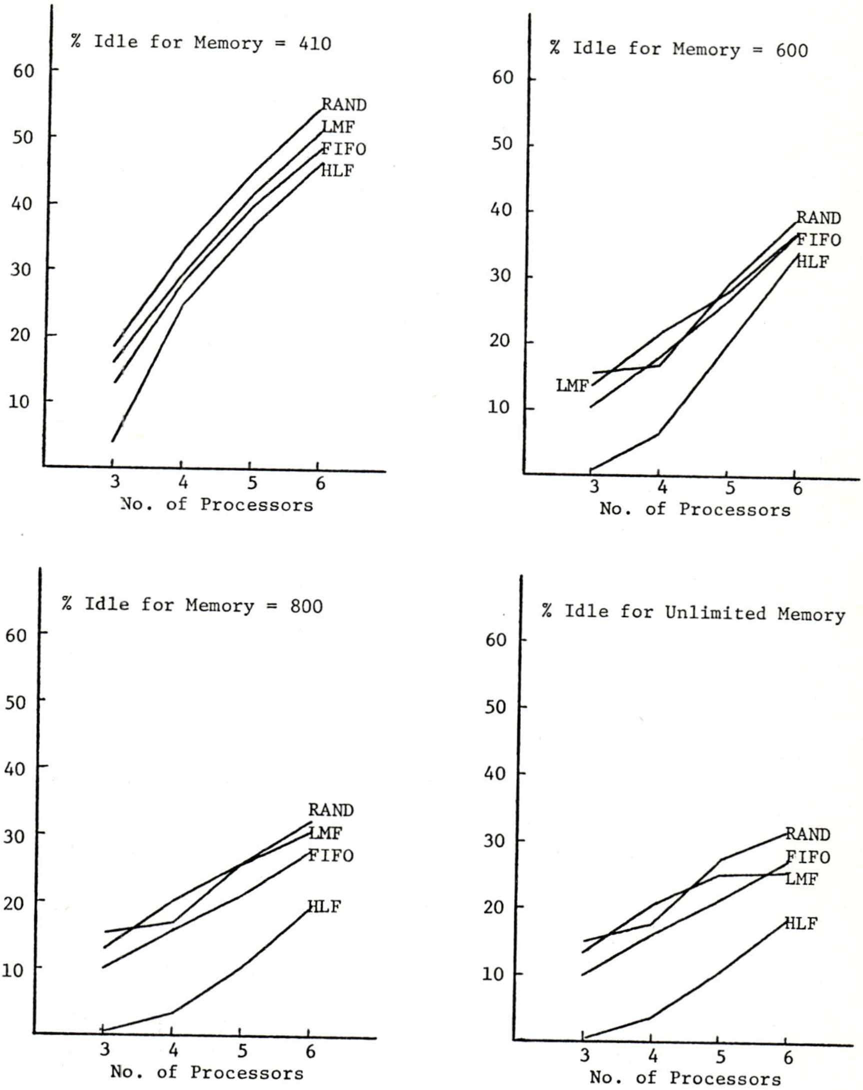

It is to be noted that we performed these experiments on several graphs and consistently found the same results. In particular the abundance or paucity of branching nodes and/or replication nodes did not alter the general ranking of the algorithms. A possible explanation for the small difference between weighted and unweighted strategies might lie in the fact that tasks weights were of the same order of magnitude.

From these experiments we might conclude that in the way of scheduling algorithms, we have found that the local heuristics are of no help at all, that all of the global strategies listed are of equal value (therefore pick the cheapest one to implement), and that the usefulness of the global strategies is limited when the time spent on determining these priorities is a critical concern. We were also disappointed by the failure of the LMF attempt at introducing the memory constraint in an unexpansive manner.

V. Conclusion

In this paper we have presented some extensions to the GMC which make it more amenable to the modeling of tasks to be run on large multiprocessor systems. The introduction of replication nodes and of colored tokens allows the modeling of constructs such as DO PARALLEL which are important in this context. It also permits the representation of shared code. With tasks being represented in this extended GMC model we performed some simulation experiments. The two most salient results can be summarized as follows:

- Representation of tasks by an acyclic graph is justified but an evaluation of the scheduling overhead is lost in the transformation.

- Local scheduling policies fail, even when memory constraints are added to the time estimates.

References

|1| Aggerwala, T. Ph.D. Dissertation, Department of Electrical Engineering, The Johns Hopkins University, 1975.

|2| Baer, J.-L. "A Survey of Some Theoretical Aspects of Multiprocessing", Computing Surveys, 5, 1 (March 1973), 31-80.

|3| Baer, J.-L. "Modeling for Parallel Computation: A Case Study", Proceedings of the 1973 Sagamore Computer Conference on Parallel Processing, 13-22.

|4| Gardner, R. A Methodology for Digital System Design Based on Structural and Functional Modeling, Ph.D. Dissertation, U.C.L.A., 1975.

|5| Gostelow, K., Cerf, V., Estrin, G., and Volansky, S. "Proper Termination of Flow of Control in Programs Involving Concurrent Processes:. Proc. ACM National Conference, 1972, 742-754.

|6| Jensen, J. Dynamic Task Scheduling in a Shared Resource Multiprocessor. Ph.D. Dissertation, University of Washington, 1976.

|7| Jensen, J. and J.-L. Baer. "A Model of Interference in a Shared Resource Multiprocessor", Proc. 3rd Symposium on Computer Architecture, 1976, 52-57.

|8| Keller, R. "Formal Verification of Parallel Programs" Comm. ACM 19, 7 (July 1976), 371-384.

|9| Lipton, R. "Limitations of Synchronization Primitives" Proceedings of the 6th SIGACT Symposium, 1974.

|10| Noe, J.D. and G. Nutt "Macro E-Nets for Representation of Parallel Systems" IEEE Trans. Computers C-22, 8 (August 1973), 718-727.

|11| Peterson, J.L. and T.H. Bredt "A Comparison of Models of Parallel Computation" Proceedings IFIP Congress, 1974, 466-470.
|12| Postel, J. A Graph Model Analysis of Computer Communications Protocols, Ph.D. Dissertation, U.C.L.A., 1974.

Measuring, Modelling and Evaluating Computer Systems,
H. Beilner and E. Gelenbe, (eds.)
© North-Holland Publishing Company (1977)

USE OF PETRI NETS FOR PERFORMANCE EVALUATION

Joseph Sifakis
Institut de Mathématiques Appliquées, Informatique
Grenoble, France.

We study the behavior of pure timed Petri nets for constant current assignments. It is given a set of relations describing the behavior of a timed Petri net and it is shown that its maximum computation rate can be calculated by solving a set of n linear equations where n is the number of its places. These relations are estabilished between the currents, the initial marking and the delays of the network. Also, in order to better understand and use these relations, we give some results on the decompositions of a Petri net, obtained by studying the types of solutions of the equations CI = 0 and $J^tC = 0$ where C is the incidence matrix of the net. It is shown, that every consistent (resp. invariant) Petri net can be decomposed into a set of consistent (invariant) "elementary" subnets. We finally give some examples in order to illustrate the use of timed Petri nets in the study of the dynamic behavior of the systems.

INTRODUCTION

Petri nets [1][2] have been found a simple and elegant formalism for the description of asynchronous systems with concurrent evolutions. According to the adopted interpretation, they can be used to model flow phenomena of information, of energy and of materials [3][4][5]. However, this model is not complete enough for the study of system performances since no assumption is made about the firing of a transition as far as its duration and the moment at which it takes place after the transition has been enabled.

Timed Petri nets have been introduced by C. Ramchandani [6] by associating firing times to the transitions of Petri nets. He studied the steady state behavior and gave methods for calculating the throughput rate for certain classes of Petri nets. The results given in this paper are applicable to the class of pure [7] Petri nets and generalize, in some sense, those presented in [6]. The litterature on timed Petri nets is very poor : to the author's knowledge, the only works on this subjet are the Ramchandani's thesis and a paper by S. Ghosh [8] comparing the properties of boundedness and liveness for timed Petri nets and unrestricted Petri nets.

I - DEFINITIONS

Definition 1 : A Petri Net (PN) is a quadruple $\mathcal{N} = (P,T,\alpha,\beta)$ where :

P : is a set of places, $P \neq \emptyset$

T : is a set of transitions, $T \neq \emptyset$, $P \cap T = \emptyset$

α : $P \times T \to \mathbb{N}$ forward incidence function

β : $P \times T \to \mathbb{N}$ backward incidence function

($\mathbb{N}$ represents the set of natural integers : 0,1,2,3,...).

Representation : To a PN one can associate a digraph the nodes of which are the places and the transitions, represented respectively by circles and dashes. There is a directed edge from the place p_s to the transition t_j iff $\alpha(p_s,t_j) = n_{sj} \neq 0$. This edge is labeled by the value n_{sj}, called weight of the edge. There also is a directed edge from the transition t_r to the place p_w iff $\beta(p_w,t_r) = n_{wr} \neq 0$. This edge is labeled by the weight n_{wr}.

Definition 2 : Let $\mathcal{N} = (P,T,\alpha,\beta)$ a PN. We adopt the following notations :
For $t \in T$, ${}^{\bullet}t = \{p \in P \mid \alpha(p,t) \neq 0\}$ and $t^{\bullet} = \{p \in P \mid \beta(p,t) \neq 0\}$
For $p \in P$, ${}^{\bullet}p = \{t \in T \mid \beta(p,t) \neq 0\}$ and $p^{\bullet} = \{t \in T \mid \alpha(p,t) \neq 0\}$
We call ${}^{\bullet}t(t^{\bullet})$ set of input (output) places of t and by analogy, ${}^{\bullet}p(p^{\bullet})$ set of input (output) transitions of p. These notations are extended to subsets of T and P : for example, if $P_i \subset P$ then, ${}^{\bullet}P_i = \bigcup_{p_k \in P_i} {}^{\bullet}p_k$.

Definition 3 : A marking M of a PN, $\mathcal{N} = (P,T,\alpha,\beta)$, is a mapping of P into $\mathbb{N}$: $P \xrightarrow{M} \mathbb{N}$. When $|P| = n$, one can represent a marking M by a vector $M \in \mathbb{N}^n$, such that its i-th entry $m_i = M(p_i)$.

Definition 4 : A transition t of a PN is enabled for a marking M iff :
$\forall p \in {}^{\bullet}t \Rightarrow \alpha(p,t) \leq M(p)$

Definition 5 : Let $\mathcal{M}_t$ the set of markings for which a transition t of a PN is enabled. The firing of the transition t (F(t)) is a mapping of $\mathcal{M}_t$ into the set of the markings $\mathcal{M}$ defined as follows : if $F(t)\,[M_i] = M_j$ then

$$M_j(p) = \begin{cases} M_i(p), \forall p \notin {}^{\bullet}t \cup t^{\bullet} \\ M_i(p) - \alpha(p,t), \forall p \in {}^{\bullet}t - ({}^{\bullet}t \cap t^{\bullet}) \\ M_i(p) + \beta(p,t), \forall p \in t^{\bullet} - ({}^{\bullet}t \cap t^{\bullet}) \\ M_i(p) + \beta(p,t) - \alpha(p,t), \forall p \in {}^{\bullet}t \cap t^{\bullet} \end{cases}$$

Definition 6 : Let a PN, $\mathcal{N} = (P,T,\alpha,\beta)$ and M one of its markings. Consider a sequence of transitions $\sigma = t_{j_1} t_{j_2} \ldots t_{j_s}$. We say that σ is a simulation sequence or a firing sequence from M_0 iff there exists a sequence of markings $M_1, M_2, M_3, \ldots M_s$

such that $F(t_{j_i})\,[M_{i-1}] = M_i$ for $i = 1,2,3,\ldots,s$. We note : $M_0 \overset{\sigma}{\to} M_s$. M_s is the marking attained by applying σ from M_0. We denote by $\vec{M}_0$ the set of markings that can be attained from M_0. The firing vector of σ is a vector R, $R \in \mathbb{N}^m$, $m = |T|$, such that its k-th entry is equal to the number of occurrences of the transition t_k in σ.

Definition 7 : An ordinary PN, $N = (P,T,\alpha,\beta)$, is a PN such that : $\alpha : PxT \to \{0,1\}$ and $\beta : PxT \to \{0,1\}$. A marked graph is an ordinary PN such that : $\forall p \in P$, $|{}^{\bullet}p| \le 1$ and $|p^{\bullet}| \le 1$. A state graph is an ordinary PN such that : $\forall t \in T$, $|t^{\bullet}| \le 1$ and $|{}^{\bullet}t| \le 1$.

Definition 8 : Let a PN and one of its markings M_0.
We say that a place p is bounded for M_0 iff $\exists k \in \mathbb{N}$ such that : $\forall M \in \vec{M}_0$, $M(p) < k$. A PN is bounded for M_0 iff all its places are bounded. We say that a transition t is live for M_0 iff for every marking M, $M \in \vec{M}_0$, there exists a sequence σ, $\sigma \in T^*$ such that σt is a firing sequence from M. A net having all its transitions live for a marking M_0, is called live for M_0.

Definition 9 : A pure PN is a PN such that $\forall t \in T$, $\{{}^{\bullet}t\} \cap \{t^{\bullet}\} = \emptyset$.
For a pure PN, $N = (P,T,\alpha,\beta)$, $|P| = n$, $|T| = m$, one can define the matrices :

$$- C = [c_{ij}]_{nxm} \quad \text{with } c_{ij} = \begin{cases} \beta(p_i,t_j) & \text{if } \beta(p_i,t_j) \ne 0 \\ -\alpha(p_i,t_j) & \text{if } \alpha(p_i,t_j) \ne 0 \\ 0 \text{ if not} \end{cases}$$

C is called incidence matrix of the net [7].

$$- C^+ = [c^+_{ij}]_{nxm} \quad \text{with } c^+_{ij} = \begin{cases} \beta(p_i,t_j) & \text{if } \beta(p_i,t_j) \ne 0 \\ 0 \text{ if not} \end{cases}$$

$$- C^- = [c^-_{ij}]_{nxm} \quad \text{with } c^-_{ij} = \begin{cases} \alpha(p_i,t_j) & \text{if } \alpha(p_i,t_j) \ne 0 \\ 0 \text{ if not} \end{cases}$$

Remark : $C = C^+ - C^-$

II - TIMED PETRI NETS

II.1 - Definitions

Definition 10 : A Timed Petri Net (TPN) consists in giving :
- a Petri net $N = (P,T,\alpha,\beta)$
- $\mathcal{T} = (\tau_1,\tau_2,\ldots,\tau_i,\ldots)$ an increasing sequence of real numbers called time base
- a mapping $\nu : P \times \mathcal{T} \to \mathcal{T}$ such that, $\forall (p,\tau_i) \in P \times \mathcal{T} : \nu(p,\tau_i) = \tau_j \Rightarrow \tau_j \ge \tau_i$

Simulation Rules

a) A marker in a TPN may be in one of the two following states : available or unavailable. Initially each place p contains $M_0(p)$ available markers.

b) A transition t is enabled iff every place p_s, $p_s \in {}^{\bullet}t$, contains $\alpha(p_s,t)$ available markers at least.

c) The firing of a transition t has to take place instantaneously as soon as t is enabled. It consists in removing $\alpha(p_s,t)$ available markers from each place p_s, $p_s \in {}^{\bullet}t$ and in placing $\beta(p_w,t)$ markers in each place $p_w \in t^{\bullet}$.

d) A marker remains unavailable in a place p_s during the time interval between the instant of its arrival τ_i and the instant $\nu(p_s,\tau_i)$; then it becomes available.

Remark : According to the above definition, firings in a TPN take place only at moments of $\mathcal{T}$.

In what follows we study the behavior of pure TPN's such that $\forall(p_i,\tau) \in P \times \mathcal{T} : \tau(p_i,\tau) - \tau = z_i$ = constant. That is, each marker is delayed by z_i in the place independently of the instant of its arrival.

Definition 11 : Let a TPN, $M_1 M_2 \ldots M_s$ the markings attained successively from an initial marking M_0 by applying a firing sequence $\sigma = t_{i_0}, t_{i_1}, \ldots, t_{i_{s-1}}$ and $\tau_{i_0}, \tau_{i_1}, \ldots, \tau_{i_{s-1}}$ the moments of firing of the transitions $t_{i_0}, t_{i_1}, \ldots, t_{i_{s-1}}$ respectively. The marking of the net at a moment τ_{i_k} will be by definition the marking of the net in the interval $\tau_{i_{k-1}} \leq \tau < \tau_{i_k}$. Generally, the marking of a TPN with $\mathcal{T} = (\tau_0, \tau_1, \tau_2, \ldots, \tau_i, \ldots)$ at a moment $\tau_i \in \mathcal{T}$ will be the marking of the net at the interval $\tau_{i-1} \leq \tau < \tau_i$, i = 1,2,3,... The marking at τ_0 corresponds to the initial marking. For a TPN with n places we define a general temporal variable $Q^t(\tau) = [q_1(\tau), q_2(\tau), \ldots, q_n(\tau)]$, ($Q^t$ denotes the transpose of a matrix Q), such that $\forall \tau_i \in \mathcal{T}$, $Q(\tau_i) = M$ where M is the marking at the moment τ_i. The variable $Q(\tau)$ will be called charge variable.

Let M_i be a marking attained from a marking M by applying a sequence $\sigma, (M_0 \overset{\sigma}{\to} M)$ in a PN defined by its incidence matrix C. Then

$$M_s = M_0 + CR \qquad \text{(I)}$$

where $R \in \mathbb{N}^m$, $m = |T|$, is the firing vector of σ. Equation (I) can be written for a TPN

$$Q(\tau) = Q(\tau_0) + CR(\tau) \qquad \text{(II)}$$

Let us suppose now, that $\tau \neq \tau_0$ and put $\Delta\tau = \tau - \tau_0$. We have from (II)

$$\frac{\Delta Q(\tau)}{\Delta\tau} = \frac{Q(\tau) - Q(\tau_0)}{\Delta\tau} = C\,\frac{R(\tau)}{\Delta\tau} = CI(\tau) \Rightarrow \frac{\Delta Q(\tau)}{\Delta\tau} = CI(\tau) \qquad \text{(III)}$$

where :

- $\frac{Q(\tau)}{\Delta\tau}$ is a vector representing the mean variation of the charge of the net in the interval $\Delta\tau$.

- the kth entry of the vector I, $i_k = \frac{r_k(\tau)}{\Delta\tau}$ represents the mean frequence of firing of the transition t_k during $\Delta\tau$.

The vector $I(\tau)$ will be called <u>current vector</u> and evidently $\forall\tau_j \in T$, $I(\tau_j) > 0$.

II.2 - Description of the Behavior for Constant Currents

II.2.1 - General Case

We are interested in the cases of functioning with constant currents for which the total charge of the net remains bounded. This amounts to searching for solutions of the equation :

$$CI = 0 \qquad I > 0 \qquad \text{(IV)}$$

Those solutions correspond to cyclic firing sequences in the net as it is shown in [6]. We give additional relations that the current vector I, must satisfy in terms of the initial marking and of the delays associated to the places.

<u>Definition 12</u> : Let C a matrix of order $n \times m$ on $\mathbb{Q}$. We denote by $\mathcal{C}$ (respectively $\mathcal{C}^t$) the set of non negative solutions of $CX = 0$, $(C^tX = 0)$. A <u>generator</u> of $\mathcal{C}(\mathcal{C}^t)$ is a set of vectors $\{X_j\}^s_{j=1}$, $X_j \in \mathbb{N}^m$, $(X_j \in \mathbb{N}^n)$ such that any element X_0 of $\mathcal{C}(\mathcal{C}^t)$ could be expressed as the linear combination of elements of $\{X_j\}^s_{j=1}$ with non negative rational coefficients. That is, $X_0 = \sum_{j=1} \lambda_j X_j$, where λ_j are non negative rational numbers.

If we assign constant currents to the transitions of a bounded TPN, we have a periodic functioning and let $Q(\tau_{k_0})$, $Q(\tau_{k_1})\ldots Q(\tau_{k_s})$ the successive markings of the net during a period. Then, the mean value $\bar{Q}$ of the charge variable $Q(\tau)$ is given by :

$$\bar{Q} = \frac{Q(\tau_{k_0}) + Q(\tau_{k_1}) + Q(\tau_{k_2}) + \ldots + Q(\tau_{k_s})}{s + 1}$$

If we multiply this last equation by J_0^t, $J_0^t \in \mathcal{C}^t$, we obtain :

$$J_0^t\bar{Q} = J_0^tQ(\tau_0) \qquad \text{(Va)}$$

But the mean value $\bar{q}_w$ of the charge of a place p_w satisfies the inequality

$$\bar{q}_w \geq z_w\, C_w^+\, I$$

where C_w^+ is the wth line of the matrix C^+ and the product C_w^+I represents the mean frequence of the arrivals of markers at the place p_w.

Let Z the square matrix of order n :

$$Z = \begin{bmatrix} z_1 & 0 & 0 & 0 & 0 \ldots 0 \\ 0 & z_2 & 0 & 0 & 0 \ldots 0 \\ 0 & 0 & z_3 & 0 & 0 \ldots 0 \\ \cdots & \cdots & \cdots & \cdots & \cdots \\ 0 & 0 & 0 & 0 & 0 \ldots z_n \end{bmatrix}$$

Then, the set of the inequalities $\{\bar{q}_w \geq z_w\, C_w^+\, I\}_{w=1}^{n}$ can be written in the form :

$$\bar{Q} \geq Z\, C^+\, I = Z\, C^-\, I \qquad \text{(Vb)}$$

Let J_0^t a positive solution of $J^tC = 0$. One can obtain from (Va) and (Vb) :

$$J_0^t Q(\tau_0) \geq Z\, C^+ = Z\, C^-\, I \qquad \text{(Vc)}$$

This last inequality estabilishes a relation between the initial marking, the current vector and the delays associated to the places of a TPN.

Let $\mathcal{J} = \{J_1^t, J_2^t, \ldots, J_k^t\}$ a generator of $\mathcal{C}^t$. Then, if $J_0^t \in \mathcal{C}^t$, any inequality $J_0^t Q(\tau_0) \geq J_0^t\, Z\, C^+\, I$ can be expressed as a linear combination of the set of inequalities $\{J_s^t Q(\tau_0) \geq J_s^t\, Z\, C^+\, I\}_{s=1}^{k}$

The relations

$$CI = 0, \quad I > 0 \qquad \text{(IV)}$$

$$\{J_s^t Q(\tau_0) \geq J_s^t Z\, C^+\, I\}_{j=1}^{k} \qquad \text{(V)}$$

describe the functioning of a timed Petri Net for constant currents.

II.2.2 - Functioning of TPN at its natural rate

Definition 13 : Given a TPN by its incidence matrix C and its delay matrix Z, we say that it functions at its natural rate for a given current vector I_0, iff I_0 satisfies the equations $CI = 0$ (IV) and $\{J_s^t Q(\tau_0) = J_s^t Z\, C^+\, I\}_{s=1}^{k}$ (VI), where $\{J_s^t\}_{s=1}^{k}$ is a generator of $\mathcal{C}^t$.

Proposition 1 : There exists at most n linearly independent equations describing the functioning at natural rate of a TPN with n places.

Proof : Suppose that the rank of C is equal to ρ. Then (IV) contains ρ linearly independent equations at most. Also, the dimension of the space of the solutions of $J^tC = 0$ is $n-\rho$. Thus (VI) has at most $n-\rho$ linearly independent equations and consequently there exists at most n linearly independent equations in the system (IV)(VI).

Example 1 : Let the TPN of figure 1. We want to calculate the current vectors, (if there exists any), corresponding to functionings at natural rate. $Q(\tau_0)$ and Z are supposed given.

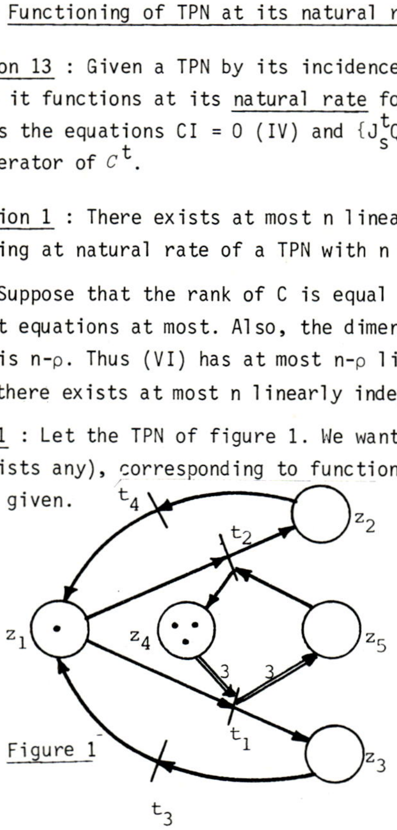

Figure 1

$$C = \begin{bmatrix} -1 & -1 & 1 & 1 \\ 0 & 1 & 0 & -1 \\ 1 & 0 & -1 & 0 \\ -3 & 1 & 0 & 0 \\ 3 & -1 & 0 & 0 \end{bmatrix}$$

Solution of $CI = 0$: we find $i_2 = i_4 = 3i_1$, $i_1 = i_3$

A generator of C^t is : $J_1^t = [1\ 1\ 1\ 0\ 0]$ $J_2^t = [0\ 0\ 0\ 1\ 1]$

$J_1^t Z C^+ I = J_1^t Q_0 \Rightarrow q_{0_1} + q_{0_2} + q_{0_3} = z_1 i_3 + z_1 i_4 + z_2 i_2 + z_3 i_1$

$J_2^t Z C^+ I = J_2^t Q_0 \Rightarrow q_{0_4} + q_{0_5} = i_2 z_4 + 3 i_1 z_5$

The condition for the existence of a solution is : $\dfrac{q_{0_1} + q_{0_2} + q_{0_3}}{4z_1 + 3z_2 + z_3} = \dfrac{q_{0_4} + q_{0_5}}{3(z_4 + z_5)}$ (α)

In this case $i_1 = \dfrac{q_{0_4} + q_{0_5}}{3(z_4 + z_5)}$, $i_2 = \dfrac{q_{0_4} + q_{0_5}}{z_4 + z_5}$

Suppose now, that we have $z_1 = z_2 = z_3 = z_4 = z_5 = 1$ and $Q_0^t = [1\ 0\ 0\ 3\ 0]$ then the equation (α) is not verified and there is no functioning at natural rate possible. The inequalities (V) give :

$q_{0_1} + q_{0_2} + q_{0_3} \geq z_1(i_3 + i_4) + z_2 i_2 + z_3 i_1 \Rightarrow 1 \geq 8i_1$

$q_{0_4} + q_{0_5} \geq i_2 z_4 + 3i_1 z_5 \Rightarrow 3 \geq 6i_1$

which gives : $i_{1\,max} = \min\{\frac{1}{8}, \frac{1}{2}\} = \frac{1}{8}$ and $i_{2\,max} = \frac{3}{8}$.

III - SOLUTION OF CI = 0 AND $J^tC = 0$. DECOMPOSITION

In this section we present some results relative to the properties of non negative solutions of $CI = 0$ and $J^tC = 0$, where C is the incidence matrix of a PN. Many authors have used linear equations for the study of the properties of PN's [6][7][9][10][11][12][14]. In particular, a part of the results on the decomposition of PN's exposed in this section have been developped independently by Memmi [10] Crespi-Reghizzi and Mandrioli [9] and the author [14]. Also, similar results, in a less restrained context, are well known since several years (see for example [13]). Our contribution consists in making evident the relations between the structure of the net (decomposability into consistent and invariant components) and the solutions of $CI = 0$ and $J^tC = 0$. We borrowed the terms "consistent" and "invariant" from [6] and [7] respectively and the term "support" from FulKerson [13], although it is used in a slightly different sense. This study is limited to pure and strongly connected PN's. Pureness is imposed by the fact that we use the incidence matrix for representing PN's and strong connexity by the fact that it is a necessary condition for a net to be bounded [6]. In what follows, the term "PN" denotes a strongly connected and pure PN.

Definition 14 : Being given a PN, $N = (P,T,\alpha,\beta)$ a subnet of N is a PN $N_1 = (P_1,T_1,\alpha_1,\beta_1)$ such that $P_1 \subset P$, $T_1 \subset T$ and

$\alpha_1 : P_1 \times T_1 \to \mathbb{N}$ such that $\alpha_1(p,t) = \begin{cases} \alpha(p,t) \text{ if } (p,t) \in P_1 \times T_1 \\ 0 \text{ if not} \end{cases}$

$\beta_1 = P_1 \times T_1 \to \mathbb{N}$ such that $\beta_1(p,t) = \begin{cases} \beta(p,t) \text{ if } (p,t) \in P_1 \times T_1 \\ 0 \text{ if not} \end{cases}$

Definition 15 : The union of two subnets $\mathcal{N}_1 = (P_1,T_1,\alpha_1,\beta_1)$, $\mathcal{N}_2 = (P_2,T_2,\alpha_2,\beta_2)$ of a PN $\mathcal{N} = (P,T,\alpha,\beta)$ is a subnet of $\mathcal{N}$, $\mathcal{N}_3 = (P_3,T_3,\alpha_3,\beta_3)$, with $P_3 = P_1 \cup P_2$ and $T_3 = T_1 \cup T_2$.

Definition 16 : Let $\mathcal{N} = (P,T,\alpha,\beta)$ a PN and $S = \{\mathcal{N}_i = (P_i,T_i,\alpha_i,\beta_i)\}_{i=1}^{k}$ a set of subnets of $\mathcal{N}$. $\mathcal{N}$ is covered by S or S is a decomposition of $\mathcal{N}$ if $P = \bigcup_{i=1}^{k} P_i$ and $T = \bigcup_{i=1}^{k} T_i$.

III.1 - Non negative solutions of CI = 0. Decomposition into consistent components

Definition 17 : Let $\mathcal{N} = (P,T,\alpha,\beta)$ a PN. Then a set $T_1 \subset T$ defines a t-complete subnet of $\mathcal{N}$, $\mathcal{N}_1 = (P_1,T_1,\alpha_1,\beta_1)$ if $P_1 = {}^{\bullet}T_1 = T_1^{\bullet}$.

Proposition 2 : Let C the incidence matrix of a PN and $I_0 \in \mathcal{C}$. Then, the set $T_1 = \{t_j | i_{0_j} \neq 0\}$ defines a t-complete subnet of the net having C as incidence matrix.

Proof : Consider the subnet with $T_1 = \{t_j | i_{0_j} \neq 0\}$ and $P_1 = {}^{\bullet}T_1 \cup T_1^{\bullet}$. Then each place p of P_1 has at least one input transition or one output transition (by construction of the set P_1). Suppose that a place p_w, $p_w \in P_1$, has the input transitions $t_{i_1}, t_{i_2},\dots,t_{i_r}$ but no output transition in the subnet defined by P_1 and T_1. Then we have : $\sum_j i_{0_{ij}} \beta(p_w,t_{i_j}) = 0$ where $i_{0_{ij}}$ and $\beta(p_w,t_{i_j})$ are rational positive numbers (absurde). So, p_w must have an output transition belonging to T_1. In the same manner one can prove that if a place p_w has an output transition belonging to T_1 then it has an input transition belonging to T_1.

Definition 18 : Let C the incidence matrix of a PN, $\mathcal{N}$. A consistent component of $\mathcal{N}$ is any t-complete subnet $\mathcal{N}_1$ defined by the set of transitions corresponding to the positive entries of a vector I_1, $I_1 \in \mathcal{C}$. $\mathcal{N}_1$ is the support of I_1, (we note $\mathcal{N}_1 = S(I_1)$). If there exists I_0 such that $S(I_0) = \mathcal{N}$ then, we say that $\mathcal{N}$ is consistent.

Definition 19 : Let a PN with an initial marking M. A firing sequence σ is a cyclic firing sequence from M iff $M \xrightarrow{\sigma} M$.

Proposition 3 [6] : A PN having a live and bounded marking is consistent.

Proposition 4 [6] : Let $\mathcal{N}_1 = (P_1,T_1,\alpha_1,\beta_1)$ a consistent component of a net $\mathcal{N}$. Then $\mathcal{N}_1$ has a marking M from which there exists a cyclic firing sequence $\sigma = t_{k_1},t_{k_2},\dots,t_{k_s}$ such that $\bigcup_{j=1}^{s} t_{k_j} = T_1$. Inversely, each cyclic firing sequence in $\mathcal{N}$, $\sigma = t_{k_1},t_{k_2},\dots,t_{k_s}$, defines a consistent component of $\mathcal{N}$ having as set of transitions $T_1 = \bigcup_{j=1}^{s} t_{k_j}$.

Proposition 5 : The union of two consistent components of a net is a consistent component.

Proof : Let I_1, I_2 two elements of C defining two consistent components $S(I_1)$ and $S(I_2)$. Then, $I_1 + I_2 \in C$ defines the consistent component $S(I_1) \cup S(I_2)$.

Definition 20 : Let $I_1 \in C$, C being the incidence matrix of a PN, N. Then, $S(I_1)$ is an elementary consistent component of N iff there exists no I_2, $I_2 \neq 0$, $I_2 \in C$, such that $S(I_2) \subsetneq S(I_1)$. A vector I_1 defining an elementary consistent component $S(I_1)$ is called elementary vector of C.

Proposition 6 : If C is the incidence matrix of a PN and I_1, I_2 two elementary vectors of C such that $S(I_1) = S(I_2)$ then, I_1, I_2 are linearly dependent.

Proof : Suppose that I_1 and I_2 are linearly independent and $S(I_1) = S(I_2)$. Let $\lambda = \min_{i_{2j} \neq 0} \{\frac{i_{1j}}{i_{2j}}\}$ and $I_3' = I_1 - \lambda I_2$. Then, $I_3' \neq 0$ and there exists a scalar μ such that $I_3 = \mu I_3' \in C$. We have $S(I_3) \subsetneq S(I_1)$. So, $S(I_1)$ is not elementary.

Proposition 7 : Every consistent PN, N, can be decomposed into a set of elementary consistent components.

Proof : Let $I_0 \in C$, $S(I_0) = N$ and suppose that N is not elementary. Then, there exists a consistent component N_1, $N_1 \subsetneq N$ and I_1 such that $S(I_1) = N_1$. Let $\lambda = \min_{i_{1j} \neq 0} \{\frac{i_{0j}}{i_{1j}}\}$ and $I_2' = I_0 - \lambda I_1$. Then, it is easy to verify that there exists a scalar μ such that $I_2 = \mu I_2' \in C$ and if $N_2 = S(I_2)$ then $N = N_1 \cup N_2$.

Corollary 1 : The set of elementary vectors of C is a generator.

Definition 21 : Let a PN, N, with incidence matrix C and S a set of elementary vectors of C. Then, S is a t-base of N iff S is a generator (of C) of minimal cardinality.

Proposition 8 : Let $B = [I_1, I_2, \ldots, I_S]$ a matrix of order $m \times s$ such that $\{I_j\}_{j=1}^{s}$ is a t-base of a PN. Then, the rank of B is less or equal to $m - \rho$ where ρ is the rank of the incidence matrix of the net. Furthermore, if the net is consistent, then the rank of B is equal to $m - \rho$.

Proof : The fact that rank $[B] \leq m - \rho$ is obvious because the space of the solutions of $CI = 0$ is of dimension $m - \rho$. In order to prove that rank $[B] = m - \rho$, in the case of a consistent net, it is sufficient to prove that any solution I_0 of $CI = 0$ can be expressed as the linear combination of $I_1, I_2, \ldots, I_S$ (columns of B). If $I_0 > 0$ this is always possible according to corollary 1. If not, one can obtain from I_0, a vector $\tilde{I}$, $\tilde{I} > 0$ such that $\tilde{I} = \sum_{j=1}^{S} \beta_j I_j + I_0$ where the β_j's are non negative rational numbers. But $C\tilde{I} = 0$ and $\tilde{I}$ defines a consistent component. So, according to the corollary 1, we can write $\tilde{I} = \sum_{j=1}^{s} \gamma_j I_j$. This gives $I_0 = \sum_{j=1}^{s} (\gamma_j - \beta_j) I_j$.

Remark : $C\,B = 0$. For any current vector $I \in \mathcal{C}$, $I = B\,I_b$, the k-th entry of I_b being the "loop current" associated to the elementary component corresponding to the k-th column of B.

III.2 - Non negative solutions of $J^tC = 0$. Decomposition into invariant components

The following definitions and propositions are dual of those in III.1.

Definition 22 : Let $N = (P,T,\alpha,\beta)$ a PN. Then a set P_1, $P_1 \subset P$, defines a p-complete subnet of N, $N_1 = (P_1,T_1,\alpha_1,\beta_1)$, if $T_1 = {}^{\cdot}P_1 = P_1^{\cdot}$.

Proposition 9 : Let C the incidence matrix of a PN and $J_0^t \in \mathcal{C}^t$. Then, the set $P_1 = \{p_i | j_{0_i} \neq 0\}$ defines a p-complete subnet of the net having C as incidence matrix.

Definition 23 : Let C the incidence matrix of a PN, N. An invariant component of N is any p-complete subnet N_1 defined by the set of places corresponding to the positive entries of a vector J_1^t, $J_1^t \in \mathcal{C}^t$. N_1 is the support of J_1^t, (we note $N_1 = S(J_1^t)$). If there exists J_0^t such that $S(J_0^t) = N$ then, we say that N is invariant.

Proposition 10 : The union of two invariant components is an invariant component.

Definition 24 : Let $J_1^t \in \mathcal{C}^t$, C being the incidence matrix of a PN, N. Then, $S(J_1^t)$ is an elementary invariant component of N iff there exists no J_2^t, $J_2^t \neq 0$, $J_2^t \in \mathcal{C}^t$, such that $S(J_2^t) \subsetneq S(J_1^t)$. A vector J_1^t defining an elementary invariant component $S(J_1^t)$ is called elementary vector of $\mathcal{C}^t$.

Proposition 11 : If C is the incidence matrix of a PN and J_1^t, J_2^t two elementary vectors of $\mathcal{C}^t$ such that $S(J_1^t) = S(J_2^t)$ then, J_1^t, J_2^t are linearly dependent.

Proposition 12 : Every invariant PN, N, can be decomposed into a set of elementary invariant components.

Corollary 2 : The set of elementary vectors of $\mathcal{C}^t$ is a generator (of $\mathcal{C}^t$).

Definition 25 : Let a PN, N, with incidence matrix C and S a set of elementary vectors of $\mathcal{C}^t$. Then, S is a p-base of N iff S is a generator (of $\mathcal{C}^t$) of minimal cardinality.

Proposition 13 : Let $D = [J_1, J_2, \ldots, J_s]$ a matrix of order $n \times s$ such that $\{J_i^t\}_{i=1}^{s}$

is a p-base of a PN. Then, the rank of D is less than or equal to $n - \rho$ where ρ is the rank of the incidence matrix of the net. Furthermore, if the net is invariant, then, rank $[D] = n - \rho$.

III.3 - Particular cases : State Graphs and Marked Graphs

Proposition 14 : Let C the incidence matrix of a pure and strongly connected state graph with n places and m transitions. Then,

a) rank $[C] = n - 1$

b) the space of solutions of $CI = 0$ is of dimension $m - n + 1$

c) the space of solutions of $J^tC = 0$ is of dimension 1 and the vector $J_0^t = [1\ 1\ 1\ \ldots\ 1]$ is a base of this space.

Proof : Well known results of the net theory.

Remarks : - A t-base for a state graph is a circuit base
- The proposition 14c expresses the fact that any strongly connected state graph is an elementary invariant component.

Proposition 15 : Let C the incidence matrix of a pure strongly connected marked graph with n-places and m transitions. Then,

a) rank $[C] = m - 1$

b) the space of the solutions of $CI = 0$ is of dimension 1 and the vector $I_0^t = [1\ 1\ 1\ \ldots\ 1]$ is a base of this space.

c) the space of solutions of $J^tC = 0$ is of dimension $n - m + 1$

Proof : This proposition is dual of the preceding one.

Remarks : - A t-base for a marked graph is a circuit base
- The proposition 15b expresses the fact that any strongly connected marked graph is an elementary consistent component.

IV - RESOLUTION OF THE EQUATIONS (IV) AND (VI) BEING GIVEN $Q(\tau_0)$ AND Z

In this section we show that the problem of determining the currents of a TPN for functioning at natural rate, when we know $Q(\tau_0)$ and Z may have either several solutions or no solution at all. The extreme cases correspond to state graphs and marked graphs.

Example 2 : For the TPN of the figure 2 the system of the equations (IV) (VI) generally has a unique solution for I. We have : $B^t = \begin{bmatrix} 2 & 1 & 1 & 0 & 1 & 1 \\ 2 & 1 & 1 & 1 & 2 & 0 \end{bmatrix}$ and $D = \begin{bmatrix} 1 & 1 & 1 & 0 & 0 \\ 0 & 0 & 0 & 1 & 1 \end{bmatrix}$.
If i_x and i_y are the currents associated respectively to the two elementary consistent components of the net, we have, $I = B \begin{vmatrix} i_x \\ i_y \end{vmatrix}$.

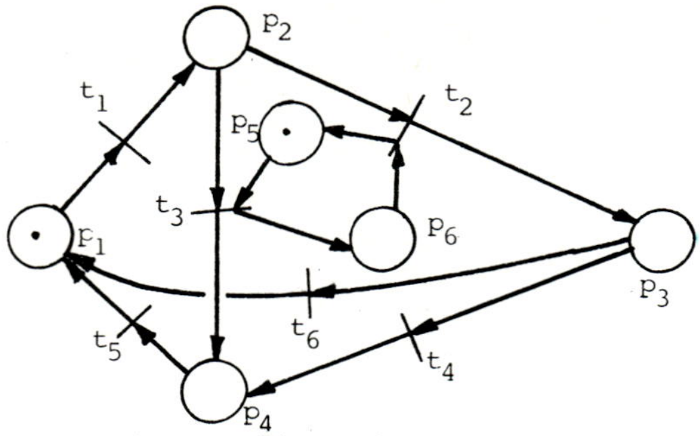

Figure 2

On the other hand, we have two equations expressing the charge conservation in the state graphs defined by the lines of D.

$$(i_x + i_y)\, 2z_0 = 1 \quad (\text{we put } z_0 = z_5 = z_6)$$

$$2(i_x + i_y)\, z_1 + 2(i_x + i_y)\, z_2 + (i_x + i_y)\, z_3 + (2i_y + i_x)\, z_4 = 1$$

By resolving this system we obtain :

$$i_x = \frac{2(z_1 + z_2 + z_4) + z_3 - 2z_0}{2z_0\, z_4}, \qquad i_y = \frac{2z_0 - 2(z_1 + z_2) - z_3 - z_4}{2z_0\, z_4}$$

where i_x and i_y must satisfy the inequalities $i_y > 0$ and $i_x + i_y > 0$. The second inequality is always verified and the first gives the condition :

$$z_0 > \frac{2(z_1 + z_2) + z_3 + z_4}{2}$$

Timed Marked Graphs : In this case we have $n \geq m$ ($n = |P|$, $m = |T|$, the equality is verified only if the marked graph is a circuit). So, the currents determined by solving m among the n equations (IV) (VI), must satisfy the remaining $n-m$ equations in order to have a functioning at natural rate. If not, it is sufficient to search for the solutions of :

$$\{J_r^t\, Q_0 \geq J_r^t\, Z\, C^+\, I\}_{r=1}^{n-m+1}$$

where, $\{J_r^t\}_{r=1}^{n-m+1}$ is a p-base (base of circuits in this case) and $I^t = [ii\ldots i]$ solution of $CI = 0$.

The rth inequality can be written in the form : $\sum_{K_r} q_{0_i} \geq (\sum_{K_r} z_i)i$, where $\sum_{K_r} q_{0_i}$ is the sum of the markers in the circuit K_r, $K_r = S(J_r^t)$ and $\sum_{K_r} z_i$ is the sum of the delays associated to the places of this circuit. Therefore,

$$i_{max} = \min_{r=1}^{n-m+1} \{(\sum_{K_r} q_{0_i})/(\sum_{K_r} z_i)\}.$$ This result is given in [6].

Timed State Graphs : In this case $m \geq n$ and it is always possible to solve for I the system (IV) (VI). One can construct a system having a unique solution for I by giving additional equations imposing a constant ratio between the currents of the transitions having the same input place. There exists exactly $m-n$ linearly independent equations of this kind for any state graph.

Example 3 : Let the timed state graph of figure 3. The solution of CI = 0 gives :

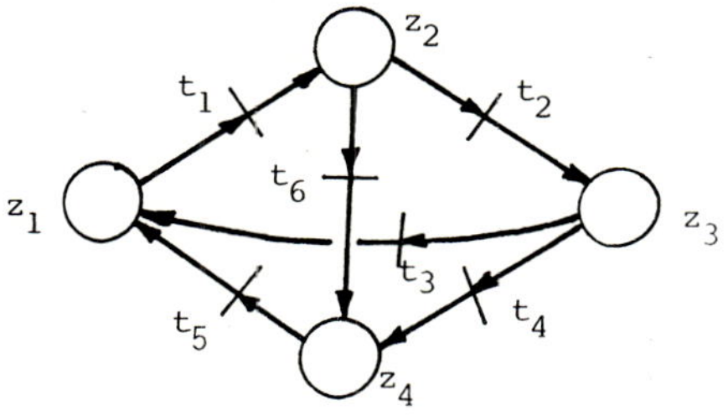

Figure 3

$$i_1 = i_3 + i_4 + i_6$$

$$i_2 = i_3 + i_4$$

$$i_5 = i_6 + i_4$$

The equation of conservation of the charge in the graph is

$$(i_6+i_3+i_4)(z_1+z_2)+(i_3+i_4)z_3+(i_4+i_6)z_4 = \sum_{j=1}^{4} q_{0_j}$$

If we impose $\frac{i_2}{i_6} = \lambda_1$ and $\frac{i_3}{i_4} = \lambda_2$ we have :

$$i_2 = \frac{\lambda_1 i_1}{\lambda_1+1}, \quad i_3 = \frac{\lambda_1 \lambda_2 i_1}{(1+\lambda_1)(1+\lambda_2)}, \quad i_4 = \frac{\lambda_1 i_1}{(1+\lambda_1)(1+\lambda_2)}, \quad i_5 = \frac{(1+\lambda_1+\lambda_2) i_1}{(1+\lambda_1)(1+\lambda_2)}, \quad i_6 = \frac{i_1}{1+\lambda_1}$$

We can now uniquely determine the currents in terms of Q_0, Z, and of the parameters λ_1 and λ_2. For example solving for i_1 we obtain :

$$i_1 \left[(z_1+z_2) + \frac{\lambda_1}{1+\lambda_1} z_3 + \frac{1+\lambda_1+\lambda_2}{(1+\lambda_1)(1+\lambda_2)} z_4\right] = \sum_{i=1}^{4} q_{0_i}$$

Remark : One can construct a system having a unique solution for I, from the system of the equations (IV) (VI) by imposing the additional constraint that the sum of the charge of each circuit of a base of circuits of the state graph is constant. In this case, we have (n-1) linearly independent equations from the system CI = 0 and m-n+1 linearly independent equations by application of this constraint. So we have m equations describing the behavior of the net. (The equation $[1\ 1\ 1\ \ldots\ 1]\ Q_0 = [1\ 1\ 1\ \ldots\ 1]\ ZC^{+}I$ can be obtained as the linear combination of the n-m+1 equations). The analogy with the electrical circuits is obvious. The m-n+1 equations express the application of the Kirchhoff's voltage law : the sum of $i_j\ z_j$ (voltage drops) for a circuit is equal to its total charge (electromotive force).

IV - APPLICATIONS

Example 4 : Producer-Consumer System

Consider the producer-consumer problem with a buffer of bounded capacity N_0. We suppose that the producer and the consumer do not try to access the buffer at the same time. The producer deposits items in the buffer as long as it is not full and the consumer does not try to take an item from the buffer when it is empty. Items are produced, deposited, taken and consumed one by one.

The TPN of figure 4 describes the system producer-consumer with a possible initial marking. Interpretation of the delays associated to the places :

z_p : mean time of producing an item
z_d : mean time of depositing an item
z_t : mean time of taking an item
z_c : mean time of consuming an item.

We suppose that the z_i' s associated to the other places are equal to zero. That is, the producer and the consumer are functioning at maximum speed : the producer is allowed to deposit an item right after having produced one and he always finds the access to the buffer free. Also, the consumer is allowed to take an item right after having consumed one and he always finds the access to the buffer free.

By solving the equation CI=0 we find that the same current i must be associated to all the transitions. Also, a cover by elementary invariant components (state graphs in this case) is given in figure 5.

Problem : If we consider as initial marking this one given in figure 4 find the conditions for functioning at natural rate.

The inequality (V) applied for SG1, SG2, SG3, SG4 gives respectively :

$$i \le \frac{1}{z_p+z_d}, \quad i \le \frac{1}{z_d+z_t+z_s}, \quad i \le \frac{1}{z_c+z_t}, \quad i \le \frac{N_0}{z_d+z_t+z_a}$$

which gives : $i_{max} = \min \{\frac{1}{z_p+z_d}, \frac{1}{z_d+z_t+z_s}, \frac{1}{z_c+z_t}, \frac{N_0}{z_d+z_t+z_a}\}$

Conditions for functioning at natural rate :

$$z_s = z_p - z_t = z_c - z_d > 0 \quad \text{and} \quad N_0 - 1 = \frac{z_a - z_s}{z_p + z_d} = \frac{z_a - z_s}{z_c + z_t}$$

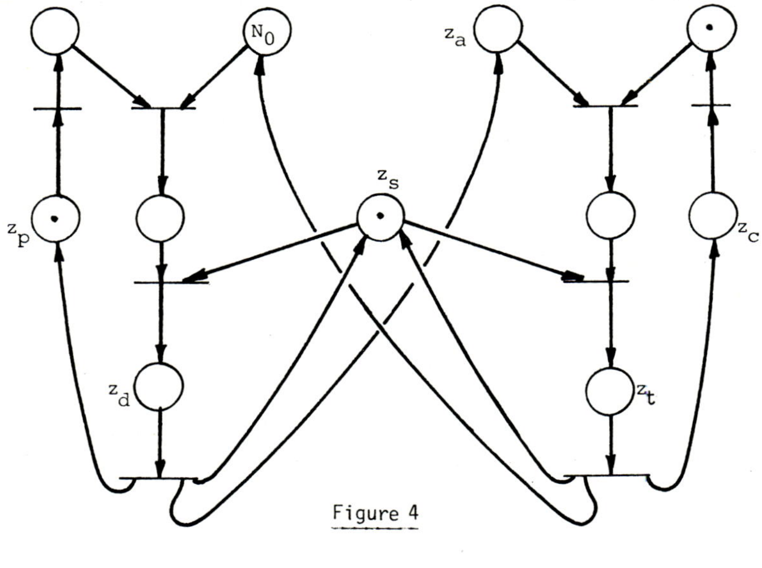

Figure 4

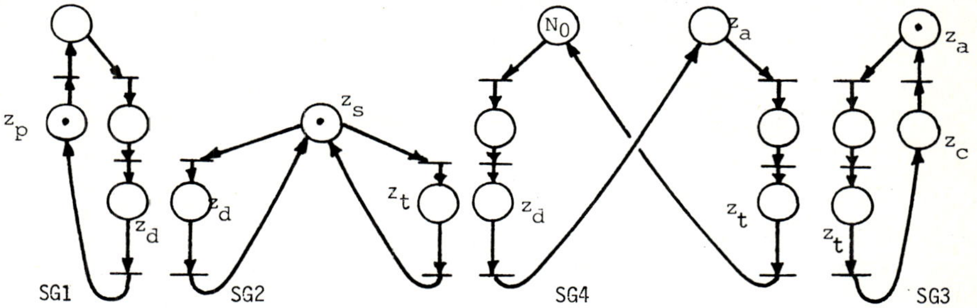

Figure 5

Conclusion : The producer's and consumer's periods must be equal : $z = z_p + z_d = z_c + z_t$. Also, z_s, the mean time between two successive accesses, is given by $z_s = z_p - z_t = z_c - z_d > 0$. From $N_0 - 1 = \frac{z_a - z_s}{z}$ we deduce that :

a) for $z_a < z_s$, a functioning at natural rate is impossible,

b) if $z_a = z_s$, a minimum capacity $N_0 = 1$ is necessary,

c) if $z_a > z_s$, a minimum capacity of $N_0 = 1 + \frac{z_a - z_s}{z}$ is necessary.

Example 5 : System of r producers and w consumers

Let a system of r producers and w consumers connected with a buffer of capacity N_0. The simultaneous access to the buffer is not allowed. We consider for the delays associated to the places the same notations as in the preceding example by adding an index in order to distinguish the producers and the consumers among them. So, z_{d_i} is the time for the deposit of an item by the i-th producer and z_{c_j} is the time of consuming an item by the j-th consumer. We consider the case in which procuders and consumers are functioning at maximum speed, which implies zero waiting times before the deposit or before taking an item (figure 6).

In figure 7, we give a decomposition of the PN representing the system, into elementary invariant components.

If i_{0_j} and i_{0_j} are the currents associated to the cycles of the j-th producer and j-th consumer respectively, we have :

$$\{i_{1_j} \leq \frac{1}{z_{d_j} + z_{p_j}}\}_{j=1}^{r} \qquad \{i_{2_j} \leq \frac{1}{z_{c_j} + z_{t_j}}\}_{j=1}^{w}$$

Furthermore, $\sum_{j=1}^{r} i_{1_j} = \sum_{j=1}^{w} i_{2_j} = i_0$ where i_0 is the current throughout the buffer.

So, $i_0 = \min \{ \sum_{j=1}^{r} \frac{1}{z_{d_j} + z_{p_j}}, \quad \sum_{j=1}^{w} \frac{1}{z_{c_j} + z_{t_j}} \}$

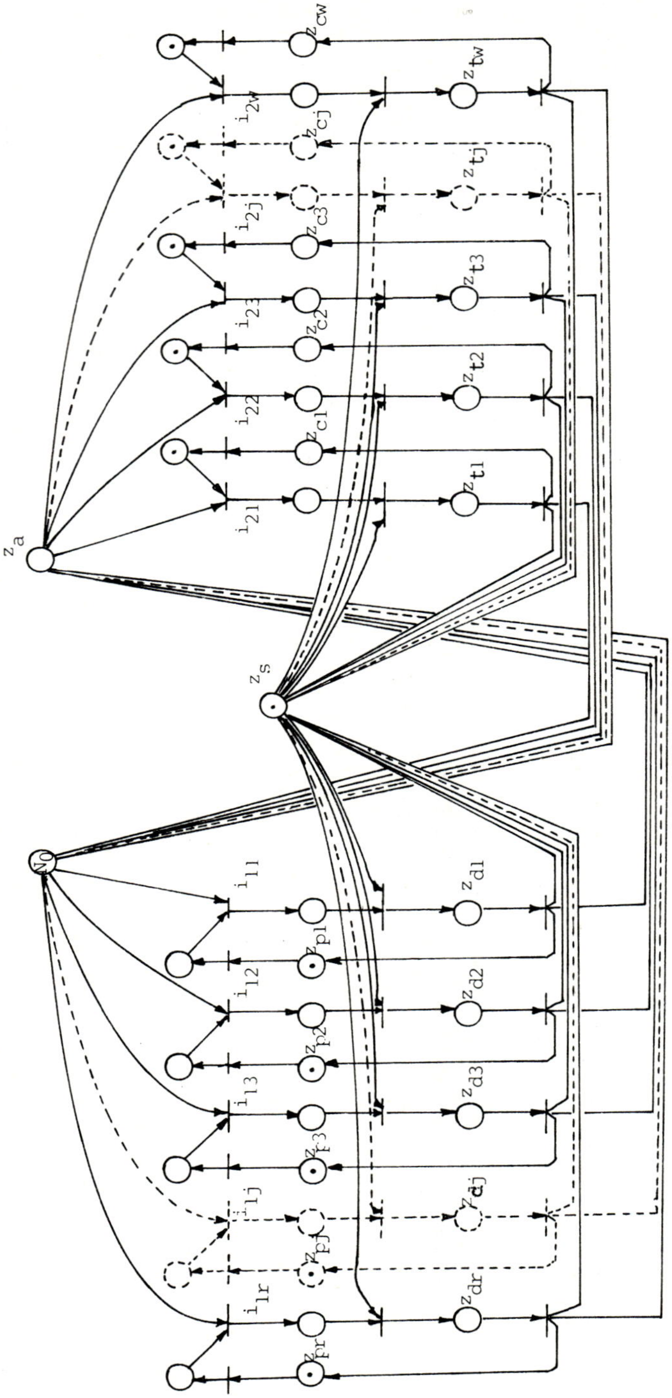
z_{cw}
z_{tw}
i_{2w}
z_{cj}
z_{tj}
i_{2j}
z_{c3}
z_{t3}
i_{23}
z_{c2}
z_{t2}
i_{22}
z_{c1}
z_{t1}
i_{21}
z_a
z_s
N0
i_{11}
z_{d1}
z_{p1}
i_{12}
z_{d2}
z_{p2}
i_{13}
z_{d3}
z_{p3}
i_{1j}
z_{dj}
z_{pj}
i_{1r}
z_{dr}
z_{pr}

Figure 6

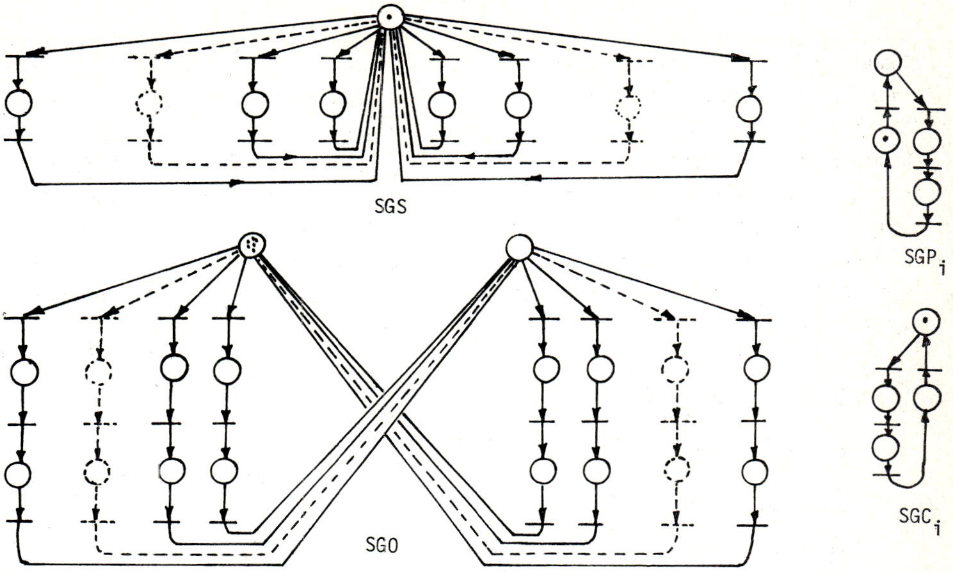

Figure 7

The equation of conservation of the charge is SGS is :

$$\sum_{j=1}^{r} i_{1_j} z_{d_j} + \sum_{j=1}^{w} i_{2j} z_{t_j} + i_0 z_s = 1 \Rightarrow z_s = \frac{1 - \sum_{j=1}^{r} i_{1_j} z_{dj} - \sum_{j=1}^{w} i_{2_j} z_{tj}}{i_0} \quad \text{(a)}$$

But, $\sum_{j=1}^{r} i_{1_j} z_{d_j} \leq \sum_{j=1}^{r} \frac{z_{d_j}}{z_{d_j} + z_{p_j}}$ and $\sum_{j=1}^{w} i_{2_j} z_{t_j} \leq \sum_{j=1}^{w} \frac{z_{t_j}}{z_{c_j} + z_{t_j}}$

From the two preceding inequalities and (a) we find :

$$z_s \geq \frac{1}{i_0} \left(1 - \Sigma \frac{z_{d_j}}{z_{d_j} + z_{p_j}} - \Sigma \frac{z_{t_j}}{z_{t_j} + z_{c_j}}\right) \quad \text{(b)}$$

Finally, for SGO (figure 7) we have :

$$\sum_{j=1}^{r} i_{1_j} z_{d_j} + \sum_{j=1}^{w} i_{2_j} z_{t_j} + z_a i_0 = N_0 \Rightarrow 1 - i_0 z_s + i_0 z_a = N_0 \Rightarrow$$

$$\Rightarrow N_0 - 1 = (z_a - z_s) i_0$$

From this last equation and the inequality (b) we find :

$$z_a \geq \frac{1}{i_0} \left(N_0 - \sum_{j=1}^{r} \frac{z_{d_j}}{z_{d_j} + z_{p_j}} - \sum_{j=1}^{w} \frac{z_{t_j}}{z_{t_j} + z_{c_j}}\right) \quad \text{(c)}$$

The inequalities (b) and (c) give least bounds for the mean time between two successive accesses to the buffer (z_s) and for the mean waiting time (z_a) of an item in the buffer.

Example 6 : Let the TPN of figure 8. One could imagine that it represents the functioning of an enterprise of car location having customers of two types. Customers of type 1, whose number is N_1, have a mean location time z_1 and a mean time between two successive demands for location z_{a_1}. Also, customers of type 2, whose number is N_2, have a mean location time z_2 and a mean time between two successive demands for location z_{a_2}. We suppose that the total number of cars of the enterprise is N_0 and that after location, a service of mean duration z_s is done to each car. We finally admit that a car ready for location waits during z_0 before a customer demands it.

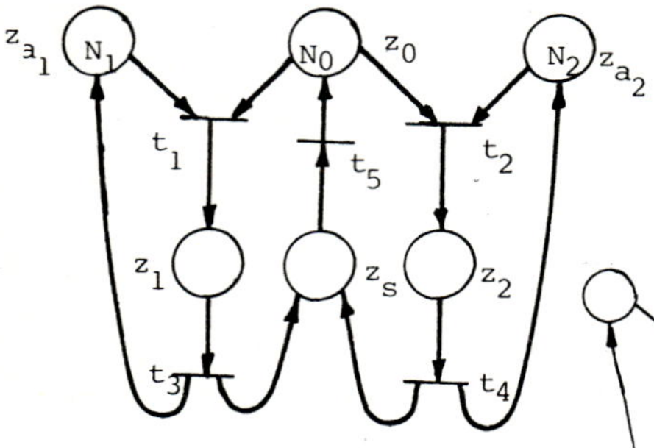

Figure 8

By solving CI = 0, we have : $i_1 = i_3$, $i_2 = i_4$, $i_5 = i_1 + i_2$. Furthermore, the resolution of $J^tC = 0$ gives a decomposition into state graphs (figure 9).

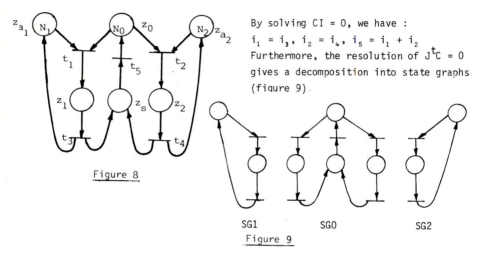

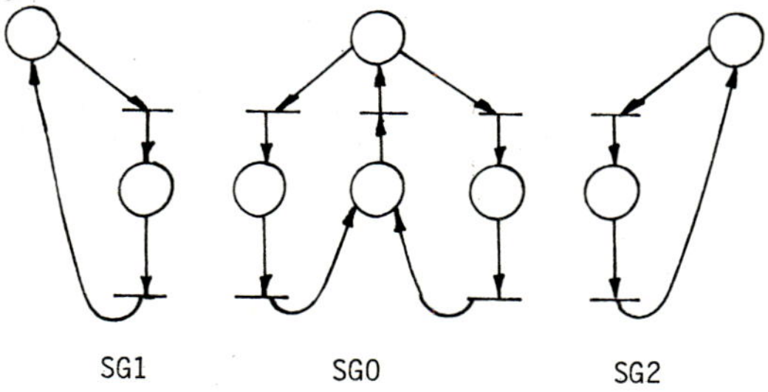

Figure 9

Problem : If we know N_1 and N_2 as well as the delays associated to the places, determine N_0 such that a functioning at natural rate be possible.

The equations of charge conservation for SG1 and SG2 are respectively :

$$i_1 = \frac{N_1}{z_1 + z_{a_1}} \qquad i_2 = \frac{N_2}{z_2 + z_{a_2}}$$

For SG0, we have : $N_0 = (i_1+i_2)(z_0+z_s) + i_1 z_1 + i_2 z_2 \Rightarrow$

$$\Rightarrow N_0 = \frac{N_1(z_0+z_1+z_s)}{z_{a_1} + z_1} + N_2 \frac{(z_0+z_s+z_2)}{z_{a_2} + z_2}$$

N_0 is the minimum number of cars in order to satisfy the demands of the $(N_1 + N_2)$ customers.

References :

[1] C.A. PETRI : "Communication with automata", Techn. Rep. n° RADC-TR-65-377 vol.1, Rome Air Develop. Center, N.Y., Jan. 1966.

[2] A.W. HOLT : "Information Systems Theory Project", Applied Data Research Incorporated Princeton, N.J., AD.676.972, Sept. 1968.

[3] M. HACK : "Analysis of Production Schemata by Petri Nets", MIT - Project MAC, TR-94 (1972).

[4] C.A. PETRI : "Concepts of Net Theory", Proc. of Symp. on Math. Foundations of Comp. Science, pp. 137-146, High Tatras, Sept. 1973.

[5] C.A. PETRI : "Interpretations of Net Theory", Interner Bericht 75-07, G.M.D. Bonn, July 1975.

[6] C. RAMCHANDANI : "Analysis of Asynchronous Concurrent Systems by Timed Petri Nets", PhD. Thesis MIT, Sept. 1973.

[7] K. LAUTENBACH, H.A. SCHMIDT : "Use of Petri Nets for Proving Correctness of Concurrent Process Systems", IFIP 1974, North Holland Publ. Co., 1974, pp. 187-191.

[8] S. GHOSH : "Some Comments on Timed Petri Nets" Journées sur les Réseaux de Petri, March 1977, Paris, pp 151-163.

[9] S. CRESPI-REGHIZZI, D. MANDRIOLI : "Some Algebraic Properties of Petri Nets" Alta Frequenza, N° 2, Vol XLV, pp 130-137.

[10] G. MEMMI : "Semiflows and Invariants. Applications in Petri Nets Theory" Journées sur les Réseaux de Petri, March 1977, Paris, pp 145-150.

[11] Y.E. LIEN : "Termination Properties of Generalized Petri Nets" S.I.A.M. J. Comput. Vol 5, N° 2, June 1976, pp 251-265.

[12] T. MURATA, R.W. CHURCH : "Analysis of Marked Graphs and Petri Nets by Matrix Equations" R.R. N° M.D.C. 1.1.8 Univ. of Illinois, Nov. 1975.

[13] D.R. FULKERSON : "Networks, Frames, Blocking Systems" in Mathematics for decision sciences. Vol 11 of Lectures in Applied Mathematics (1968), the American Mathematical Society, Providence, Rhode Island.

[14] J. SIFAKIS : "Etude du Comportement Permanent des Réseaux de Petri Temporisés" Journées sur les Réseaux de Petri, March 1977, Paris, pp 165-185.

Measuring, Modelling and Evaluating Computer Systems,
H. Beilner and E. Gelenbe, (eds.)
© North-Holland Publishing Company (1977)

AN EVALUATION NET MODEL FOR THE PERFORMANCE EVALUATION OF A COMPUTER NETWORK

R. Winter
Philips GmbH Forschungslaboratorium Hamburg
2000 Hamburg 54, Germany

This paper discusses the use of the evaluation nets for the description of the simulation model of a computer network, it presents the simulation experiments defined for the performance evaluation of the system and some of the simulation results. The model has been used to support the configuration planning of a terminal system for inventory control in a machine factory.

A three-partite approach was followed to model the hardware parts, the operating system and the application software of the computer network in isolated modules which are synchronized via predefined interfaces thus permitting easy exchange of parts of the model. The investigations which led to this approach are discussed. The modules of the system model were calibrated and validated.

1 INTRODUCTION

For the performance evaluation of complex systems such as computer networks, large and complicated models may be needed. Consequently, the simulation runs will require much computer time. But also the model preparation will become time-consuming if not modelling and simulation tools are available which take care of most of the routine work of the model builder.

In the course of our project "Optimization of Computer Networks with Intelligent Terminals"* several tools and methods for deterministic simulation of complex models were developed or extended for this purpose. These tools include the simulation program package SAMO, the evaluation-nets adapter SAMEN, the application modelling system AMOS, the methodology of deterministic model building by functional language elements, the dialogue implementation program DIMPLE and an appropriate method of collecting and evaluating simulation results.

Using these tools, a computer network was modelled and simulated. The model and the tools used will be introduced, aims and approaches will be described.

---

* The described work was sponsored by the German Federal Ministry for Research and Technology (BMFT) under no. 082 2008 72. Only the author is responsible for the contents of this publication.

WATERFORD REGIONAL TECHNICAL COLLEGE LIBRARY

2 METHODOLOGY AND TOOLS FOR DETERMINISTIC MODEL BUILDING

2.1 Formal description by functional language elements

For the determination of the structure and the functions of the model rules of the deterministic model building have been worked out [1].

In a first step the model builder should determine the components of the entire model and the interfaces between them. According to the interfaces input and output language elements (model commands) and the operation of the model components induced by the input language elements have to be defined in a second step. All components are then specified by their input commands A, their inner states Σ and their answers B, if there are any (Fig. 1).

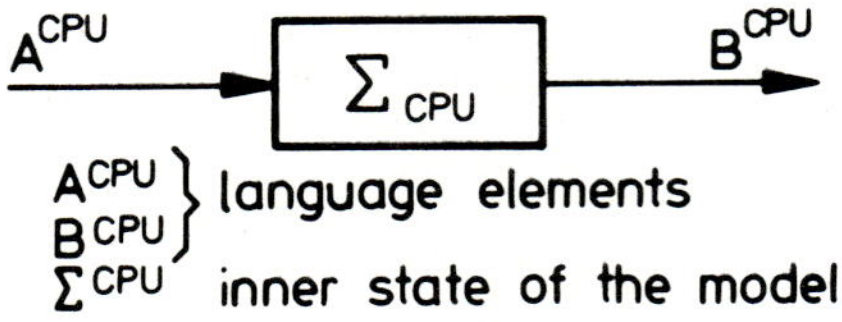

FIGURE 1: The CPU model described by functional language elements

For instance a special input command may switch the actual state of the CPU (unmasked into masked), induce an action, and perhaps after elapsed time transmit an output command to another component (operating system).

These functions are defined by the two mappings σ and τ:

$\sigma: A \times \Sigma \rightarrow \Sigma$ new state caused by a language element and the old state.

$\tau: A \times \Sigma \rightarrow B$ output language element caused by an input language element and the old inner state.

The language elements A and B describe model commands consisting of several parameters of information such as command code, device no., partition no. etc.

2.2 Modelling with Evaluation Nets

The evaluation nets (E-nets) originally defined by Nutt [2] have been further developed [3,4] for the purpose of modelling computer systems. The E-nets are very well suited for the description of the inner structure of any transaction-oriented simulation model. The advantages of this model description tool result from the capability of representing information flows and parallelism in an arbitrary complex structure. Sequences of functions or the logic structure of programs may be modelled in an easy way. A useful feature of the E-net is its deterministic character:

> Packages of information may be transported through the net. The temporal and functional behaviour of the information flow may be determined depending on this information.

A formal description of the E-nets may serve as input for their implementation on a computer. A short introduction should show the main elements of an E-net model and their functions. The E-net elements are tokens, locations and transitions, see Fig. 2.

FIGURE 2: Elements of evaluation nets

Tokens carry the actual information, parts of which are allocated to their attributes. Tokens reside in locations. Each location may contain one token at a time only, thus blocking subsequent tokens. The motion of a token from one location to the next ("firing") follows a defined transition schema showing four phases:

passive: the token is blocked, or the firing conditions of the transition are not fulfilled

enabled: the firing conditions are fulfilled, the transition time is evaluated

active: the transition time is running

terminate: the tokens are actually moved from the input to the output locations of the transition, and the transition procedure programmed by the user is executed.

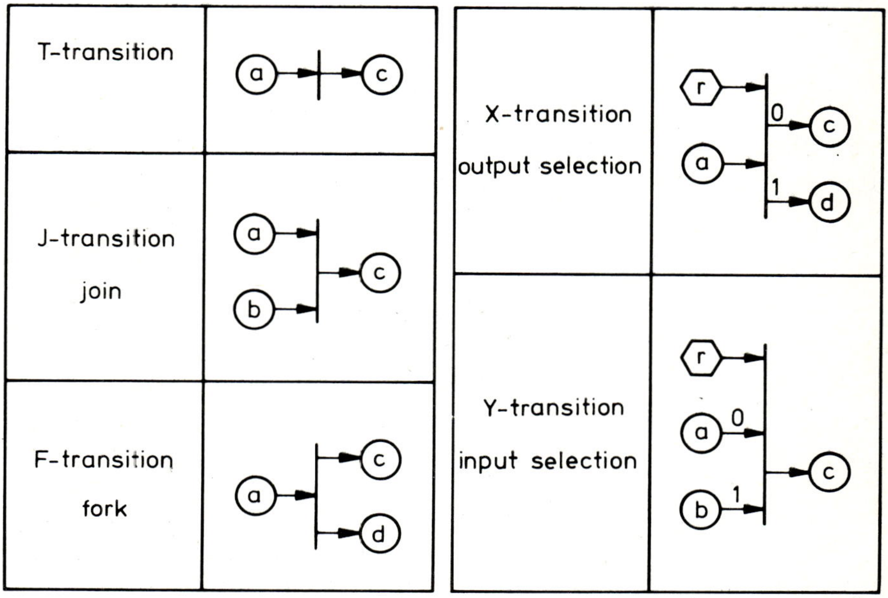

FIGURE 3: The five basic transition types

Fig. 3 shows the five basic transition types. The T-transition symbolizes the execution of an action represented by motion of a token from one location to another and characterized by its time. It also contains a user-defined transition procedure which for example may change the values of token attributes.

The J- and F-transitions differ from the T-transition only by the fact that two input tokens are joining in the case of a J-transition resp. one input token is forked in the case of an F-transition. The conflict transitions X and Y require an additional resolution procedure, controlling the direction of firing. In this way logical branching is realized depending on the status of the net or the actual values of the token attributes.

The five basic transition types were extended [3] by adding macro transitions such as MX- and MY-transitions, generators (ge) and absorbers (ab) (see Fig. 4).

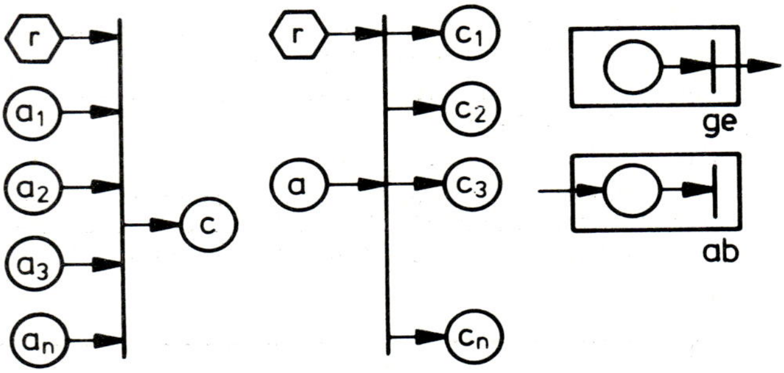

FIGURE 4: Some macro transitions

As a very important type of transition the interruptable T-transition called TI-transition was found [5], because the former types do not support the modelling of interrupts and time outs. But this was an indispensable function for modelling the CPU of a multiprogramming system. In Fig. 5 the TI-transition is shown with its transition schema.

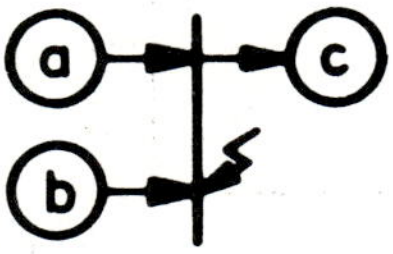

FIGURE 5: TI-transition

Location a is the normal input location and c is the normal output location of this extended T-transition. If a token occurs in b while the transition is in the active phase it is immediately switched to the terminate phase regardless of the remaining transition time. The token of a then is moved to c while the interrupt token in b is absorbed.

2.3 Application modelling system AMOS

Applications are described in terms of tasks and data flow. Tasks contain the functional sequences of operations to be performed, the data flow contains the data elements connecting two tasks or serving as input or output data [1]. Fig. 6 illustrates the representation of the application "inventory".

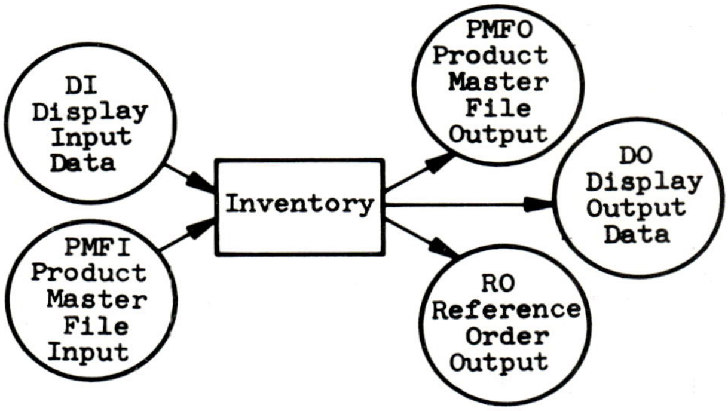

FIGURE 6: Description of inventory

For the documentation of application description and for the generation of a model program which serves as the application load for the simulated computer system, an application modelling system AMOS was conceived (Fig. 7).

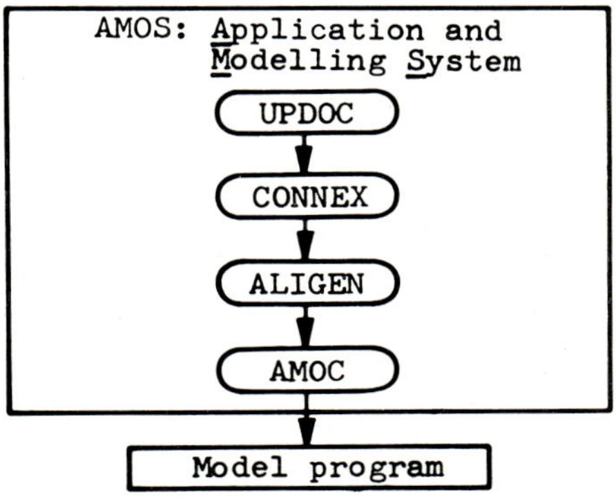

FIGURE 7: Application model

The module UPDOC is used for the storage of task and data element descriptions and their structural relations. The module CONNEX allows the definition of input-output relationship R = (A,B,η) within tasks.

A: set of input data element

B: set of output data element

η: operation (=,-,+,*,etc.).

The module ALIGEN generates a model of the specified application consisting of model commands like e.g.

BOLOOP [<Taskname> |<Filename>]$_0^1$ <No of repetitions>

OPEN <Filename><No of groups or elements>

JUMPOFF <condition>

ARITHM [= |+ |- |* |/]$_1^1$

The ALIGEN commands are converted by the program AMOC according to the actual configuration and special parameters of the modelled system. The results will serve as input data for the application software model at simulation run time.

2.4 Simulation program package SAMO

The simulation and modelling program package SAMO supports event controlled simulation of time discrete systems [6]. The object to be simulated is represented as a system of black boxes and interconnections transmitting information only at discrete times. The entire model is generated in two steps. In the first step the black box structure of the model is defined by describing the connection net using the connection model description language COMOL. In the second step the functional behaviour of each black box type has to be defined. For this a black box input format BOMOL (box modelling language) is used. BOMOL is based on ALGOL 60 supplementing it by some simple rules for the description of delay times and time-parallel operations. The black boxes and the connection net are then converted to an ALGOL program by the SAMO-translator. Each step in creating this simulation program is initiated by a statement of the SAMO control language SAMCOL. Further extensions are applied to interactive parameter variation during run time and step-by-step simulation. The latter feature is used for the segmentation of very long simulation runs.

2.5 Evaluation nets adapter SAMEN

Choosing evaluation nets as model description method and SAMO for simulation led to the demand for an E-net adapter [7]. A simple approach for the implementation of E-nets appears if its formal description is compared with an ALGOL program. It contains a kind of declaration part which defines the locations and transitions. The description of a single transition is similar to a procedure call. The specifications of resolution and transition procedures are similar to procedure declarations in ALGOL. Following this approach a very simple pattern for the description of E-nets was defined in the SAMEN (simulation and modelling with evaluation nets) implementation module, according to the formal description of E-nets and to the black box input format BOMOL of the SAMO simulation program package.

The usage of SAMEN and SAMO allows the network to be decomposed into several subnets, independently described. Each subnet is implemented as one black box.

Each black box contains its own local simulation routine which controls the token flow in the box. The transitions are represented by transition type procedures which imitate their logical behaviour. Special interfaces connecting the peripheral locations of the subnets and the SAMO connections organize the token flow between the boxes by a handshaking mechanism. The information flow via the box connections as well as the model time are controlled by the SAMO package.

3 THE MODEL OF THE COMPUTER NETWORK

3.1 Aspects of model representation

The objective of performance evaluation by simulation is always to save costs and time in comparison with tuning a system in the field. Therefore the expenses for shifting the evaluation procedure from the real object to an abstract level are of importance. These expenses depend on the degree of abstraction or detail of the model which affects model preparation time, simulation time and storage demand.

If a model contains more details of the object, this results in

- a larger number or extent of model description statements,
- a larger number of input data,
- a larger number of transition time calculations to be executed,
- splitting up of simulation events (simulation overhead) and
- extension of the modelling phase.

But even if we try to shorten the modelling phase by developing modelling tools, as we did, the other points are left and we are forced to find an acceptable compromise between detail of model (development and simulation time) and the quality of the answers we want to get from simulation results.

Nevertheless detailed models are often desired, even if complex systems of computer networks are investigated. So Teory and Merten proposed the simulation of a model with different levels of detail [8]. Interesting components, for instance the bottle-necks of the system, may be represented in very fine detail. However, difficulties then arise at the interface of two differently detailed models if model instructions are of different detail.

Of course there exist several kinds of detailed representation. The first way is, to concentrate all the functions, i.e. the program describing them, in one or at most a few transition procedures depending on the number of inputs and outputs of a black box. In the second way the structure of the functional description of a system (or program) is made visible. Branches of programs or functions may be represented by several T-transitions concatenated by locations. The respective program parts then have to be allocated to the separated transitions.

In both ways the model is described on the same level of detail, but nevertheless there may exist a great difference in simulation time and core demand. Processing the E-net structure causes simulation overhead. Besides this disadvantage of model structuring the importance of visibility, extension of the number of visible measuring points and the possibility of functional tracing in the test phase should not be underestimated. The differences in simulation run time result from different influences of E-nets extension:

Separation of models into several black boxes. The SAMO simulator more frequently has to handle interface information and box activation.

Splitting into many single events. The SAMO simulator is more frequently called, so simulation overhead increases.

Replacement of program structure by E-net structure. The organisational overhead of transition handling takes more time than for instance a program branch.

Increase of redundancy.
Programs mostly contain general parts or statements, providing some results or initializations needed in several branches. Separating these branches requires repetition of the general part. Also repeated calls of procedures need more time than one does.

Choosing E-nets as model description method, a further compromise between clearness of representation of the model and limited simulation time is inevitable.

The following phases of model building have to be passed through:

Determination of the coarse structure of the entire model with all attached black boxes.

Choice of level of detail and E-nets representation for the entire model and decision which functions of the component should be represented in this special environment of simulation.

Choice of simulation period depending on system load etc.

Estimation of the required simulation run time [8] and storage demand and relation to the expected benefits. Eventually going back to choice of level of detail.

3.2 The model configuration

The model of the computer network represents the configuration of a planned computer net for inventory control in a machine factory composed of two Philips small business computers of the series P400, a P300 office computer and terminals. We aimed at the simulation of the peak load period of the central computer. Therefore the extent of application and configuration could be reduced to the requirements of the interesting applications during this period. Fig. 8 shows the selected configuration elements of the entire model.

The configuration with each module modelled in a separate SAMO black box comprises the models of the central computer P400 serving as control station, 2 disk drives, a line printer, 2 synchronous line

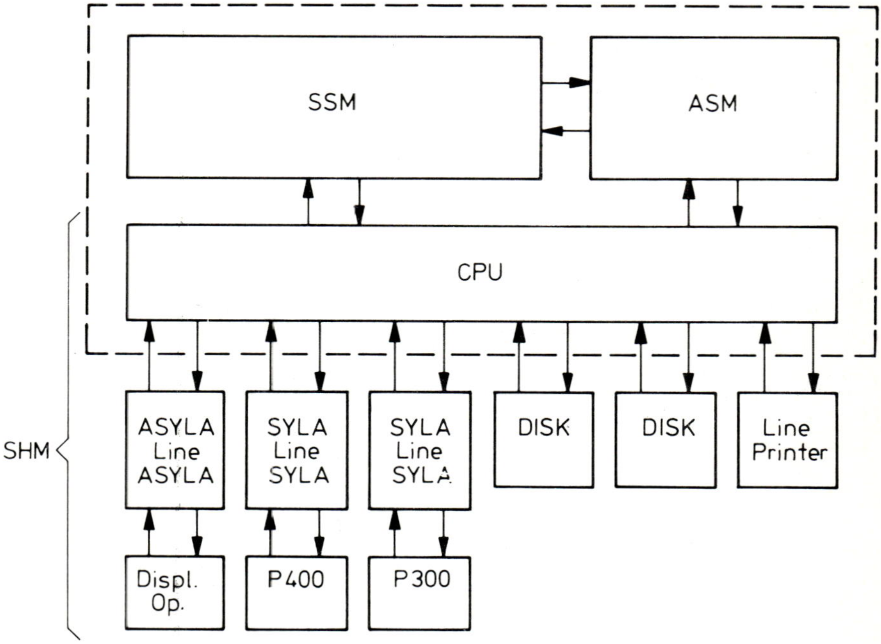

FIGURE 8: Model configuration

adapters (SYLA) respectively 2 asynchronous line adapters (ASYLA) on both ends of the in-house transmission lines, a display together with its operator, a P300 and P400 computer used as tributary stations.

In former models of a stand-alone P400 system experiences were gained in modelling with E-nets. From these models the principle of the three-partite model was taken over. In this configuration mainly the control station should be investigated in detail, and was subdivided into three modules representing hardware, operating system and application program. As could be concluded from the earlier models, maintaining this level of detail for the complete network model would lead to unacceptable simulation time and storage demand. Therefore several parts of the net had to be modelled in less detail. The control station as the interesting part of the entire system should be represented as a generally applicable model of a P400 office computer, whereas the tributary stations of P400 and P300 could only be represented by their coarse behaviour. Following the rules of chapter 3.1 the level of detail was determined on the level of the so-called hardware-software interface (HSI). The simulation period should cover some minutes. The estimated simulation time would then amount to about 2 hours.

The E-net structure of the IO-device models and those of the tributary stations had to be as simple as possible to keep within these limits. As example Fig. 9 shows the model of the disk in its graphic-

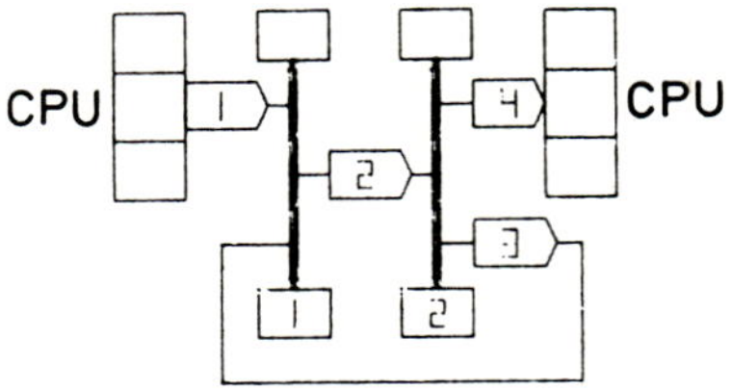

FIGURE 9: Model of a disk drive

al representation. It was mentioned in 3.1 that not only the chosen level of detail is influencing the models' complexity. The complexity may be delimited by representing only the needed functions of the real system. Also the sequence of functions if it is never changed and not influenced by other actions may be concentrated in a time procedure of an E-net transition. This is done in the case of the P300 and P400 tributary stations (Fig. 10).

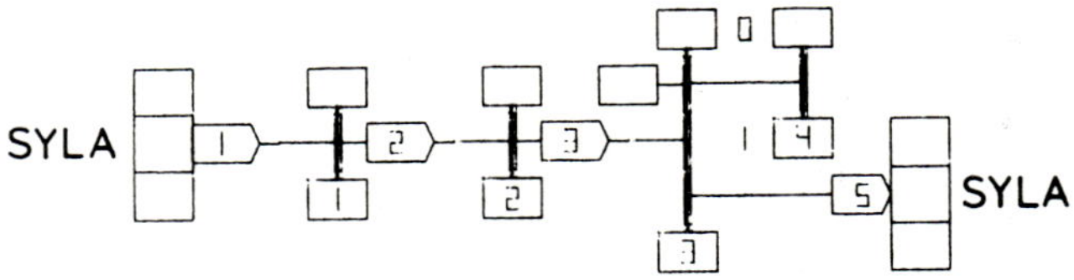

FIGURE 10: Model of the tributary station (P300/P400)

Some additional remarks on the model configuration should be made. Although the entire model is tailored to the chosen environment, application, and questions presented to it, we considered to make the structure variable and keep the more complex models reusable for other configurations. So an exchange of the IO-devices is possible only by defining a new SAMO connection net. (Of course a suitable application program must be available.) Besides simulation of a stand-alone P400 connection between two detailed P400 models by a SYLA model would be imaginable and realizable. For realizing this variability a standardized IO-interface was defined. This modular modelling scheme allows separate work of several specialists all working on their own models.

As an example the language elements of the interface between CPU and IO-devices are given:

SIO = {<device no.><partition no.><IO-code><number of characters/line>[<sectoraddress><volume no.>]$_0^1$}

IOC = {<device no.><partition no.><interrupt code>}

Table 1 contains all possible IO-codes of this interface.

	MNEMO	CODE	IO-device
⟨IOcode⟩ ::=	I-READ	10	
	O-WRITE	50	DK
	O-SEARCH	51	
	O-MOVETOP	55	
	O-WRITEMOVE	56	LP
	O-MOVE	57	
		58	
	OUTCLOSE	8070	
	OUTCLOSEOPEN	208070	
	OUTOPEN	2070	
	O-OUTPUT	70	
	I-INPUT	30	DC
	INCLOSE	4030	
	O-CLOSE	80	
	I-OPEN	20	
	I-CLOSE	40	

TABLE 1: List of possible IO-codes

3.3 The model of the central computer

Following the three-partite model concept the interfaces and the functions of these modules were determined. The system hardware model (SHM) includes all physical components of the entire model i.e. CPU of the control station, IO-devices and the connected tributary stations. The system software model (SSM) realizes the administration tasks. The application software model (ASM) generates model commands corresponding to the HSI-statements of the user's program. Experiences with our first model of a P400 computer had shown that some problems would arise if these three components were separated. For in the reality the three parts of the system are not completely decoupled as desired for model building.

The modelling of the application is influenced by the selection of the hardware components (dimension of buffers and store and configuration). Other dependencies exist between the operating system and the hardware. The operating system presents a load to the hardware (CPU), so activities of the first are coupled with activities of the last one. Which consequences on modelling of both parts will result from this fact? Two alternatives have been tested in the former model:

every time-consuming action of the SSM is transferred to the SHM for execution;

every time-consuming action is executed in the SSM while the SHM is blocked.

The second way is chosen because box transitions are less frequent. If the CPU model branches a model command to the SSM, the CPU is blocked. No further interrupts can enter. Blocking is raised if SSM has given its answer.

Besides these couplings the three system components are modelled separately.

The application software model ASM is prepared by using the application and modelling system AMOS - presented in 2.3. At the beginning of the simulation run the ALIGEN statements are interpreted by the ASM and converted to a model program and some control lists. In the presented model, the system load consists of 4 programs of an inventory control application package. The first program represents the update of two files initiated by the user at the display. The synthetic code contains a program loop with 10 blocks of dc-transactions, 4 attachments to disk including data management facilities, and a number of arithmetic commands.

In the second program the generation of an inventory report and its transmission to a tributary station is modelled by a program loop containing 2 attachments to disk, one block of dc-commands and several arithmetics.

The third model program consisting of a loop of 8 printer and 2 disk commands (including data management) prints the contents of a disk file.

In the fourth program, the contents of a disk file are transmitted to the tributary station in the purchasing department. The program loop contains a disk attachment and a dc-transmission block. There are two files on disk. The programs of partition 1, 2 and 3 are working on the first indexed file and partition 1 and 4 on the second file. The program statements are composed of ARITHMETIC and CALL MONITOR commands. After program conversion the ASM realizes the following facilities:

Start of simulation.

Initializing of the file description table of the SSM.

Control functions for the command generation, execution of program loops or branches.

After a RUN command of the SSM the desired partition is activated and the next string of arithmetic commands together with the subsequent monitor call of this partition is given to the CPU model.

Interrupted strings of arithmetic commands coming back from the CPU are entered into a queue and later started again by the respective RUN statement of the SSM.

Data management routines are linked to the programs.

The E-net structure of the ASM is coarsely representing the coupling mechanism between ASM, SSM and CPU model and the functional activities.

The disk-oriented operating system (DOS 400) with multiprogramming (max. 4 partitions) and data communication facilities of a control station is modelled as several E-net modules comprising interrupt handler, multifunc, dc-scheduler, scheduler, a part of the stepmanager, general SIO and section load. The last module represents the overlay mechanism of the operating system.

CALM(CALL MONITOR) and IOC(INPUT-OUTPUT-COMPLETED) commands cause an interrupt and activities of the operating system modules after passing the CPU model.

Each module of the SSM consists of an evaluation net which describes the logical structure of that module so that for each distinguishable sequence of system software operations the execution time can be determined, and the appropriate control information can be sent to the ASM and the SHM. Thus depending on the kind of interrupt the model command has to pass through specific paths of the E-net modules of the SSM causing the following actions of the operating system in the E-net transitions:

CALM EXIOC:	interrupt, monitor call, management of the corresponding device (e.g. blocking of update files on disk), IO-handling.
CALM WAITIO:	interrupt, monitor call, the program is set into wait status.
CALM WMTERM:	interrupt, monitor call, dc-management (e.g. waiting queue for several dc-commands), IO-handling, output of data to line-adapter.
CALM RMIQ:	interrupt, monitor call, IO-handling, input of data from line-adapters.
CALM STOP:	interrupt, monitor call, execution of the corresponding partition is stopped.
INT:	interrupt, interrupt handling corresponding to the interrupt class (INPUT-OUTPUT-COMPLETED or PERIPHERAL-ATTENTION-INTERRUPT), reset of the wait status of the corresponding partition.

After finishing its operation the SSM starts a scheduling algorithm to select the next partition to be activated.

As the most interesting part of the entire model the SSM is rather detailed, and the E-nets of the individual modules within the SSM are extensively structured. So a great deal of the simulation time is caused by this model.

The model of the CPU is a rigid direct representation of the CPU functions. The facilities to be realized by the CPU model are

- times for arithmetic statements execution,
- branching of IO-commands to the IO-devices,
- representation of interrupt behaviour,
- handling IOC-priorities,
- masking of CPU activities during SSM actions,
- handling of commands from and to SSM and ASM.

As an example a part of the interrupt behaviour of the CPU model will be explained by means of Fig. 11.

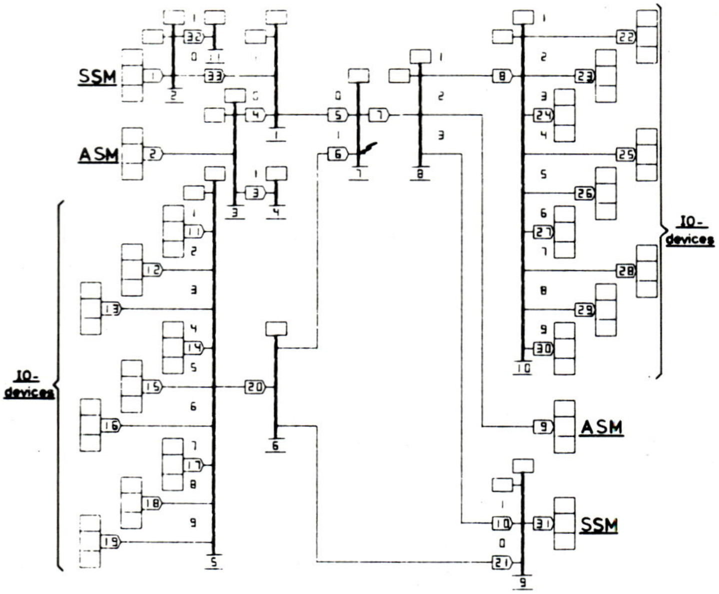

FIGURE 11: Evaluation-net model of the CPU

This E-net shows the CPU model with its interfaces to SSM, ASM and the IO-devices. A token may reside in location 5 where the arithmetic instruction execution time is elapsing and a second token may arrive from an IO-device. The CPU is not masked, so the token signalling the completion of an input/output operation (IOC) proceeds via location 20 to transition 6 where an additional token is generated in location 6. This token interrupts the elapsing arithmetic instruction execution time. After calculation of the remaining execution time the token of location 5 leaves the model passing the locations 7 and 9. The token in 6 disappears and that in 21 reaches the box output (location 31) after the time for IOC-handling has elapsed in transition 9.

4 CONSIDERATIONS AND TOOLS FOR THE PERFORMANCE EVALUATION

4.1 System characteristics

Simulating the presented computer net, aimed at the measuring of influences of system and configuration parameters on system characteristics of the entire net and especially on the central computer, these characteristics had to be specified with regard to the given environment and the chosen application.

Performance characteristics are the answers to the interesting questions presented to the real system or the model. So after formulating of relevant questions, parameters should be specified which may have influence on system performance or which may deliver helpful hints on possible optimization steps, as does the utilization of all system components. In our case the questions are centred around the model of the control station. The periphery of the central computer only delivers influences by parameter variation. Fig. 12 shows the performance characteristics and the associated parameters which are expected to directly influence the system performance.

parameters / performance characteristics	mean instruction execution time	section load interval	priority assignment	file characteristics size blocking factor	device characteristics disk printer DC
system response time			x	x	x
job time		x	x	x	x
parallelism	x	x			x
frequency of interrupts		x		x	
frequency of disk-accesses		x		x	
utilization of CPU and devices	x		x		

FIGURE 12: Performance characteristics and parameters

The utilization of the CPU, of the devices disk (employed by SSM), disk (employed by ASM), line printer and the dc-devices are measured. The CPU activity is splitted into two parts, that of SSM and that of ASM activity.

Looking at the parameters to be varied a great number of simulation runs can be expected. There is a wide range of possible variation steps, even if only one parameter is regarded (priority assignment: 16 variations, file blocking factor: 5 to 10). An optimization technique requiring all possible permutations would not be feasible. Even the variation of only one parameter while all other parameters are held in initial position would take 70 or more simulations. In order to reduce the amount of simulation run time we limited the number of the variations of a single parameter to 5. Even now 30 variations are necessary. A further reduction of simulation time is seen in the possibility of parameter variation during simulation run.

4.2 Measurements and evaluation

The determination of parameter influences for system optimization requires some appropriate measuring and evaluating tools. The "token flow", a protocol of E-nets activities delivered by SAMEN, only allows to observe the actions of the simulator and that of the E-net adapter but does not provide information in a form that may be used as input to subsequent evaluations. Hence some considerations on additional tools became necessary. The aim was to achieve a measuring tool fulfilling the following requirements:

- optional choice of measuring points (switchable),
- accessibility of every value of simulation data and program variable,
- all values should be accessible in every part of the E-net,
- representation of the values in a clear perhaps sorted table suited for further evaluations.

These demands also account for the request of representing simulation runs as activity sequences of modules. The entire simulation is protocolled by an activity diagram (Fig. 13).

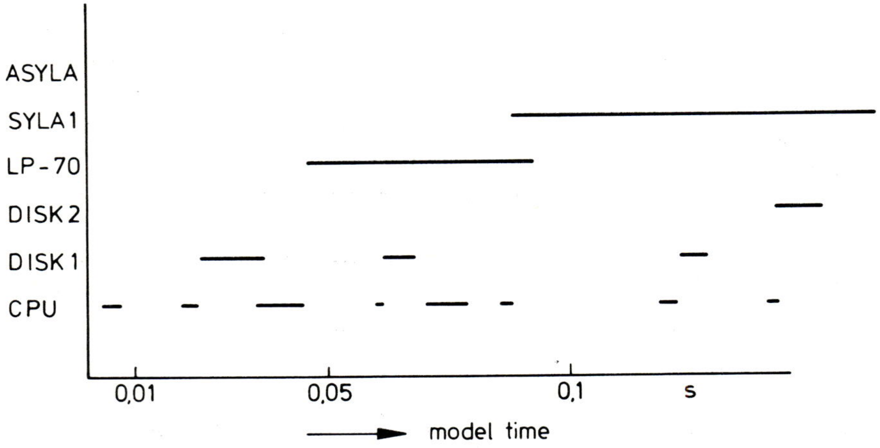

FIGURE 13: Activity diagram

Measuring is simply activated by calling one of the procedures:

sto1(mp) or sto3(mp,mv,mv) - mp::=<no. of measuring point>,
mv::=<value to be measured>.

If one of these procedures is called, simulation time, box identification, number of measuring points and in the case of sto3 two additional values of optional variables are written into a table which is transferred to a disk file after every 100 measurements. So after simulation has come to an end all measured data are available independent of other simulation activities. The tool of "token flow" is then only used in the test phase of the model, when also functional correctness is analysed.

The evaluation is carried out in four steps. Measured data are sorted in the first step according to their box and measuring point identities. They are now suited for the evaluation programs. The following step delivers an activity diagram of the model. Within this plotted diagram (Fig. 13) all time-consuming activities of the modules are represented by a time-proportional length of a horizontal bar. The whole simulation protocol may be plotted, interesting short periods may be spread by giving an extended scale.

For the third evaluation step an interactive program has been realized offering the command set of a common programmable pocket calculator. The user may give his individual program using the sorted data as input data denoted by the number of their boxes and measuring points.

Execution of this program delivers a list of computed values and their denominations. The list gives a survey of the mentioned system characteristics.

5 SOME SIMULATION RESULTS

The representation of modelling methods and tools was the main objective of this proceeding. Nevertheless some results of the first simulation run should be given. Models and tools were implemented on the Philips computer P1400 with multiprogramming dialogue system (Release 18).

The entire simulation program required about 350 K Bytes. The single models contribute the following values of storage demand:

SSM	:	120 K Bytes	LP	:	7 K Bytes
ASM	:	47 K Bytes	Display	:	5 K Bytes
SHM	:	24 K Bytes	P300	:	5 K Bytes
Disk	:	5 K Bytes	P400	:	5 K Bytes
SYLA	:	11 K Bytes			
ASYLA	:	7 K Bytes			

The simulation run took about 150 minutes while model time reached about 80 seconds. So including the initializing phase of about 30 seconds a ratio of simulation time to model time of about 120:1 was recognized.

In a first simulation the system characteristics of the originally chosen configuration described by the following initialization parameters of the components have been determined.

CPU	:	P400
Disk	:	2400 rotations per minute
		200 cylinders
		2 tracks per cylinder
		22 sectors per track
		256 Bytes per sector

Lineprinter	:	200 lines per minute
Transmission line line with SYLA	:	4800 bit/s transmission rate 10^{-5} error rate 30 ms modem switching time
Transmission line with ASYLA	:	2400 bit/s transmission rate
SSM	:	high priority for the 1. partition (display) section load every 7th interrupt 20 data set control areas
ASM	:	blocking factor for the 1. disk file: 1 2. disk file: 3

The simulation run delivered the following results:

average interval between interrupts:			22 ms
utilization of	Disk	:	28 percent
	Line Printer	:	98 percent
	SYLA (P300)	:	30 percent
	SYLA (P400)	:	82 percent
	ASYLA	:	26 percent
average access time (Disk)		:	52 ms
including the time for reading or writing (without data management)			
program loop time of	partition 1	:	5,1 s
	partition 2	:	0,72 s
	partition 3	:	4,1 s
	partition 4	:	0,24 s
average system response time seen from the operator at the display		:	0,38 s
worst case of system response time seen from the operator		:	0,73 s

REFERENCES

[1] Seidel, H., v. Studnitz, P.: A methodology for deterministic model building and simulation of computer systems. Simulation '77, Montreux, June 22-24, 1977. Proceedings.

[2] Nutt, G.J.: The formulation and application of evaluation nets. Ph. D. Dissertation, University of Washington, Computer Science (1972).

[3] Noe, J.D., Nutt, G.J.: Macro E-nets for representation of parallel systems. IEEE Trans. on Comp. C-22 (1973) no. 8, p. 718-727.

[4] Behr, J.-P., Isernhagen, R., Pernards, P., Stewen, L.: Modellbeschreibung mit Auswertungsnetzen. Angewandte Informatik 17 (1975) 9, p. 375-382.
Behr, J.-P., Isernhagen, R., Pernards, P., Stewen, L.: Erfahrungen mit Auswertungsnetzen - Implementierung, Alternativen. Angewandte Informatik 17 (1975) 10, p. 427-432.

[5] Stewen, L.: Auswertungsnetze als Hilfsmittel zur Modellbildung - Probleme und deren Lösungen. GI - 5. Jahrestagung Dortmund, Oct. 8-10, 1975. Lecture Notes in Computer Sci., Vol. 34, p. 462-474.

[6] Lagemann, K.: Das Simulationsprogrammpaket "SAMO". Angewandte Informatik, 16 (1974) 11, p. 488-492.
[7] Behr, J.-P.: Implementierung von Auswertungsnetzen mit interaktiven grafischen Methoden. GI Workshop über Modelle für Rechensysteme, Bonn, March 31 - April 1. 1977, Informatik-Fachberichte, Vol. 9, p. 199-210.
[8] Merten, A.G., Teorey, T.J.: Considerations on the level of detail in simulation. Symposium on the simulation of computer systems 1973.

Measuring, Modelling and Evaluating Computer Systems,
H. Beilner and E. Gelenbe, (eds.)
© North-Holland Publishing Company (1977)

TASK SCHEDULING IN SYSTEMS WITH NONPREEMPTIBLE RESOURCES

W. Cellary
Institute of Control Engineering
Technical University of Poznan
Poznań , Poland

A strategy of resource allocation in computer systems with many nonpreemptible resources of a single type to improve system throughput, is described. A new approach to avoiding deadlocks, which radically reduces overhead involved, is used. Also, the problem of permanent blocking is solved. The improvement of system throughput is reached by the use of the idea of SPT-rule in granting resource requests. The precise algorithms which can be directly used in resource allocation routines are presented.

1. INTRODUCTION

The paper deals with scheduling strategies in systems with nonpreemptible resources. In this case, the problem of system performance failures, such as deadlock and permanent blocking, must be solved. As is known, there are three general approaches to dealing with deadlocks: detection and recovery, prevention, and avoidance. From among these approaches, the avoidance methods are characterized by the highest system throughput and resource utilization. However, a cost which is paid in these methods is the large overhead involved.

The problem of permanent blocking was first stated and solved by Holt [5]. His approach to the solution of this problem consists in the detection of permanent blocking and the cutting off of the input stream of tasks until the completion of blocked tasks.

A new approach to the avoidance of system deadlocks proposed by Habermann in [3] reduces the overhead involved without losing the benefit of improved resource utilization. This is reached by the application of an admission test which cuts out many undesirable allocation states, and as a result, reduces the number of tasks examined by the safety test.

However further improvement of the system throughput, based on additional, prior information about tasks is possible and should be considered. This point is the subject of this paper. The presented approach also includes the permanent blocking problem.

In Section 2 of this paper we introduce basic definitions used and formulate the problem precisely. Section 3 contains the algorithms of resource allocation to improve system throughput. In Section 4 we present the concept of permanent blocking prevention, and in Section 5 some conclusions.

2. BASIC DEFINITIONS AND PROBLEM FORMULATION

Let us consider a system with many nonpreemptible resources of one kind [3] . The number of resources in the system will be denoted by t.

Every task T in the system will be characterized by the following:

1°. Claim - C(T) - which represents the number of resources that task T ultimately needs in order to finish;

2°. Rank - R(T) - which represents the difference between the claim of task T and the number of resources currently allocated to T;

3°. Remaining performance time - $\tau(T)$ - the time needed by task T to completion;

4°. Blocked-free time - $\eta(T)$ - time elapsed from task arrival after which task T is treated as permanently blocked. (This value has to be assumed with care - the priority of the task, and mean rate of performance time to turn-around time must be taken into account).

Moreover we assume that every task will terminate when it has been allocated all resources claimed, and after completion it releases all resources held.

The set of tasks which hold at least one resource we will denote by SCO (Set of COmpetitors); the set of tasks which enter the system and pass through the admission test (see below), but hold no resource will be denoted by SCA (Set of CAndidates). Finally, the remaining tasks which enter the system compose the Set of Potential Candidates (SPC).

Let us pass now to the safety and admission tests [3].

First let us define the promotion of a task T which consists of allocating a resource to the task T and decrementing its rank by one. The allocation state of a task can be described by the number of promotions starting from the fictitious initial state in which no resources are allocated to it (i.e. $R(T)=C(T)$) until its current rank.

The allocation state of the system can be stored in a vector, denoted by $\bar{x}$, where x_k is the total number of promotions of all competitors from rank = k to rank = k-1, (k=1,...,t).

As an example, let us consider the following system.

t=6 CLAIM = (2,4,4) RANK = (1,1,3)

then

$$\bar{x} = (0,2,1,2,0,0)$$

since task T_1 was promoted from rank = 2 to rank = 1, task T_2 from rank = 4 to rank = 3, from rank = 3 to rank = 2, and from rank = 2 to rank = 1; and task T_3 was promoted from rank = 4 to rank = 3.

For the formulation of the safety test let us define vector $\bar{p} = (p_1,...p_t)$, in the following way:

$$p_k = \sum_{j=k}^{t} x_j \quad , \quad k=1,...,t \; .$$

Vector $\bar{p}$ for the above example is as follows:

$$\bar{p} = (5,5,3,2,0,0)$$

The safety test can be explained as follows [3] .

Theorem 1. A realizable allocation state is safe if and only if

$$\bar{p} \leqslant \bar{t}$$

where $\bar{t} = (t, t-1,t-2,...,1)$.

Proof - see [3] .

Let us note that a state is realizable if $p_k \geqslant 0$, k=1.,,,,.t [3].

It is easy to verify that allocation state in our example is safe, since

$$\bar{p} = (5,5,3,2,0,0) \leq \bar{t} = (6,5,4,3,2,1)$$

The admission test is a necessary condition for safety. It is applied for admitting tasks to the set of competitors. In this way, competitor sets with only unsafe states are precluded.

Analogous to vector $\bar{p}$ we define vector $\bar{n} = (n_1, n_2, \ldots, n_t)$:

$$n_k = \sum_{j=k}^{t} y_j \quad , \quad k=1,\ldots,t ,$$

where y_j is the number of tasks whose claim = j.

In the example vectors $\bar{y}$ and $\bar{n}$ are as follows:

$$\bar{y} = (0,1,0,2,0,0)$$
$$\bar{n} = (3,3,2,2,0,0)$$

The admission test can be now formulated.

Theorem 2. If a realizable allocation state is safe then

$$\bar{n} \leq \bar{t}$$

Proof - see [3].

A valuable property of this test is that it depends entirely on claims and not on ranks, so it is applied only either when a new task enters the system, or a competitor has been completed; and not when resources are allocated or released.

On the basis of the above theorems one can construct the policy of nonpreemptible resource allocation to avoid deadlocks, which involves much lower overhead than the classical avoidance method [4], without decreasing system throughput and resource utilization. However, the addition assumption about prior knowledge of tasks performance times allows one for further improvement of system throughput. Our concept is the use of the idea of SPT-rule (Shortest Processing Times) [1] in the general strategy of scheduling tasks to resource allocation. This idea is used in searching both the set of tasks which wait for granting of their resource requests, and the set of potential candidates which waits for moving to the set of candidates. Of course, such approach increase system throughput. Moreover, in our policy we solve the problem of permanent blocking, i.e. such situation when request of a task cannot be granted, because of the infinite stream of "better" tasks. The proposed approach to the solution of this problem tends to minimize time elapsed since the detection of permanent blocking until completion of a blocked task. Moreover, the cutting off of the input stream is not assumed.

3. RESOURCE ALLOCATION ALGORITHMS

Let us note that if we assume the following:

- there is only a finite set of tasks among which resources are allocated;
- all the tasks arrive at the system at the same moment;
- no task releases the processor until completion;
- processing time of every task is equal to unit time;

then system throughput is independent of resource allocation and task processing order.

If we assume arbitrary task performance times, we can find the optimal schedule using the SPT-rule (Shortest Processing Times) [1].

If we assume that the processor can be preempted befor the completion of a task (e.g. during delays caused by the use of resources) and then assigned to another task, we can prove that the problem of minimizing system throughput is NP-complete.

Theorem 3. Problem P of minimizing mean flow time (maximizing throughput) for the set of m tasks for which times of the use of the processor and every resource are known, is NP-complete.

Proof. It is clear that our problem P belongs to *NP*. In order to prove that P is NP-complete we will polynomially reduce to it the NP-complete problem (it will be denoted by F) of flowshop scheduling with two machines to minimize mean flow time [2]. Namely, given an instance of F (i.e. number of tasks - m' , number of machines - - 2, vectors of processing times on the first and the second machine, respectively $[\tau_1]$ and $[\tau_2]$) with value K for which a "yes - no" question is answered, we can construct an instance to P in the following way.

Set:

$$m = m'$$

$$t = 1,\ C(T_i) = 1\ ,\ i=1\dots,m'$$

and assume that each task T_i needs for its performance first the processor only (for τ_{1i} time units) and then this resource (for τ_{2i} time units) . Take the value of the objective function equal to K. It is then obvious that problem F has a solution with the value of mean flow time K if and only if problem P has the solution with value of mean flow time K. The theorem then follows. □

Further we will consider the more general case, when there is an infinite stream of tasks which arrive at the system at arbitrary, a priori unknown time moments. We will assume nothing more about the tasks than was specified in Section 2. We assume that a resource request concerns only one resource, however, a resource release concerns a number of resources greater or equal to one. We distinguish four situations which may arise in the system.

Situation 1. The occurence of a request of a competitor or the arrival of a candidate.

Deadlock states can be avoided if the allocations move from one safe state to another. It was shown in [4] that the state is safe if tasks can be placed in line for successive allocation. For testing state transition, Theorem 1 from Section 2 will be used, but in a modified form. Let us define vector

$$\bar{q} = \bar{t} - \bar{p} \quad , \quad \text{i.e.,} \quad q_k = t_k - p_k \quad , \quad k=1,\dots,t \quad ,$$

and pointer

$$I_q = \min_{q_k=0} \{k\} \quad .$$

In the example given in Section 2

$$\bar{q} = (1,0,1,1,2,1)$$

$$I_q = 2 \quad .$$

Theorem 4. Let the initial state be safe. A state transition is safe if and only if

$$R(T) < I_q$$

where $R(T)$ is the rank of a task which requests a resource.

Proof. It results from Theorem 1 that a state is safe if and only if $\bar{q} \geqslant 0$. Promotion of T from rank $R(T) = k$ to rank $= k-1$ implies the increase of x_k by one and as a result, increasing by one p_i for $i=1,\dots,k$. Since elements of $\bar{t}$ remain constant, it is equivalent to decreasing q_i, for $i=1,\dots k$, by one. Since the initial state was safe, the new state is safe if the new values of q_i for $i=1,\dots,k$ are not less than zero, i.e. if the initial values of q_i, $i=1,\dots,k$, are not less than one, or the index (I_q) of the leftmost $\bar{q}$'s element equal to zero is greater than k. □

Corollary. Element q_1 is equal to the number of resources currently available in the system.

Proof. Since $p_1 = \sum_{k=1}^{t} x_k$, represents the total number of promotions, which is equivalent to number of allocated resources. The difference $q_1 = t - p_1$ is equal to the number of currently available resources in the system. □

As a conclusion from Theorem 3, it is found that for the examination of state transition, it is sufficient to compare only two numbers R(T) and I_q . If the examination is successful the resource is allocated and the following algorithm is performed:

Algorithm 1.

```
Iq,i:=1;
while i ≤ R(T) do
  begin
    qi:=qi-1;
    i:=i+1
  end;
while qIq > 0 and Iq ≤ t do Iq:=Iq+1;
R(T):=R(T)-1;
```

The first while statement calculates new values of vector $\bar{q}$, and the second one - the new value of I_q.

As an example let us consider the system state :

t=5 CLAIM = (2,4,5) RANK = (1,3,4)

Then:

$$\bar{x} = (0,1,0,1,1)$$
$$\bar{p} = (3,3,2,2,1)$$
$$\bar{q} = (2,1,1,0,0)$$
$$I_q = 4$$

As may be seen, in accordance with Theorem 2 and 4 we can grant only the request of either task T_1 or T_2. The allocation of a resource to task T_3 could cause deadlock, since even after the completion of T_1, there may not be enough resources to complete either T_2 or T_3 .

Situation 2. The release of resources.

In this case, the new allocation state must be calculated. For this reason we use the following algorithm.

Algorithm 2.

Let A be the number of released resources.

```
i:=1;
while i ≤ R(T) do
  begin
    q_i:=q_i+A;
    i:=i+1
  end;
  I_q,R(T):=R(T)+A;
while A > 0 do
  begin
    q_i:=q_i+A;
    i:=i+1;
    A:=A-1
  end;
while q_{I_q} > 0 and I_q ≤ t do I_q:=I_q+1;
```

This algorithm calculates the values which must be added to the appropriate elements of $\bar{q}$ and finds the new values of I_q.

Let task T_2 from the above example release one resource. Then $A=1$, $R(T)=3$. After execution of the first while statement we obtain:

$$\bar{q} = (3,2,2,0,0)$$
$$I_q = 4,$$
$$R(T) = 4 .$$

Finally, after execution of the second and third while statement we obtain:

$$\bar{q} = (3,2,2,1,0)$$
$$I_q = 5 .$$

After performance of Algorithm 2, we should try to grant the requests, which up to now could not be granted because of the safety of state transition. This can be done by the following algorithm.

Algorithm 3.

1°. Search for tasks with ranks less than I_q, from among candidates and those competitors which are waiting for the granting of requests. If no such task can be found, stop the algorithm.

2°. Choose the task with minimum $\tau(T)$ and grant its request (use Algorithm 1).

3°. Repeat from step 1°.

In the first step of this algorithm we search for tasks whose requests can be granted safely. This searching is applied only for candidates and competitors since potential candidates certainly could not have their requests granted (they do not fulfill the necessary condition for safety). Thus, the number of examined tasks is greatly reduced.

We can further improve the search procedure, if we keep the mentioned sets ordered in ascending rank order. Moreover, it is easy to prove that this algorithm will have to be repeated at most as many times as the number of released resources. The choice of the task with the minimum remaining performance time guarantees the improvement of system throughput.

Situation 3. The arrival of a new potential candidate.

In this situation we must decide if the potential candidate can be moved to the set of candidates or not.

Analogous to vector $\bar{q}$ and pointer I_q let us define vector $\bar{s}$

$$\bar{s} = \bar{t} - \bar{n} \quad \text{i.e.} \quad s_k = t_k - n_k \;, \; k=1,\ldots,t \;,$$

and pointer I_s

$$I_s = \min_{s_k=0} \{k\} \;.$$

The necessary condition for safety may be now formulated as an inequality:

$$C(T) < I_s \;.$$

Vector $\bar{s}$ and pointer I_s change their values when the request of a candidate is granted, i.e. when a candidate is moved to the set of competitors. The new values of $\bar{s}$ and I_s are calculated in the following way.

Algorithm 4.

```
I_s,i:=1;
while i ≤ C(T) do
  begin
    s_i:=s_i-1;
    i:=i+1
  end;
while s_{I_s} > 0 and I_s ≤ t do I_s:=I_s+1;
```

Since vectors $\bar{n}$ and $\bar{s}$ are calculated only for competitors, let us introduce the analogous vectors $\bar{n}^*$ and $\bar{s}^*$ and pointer I_{s*} calculated both for competitors and candidates.

The algorithm of admission of a new potential candidate T is as follows.

Algorithm 5.

1°. If $C(T) < I_{s*}$ move T to the set of candidates and calculate the new values of $\bar{s}^*$ and I_{s*} using Algorithm 4; then stop the algorithm.

2°. If $C(T) \geqslant I_s$ stop the algorithm.

3°. Search for the task with rank greater then or equal to C(T) and with performance time at the maximum. If this time is less than or equal to $\tau(T)$, or no such task can be found, stop the algorithm, otherwise replace the chosen task by T in the set of candidates. Calculate the new values of $\bar{s}^*$ and I_{s*} using Algorithm 6. Then stop the algorithm.

Algorithm 6.

Let T_r be the replaced task.

```
i:=C(T)+1;
while i ≤ C(T_r) do
  begin
    s*_i:=s*_i+1;
    i:=i+1
  end;
I_s*:=i;
while s_{I_s*} > 0 do I_s*:=I_s*+1;
```

In the first step of Algorithm 5 we ask if a new potential candidate can be admitted with regard both to competitors and candidates. In the second step we take into account only the set of competitors. If this testing is successful we must find the candidate which can be replaced. Then we check to see if such a replacement will be good for system throughput.

Situation 4. The completion of a competitor.

In this situation we should

- try to move a potential candidate to the set of candidates (it can be easily proved that there will be at most one such potential candidate),
- try to allocate resources released by the completed competitor.

The allocation of the resources should not precede the possible introduction of a new candidate since this candidate should not be overlooked in request granting.

Now, values of vectors $\bar{s}$, $\bar{s}^*$, and pointers I_s, I_{s^*}, after the completion of competitor T can be calculated by the use of Algorithm 4 if we replace the substraction of 1 by the addition of 1.

For searching the set of potential candidates in order to move a potential candidate to the set of candidates we use Algorithm 7.

Algorithm 7.

1°. Search for a potential candidate T with $C(T) < I_{s*}$ and with $\tau(T)$ at the minimum. If no such task can be found, stop the algorithm.

2°. Move T to the set of candidates and use Algorithm 4 for calculating new values of $\bar{s}*$ and I_{s*}. Then, stop the algorithm.

4. PREVENTION OF PERMANENT BLOCKING.

The problem of permanent blocking can be solved by the detection of blocked tasks and the activation of a special strategy of resource allocation to grant the request of blocked tasks. The periodical examination, of whether the time elapsed since the arrival of task T exceeds $\eta(T)$, allows for the detection of blocked tasks.

First, let us assume that the blocked task T_b is a competitor. If the detection of the permanent blocking of task T_b occurs in a state of resource allocation such that rank $R(T_b)$ is less then or equal to the number of resources currently available, then it means that T_b is not really blocked now, and we only need to prevent its possible blocking in the future. It can be reached by the allocation to T_b (or rather reservation for T_b) of the number of resources equal to its rank $R(T_b)$. Permanent blocking is then prevented since task T_b holds all the resources necessary for its completion.

A more complex situation occurs if a state of resource allocation does not allows for the promotion task T_b to rank $R(T_b) = 0$. Then we must look for a sequence of tasks,which we will denote by L, whose completion is necessary for the safe granting of the rest of the blocked task's claim. We propose the following algorithm for finding this sequence.

Algorithm 8.

1°. Let the subsidiary variable A equal 0.
Let sequence L be an initially empty list.

2°. Find the subset of SCO, of tasks whose rank is less than or equal to the sum of A and the number (AV) of available resources. From among them, search for task T_i for which

$C(T_i) \geqslant R(T_b)-A-AV$ and $\tau(T_i)$ is at the minimum. If no such task can be found, search for the task whose claim $C(T_i)$ is at the maximum.
If the difference $R(T_i) - A$ is a positive number calculate $AV=AV-R(T_i)+A$; $A=C(T_i)$, otherwise $A=A-R(T_i)+C(T_i)$. Add T_i as the next task to sequence L, and disregard it in the rest of the algorithm.

3°. Repeat from step 2° until sum of A and the number of available resources is less than rank $R(T_b)$.

Let us note first that Algorithm 8 find a safe sequence of tasks. Indeed, in every pass of step 2° of this algorithm we look for tasks which can be promoted to the rank equal to 0 and then completed, after completion of the task found in the previous pass. Of course, in the first pass we look for a task for which there are enough currently available resources. The sum of A and the number of available resources is equal to the number of resources that will be available after the completion of a given task. Moreover, the sequence found by Algorithm 8 is the shortest one. This results from that we choose, in every pass, the task which releases the maximum number of resources after its completion. However it is sufficient that the last task in the sequence releases only the remaining number of resources necessary for promoting T_b to rank = 0. This task should be as short as possible.

Of course, the minimization of the length of sequence L tends to shorten the time of resource reservation in order to complete the blocked task, and thus to increase system throughput. After application of the proposed algorithm, we obtain the reduced number of available resources. This number can be used for granting request from all tasks in the system (which compose sequence L or not), in contrast to the resources released by the tasks composing sequence L, which are reserved until task completion, and then allocated to the next task in L.

As an example let us consider the following system:

$$t = 6 \qquad CLAIM = (3,2,4,5) \qquad RANK = (1,1,3,4)$$

Let $T_b = T_4$ be the blocked task, and let $\tau(T_2) = 1$, $\tau(T_3) = 2$.
In the first pass through the algorithm we obtain :

$$L = \emptyset$$
$$A = 0$$

$$AV = 1$$
$$R(T_b) - A - AV = 4 - 0 - 1 = 3$$
$$T_i = T_1$$
$$R(T_1) - A = 1 - 0 = 1 \quad \text{(positive number)}$$
$$AV = 1 - 1 = 0$$
$$A = 3$$
$$L = T_1$$

Since $A+AV = 3+0 = 3$ is less than $R(T_b) = 4$ we must repeat the algorithm.

$$R(T_b) - A - AV = 4 - 3 - 0 = 1$$
$$T_i = T_2$$
$$R(T_2) - A = 1 - 3 = -2 \quad \text{(negative number)}$$
$$AV = 0$$
$$A = A - R(T_2) + C(T_2) = 3 - 1 + 2 = 4$$
$$L = T_1, T_2$$

Now, $A+AV = 4$ is enough to promoting T_b to rank $= 0$.

If the blocked task is not a competitor we add it to the set of competitors without regard to the admission test, and use the proposed Algorithm 8. In the worst case (if the blocked task request all resources available in the system) no other task can enter SCO until this task is completed.

Let us note that the proposed approach to permanent blocking prevention, in contrary to [4,5] , does not cut off the possibility of granting the requests of tasks which hold no resources (if it can be done safely) and thus keeps system throughput high.

5. CONCLUSIONS.

In the commonly used approaches to systems with nonpreemptible resources the rules improving system throughput have been applied for tasks whose nonpreemptible resource requests have been previously granted. Of course, the use of these rules, together with a nonpreemptible resource allocation policy, will lead to much better results.

The algorithms of resource allocation proposed here constitute a policy which fulfills the above postulate. Besides the deadlock problem, the problem of permanent blocking is also solved in this policy. The presented algorithms can be easily implemented in operating systems because of their simplicity and the low overhead involved.

References

[1] R.W. Conway, W.L. Maxwell, L.W. Miller: Theory of Scheduling, Addison-Wesley, Reading Mass, (1967).

[2] M.R. Garey, D.S. Johnson, R. Sethi: The complexity of flowshop and jobshop scheduling, Math. Operations Res. (to appear).

[3] A.N. Habermann: A new approach to avoidance of system deadlocks; Revue Francaise d'Automatique, Informatique et Recherche Opérationelle, 9 (1975) pp. 19-28.

[4] A.N. Habermann: Prevention of system deadlocks, Comm. ACM 12,7 (1969) pp. 373-377, 385.

[5] R.C. Holt : Comments on prevention of system deadlocks, Comm. ACM 14, 1 (1971) pp. 36-38.

[6] D.L. Parnas, A.N. Habermann: Comment on deadlock prevention method (with a reply by R.C. Holt) , Comm. ACM 15, 9 (1972) pp. 840-841.

Measuring, Modelling and Evaluating Computer Systems,
H. Beilner and E. Gelenbe, (eds.)
© North-Holland Publishing Company (1977)

IMPLEMENTATION OF ALGORITHMS FOR PERFORMANCE ANALYSIS OF A CLASS OF MULTIPROGRAMMED COMPUTERS

Mauro Brizzi, Davide Grillo
Fondazione Ugo Bordoni
Roma, Italy

The description of a package for the numerical evaluation of queueing networks performance figures is presented. The package is based on the application of the generating function approach for analyzing models characterized by product form solutions. Output performance figures are: utilization, throughput, queue length, job renewal rate and response time. The package pursues flexibility in modelling the network, efficiency in terms of running time and control over the detail level in investigating network behaviour.

1. Introduction

In /1/ and /2/ a class of queueing networks is defined for which the generic state probability may be factorized into as many terms as there are service stations in the network (product form solution). Such a class is finding extensive application and reference - especially in the field of computer systems - due to the quite satisfactory closeness with which many situations of competing demands on a limited number of resources can be modelled.
In this paper only closed queueing networks belonging to that class will be considered. For closed networks the amount of work required to compute performance figures grows very rapidly with the number of jobs and the number of distinct job streams flowing in the system.
The generating function approach proposed in /3/ for networks with RR-Processor Sharing discipline through all service stations, shortens greatly the computational effort otherwise needed. Moreover this powerful approach need not be restricted to one type of scheduling since it is also warranted by FCFS and LCFS-Preemptive Resume scheduling algorithms as well, /4/.
The aim of the paper is to describe a package - called CQNA-1, /11/ - for the numerical evaluation of network performance derived from the abovementioned exact, closed form solutions. Other efforts in this direction are known, /5/, /6/ and /10/; this package is based on the application of the generating function approach which allows easy attainment of the detail level with which a network can be analyzed.

Service stations belonging to the considered networks may have one of the three servicing disciplines: RR–Processor Sharing, FCFS, LCFS–Preemptive Resume. Service rates throughout all service stations are assumed to be state independent.
Routing in the networks is described by Markov chains. The pattern followed by a job within each job stream depends on the pair "service center–job class". The package pursues flexibility in modelling the network, efficiency in terms of running time and control over the detail level in investigating network behaviour.

2. Notations

$\{b_1, b_2, \dots b_K\}$	set consisting of the elements b_1, $b_2, \dots, b_K$ or, when no confusion arises, ordered collection of elements b_1, $b_2, \dots$, b_K; to refer to the latter meaning the word "sequence" is conventionally used in this paper;
$\{b \in \mathcal{B} \mid \dots\}$	set consisting of all elements b belonging to a set $\mathcal{B}$ such that ... ;
$\sum_{b \in \mathcal{B}} \; (\prod_{b \in \mathcal{B}})$	sum (product) extended to all elements b of a set $\mathcal{B}$;
m_{ierl} $(\{m_{ierl}\})$	number (sequence) of jobs labelled "ierl", $m_{ierl} \geq 0$;
δ_{hk}	Kronecker delta ($\delta_{hk}=0$ if $h \neq k$, $\delta_{hk}=1$ if $h=k$);
$\mathcal{M}$	$\{m_1, m_2, \dots, m_E\}$ or equivalently $\{m_h\}$ $h=1(1)E$, sequence;
$\mathcal{S}$	set of all network feasible states;
s	$\in \mathcal{S}$;
$\mathcal{S}_{\{m_{ierl}\}}$	aggregate state $\{s \in \mathcal{S} \mid s$ is described by the sequence $\{m_{ierl}\}\}$, $l=1(1)u_{ier}$, $\forall r \in \mathcal{R}(i, e)$, $\forall e \in \mathcal{E}_i$, $\forall i \in \mathcal{N}$;
$\mathcal{S}_{\{m_{\underline{i}erl}\}}$	aggregate state $\{s \in \mathcal{S} \mid s$ is described by $\{m_{ierl}\}$, i fixed$\}$, $\mathcal{S}_{\{m_{\underline{i}erl}\}} \supseteq \mathcal{S}_{\{m_{ierl}\}}$;

t_e	generating function variable attached to ergodic subchain e, $\forall e \in \mathscr{E}$;
$\mathscr{T}$	$\{t_1, t_2, \ldots, t_E\}$, sequence;
$\mathscr{T}_i$	$\{t_e \in \mathscr{T} \mid e \in \mathscr{E}_i\}$, $\forall i \in \mathscr{N}$, sequence;
$\mathscr{T}^*_h$	$\bigcup_{i=1}^{h} \mathscr{T}_i$, h=1(1)N, sequence;
$\triangleq$	equal by definition;
$\propto$	proportional to;
s. d.	servicing discipline;
X	cartesian product;
$\emptyset$	empty set.

3. The model

The class of closed queueing networks considered in this paper is a subclass of that one defined in /2/. In what follows notations are introduced that will help in defining the class.
Be: $\mathscr{N}$ a set of service stations - each service station consisting of one queue and one server (processor) - , $\mathscr{N} = \{1, 2, \ldots, N\}$, and $i \in \mathscr{N}$; $\mathscr{E}$ a set of job streams flowing through the N service stations, $\mathscr{E} = \{1, 2, \ldots, E\}$, and $e \in \mathscr{E}$; $\mathscr{E}_i \subseteq \mathscr{E}$ the subset of job streams flowing through the service station i, $\forall i \in \mathscr{N}$; m_e the number of jobs in each job stream.
The network of the N processors is closed for each job stream, that is m_e = constant, $\forall e \in \mathscr{E}$. At any instant of time during its existence in the network, to each job is attached a class r, $r \in \mathscr{R}$ with $\mathscr{R} = \{1, 2, \ldots, R\}$.
Routing of jobs is described by a Markov chain $\left[p^{(e)}_{(i_1r_1)(i_2r_2)}\right]$, $\forall e \in \mathscr{E}$; $p^{(e)}_{(i_1r_1)(i_2r_2)}$ is the probability that a job belonging to stream e leaving station i_1 in class r_1 will enter station i_2 in class r_2, $i_1, i_2 \in \mathscr{N}_e$ and $r_h \in \mathscr{R}(i_h, e)$, h = 1, 2, where $\mathscr{N}_e = \{ i \in \mathscr{N} \mid e \in \mathscr{E}_i \}$ and $\mathscr{R}(i_h, e) \subseteq \mathscr{R}$ is the subset

of job classes in service station i_h attached to stream e. $\mathcal{R}(i,e)$ is defined for $\forall e \in \mathcal{E}$ and $i = 1(1)N$.
A service station may have one of the following three types of servicing disciplines:

FCFS : First Come First Served; all jobs have the same service time distribution. The distribution is negative exponential;

LCFS-PR : Last Come First Served - Preemptive Resume; each class of jobs may have a distinct service distribution. The service time distributions have rational Laplace transforms;

RR-PS : Round Robin - Processor Sharing: when there are n jobs in the service center each is receiving service at a rate n^{-1} sec/sec; each class of jobs may have a distinct service time distribution. The service time distributions have rational Laplace transforms.

The service time distributions having rational Laplace transforms, may be represented by a tandem of u_{ier} exponential stages having average service rate μ_{ierl}, and by introducing the probability a_{ierl} that a job joins the stage l after being processed in the stage l - 1, $l = 1(1)u_{ier}$, and $a_{ier1} = 1$.

4. Extension of the Generating Function Approach

The class of queueing networks defined in /2/ is known to be the largest one for which exact, closed form solution for the generic state probabilities may be obtained. Such a class, explicitly motivated by problems of computer system modelling but of far wider applications, embodies a number of network models.
The ease of access to exact solutions has made it more appealing for practitioners to investigate scheduling problems by analytical tools as opposed to simulation, at least in the project stages where no full scale reproduction of reality is needed.
The expression of the probability attached to a single state or to a set of states (for the whole or a part) of a network belonging to that class can be easily written down.
However it may become a hard task to handle expressions of aggregate of states that are relevant to the evaluation of network performance figures, such as utilization, throughput and so on.
Analysts and designers concerned with the evaluation of computer operating systems are interested in methods or tools for rapidly testing the impact of design changes.
In /3/, an orderly and unified way of approaching the problem of determining per-

formance figures for closed networks belonging to the class defined in /2/ has been devised by means of generating functions and by making use of results due to Buzen, /7/ and /8/. The approach is particularly amenable to mechanization and need not be restricted to closed queueing networks with service stations characterized by RR-Processor Sharing service discipline but may be extended, /4/, to (closed) networks where service stations have one of the following "work conserving" servicing algorithms: RR-Processor Sharing, FCFS and LCFS-Preemptive Resume. In what follows a proof of the above statement is outlined. More details are found in /4/.

Taking

$$A_{ierl} \triangleq \prod_{h=1}^{l} a_{ierh} \tag{4-1}$$

$$l = 1(1)u_{ier} \quad \forall r \in \mathscr{R}(i,e) \quad \forall e \in \mathscr{E}_i \quad i = 1(1)N$$

and

$$\varphi^{(e)}_{(i_1 r_1)} \triangleq \sum_{i_2 \in \mathscr{N}_e} \sum_{r_2 \in \mathscr{R}(i_2, e)} \varphi^{(e)}_{(i_2 r_2)} \, p^{(e)}_{(i_2 r_2)(i_1 r_1)}$$

$$i_1 \in \mathscr{N}_e \text{ and } r_1 \in \mathscr{R}(i_1, e) \tag{4-2}$$

$$\forall r_1 \in \mathscr{R}(i_1, e) \quad \forall e \in \mathscr{E}_{i_1} \quad i_1 = 1(1)N$$

in /2/ it is shown that the state probability of a closed queueing network matching the conditions for applying "local balance" may be factorized, to within a normalizing coefficient, into

$$\text{Prob}\{s\} \propto \prod_{i \in \mathscr{N}} \left\{ \left(\sum_{e \in \mathscr{E}_i} \sum_{r \in \mathscr{R}(i,e)} \sum_{l=1}^{u_{ier}} m_{ierl} \right)^{\xi} ! \times \right.$$

$$\left. \times \prod_{e \in \mathscr{E}_i} \prod_{r \in \mathscr{R}(i,e)} \prod_{l=1}^{u_{ier}} \frac{\left(\varphi^{(e)}_{(i,r)} \dfrac{A_{ierl}}{\mu_{ierl}} \right)^{m_{ierl}}}{(m_{ierl})^{\xi} \, !} \right\} \tag{4-3}$$

$$\forall s \in \mathscr{S}$$

with:

$$\xi = \begin{cases} 0 \text{ if i has FCFS or LCFS-PR s. d.} \\ 1 \text{ if i has RR-PS s. d.} \end{cases} \qquad u_{ier} = \begin{cases} 1 \text{ if i has FCFS s. d.} \\ \geq 1 \text{ if i has LCFS-PR or RR-PS s. d.} \end{cases}$$

$$\mu_{ierl} = \mu_i \text{ if i has FCFS s. d.}$$

Singling out in (4 – 3 the term $\varphi^{(e)}_{(i,r)} A_{ierl}/\mu_{ierl}$, the generating function for the processor i, $f_i(\mathcal{T}_i)$, extension of that defined in /3/ is

$$f_i(\mathcal{T}_i) \triangleq \begin{cases} \sum_{k_i=0}^{\infty} \left\{ \sum_{e \in \mathcal{E}_i} \left(\sum_{r \in \mathcal{R}(i,r)} \frac{\varphi^{(e)}_{(i,r)}}{\mu_{ier}} \right) t_e \right\}^{k_i} \\ \text{if i has FCFS or LCFS-PR s. d.} \\ \sum_{k_i=0}^{\infty} \left\{ \sum_{e \in \mathcal{E}_i} \left(\sum_{r \in \mathcal{R}(i,e)} \sum_{l=1}^{u_{ier}} \varphi^{(e)}_{(i,r)} \frac{A_{ierl}}{\mu_{ierl}} \right) t_e \right\}^{k_i} \\ \text{if i has RR-PS s. d.} \end{cases}$$

$$= \begin{cases} \sum_{k_i=0}^{\infty} \sum_{H\binom{m_{ie}}{k_i}} \sum_{H\binom{m_{ier}}{m_{ie}}} k_i! \prod_{e \in \mathcal{E}_i} \prod_{r \in \mathcal{R}(i,e)} \frac{1}{(m_{ier})!} \left(\frac{\varphi^{(e)}_{(i,r)}}{\mu_{ier}} \right)^{m_{ier}} t_e^{m_{ier}} & \text{(4 – 4 – a} \\ \text{if i has FCFS or LCFS-PR s. d.} \\ \sum_{k_i=0}^{\infty} \sum_{H\binom{m_{ie}}{k_i}} \sum_{H\binom{m_{ier}}{m_{ie}}} \sum_{H\binom{m_{ierl}}{m_{ier}}} k_i! \prod_{e \in \mathcal{E}_i} \prod_{r \in \mathcal{R}(i,e)} \prod_{l=1}^{u_{ier}} \frac{\left(\varphi^{(e)}_{(i,r)} \frac{A_{ierl}}{\mu_{ierl}} \right)^{m_{ierl}}}{(m_{ierl})!} t_e^{m_{ierl}} & \text{(4 – 4 – b} \\ \text{if i has RR-PS s. d.} \end{cases}$$

with

$$\frac{1}{\mu_{ier}} = \sum_{l=1}^{u_{ier}} \frac{A_{ierl}}{\mu_{ierl}}$$

and

$$H\binom{x}{y} : \text{"all } x \text{ such that } \Sigma x = y \wedge x \geq 0\text{"}$$

The coefficient of the term $t_e^{m_{ier}}$ ($t_e^{m_{ierl}}$) such that $\sum_{e \in \mathscr{E}_i} \sum_{r \in \mathscr{R}(i,e)} m_{ier}$ $\left(\sum_{e \in \mathscr{E}_i} \sum_{r \in \mathscr{R}(i,e)} \sum_{l=1}^{u_{ier}} m_{ierl} \right) = k_i$, $k_i \leq \sum_{e \in \mathscr{E}_i} m_e$ and $\sum_{i \in \mathscr{N}} k_i = \sum_{e \in \mathscr{E}} m_e$ is the probability – to within a normalizing coefficient – that the sequence $\{m_{ier}\}$ ($\{m_{ierl}\}$) of jobs is in the queue i, no matter how they all are ordered.
If i has FCFS or LCFS-PR s. d. this probability is Prob $\left\{\mathscr{S}_{\{m_{ier}\}}\right\}$, if i has RR-PS s. d. this probability equals Prob $\left\{\mathscr{S}_{\{m_{ierl}\}}\right\}$, as it is stated in /2/.

For all the three disciplines it is possible to write $f_i(\mathscr{T}_i)$ in the following alternative forms:

$$f_i(\mathscr{T}_i) = \sum_{k_i=0}^{\infty} \left\{ \sum_{e \in \mathscr{E}_i} \left(\sum_{r \in \mathscr{R}(i,e)} x_{r(i,e)} \right) t_e \right\}^{k_i}$$

where (4 – 5

$$x_{r(i,e)} = \varphi_{(i,r)}^{(e)} \frac{1}{\mu_{ier}} = \sum_{l=1}^{u_{ier}} \varphi_{(i,r)}^{(e)} \frac{A_{ierl}}{\mu_{ierl}}$$

and

$$f_i(\mathscr{T}_i) = \sum_{k_i=0}^{\infty} \left\{ \sum_{e \in \mathscr{E}_i} x_{\mathscr{R}(i,e)} t_e \right\}^{k_i}$$

where (4 – 6

$$x_{\mathscr{R}(i,e)} = \sum_{r \in \mathscr{R}(i,e)} x_{r(i,e)}$$

All expressions above do not differ formally from those reported in /3/, when processor service times are not state dependent, thus allowing the extension of the class of closed queueing networks to which the generating function approach is applicable. With respect to results in /3/ the extension is twofold: 1) FCFS and LCFS-PR servicing algorithms are permissible; 2) job routing may be specified on the basis of the pair "node - job class".
The three alternative ways, (4 - 4 - b, (4 - 5, (4 - 6, of expressing $f_i(\mathcal{T}_i)$ may be put in correspondence with different degrees of detail with which the network performance can be investigated.
Expression (4 - 6, formally identical - to within an obvious generalization - with that in /3/, copes with evaluation of the network that accounts for the effect due to different job streams. Expression (4 - 5 allows a level of investigation that explicitly evidences the influence of different job classes inside each job stream.
Expression (4 - 4 - b, valid if the service station has RR-PS service discipline, allows a degree of investigation that descends into such details as the exponential stages mix that realize the prescribed service distribution.
This level of detail will not be further considered in this paper.

5. Output Network Performance Figures

In the same way as in /3/, by setting

$$g_i(\mathcal{T}_i^*) \triangleq \prod_{h=1}^{i} f_h(\mathcal{T}_h) \qquad i = 1(1)N \qquad (5 - 1$$

the generating function for the whole network is given by $g_N(\mathcal{T})$. The coefficient of the term $\prod_{e\in\mathcal{E}} t_e^{m_e}$ of $g_N(\mathcal{T})$, that is $G_N(\mathcal{M})$, /8/, is the reciprocal of the normalizing coefficient for the expressions of Section 4. As an example of application of the results obtained in /3/ and /4/, consider the utilization of processor i, i = 1(1)N. Since (4 - 4 - a may also be written as

$$f_i(\mathcal{T}_i) = \left\{1 - \sum_{e\in\mathcal{E}} \sum_{r\in\mathcal{R}(i,e)} \varphi_{(i,r)}^{(e)} \frac{1}{\mu_{ier}} t_e\right\}^{-1} \qquad (5 - 2$$

(for suitably chosen t_e's), following /3/, the utilization generating function for the processor i is

$$h_i(\mathcal{T}) \triangleq g_N(\mathcal{T}) \frac{f_i(\mathcal{T}_i) - 1}{f_i(\mathcal{T}_i)}$$

$$= g_N(\mathcal{T}) \sum_{e \in \mathcal{E}_i} \left\{ \sum_{r \in \mathcal{R}(i,e)} \varphi^{(e)}_{(i,r)} \frac{1}{\mu_{ier}} \right\} t_e \qquad (5-3$$

and the utilization of the processor i, $U_i(\mathcal{M})$ – percentage of the time during which the processor i is not idle – is the coefficient of $\prod_{e \in \mathcal{E}_i} t_e^{m_e}$ in $h_i(\mathcal{T})$ divided by the coefficient of the same term in $g_N(\mathcal{T})$, that is

$$U_i(\mathcal{M}) = \frac{\sum_{e \in \mathcal{E}_i} G_N(\mathcal{M}_e) \times_{\mathcal{R}(i,e)}}{G_N(\mathcal{M})} \qquad \forall i \in \mathcal{N}$$

with (5 – 4

$$\mathcal{M}_e = \left\{ m_h - \delta_{eh} \right\} \qquad h = 1(1)E$$

The utilization of the processor i can be broken down into various components, according to the desired degree of detail. Proceeding similarly as in (5 – 3, the following expressions can be derived

$$U_{ie}(\mathcal{M}) = \frac{G_N(\mathcal{M}_e) \times_{\mathcal{R}(i,e)}}{G_N(\mathcal{M})}$$

(5 – 5

$$U_{ier}(\mathcal{M}) = \frac{G_N(\mathcal{M}_e)\, x_{r(i,e)}}{G_N(\mathcal{M})}$$

which, in the order, stand for the percentage of time during which the processor i is executing: jobs belonging to stream e, $\forall e \in \mathcal{E}_i$; jobs of class r in stream e, $\forall r \in \mathcal{R}(i,e)$.

Combining results obtained in /2/ to /4/ and /7/ to /9/, the following list of network performance figures can be produced by the package.

Processor-bound figures

(all entries to be divided by $G_N(\mathcal{M})$)

	(i)	(i, e)	(i, e, r)
U utilization	$\sum_{e \in \mathcal{E}_i} G_N(\mathcal{M}_e) \times_{\mathcal{R}(i,e)}$	$G_N(\mathcal{M}_e) \times_{\mathcal{R}(i,e)}$	$G_N(\mathcal{M}_e) \times_{r(i,e)}$
T throughput	$\sum_{e \in \mathcal{E}_i} G_N(\mathcal{M}_e) \sum_{r \in \mathcal{R}(i,e)} \varphi^{(e)}_{(i,r)}$	$G_N(\mathcal{M}_e) \sum_{r \in \mathcal{R}(i,e)} \varphi^{(e)}_{(i,r)}$	$G_N(\mathcal{M}_e)\, \varphi^{(e)}_{(i,r)}$
Q queue length	$\sum_{e \in \mathcal{E}_i} G_{N+i}(\mathcal{M}_e) \times_{\mathcal{R}(i,e)}$	$G_{N+i}(\mathcal{M}_e) \times_{\mathcal{R}(i,e)}$	$G_{N+i}(\mathcal{M}_e) \times_{r(i,e)}$

Coefficients $G_{N+i}(\mathcal{M}_e)$ are explained in Section 7.

Job stream-bound figures

JRR(e) job renewal rate	$\varphi^{(e)}_{(i'_e, r'_e)} \dfrac{G_N(\mathcal{M}_e)}{G_N(\mathcal{M})}$
RT(e) response time	$\dfrac{m_e}{JRR(e)}$

In the considered model, jobs belonging to stream e enter the network at origin service station i'_e in class r'_e and leave the network from the set

$$\left\{ (i,r) \in \mathcal{N}_e \times \bigcup_{i \in \mathcal{N}_e} \mathcal{R}(i,e) \,\middle|\, p^{(e)}_{(i,r)(i'_e, r'_e)} \neq 0 \right\}$$

JRR(e) is the rate at which jobs leave this set reaching (i'_e, r'_e); RT(e) is the time elapsed from the instant of job entry into the network to the instant of its departure, $\forall e \in \mathscr{E}$.

6. Package Features

The package is capable of modelling the class of closed queueing networks defined in the preceding Sections. The following performance figures are produced: utilization, throughput, average queue length, job renewal rate and response time. The first three of them are processor bound and may be further specified according to the combinations processor-job stream or processor-job stream-class. The degree of detail attached to the results is controlled by the user; it is in any case automatically adjusted to be compatible with the service stations scheduling algorithms. Output data are displayed in tabular form, as will be illustrated in Section 8.

Once fed with the ultimate values of the multiprogramming grades attached to each job stream, the package may produce the whole set of network performance figures also for any combinations of intermediate multiprogramming values. This is made possible by the structure of the algorithm employed for the G(.) coefficients computation. The amount of output data may be suitably limited by the user, as will be discussed in Section 7.

The average service rates may be specified according to the service station, (i), or - for service stations with LCFS-PR or RR-PS scheduling algorithms - on the basis of the pair processor-job stream, (i, e), or of the triplet processor-job stream-class, (i, e, r). Moreover it is possible to attach to each level of specification, whether (i), (i, e) or (i, e, r), a finite range of service rates by feeding the minimum and the maximum value and the total number of rate values to be scanned. The incremental, multiplicative or additive steps are automatically computed. Network performance figures can be produced for any combination of service rate values coupled with any combination of multiprogramming grades.

The amount of performance figures sets displayed in one run may further be limited by linking together in one group several service rate specifications and by forcing the current values inside the ranges grouped together to advance jointly. In such a way, the number of output data due to the service rates variation equals the product among the number of values pertaining to each group. Feeding service rate specifications is eased by a data format design that will be described in Section 8.

Compatibility and completeness of input data are checked by diagnostic routines that are activated in the initial stage of each run. More specifically, all of the following tests have to be passed before performance figures may be produced:

- all job streams are associated ergodic chains;
- all branching probabilities attached to each service station, inside each job stream, sum to unity;
- the detail of service rates specifications is compatible with the service station scheduling algorithm;
- all feasible combinations (i, e, r) have been assigned a service rate value.

In addition to user determined issues, like accessibility to and flexibility in network description, the package pursues portability and efficiency. Portability was attempted in the actual version by adopting an "intersection" between FORTRAN IV and FORTRAN V to code the package. The portability issue is in any case hard to meet fully: the chosen instruction repertoire is a widespread one and should allow the package to be run on a number of computers.
As for the second objective, one might distinguish between two aspects: core and time efficiency. The major contribution to core occupancy is due to G(.) coefficients storage. A method has been envisaged which allows progressive overlapping of no more recalled G(.) array space by newly produced information, so that core saving results. The method works when no service rate changes are specified. Every time there is a service rate change inside a group of specifications, a variable number of G(.)'s, depending on the group, have to be updated. Therefore, the total number of updated coefficients in one run may depend on what groups of specifications are more rapidly scanned in order to generate the combinations of rate values. An algorithm has been set up which minimizes the total updated coefficients so that time saving results.

7. Algorithms

The rapid determination of the G(.)'s is central for the computational efficiency of the generating function approach. To this end the recurrence relations due to Buzen /8/ may be utilized. Recalling (5 - 1

$$g_1(\mathcal{T}_1^*) = f_1(\mathcal{T}_1)$$

$$g_i(\mathcal{T}_i^*) = \prod_{h=1}^{i} f_h(\mathcal{T}_h) = g_{i-1}(\mathcal{T}_{i-1}^*) f_i(\mathcal{T}_i) \qquad (7-1$$

and by making use of (5 - 2 and (7 - 1, one obtains

$$g_i(\mathcal{T}_i^*) = \frac{g_{i-1}(\mathcal{T}_{i-1}^*)}{1 - \sum_{e \in \mathcal{E}_i} \sum_{r \in \mathcal{R}(i,e)} \varphi_{(i,r)}^{(e)} \frac{1}{\mu_{ier}}} \qquad (7-2$$

that is

$$g_i(\mathcal{T}_i^*) = g_{i-1}(\mathcal{T}_{i-1}^*) + g_i(\mathcal{T}_i^*) \sum_{e \in \mathcal{E}_i} x_{\mathcal{R}(i,e)}\, t_e \qquad (7-3$$

therefore

$$G_i(\mathcal{M}_{\{\cdot\}}) = G_{i-1}(\mathcal{M}_{\{\cdot\}}) + \sum_{e \in \mathcal{E}_i} G_i(\mathcal{M}'_{\{\cdot\}}) \times \mathcal{R}(i, e) \qquad (7-4$$

with

$$\mathcal{M}_{\{\cdot\}} = \{n_h\} \qquad 0 \le n_h \le m_h$$

$$\mathcal{M}'_{\{\cdot\}} = \{n_h - \delta_{eh}\} \qquad h = 1(1)E$$

and

$$G_0(\{n_h\}) = 0 \quad , \quad G_i(\{0, 0, \ldots, 0\}) = 1 \qquad i = 1(1)N$$

The coefficients $G_{N+i}(.)$, necessary to compute the average queue lengths, are defined in /9/ as

$$G_{N+i}(\mathcal{M}_{\{\cdot\}}) = G_N(\mathcal{M}_{\{\cdot\}}) + \sum_{e \in \mathcal{E}_i} G_{N+i}(\mathcal{M}'_{\{\cdot\}}) \times \mathcal{R}(i, e) \qquad (7-5$$

and

$$G_{N+i}(\{0, 0, \ldots, 0\}) = 1 \qquad i = 1(1)N$$

The G(.)'s are stored in a 3-dimensional G-ARRAY. The first coordinate stands for the service station, the second one for the multiprogramming values mix. Technical grounds advise to address the $G_i(.)$'s and the $G_{N+i}(.)$'s only through index i. The third coordinate of G-ARRAY discriminates between $G_i(.)$ and $G_{N+i}(.)$. The core required to store the G(.)'s is $N \times \prod_{h=1}^{E} (m_h + 1) \times 2$.

To ease the implementation of the algorithm for the G(.)'s computation, entries of G - ARRAY are addressed as if it had E + 2 dimensions; so a two-way correspondence is set up between G-ARRAY and a virtual matrix $(N, m_1 + 1, m_2 + 1, \ldots, m_E + 1, 2)$. Access to a particular entry with coordinates $(i, n_1, n_2, \ldots, n_E, \xi)$ in the virtual matrix, $i \in \mathcal{N}, 0 \le n_h \le m_h$, $h = 1(1)E$, $\xi = 1, 2$, is obtained by referring to the entry with coordinates

$$(i,\ 1 + \sum_{h=1}^{E} n_h b_h,\ \xi)$$

with

$$\begin{cases} b_h = \sum_{k=1}^{h-1} (m_k + 1) & h = 2(1)E \\ b_1 = 1 \end{cases}$$

of the G - ARRAY.

The exhaustive generation of the $\{n_h\}$ multiprogramming mixes is obtained by means of a back tracking algorithm. Considering (6 - 4, it appears that the G(.)'s can be produced either "row - wise" or "column -wise", depending on which of the two items i or $\{n_h\}$ varies more slowly. Since by row -wise production only information related to service stations i and i - 1 need be simultaneously stored, the range of the first coordinates of G - ARRAY may be reduced from N to 2 ($N \geq 2$) for $\xi = 1$.

Column - wise production may require only the storage of the last $\prod_{k=1}^{E-1} (m_k + 1)$ $\{n_h\}$'s with respect to the actual one, because the preceding $\{n_h\}$ E - tuples will no longer be referred to by any subsequently generated one. Thus, as soon as $1 + \prod_{k=1}^{E-1} (m_k + 1)$ $\{n_h\}$ E - tuples have been generated, information related to the next ones may begin to overlap G - ARRAY, allowing in this way a "folded" use of the dedicated core. More specifically, an entry $(i, n_1, n_2, \ldots, n_E, \xi)$ in the virtual matrix will be allocated into G - ARRAY according to the coordinates

$$\left(i,\ 1 + \left\{\sum_{h=1}^{E} n_h b_h \left[\text{modulo}\left(1 + \prod_{h=1}^{E-1} (m_h + 1)\right)\right]\right\},\ \xi\right)$$

In this way an appreciable saving in core may be achieved by reordering the m_h's inside the $\{m_h\}$ E - tuple so that m_E has the maximum value. This is possible since, for the G(.)'s computation, the ordering inside $\{m_h\}$ is immaterial.

The computation of the $G_{N+i}(.)$'s is kept in step with that of the $G_i(.)$'s.
The abovementioned G-ARRAY handling patterns work when no service rate changes are allowed in one run. If it is not the case, neither row-wise nor column-wise with folded use of core are applicable. Indeed, all entries attached to processors affected by service rate changes, whatever the level (i), (i, e) or (i, e, r), have to be recomputed.
The problem of how to arrange the sequence of combinations of service rate changes through all groups, so as to minimize the total number of computations, becomes then a vital one.
More formally, denoting with $\mathscr{C}$ the set of all feasible triplets (i, e, r), that is $(i, e, r) \in \mathscr{C}$, with g the number of groups of service rate specifications as explained in Section 6, with $\mathscr{C}_l$, $l = 1(1)g$, the subset of triplets belonging to each group, such that

$$\left(\bigcup_{l=1}^{g} \mathscr{C}_l = \mathscr{C}\right) \wedge \left(\mathscr{C}_m \cap \mathscr{C}_n = \emptyset \quad m=1(1)g, \; n=1(1)g, \; m \neq n\right) \qquad (7-6$$

to each $\mathscr{C}_l$ is attached a set $\mathscr{N}_l$ such that

$$\mathscr{N}_l = \left\{ i \in \mathscr{N} \,\middle|\, (i, e, r) \in \mathscr{C}_l \right\} \qquad l = 1(1)g \qquad (7-7$$

(Obviously $\mathscr{N}_l \subseteq \mathscr{N}$, $l = 1(1)g$, and $\bigcup_{l=1}^{g} \mathscr{N}_l = \mathscr{N}$).
Be further

$$\begin{cases} \mathscr{N}'_l \triangleq \mathscr{N}_l - \mathscr{N}_l \cap \left(\bigcup_{m=1}^{l-1} \mathscr{N}_m \right) & \\ & l = 2(1)g \\ \mathscr{N}'_1 \triangleq \mathscr{N}_1 & \end{cases} \qquad (7-8$$

(Obviously $\mathscr{N}'_m \cap \mathscr{N}'_n = \emptyset$, $m = 1(1)g$, $n = 1(1)g$, $m \neq n$).
Lastly, denoting with N'_l the cardinality of $\mathscr{N}'_l$ and with v_l the number of different service rates attached to each group, $l = 1(1)g$, and with $\langle h_1, h_2, \ldots, h_g \rangle$ any arrangement of the integers 1 to g, the objective is to find an arrangement $\langle h_1, h_2, \ldots, h_g \rangle$ such that

$$\sum_{l=1}^{g} N'_{h_l} \prod_{m=l}^{g} v_{h_m} = \min \qquad (7-9$$

In the present version of the package the objective (7 – 9 is achieved by axhausting all arrangements $\langle h_1, h_2, \ldots, h_g \rangle$. For moderate values of g, that is in many practical cases, this procedure guarantees the package overall run time efficiency. Should g become very large, that is more than ten, the time spent in exhausting all arrangements might offset the advantage of achieving (7 – 9. Considering the rareness of such values and the difficulty of supervising the amount of data produced consequently, 10 is the upper limit for g in the package.

8. Data Input and Output

The present version of the package runs in batch mode. Input data are fed by cards. Informations regarding amplitude of the service stations set and normalizing mode to solve the set of linear equations systems defined by (4 – 2 are introduced first. So many card blocks follow as job streams are involved. Each block is descriptive of the job stream routing and of the associated branching probabilities. Blocks are completed with information regarding (eventual) jobs renewal mode, ultimate multiprogramming grade, step according to which performance figures are produced from an initial value to be selected among 0, 1 or the step itself to the ultimate multiprogramming grade.

A subsequent set of specifications label each service station with a scheduling algorithm, assign each feasible triplet (i, e, r) a range of service rates and specify which ranges are linked in which groups. Marginalization of service rate specifications is also pursued: namely, it is possible to assign by a unique card service rates pertaining to all the feasible values of one, two, or all the three elements of the triplet (i, e, r). This eases to a great extent the system description, provided there is appreciable simmetry in the service rates. If overlapping assignments occur, conflict cases will be resolved by retaining the latest assignments. Feeding service rate specifications may further be eased by a clever use of this property.

Output data are at present displayed in tabular form. Performance figures such as utilization, throughput, queue lenghts, job renewal rate and response time are produced according to any desired degree of detail compatible with the nature of the figure and with the scheduling algorithm. Things can be arranged in such a way that several sets of performance figures can be displayed in one table. In each table all multiprogramming grades and service rates are held frozen but one. The current value may be either a multiprogramming grade or a service rate. A set of logical switches accessible to the user control the output data production. Figure 1 shows a queueing network of a certain complexity. Rectangles stand for service stations and routing of the jobs is indicated in the same figure. So many job streams flow through the network as many service stations there are in stage 1. Jobs belonging to every stream may mix in service stations of stage 3, whereas mixing in stage 2 is limited.

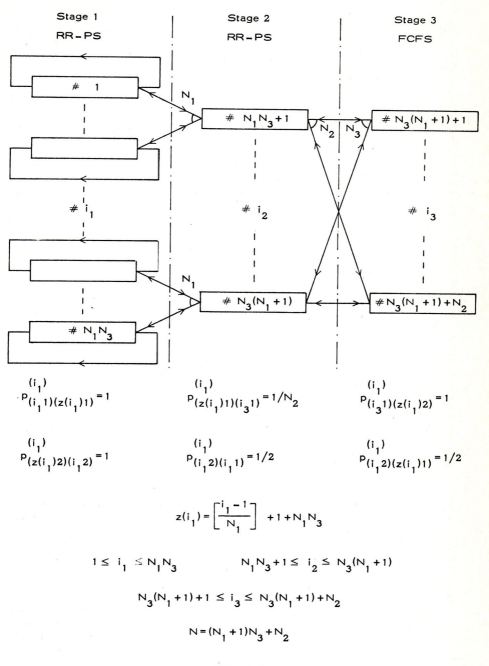

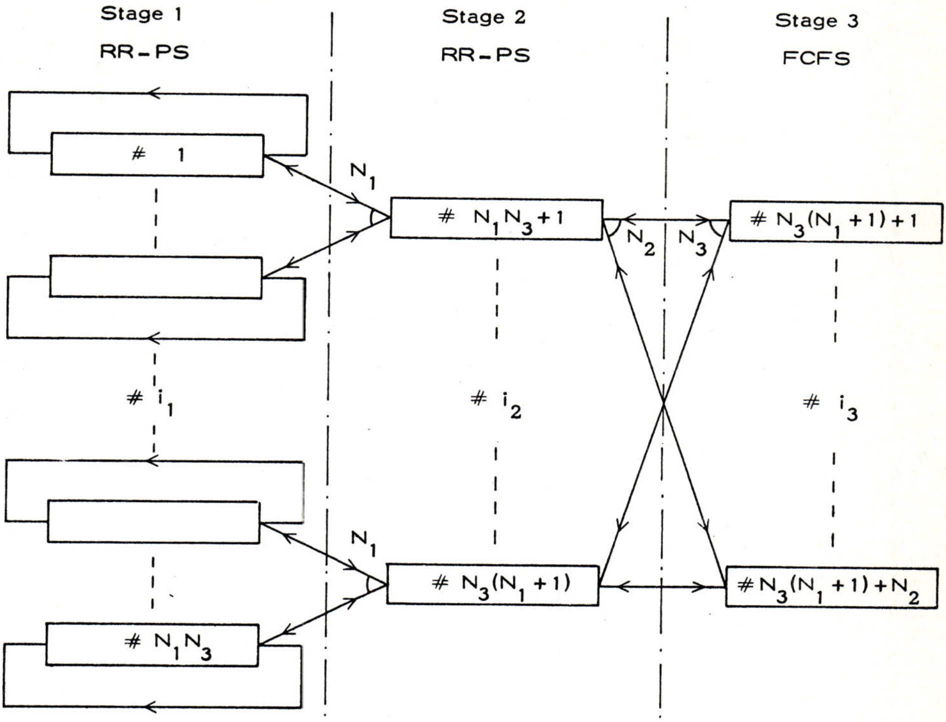

$$p^{(i_1)}_{(i_1 1)(z(i_1)1)} = 1 \qquad p^{(i_1)}_{(z(i_1)1)(i_3 1)} = 1/N_2 \qquad p^{(i_1)}_{(i_3 1)(z(i_1)2)} = 1$$

$$p^{(i_1)}_{(z(i_1)2)(i_1 2)} = 1 \qquad p^{(i_1)}_{(i_1 2)(i_1 1)} = 1/2 \qquad p^{(i_1)}_{(i_1 2)(z(i_1)1)} = 1/2$$

$$z(i_1) = \left[\frac{i_1 - 1}{N_1}\right] + 1 + N_1 N_3$$

$$1 \leq i_1 \leq N_1 N_3 \qquad N_1 N_3 + 1 \leq i_2 \leq N_3(N_1 + 1)$$

$$N_3(N_1 + 1) + 1 \leq i_3 \leq N_3(N_1 + 1) + N_2$$

$$N = (N_1 + 1)N_3 + N_2$$

Figure 1

Table 1 shows a typical package output. The results refer to the network of Figure 1, assuming $N_1 = 2$, $N_2 = 3$ and $N_3 = 1$, and may help in detecting a lower bound for the service rate of the processor in stage 2 so that it does not act as the system bottleneck.

9. Package Performance

A wide repertoire of selfexplanatory diagnostic messages to the user helps in removing eventual errors in input data. If input data are invalid, execution of test routines continues until further processing leads to nonsensical operations. In this way the greatest number of meaningful diagnostic messages is produced.
The package consists of about 1800 instruction cards and about 200 comment cards. The core required to store the set of instructions is 16K memory words on a UNIVAC 1106 and 21K memory words on a IBM 370/168.
The memory space needed to allocate the data bank is very closely upper bounded by the following expression (in memory words)

$$1000 + N\left[E(4+2R) + g + 3R\right] + NR \max\left\{NR,\ 8E\right\} + N \max\left\{NR^2,\ 2\frac{\prod_{l=1}^{E}(m_l+1)}{\psi}\right\}$$

with

$$\psi = \begin{cases} \max\left\{m_1+1,\ m_2+1, \ldots,\ m_E+1\right\} & \text{if folded use of core is allowed for computing } G(.) \text{ coefficients} \\ 1 & \text{otherwise} \end{cases}$$

Execution time depends on many factors, such as number of service stations, number of job streams, multiprogramming values and number of alternative service rate values to be combined.
With reference to the network of Figure 1, Table 2 summarizes execution time and data core requirement for some combinations of the parameters N_1, N_2 and N_3.

10. Conclusions

A package for the numerical determination of closed queueing networks performance figures has been developed. The class of analyzable networks is a subset of that defined in /2/, main characterizations being FCFS, LCFS-PR and RR-PS

Table 1 (*)

	$\mu(4,0,0) = (5,0,0) = (6,0,0) = 1$					
	$\mu(1,1,1) = 2/3$ $\mu(1,1,2) = 2$			$\mu(2,2,1) = 4/3$ $\mu(2,2,2) = 4$		
	$m_1 = 5$ $m_2 = 10$			$m_1 = 10$ $m_2 = 15$		
$\mu(3,0,0)$	4	8	16	4	8	16
U (4, 0, 0)	.6249	.7277	.7370	;6580	.7796	.7829
U (1, 1, 0)	.7401	.8736	.8879	.8735	.9838	.9864
U (2, 2, 0)	.8016	.9276	.9380	.7970	.9698	.9748
U (3, 0, 0)	.9373	.5458	.2763	.9870	.5847	.2936
T (4, 0, 0)	.62	.73	.74	.66	.78	.78
T (1, 1, 0)	.89	1.05	1.07	1.05	1.18	1.18
T (2, 2, 0)	1.92	2.23	2.25	1.91	2.33	2.34
T (3, 0, 0)	3.75	4.37	4.42	3.95	4.68	4.70
Q (4, 0, 0)	1.56	2.31	2.43	1.88	3.25	3.33
Q (1, 1, 0)	1.65	2.43	2.56	3.38	6.22	6.47
Q (2, 2, 0)	2.72	4.48	4.78	3.14	7.62	8.10
Q (3, 0, 0)	5.92	1.15	.37	12.60	1.38	.41
JRR (1)	.296	.349	.355	.349	.394	.395
JRR (2)	.641	.742	.750	.638	.776	.780
RT (1)	16.89	14.30	14.07	28.61	25.41	25.34
RT (2)	15.59	13.47	13.32	23.53	19.37	19.24

(*) A zero in any position in the triplets stands for all the feasible values.

Table 2 (*)

	$N_1 = 2$	
	$m_e = 5$ $e = 1(1)N_1N_3$	$m_e = 4$ $e = 1(1)N_1N_3$
N_2 \ N_3	2	3
3	N= 9 CPU time: i) 16 sec; ii) 5 sec Core: 25 Kwords	N= 12 CPU time: i) 184 sec; ii) 61 sec Core: 78 Kwords
6	N= 12 CPU time: i) 23 sec; ii) 8 sec Core: 33 Kwords	N= 15 CPU time: i) 270 sec; ii) 91 sec Core: 97 Kwords

Executions characterized by $N_3 = 2$ were run with service rate changes, whereas those characterized by $N_3 = 3$ were run without.

(*) Host computer: i) UNIVAC 1106 under EXEC-8, ii) IBM 370/168 under OS/VS1

servicing disciplines and state independent service rates. The package takes advantage of the positive computational features of the generating function approach. In this way the desirable objective of handling any mixture of detail levels in producing network performance figures can be easily obtained in the framework of a unified treatment. Aids to the user are also implemented in order to ease the description of the network model.
Further work is planned to remove the limitation of state independent service rates and to reduce core requirement for particular network topologies.

References

/1/ K. M. Chandy, "The analysis and Solutions for General Queueing Networks" Proceedings of the Sixth Annual Princeton Conference on Information Sciences and Systems, Princeton University, 224 - 228, March 1972

/2/ F. Baskett, K. M. Chandy, R. R. Muntz and F. G. Palacios, "Open, Closed and Mixed Networks of Queues with Different Classes of Customers", Journal of the Association for Computing Machinery, Vol. 22, No. 2, 248 - 260, April 1975

/3/ A. C. Williams and R. A. Bhandiwad, "A Generating Function Approach to Queueing Network Analysis of Multiprogrammed Computers", Networks, Vol. 6, No. 1, 1 - 22, 1976

/4/ D. Grillo, "Use of Generating Functions for Performance Analysis of a Class of Multiprogrammed Computers", Fondazione U. Bordoni Monograph, IIIEz1, February 1977

/5/ K. B. Irani and V. L. Wallace, "On Network Linguistics and the Conversational Design of Queueing Networks", Journal of the Association for Computing Machinery, Vol. 18, No. 4, 616 - 629, October 1971

/6/ K. M. Chandy, J. W. Keller and J. C. Browne, "Design Automation and Queueing Networks: an Interactive System for the Evaluation of Computer Queueing Models", Ninth Annual Design Automation Workshop, Dallas, Texas, June 26 - 27, 1972

/7/ J. P. Buzen, "Queueing Network Models of Multiprogramming", Ph. - D. Dissertation, Division of Engineering and Applied Phisics, Harward University, Cambridge, Mass., June 1971

/8/ J. P. Buzen, "Computational Algorithms for Closed Queueing Networks with Exponential Services", Communications of the Association for Computing Machinery, Vol. 16, No. 9, 527 - 531, September 1973

/9/ M. Reiser and H. Kobayashi, "Horner's Rule for the Evaluation of General Closed Queueing Networks", Communications of the Association for Computing Machinery, Vol. 18, No. 10, 592 - 593, October 1975

/10/ M. Reiser, "Interactive Modeling of Computer Systems", IBM Systems Journal, Vol. 15, No. 4, 309 - 327, 1976

/11/ M. Brizzi, D. Grillo, "CQNA - 1, A Package for Analyzing Closed Queueing Networks. Description and User's Guide", Fondazione U. Bordoni Monograph, IIILz2, May 1977

Measuring, Modelling and Evaluating Computer Systems,
H. Beilner and E. Gelenbe, (eds.)
© North-Holland Publishing Company (1977)

OPERATIONAL ANALYSIS OF QUEUEING NETWORKS[1]

Peter J. Denning[2]

Jeffrey P. Buzen[3]

The first step in analyzing a queueing network model is to obtain a set of equations which express $p(\underline{n})$, the steady state distribution of customers in the network, in terms of basic network parameters such as mean service times or routing probabilities. When applying these equations, the analyst usually identifies $p(\underline{n})$ with an operational (i.e., directly measurable) quantity, the proportion of time the system spends in state $\underline{n}$. The analyst also identifies network parameters with operational quantities; for example, he uses measured average service times as values for stochastic means, or relative transition frequencies for routing probabilities. In this paper, we show that the equations relating the operational values of $p(\underline{n})$ to the operational values of the queueing network parameters are considerably more general than in Markovian queueing network theory. In operational queueing network theory, these equations depend only on four assumptions: the number of jobs which are observed to arrive at a given device is (almost) the same as the number observed to depart; the number of transitions into a given system state is (almost) the same as the number out; the number simultaneous interdevice transitions is negligible; the on-line service functions of devices are (almost) the same as the off-line service functions. The last assumption, called "homogeneity", is the major approximation, on account of which queueing network results are not exact. It is closely related to the principle of decomposability.

1 INTRODUCTION

1.1 Background

Queueing networks have become a widely used analytic tool for multiple resource computer system performance studies. The theoretical results have been known for a long time. In 1957, Jackson published a paper showing the analysis of a multiple device system wherein each device contained one or more parallel servers and new jobs could enter or exit the system at any device [JACK57]. In 1963 Jackson extended his analysis to open and closed systems with arbitrary queue dependent service rates at all devices in the system [JACK63]. In 1967, Gordon and Newell simplified the notational structure of these results for the special case of closed systems, wherein the number of jobs was held fixed [GORD67]. In 1971, Buzen showed how to apply these models to computer systems [BUZE71]; he

---

(1) Supported in part by NSF Grant GJ-41289 at Purdue University.

(2) Computer Sciences Dept., Purdue University, W. Lafayette, IN 47907 USA.

(3) BGS Systems, Inc., Box 128, Lincoln, MA 01773 USA.

also developed efficient procedures for calculating performance quantities from these models [BUZE73]. Extensive validation since 1971 has verified that these models predict observed performance quantities with remarkable accuracy [BUZE75, GIAM76].

Most analysts have expressed puzzlement at the accuracy of queueing network models. The traditional approach to deriving them depends on a series of concepts from the theory of stochastic processes; for example:

- The system is modeled by a stationary stochastic process;
- Jobs are stochastically independent;
- Transitions from device to device follow a Markov Chain;
- The system is in stochastic equilibrium;
- The service time requirements at each device follow an exponential distribution; and
- The system is ergodic -- i.e., long term time averages converge to the mean values computed for stochastic equilibrium.

The theory of queueing networks based on these assumptions is usually called "Markovian queueing network theory" [KLEI76a]. The underlined words in this list of assumptions illustrate concepts that the analyst must understand to be able to use the models confidently. Some of these concepts are difficult. Others can be disproved empirically -- for example, system parameters change over time, jobs are dependent, device to device transitions do not follow Markov chains, systems are observable only for short intervals, service distributions are seldom exponential. It is no wonder that many people are surprised that these models succeed, when applied to systems that violate so many assumptions of the analysis!

Operational analysis explains these observations by showing a much weaker set of assumptions on which the validated results rely. (See BUZE76a,b,c;DENN75.)

1.2 Typical Form of Validations

Let $i = 1,\ldots,K$ denote a device in the system, n_i denote the number of jobs present at the ith device, and $\underline{n} = (n_1,\ldots,n_K)$ denote a "state" of the system. In general, $\underline{n}$ changes over time as jobs move among the devices, or enter and exit the system. Let $p(\underline{n})$ denote the proportion of time during which the state is observed to be $\underline{n}$; the $p(\underline{n})$ sum to 1 over all possible values of $\underline{n}$.

An analyst normally uses a model -- whether simulation or analytic -- to define a method for computing, in terms of workload and device parameters, either $p(\underline{n})$ or quantities derived from $p(\underline{n})$. Three important derived quantities are the queue distributions, the mean queue lengths, and the device utilizations. The queue distribution $p_i(n)$ for device i measures the proportion of time $n_i = n$:

$$p_i(n) = \sum_{\underline{n},\ n_i=n} p(\underline{n}) .$$

The mean queue length at device i is

$$\bar{n}_i = \sum_{n>0} n\ p_i(n) .$$

The utilization of device i is the proportion of time $n_i > 0$:

$$U_i = \sum_{n>0} p_i(n) .$$

In a typical validation, the analyst will use physical properties of the devices, together with empirical data on request sizes, to determine the mean service time for one task at a device. He will use empirical data on the workload to determine how often jobs generate tasks for the various devices. He will use the model, applied to these parameters, to compute values for quantities like U_i and $\bar{n}_i$. If, over many different observation periods, these computed values compare well with actual (measured) values, he will conclude that the model is good. (See Figure 1.) Thereafter, he will employ it confidently for predicting future behavior or evaluating proposed changes in the system.

The important observation is that most practical validations interpret model $p(\underline{n})$ as proportions of time rather than as probabilities. Though stochastic assumptions are sufficient to calculate the $p(\underline{n})$, they are stronger than needed for this purpose.

Three simple, operational, assumptions define weak conditions under which $p(\underline{n})$ can be computed from device and workload parameters:

- All quantities should be precisely measurable in finite observation periods -- the precision of results should not depend on an assumption of "stationarity" or "steady state".
- The system must be work conservative -- i.e., the number of entries to a given device (or system state) must be (almost) the same as the number of exits from that device (state) during the observation period.
- The system must be homogeneous -- i.e., the mean service time of each device for given queue length is the same whether the device is on line or off line. (When a device is off line, its output rate for given queue length is measured by subjecting it to constant load.)

Our interest in this paper is showing how the operational assumptions are employed to set up the familiar "local balance equations" of queueing network analysis. The usual product form solutions and computational procedures are then

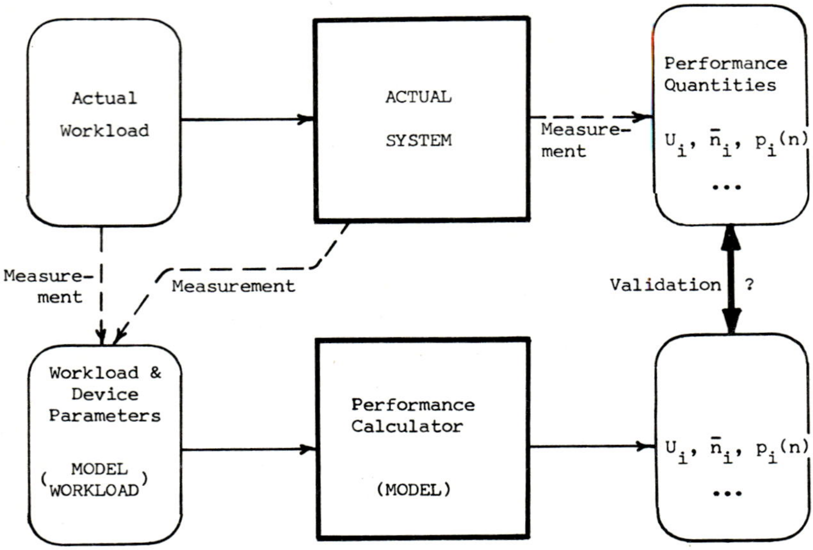

FIGURE 1. Typical validation scheme.

applicable. The conclusion is that the p(n), and quantities derived from them, actually depend only on the operational assumptions, which are weaker than the stochastic ones traditionally used.

The weaker assumptions of operational queueing network theory allow the p(n) to be interpreted only as proportions of time. The stronger assumptions of Markovian queueing network theory are required to answer questions in which the p(n) are interpreted as probabilities. The limitations of operational analysis are discussed at the end of the paper.

2 OPERATIONAL QUANTITIES IN NETWORKS

2.1 Basic Device and Routing Measures

Figure 2 shows two of the K devices in a multiple resource network. A device may depend on load to the extent that its work completion rate is a function of n_i, the number of jobs present there. All jobs of this system are of one class -- i.e., they exhibit similar patterns of demand. A job enters the system at the

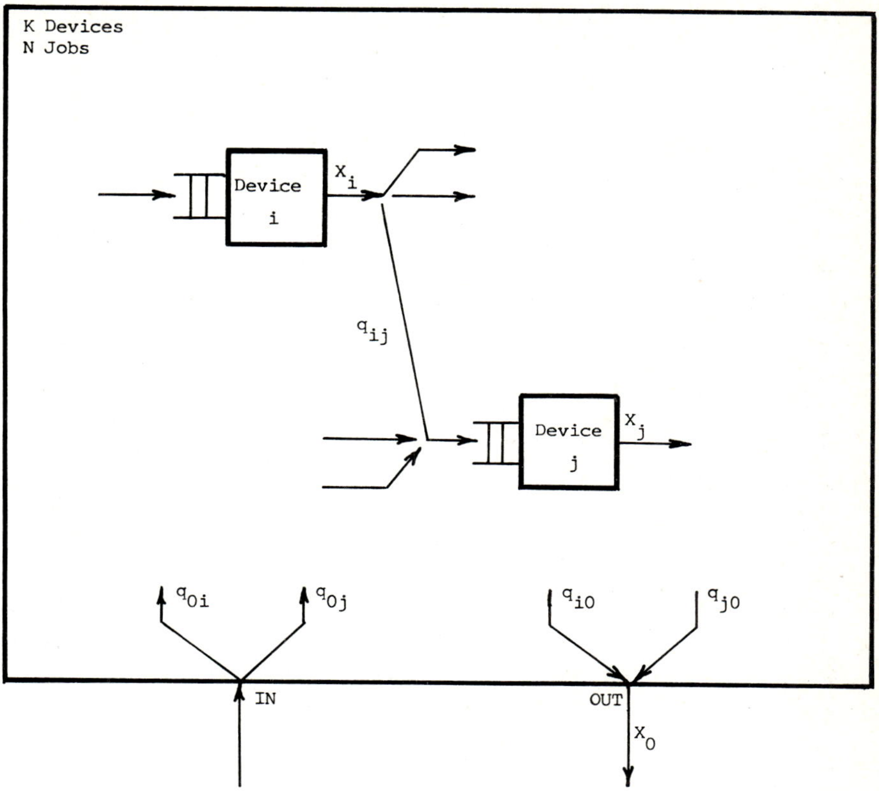

FIGURE 2. Portion of a queueing network.

point 'IN'; whereupon it circulates through the network, waiting in queues and having service requests processed at various devices; when done, it exits at 'OUT'.

The model assumes no job overlaps its use of different devices. In practice, few applications ever achieve more than 2 or 3 per cent overlap between central processor (CPU) and input/output (I/O) devices: the error introduced by this model assumption is usually not significant.

If n_i is the number of jobs present at device i, then $N = n_1 + \ldots + n_K$ is the total in the system. If N is fixed, the system is closed; this is modeled by connecting the output back to the input. The system output rate, X_0, is the number of jobs per unit time leaving the system; it is a function of N.

Suppose the system is observed for a time interval [0,T], wherein these data are collected ($i = 1, \ldots, K$):

$A_i(n)$, number of arrivals at device i when $n_i = n$;+

$C_{ij}(n)$, number of times a job requests service at device j immediately after completing a service request at device i, when n_i=n;+ and

$T_i(n)$, total time during which $n_i = n$.

If we treat the "outside world" as device "0" we can define also

$C_{0i}(n)$, number of jobs whose first service request is for device i when N = n;+ and

$C_{i0}(n)$, number of jobs whose last service request is for device i when $n_i = n$.+

Note that $C_{00}(n) = 0$ for all n. The number of completions at device i is computed as

$$C_i(n) = \sum_{j=0}^{K} C_{ij}(n) , \qquad i = 1,\ldots,K.$$

The number of arrivals to the system when N=n is

$$A_0(n) = \sum_{i=1}^{K} C_{0i}(n) .$$

The method of partitioning the data according to time intervals in which n_i=n is called <u>stratified sampling</u>. The sets of intervals in which n_i=n are sometimes called the "strata" of the sample. This technique aggregates data in the same stratum.

In terms of the (stratified) data, these operational quantities are defined:

$X_i(n)$, request completion rate from device i when n_i=n, $X_i(n)=C_i(n)/T_i(n)$

$p_i(n)$, proportion of time when n_i=n, $p_i(n)=T_i(n)/T$

$S_i(n)$, mean service time when n_i=n, $S_i(n)=T_i(n)/C_i(n)$

(None of these quantities is defined if its denominator is 0.) Define the total number of completions at device i to be

$$C_i = \sum_{n>0} C_i(n) ,$$

and the <u>overall request completion rate</u> of device i to be

$$X_i = C_i/T .$$

+More precisely, these counters register the number of times t at which the given event occurred, such that $n_i(t^-) = n$, or $N(t^-) = n$.

It is easily verified from the definitions that

$$X_i = \sum_{n>0} p_i(n)\, X_i(n) .$$

Define the total busy time of device i to be

$$B_i = \sum_{n>0} T_i(n) .$$

The <u>mean service time</u> over all tasks completed at device i is

$$S_i = B_i / C_i .$$

These definitions imply the <u>operational utilization formula</u>:

$$U_i = X_i S_i , \qquad i = 1,\ldots,K.$$

(See also BUZE76c.)

Let J_i denote the total job-seconds accumulated at device i, that is,

$$J_i = \sum_{n>0} n\, T_i(n) .$$

Two more operational quantities follow:

$\bar{n}_i$ = mean queue length, $\bar{n}_i = J_i/T$

R_i = mean response time of a request, $R_i = J_i/C_i$

These definitions imply the <u>operational Little's Formula</u>:

$$\bar{n}_i = R_i X_i , \qquad i = 1,\ldots,K.$$

(See also BUZE76c.)

In the special case of a load independent system, the load parameter, n, can be dropped from the service times and work rates; thus $S_i(n) = S_i$, and $X_i(n) = X_i$. In this case, data collection is simpler because the data do not need to be stratified.

Congestion in a queueing network depends not only on the service functions $S_i(n)$ of devices, but also on the frequencies at which jobs generate tasks for the devices. We define a <u>routing frequency</u> as

$$q_{ij} = \frac{1}{C_i} \sum_{n>0} C_{ij}(n) ,$$

which is the fraction of the completions at device i which are followed immediately by requests for device j. In most cases the routing frequencies depend only on intrinsic job characteristics; they are independent of queue lengths. Thus quantities like $q_{ij}(n) = C_{ij}(n)/C_i(n)$ are of no interest. In some systems, the routing frequencies depend on the total load, N; for example, the relative frequency of swapping requests will increase as N increases in a multiprogrammed memory fixed in size [DENN76]. We will not consider this case further here.

2.2 On Line and Off Line Behavior

The method of stratified sampling defines a (load dependent) service function, $S_i(n)$, for each device i. It is defined so that $X_i(n) = 1/S_i(n)$ is the number of tasks per unit time leaving device i, over all time periods in which $n_i = n$. We call this the on line service function of the device.

The analyst can also measure an off line service function, $S_i^*(n)$. He does this with a "constant load" controlled experiment -- in which, for given n, he maintains n_i=n. The rule of the experiment is, simply, that a new job of the given class is added to the device's queue just after a previous job completes service. If, during T seconds of such an experiment, the analyst observes C jobs leaving the device, he assigns

$$S_i^*(n) = T/C .$$

Off line behavior is often easier to determine than on line behavior because, off line, the device is isolated from possible interactions with the rest of the system. Off line behavior can often be determined from simple analysis or simulation. Analysts frequently use off line characteristics as approximations to the true behavior when a device is on line.

The concept of off line behavior can be extended to an entire subsystem. We will return to this in the section on decomposability.

3 JOB FLOW AND BOTTLENECK ANALYSIS

Suppose that we know the overall mean service times (S_i) and the routing frequencies (q_{ij}); how much can we determine about overall device output rates (X_i)? This question is usually approached through the approximation known as the

Principle of Job Flow Balance. For each device i, X_i is the same as the total input rate to device i.

This principle will give a good approximation when the difference between arrivals and completions, $A_i - C_i$, is small compared to C_i. When it holds, we refer to the X_i as device throughputs. Expressing it as an equation,

$$C_j = A_j = \sum_{i=0}^{K} C_{ij} \qquad j = 0,\ldots,K .$$

(The dependence of C_{ij} and A_i on n_i has been removed by summing over all observed values of n_i.) The definition $q_{ij} = C_{ij}/C_i$ allows writing

$$C_j = \sum_{i=0}^{K} C_i \, q_{ij} .$$

Employing the definition $X_i = C_i/T$, we obtain

Job Flow Balance Equations

$$X_j = \sum_{i=0}^{K} X_i \, q_{ij} \qquad j = 0,\ldots,K$$

If the network is open, X_0 will have a value determined by the environment and these equations will have a unique solution for the unknowns X_i. However, if the system is closed, X_0 is unknown and the equations have no unique solution; it is easy to verify that the sum of the X_j-equations for $j = 1,\ldots,K$ reduces to the equation for $j=0$. In a closed network, there are K independent equations and $K+1$ unknowns.

Even when the job flow equations cannot be solved for a unique set of X_i, they still contain information of considerable value. Define

$$V_i = X_i/X_0 ,$$

which is the job flow through device i relative to the system throughput. Our definitions imply that $V_i = C_i/C_0$, which is the number of completions at device i for each completion at the system: V_i is the mean number of requests per job for device i. We refer to V_i as the visit count of a for device i. Substituting into the job flow balance equations, we obtain the

Job Visit Count Equations

$$V_0 = 1$$

$$V_j = q_{0j} + \sum_{i=1}^{K} V_i \, q_{ij} \qquad j = 1,\ldots,K$$

A unique solution of these equations is always possible. If X_0 is known, we can compute $X_i = V_i X_0$.

The solution of the p(n) of a queueing network will, as we shall see, require knowledge of the visit counts, V_i, and of the service functions, $S_i(n)$. The routing frequencies are used in the proofs to show that this is so. In practice, the analyst needs only to extract the K visit counts from workload data, rather then as many as $(K+1)^2$ values of q_{ij}.

If, besides job flow balance, we assume that the service time and routing parameters are all independent of load, we can prove that system throughput X_0 increases in N toward the asymptote 1/W, where

$$W = \max\{V_1 S_1, \ldots, V_K S_K\} .$$

This property was first observed by Buzen for the special case of central server networks with exponential service times [BUZE71]. It was shown to hold under very general conditions by Chang and Lavenberg [CHAN72]. Muntz and Wong used it in bottleneck analysis of general queueing networks, to compute response time asymptotes and to evaluate effects of device speed-up [MUNT74; also DENN75, KLEI76b, MUNT75].

4 SOLUTIONS FOR STATE OCCUPANCIES

4.1 State Transition Balance

Let $T(\underline{n})$ denote the total time during which state $\underline{n} = (n_1, \ldots, n_K)$ is observed in a network over an interval [0,T]; the $T(\underline{n})$ sum to T over all $\underline{n}$. The time proportion for $\underline{n}$ is $p(\underline{n}) = T(\underline{n})/T$.

In the following discussion, $\underline{k}$, $\underline{n}$, and $\underline{m}$ denote distinct system states. Let $Q(\underline{n},\underline{m})$ denote the number of one-step transitions observed from $\underline{n}$ to $\underline{m}$; since the system's remaining in a state is not counted as a transition, $Q(\underline{n},\underline{n}) = 0$. We make the approximation,

> Principle of State Transition Balance. The number of entries to every state is the same as the number of exits from that state during the observation period.

With this, we can write "conservation of transition" equations:

$$\sum_{\underline{k}} Q(\underline{k},\underline{n}) = \sum_{\underline{m}} Q(\underline{n},\underline{m}) , \qquad \text{all } \underline{n} .$$

The only error in these equations is a +1 (or -1) term missing on the right side if $\underline{n}$ is the final (or initial) state of the system for the observation period. This error is not significant if the initial and final states are visited frequently; it is zero if the initial and final states are the same. For given $\underline{n}$ both sides of the equation are zero if and only if $T(\underline{n}) = 0$.

The transition rate from $\underline{n}$ to $\underline{m}$ is the number of transitions per unit time $\underline{n}$ is occupied:

$$H(\underline{n},\underline{m}) = Q(\underline{n},\underline{m})/T(\underline{n}), \qquad T(\underline{n}) \neq 0;$$

it is not defined if $T(\underline{n}) = 0$. The conservation equations can be reexpressed as

$$\sum_{\underline{k}} T(\underline{k})\ H(\underline{k},\underline{n}) = T(\underline{n}) \sum_{\underline{m}} H(\underline{n},\underline{m}) ,$$

for all $\underline{n}$ in which $H(\underline{n},\underline{m})$ is defined; note $T(\underline{n})=0$ when $H(\underline{n},\underline{m})$ is not defined. If we substitute $T(\underline{n}) = p(\underline{n})T$ and cancel T, we obtain the

State Space Balance Equations

$$\sum_{\underline{k}} p(\underline{k})\ H(\underline{k},\underline{n}) = p(\underline{n}) \sum_{\underline{m}} H(\underline{n},\underline{m})$$

for all $\underline{n}$ in which each $H(\underline{n},.)$ is defined.

Because the $T(\underline{n})$ sum to T, we can augment these equations with the normalizing condition

$$\sum_{\underline{n}} p(\underline{n}) = 1 ,$$

which will guarantee that only one set of $p(\underline{n})$ can satisfy them. (Our definitions imply $p(\underline{n}) = 0$ for states $\underline{n}$ not included in the balance equations.)

4.2 Solving the Balance Equations

The state space balance equations are nothing more than algebraic identities on the operational definitions of $p(\underline{n})$ and $H(\underline{n},\underline{m})$. An analyst would hardly use these equations to "solve" for the $p(\underline{n})$. He would instead express the $H(\underline{n},\underline{m})$ in terms of device and workload parameters, and seek a unique solution for the $p(\underline{n})$ in terms of these parameters.

The system state space contains a large number, L, of possible $\underline{n}$ values. If N is the maximum number of jobs ever observed in any queue in the system, L may be as large as $(N+1)^K$ in an open system, and as large as $\binom{N+K-1}{K-1}$ in a closed system.

To render the balance equations more manageable, analysts often make this assumption:

> <u>One Step Behavior</u>. The only observable state changes result from single jobs either entering the system, or moving between pairs of devices in the system, or exiting from the system.

This assumption reduces the number of nonzero transition rates to about K^2 in a load-independent system, and to about NK^2 in a load-dependent system. In most computer modeling, this assumption introduces little or no error. Let

$$\underline{n}_{ij} = (n_1,\ldots,n_i+1,\ldots,n_j-1,\ldots,n_K)$$
$$\underline{n}_{i0} = (n_1,\ldots,n_i+1,\ldots,n_K)$$
$$\underline{n}_{0j} = (n_1,\ldots,n_j-1,\ldots,n_K)$$

denote states which are "neighbors" of $\underline{n}$ relative to the one step assumption. Under this assumption, the state space balance equations reduce to (for all $\underline{n}$):

$$\sum_{i,j} p(\underline{n}_{ij})H(\underline{n}_{ij},\underline{n}) + \sum_i p(\underline{n}_{i0})H(\underline{n}_{i0},\underline{n}) + \sum_j p(\underline{n}_{0j})H(\underline{n}_{0j},\underline{n})$$
$$= p(\underline{n})\left(\sum_{i,j} H(\underline{n},\underline{n}_{ji}) + \sum_i H(\underline{n},\underline{n}_{0i}) + \sum_j H(\underline{n},\underline{n}_{j0})\right)$$

The first terms on left and right correspond to jobs making (i,j) transitions within the system; the second terms on left and right correspond to jobs exiting the system from device i; the third terms on left and right correspond to jobs entering the system at device j. All sums on i and j use values 1,...,K. (For a closed system, the second and third terms on left and right are dropped, and q_{ij} is increased by $q_{i0}q_{0j}$.) Relative to the one step assumption, these equations are algebraic identities over the $p(\underline{n})$ and $H(\underline{n},\underline{m})$.

To obtain solutions of these equations from device and workload parameters, analysts frequently use routing frequencies and off line device characteristics to determine the transition rates. Substituting the off line characteristics for the on line is a major approximation. In doing it, the analyst is asserting

> <u>Homogeneity</u>. The off line service function, $S_i^*(n)$, of each device i is the same as its on line service function, $S_i(n)$.

The substitutions implied by this assumption are summarized in Table I. We have defined the binary indicator variable, I_i, to be 1 when $n_i > 0$ and 0 when $n_i = 0$; this variable sets transition rates between pairs of states to zero when one of the states is illegitimate. Under the substitutions of Table I, together with the identities $q_{01}+\ldots+q_{0K} = 1$ and $q_{i0}+q_{i1}+\ldots+q_{iK} = 1$, the balance equations reduce to

<u>Homogenized Balance Equations</u>

$$\sum_{i,j} p(\underline{n}_{ij}) \frac{q_{ij}I_j}{S_i(n_i+1)} + \sum_i p(\underline{n}_{i0}) \frac{q_{i0}}{S_i(n_i)} + \sum_j p(\underline{n}_{0j}) X_0 q_{0j} I_j$$

$$= p(\underline{n}) \left(\sum_i \frac{I_i}{S_i(n_i)} + X_0 \right), \qquad \text{all } \underline{n}$$

These equations are identical in form to the "local balance equations" of Markovian queueing networks [KLEI76a]. The analyst can solve them for the $p(\underline{n})$ without measuring the state space. Note that the solution is exact if the assumptions of job flow balance, state transition balance, one step behavior, and homogeneity are all precisely satisfied. In practice, these assumptions may only be satisfied approximately, whereupon the solution may only be approximate. Homogeneity is the assumption most likely to be violated in practice. Experience has been good: errors are usually small, the assumptions reasonable.

<u>Table I</u>. Homogeneous Transition Rates.

Type of Job Transition	Type of State Transition	Homogeneous Rate
$i \to j$	$\underline{n}_{ij} \to \underline{n}$	$H(\underline{n}_{ij},\underline{n}) = q_{ij}I_j/S_i(n_i+1)$
	$\underline{n} \to \underline{n}_{ji}$	$H(\underline{n},\underline{n}_{ji}) = q_{ij}I_i/S_i(n_i)$
$i \to 0$	$\underline{n}_{i0} \to \underline{n}$	$H(\underline{n}_{i0},\underline{n}) = q_{i0}/S_i(n_i+1)$
	$\underline{n} \to \underline{n}_{0i}$	$H(\underline{n},\underline{n}_{0i}) = q_{i0}I_i/S_i(n_i)$
$0 \to j$	$\underline{n}_{0j} \to \underline{n}$	$H(\underline{n}_{0j},\underline{n}) = X_0 q_{0j} I_j$
	$\underline{n} \to \underline{n}_{j0}$	$H(\underline{n},\underline{n}_{j0}) = X_0 q_{0j}$

As shown by Jackson [JACK63], the solution of the homogenized balance equations is of the "product form"

$$p(\underline{n}) = \frac{1}{G} \prod_{i=1}^{K} F_i(n_i).$$

The term corresponding to device i is

$$F_i(n) = \begin{cases} 1, & n = 0 \\ X_i S_i(n) F_i(n-1), & n > 0 \end{cases}$$

The X_i are a solution of the job flow balance equations and G is a normalizing constant. (See COFF73, GELE76, KLEI76a.) Efficient procedures are available for computing G and the queue distributions $p_i(n)$ [BUZE73, GELE76].

Our assumptions -- queueing network connectedness, job and state flow balance, and homogeneity -- imply a nonzero transition rate in and out of every possible state $\underline{n}$ of the network. The model will therefore assign nonzero values to all $p(\underline{n})$ even though the actual system may not enter all its possible states. The model of a closed system thus determines $\binom{N+K-1}{K-1}$ values of $p(\underline{n})$; the model of an open system, with a maximum of N jobs observable in any queue, determines $(N+1)^K$ values of $p(\underline{n})$.

Assuming a maximum of N jobs in any queue of an open system, the normalizing constant can be expressed as a product of normalizing constants:

$$G = \sum_{n_1=0}^{N} \cdots \sum_{n_K=0}^{N} \prod_{i=1}^{K} F_i(n_i) = \prod_{i=1}^{K} \sum_{n_i=0}^{N} F_i(n_i) = \prod_{i=1}^{K} G_i$$

Now: the solution of a network containing only device i, and having throughput X_i, is

$$p_i(n_i) = F_i(n_i)/G_i \qquad G_i = \sum_{n_i=0}^{N} F_i(n_i)$$

(See also BUZE76a,b.) This implies that, for an open system,

$$p(\underline{n}) = \prod_{i=1}^{K} p_i(n_i).$$

In other words, $p(\underline{n})$ is the product of the (marginal) queue distributions of the devices, the marginal distribution being determined as if the device were off line with job flow X_i identical to the job flow it experiences on line. This is the operational counterpart of Jackson's Theorem [JACK63; also GELE76]. No similar property holds for closed networks.

4.3 An Example

Figure 3 illustrates a simple system with K=2 and N=2. The timing diagram shows a possible behavior that can be observed. The numbers within the diagram

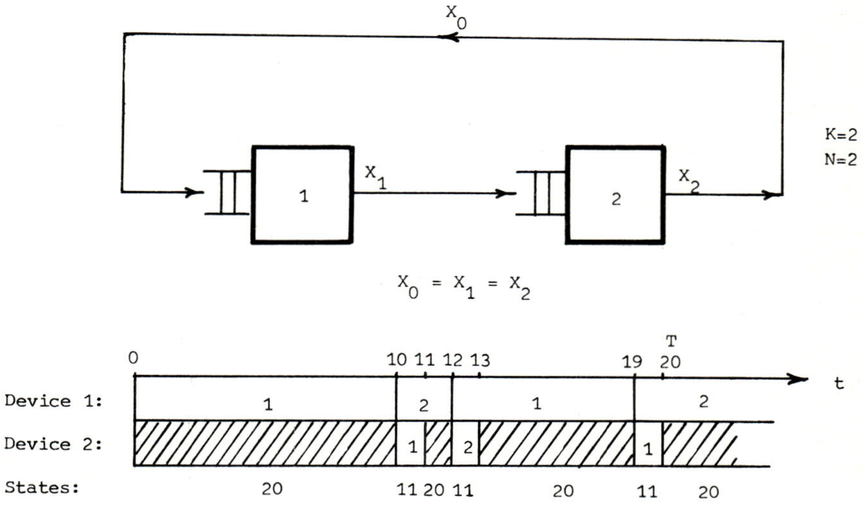

FIGURE 3. Two device system and observed behavior.

show which job is using the device, and shaded portions indicate idleness. The observed states $(n_1 n_2)$ are shown below the timing diagram. The devices are load independent. The observation period is [0,20].

We will compare the model solutions with the actual behavior of this system. The basic operational quantities are

$$S_1 = B_1/C_1 = 20/3 \qquad U_1 = B_1/T = 1 \qquad X_1 = C_1/T = 3/20$$

$$S_2 = B_2/C_2 = 1 \qquad U_2 = B_2/T = 3/20 \qquad X_2 = C_2/T = 3/20$$

The proportions of time of state occupancy are

$$p(20) = T(20)/T = 17/20 \qquad p(11) = T(11)/T = 3/20$$

The transition rates are

$$H(20,11) = Q(20,11)/T(20) = 3/17$$

$$H(11,20) = Q(11,20)/T(11) = 1$$

The balance equations are

$$p(20)(3/17) = p(11)(1)$$

$$p(11)(1) = p(20)(3/17)$$

$$p(11) + p(20) = 1$$

It is easily verified that the observed p($\underline{n}$) satisfy these equations.

The system is not homogeneous. Homogeneity assigns transition rates as follows:

$$H(20,11) = 1/S_1 = 3/20 \qquad H(11,20) = 1/S_2 = 1$$

$$H(11,02) = 1/S_1 = 3/20 \qquad H(02,11) = 1/S_2 = 1$$

These rates allow state 02 to be occupied, which is not observed in the actual system. The balance equations become

$$p(11)(1) \qquad p(20)(3/20)$$

$$p(20)(3/20) + p(02)(1) = p(11)(1 + 3/20)$$

$$p(11)(3/20) = p(02)(1)$$

$$p(20) + p(11) + p(02) = 1$$

For which the solution is

$$p(20) = 400/469 \qquad p(11) = 60/469 \qquad p(02) = 9/469$$

This solution differs from the observed p($\underline{n}$). The predicted utilizations are:

$$U_1 = p(20) + p(11) = 460/469$$

$$U_2 = p(11) + p(02) = 69/469$$

which yield $X_1 = X_2 = U_1/S_1 = 69/469$. The error between these predictions are the true values is under 2%: homogeneity enabled a solution agreeing closely with the observations.

Since $X_0 = X_1 = X_2$, the visit counts are $V_1 = V_2 = 1$. The product form solution specifies

$$p(n_1 n_2) = (V_1 S_1)^{n_1} (V_2 S_2)^{n_2}/G = (20/3)^{n_1} (1)^{n_2}/G = (20/3)^{n_1}/G$$

where

$$G = (20/3)^0 + (20/3)^1 + 20/3)^2 = 469/9.$$

Then, as before,

$$p(20) = (20/3)^2/G = 400/469$$

$$p(11) = (20/3)^1/G = 60/469$$

$$p(02) = (20/3)^0/G = 9/469 .$$

5 DECOMPOSABILITY

The concept of decomposability is often used to simplify the analyses of stochastic processes that model real systems. The concept is straightforward. If a subsystem interacts weakly with its environment, the transient behavior of the subsystem (following an interaction with the environment) will have little effect on the long run dynamics of the total system. Thus, very little error will be introduced by supposing that the subsystem is in equilibrium for the entire interval between two interactions with the environment. The principle of decomposability allows an analyst to decouple a subsystem from its environment, determine its equilibria in isolation, then substitute the equilibria for the true behaviors when the subsystem is embedded in its environment. It is a powerful approximation tool. (See COUR75; COUR77.)

Operationally, decomposability allows an analyst to begin an analysis of a complex system by studying one of its subsystems in isolation. To do this, he subjects the subsystem in question to a series of controlled experiments. In one of these experiments, the subsystem is operated under a constant load (n jobs of the given type) for some time interval of length T. Immediately after each completion in the controlled experiment, the analyst adds another job, to keep the load equal to n. The analyst counts the number of completions, C, and assigns $S(n) = T/C$. The subsystem is then replaced by a single load dependent device of service function $S(n)$, thereby simplifying the overall problem. If indeed the subsystem interacted weakly with its environment, the principle of decomposability holds that the marginal distribution $p_i(n_i)$ of any device in the environment will not be significantly affected by this replacement.

Operationally, decomposability asserts that off line behavior of a subsystem or device is nearly the same as its on line behavior: interactions are too weak to alter the off line behavior substantially. The homogeneity assumption is nothing more than an assertion of perfect decomposability.

Chandy, Herzog, and Woo proved a theorem for systems whose $p(\underline{n})$ satisfy the "local balance equations" (homogenized balance equations) [CHAN75]. Their theorem implies that, under local balance, a subsystem can be replaced by a single load dependent device, whose service function is obtained by studying the subsystem off line; this replacement has no effect on the marginal distribution $p_i(n_i)$ of any device outside the subsystem. Actually, this theorem only depends on the product form of $p(\underline{n})$; consequently it works in the operational case as well. In other words, a network of homogeneous devices is itself homogeneous relative to the environment in which it is embedded.

6 LIMITATIONS OF OPERATIONAL ANALYSIS

Using a relatively weak set of assumptions, operational analysis makes it possible to derive the proportions of time $p(\underline{n})$ a queueing network occupies each state $\underline{n}$, when only the empirical mean service functions of devices and the job visit counts are known. To the extent that operational assumptions resemble practical conditions more closely than Markovian assumptions, they explain the success of typical queueing network validations. To the extent that operational assumptions are intuitive, more analysts can use the queueing network models with confidence and understanding.

Operational queueing network theory has been well validated. All the reported queueing network validations use measured mean service time functions and measured job visit counts to compute $p(\underline{n})$, which are then compared against actual proportions of time the system spends in state $\underline{n}$. (See, e.g., BUZE75, GIAM76.) Analysts have, all along, been validating operational analyses.

The operational results of this paper need not produce exact answers. This is because the principles of job flow balance, state transition balance, one step behavior, and homogeneity are not met exactly in actual systems during finite intervals. The error introduced by assuming that the first three principles are exact is generally not significant. The greatest error is introduced by the homogeneity principle. In practice, devices do interact; their on line service functions, measured by stratified sampling, may differ significantly from their service functions measured off line under fixed load. Homogeneity predicts that all model states will be occupied, even if some actual system states are not. The principle of homogeneity can be extended, with improvements in accuracy. Shum and Buzen, for example, show how off line characteristics of M/G/1 systems can be used to determine on line service functions with improved accuracy [SHUM77]. Cox's method of stages can be used to deal with very general service distributions in an operational context. (See BASK75, GELE76, KLEI76a.)

Operational assumptions do restrict the set of questions that can be answered about queueing networks. These assumptions produce a theory of queueing networks just powerful enough to answer questions about the $p(\underline{n})$ interpreted only as proportions of time. The Markovian assumptions in the stochastic queueing network theory considerably broaden the set of answerable questions by allowing the $p(\underline{n})$ to be interpreted as probabilities.

Operational analysis, for example, has nothing to say about the state of the system at time t (except to the extent that $p(\underline{n})$ is the probability of observing state $\underline{n}$ at a "random" time t). Markovian assumptions allow constructing differential equations relating state probabilities $p(\underline{n},t)$. These equations can, in principle, be solved for the transient behavior of the system; they can be used to study $p(\underline{n},t_2)$ given $\underline{n}(t_1)$.

Operational analysis is sometimes criticized on the grounds that the homogeneous assumption "hides" a Markovian assumption -- with the implication that it is equivalent to Markovian queueing network theory. That operational queueing network theory cannot answer questions about transient behavior, or about system state correlations, disproves this assertion. Moreover, operational analysis can be applied with full precision in finite time periods; steady-state Markovian analysis cannot. Operational analysis assumes measured parameters are used directly; Markovian analysis assumes stochastic parameters are known which, in practice, often cannot be done without difficult methods of parameter estimation.

Operational analysis is also criticized on the grounds that the lack of "stochastic regularity" makes the models useless in performance prediction. To study this assertion, consider a typical scheme of prediction, shown in Figure 4. The analyst begins with a model and model workload validated against an actual system (as in Figure 1). He constructs a projected set of workload and device parameters under the future conditions -- e.g., the same system with a new workload at a future time, or the same workload in a different system. He applies the same model to calculate projected performance quantities. If the modified system is ever built, he validates the predictions by comparing the actual workload against the projection (#1), and the actual performance quantities against the projected (#2). Serious errors in validation #2 almost always result from errors in workload prediction. After all, previous validations established the ability of the model to compute performance quantities when applied to measured parameters.

The central point here is that the difficulty in performance prediction is not the model. It is, rather, predicting the workload. This is a very important problem, but it has nothing to do with whether the analyst uses operational or stochastic assumptions to derive relations between the $p(\underline{n})$ and device or workload parameters.

Operational analysis defines a mathematical system weaker than stochastic analysis. Because it is weaker, it applies to a larger class of systems; but it answers fewer questions. Even as there is a hierarchy of algebraic systems in mathematics -- semigroups, groups, fields -- so there is a hierarchy of

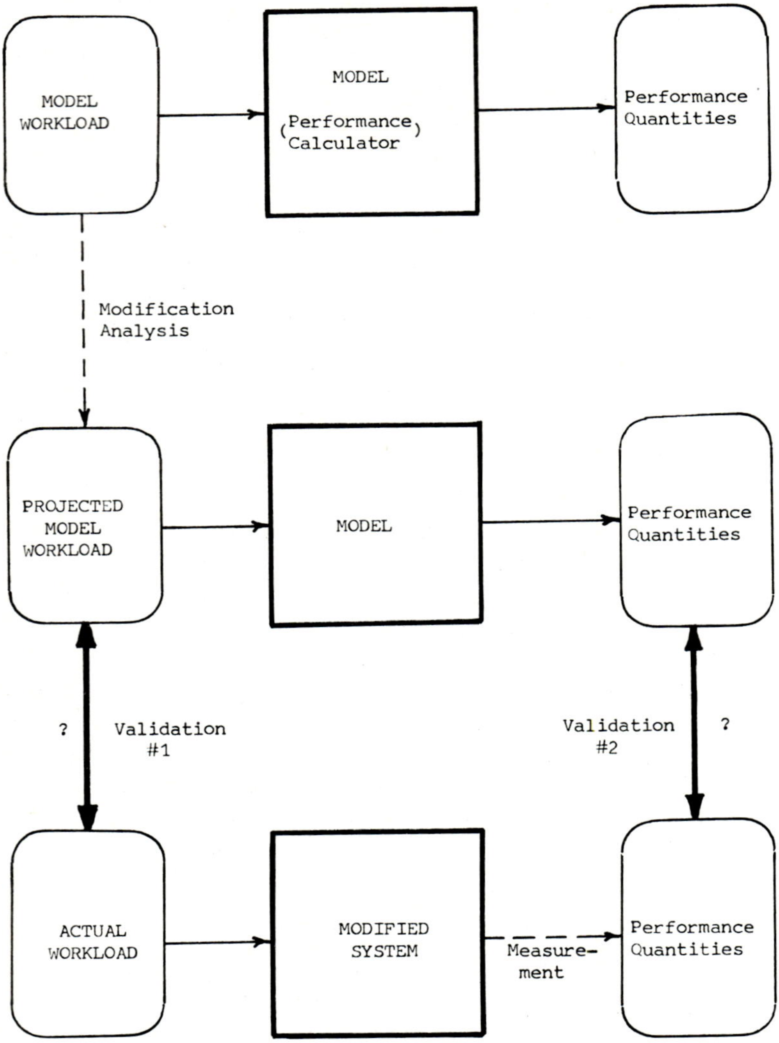

FIGURE 4. Typical performance prediction scheme.

mathematical systems for performance analysis. At the lowest level is bottleneck analysis, which assumes only that the visit counts and service functions are known and that job flow is conserved. At the next level is the network state space analysis of this paper, which adds the assumptions of state transition conservation and device homogeneity. At the highest level is Markovian queueing network analysis.

REFERENCES

BASK75 Baskett, F., Chandy, M., Muntz, R., and Palacios, J., "Open, closed, and mixed networks of queues with different classes of customers," J. ACM 22, 2 (April 1975), 248-260.

BUZE71 Buzen, J. P., "Analysis of system bottlenecks using a queueing network model," Proc. ACM SIGOPS Workshop on System Performance Evaluation (April 1971), 82-103.

BUZE73 Buzen, J. P., "Computational algorithms for closed queueing networks with exponential servers," Comm. ACM 16, 9 (September 1973), 527-531.

BUZE75 Buzen, J. P., "Cost effective analytic tools for computer performance evaluation," Proc. IEEE Compcon (September 1975), 293-296.

BUZE76a Buzen, J. P., "Operational analysis: the key to the new generation of performance prediction tools," Proc. IEEE Compcon (September 1976).

BUZE76b Buzen, J. P., "Operational analysis: an alternative to stochastic modeling," Technical report, BGS Systems, Inc., Box 128, Lincoln, MA 01773 (October 1976).

BUZE76c Buzen, J. P., "Fundamental operational laws of computer system performance," Acta Informatica 7, 2 (1976), 167-182.

CHAN72 Chang, A., and Lavenberg, S., "Work rates in closed queueing networks with general independent servers," IBM Research Report RJ989 (1972).

CHAN75 Chandy, M., Herzog, U., and Woo, L., "Parametric analysis of queueing networks," IBM J R & D 19, 1 (January 1975), 36-42.

COFF73 Coffman, E. G., Jr., and Denning, P. J., Operating Systems Theory, Prentice-Hall (1973).

COUR75 Courtois, P. J., "Decomposability, instabilities, and saturation in multiprogrammed systems," Comm. ACM 18, 7 (July 1975), 371-377.

COUR77 Courtois, P. J., Decomposability, ACM Monograph Series, Academic Press (1977).

DENN75 Denning, P. J., and Kahn, K. C., "Some distribution free properties of throughput and response time," Computer Sciences Dept., Purdue University, W Lafayette, IN 47907 USA, TR-159 (May 1975).

DENN76 Denning, P. J., Kahn, K. C., Leroudier, J., Potier, D., and Suri, R., "Optimal multiprogramming," Acta Informatica 7, 2 (1976).

GELE76 Gelenbe, E., and Muntz, R., "Probability models of computer systems - Part I (Exact results)," Acta Informatica 7, 1 (1976), 35-60.

GIAM76 Giammo, T., "Validation of a computer performance model of the exponential queueing network family," Acta Informatica 7, 2 (1976), 137-152.

GORD67 Gordon, W. J., and Newell, G. F., "Closed queueing systems with exponential servers," Operations Research 15 (1967), 254-265.

JACK57 Jackson, J. R., "Networks of waiting lines," Operations Research 5 (1957), 518-521.

JACK63 Jackson, J. R., "Job shop like queueing systems," Management Science 10 (1963), 131-142.

KLEI76a Kleinrock, L., Queueing Systems, Vol. I, Wiley (1976).

KLEI76b Ibid., Vol. II.

MUNT75 Muntz, R., "Analytic modeling of interactive systems," Proc. IEEE 63 (June 1975), 946-953.

MUNT74 Muntz, R., and Wong, J., "Asymptotic properties of closed queueing network models," Proc. 8th Princeton Conf. on Infor. Scis. and Systs., Dept EECS, Princeton University, Princeton, NJ 08540 USA (March 1974), 348-352.

SHUM77 Shum, A., and Buzen, J. P., "The EPF Technique: a method for obtaining approximate solutions to closed queueing networks with general service times," Proc. 3rd Int'l Symp. on Modelling and Performance Evaluation of Computer Systems, Bonn, Germany (October 1977).

Measuring, Modelling and Evaluating Computer Systems,
H. Beilner and E. Gelenbe, (eds.)
© North-Holland Publishing Company (1977)

A HYBRID ITERATIVE-NUMERICAL METHOD FOR THE SOLUTION OF A GENERAL QUEUEING NETWORK

Raymond MARIE and William J. STEWART
IRISA
Université de Rennes
35031 Rennes
France

1. INTRODUCTION

Over the past years, a considerable research effort has been devoted to the problem of obtaining exact analytic solutions for queueing networks, and with only a few notable exceptions (e.g. Baskett et al, [1]) such research has been crowned with only limited success. System analysts have therefore been obliged to turn to other methods of solution and in particular, to simulation. However, this is a very expensive alternative, requiring large amounts of computer time and yielding results which are often less than accurate. It is chiefly for this reason that intermediate methods have become increasingly popular. Methods such as the iterative techniques based on the theorems of Norton [11], (Chandy et al [2], Marie, [9]), and diffusion techniques, (e.g. Gelenbe, [5], Kobayashi, [8]) may be used to obtain approximate solutions to a considerably larger class of problem than that which is amenable to solution using analytic techniques, and in general, these methods require very little computer time. On the other hand, numerical techniques (e.g. Stewart, [12]) may be used to determine the exact solution for practically any class of queueing network, but suffer from the disadvantage that when the network has a very large state space, the time required to determine this solution becomes excessive.

The purpose of this paper is to present a novel hybrid approach — embedding the numerical technique into an iterative method — to permit solutions to be obtained for networks in which one or more of the stations contain non-exponential servers. We will consider closed queueing networks, R, containing M service facilities and N customers for which the following assumptions apply :

(a) The transition matrix $Q = (q_{ij})$ is fixed ; i.e. the probability that a customer leaving station i will enter station j is independent of the state of the system. (As will be seen, however, service rates are allowed to the state dependent).

(b) The service time distribution at station i, $F_i(t)$, (i = 1,2,...,M) has a rational Laplace transform, and finite mean $\bar{u}_i$, $(0 < \bar{u}_i < +\infty)$. Further, station i contains r_i servers.

(c) Within each station, the queueing discipline is first-come, first-served.

The equilibrium distribution of customers in such a network cannot be determined using existing analytic tools because of the non-exponential nature of the servers. Existing iterative methods must also be eliminated from consideration since these can only be used for the analysis of networks in which each station contains a single server, or if the stations which contain more than one server have exponential service times. In addition, it would appear that the relatively large number of stations and servers considered would make simulation too expensive. Similar considerations rule out a purely numerical approach. Consequently, this paper will propose a method of determining the marginal probability distribution $\tilde{P}_i(n_i)$ of the states of each station in a network not previously amenable to solution. The class of "solvable" queueing networks will therefore be considerably enlarged.

Note that when the analysis is required for an open network in which the arrival rate is state dependent, the correct results may be determined by considering the canonically associated closed network in which the number of customers is sufficiently large to ensure that the probability of the source containing zero customers is negligible.

2. BASIC ITERATIVE CONSIDERATIONS

Each station of the network is studied seperately as a $\lambda(n)/K/r$ queue, i.e. an $M/K/r$ queue in which the arrival process $\lambda(n)$ depends on the state of the station. Here K denotes service time distribution functions with rational Laplace transforms. For each station, the only unknown is the sequence of arrival rates $\{\lambda(n)\}_{n = 1,2,...,N}$. If this can be determined exactly, then a numerical analysis of the station will yield the exact stationary probability distribution of that station. The purpose of the iterative method is therefore to determine a sequence $\{\lambda(n)\}$ so that the computed behaviour of the station approximates its exact behaviour in the networks. The proximity of the computed results to the exact results is evaluated by means of the test-termination conditions which are discussed below. Schematically, we have :

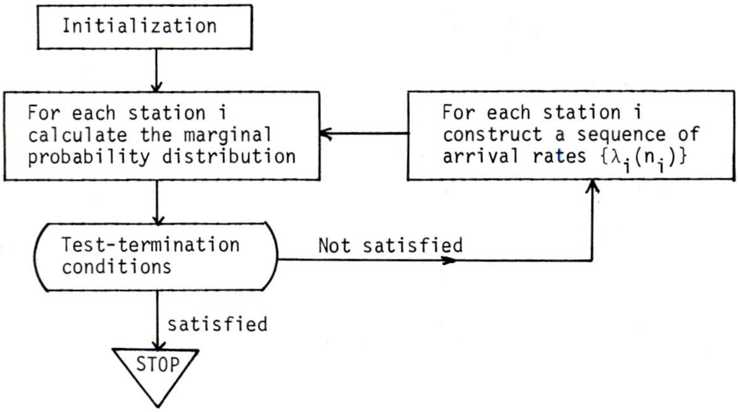

Initialization :

The initial values for the sequence of arrival rates $\{\lambda_i(n_i)\}$ are determined by considering the exponential network R' canonically associated with the network R. This network R' possesses the same number of stations M, the same matrix of transitions Q and the same number of customers N as the network R. The difference resides in the fact that although each station i of R' possesses the same number of servers r_i as the network R, these servers have exponential, rather than Coxian service time distribution of mean $\bar{u}_i$. If $\nu_{\bar{i}}(j)$ is the conditional throughput of the complementary network of station i in R', then the initial approximations to the sequences of arrival rates is taken as $\lambda^{(0)}(n_i)=\nu_{\bar{i}}(N-n_i)$ for $n_i = 0,1,\dots,N$ and $i = 1,2,\dots,M$.

Determination of arrival rates $\{\lambda_i(n_i)\}$

Consider a $\lambda(n)/K/1$ queue. Cox [4] has shown that it is possible to represent such a distribution by means of fictitious stages as :

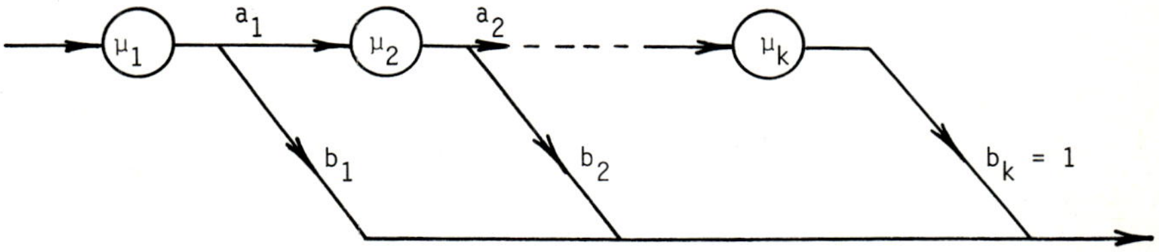

Let p(n,j) be the stationary probability of the Markovian process naturally associated with this queue when it is in state j and when the queue contains n customers. It has been shown by Marie [10] that :

$$\tilde{P}(n).\nu(n) = \lambda(n-1).\tilde{P}(n-1)$$

where $\tilde{P}(n) = \sum_{j=1}^{k} p(n,j)$ is the marginal probability that the queue possesses n customers and

$$\nu(n) = \frac{\sum_{J=1}^{k} b_j \mu_j p(n,j)}{\tilde{P}(n)}$$ is the conditional throughput of the queue when the number of customers equals n.

It is therefore meaningful in this context to speak of the conditional throughput of a non-exponential queue. In the appendix, it is shown that the relationship (1) holds for any $\lambda(n)/K/r$ queue.

Let I be the set of positive integers $\{1,2,\dots,M\}$, and let $\{\lambda_i^{(\ell)}(n_i)\}$ and $\tilde{P}_i^{(\ell)}(n_i)$ for $n_i = 0,1,\dots,N$ and $i \in I$, be respectively the sequences of arrival rates and the marginal probabilities computed during the ℓ-th iteration. By means of equation (1) the conditional throughput $\nu_i^{(\ell)}(n_i)$ for $n_i = 0,1,\ldots,N$ and $i \in I$ may be easily computed. Let $e = (n_1,n_2,\ldots,n_M)$ be a vector of non-negative integers in which n_i represents the number of customers in station i ; the states e are defined as elements of the set $H_N = \{(n_1,n_2,\ldots,n_M) \mid \sum_{i=1}^{M} n_i = N\}$.

Let P(e) be the stationary probability of state e. Although no known analytic method is available for the determination of this equilibrium probability, it is possible (see MARIE [10]) to obtain an approximate result by assuring that

$$P^{(\ell)}(n_1,n_2,\ldots,n_M) = \frac{\prod_{i=1}^{M} \frac{x_i^{n_i}}{\Gamma_i^{(\ell)}(n_i)}}{\sum_{e \in H_N} \left(\prod_{i=1}^{M} \frac{x_i^{n_i}}{\Gamma_i^{(\ell)}(n_i)} \right)}$$

where $\Gamma_i^{(\ell)}(n_i)$, defined for any station of the type K, is given by

$$\begin{cases} \Gamma_i(0) = 1 \\ \Gamma_i^{(\ell)}(n_i) = \Gamma_i^{(\ell)}(n_i-1).\nu_i^{(\ell)}(n_i) \end{cases}$$

and x_i is the i-th component of the normalized vector $\underset{\sim}{X}$ which satisfies $\underset{\sim}{XQ} = \underset{\sim}{X}$.

Consequently, to determine an approximation to the conditional throughput $\eta_{\bar{i}}(j)$ of the complementary network of station i, when this station contains (N-j) customers, we proceed as follows.

Let $\rho_{\bar{i}}(e)$ be the conditional throughput of the complementary network of station i, when the network R is in state e.

It is assumed that

$$\rho_{\bar{i}}^{(\ell)}(e) = \sum_{j \neq i}^{M} \nu_j^{(\ell)}(n_j).q_{ji}$$

which implies

$$\eta_{\bar{i}}^{(\ell)}(N-m) = \frac{\Sigma\, \rho_{\bar{i}}^{(\ell)}(e).P^{(\ell)}(e)}{\Sigma\, P^{(\ell)}(e)}$$

where the summations are taken over all values of $e \in H_N$ such that $n_i = m$.

Note that $\rho_{\bar{i}}(e)$ and $\eta_{\bar{i}}(j)$ are <u>defined</u> by means of the Markovian process naturally associated with the entire network R, but are <u>computed</u> by means of approximations on this network.

The sequence of arrival rates for the $(\ell+1)$-th iteration may therefore be taken as

$$\lambda_i^{(\ell+1)}(n_i) = \eta_{\bar{i}}^{(\ell)}(N-n_i)$$

for $n_i = 0,1,\ldots,N$ and $i \in I$.

Determination of Marginal Probability Distributions $\tilde{P}_i(n_i)$:

For each station i, the marginal probability distribution $\tilde{P}_i(n_i)$ is obtained by means of the numerical method discussed in the following section. The states of the Markovian process naturally associated with the queue $\lambda(n)/K/r$ representing station i, are defined by the (r+1)- tuples $(m,h_1,h_2,\ldots,h_{r_i})$ where h_i is the state of the i-th server and m is the number of customers waiting for a server. The servers are supposed to have identical service time distribution function. Then $h_i \in \{1,2,\ldots,k\}\ \forall_i$, and the number of states of the Markovian process is given by $n = (k+1)^r + (N-r) \times k^r$.

Let $\underset{\sim}{Z}$ be the row probability vector with n components which denote the stationary probabilities of the states of this Markovian process. The first component z_1 of $\underset{\sim}{Z}$ denotes the stationary probability of the state $(0,0,\ldots,0)$ and the last component z_n denotes the probability of the state $(N-r,k,k,\ldots,k)$. Between these two extremes, the components are ordered in ascending order. It is this vector $\underset{\sim}{Z}$ which is calculated by the numerical method.

Test-termination conditions :

The test-termination conditions used in this method are the same as those given by Chandy, Herzog and Woo [2].

Let $\bar{n}_i$ be the mean queue length and t_i the mean throughput of queue i, as calculated from :

$$\bar{n}_i = \sum_{n_i=1}^{N} n_i \tilde{P}_i(n_i) \quad \text{and}$$

$$t_i = \sum_{n_i=0}^{N} \lambda_i(n_i)\tilde{P}_i(n_i) \quad \text{respectively.}$$

In such a closed queueing network, with fixed transitions matrix Q, it is normally expected that

$$\sum_{i=1}^{M} \bar{n}_i = N$$

and

$$\sum_{i=1}^{M} t_i q_{ij} = t_j \qquad j = 1,2,\ldots,M$$

The test-termination conditions therefore demand that the inequalities

$$\left| \frac{N - \sum_{i=1}^{M} \bar{n}_i}{N} \right| < \varepsilon$$

and

$$\left| \frac{\frac{t_i}{x_i} - \frac{1}{M} \sum_{j=1}^{M} \frac{t_j}{x_j}}{\frac{1}{M} \sum_{j=1}^{M} \frac{t_j}{x_j}} \right| < \varepsilon \qquad i = 1,2,\ldots,M$$

in which ε is the specified tolerance criterion, be satisfied.

3. NUMERICAL CONSIDERATIONS

In this section the problem of obtaining the marginal probability distribution of customers in a given station i will be considered. This distribution may the calculated from the stationary probability vector associated with the transition probability matrix of the station, i.e. the stochastic matrix $\underset{\sim}{W}$ whose elements w_{ij} denote the probability of the station changing from state i to state j.

Two different phases in the determination of this vector may be distinguished, the first concerning the generation of the transition probability matrix, and the second concerning the actual determination of the vector from the matrix. In the both phases the time factor is of prime importance. In each iteration of the enclosing iterative method, the numerical analysis must be performed for each of the stations, so that it is vital that the time spent in obtaining the solution for a single station be kept as short as possible.

Let $z_i(t)$ be the probability that the station is in state i at time t, then we have the Chapmann-Komogorov equation :

$$z_i(t+\delta t) = z_i(t) \left\{ 1 - \sum_{j \neq i}^{n} S_{ij} \, \delta t \right\} + \left\{ \sum_{k \neq i}^{n} S_{ki} \, z_k(t) \right\} \delta t + O(\delta t)$$

where S_{ki} is the rate of transition from state k to state i, and n is the total number of states.

Let $S_{ii} = - \sum_{j \neq i}^{n} S_{ij}$, then $z_i(t+\delta t) = z_i(t) + \left\{ \sum_{k=1}^{n} S_{ki} \, z_k(t) \right\} \delta t + O(\delta t)$

$$\lim_{\delta t \to 0} \frac{z_i(t+\delta t) - z_i(t)}{\delta t} = z_i(t) = \sum_{k=1}^{n} S_{ki} \, z_k(t)$$

In matrix notation $\dot{\underset{\sim}{z}}(t) = \underset{\sim}{S}^T \underset{\sim}{z}(t)$

At steady state, the rate of change of $\underset{\sim}{Z}(t)$ is zero, and therefore :

$$\underset{\sim}{S}^T \underset{\sim}{Z} = 0 \qquad (2)$$

where $\underset{\sim}{Z}(t)$ is now written as $\underset{\sim}{Z}$.

From equation (2) $\underset{\sim}{S}^T \Delta t \underset{\sim}{Z} + \underset{\sim}{Z} = \underset{\sim}{Z}$ where Δt is arbitrary, $(\underset{\sim}{S}^T \Delta t + \underset{\sim}{I}) \underset{\sim}{Z} = \underset{\sim}{Z}$,
i.e. $\underset{\sim}{W}^T \underset{\sim}{Z} = \underset{\sim}{Z}$ where $\underset{\sim}{W}^T = (\underset{\sim}{S}^T \Delta t + \underset{\sim}{I})$.

If Δt is chosen such that $\Delta t \leqslant (\max_i |S_{ii}|)^{-1}$, then the matrix $\underset{\sim}{W}$ is a stochastic matrix and may be regarded as the transition probability matrix for a discrete time Markov system in which transitions take place at intervals of Δt, Δt being sufficiently small to ensure that the possibility of two changes of state within this interval is negligible. From the method of construction of this matrix, it may be shown that there always exists a unit eigenvalue and that no other exceeds this in modulus. The required vector $\underset{\sim}{Z}$ is therefore the left eigenvector corresponding to the dominant eigenvalue of the stochastic matrix $\underset{\sim}{W}$.

Generation of transition probability matrix

We will now consider how this matrix may be efficiently generated. This is achieved by considering each possible state of the system, one at a time, and constructing its corresponding row. Due to the unique manner in which the states are arranged (see preceding section) it is possible to determine for each row, the correct possition in which to place the non-zero transition rates. Thus, for example, if state "a" has transitions to states "x", "y" and "z" with rates r_x, r_y, r_z respectively, then it is possible, merely by an examination of the states "x", "y" and "z" to determine the correct position in which to place the values r_x, r_y and r_z in row a. It should also be noted that a semi-systematic row-wise packing scheme is employed, in which only the non-zero elements of each row are stored.

Further savings both in time and in core may be effected by realizing that after the initialization, i.e. after the state (0,k,k,...,k) has been treated, be remaining portion consists of blocks of k^r states for which all the transition rates are identical, except the value which denotes the rate of entry, since these may depend on the number of customers in the station. Due to the similarity of these blocks, it is sufficient to generate and store only the first and to take appropriate action for the single value which varies. This procedure thereby gives the transition rate matrix $\underset{\sim}{S}$, which may readily be normalized and converted to the stochastic matrix $\underset{\sim}{W}$.

Numerical iterative methods for $\underset{\sim}{Z}$

Consider now the determination of the stationary probability vector $\underset{\sim}{Z}$ from the transition probability matrix. Numerical iterative methods are normally recommended since the stochastic matrices involved are usually large and very sparse, and consequently compact storage schemes may be conveniently implemented and used, resulting therefore in a considerable saving in core store. The saving already referred to above would not be possible with a direct method. In the particular networks being studied in this paper, numerical iterative methods have several additional advantages.

(1) Since the numerical method is already embedded in an "outer" iterative process which normally will not achieve an accuracy better than one part in 1000, there is

little benefit in obtaining a very accurate numerical solution. Time spent in obtaining an accuracy of better than one part in 1000 will only be wasted. In addition, during the initial iterations of the outer iterative procedure, an accuracy of less then 1 part in 1000 may be acceptable. In fact it is possible to envisage a schema in which the accuracy asked of the numerical method is a function of the iteration number of the outer iterative loop. Such a procedure could result in a considerable saving of time.

(2) For each station, it is conceivable that, from one outer iteration to the next, the numerical solution will differ by only a relatively small amount, so that it may be possible for each station to keep the solution of the previous analysis and to use it as an initial approximation for the following analysis. Under such circumstances, the time required to obtain the numerical solution will diminish from iteration to iteration.

The power method and simultaneous iteration

When the dominant eigenvalue and corresponding eigenvector of a matrix are required then, the power method [6] is the usual iterative technique employed. This method involves successively premultiplying an arbitrary trial vector until the results obtained from consecutive iterations become proportional to one another. The vector thus obtained is the dominant right eigenvector and the constant of proportionality, the dominant eigenvalue. If we let $\underset{\sim}{A}$ be a square matrix of order n with eigensolution $\underset{\sim}{A}\underset{\sim}{x}_i = \lambda_i \underset{\sim}{x}_i \quad i = 1,2,\ldots,n$ and if we suppose $|\lambda_1| > |\lambda_2| \geqslant |\lambda_3| \geqslant \ldots\ldots \geqslant |\lambda_n|$ then the power method is described by the iterative procedure : $\underset{\sim}{y}_k = \underset{\sim}{A}\underset{\sim}{y}_{k-1}$ with $\underset{\sim}{y}_o$ arbitrary and its rate of convergence may be determined from the relationship

$$\underset{\sim}{y}_k = \underset{\sim}{A}^k \underset{\sim}{y}_o = \sum_{i=1}^{n} \alpha_i \lambda_i^k \underset{\sim}{x}_i = \lambda_1^k \left\{ \alpha_1 \underset{\sim}{x}_1 + \sum_{i=2}^{n} \left(\frac{\lambda_i}{\lambda_1}\right)^k \underset{\sim}{x}_i \right\} \qquad (3)$$

It may be observed that the process converges onto the dominant eigenvector $\underset{\sim}{x}_1$, and that the rate of convergence depends on the ratios $|\lambda_i|/|\lambda_1|$ for $i = 2,3,\ldots,n$ since the smaller these ratios are, the quicker the summation on the right-hand side of equation (3) goes to zero. It is, in particular, the magnitude of the subdominant eigenvalue, λ_2 which determines the convergence rate, so that the power method will not perform satisfactorily when $\lambda_2 \simeq \lambda_1$. This situation, unfortunately arises relatively frequently in stochastic matrices of large dimension.

This problem can be largely overcome by using simultaneous iteration methods. Such methods are extensions of the power method in which iteration is carried out with m trial vectors, which converge onto the eigenvectors corresponding to the m dominant eigenvalues. Within each iteration cycle, these methods usually include a premultiplication and a reorientation, followed by normalization and a tolerance test. Of these the normalization and tolerance test are trivial as far as the amount of computation is concerned. The purpose of the premultiplication phase is to wash out the components of the lower eigenvectors in the approximations to the dominant eigenvectors, in much the same way as occurs in the power method. However, if this was the only operation involved, then all m trial vectors would converge onto the dominant eigenvector. It is the purpose of the reorientation to prevent this happening by eleminating the components of the dominant eigenvectors from those subdominant to them, in the set of m trial vectors. This is sometimes called the interaction analysis since it eliminates the mutual "interactions" among approximations to the dominant eigenvectors.

Although simultaneous iteration methods have been most highly developed for the real symmetric eigenvalue problem, there now exists several algorithms for the real unsymmetric case [3, 7, 14]. Among these latter, the lop-sided method developed by Jennings and Stewart [7], has several characteristics which make it highly recommendable for the present problem.

(1) Only one set of dominant eigenvectors (either the right or left eigenvector set) is obtained. This is in contrast with other simultaneous iteration techniques in which both left and right sets of vectors are simultaneously derived. The iteration cycle for the lop-sided method is therefore greatly simplified, and since the rate of convergence of the eigenvectors is not affected, the stationary probability vector for the station may be determined in approximately half the time required by other simultaneous iteration methods. In addition, the lop-sided method requires only half the core used by other methods.

(2) The lop-sided algorithm presented in Stewart and Jennings [14] includes several features designed to reduce the average time required per iteration. Notably, the possibility of performing several consecutive premultiplications before a reorientation, greatly reduces the time required for slowly converging matrices of the type considered in this paper.

It is believed that the lop-sided iteration method offers the best possibility of obtaining the stationary probabilities of the states of the system in the shortest possible time. This combined with the fast generation of the transition probability matrix should permit relative large stations to be analysed quickly and efficiently. For example, with 40 customers, a station consisting of five hyperexponentiel or Erlang servers of order 2 may be analysed in less than 2 minutes on the CII IRIS 80 computer of the University of Rennes, France. If the number of clients is reduced to 20, then the same station requires approximately 30 seconds to analyse.

Note that if the number of customers becomes too large to permit an exact numerical solution to be obtained in a short period of time, then an approximate analysis can be performed by halving the number of customers in the station, and doubling the service rates at the servers.

4. TEST RESULTS AND CONCLUSIONS

The initial tests on the hybrid method were conducted with a view to determining a measure of the accuracy of the method. This necessitated using models whose state space were sufficiently small to allow an exact numerical solution to be obtained. The first model employed was of the central server-type i.e. it consists of a central-station with three hyperexponential servers each of order 2, which serves the requests which emanate from two exponential servers. The exponential servers have mean service time equal to 1.0 and 2.0 respectively, while the service time at each of the servers in the central station was taken to be 1.0. The parameter K^2 (=variance/mean^2) of each of the hyperexponential servers in the central station was chosen to be 10. Tests were conducted for the number of customers equal to 4,5,...,10. The exact results for this model were obtained from the numerical package MARCA [13]. For the purpose of comparison, results were also obtained for the canonically associated exponential network.

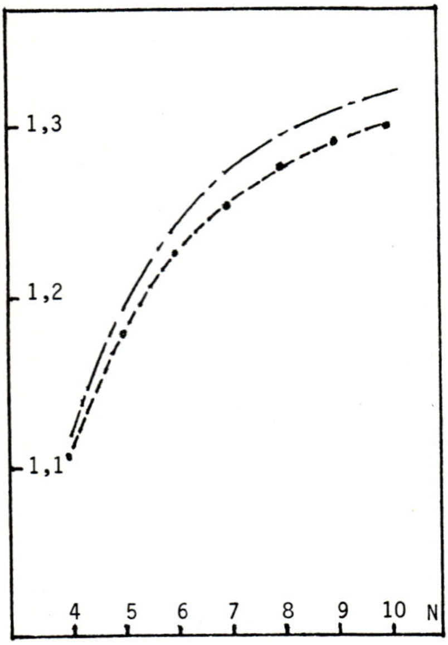

Fig 1a : Mean throughput of station N°1

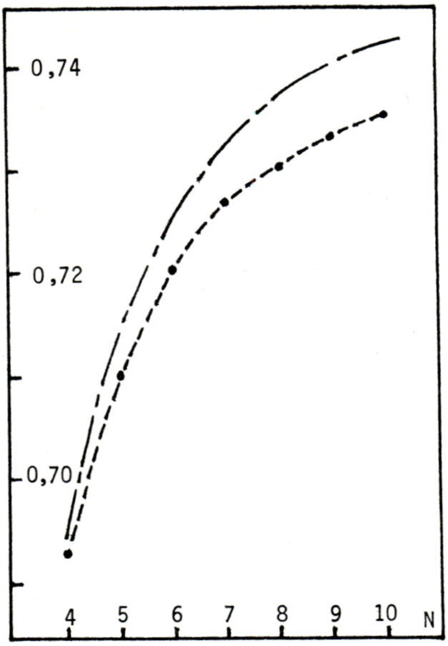

Fig 1b : Busy rate of station N°1

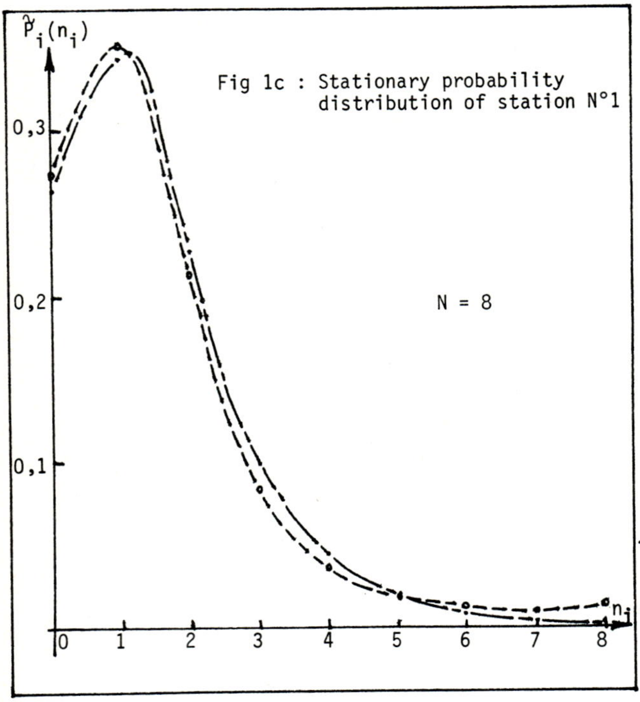

Fig 1c : Stationary probability distribution of station N°1

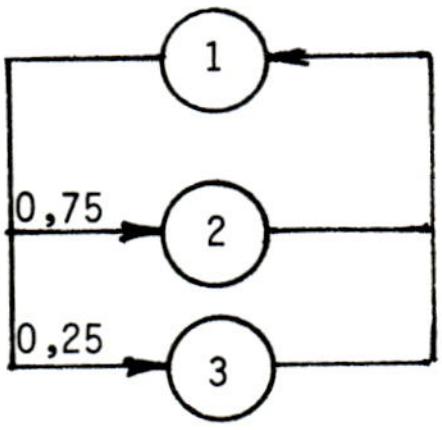

Parameters \ Stations	1	2	3
Type of law	H_2	M	M
Mean	1	1	2
Nb.of servers	3	1	1
Coeff. K^2	10	1	1

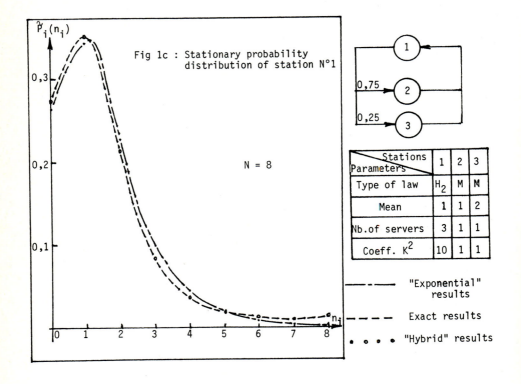

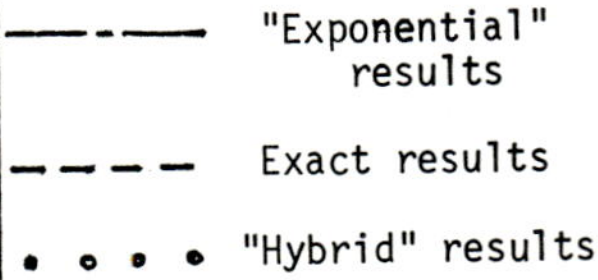

The results obtained for this example are shown in figures 1a, 1b and 1c. Figure 1a shows the mean throughput and figure 1b the busy rate of the central station, as the number of customers in the network is varied. It may be observed that the results obtained by the hybrid method differ hardly at all from the exact results, while the results of the canonically associated exponential network display a relatively large difference. Figure 1c shows the stationary probability distribution of the central station when the number of users in the network is 8. Once again, the difference in the results obtained by the hybrid method and the exact results are so small that they cannot be observed on the graph. Finally it should be pointed out that the results obtained by the hybrid method were determined in only a few iterations.

The second model consists of two stations, one of which contains two servers and the second a single server. All three servers were considered to have hyper-exponentially distributed service times, the two servers belonging to the first station each having a mean of 3.0 and the remaining server having a mean of 2.0. The parameter K^2 (=variance/mean^2) was taken to be 10 for all servers. This model was analysed largely because it was thought that the difference between the results produced by the hybrid method and the exact numerical results would be as large as that obtained for a great number of models, in other words, it would yield an estimate of the greatest error which should be expected of the hybrid method. The reason for making such an estimation not only lies in the fact that a large value was chosen for K^2, to move as far away from exponential distributions as possible, but also because the number of stations was limited to two ; many additional servers having an apparent overall effect of mutually eliminating the non-exponential properties.

Tests were conducted on this model for 2,3,...,10 customers. As for the first model, the exact results were obtained numerically from MARCA, while for comparison purposes only, the canonically associated exponential network was also analysed. The results obtained for the mean throughput and the busy rate of the station with two servers are shown in tables 2a and 2b respectively.

The results produced by the hybrid method are, as expected, not as good as those obtained for the first model, but nevertheless are accurate to approximately 4 %. Note however that the results lie outside the interval between the exact numerical results and those of the canonically associated exponential network. This is contrary to what had been anticipated. The probability distribution obtained for the particular instance of the model having eight customers is shown in figure 2c. It may be observed that the hybrid method approximates quite closely the exact results while the curve obtained by the canonically associated exponential network is completely incorrect.

It is perhaps rather premature to draw conclusions about the performance of the hybrid method but it would appear that it offers considerable advantages over other methods. Timing experiments suggest that networks consisting of up to ten stations each consisting of several servers may be analysed without difficulty while a high degree of accuracy is achieved.

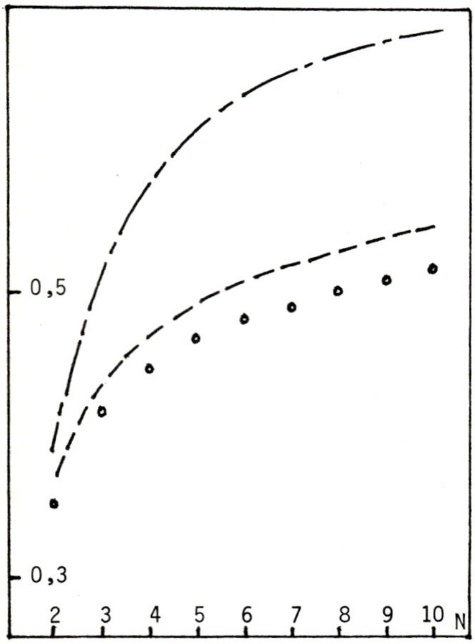

Fig 2a : Mean throughput of station N°1

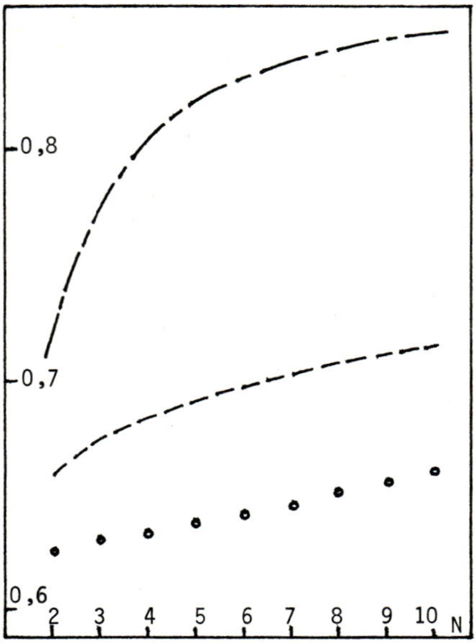

Fig 2b : Busy rate of station N°1

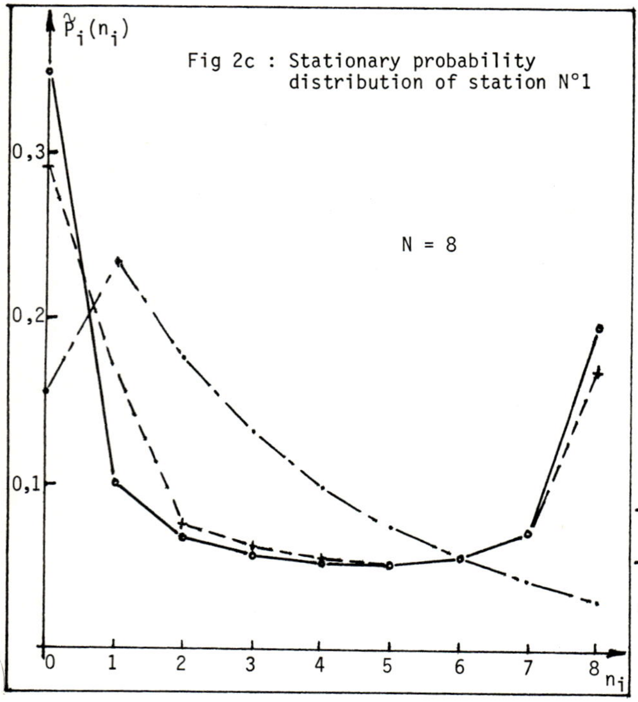

Fig 2c : Stationary probability distribution of station N°1

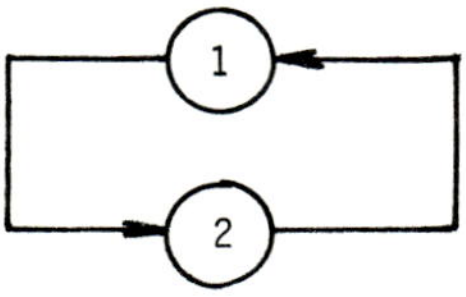

Parameters \ Stations	1	2
Type of lax	H_2	H_2
Mean	3	2
Nb.of servers	2	1
Coeff. K^2	10	10

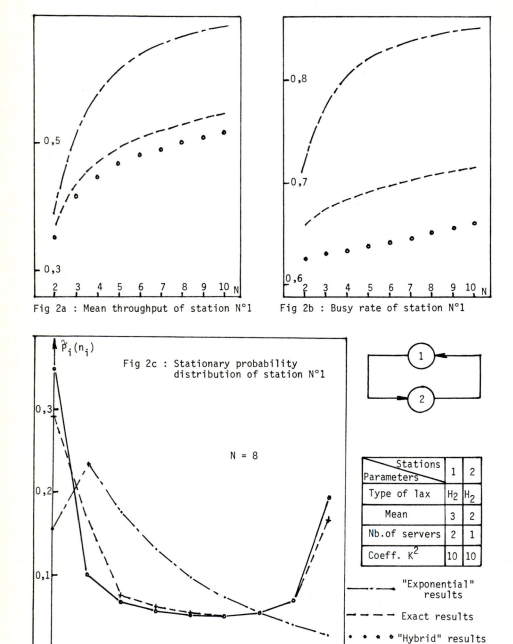

APPENDIX Proof of the relationship $P(i)\lambda(i) = \nu(i+1)P(i+1)$

General Analysis

The stationary behaviour of an irreducible and ergotic Markovian system S, whose state space is denoted by E, and which satisfies hypothesis H1 below, is considered.

Hypothesis H1

There exists a partition $(E_i)_{0 \leq i \leq n}$ of E such that

$$\forall i,\ \forall j \in \mathbb{Z} \quad \text{and} \quad |j| > 1$$

$$\text{Prob}\ \{\xi(t+dt) = i+j \mid \xi(t) = i\} = \sigma(dt)$$

Here $\xi(t)$ is the stochastic process associated with the states E_i of the partition $(E_i)_{0 \leq i \leq n}$, and $\sigma(dt)$ denotes a quantity for which $\lim\limits_{dt \searrow 0} \frac{\sigma(dt)}{dt} = 0$.

Definitions

Let P(i) be the stationary probability that the state e of the system S belongs to E_i, and let

$$[\lambda(i)dt + \sigma(dt)] = \text{Prob}\ \{\xi(t+dt) = i+1 \mid \xi(t) = i\}$$

$$[\nu(i)dt + \sigma(dt)] = \text{Prob}\ \{\xi(t+dt) = i-1 \mid \xi(t) = i\}$$

Theorem

In any Markovian system which satisfies hypothesis H1,

$$\lambda(i)P(i) = \nu(i+1)P(i+1)$$

Proof

Since only stationary probabilities are considered,

$$\text{Prob}\ \{\xi(t) = i \ \underline{\text{and}}\ \xi(t+dt) \neq i\} = \text{Prob}\ \{\xi(t) \neq i \ \underline{\text{and}}\ \xi(t+dt) = i\} + \sigma(dt)$$

this may be written in the form

$$\sum_{\substack{j \in Z \\ j \neq 0 \\ i-n \leq j \leq i}} \text{Prob}\ \{\xi(t) = i \ \underline{\text{and}}\ \xi(t+dt) = i-j\}$$

$$\sum_{\substack{j \in Z \\ j \neq 0 \\ i-n \leq j \leq i}} \text{Prob}\ \{\xi(t) = i-j \ \underline{\text{and}}\ \xi(t+dt) = i\} + \sigma(dt)$$

i.e.

$$\sum_{\substack{j \in Z \\ j \neq 0 \\ i-n \leqslant j \leqslant i}} \{ P(i) \text{ Prob } [\xi(t+dt) = i-j \mid \xi(t) = i] \}$$

$$\sum_{\substack{j \in Z \\ j \neq 0 \\ i-n \leqslant j \leqslant i}} \{ P(i-j).\text{Prob } [\xi(t+dt) = i \mid \xi(t) = i-j] \} + \sigma(dt)$$

As a result of hypothesis H1, this yields

a) for $i > 0$

$$P(i) \{[\lambda(i)dt + \sigma(dt)] + [\nu(i)dt + \sigma(dt)]\} + \sigma(dt) =$$

$$P(i-1).[\lambda(i-1)dt + \sigma(dt)] + P(i-1) [\nu(i+1)dt + \sigma(dt)] + \sigma(dt)$$

and since $\lim_{dt \searrow 0} \frac{\sigma(dt)}{dt} = 0$

$$P(i)\lambda(i) + P(i)\nu(i) = P(i-1)\lambda(i-1) + P(i-1)\nu(i-1) \qquad (1)$$

b) for $i = 0$

$$P(0) [\lambda(0) + \sigma(dt)] + \sigma(dt) = P(1) [\nu(1)dt + \sigma(dt)] + \sigma(dt)$$

which yields $P(0)\lambda(0) = P(1)\nu(1)$ (2)

when $\lim_{dt \searrow 0} \frac{\sigma(dt)}{dt} = 0$ is applied

Substituting $i = 1$ into equation (1) and using equation (2) we obtain

$$\lambda(1)P(1) = \nu(2)P(2)$$

Now suppose that the relationship

$\lambda(i-2)P(i-2) = \nu(i-1)P(i-1)$ is true,

Using equation (1) this immediately yields

$$\lambda(i-1)P(i-1) = \nu(i)P(i)$$

which, by recurrence, completes the proof.

Application to the queue $\lambda(i)/K/r$

For such a queue

1) the arrivals are Markovian with rate $\lambda(i)$ which depends on the number of customers i in the queue.

2) the service time distribution of each server v, $v = 1,2,\dots,r$ is Coxian of order K_v.

This station, whose service time distributions have rational Laplace transforms may be studied by means of the Markovian graph with fictive states which is normally associated with the queue.

Let $p(i,j_1 \ldots j_r)$ be the stationary probability of state $e(i,j_1 \ldots j_r)$ in this Markovian system.
Here i denotes the number of customers in the station and j_v denotes the phase of the server v.
By convention $j_v = 0$ if the server v is idle.

Let E be the set of states of the Markovian system and E_i the set of states having i customers.

$$E_i = \{ (u,j_1 \ldots j_r) : (u,j_1 \ldots j_r) \in E \ , \ u = i \}$$

Hypothesis H1 of the preceding paragraph is obviously satisfied for the partition $(E_i)_{0 \leq i \leq N}$. Further, for stationary probabilities,

$$\text{Prob } \{\xi(t+dt) = i-1 | \xi(t) = i\} = \frac{\sum_{e \in E_i} \left(\sum_{v=1}^{r} \mu_v(j_v).b_v(j_v).dt \right) p(e)}{\sum_{e \in E_i} p(e)}$$

Using the definitions and the theorem of the preceding paragraph immediately yields

$$\nu(i).P(i) = \lambda(i-1).P(i-1)$$

$$\text{where} \quad \nu(i) = \frac{\sum_{e \in E_i} \left(\sum_{v=1}^{r} \mu_v(j_v).b_v(j_v) \right).p(e)}{P(i)}$$

REFERENCES

[1] BASKETT,F., CHANDY,K.M., MUNTZ,R.R., PALACIOS,F.G. (1975). *Open, Closed and Mixed Networks of Queues with different classes of Customers.* J. ACM. Vol. 22, n° 2, April, pp. 248-260.

[2] CHANDY,K.M., HERZOG,U. and WOO,L. (1975). *Approximate Analysis of General Queuing Networks.* IBM, J. Res. Develop. Jan, pp. 43-49.

[3] CLINT,M. and JENNINGS,A. (1971). *A Simultaneous Iteration Method for the Unsymmetric Eigenvalue Problem.* J. Inst. Maths. Applics. Vol. 8, pp. 111-121.

[4] COX,D.R. (1955). *A use of Complex Probabilities in the theory of stochastic Processes.* Proc. Camb. Phil. Soc. Vol. 51, pp. 313-319.

[5] GELENBE,E. (1975). *On approximate Computer System Models.* J. ACM. Vol. 22, n°2 April, pp. 261-269.

[6] JENNINGS,A. (1977). *Matrix Computation for Engineers and Scientists.* John Wiley and Sons.

[7] JENNINGS,A. and STEWART,W.J. (1975). *Simultaneous Iteration for Partial Eigensolution of Real Matrices.* J. Inst. Maths. Applics, Vol. 15, pp. 351-361.

[8] KOBAYASHI,H. (1974). *Application of the Diffusion Approximation to Queuing Networks, Part 1 : Equilibrium Queue distributions.* J. ACM. Vol. 21, n° 2, April, pp. 316-328.

[9] MARIE,R. (1976). *Méthodes Itératives de Résolution de Modèles Mathématiques pour Systèmes Informatiques*. Séminaire IRIA, November. Domaine de Voluceau 78150 FRANCE.

[10] MARIE,R. (1976). *Approximations et Applications de Réseaux de Files d'attente*. IRISA, Rapport interne n° 65. Université de Rennes. 35031 RENNES - FRANCE

[11] SMITH,C.E. (1949). *Communication Circuit Fundamentals*. Mc Graw Hill Book Co. Inc. New-York.

[12] STEWART,W.J. (1976). *Practical Considerations in the Numerical Analysis of Markovian Models*. Modelling and Performance Anal. of Computer Science. E. Gelenbe (ed.) North Holland Publishing Co.

[13] STEWART,W.J. (1976). *MARCA : Markov Chain Analyser*. IRISA, Publication Interne n° 45, Université de Rennes. FRANCE 35031.

[14] STEWART,W.J. and JENNINGS,A. (1977). *LOPSI : A lop-sided Simultaneous Iteration Algorithm*. IRISA, Rapport Interne, Université de Rennes. 35031 FRANCE.

Measuring, Modelling and Evaluating Computer Systems,
H. Beilner and E. Gelenbe, (eds.)
© North-Holland Publishing Company (1977)

A DIFFUSION MODEL FOR MULTIPLE CLASS QUEUEING NETWORKS

E. GELENBE
Dept. de Mathématiques
Université Paris-Nord
Ave. J.B. Clément
93 Villetaneuse
FRANCE

G. PUJOLLE
IRIA/LABORIA
B.P. 105
78150 Le Chesnay
FRANCE

We obtain a simple and analytically tractable diffusion process model for treating open networks of queues with FIFO service and multiple classes. The model, which provides approximate explicit stationary distributions for queue lengths of a case for which exact results are unavailable, is applied to a model of a packet switching computer network. In such networks short and long packets, corresponding to time-sharing usage and file transfers respectively, are frequent and we study this phenomenon with a diffusion model.

1 - INTRODUCTION

The panoply of existing mathematical tools for the modelling of computer systems does not include solution techniques for systems with FIFO service and multiple distinct classes of customers, even when service times are exponentially distributed and arrival processes are Poisson.

The purpose of this paper is to extend our previous work [4] to the case of general service times with multiple classes of customers, FIFO service at each service station and renewal processes representing the arrivals. Our approach uses a diffusion process model [3, 4, 5] for which we provide an analytical solution.

The theoretical results are then applied to a model of CIGALE [6], the packet-switching subnetwork of the CYCLADES computer network with two classes of traffic. The first class represents packets which arrive irregularly and which are of widely differing lengths : these represent packets originating from time-shared computation on the network. The second class arrives in long batches and in bursts and are of a constant length : they represent file transfers through the network.

We also present numerical results and validations (using simulation results) for a model of an interactive system.

2 - BEHAVIOUR OF A SINGLE QUEUE IN A NETWORK WITH MULTIPLE CLASSES

In this section we are concerned with an open network containing n stations. Each station contains one server. Customers of the network are divided into R classes : at each station, service is rendered in strict FIFO order with no priorities between classes.

The r-th class, $1 \le r \le R$, is characterized by :

i) a stream of arrivals to the network which is a renewal process : its rate is $\lambda_{0,r}$ and the squared coefficient of variation of interarrival times is $Ka_{0,r}$

ii) a general service time distribution function $G_r^i(x)$ at the i-th service station, $1 \le i \le n$.

Furthermore, transitions of customers through the network are described by a Markov chain $(p_{i,r;j,r'})$ where $1 \le i \le n$, $1 \le r,r' \le R$, $1 \le j \le n+1$. $p_{i,r;j,r'}$ is the probability that a class r customers leaving station i enters station j in class r'. The fictitious stations (n+1) denotes a departure from the network. We shall note $q_{i,r}$ the probability that an arriving customer of class r enters station i of the network.

The reader will notice that the QN (queueing network) we have thus defined cannot be solved by any of the available exact solution methods [1]. In particular, FIFO service with general service times cannot be treated by the classical BCMP [2] result though it can be handled by the approximate method of [3], [4]. Thus the model we are treating in this paper extends our previous work [4] to the case of multiple classes. Such models are of particular interest in performance evaluation studies of computer systems which take into account the existence of multiple job classes. In the area of computer networks they reflect well the presence of "short" and "long" packets : the former can represent interactive processing while the latter can represent the transfer of files.

As in the approach we had taken earlier [4] our analysis proceeds in two parts : the first concerns the computation of the parameters of the arrival process to each queue while the second part uses the results of the first part in the queue length computations using diffusion approximations [3].

2.1 - The interarrival statistics to each queues

Let $Ks_{i,r}$ denote the squared coefficient of variation of the service time at queue i, and $Ka_{i,r}$ the squared coefficient of variation of interarrival times to the queue i, for customers of class r. $\lambda_{i,r}$ will be the arrival rate of class r customers to queue i, and $\mu_{i,r}^{-1}$ will be their average service time.

From conservation of flow arguments we have the system of equations

$$(1) \qquad \lambda_{i,r} = \lambda_{0,r} q_{i,r} + \sum_{i=1}^{n} \sum_{r=1}^{R} \lambda_{j,r'}\, p_{j,r';i,r}$$

for $1 \le i \le n$, $1 \le r \le R$. These equations may also be obtained by first considering $e_{i,r}$, the average number of times that a customer of class r passes through the station i before leaving the QN. Notice that $e_{i,r} = \lambda_{i,r}/\lambda_{0,r}$ so that (1) can be interpreted as a system of equations for the $e_{i,r}$. Clearly, using (1), we have a unique solution for the $\lambda_{i,r}$.

Let us denote $u_{i,r} = \lambda_{i,r}/\mu_{i,r}$: it can be viewed as the load imposed by class r customers to station i. We shall define

(2) $$u_i = \sum_{r=1}^{R} u_{i,r}$$

and

(3) $$\lambda_i = \sum_{r=1}^{R} \lambda_{i,r}\ ,\ \Pi_{i,r} = \lambda_{i,r}/\lambda_i$$

where u_i is the utilization (steady-state probability that the queue is busy), and λ_i is the total arrival rate, associated with station i.

Having obtained the $\lambda_{i,r}$, from (1) we need to compute the $Ka_{i,r}$ (already defined as the squared coefficients of variation of the interarrival times of class r customers to station i). These are obtained by assuming that the arrival and departure processes of class r customers to and from each queue are renewal processes. Although this assumption is not always true, it has provided very accurate predictions of interarrival statistics in a previous study [4], as well as exact results in all known cases including for very light or very heavy traffic.

Let τ_i be the time separating two successive departures from station i. We shall write :

(4) $$\tau_i = \begin{cases} S_i \text{ with probability } u_i \\ S_i + A_i \text{ with probability } (1-u_i) \end{cases}$$

where A_i is an interarrival time to queue i, and S_i is $S_{i,r}$ with probability $\lambda_{i,r}/\lambda_i$, $S_{i,r}$ being the service time of class r customer at station i. Therefore, as expected from the conservation of flow :

$$E[\tau_i] = E[S_i] + E[A_i]\ (1-u_i)$$
$$= \sum_{r=1}^{R} \mu_{i,r}^{-1}\ \Pi_{i,r} + \lambda_i^{-1}\ (1-u_i)$$
$$= \lambda_i^{-1} = (\sum_{i=1}^{R} \lambda_{i,r})^{-1}$$

Also, we obtain :

$$E[\tau_i^2] = u_i\ E[S_i^2] + (1-u_i)\ E[S_i^2 + 2A_i\ S_i + A_i^2]$$
$$= E[S_i^2] + 2(1-u_i)\ \lambda_i^{-1} \sum_{r=1}^{R} \mu_{i,r}^{-1}\ \Pi_{i,r} + (1-u_i)\ E[A_i^2]$$

Denote by $C_i = \lambda_i^2\ \{E[\tau_i^2] - (E[\tau_i])^2\}$ the squared coefficient of variation of interdeparture times at the i-th queue, and let K_i be the squared coefficient of variation of interarrival times to the i-th queue. We then have

(5) $$C_i+1 = \lambda_i^2 E[S_i^2] + (1-u_i)(K_i+1) + 2u_i(1-u_i)$$

$$= \lambda_i \sum_{i=r}^{R} u_{i,r} \mu_{i,r}^{-1} (Ks_{i,r}+1) + (1-u_i)(K_i+1+2u_i)$$

But the input process to the queue is obtained as the superposition of the process of external arrivals plus the output process of the queues. In fact, assuming that the output of the j-th queue is a renewal process, the arrival process to the i-th queue from the j-th queue is characterized by a rate and a squared coefficient of variation which are respectively

(6) $$\lambda_j P_{ij} , [(C_j-1) P_{ji} + 1]$$

where P_{ji}, the probability that a customer leaving station j enters queue i, is given by

(7) $$P_{ji} = \sum_{r=1}^{R} \sum_{r'=1}^{R} (\lambda_{j,r}/\lambda_j) p_{j,r;i,r'}$$

Let $\mathcal{a}_i(t)$ be the total number of arrivals to the i-th queue in the interval (0,t); its variance will then be (asymptotically, for large t) [4]

(8) $$\sum_{j=0}^{n} [(C_j-1) P_{ji} + 1] \lambda_j P_{ji} t = \lambda_i^3 \{E[A_i^2] - (E[A_i]^2\} t$$

where C_0 is obtained from the superposition of the R input processes as shown below. From (8) and (5) we obtain the system of n equations for the C_i

(9) $$C_i = \lambda_i \sum_{r=1}^{R} u_{i,r} \mu_{i,r}^{-1} (Ks_{i,r}+1) + (1-u_i)(K_i+1+2u_i) - 1$$

where

(10) $$K_i = \lambda_i^{-1} \sum_{j=0}^{n} [(C_j-1) P_{ji} + 1] \lambda_j P_{ji} t$$

where $1 \leq i \leq n$. Concerning C_0 which is the squared coefficient of variation of external interarrival times to the network, notice that the variance of the number of arrivals in (0,t) is, asymptotically for large t,

$$(\sum_{r=1}^{R} \lambda_{0,r}) C_0 t = \sum_{r=1}^{R} \lambda_{0,r} Ka_{0,r}$$

so that we compute C_0 from

(11) $$C_0 = \sum_{r=1}^{R} \lambda_{0,r} Ka_{0,r} / \sum_{r=1}^{R} \lambda_{0,r}$$

We can now solve for $C_1,\dots,C_n$ from (9). The $K_1,\dots,K_n$ will then be immediately available from (10).

In the arrival process to queue i, $\Pi_{i,r} = \lambda_{i,r}/\lambda_i$ is the probability that an arriving customer is of class r. Therefore, the squared coefficient of variation of interarrival times of class r customers to queue i will be

(12) $$Ka_{i,r} = (K_i-1) \Pi_{i,r} + 1$$

Thus $\lambda_{i,r}$ obtained from (1) and $Ka_{i,r}$ obtained from (12) (after solving (9) and using (11)) characterize the arrival stream of class r processes to station i, $1 \le i \le n$, $1 \le r \le R$.

2.2 - Diffusion approximation to the queue length process

We now consider the behaviour of any queue, say the i-th, in the network and we propose to approximate the queue length process by a diffusion process.

Just before a service begins at the queue, the probability that the customer at the head of the queue is of class r is $\Pi_{i,r}$. Therefore its service time distribution will be $\Sigma_1^R G_r^i(x)\Pi_{i,r}$: let μ_i^{-1} denote the mean of this distribution and V_i its variance.

As in [3, 4] the queue length probability function $f_i(x, t)$ is assumed to satisfy the diffusion equations

$$(13) \qquad -\frac{\partial f_i}{\partial t} - b_i \frac{\partial f_i}{\partial x} + \frac{1}{2}\alpha_i \frac{\partial^2 f_i}{\partial x^2} + \lambda_i P_i(t)\, \delta(x-1) = 0$$

$$(14) \qquad \frac{d}{dt} P_i(t) = -\lambda_i P_i(t) + \lim_{x\to 0^+} [-b_i f_i + \frac{1}{2}\alpha_i \frac{\partial f_i}{\partial x_i}]$$

where $P_i(t)$ is the empty queue probability at time t. The parameter b_i is the "drift" of the diffusion model, while α_i is the rate of change of the variance :

$$(15) \qquad b_i = \lambda_i - \mu_i \,, \quad \alpha_i = \lambda_i K_i + \mu_i^3 V_i$$

The stationary solution is readily obtained from (13), (14)

$$P_i = \lim_{t\to\infty} P_i(t) \quad , \quad f_i(x) = \lim_{t\to\infty} f_i(x, t)$$

$$(16) \qquad P_i = 1 - \lambda_i/\mu_i = 1 - u_i$$

$$(17) \qquad f_i(x) = \begin{cases} u_i[1 - e^{\gamma_i x}] \,, & 0 \le x \le 1 \\ u_i[1 - e^{-\gamma_i}]\, e^{\gamma_i x} \,, & x \ge 1 \end{cases}$$

where $\gamma_i = 2b_i/\alpha_i$ for $\gamma_i < 0$ (which is true and only if $\lambda_i < \mu_i$).

The average length L_i of queue i is given by

$$(18) \qquad L_i = u_i[1 + \frac{u_i K_i + Ks_i}{2(1-u_i)}]$$

where $Ks_i = \mu_i^2 V_i$ is the squared coefficient of variation of service time at station i.

A formula for the average transit time T of a customer through the network is particularly useful. We then have

(19) $$T = \sum_{i=1}^{n} L_i/\lambda_i = \sum_{i=1}^{n} \mu_i^{-1} \left[1 + \frac{u_i K_i + K s_i}{2(1-u_i)}\right]$$

2.3 - The number in queue for each class

From the distribution for the total number in queue we will now work back to the distribution of the number of customers of each class in queue. We proceed as follows. Discretize the probability density function $f_i(x)$ by defining

$$p_i(n) = \int_{(n-1)}^{n} f_i(x)\,dx \quad , \quad n = 1, 2, \ldots$$

and

$$p_i(0) = 1-u_i$$

$p_i(n)$ will be the discrete approximation to the stationary queue length distribution at station i. Let $p_{i,r}(\ell)$ be the probability of finding ℓ customers of class r at station i ; we take

(20) $$p_{i,r}(\ell) = \sum_{n\geq\ell} \binom{n}{\ell} \Pi_{i,r}^{\ell} (1 - \Pi_{i,r})^{n-\ell} p_i(n)$$

since each customer in queue i belongs to class r with probability $\Pi_{i,r}$.

2.4 - The average response time for a class r customer

A quantity of interest is the average response (or transit) time through the network for customers of each class. Denote this quantity by T_r for class r : T_r is the average time spent by a customer of class r between the instant at which it enters the network and when it leaves it. Clearly, a customer's waiting time at each queue does not depend on its class ; let $T_{i,r}$ be the response (or transit) time of a class r customer through station i and $W_{i,r}$ the waiting time. We have

$$W_{i,r} = L_i/\lambda_i - \mu_i^{-1}$$

and

(21) $$T_{i,r} = L_i/\lambda_i - \mu_i^{-1} + \mu_{i,r}^{-1}$$

Therefore

(22) $$T_r = \sum_{i=1}^{n} T_{i,r}\, \lambda_{i,r}/\lambda_{0,r}$$

since a class r customer will visit station i on the average $\lambda_{i,r}/\lambda_{0,r}$ times.

3 - APPLICATION TO A PACKET SWITCHING NETWORK

In this section we apply the diffusion approximation method with classes of customers to the analysis of the packet switching sub-network CIGALE of the computer network CYCLADES [6]. We take the 7-node network described on Figure 1. Nodes A through G are minicomputers used for packet buffering and switching. Packet routing is assumed fixed and summarized in Table 1. The routes which are not indicated on Table 1 are chosen by the smallest number of nodes which are traversed. We assume two classes of customers : a class of short packets or interactive packets and a class of large packets (transfer of files, for example). The characteristics of these classes are given in Table 1 and 2. These assumptions are chosen so that large packets have all the same length and arrive in bursts of a large group of packets. Short packets arrive singly and irregularly (Poisson traffic) and their length is exponentially distributed. This traffic is reported as being typical of computer network applications [7]. We assume that packets (short or long) arriving from the outside of the network have identical routing probabilities.

The packet switching network of Figure 1 can be represented as a queueing network with 16 queues. Routing probabilities can be computed from external arrivals and the routing table.

The method described in section 2 is used to compute the expected number of customers with Jackson's [1] formula which assumes Poisson traffic for a single class of packets whose length is exponentially distributed. If μ_i^{-1} is the average service time for a customer at station i in Jackson's model, we have taken :

$$\mu_i^{-1} = \frac{\lambda_i}{\lambda_{i,1}} \mu_{i,1}^{-1} + \frac{\lambda_i}{\lambda_{i,2}} \mu_{i,2}^{-1}$$

Numerical results are given in Table 3.

4 - APPLICATION TO A MODEL OF AN INTERACTIVE SYSTEM

The model of an interactive computer system examined by Anderson and Sargent is described in Figure 2.

It has already been used by Reiser and Kobayashi [8] and Gelenbe and Pujolle [4] to examine the accuracy of diffusion approximations for one customer class.

We shall apply our method to this model with two classes of customers. Jobs of class 1 and 2 arrive to the system according to Poisson processes of parameters $\lambda_1 = 0.5$ and $\lambda_2 = 0.25$, respectively. After passing through server 1, they leave the system with probability 0.5 or enter the queue of server 2 with probability 0.5. At the output of server 2 the customers feed-back into queue 2 with probability 0.5 or they go to queue 1.

We shall study this model assuming several sets of service time distributions server 1 and 2. These are indicated in Table 4 with the results. In this table we present average queue lengths which are compared with those obtained from simulations which have been carried out with a package developped by Merle and Veran [9] We give only the estimated average length obtained from the simulations.

The results described in Table 4 provide an indication of accuracy of the approximation by diffusion process with several classes. We also tabulate the relative error in each case, under the assumption that the "correct" result is obtained from the simulation. Together with a number of other authors [8,10] we notice that the queue with feed-back is where the largest errors seem to occur. A new treatment of this case will be given so as to obtain more accurate results (following an idea of Kühn [10] but with diffusion approximation).

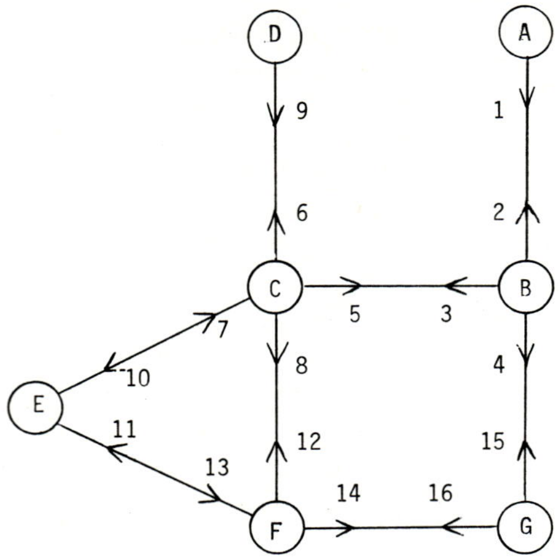

Figure 1

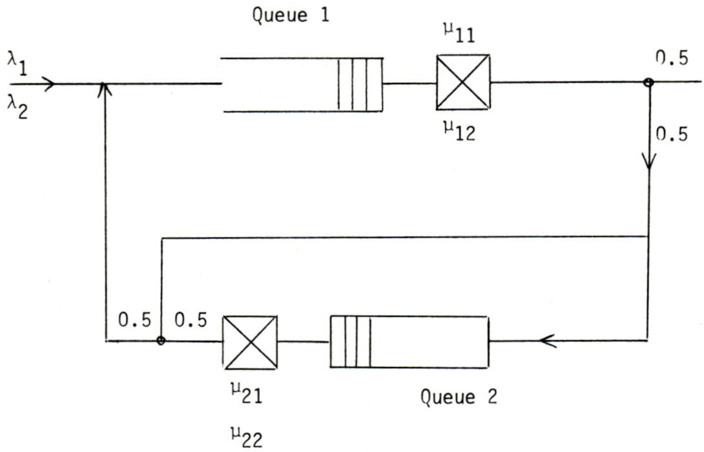

Figure 2

Source	Destination	Via Node	Input rate class short packets	Input large packets
A	F	C	1.5	1.
B	F	C	1.	1.
C	G	F	1.	1.
D	G	F	2.	0.5
E			1.5	0.5
F	C,D	B	1.	2.
G	A,B	C	0.5	2.

Table 1

	Squared coefficient of var. external arrival	Squared coefficient of service times	Service rate link 1,2,3,5	Others
Class 1 short packets	1.	1. (exponential)	15.	10.
Class 2 large packets	5.	0. (constant)	3.	2.

Table 2

	Diffusion method	Jackson
1	0.81	0.76
2	0.77	0.88
3	3.57	3.73
4	0.24	0.27
5	1.21	1.30
6	2.81	3.25
7	0.53	0.57
8	1.02	1.07
9	0.67	0.56
10	0.49	0.50
11	0.19	0.20
12	3.35	2.77
13	0.43	0.56
14	0.69	0.74
15	2.98	2.33
16	0.45	0.54

Table 3

			DIFFUSION		SIMULATION	
			Mean number in queue 1	Mean number in queue 2	Mean number in queue 1	Mean number in queue 2
server 1	EXP	$\mu_{11}^{-1} = 0.5$	2.54	2.86	2.66	2.79
	EXP	$\mu_{12}^{-1} = 0.4$				
server 2	EXP	$\mu_{21}^{-1} = 0.5$	5.6 %	2.5 %		
	EXP	$\mu_{22}^{-1} = 0.4$				
server 1	EXP	$\mu_{11}^{-1} = 0.5$	2.61	0.95	2.63	.96
	EXP	$\mu_{12}^{-1} = 0.4$				
server 2	EXP	$\mu_{21}^{-1} = 0.3$	0.76 %	1.04 %		
	EXP	$\mu_{22}^{-1} = 0.4$				
server 1	EXP	$\mu_{11}^{-1} = 0.5$	2.39	8.86	2.22	8.68
	EXP	$\mu_{12}^{-1} = 0.4$				
server 2	EXP	$\mu_{21}^{-1} = 0.7$	7.6 %	2.07 %		
	EXP	$\mu_{22}^{-1} = 0.4$				
server 1	ERLANG 2	$\mu_{11}^{-1} = 0.5$	2.12	0.77	2.29	0.91
	EXP	$\mu_{12}^{-1} = 0.4$				
server 2	CONSTANT	$\mu_{11}^{-1} = 0.3$	7.4 %	15 %		
	EXP	$\mu_{22}^{-1} = 0.4$				
server 1	ERLANG 2	$\mu_{11}^{-1} = 0.5$	1.89	1.56	2.03	2.08
	EXP	$\mu_{12}^{-1} = 0.4$				
server 2	CONSTANT	$\mu_{21}^{-1} = 0.5$	6.9 %	25 %		
	EXP	$\mu_{22}^{-1} = 0.4$				
server 1	ERLANG 2	$\mu_{11}^{-1} = 0.5$	1.76	7.55	1.92	8.19
	EXP	$\mu_{12}^{-1} = 0.4$				
server 2	CONSTANT	$\mu_{21}^{-1} = 0.7$	8.3 %	7.8 %		
	EXP	$\mu_{22}^{-1} = 0.4$				

REFERENCES

[1] Gelenbe E., Muntz R.R. - "Probabilistic models of computer systems, Part I" - (Exact Results) - Acta Informatica 7 - 35-60 - 1976.

[2] Baskett F., Chandy K.M., Muntz R.R., Palacios F.G. - "Open, closed, and mixed networks of queues with different classes of customers" - J.ACM 22 - 248-260 - 1975.

[3] Gelenbe E. - "On approximate computer system models" - J.ACM 22 - 261-263 - 1975.

[4] Gelenbe E., Pujolle G. - "The behaviour of a single queue in a general queueing network" - Acta Informatica 7 - 123-160 - 1976.

[5] Kobayashi H. - "Application of the diffusion approximation to queueing networks : Part I and II" - J.ACM 21 - 316-328 - 459-469 - 1974.

[6] Pouzin L. - "CIGALE, the packet-switching machine of the Cyclade computer network" - Proc. IFIP Congress 74 - North-Holland - 155-159 - 1974.

[7] Kleinrock L., Opderbeck H. - "Throughput in the Arpanet-protocols and measurement" - Proc. Data Comm. Symp. Quebec City - Canada - 1975.

[8] Reiser M., Kobayashi H. - "Accuracy of the diffusion approximation for some queueing systems" - IBM J.R. and D. 18 - 110-124 - 1974.

[9] Merle D., Véran M., Stewart W. - "A queueing network analysis package (QNAP)" Research Report IRIA - 1977.

[10] Kühn P. - "Analysis of complex queueing networks by decomposition" - Proc. of International Teletraffic Congress - Melbourne - 1976.

Measuring, Modelling and Evaluating Computer Systems,
H. Beilner and E. Gelenbe, (eds.)
© North-Holland Publishing Company (1977)

THE EPF TECHNIQUE: A METHOD FOR OBTAINING APPROXIMATE SOLUTIONS TO CLOSED QUEUEING NETWORKS WITH GENERAL SERVICE TIMES

A.W. Shum* and J.P. Buzen

BGS Systems, Inc.
Lincoln, MA, USA

and

Harvard University
Cambridge, MA, USA

A general technique is presented for obtaining approximate numerical solutions to closed queueing networks which are composed of servers with generally distributed service times and first come, first served scheduling. The technique is computationally efficient and can be applied in a routine manner to a large class of queueing networks. Server utilization and expected queue length values obtained using the technique were generally within 2% of exact values in an initial series of more than 2000 case studies.

INTRODUCTION

This paper presents a method for obtaining approximations to the steady state distributions of closed queueing networks containing servers with general service time distributions and "first come, first served" scheduling. The method, which is known as the Extended Product Form (EPF) solution technique, has been evaluated through a series of case studies and has consistently produced estimates of server utilization and expected queue length which are within 2% of exact values. The most important characteristics of the EPF technique are summarized below:

1. The EPF technique is conceptually simple and can be applied in a straightforward manner to networks of arbitrary size and complexity. Special case analyses are not required each time the number of servers or the topology of the network is altered, and distributional characteristics are incorporated in a routine manner.

2. The errors associated with the EPF technique are not overly sensitive to the second moments of the service time distributions in the network, and the technique works well with both very large and very small coefficients of variation.

3. The EPF technique preserves the exact analytic solution in the case where all service times are exponentially distributed: furthermore, the cost of generating the EPF approximate solution in these cases is almost identical to the cost of generating the exact solution using conventional techniques.

---

* Now at IBM Corporation, San Jose, CA, USA

4. The EPF technique enables the analyst to compute marginal distributions (e.g., server utilization and queue length) using computational algorithms that are direct generalizations of the highly efficient algorithms previously derived for exponential networks (1, 2).

5. The EPF technique provides a unified conceptual framework for understanding the properties of a large class of closed queueing networks.

The next section of this paper presents a detailed review of previously derived solutions for exponential queueing networks. This review is essential to understand the rationale behind the EPF technique. Following this, the EPF technique is presented on a conceptual level, some technical issues are discussed, and the results of some case study error investigations are reported. Finally, an interpretation of the remarkable accuracy of the EPF technique is offered and some considerations for further extensions of the technique are outlined.

MOTIVATION FOR THE EPF METHOD

In order to gain insight into the general problem, it is helpful to first review the solutions obtained by Jackson (8) and by Gordon and Newell (7). Consider a closed queueing network with exponential service times at all servers, "first come, first served" scheduling, and a single class of customers.

Let M = number of servers
N = number of customers
p_{ji} = probability that a customer who completes service at server j will proceed next to server i ($j = 1, \ldots, M$; $i = 1, \ldots, M$)
s_i = mean service time at server i ($i = 1, \ldots, M$)

Assuming that the values of M, N, p_{ji} and s_i are given, the first step in the solution process involves determining the average arrival rate at each server. Let a_i equal the average arrival rate at server i for $i = 1, \ldots, M$. Since the network is closed, an arrival at server i occurs only if there is a departure from some server j ($j = 1, \ldots, M$) and the departing customer proceeds next to server i. Since the stochastic process that corresponds to the network is assumed to be in statistical equilibrium, the average departure rate from each server will be equal to the average arrival rate at that server. Thus, a_j is also the average departure rate from server j, and $a_j p_{ji}$ is the average arrival rate at server i generated by departures from server j.

Since departures from any server can contribute to the total arrival rate at server i, a_i is given as

$$a_i = \sum_{j=1}^{M} a_j p_{ji} \qquad i = 1,\ldots,M \tag{1}$$

The steady state distribution of customers in the network is then given as

$$P(n_1, \ldots, n_M) = \frac{1}{G(N)} P_1(n_1) \cdot P_2(n_2) \cdot \ldots \cdot P_M(n_M) \tag{2}$$

where G(N) is a normalizing constant chosen so that equation (3) is satisfied

$$\sum_{\substack{\text{ALL}\\ \text{STATES}}} P(n_1, \ldots, n_M) = 1 \tag{3}$$

and each function $P_i(n_i)$ has the form given in equation (4) below.

$$P_i(n_i) = K_i \cdot (a_i s_i)^{n_i} \tag{4}$$

The term K_i in equation (4) represents an arbitrary constant whose value has no impact on the ultimate values of $P(n_1, \ldots, n_M)$. To demonstrate this point let $G^*(N)$ denote the value of the normalizing constant $G(N)$ when all the K_i are equal to 1. That is,

$$G^*(N) = \sum_{\substack{\text{ALL} \\ \text{STATES}}} \prod_{i=1}^{M} (a_i s_i)^{n_i} \tag{5}$$

and

$$P(n_1, \ldots, n_M) = \frac{1}{G^*(N)} \prod_{i=1}^{M} (a_i s_i)^{n_i} \tag{6}$$

Now suppose the K_i are assigned arbitrary values. The resulting value for $G(N)$ is

$$\begin{aligned} G(N) &= \sum_{\substack{\text{ALL} \\ \text{STATES}}} \prod_{i=1}^{M} K_i (a_i s_i)^{n_i} \\ &= \left[\prod_{i=1}^{M} K_i \right] \cdot G^*(N) \end{aligned} \tag{7}$$

The values of $P(n_1, \ldots, n_M)$ are then given as follows

$$\begin{aligned} P(n_1, \ldots, n_M) &= \frac{1}{G(N)} \prod_{i=1}^{M} K_i (a_i s_i)^{n_i} \\ &= \frac{1}{G^*(N)} \prod_{i=1}^{M} (a_i s_i)^{n_i} \end{aligned} \tag{8}$$

Thus, $P(n_1, \ldots, n_M)$ will have the same value regardless of the values assigned to $K_1, K_2, \ldots, K_M$.

If K_i is assigned the value $1 - a_i s_i$, $P_i(n_i)$ has the following form

$$P_i(n_i) = (1 - a_i s_i) \cdot (a_i s_i)^{n_i} \tag{9}$$

Thus, $P_i(n_i)$ can be regarded as the solution of an M/M/1 queueing model with arrival rate a_i and mean service time s_i.

On the other hand, K_i could be assigned the value $1/\sum_{k=0}^{N}(a_i s_i)^k$. In this case $P_i(n_i)$ is given as

$$P_i(n_i) = (a_i s_i)^{n_i} \Big/ \sum_{k=0}^{N} (a_i s_i)^k \qquad (10)$$

Equation (10) represents the solution of an M/M/1/N queueing model with average arrival rate a_i, average service time s_i, and finite waiting room equal to N (Figure 1 presents a cyclic queueing model that is isomorphic to M/M/1/N to clarify this definition). Thus, the values of $P_i(n_i)$ in equation (2) can be regarded as terms from the solutions of either the M/M/1 or the M/M/1/N queueing models.

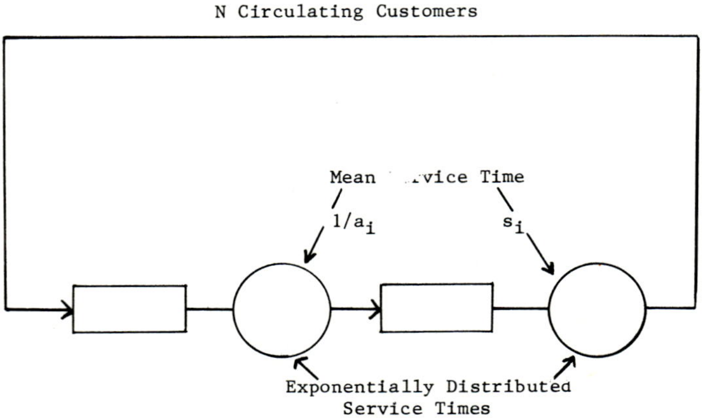

FIGURE 1

Cyclic Queueing Model Isomorphic to M/M/1/N

The next important point to note regarding equations (2) and (4) is that the values $(a_1, a_2, \ldots, a_M)$ can be replaced by any scalar multiple $(\lambda a_1, \lambda a_2, \ldots, \lambda a_M)$ without affecting the value of $P(n_1, \ldots, n_M)$. To prove this, note that if all the values of a_i are multiplied by the constant λ, G(N) will become

$$G(N) = \sum_{\substack{\text{ALL} \\ \text{STATES}}} \prod_{i=1}^{M} (\lambda a_i s_i)^{n_i}$$

$$= \lambda^N \; G^*(N) \qquad (11)$$

Equation (11) follows from the fact that the sum of the n_i must be equal to N for each state $(n_1, n_2, \ldots, n_M)$.

Applying equation (2) to this case,

$$P(n_1, \ldots, n_M) = \frac{1}{G(N)} \sum_{i=1}^{M} (\lambda a_i s_i)^{n_i}$$

$$= \frac{1}{G^*(N)} \sum_{i=1}^{M} (a_i s_i)^{n_i} \qquad (12)$$

Thus, the choice of λ does not affect the values of $P(n_1, \ldots, n_M)$. Note that equation (1) only enables the values of $(a_1, \ldots, a_M)$ to be determined up to a multiplicative constant. The fact that the values of $P(n_1, \ldots, n_M)$ are independent of λ implies that any solution of equation (1) can be used in equations (2) and (4) with equivalent results. If this were not the case, the analysis of separable closed queueing networks would be more complex since it would be necessary to determine which specific solution of equation (1) to use in forming the steady state distribution.

THE EPF HYPOTHESIS

Now consider a similar queueing network, but suppose that service times have general rather than exponential distributions. In this case, we hypothesize that the steady state distribution can be closely approximated by a function of the following form:

$$P(n_1, \ldots, n_M) = \frac{1}{G(N)} P_1(n_1) \cdot P_2(n_2) \cdot \ldots \cdot P_M(n_M) \qquad (13)$$

where $G(N)$ is a normalizing constant as defined by equation (3) and $P_i(n_i)$ is the solution of either an M/G/1 or an M/G/1/N queueing system having the same service time distribution as the i-th server in the network and an arrival rate a_i which satisfies equation (1).

It is worth pointing out that equation (13) represents a direct extension of equation (2); in particular, equation (13) retains the overall product form that is characteristic of the solutions of all separable queueing networks. Hence, the approximate solution developed using equation (13) will be referred to as the Extended Product Form or EPF solution.

Note that in the case of networks containing servers which all have exponential service times, the EPF solution is, in fact, the exact solution. Thus, the EPF solution includes the solution derived by Jackson (8) and by Gordon and Newell (7) as a special case.

When service time distributions are not exponential, two important issues must be resolved. These are: the choice between the M/G/1 and the M/G/1/N solutions for use in the $P_i(n_i)$ expressions; the choice of a specific solution $(a_1. \ldots. a_M)$ to equation (1) for use in forming the M/G/1 or M/G/1/N solutions. Note that neither of these issues arise in the exponential case. As shown in the preceding section, the M/M/1 and M/M/1/N solutions produce identical values for $P(n_1, \ldots, n_M)$ thus removing the first issue. Also, any (non-zero) solution to equation (1) produces identical values for $P(n_1, \ldots, n_M)$ which removes the second issue.

In the case of generally distributed service times, both issues affect the resulting value of $P(n_1, \ldots, n_M)$. Thus, the analyst must make each choice carefully. The key to the EPF solution technique is the manner in which a solution to equation (1) is selected. However, before addressing this issue, we will first examine the choice between the M/G/1 and M/G/1/N solution forms.

PREFERENCE FOR THE M/G/1/N SOLUTION

The EPF solution method makes use of the M/G/1/N rather than the M/G/1 solution form. The reasons for this are basically pragmatic: that is, the M/G/1/N option has produced smaller relative errors than the M/G/1 option in almost all case studies which have been investigated thus far (13). In addition, use of the M/G/1/N option enables the EPF method to provide exact solutions to certain non-exponential networks with FCFS scheduling. These include cyclic networks with one general and one exponential server, and "machine repair" networks with a total of two customers (machines). For proofs that the EPF method provides exact solutions in these special cases, see (13).

On philosophical and conceptual grounds, the M/G/1/N option offers an advantage over the M/G/1 option with respect to the issue of population size. In an M/G/1 system, population size is assumed to be infinite in the sense that the maximum queue length at the server is unbounded. In contrast, the maximum queue length at any server in a closed network is bounded by N, the number of customers present. The M/G/1/N solution reflects this bound and would thus appear to be more appropriate for closed networks.

The finite bound on queue length which is incorporated into the M/G/1/N solution becomes more significant as the coefficient of variation of the server increases. To see this, note that an increase in the coefficient of variation is generally accompanied by an increase in the relative frequency with which extremely long service times occur. In infinite population models such as M/G/1, these extremely long service times cause very long queues to build up and thus have a major impact on average queue length and average response time. On the other hand, the impact of an extremely long service time is much less significant in a finite population system since maximum queue length is bounded. This helps to explain why the M/G/1/N solution has proven superior to the M/G/1 solution for use in the analysis of closed queueing networks with finite populations, and why the advantages of the M/G/1/N option become more significant as the coefficients of variation increase throughout the network.

THE THROUGHPUT CONSTRAINT IN CLOSED NETWORKS

Recall that equation (1) was originally formulated to express an invariant relationship between the arrival rates at the individual servers in a closed queueing network. Since the arrival rate at any server must be equal to the throughput (i.e., the departure rate) of that server if the system is in equilibrium, equation (1) will be referred to as the <u>throughput constraint</u> for the network.

Note that the throughput (or arrival rate) of server i can be expressed in terms of the steady state distribution of the network as follows:

$$a_i = \frac{1}{s_i}\left[\text{utilization of server } i\right]$$

$$= \frac{1}{s_i} \sum_{n_i \geq 1} P(n_1, \ldots, n_M) \tag{14}$$

where the sum in equation (14) is taken over all states for which $n_i \geq 1$.

In order for the values of $P(n_1, \ldots, n_M)$ to represent the actual steady state distribution of the network, it is clear that the values of a_i obtained from equation (14) must satisfy the throughput constraint expressed by equation (1). This observation is crucially important since it provides a basis for determining the specific solution to equation (1) which is used in forming the EPF solution. Essentially, the EPF solution is derived as follows:

1. Select $e_1, e_2, \ldots, e_M$ so that equation (1) is satisfied and $\sum_{i=1}^{M} e_i = 1$. Note that the e_i are uniquely determined (assuming the network is connected), and note also that any scalar multiple $\lambda e_1, \lambda e_2, \ldots, \lambda e_M$ will also satisfy equation (1).

2. Assume that the steady state distribution for the network is given by equation (13) where $P_i(n_i)$ is the solution of an M/G/1/N queue having one general server that is identical to server i, an arrival rate of λe_i, and finite waiting room equal to N.

3. Adjust the value of λ until the values of a_i obtained by equation (14) satisfy the throughput constraint as closely as possible.

In the case where all service times are exponential, any value of λ will produce the same values of $P(n_1, \ldots, n_M)$, and consequently the same values of $a_1, \ldots, a_M$ via equation (14). Furthermore, it is easy to verify that these values of $a_1, a_2, \ldots, a_M$ will in fact satisfy the throughput constraint.

When service times are not exponential, different values of λ will produce different values of $P(n_1, \ldots, n_M)$ and different values of $a_1, a_2, \ldots, a_M$ via equation (14). Since the EPF does not necessarily produce exact solutions, the resulting values of $a_1, a_2, \ldots, a_M$ will not necessarily satisfy the throughput constraint. However, by adjusting λ so that the throughput constraint is closely satisfied, we have found that the corresponding values of $P(n_1, \ldots, n_M)$ provide an excellent approximation to the actual steady state distribution for a great many cases of interest.

TECHNICAL CONSIDERATIONS

ERROR FUNCTIONS

In order for the values of a_i produced by equation (14) to satisfy the throughput constraint, there must be a constant k such that

$$a_i = k \cdot e_i \qquad \text{for } i = 1, \ldots, M \tag{15}$$

Note that the constant k is not the same as the constant λ which is used in forming the EPF solution.

For any value of λ, it is possible to form a steady state distribution and derive a set of values $a_1, a_2, \ldots, a_M$ using equation (14). Assuming this has been done, define the values $k_1, k_2, \ldots, k_M$ as follows:

$$k_i = a_i/e_i \qquad \text{for } i = 1, \ldots, M \tag{16}$$

Clearly, adjusting λ so that the values of a_i satisfy the throughput constraint is equivalent to adjusting λ so that all values of k_i are equal.

Define $\overline{k}$, the average of $k_1, k_2, \ldots, k_M$, as indicated in equation (17).

$$\overline{k} = \frac{1}{M} \sum_{i=1}^{M} k_i \tag{17}$$

Then one possible measure of how closely the values of $a_1, a_2, \ldots, a_M$ satisfy the throughput constraint for a specific value of λ is given by $\sum_{i=1}^{M} (k_i - \bar{k})^2$. Rather than using this conventional error function as a measure of "goodness of fit", we use the slightly modified error function $L(\lambda)$ which is given in equation (18) below.

$$L(\lambda) = \sum_{i=1}^{M} (e_i s_i) \quad (k_i - k^*)^2 \tag{18}$$

In equation (18), k^* indicates the value of k_i for the most heavily saturated server, specifically the server with the largest value of $e_i s_i$. In addition to replacing $\bar{k}$ by k^*, a set of weighting factors $e_i s_i$ are introduced into the error function to reflect the relative utilization of each server. The intended effect of both these modifications is to achieve better fits at the more highly saturated servers, and to achieve the best fit of all at the server that is most highly saturated. This is motivated by the observation that the activity of the most saturated server is extremely critical in determining overall system performance. In situations where other considerations make it desirable to use a different set of weighting factors and a different replacement for $\bar{k}$, the EPF procedure could of course be modified.

SEARCH ALGORITHMS

Ideally, the EPF solution is formed by adjusting λ until the value of $L(\lambda)$ in equation (18) is equal to zero. However, it is frequently impossible to determine such a λ. This leaves us with two alternatives: either adjust λ until $L(\lambda)$ falls below some pre-specified tolerance level $\varepsilon > 0$, or attempt to minimize $L(\lambda)$ over some range $(0,\Lambda)$. In our case studies we adopted the latter approach and defined Λ as follows:

$$\Lambda = \max_{1 \leq i \leq M} \left\{ \frac{m_i}{e_i s_i} \right\} \tag{19}$$

where m_i is the number of parallel servers at service center i. A more detailed discussion of the search algorithms can be found in (13).

COMPARISON WITH THE DIFFUSION APPROXIMATION

Our evaluations of the EPF method are primarily based on comparisons between exact solutions to non-exponential networks and the solutions obtained using EPF. Before presenting these results, we will first compare the accuracy of the EPF method with that of another widely used approximation technique, the so-called diffusion approximation (16, 9). We use the specific version of the diffusion approximation presented by Reiser and Kobayashi (10) for this comparison.

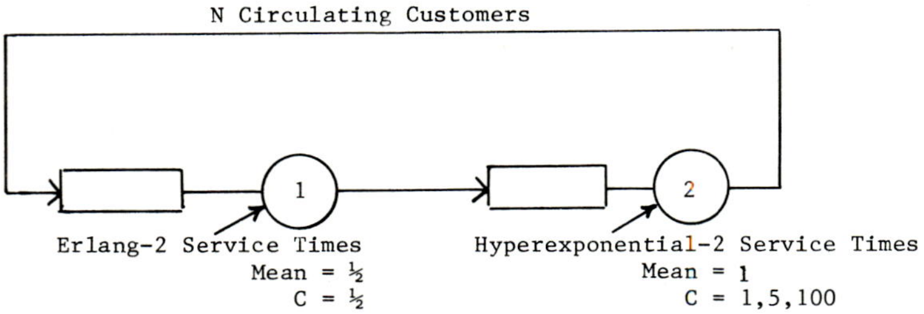

FIGURE 2
Cyclic Queueing Network

Consider the closed cyclic network containing two servers that is illustrated in Figure 2. The mean service time of server 1 is one half the mean service time of server 2; server 1 has an Erlang-2 distribution with coefficient of variation equal to .5, and server 2 has a hyperexponential distribution. Table 1 presents the relative errors in the utilization of each server for cases where the coefficient of variation for server 2 steps through the range 1, 5 and 100, and where the number of customers in the network varies from 2 to 7. Table 2 presents relative queue length error for the same cases.

		C = 1.0		
	SERVER 1		SERVER 2	
N	EPF	DIFF	EPF	DIFF
2	0	3.11	0	2.91
3	0	1.61	0	1.61
4	0	0.77	0	0.81
5	0	0.36	0	0.40
7	0	0.07	0	0.09
		C = 5.0		
	SERVER 1		SERVER 2	
N	EPF	DIFF	EPF	DIFF
2	0.26	-18.15	0.26	10.58
3	0.25	-13.35	0.25	3.29
4	0.17	- 9.78	0.17	1.12
5	0.09	- 7.18	0.09	0.35
7	0.01	- 3.87	0.01	-0.09
		C = 100.0		
	SERVER 1		SERVER 2	
N	EPF	DIFF	EPF	DIFF
2	0.08	-41.79	0.08	29.91
3	0.21	-42.31	0.21	16.48
4	0.24	-42.29	0.24	10.69
5	0.23	-42.05	0.23	7.64
7	0.20	-41.22	0.20	4.64

TABLE 1

ERROR IN SERVER UTILIZATION

		C = 1.0		
	SERVER 1		SERVER 2	
N	EPF	DIFF	EPF	DIFF
2	0	1.01	0	-2.58
3	0	1.57	0	-5.10
4	0	1.68	0	-6.86
5	0	1.60	0	-8.01
7	0	1.29	0	-9.13
		C = 5.0		
	SERVER 1		SERVER 2	
N	EPF	DIFF	EPF	DIFF
2	0.08	-13.84	-0.19	33.80
3	0.17	- 9.39	-0.47	26.06
4	0.18	- 6.89	-0.57	21.49
5	0.15	- 5.34	-0.54	18.70
7	0.08	- 3.65	-0.36	15.99
		C = 100.0		
	SERVER 1		SERVER 2	
N	EPF	DIFF	EPF	DIFF
2	0.03	-32.98	-0.06	78.75
3	0.17	-30.79	-0.43	78.80
4	0.28	-29.75	-0.74	79.30
5	0.35	-29.15	-0.96	80.03
7	0.42	-28.41	-1.21	81.67

TABLE 2

ERRORS IN AVERAGE QUEUE LENGTH

NOTE: ALL ERRORS ARE EXPRESSED AS PERCENT DEVIATIONS FROM THE CORRESPONDING EXACT VALUES

GENERAL ERROR ANALYSIS

Having verified that EPF approximations compare favorably to those generated by another popular approximation method, we now turn to a more detailed evaluation of the EPF technique itself. Specifically, this section presents the results of a series of case studies in which EPF approximations are compared with exact solutions for a range of parameter values and network structures.

Unfortunately, only a limited number of network structures have been investigated because of the difficulty in obtaining the exact numerical solutions needed to determine actual error levels. However, we have examined two specific structures which are representative of the models typically developed to analyze computer system performance. These are:

1. The machine repairman model with exponentially distributed "times between repair requests" and generally distributed "repairman service times". See Figure 3.
2. The central server model with hyperexponentially distributed CPU processing times and two I/O devices with Erlang-2 service time distribution. See Figure 4.

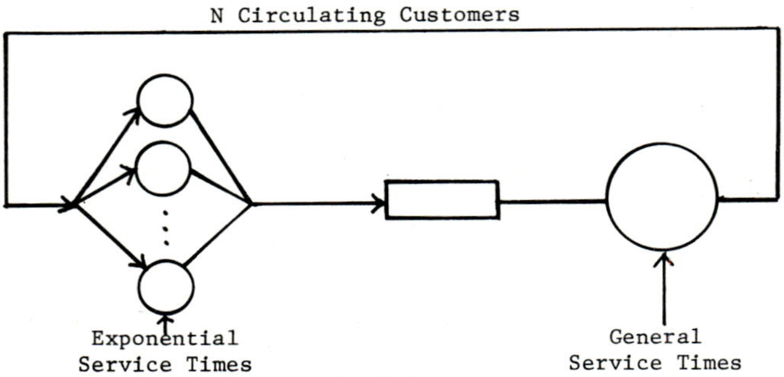

FIGURE 3
Machine Repairman Model

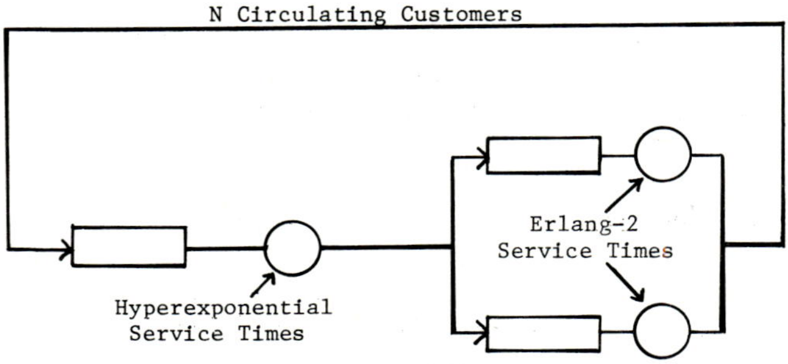

FIGURE 4
Central Server Model

The machine repairman model is the basis for some of the earliest successful models of time sharing systems (11) and has also been used in more recent analyses which employ decomposition (3) and hierarchic modeling (12). The exact closed form solution utilized to assess error levels for this model was originally developed by Takacs (14).

In the case of the central server model, exact numerical solutions were obtained (for the specific distributions involved) via the method of stages (4). The central server model was selected for investigation because it has proven itself to be extremely useful for analyzing the resource contention effects that arise in almost any multiprogramming system (1).

It should be noted that analysts may have to turn to simulation for comparison purposes when more complex network structures are considered. This will have to be done with great care since the accuracy of the EPF technique has proven to be roughly equivalent to the accuracy of conventional simulation studies for the range of cases that we have investigated.

MACHINE REPAIRMAN ANALYSIS

In these case studies, three different families of service time distributions were assigned to server 2. These were: constant, Erlang-2, and hyperexponential-2. The corresponding values of C, the coefficient of variation, were 0 (for constant), 1/2 (for Erlang-2), and values ranging from 2 to 2000 (for hyperexponential). The number of customers in the network was varied from 2 to 8, and the service times of the two servers were varied from a 1:1 ratio to a 10:1 ratio.

It was pointed out previously that, when the number of customers in the network is equal to one or two, the EPF method produced exact solutions for all distributions that were considered. Graphs 1-6 illustrate typical relative error values for utilization (throughput) and expected queue length for each of the three service time distributions that were investigated.

CENTRAL SERVER ANALYSIS

In addition to examining the case of hyperexponential-2 CPU service times and Erlang-2 I/O service times, we also evaluated exponential CPU with hyperexponential I/O, exponential CPU with Erlang I/O, and hyperexponential CPU with exponential I/O. The service times of the CPU and one of the I/O devices were kept equal, and the other I/O service time was varied from one tenth to ten times the CPU service time. Each I/O device was selected with probability 1/2, and the number of customers was varied from 2 to 7.

In general, the smallest errors occured at the most saturated server(s) and the relative errors for these servers were very small, less than 1%. The maximum errors occur at the least utilized server(s). This observation is important because it is consistent with our desired objective for the EPF solution method to maximize the accuracy of the most critical resources (i.e., the system bottlenecks and most saturated servers). Graphs 7 and 8 are typical of the utilization and expected queue length errors that were observed at the most saturated servers.

SENSITIVITY TO C

It is important to observe from all the error graphs that the accuracy of the EPF solution method does not decrease monotonically with increasing values of C. The graphs indicate that in general errors are very small for C close to 1. The highest errors occur in the range of 10 to 25 and then decrease monotonically as C increases again. This represents a significant advantage over some other approximation methods whose accuracy decreases monotonically with increasing value of $C > 1$. Graphs 9-12 illustrate typical relative error values for utilization and expected queue length errors in the case of the machine repairman and central server models.

DISCUSSION

This section presents an intuitive explanation for the surprising accuracy of the EPF approximation technique. Note that the EPF technique relies on a form of decomposition in which each server is analyzed individually, given only its service time distribution, average arrival rate, and maximum queue length (these are the parameters of the M/G/1/N model). In effect, each server is "decoupled" from the network and analyzed under the assumption that its behavior is more or less independent of specific activities elsewhere in the network. The intuitive concept of decoupling corresponds to the precise operational concept of server homogeneity (i.e., off-line service function equals on-line service function) as discussed in Denning and Buzen (5).

After carrying out the individual decoupled analyses, the overall distribution of customers in the network is built up using a product form solution. Once again, a type of independence is implicitly assumed since the product form solution essentially allows each server to operate independently of the other servers in the network. Since such independence is intuitively reasonable, we would expect the full steady state distribution to have such a product form (at least approximately). The nature of product form solutions is discussed further in (5).

Finally, after developing the general product form solution, attention is directed towards the specific constraints which arise because the network is closed and contains a finite number of customers. Only two constraints have to be taken into account. The first is that the sum of the number of customers present in the network must be equal to N. This constraint is satisfied by assigning a zero probability to all states where the sum is not equal to N and then selecting G(N) so that equation (3) is satisfied.

The second constraint which must be satisfied is the throughput constraint given by equation (1), with the values of a_i given by equation (14). The EPF technique is based on adjusting the parameter λ so that this constraint is satisfied as closely as possible. The explicit use of the throughput constraint in conjunction with equation (14) to assign a value to λ is the essential technical feature that distinguishes EPF from the techniques used to solve separable (i.e., Markovian) queueing networks.

The success of the EPF approximation technique suggests that each server in the network does operate in a more or less independent manner, and that the only interactions between the servers which have major system impact are the two constraints described above. If this hypothesis is correct, we would expect the EPF technique to work well in other situations where these conditions appear likely to hold. Examples include: networks with service centers containing multiple parallel servers which are individually analyzed as M/G/n/N systems; networks with various forms of queue dependent servers; networks with multiple classes of customers; networks with priority scheduling. A more detailed discussion of these extensions is provided in (13).

On the other hand, our intuitive explanation also leads us to conclude that there may be cases where the EPF technique will not work well. For example, consider a situation where a server has customers waiting, but is blocked because of the activity of some other server in the network. If such an effect has a significant impact on overall network performance, one would not expect the EPF technique to provide an accurate approximation to actual system behavior.

In summary, the EPF technique holds considerable promise for the analysis of a wide class of closed queueing networks, but further validation studies are required in order to gain confidence in the method. These studies present certain technical difficulties since they require that the analyst have access to the exact numerical solutions to networks with general service time distributions. However, there are several reasons for believing that such studies will prove successful:

1. The idea of adjusting λ to satisfy the throughput constraint serves the same function in large networks as it does in the small networks we have investigated.
2. The concept of decoupling a server from the rest of a network and analyzing it in isolation should not depend to any significant extent on the total size of the network. Denning and Buzen (5) show how the related operational concept of server homogeneity can be applied to networks of arbitrary size.
3. By using the concept of decomposability as described by Courtois (3), large networks can be reduced to approximately equivalent smaller networks of aggregated servers. Thus, our success in applying the EPF technique to small networks can be regarded as success for the case of aggregated servers in large networks.

We feel these arguments strongly imply that the EPF technique will prove equally accurate in larger networks. However, we fully agree with those who have stated that further validations are necessary, and we would encourage others to investigate this area.

References

(1) Buzen, J.P., Queueing Network Models in Multiprogramming, Ph.D. Thesis, Division of Engineering and Applied Physics, Harvard University, Cambridge, Massachusetts, May 1971.

(2) Buzen, J.P., "Computational Algorithms for Closed Queueing Networks with Exponential Servers", C. ACM Vol. 16, No. 9, September 1973, pp. 527-521.

(3) Courtois, P.J., On the Near-Complete Decomposability of Network of Queues and of Stochastic Models of Multi-programming Computer Systems, Technical Report, Department of Computer Science, Carnegie-Mellon University, Pittsburgh, Pennsylvania, November 1972.

(4) Cox, D.R., "A Use of Complex Probabilities in the Theory of Stochastic Processes", Proceedings of the Cambridge Philosophical Society, 1955, pp. 313-319.

(5) Denning, P.J. and Buzen, J.P., "Operational Analysis of Queueing Networks", appears in this volume.

(6) Gelenbe, E., "On Approximate Computer System Models", J.ACM, Vol. 22, No. 2, 1975, pp. 261-263.

(7) Gordon, W.J. and Newell, G.F., "Closed Queueing Systems with Exponential Servers", Operations Research, Vol. 15, No. 2, April 1967, pp. 254-265.

(8) Jackson, J.R., "Jobshop-Like Queueing Systems", Management Science, Vol. 10, No. 1, October 1963, pp. 131-142.

(9) Newell, G.F., Applications of Queueing Theory, Chapman and Hall, Ltd., London, 1971 (Chapter 6).

(10) Reiser, M. and Kobayashi, H., "Accuracy of the Diffusion Approximation for Some Queueing Systems", IBM J. Research Development, Vol. 18, No. 2, March 1974, pp. 110-124.

(11) Scherr, A., An Analysis of Time-Shared Computer Systems, Research Monograph 36, MIT Press, Cambridge, Massachusetts, 1967.

(12) Sekino, A., "Performance Evaluation of Multiprogrammed Time-Shared Computer System", Project MAC, MIT, Cambridge, Massachusetts, MAC-TR-103, September 1972.

(13) Shum, A.W., Queueing Models for Computer Systems with General Service Time Distributions, Ph.D. Thesis, Division of Engineering and Applied Physics, Harvard University, Cambridge, Massachusetts, December 1976.

(14) Takacs, L., "On a Stochastic Process Concerning some Waiting Time Problems", The Theory of Probability and its Applications, Vol. 2, No. 1, 1957, pp. 90-103.

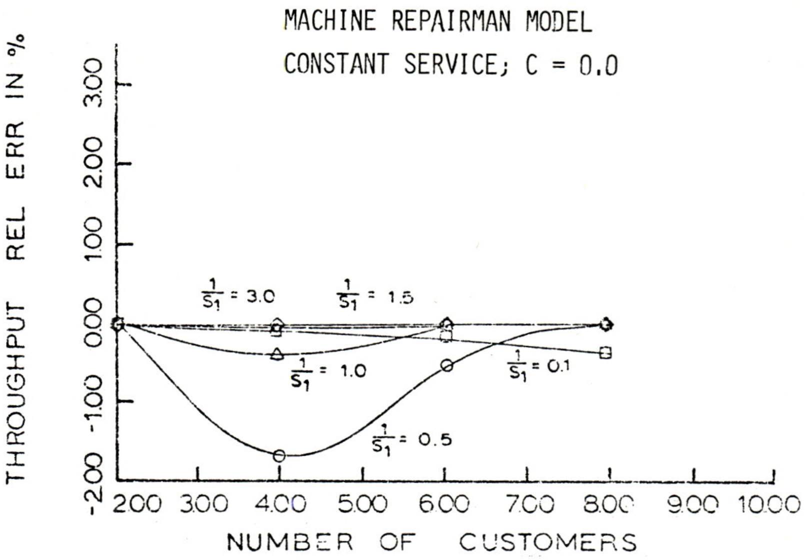

GRAPH 1

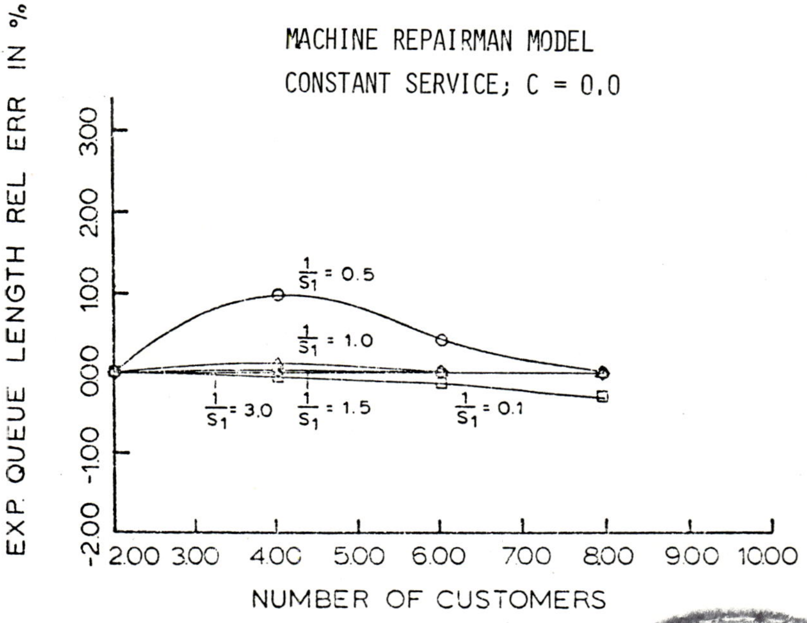

GRAPH 2

WATERFORD REGIONAL LIBRARY

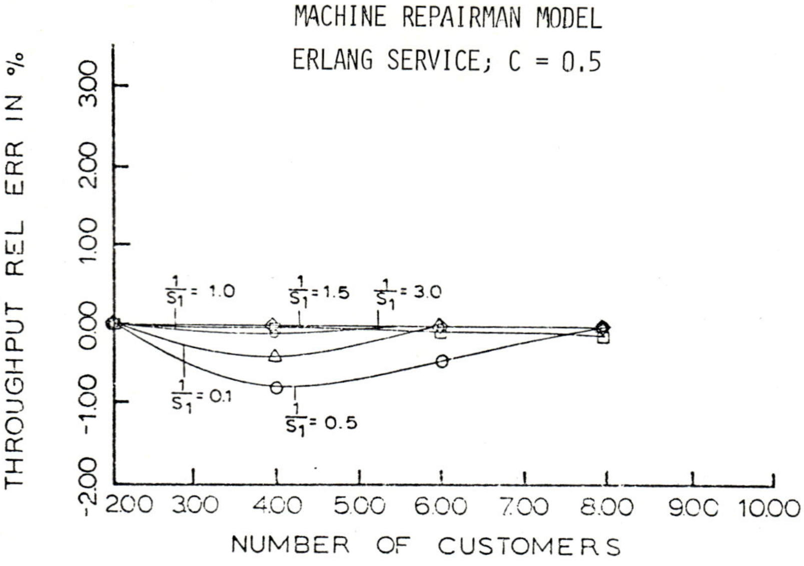

GRAPH 3

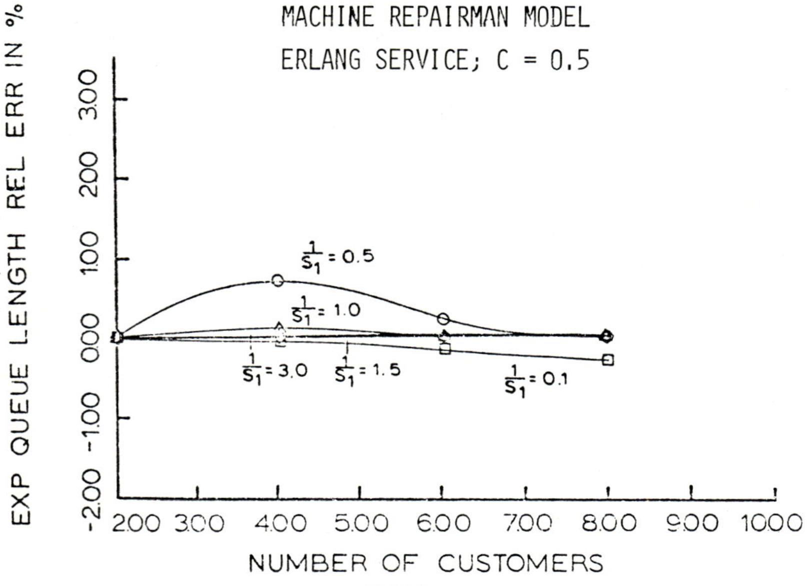

GRAPH 4

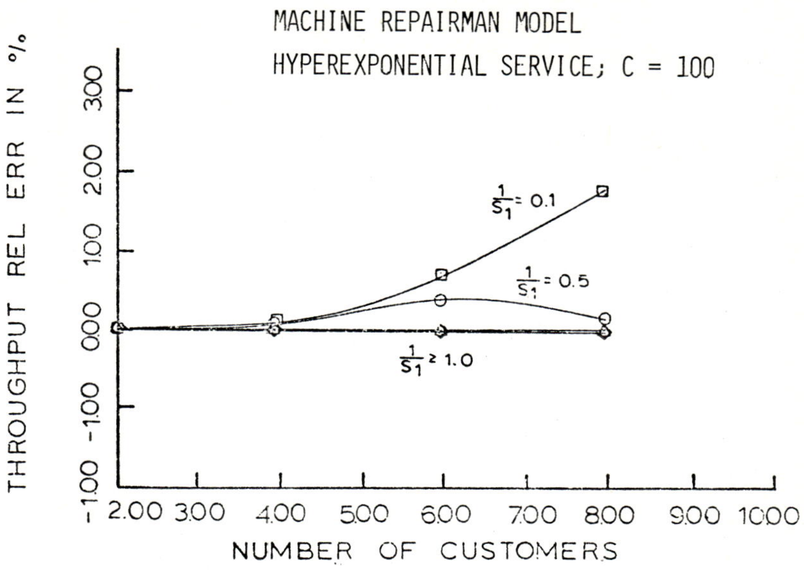

GRAPH 5

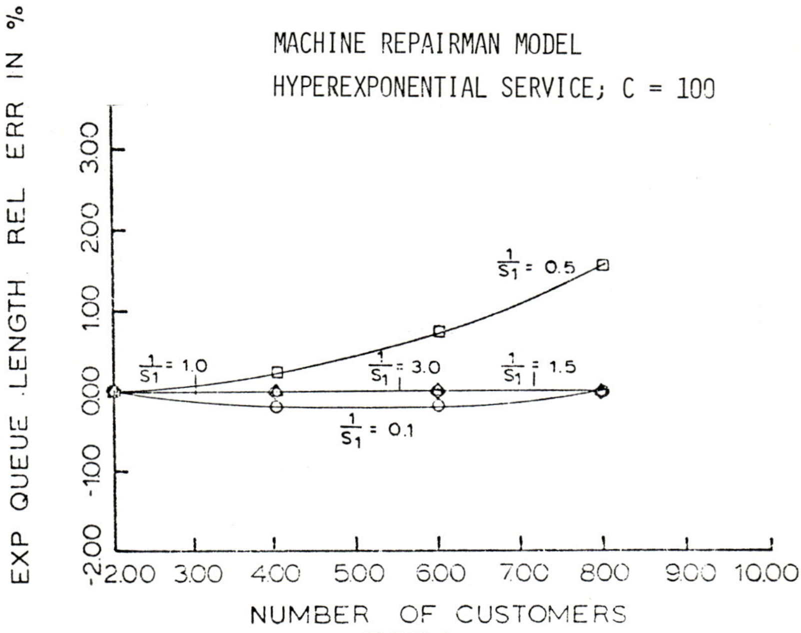

GRAPH 6

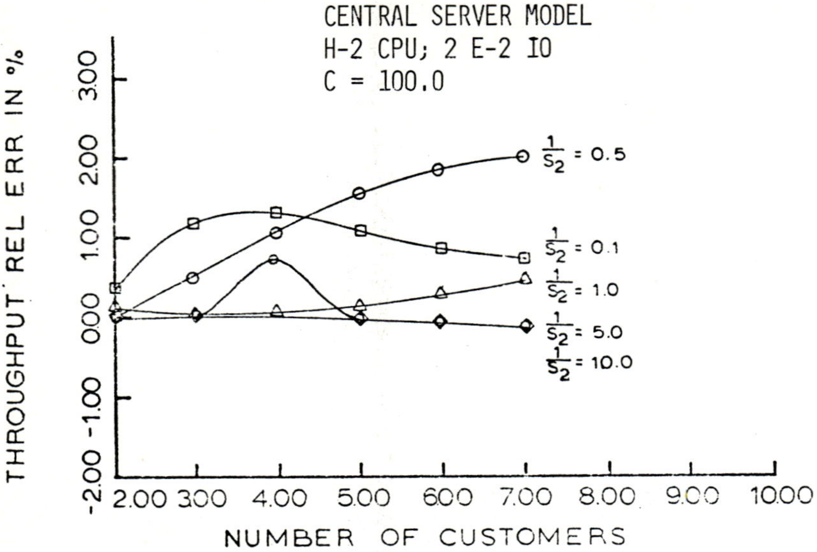

GRAPH 7

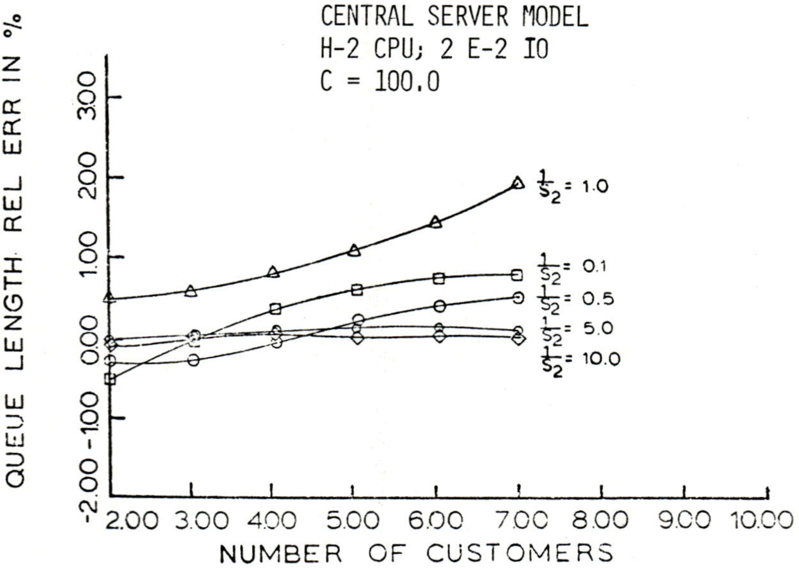

GRAPH 8

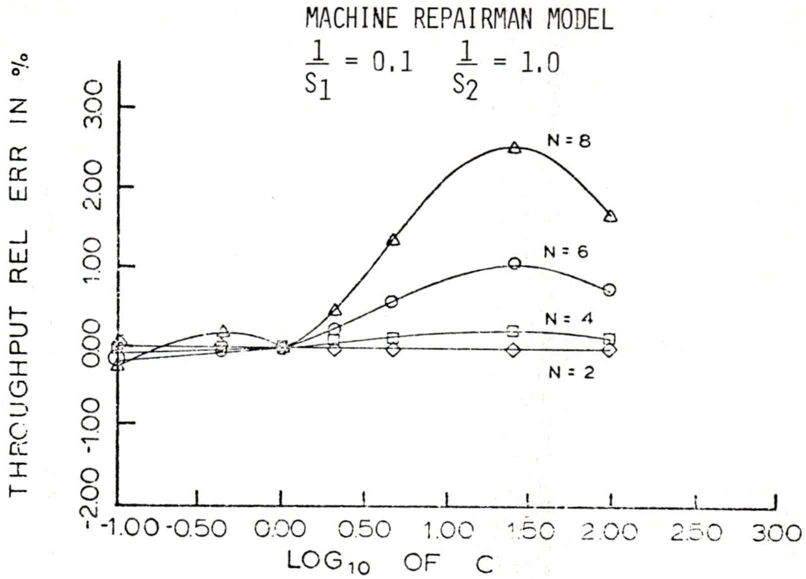

GRAPH 9

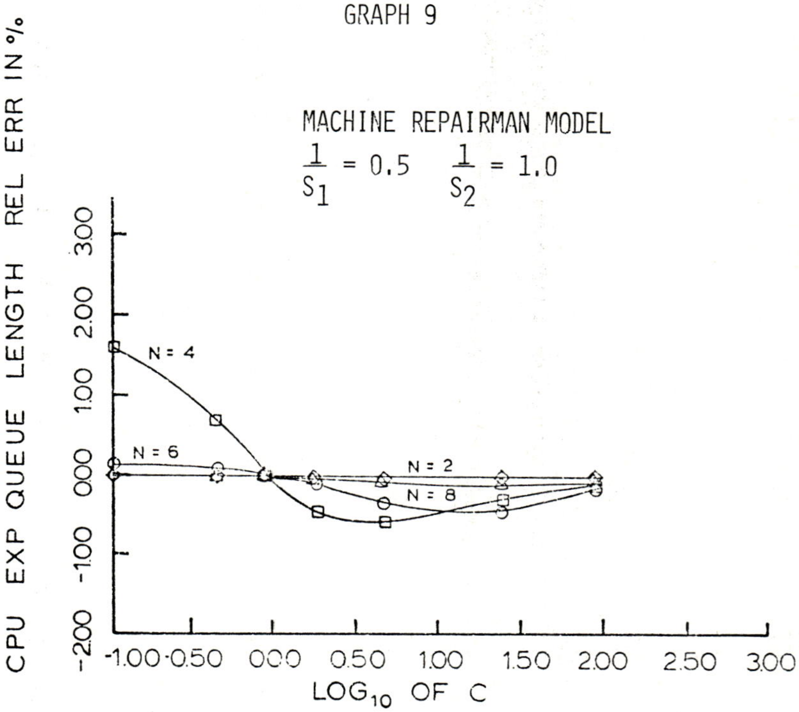

GRAPH 10

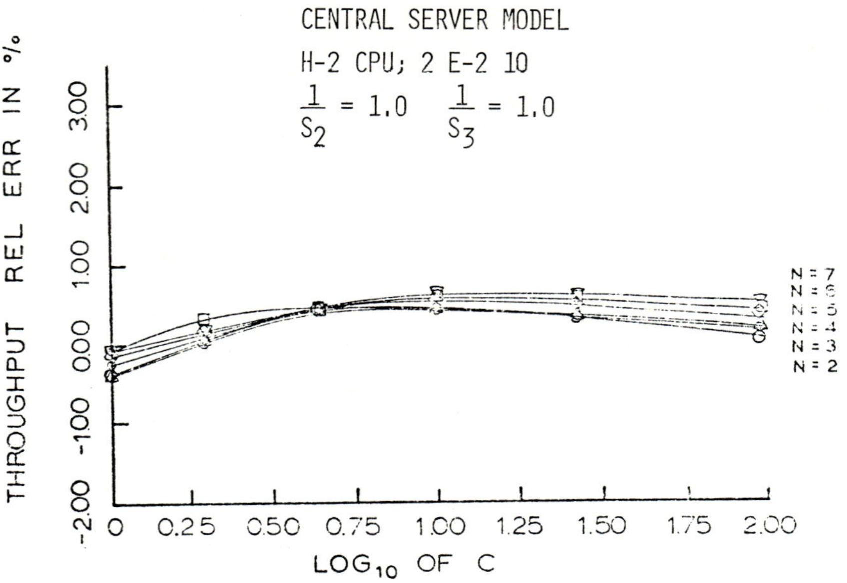

GRAPH 11

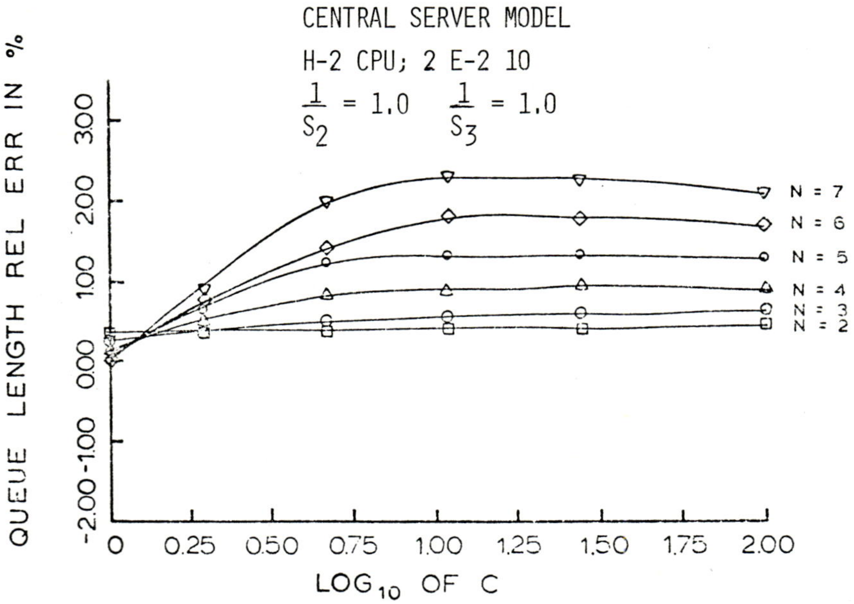

GRAPH 12

Measuring, Modelling and Evaluating Computer Systems,
H. Beilner and E. Gelenbe, (eds.)
© North-Holland Publishing Company (1977)

STRUCTURE WITHIN LOCALITY INTERVALS†

A. P. Batson, D. W. E. Blatt*, and J. P. Kearns
Department of Applied Mathematics and Computer Science
University of Virginia
Charlottesville, Virginia 22901

A new definition of an interval of localized information referencing is presented and is compared with the Bounded Locality Interval (BLI) defined by Batson and Madison. The internal structure of these locality intervals is characterized in terms of the cyclic patterns of reference to the entire locality set. We show that the properties of these cycles impose limits on the substructure which is possible within the locality interval. We define a "structure parameter" which is a good predictor for the extent of significant or useful substructure within a locality interval. Experimental data obtained from symbolic data reference strings are presented, and we discuss the potential utilization of these concepts in predictive memory management algorithms.

1. INTRODUCTION

The development of virtual memory systems has generated a great deal of interest in the phenomenon of "locality of reference", first described by Belady |1| in 1966. Loosely speaking, a program is said to exhibit locality of reference if it makes references to only a subset of its information space over tims periods of significant duration. We refer here to such periods as <u>locality intervals</u>. A program with "good" locality of reference is one in which such locality intervals cover a large fraction of its execution period, and moreover is one in which the various locality intervals involve references to a relatively small fraction of the program's information space. Programs with good locality of reference will usually perform efficiently on virtual memory systems when the executable memory allocated to the program is significantly smaller than the maximum amount of virtual memory associated with program execution. Equally, the phenomenon leads to improved performance on hardware systems which incorporate a cache, or high speed buffer store, between a processor and main memory.

The first conceptual model which identified locality intervals as stages in a program's sequence of information references was given by Denning |2| in 1972. This model represented the course of program execution as a sequence of pairs:

$$(\ell_1, \tau_1), (\ell_2, \tau_2), \ldots\ldots (\ell_i, \tau_i), \ldots\ldots$$

where ℓ_i is the set of pages or segments referenced during the ith locality interval which has duration τ_i. This simple and intuitively attractive characterization of program behavior has recently been developed and extended by Denning and Kahn |3|, and Batson and Madison |4,5|. These later models allow for

*Current address: New South Wales Institute of Technology
Broadway, NSW 2007, Australia.

†This research is supported by NSF Grant MCS76-15566

the possible existence of transitional periods between distinctive locality intervals, i.e. they recognize that there may exist unstructured or haphazard referencing activity during certain periods of program execution. Well-defined locality intervals have been described as phases or major phases |4,5| or regimes |6|. One attractive feature of such "phase-transition" models is that they provide a macroscopic model for program behavior, as distinct from a reference-by-reference description. Well-parameterized macroscopic models of this kind can be used effectively in performance evaluation studies of virtual memory systems.

A basic difficulty with the class of models described above is that, given a specific reference string, it is difficult to formulate a procedure which will identify distinctive locality intervals. Moreover, it has been shown that at any given time there exists a potential hierarchy of locality intervals |4|. The choice of one particular one of these as the "major phase" active at that time is a decision whose outcome may be dependent on the characteristics of the computer system supporting the program's execution |5|.

While it is evident that the characteristics of a particular computing system will inevitably be crucial in performance evaluation studies, our interest here lies in system-independent modelling of program behavior. One such system-independent model is based upon the Bounded Locality Interval concept introduced by Madison and Batson |4|, and this paper describes some recent investigations of the structural properties of these locality intervals.

2. BOUNDED LOCALITY INTERVALS

The concept of the Bounded Locality Interval (BLI) was introduced by Madison and Batson |4| as a mechanism through which an arbitrary reference string could be partitioned into intervals of distinctive referencing behavior. The least-recently-used (LRU) vector contains, at any time t, the segment names arranged in order of recency of reference, with the most-recently-used segment being in the first position of the vector. Informally, an activity set is defined as follows: an activity set of size i exists at time t if every element in the first i positions of the LRU vector have been referenced more than once whilst this set has occupied the first i vector positions. A BLI was then defined as the two-tuple (A_i,τ_i), where A_i is the activity set and τ_i is its lifetime at the head of the LRU vector. This definition allows for a hierarchy of BLI's to exist over a given time period, as illustrated in |4|, and additional procedures are required to reduce this representation of program behavior to a linear sequence of major phases and transitions as described in the previous section. The central issue is that, at any given time, some of the existing BLI's are more likely candidates for major phases than are others. One class of methods for selecting a particular BLI as being the most "distinctive" makes use of information about the memory hierarchy on which the program is to execute. For example Batson and Madison |5| explored the use of an approximation to a minimum space-realtime cost pathway through the BLI hierarchy to achieve this purpose. The determination of this pathway required assumptions about the relative access times to executable and secondary memory, and involved arguments similar to those utilized by Prieve and Fabry's VMIN algorithm |7|. Our approach in this paper is to defer this system-dependent procedure and to explore ways in which the internal structure of the BLI's themselves can be used to identify more significant phases of program behavior.

3. CYCLES IN LOCALITY INTERVALS

Most computer programs for non-trivial tasks make extensive use of iteration or looping techniques. Our intuition leads us to speculate that computational loops in a program might correspond to the more significant locality intervals, and that it may be possible to recognize such intervals by analysis of their internal structure.

The first concept to be developed is that of a cycle of references within a locality interval. Figure 1 shows a sample reference string containing the substring $(ABC)^6$, and also the BLI associated with this substring.

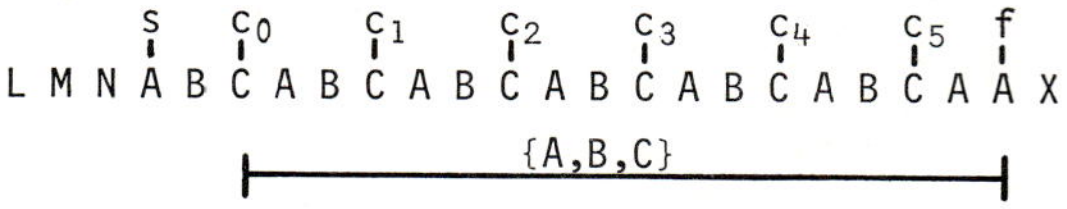

Figure 1. Example Reference String with Cycle Points and BLI.

The times c_0, c_1, c_2, ..., c_5 in the figure correspond to the ends of successive cycles of reference to members of the activity set, and we refer to such times as cycle points. Informally, we can define c_0 as the time at which the activity set first appears at the head of the LRU vector, and c_k as the minimum time at which all members of the activity set have been referenced since c_{k-1}.

Referring again to Figure 1, we point out that:

(i) during the interval [s,f] all references are to members of the activity set

(ii) the BLI is recognized at time c_1, and extends over the interval $[c_0,f]$,

and (iii) At least two complete cycles must occur for a BLI to exist, and the BLI begins at the end of the first cycle.

There are three distincitve periods during the interval [s,f]. The first occurs during $[s,c_0]$, when the activity set is being built up at the head of the LRU vector. The second period, $(c_0,c_5]$ in the example, is the "body" of the locality interval, consisting of one or more complete cycles of reference to the members of the activity set. Finally there exists in general a "tail" to the locality interval consisting of an incomplete cycle. The number of cycles in the body of the locality interval is referred to as its rank.

It seems reasonable to suppose that the rank of a locality interval is in some way related to its significance as a characterization of a phase of distinctive referencing behavior. The BLI for Figure 1 for example, with rank 5, has no substructure. By way of contrast, Figure 2 shows a substring which contains the same number of references to the set {A,B,C}, but which exhibits much less cyclic structure. Cycle points are denoted in the figure by an "x" for the upper-level BLI's.

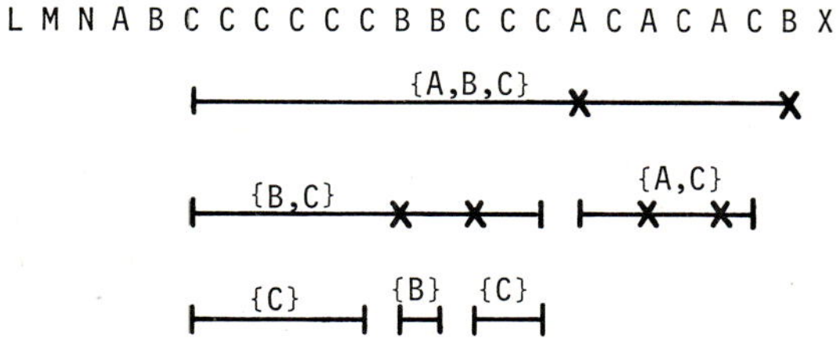

Figure 2. Example Reference String with BLI Hierarchy

Here the BLI at level one (see |4|) has a rank of only two for the same number of references as the rank five BLI of Figure 1, and this lower rank is reflected in the existence of substructure in the BLI hierarchy.

Clearly the likelihood of finding sub-structure beneath any particular BLI is related to its rank, the number of references within the BLI, and the size of its activity set. We defer further consideration of this observation until section 5 below, and first consider some formal properties relating cycle points to the structure of the BLI hierarchy.

4. CYCLE POINTS AND BLI STRUCTURE

Inspection of Figure 2 reveals that no cycle point at level one, shown by an "x" in the figure, is overlapped by any BLI in the structure below level one. We now show that no cycle point at level q can be overlapped by any BLI "beneath" it in the hierarchy of localities.

Figure 3 shows a BLI at level q, with successive cycle points c_{k-1}, c_k, and c_{k+1}. Suppose that its activity set is A_q, with size Q, and suppose that segment $\sigma \in A_q$ is referenced at time c_k.

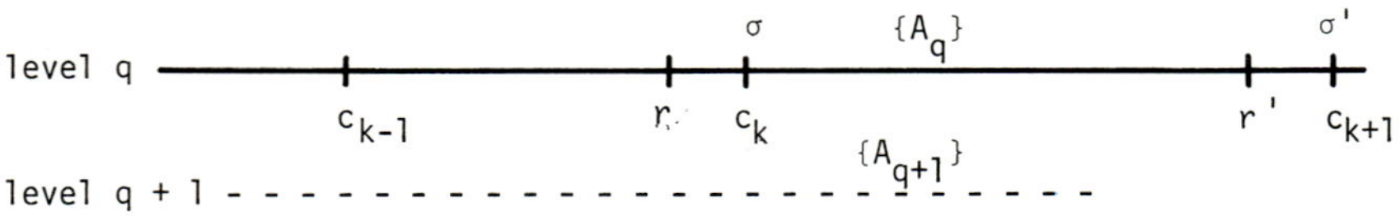

Figure 3. Cycle Points and Substructure

Let the reference immediately preceding that at c_k occur at time r. We now suppose that a BLI exists at level q + 1 with activity set $A_{q+1} \subset A_q$, with a size less than Q. It follows that:

(i) since c_k is a cycle point, the reference to σ at that time completes a cycle, i.e. this is the only reference to σ during $(c_{k-1}, c_k]$.

(ii) thus, at time r, segment σ is in the Qth position of the LRU vector.

(iii) whence, a) if $\sigma \in A_{q+1}$, the BLI at level q + 1, with activity set size less than Q, can begin no earlier than time c_k,
else b) if $\sigma \notin A_{q+1}$, the BLI at level q + 1 must begin after c_k, since at time c_k the segment σ is at the head of the LRU vector.

Thus our first result is that the beginning of a BLI cannot occur earlier than the time of any upper-level cycle point. We now suppose that segment σ' is referenced at the cycle point c_{k+1}. Using the same argument as given above in (i) and (ii), we see that at time r', one reference before c_{k+1}, segment σ' is in position Q of the LRU vector. Thus the reference at c_{k+1} terminates all activity sets of size less than Q, i.e. all BLI's below level q in the hierarchy.

We have shown that the cycle points c_k, $0 \leq k < r$ in a BLI of rank r at any level delimit the duration of BLI's at a lower level to the interval $[c_k, c_{k+1})$. This simple result suggests that the detection of cycles of reference may be an important factor in memory management studies.

5. A STRUCTURE PARAMETER FOR CYCLIC LOCALITY INTERVALS

The objective of this research is to detect those locality intervals which have little significant or useful substructure, and the result given in the previous section illustrates the important role that cycle length must play in this detection process. The minimum length of a cycle, in references, for an activity set of size m, is m references. This minimum length cycle can have no substructure, as no repetitions of segment references occur within the cycle. As the number of references in the cycle becomes larger, the probability of finding substructure at lower levels of the hierarchy must increase. This suggests that, for a cycle consisting of n references to an activity set of size m, that a structure parameter equal to $n/m \geq 1$ may be a useful predictor for the degree of substructure in lower levels of the hierarchy.

Since our interest here lies in the effects of cyclic structure, we define a new kind of locality interval, called a cyclic locality interval, which consists of an integral number of cycles and corresponds to what was referred to as the "body" of the locality interval in section 3. Thus it begins at the reference following c_0 (Figure 1) and terminates at the final cycle point of the BLI. For the example given in Figure 1, it extends over the interval $(c_0, c_5]$. These cyclic locality intervals differ from the BLI's of Madison and Batson in several respects - they begin one reference later, the tail region of the BLI is omitted, and as stated above they represent one or more complete cycles of reference to all members of the activity set. A further trivial difference is that a BLI generated by a double reference (e.g. X Y Y Z) does not give rise to a cyclic locality interval. The result of section 4 concerning cycle points and BLI overlap is also valid for cyclic locality intervals.

We can now define a structure parameter, α, for an entire cyclic locality interval, since it exists for an integral number of cycles. If now m is the size of the activity set for a cyclic locality interval of rank r, and if this interval has a lifetime of N references, then the structure parameter, α is defined by:

$$\alpha = \frac{N}{rm} \geq 1$$

For $\alpha = 1$, there can be no locality interval at a lower level of the hierarchy. For large values of α, we would expect to find significant substructure. Thus we may well be able to use the structure parameter to help identify a major phase of referencing activity amongst several different locality intervals at different levels of the hierarchy of localities. We now describe some experimental investigations of this hypothesis using actual reference strings from a sample of production programs.

6. SOME EXPERIMENTAL RESULTS - THE SAMPLE

Symbolic reference strings from 39 Algol-60 production programs were used to investigate the usefulness of the ideas developed in the previous sections. This sample was the same as that described in |4|, augmented by the addition of reference strings from four additional programs which satisfied the same selection criteria. Each reference of the symbolic reference string corresponds to a reference to an element of a specific array as declared in the source language program, i.e., there is a one-to-one correspondence between array names in the program being monitored and the segment identifiers of the reference string.

The reference strings were processed to identify the cyclic locality intervals at all levels of the hierarchy. This does not yield exactly the same structure as that shown by BLI's, mainly because the tail region of the BLI is eliminated, and its underlying substructure will ascend one level in the hierarchy. For a given symbolic reference string the corresponding cyclic locality interval structure will consist of a sequence of cyclic localities at level-one with their associated substructure. The level-one cyclic localities will be separated by "gaps" during which there are no active localities. Figure 4 shows a typical cyclic locality hierarchy for a reference string over the set of segments {A,B,C,D,E}.

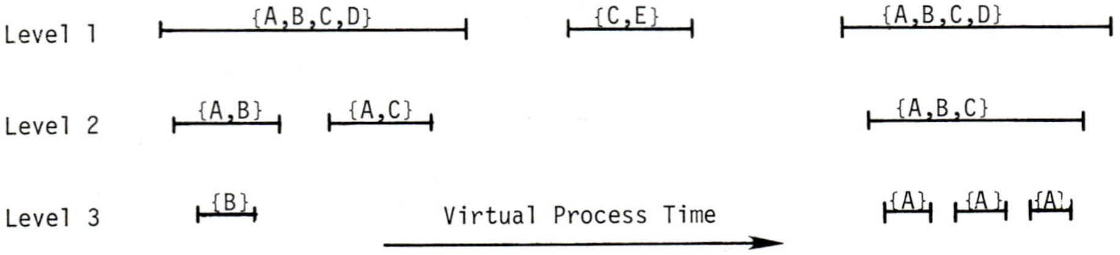

Figure 4. Typical Cyclic Locality Hierarchy

The choice of "the best current locality" at all points during the execution epoch of a program is equivalent to finding a "path" through the cyclic locality hierarchy which minimizes some cost function. We need to determine some such optimum path in order to test out the ideas described earlier, and we have chosen to adopt the space-time cost function for this purpose.

7. THE DETERMINATION OF A MINIMUM-COST PATH

Given a particular hierarchy of cyclic locality intervals, as illustrated in Figure 4, each level one interval, together with its substructure, is considered as an independent entity over which the minimum cost path is determined. The gaps between level one cyclic locality intervals are not considered, and thus each execution period covered by a level one interval will constitute a member of an ensemble whose properties are to be examined.

The path determination algorithm used is essentially the same as that described by Batson and Madison |5|. The basic assumption is that, whenever a particular cyclic locality interval lies on the minimum cost pathway, then it is retained in executable memory and there are no memory faults. The costs assumed for level transitions in the hierarchy are:

(i) The cost of retaining a locality of m segments in memory for t units of process time is mt.

(ii) Descent to a lower cyclic locality interval may occur only at the beginning of the lower locality interval. The descent costs nothing.

(iii) At the termination of a cyclic locality interval the path must continue at the immediately superior locality interval (except at the termination of a level one interval, which ends the computation for that member of the ensemble). If there are m_{q+1} segments in the locality interval at level q+1, and m_q at the superior level, then the cost associated with the ascent in the hierarchy is $m_q \cdot (m_q - m_{q+1}) \cdot \rho$ where ρ is the average real time required to transfer a segment from secondary to primary memory.

(iv) Cyclic locality intervals of duration less than ρ are ignored in the determination of the minimum cost path.

Minimum cost paths were exhaustively determined for the cyclic locality intervals in the sample of symbolic reference strings for three values of ρ-1ms., 10ms., and 50ms. These average transfer times correspond roughly to those for bulk core, fast drum, and disk, respectively.

8. THE STRUCTURE PARAMETER AS A PREDICTOR OF USEFUL SUBSTRUCTURE

The minimum-cost path described above gives an indication of the degree of useful substructure in the members of the ensemble defined by the level one cyclic locality intervals, in the context of a particular system characterized by its ρ value. We now investigate the degree to which the structure parameter, α, of these ensemble members is related to the degree of substructure.

For a given ensemble member and value of ρ let $\bar{m}$ denote the time average number of segments on the minimum cost pathway through the hierarchy. If m_o is the number of segments in the level-one activity set, then $\bar{m}/m_o$ is one measure of the degree of useful substructure, for a given value of ρ. Another measure can be obtained by comparing the cost χ_o associated with retaining the level-one activity set in memory for the duration of the locality interval with χ_{min}, that of the minimum-cost pathway.

Turning now to the structure parameter, α, as defined in Section 5, we would expect that those cyclic locality intervals with an α value close to one would exhibit little useful substructure, and thus would expect to find value of $\bar{m}/m_o$ close to one for the minimum cost pathways through such intervals. Conversely, a locality whose level one value of α were "large" should yield an $\bar{m}/m_o$ value which is significantly less than unity, since it should contain significant substructure. Equally, we can define the relative cost savings occassioned by descent into the substructure on the minimum cost pathway by the ratio $(\chi_o - \chi_{min})/\chi_o$. This ratio should be close to zero for those locality intervals with α close to one, and should become greater for larger values of α.

In Table 1 we show the experimentally determined average values of $\bar{m}/m_o$ and $(\chi_o - \chi_{min})/\chi_o$ for the minimum cost path through members of the ensemble of locality intervals for ρ = 1ms., 10ms., and 50ms., as a function of the α determined for the level one cyclic locality interval. Because of the wide range of α values, the results are displayed in equal sized intervals of $\log_{10} \alpha$, and begin at the value α = 10. For α in the range [1,10) the mean values of $\bar{m}/m_o$ are extremely close to one and the cost savings are essentially zero for ρ = 10 and 50ms. For each value of ρ, only those intervals with duration greater than ρ were considered, as described above.

Range of Log_{10} (α)	Average m/m_o			Average $(\chi-\chi_{min})/\chi_o$		
	ρ = 1ms.	10ms	50ms	ρ = 1ms	10ms	50ms
(1, 1.2]	.89	.98	.99	.08	.02	.02
(1.2, 1.4]	.81	.94	1.00	.12	.02	.00
(1.4, 1.6]	.72	.94	.98	.15	.04	.03
(1.6, 1.8]	.81	.96	.95	.14	.03	.03
(1.8, 2.0]	.73	.91	.99	.27	.07	.02
(2.0, 2.2]	.75	.85	.97	.29	.09	.006
(2.2, 2.4]	.67	.80	.88	.39	.17	.08
(2.4, 2.6]	.71	.81	.83	.43	.23	.09
(2.6, 2.8]	.69	.73	.90	.44	.23	.05
(2.8, 3.0]	.76	.77	.82	.40	.29	.16

Table 1. Variation of $\overline{m}/m_o$ and $(\chi_o-\chi_{min})$ as a Function of Log_{10} α.

The results indeed demonstrate that the system-independent parameter α is a good predictor for the degree of useful substructure in the hierarchy - the results show an unmistakeable trend of diminishing $\overline{m}/m_o$ and increased potential cost savings as the value of α increases.

A noticeable feature of the results presented in Table 1 is that the savings associated with descent into the hierarchy are more noticeable, and begin at lower values of α, for the smaller values of ρ. This is to be expected, since faster secondary memory imposes a smaller cost penalty per memory fault. Thus, although α is a completely system-independent parameter which is determined by the reference string itself, the value of α at which useful substructure is likely is inevitably related to the value of ρ which is a system characteristic.

We now develop a formula which determines, for a given system, a critical value for the structure parameter α. Level one cyclic locality intervals with α greater than this critical value are more likely to exhibit useful substructure which can be exploited by a memory management algorithm.

9. A CRITICAL VALUE FOR THE STRUCTURE PARAMETER

Suppose that a cyclic locality interval of m segments has a structure parameter value equal to α'. Then the average cycle in this interval contains mα' references. We have shown (Section 4) that any cyclic locality interval in the substructure must be bounded by the cycle points of the immediately superior locality interval. Figure 5 illustrates this fact, showing a cyclic locality interval of size n segments (n<m) which is bounded by the cycle points c_k, c_{k+1} of the upper level locality of size m.

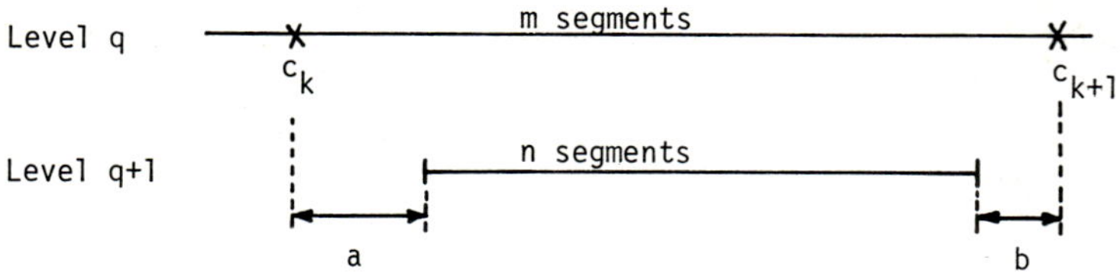

Figure 5. Estimation of Substructure

The cost χ_q of remaining at level q over the average cycle period $(c_k, c_{k+1}]$ is given by:

$$\chi_q = m\left(\frac{m\alpha'}{\delta}\right)$$

where δ is the number of references per unit of process time. The cost involved for a path which descends to level q + 1 will be:

$$\chi_{q+1} = ma + n\left(\frac{m\alpha'}{\delta} - a - b\right) + mb + (m-n)m\rho$$

$$= (m-n)(a+b+m\rho) + \frac{n.m\alpha'}{\delta}$$

Thus, the minimum cost pathway will include the cyclic locality interval at level q + 1 if $\chi_{q+1} < \chi_q$ or if:

$$\frac{m\alpha'}{\delta} > a+b+m\rho$$

The smallest value of α which can possibly lead to savings through a descent to the underlying locality interval is found by setting a+b equal to zero (although b never equals zero), and thus we can determine a critical value for the structure parameter, α^*, given by:

$$\alpha^* \simeq \rho\delta$$

Thus, any cyclic locality interval with a structure parameter value less than α^* is unlikely to have useful substructure when executed in a system with characteristics given by ρ and δ. Many studies of paging systems assume that references are equally spaced in process time. In that case the critical value α^* is simply the ratio of mean page access time to processor inter-reference time. In this development we have ignored the costs associated with copying out dirty segments to secondary storage when they are removed from main memory, and thus in practice the critical value of α would be somewhat larger than that given above. An additional simplification made here is that only two levels of the hierarchy have been considered. In fact, whilst it may not be cheaper to drop to level q + 1 and then return to level q, it may pay to drop to level q + 1, then q + 2 ....., returning eventually back to level q. We now demonstrate the degree to which this result is verified by our experimental data.

10. EXPERIMENTAL INVESTIGATION OF THE UTILITY OF THE CRITICAL STRUCTURE PARAMETER VALUE

The relative savings associated with the minimum cost path $(x_o - x_{min})/x_o$ for all members of the ensemble of intervals defined by level one cyclic localities of duration greater than ρ is shown in Figure 6. For ρ = 1ms., for example, we see that 74% of all minimum cost paths stay at level one with no cost savings to be gained by descent into the hierarchy. Figure 7 shows the distribution of structure parameter values for all level one cyclic locality intervals of

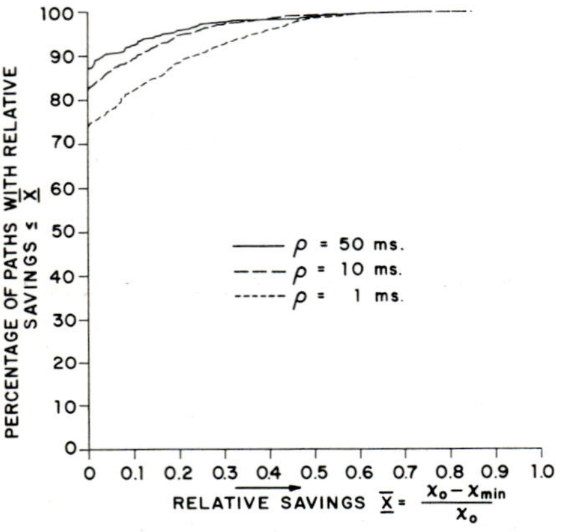

Figure 6. Distribution of Relative Savings

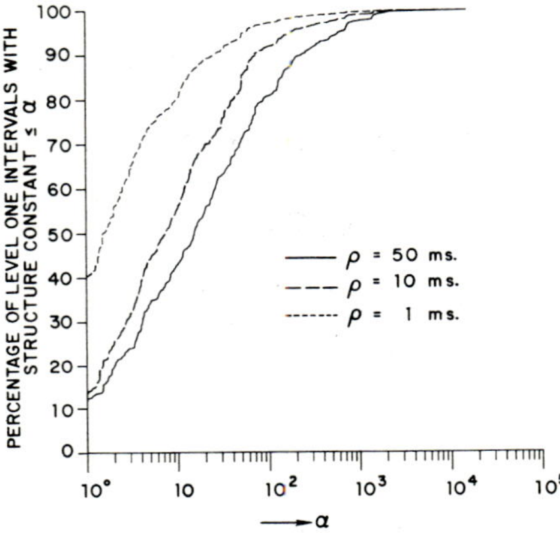

Figure 7. Distribution of Structure Values(α) for Level One Intervals of Duration >ρ

duration greater than ρ (those used in the determination of the minimum cost pathway). The reference density for our entire sample, δ, had a value of 4.6 references per millisecond-the reader is reminded that these were only references to array elements. Using that value of δ we can compute the value of α^* for our sample when ρ = 1ms., 10ms., and 50ms. From Figure 7 we can then obtain the fraction of level one locality intervals with structure constant α less than or equal to α^*, and compare this value with the experimental value shown in Figure 6. The results of this comparison are given in Table 2.

		% of level one localities with no useful substructure	
ρ	α^*	Predicted	Observed
1 ms.	4.6	73	74
10 ms.	46	82	83
50 ms.	230	89	87

Table 2. Fraction of Locality Intervals With No Useful Substructure

This close agreement is somewhat surprising in view of the fact that the computation of α^* considered only two levels in the hierarchy. The results given in Table 1 also demonstrate the significance of the critical value of the structure parameter. The cost savings for the minimum cost path, $(\chi_o - \chi_{min})/\chi_0$, only become significant for those ensemble members with a structure parameter greater than α^*. For example, for ρ = 10ms., where $\alpha^* = 46$ and $\log_{10} \alpha = 1.66$, it can be seen from the table that the cost savings appear to increase rapidly when α rises above this critical value.

11. CONCLUDING REMARKS

Iteration or looping has long been recognized as a central feature of program behavior, and several non-virtual memory computer systems contain special hardware to keep tight instruction loops in high speed buffer storage. In this research we have explored some ways in which such cycles of referencing activity to data or instruction segments, or both, impose structure constraints on a locality hierarchy. The formal results are applicable to both page and segment reference strings, and we have demonstrated their usefulness by an analysis of a sample of symbolic data reference strings. It would be interesting to see the results of a similar experimental study using page reference strings.

One of the attractive features of the kind of locality model described here and earlier is that it is system-independent and almost parameter-free. Of the class of models based on the LRU vector, the localities of Spirn and Denning |8| can be thought of as those with rank greater than zero, whereas those described here and in |4| have rank one or greater. This is the only parameter in this class of models, and they can be used to describe program behavior in a completely system-independent way. The development here of the concept of a structure parameter and its critical value enables us to apply the results to a particular computer system characterized by values of δ its processing speed, and ρ, its secondary memory speed. Although we have analysed our experimental data in terms of the ensemble of locality intervals defined by the level one structure, the results all apply at any level in the hierarchy - i.e. every cyclic locality interval has its own structure parameter and its substructure is delimited by its own cycle points.

The concepts developed here may be useful in memory management algorithms for actual computer systems. Cyclic locality intervals can be detected "on the fly" by special hardware by the time the first cycle point (c_1) has been reached. Repeated cycles of reference to the same activity set can also be recognized by the hardware, and running values of the structure parameters of all currently active locality intervals can be accumulated. Moreover, each individual cycle has its own structure parameter, and this could be used to determine whether essentially identical cycles are occurring. The value of the structure parameter can be computed at the end of each cycle and compared with the critical value for that computer system. It is conceivable that such measures could be used to control the parameters of a memory management scheme. One possibility which comes immediately to mind is that such data could be used to dynamically control the window size of a working set algorithm. We are exploring some of these applications to memory management technology.

12. REFERENCES

|1| Belady, L.A. A study of replacement algorithms for a virtual storage computer. IBM Systems J., 5 (1966) pp. 78-101.

|2| Denning, P.J. On modeling program behavior. AFIPS Conf. Proc., Vol. 40, 1972 SJCC, AFIPS Press, Montvale, N.J., 1972, pp. 937-945.

|3| Denning, P.J. and Kahn, K.C. A study of program locality and lifetime functions. Proc. 5th ACM-SIGOPS Symposium on Operating Systems Principles, Austin, Texas, 1975, pp. 207-216.

|4| Madison, A.W. and Batson, A.P. Characteristics of program localities. CACM 19 (1976), pp. 285-294.

|5| Batson, A.P. and Madison, A.W. Measurements of major locality phases in symbolic reference strings. Proc. International Symposium on Computer Performance Modeling, Measurement and Evaluation, Cambridge, Mass. 1976, pp. 75-84.

|6| Freiberger, W.F., Grenander, U. and Sampson, P.D. Patterns in program references. IBM J. of Res. and Dev. 19 (1975), pp. 230-243.

|7| Prieve, B.G. and Fabry, R.S. VMIN - an optimal variable space replacement policy. CACM 19 (1976), pp. 295-297.

|8| Spirn, J.R. and Denning, P.J. Experiments with program locality. AFIPS Conf. Proc. Vol. 41, 1972 FJCC, AFIPS Press, Montvale, N.J., 1972, pp. 611-621.

Measuring, Modelling and Evaluating Computer Systems,
H. Beilner and E. Gelenbe, (eds.)
© North-Holland Publishing Company (1977)

ANALYSIS OF DEMAND PAGING POLICIES WITH SWAPPED WORKING SETS

(Extended Abstract)*

Dominique POTIER
IRIA-LABORIA
BP 105
78150 Le Chesnay
FRANCE

The analysis of swapped working-sets policies presented in this paper is based on a simple probabilistic model of the paging behaviour of a process during its execution. A preliminary analysis conducted in the virtual time of the process indicates how these policies reduce the average page fault rate and increase the utilisation of the physical pages. These results are then used within a multiclasses queueing model of a multiprogrammed system where processes are divided into classes according to the number of their pages present in main memory. The paging drum service time characteristics and the overheads involved in the different input-output operations are taken into account. Expressions for the CPU time spent in user state and in supervisor state are obtained for paging policies ranging from pure demand paging to demand paging policies with swapped working-sets. These results are illustrated by numerical examples, and compared to measurements data obtained on a real system running with such swapping policies.

INTRODUCTION

In time-sharing multiprogrammed systems using a pure demand paging policy a page is loaded into main memory only after the occurence of a page fault. An important part of the page traffic is thus incurred when the working pages of a process are loaded on demand at the start of its execution. This effect is enhanced by the influence of such factors as the scheduling policy and slow input-output requests which cause the execution of a process to be split into several memory residence intervals, thus giving rise to as many initial loading phases. Experimental evidence [1] indicates that more than fifty percent of the page traffic comes from these page faults and the results of an analysis on the influence of process loading on the page fault presented in [4] also points out the importance of this effect.

An obvious solution to this drawback of a pure demand paging memory management policy is to preload the process active pages or working-set when the process is reactivated in the multiprogrammed set. With this technique, the effective time to load a page is reduced since the preloading of a set of several pages requires

*The full version of this paper will appear in the Proceedings of the 6th Symposium on Operating Principles, to be held at Purdue University, West Lafayette (Ind.), Nov. 16-18, 1977.

only one access to the drum rather than as many as pages for pure demand paging. Moreover, the amount of process switching and the supervisor time required for paging are smaller. On the other hand, swapping working-sets requires an efficient measurement of the process working-sets in order to minimize the amount of unused preloaded pages. There has been various attempts to implement swapped working-set policies in time-sharing multiprogrammed systems. We shall refer in the sequel of this paper to the preloading policy currently implemented in the Edinburgh Multi-Access System [2].

The analysis of demand paging policies with swapped working-set presented on this paper is based on a simple probabilistic model of the paging behaviour of a process during its execution. A preliminary analysis conducted in the virtual time of the process indicates how preloading reduces the average page fault rate and increases the utilisation of the physical pages. These results are then used within a multi-classes queueing network model of a multiprogrammed system where processes are divided into classes according to the number of their pages present in main memory. The drum service time characteristics and the overheads are taking into account. Expressions for the utilization factors of the CPU and the SM are obtained for a class of swapping policies ranging from pure demand paging to total preloading. These results are illustrated by numerical examples and discussed.

PROCESS TIME ANALYSIS

In the context of multiprogrammed page on demand computer systems, the execution of a program consists of a sequence of memory residence intervals (MRI), the number and the duration of which depends on factors such as the I/O behaviour of the program and the memory management and scheduling policies implemented in the system. Within each memory residence interval, the execution is interrupted by page faults, the interval of time between two consecutive page-faults depending on the internal behaviour of the program, the paging policy and the number of pages of the program present in main memory.

Let $X(t)$ be the number of pages of a program present in main memory at the instant t of its virtual time. The behaviour of $X(t)$ can be described in two steps. We specify in the first place the variations of $X(t)$ within a MRI and then the transitions of $X(t)$ between two consecutive MRI's. The first step consists in representing the paging behaviour of the program under a page on demand policy ; the second step in describing the swapping policy.

Let T be the mean virtual residency time of a program in main memory, q_i the mean time between two consecutive page faults conditionned to $X(t) = i$, M the maximum number of main memory page frames allocated to a process. Let (α_{ij}) be a transition matrix where α_{ij} is the probability that $X(t) = j$ at the beginning of a memory residence interval given that $X(t) = i$ at the end of the previous MRI. Assuming that T and q_i, $i = 1,\ldots,M$ are i.i.d exponential random variables, $X(t)$ is a semi-Markov process which can be simply analysed. The analysis, presented in detail in [4], yields expressions for the average time r_M between two consecutive page faults and the memory utilisation ratio ε_M as a function of the memory allotment M.

A class of demand paging policies with swapped working-sets can be simply represented by the following (α_{ij}) matrix. Consider a program which ended a given MRI with $X(t) = i$, and let β be the probability that $X(t) = 1$ at the beginning of the next MRI, $1-\beta$ the probability that $X(t) = i$. The parameter β takes into account different factors such as the proportion of new processes for which no working-set swapping can be achieved and the accuracy of the working-set estimation. Thus β defines a class of demand paging policies with swapped working-set : for $\beta=1$, no swapping is performed, for $0 < \beta < 1$, swapping is partially realized whereas for $\beta=0$

swapping is always successfull.

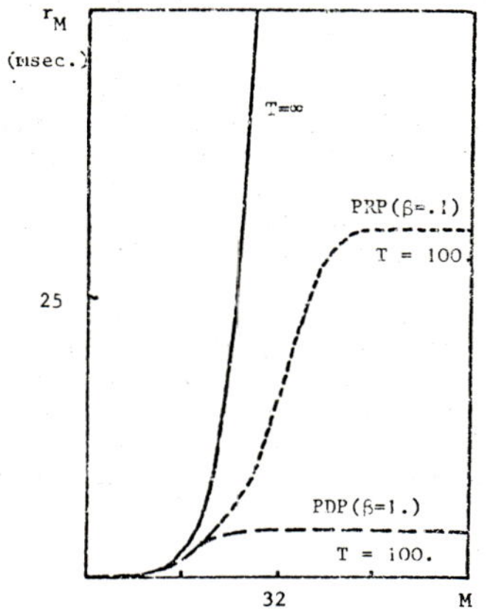

Figure 1

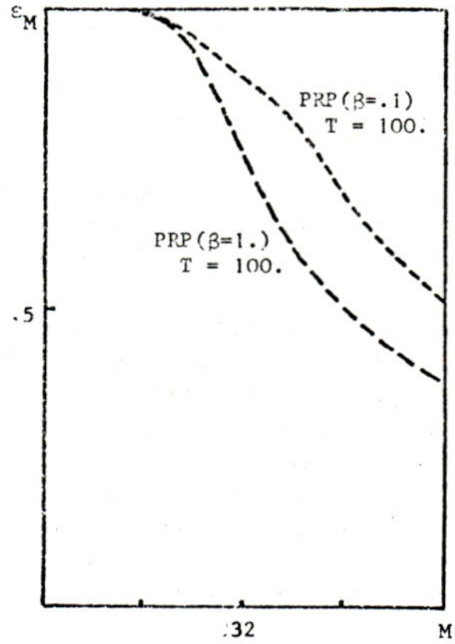

Figure 2

Numerical experiments show that a successfull swapping policy significantly reduces the paging acitivity of the programs and increases the usage of main memory page frames as illustrated in Figures 1 and 2. Moreover, they also indicate how such swapping policies reduce the number of I/O requests by generating bulk requests, although the total amount of transfered pages may increase.. The consequences of these effects on global performance, which depend mainly on the secondary memory latency characteristics, and the paging overheads are investigated in the next section.

REAL TIME ANALYSIS

We consider now a simple model of a multiprogrammed system consisting of a central processing (CPU) station and a secondary memory (SM) station as represented in Figure 3. At the end at a MRI, the execution of a process is suspended and the process leaves the CPU-SM loop and the multiprogramming set.

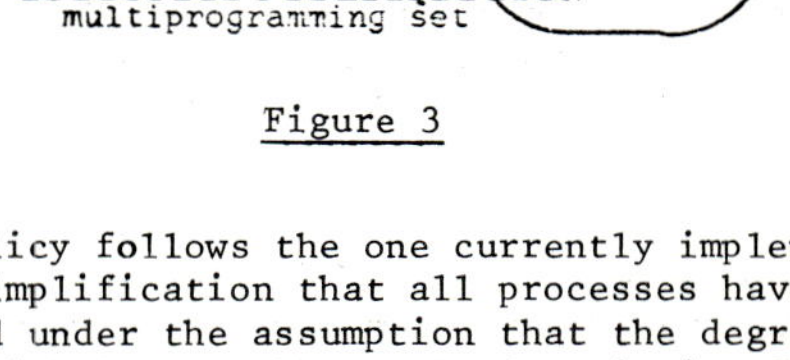

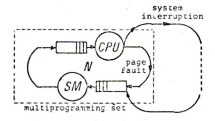

Figure 3

The memory management policy follows the one currently implemented in the EMAS system [1], with the main simplification that all processes have identical behaviour. The analysis is performed under the assumption that the degree of multiprogramming N is fixed : a process which leaves the CPU-SM loop is immediately replaced by another process. When a process enters the multiprogrammed set, it is allocated a fixed number of main memory page frames $m = M/N$, where M is the total number of main memory page frames. The working-sets of processes belonging to the multiprogramming set are periodically recorded so that when a process is reactivated in the multiprogramming set its working set can be preloaded into main memory by the SM station. The same model of swapping as in the previous section is assumed.

The basic idea of the real time analysis is to define a classification of programs being multiprogrammed according to their state X(t), to the station where they are queued or serviced, and the kind of service they are receiving from the SM station (page transfer, swapping out, swapping in), and the CPU station (execution, overheads). From these definitions and previous assumptions, the class of a program is a Markov chain, the transition diagram of which can be simply represented.

We thus obtain a multi-classes queueing network model [3]. The relative arrival rates to the different stations of the network can be easily derived from the results of the analysis presented in the previous section. The mean service times of the different classes of programs at each station are obtained by specifying the CPU overheads associated to the different I/O operations and the SM service characteristics. Let s(j) be the mean time to access and transfer j pages. For a typical paging drum s(j) would be approximated by

$$s(j) = x_a + j\, x_t$$

x_a = mean access time

x_t = mean transfer time.

The queueing network model is solved assuming that the discipline of service is processor sharing at the CPU and SM station. The solution of the model yields ρ_{CPU} the total CPU work rate ; ρ'_{CPU} the CPU work in user state ; ρ_{SPV} the CPU work rate in supervisor state ; ρ_{SM} the SM work rate ; δ the ratio of CPU time spent in user to total CPU time.

The model has been run with different sets of parameters obtained from measurements made on the EMAS system. Although the model does not describe the actual EMAS congifuration, since it is mostly restricted to the descriptions of the operations associated with the memory management policy, the results show that, as for as the influence of the swapping policy is concerned, it satisfactorily reproduces the performance improvement brought by preloading which have been observed on the real system. Moreover, it allows to investigate the sensitivity of these improvements to such factors as the overheads or the SM characteristics.

An example of the results obtained is presented in Table 1. The main observation is that the ratio δ is steadily increased by more than 10 % with prepaging as long as the system is not thrashing. Depending on the degree of multiprogramming and the utilization factor of the SM, this causes the CPU time spent in user state to increase by 2 % to 6 %. It can be noted that the maximum improvement is obtained for the optimum values of the degree of multiprogramming, i.e. the degree which maximizes ρ'_{CPU}. As already observed on measurements made on the EMAS system, the optimum degree of multiprogramming is smaller with PRP (N=3) than with PDP (N=4). Despites the service time characteristics of the SM, the utilization factor of the SM is slightly increased with prepaging, which indicates that the total amount of page transfers is greater with PRP than with PDP.

Table 1

	δ		ρ_{CPU}		ρ_{CPU}		ρ_{SPV}		ρ_{SM}	
N	PDP	PRP	PDP	PRP	PDP	PRP	PDP	PRP	PDP	PRP
1	.44	.58	.43	.41	.19	.24	.26	.17	.57	.59
2	.44	.59	.57	.54	.25	.32	.31	.22	.76	.78
3	.44	.57	.63	.61	.28	.35	.35	.27	.85	.86
4	.44	.47	.67	.62	.29	.29	.37	.34	.90	.92
5	.44	.36	.63	.59	.22	.21	.41	.39	.95	.96

CONCLUSION

The model we have presented provides a frame work for the analysis of the performance of a variety of swapping policies in page on demand multiprogramming systems. This analysis is based on a detailed characterization of the paging behavior of processes and of the system and hardware configuration. The model is computationally very simple, and we have shown that in can be used to evaluate the "trade-offs" involved in the implementation of a class of swapped working sets policy.

The results we have obtained illustrate how the different factors which have been introduced in the model interact and influence the performance of a preloading policy. As observed from the experiments we have presented, no factor is in itself determinant, but it is their combination which defines the final result. The observations we have made on the results obtained from the model corroborate the measurements made on the EMAS system. Moreover, they provide some understanding of the behavior of a swapped working sets policy, and indicate how this policy would work with other hardware configurations and in other situations.

ACKNOWLEDGEMENTS

We wish to thank Colin Adams, from the Computer Science Group at the University of Edinburgh, for many helpful discussions on the EMAS system.

BIBLIOGRAPHY

[1] J.C. ADAMS - "Evaluation of performance of the EMAS system" - Séminaires Modélisation et Mesures - IRIA-LABORIA - 1976.

[2] J.C. ADAMS, G.E. MILLIARD - "Performance measurements on the Edinburgh Multi-access system" - Proceedings of the International Computing Symposium 1975 - ACM/AFCET - Antibes - June 1975 - North-Holland Publishing Company (E. GELENBE, D. POTIER, ed.).

[3] F. BASKETT, K.M. CHANDY, R.R. MUNTZ, F.G. PALACIOS - "Open, closed and mixed networks of queues with different classes of customers" - J.ACM 22 - 2 - April 1975.

[4] M. PARENT, D. POTIER - "A note on the influence of program loading on the page fault rate" - 2nd International Workshop on Modelling and Performance Evaluation of Computer Systems - EURATOM-ISPRA - Stresa - Italy (October 1976)- North-Holland Publishing Company - To appear in Acta Informatica.

Measuring, Modelling and Evaluating Computer Systems,
H. Beilner and E. Gelenbe, (eds.)
© North-Holland Publishing Company (1977)

AN ANALYSIS OF THE PAGE SIZE PROBLEM USING A NETWORK ANALYZER

A. Krzesinski and P. Teunissen
Department of Computer Science
University of Stellenbosch
Stellenbosch, South Africa

A simple multiclass queueing network model of a demand paging computer system for determining the optimal page size is presented. The class change mechanism makes it possible to model the transient behaviour of a program as it gathers its working set. The lifetime between consecutive page faults is estimated by a Chamberlain function, modified to take the varying page size into account.

Numerical results for the analytical model are obtained with the use of SNAP, a general multiclass network analysis package.

1. INTRODUCTION

Recent developments in mixed, multiclass queueing network theory [1] have extended analytic solutions to a range of complex problems in computer systems performance evaluation. Queueing networks now afford a richness of structure that allows a detailed and realistic representation of the dynamics of program execution in a multiprogramming computer system. This paper seeks to illustrate a straight-forward multiclass network solution to a complex performance analysis problem whose solution previously required either a much simplified analytic approximation, or an expensive simulation analysis. The paper also serves to introduce an efficient, portable, multiclass network analysis program which will promote the use of multiclass network analysis amongst those who have neither the time nor the specialised mathematical skill to derive solutions for their own performance evaluation problems.

2. THE PROBLEM

The choice of page size is a central problem in the design of a demand paging computer system. Large page sizes do not cause thrashing upon program activation. However, large page sizes degrade the ability of the paging algorithm to identify the working sets and to maintain them in real storage. The consequent larger equilibrium page fault rates, together with the fact that for large page sizes, each page replacement will almost certainly require the replaced page to be copied to the paging device before the next page can be loaded, can lead to the paging device being overloaded. Small page sizes on the other hand allow the paging algorithm to identify and load the programs' working sets. Equilibrium page fault rates are correspondingly lower, and the small page sizes also place a lower page-out demand on the paging device. Nonetheless, the rapid demand for pages upon program activation can now lead to thrashing.

The effect of page size on system performance has been the subject of several studies. Belady [2] performed a simulation analysis of the problem. Gelenbe et al [3] have presented an approximate queueing analysis. A recent study by Parent and Potier [4] can be extended to give an approximate solution to the problem. A new analysis of the problem using a multiclass queueing network model demonstrates the suitability of these models for providing a simple and cost effective analysis of the dynamics of paging systems. The multiclass analysis allows the entire system to be modelled as a network of co-operating servers and customers. Global systems performance and sub-system interdependencies can be studied over a wide range of system configurations and workload compositions. Finally, the analysis provides a useful vehicle for demonstrating the capabilities of our network analysis program [5].

3. THE MODEL

Class Changes

Figures 1 and 2 represent a multiclass network model of a demand paging system. The network consists of a central CPU server, a Secondary Memory (SM) paging device, and a File Device (FD) to which the programs' I/O requests are directed.

The main storage of size M words is equipartitioned(*) amongst the N active programs so that, for a given page size p, the number W_p of pages of main storage allocated to each program is given by

$$W_p = \lfloor M/(Np) \rfloor \qquad \text{..........} \quad (1)$$

(*) It is possible to define a workload whose constituent programs have different locality, I/O and termination characteristics. Main storage could then be partitioned unequally among the N competing programs. Page stealing accross partition boundaries would still be forbidden.

where $\lfloor x \rfloor$ is the largest integer smaller than x.

The mean time between successive page faults depends upon the number of pages that the program has in main storage [6]. Each page placement therefore causes a change in the CPU service time distribution. This dependency between the CPU service rate and the main storage occupancy can readily be modelled by a system of customer classes and class changes. A program initially starts off as a customer of class 1 with only the page containing the start address loaded into main storage. Each subsequent page fault causes another page to be loaded. Thus for the i th fault $1 \leq i \leq W_p - 1$ the program changes class from class i to class i+1, returns to the CPU with an allocation of (i+1) pages, and receives CPU service appropriate to a program occupying (i+1) pages of main storage. Each customer of class i $1 \leq i \leq W_p$ therefore occupies i pages of main storage.

Fig 1 describes the behaviour of the customer classes 1 through W_p-1. These classes represent programs which do not yet occupy their full quota of W_p pages of main storage. The CPU is modelled as a Processor Sharing (PS) centre. This choice of centre is justified by noting that PS is the limiting behaviour of a time sliced round robin queue when the time slices become very small. The SM and the FD devices are modelled as exponential servers with (necessarily) FCFS service disciplines. The notation i X j is used to indicate a customer class change from class i to class j.

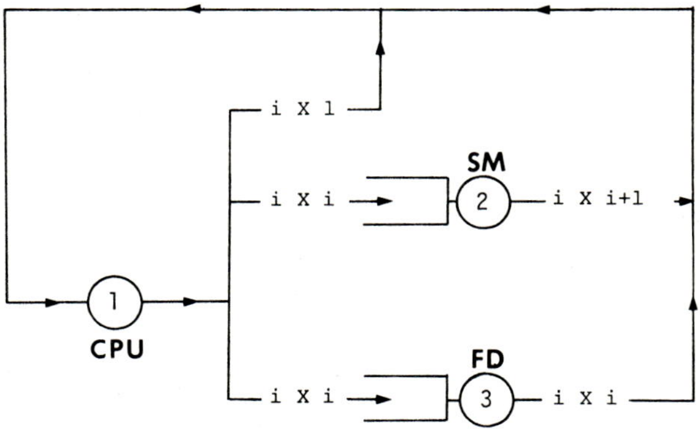

FIG 1 NETWORK MODEL WITH CLASS CHANGES
(PROGRAM LOADING PHASE)

Thus, with reference to Fig 1, if the program issues a page fault, it is routed to the SM centre, the page is loaded, and the program returns to the CPU as a customer of the next higher class. The memory allocation policy (eqn 1) restricts the first W_p faults to page-ins only. If the program issues an I/O request, it is routed to the FD centre and returns to the CPU as a customer of the same class. Program termination is modelled by a feedback route around the CPU centre. The supervisor program then activates a new program so that the number of active programs remains constant. The terminated program surrenders all its main storage to the newly activated program.

Fig 2 describes the behaviour of programs that have already loaded their full quota of W_p pages. An additional feedback route around the SM centre is now needed to model the page-outs that are necessary to free a page in main storage before a page-in can proceed. Program termination and I/O activity are as in Fig 1. Paging, I/O and termination overhead are ignored.

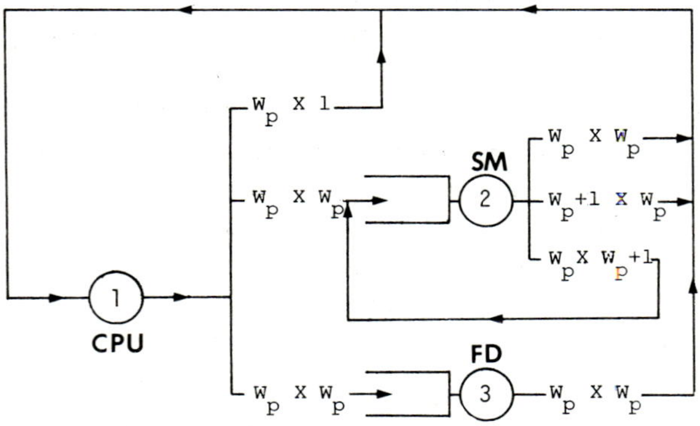

FIG 2 NETWORK MODEL WITH CLASS CHANGES
(AFTER PROGRAM LOADING PHASE)

Service Rates

The network service rates and branching probabilities are modelled as in [7]. Let D be the mean total CPU time required by the programs to complete. Let r be the mean CPU time between successive I/O transfers, and let $q_{i,p}$ be the mean CPU time between successive pages faults when the program has i pages of size p words each in main storage. Assuming the CPU times, inter I/O times and inter page fault times to be exponentially distributed, then the CPU service rate for a program of class i is an exponentially distributed random variable with mean

$$\mu_{1,i} = 1/q_{i,p} + 1/r + 1/D$$

Chamberlin et al [6] proposed the following function to estimate the mean time between page faults

$$q_i = \frac{2B}{1 + (C/i)^2} \qquad \text{..........} \quad (2)$$

where q_i is the mean time between page faults when the program has been allocated i pages of main storage. The ratio B/C is a measure of program locality such that C is the number of pages that will give a program half of its maximum expected time (2B) between page faults. However, a reference to a single word causes the entire page within which the word resides to be loaded into main storage. Many words within the page might never be referenced during the time that the page is in main storage. The presence of unreferenced words within a referenced page is referred to as "superfluity" or as "logical fragmentation", and the effect of logical fragmentation on the page fault rate is particularily evident when the page size is large, and/or when the program locality is poor. The dependence of logical fragmentation on the page size p can be approximated by means of a "pull/claim" ratio $\beta(p)$ which is defined as the ratio of the number of words paged in to the name space size of the program measured in words. Belady [2] obtained an empirical formula for $\beta(p)$.

$$\beta(p) = 0.25 + 0.06 \log_2 p$$

Consider the lifetime function (eqn 2) where C_o pages of size p_o give a program half its expected largest lifetime $2B_o$. For any other page size p, the number of words loaded will be bounded above by $C_o\, p_o\, \beta(p) \,/\, \beta(p_o)$ so that C_o pages of size p_o are equivalent to $C_p = \lfloor C_o\, p_o\, \beta(p) \,/\, p\, \beta(p_o) \rfloor$ pages of size p, where C_p has been rounded to the nearest integer.

The Chamberlin function can now be modified to take logical fragmentation into account, so that the mean time between page faults $q_{i,p}$ for a program having i pages of size p in main storage is given by

$$q_{i,p} = \frac{2B_o}{1 + (C_p/i)^2} \qquad \text{.........} \quad (3)$$

where $$C_p = \frac{C_o\, p_o\, \beta(p)}{p \quad \beta(p_o)}$$

is the number of pages of size p giving the program half its largest expected lifetime.

Fig 3 plots lifetime against memory allocated for several page sizes for a program displaying good locality of reference (B_0 = 10 msecs when C_0 = 5 pages of length 1024 words). Smaller page sizes imply less logical fragmentation. Main storage space is therefore available to contain the programs' working sets so that the mean time between page faults increases.

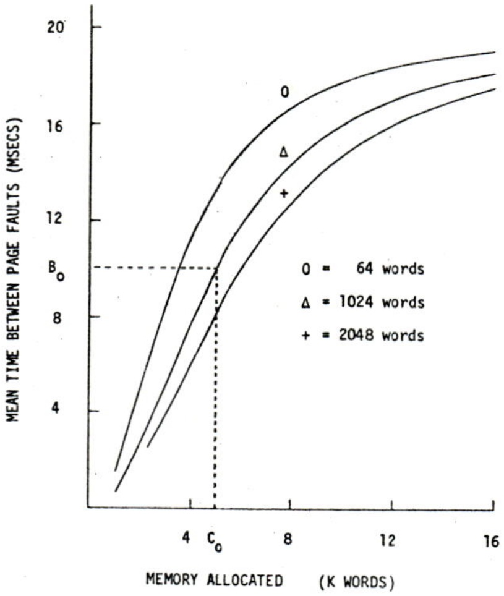

FIG 3 CHAMBERLIN FUNCTION FOR SEVERAL PAGE SIZES

The SM device is modelled either as a drum or as an Extended magnetic Core Storage unit (ECS). When modelled as a drum, if the time for one drum revolution is t msecs, and each track contains w words, then the mean service rate of the SM device is given by

$$\mu_2 = (t/2 + tw/p)^{-1}$$

where p is the page size in words. Typically, t is 8 msecs and w is 8192 words. An ECS allows d words to be transmitted per ECS memory cycle. If the initial ECS access time is a msecs, and the ECS cycle time is c msecs, then the mean service rate of the SM device is given by

$$\mu_2 = (a + pc/d)^{-1}$$

Typically, a is 3 μsecs, c is 1 μsec, and d is 10 words. The service rate of the FD is independent of the page size and is kept constant at μ_3.

Branching Probabilities

The paths followed by the programs through the network (Figs 2 and 3) are described by a stochastic transition matrix $\underset{\sim}{e}$ where

$e_{i,r;j,s}$ = Probability (upon completion of service at centre i, the customer of class r proceeds directly to centre j and changes class to class s) .... (4)

Given a page size p, the probability of a program page faulting, leaving the CPU and queueing at the paging device is given by

$$e_{1,i;2,i} = (\mu_{1,i}\ q_{i,p})^{-1}$$

The probability of a program leaving the CPU to perform an I/O operation is given by

$$e_{1,i;3,i} = (\mu_{1,i}\ r)^{-1}$$

The probability of a program terminating and a new program being immediately initiated is given by

$$e_{1,i;1,1} = (\mu_{1,i}\ D)^{-1}$$

The page-outs of modified pages are modelled by a feedback route around the SM centre. Belady [2] obtained an empirical "push/pull" ratio $\gamma(p)$ which describes the probability that a page was modified when it was last resident in main storage.

$$\gamma(p) = 0.20 + 0.06 \log_2 p$$

The probability of a modified page being replaced so that the page-in of the new page is preceeded by the page-out of the modified page, is given by

$$e_{2,W_p;2,W_p+1} = \gamma(p)$$

The probability of an unmodified page being replaced is given by

$$e_{2,W_p;1,W_p} = 1 - \gamma(p)$$

All other elements of the transition matrix $\underset{\sim}{e}$ are one or zero.

4. PERFORMANCE MEASURES

Gelenbe et al [3] introduce the Wasted Space Time Integral (WSTI) as a measure of the efficiency of a demand paging system. The WSTI is the sum of all the space-time products attributable to paging overhead that lead to an underutilisation of main storage. The WSTI is the sum of four components

- internal fragmentation: the last page of a program is, on the average, only half filled
- page table fragmentation: main storage space is required for the page tables
- logical fragmentation: words which are unnecessarily loaded cause an underutilisation of main storage
- page wait contribution: upon a page fault, the entire memory space of a program is wasted until the required page is loaded into main storage.

It must be noted that the multiclass network model differs in several important aspects from the queueing model of Gelenbe et al [3]. The multiclass model represents the paging system as an entire, synergistic network, rather than a disjoint set of independent queues. File activity is expressly taken onto account. A Chamberlin function (eqn 2) rather than a linear approximation is used to describe the lifetime curve. The lifetime curve is also adjusted to take logical fragmentation into account (eqn 3). Page-outs are explicitly accounted for. Finally, the time spent by a program in the CPU queue after a page fault has occurred is not regarded as contributing to the WSTI since this delay is considered as a multiprogramming rather than as a paging overhead.

5. NETWORK ANALYSIS PROGRAM

Figs 4 through 7 are generated by our network analysis program SNAP [5]. Written in FORTRAN IV, SNAP provides efficient solutions to mixed, multiclass queueing networks of the type analysed by Baskett et al [1]. Network parameters for SNAP are solicited and verified by an interactive data entry procedure. SNAP execution is guided by simple control directives. These statements direct repetitive executions of SNAP allowing selected network parameters to be varied in defined increments, and allowing user defined subroutines to compute network parameters at run time. SNAP output consists of a tabulated report of utilisations, queue lengths, queue delays, cycle times and throughputs per service centre per customer class. Selected subsets of the analysis results can be directed to a line printer or to a graph plotter for graphical display.

A full description of SNAP can be found in [5] and the program itself is available upon request from the authors.

The marginal distributions computed by SNAP have been reduced [8,5] so that summations over customer classes are replaced by summations over the ergodic subchains defined by the network. This greatly reduces the amount of computation required for network solutions. Recall that W_p customer classes are required to model program initiation when the page size is of length p words. The paging computer is modelled as a network of N centres serving

$$L = \sum_{i=1}^{W_p} n_i$$

customers, where n_i is the number of customers of class i. The total number of network states $|S| = |\{(S_1 .. S_i .. S_N)\}|$ where S_i = state of centre i = $(n_1 .. n_i .. n_{W_p})$ is given by

$$|S| = \binom{W_p + L - 1}{L} \binom{L + N - 1}{N}$$

Sixty four customer classes are required to model program initiation for multiprogramming level 8 in a main store of size 132 K words when the page length is 256 words. The network has 3 centres, so that $|S| = 1.3 \times 10^{12}$ states. In terms of its subchains however, the same network defines a single closed subchain with a total of only

$$\binom{L + N - 1}{N} = 120 \text{ states!}$$

SNAP makes extensive use of sparse matrix techniques to minimise the amount of main storage needed for its execution. The transition matrix $\underset{\sim}{e}$ (eqn 4) for example is largely empty, and considerable space saving results from sparse matrix encoding of the elements of $\underset{\sim}{e}$. Large networks require large sets of linear equations to be solved. These equations are too large to be held in main storage, so out-of-core solution techniques have to be employed. Sparse matrix encoding, together with the out-of-core solver allow SNAP to solve large networks without recourse to automatic or manual memory overlaying techniques. Table 1 compares the resource requirements of SNAP with and without the sparse matrix/out-of-core solver. Considerable space saving is obtained, though at the expense of CPU and I/O overhead.

Table 1 SNAP Resource Requirements

Page size	256	512	1024	2048	4096
Customer classes	64	32	16	8	4
Main store size (K words)	122 *18*	40 *15*	20 *14*	14 *13*	13 *12*
CPU time (secs)	62.53	9.79 *38.80*	2.34 *7.06*	0.94 *1.33*	0.56 *0.78*
disc time (secs)	1.13	0.95 *154.60*	0.87 *41.97*	0.81 *12.49*	0.79 *4.31*

no sparse matrix, in-core solver/*sparse matrix, out-of-core solver*

6. RESULTS

Fig 4 reveals that for short jobs, a page size of 1024 words is optimal for a drum paging device. The optimal page size is independent of the program locality measure (B_0/C_0). These results are in good agreement with those of Gelenbe et al [3]. Fig 5 however, reveals that the ratio of initial page loading time to the total compute time of a program is the primary factor that influences the optimal page size. Though smaller page sizes lead to thrashing upon program activation, the thrashing is only significant when the mean compute time between program deactivations is relatively short. As the compute time increases, the WSTI reflects more the equilibrium page fault behaviour of the workload. Smaller page sizes are now favoured since they allow the paging algorithm to better identify the programs' working sets. Furthermore, the multiclass model takes into account the limited size of the multiprogramming mix. The global page fault rate decreases as the congestion at the paging device increases. In [3] the global page fault rate is kept constant and the queue length at the paging device is therefore over estimated. The page wait contribution to the WSTI in [3] is therefore to high.

The page load approximation model of Parent and Potier [4] can easily be extended

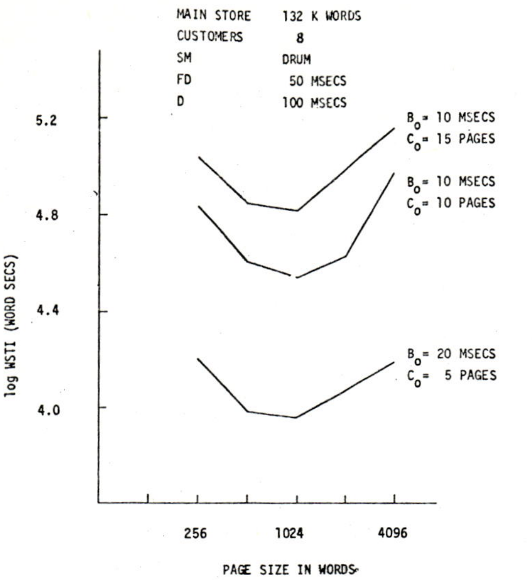

Fig 4 Optimal page size (Drum paging device)

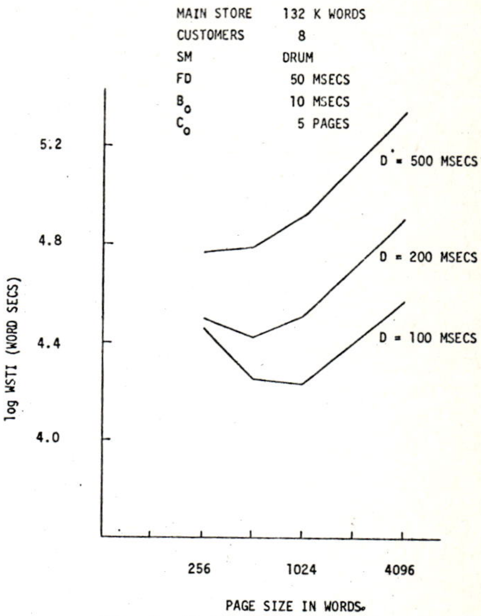

Fig 5 Optimal page size (Drum paging device)

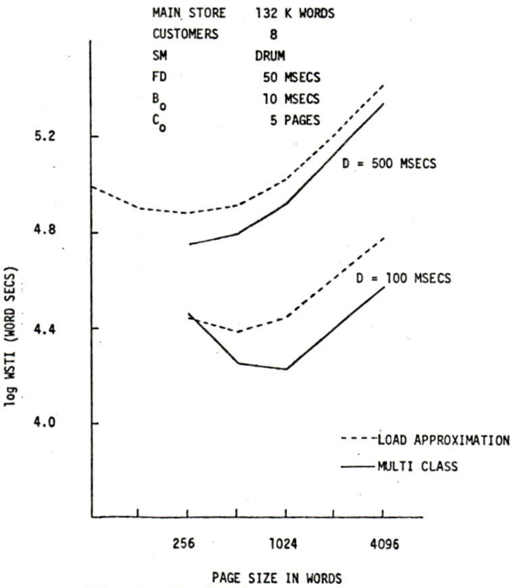

Fig 6 Optimal page size (Drum paging device)

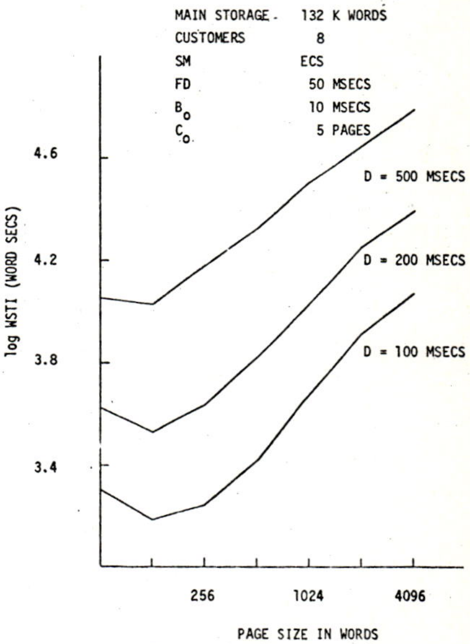

Fig 7 Optimal page size (ECS paging device)

to include the effect of page size on the Chamberlin function (eqn 3). Fig 6 reveals this simple model to be in good agreement with the multiclass model. The simple model also reveals (Fig 7) that a page size os 128 words is optimal for an ECS paging device. The higher speed of the ECS minimises the effect of thrashing so that the optimal page size is no longer dependent upon the mean CPU requirements of the workload.

References

1. Baskett, F. et al: Open, Closed and Mixed Networks of Queues with Different Classes of Customers. JACM, Vol. 22, No. 2, 248-260 (April 1975).
2. Belady, L.A.: A study of replacement algorithms for a virtual-storage computer. IBM Systems Journal, Vol. 5, No. 2, 78-160, (1966).
3. Gelenbe, E. et al: Page Size in Demand-Paging Systems. Acta Informatica, Vol. 3, 1-23 (1973).
4. Parent, M. and Potier, D.: A Note on the Influence of Program Loading on the Page Fault Rate. Proc. 2nd Int. Workshop on Modelling and Performance Evaluation of Computer Systems, 267-285 (Oct 1976).
5. Krzesinski, A. and Teunissen, P.: SNAP: Network Analysis Program User's Manual, Tech. Rep. 76/2, Dept. of Computer Science, University of Stellenbosch, South Africa.
6. Chamberlin, D.D. et al: An Analysis of Page Allocation Strategies for Multiprogramming Systems. IBM J. Res. Develop., 404-412 (Sept 1973).
7. Brandwajn, A.: A Model of a Virtual Memory System. Acta Informatica, Vol. 6, No. 4, 365-386 (1976).
8. Muntz, R.R. and Wong, J.: Efficient Computational Procedures for Closed Queueing Networks with the Product Form Solution. Modelling and Measurement Note No. 17, Computer Science Dept., School of Eng. and Applied Sci., U. of California, Los Angeles.

Measuring, Modelling and Evaluating Computer Systems,
H. Beilner and E. Gelenbe, (eds.)
© North-Holland Publishing Company (1977)

ON SCANNING-DISKS AND THE ANALYSIS OF THEIR STEADY STATE BEHAVIOR

Edward G. Coffman, Jr.
Columbia University
New York, N.Y. 10027

Micha Hofra
The Technion
Haifa, Israel

This paper describes and motivates the SCAN policy, used to schedule read/write requests at a moving-arm disk device, when fast response over the entire disk area is at a premium. Several approximate analyses that have appeared in the literature are described. A new approach is then presented, which handles precisely the dependence structure between queues accumulated at different cylinders. The arrival process of r/w requests to each cylinder is assumed Poisson, homogeneous in time. A relatively efficient algorithm, to numerically evaluate the mean waiting time at each cylinder, is presented and its complexity is analysed.

Further extensions of the model, to capture additional details of realistic situations are suggested, and some of the implications of incorporating them are discussed (these include distributed record lengths, skipping unreferenced cylinders and letting successive arrivals' targets cylinders be dependent variables).

A. INTRODUCTION

A1. The realization that the quality of service provided by a computing system depends largely, sometimes critically on the methods it uses to handle its secondary memory requirements, is now commonplace, and statements to this and similar effects are frequent. What is less easy to come by is a precise account of the performance of these memory modules, and its dependence on the physical characteristics and methods of operation. This paper presents such an account for a specific case: a disk, or disk-like device used under the so-called SCAN policy, as explained below in Paragraph B5.

A2. The term 'a disk-like device' is intended to aggregate semi-random access devices, on which the recording/reading mechanism can assume a number of positions, from which only a section of the device can be serviced continuously without further mechanical motion (in addition to the rotation of the surfaces). In the following everything is given in disk terminology, which we assume is familiar. If further specifications of these devices is desired, references [D, F and GM] may be consulted.

A3. Section B describes various methods of request scheduling for disks; Section C defines a mathematical model for the SCAN policy; Section D is a short survey of several approximate analyses of this and related models in accessible publications; Section E is a precise analysis of the model of section C; Section F deals with numerical methods to calculate moments of the waiting time and queue lenghts; Section G concludes with a description of extensions of the model and their impact on the analysis. In the references we collect several germane papers beyond those cited in the text.

B. SCHEDULING POLICIES

B1. The fact of a disk being a non-random access device manifests itself in the requirement to perform a relatively long operation - a 'seek' - between accesses to distinct cylinders; thus the time to process a batch of requests may depend on the order of service. The purpose of a scheduling policy is to devise a processing order, such as to optimize a suitable measure over the processing times. It is natural that waiting time to completion of a request is the variable most often chosen as the basis of such measures, and thus its calculation is the main thrust of the analyses we present. Usually, interest is focused on the first two moments.

B2. The simplest scheduling policy to implement, in terms of the required data structures and hardware, is a 'linear' queue - FCFS. This, as can be shown and is inituitively clear, results in many more seeks than the alternatives require, and relatively long seeks, at that.

B3. Any improvement over FCFS requires keeping track of the requests according to their target cylinders. Due to the relatively long time required to perform a seek, most of the improved policies schedule all the requests for the 'current' cylinder - this is the cylinder that can be accessed without performing a seek - before all other pending requests. (Paragraph B6 describes variants of this 'rule'.) Under these conditions the scheduling of requests reduces to selection of cylinders. Scheduling to reduce rotational latency, in the manner that is done for drums, is outside the scope of this paper.

There are two basic approaches that have been adopted for the solution of this decision problem.

B4. SSTF - an acronym for shortest-seek-time-first. Under this policy the arm performs a seek, after all the requests to the current cylinder are served, to the nearest cylinder that has a waiting request. This policy is accredited with achieving the shortest over-all mean waiting time (under certain conditions). At the same time, however, the variance of this time may be relatively large, and with many reasonable distributions of the request addresses over the disk surface, intolerably so.

B5. SCAN - under this policy the motion of the arm is systemized, so as to reduce the variance of the waiting time when compared with SSTF; naturally, a price is exacted: an increase in the mean waiting time. More specifically, at any time the arm is in one of two modes, 'in', or 'out'. In the first mode, the arm moves, when a seek is required, towards the disk spindle until a cylinder with pending requests is encountered. When no such a cylinder exists, the mode of the arm is changed, and its direction of motion reversed. Thus the arm performs a 'shuttle' service across the disk. The normal method of operation differs from this idealized description in several details; however, the only one that is of interest here is that the state of the cylinder queues is not examined en passant, but instead, before the arm starts moving; the appropriate target cylinder is determined from the state of the queues, and a seek operation is initiated which will terminate only when that cylinder is reached (i.e., arrivals during the seek operation do not alter its destination). This last item is the basis of the extension discussed in Paragraph G3.

B6. The SCAN policy gave rise to several other variants which increased its tendency to reduce the variance of the waiting time to completion of requests, at the expense of increasing the overall mean. The basis for one is that the above described SCAN policy gives preferential treatment to centrally located cylinders over the extreme ones, since the visits of the arm to the center of its span are more evenly distributed in time. In the variation called C-SCAN [T] the arm stops for reading/writing only in one mode, and the other is only used for a long return seek across the whole disk. In this fashion all the cylinders may be served with the same frequency (usually there are still differences but these result from differences in the input patterns, and do not depend on the geometry of the device.) Another variation, that curbs the increase of the variance with the load on the system, inducts to service in a given cycle only those requests that are queued when the seek to 'their' cylinder terminated; subsequent arrivals to that cylinder will be detained until the next cycle. In the sequel, except for section G, we limit the discussion to the pure SCAN policy.

C. MATHEMATICAL MODEL

C1. For the purposes of the analysis given here, the disk may be viewed as comprising M service points (cylinders) arranged along a line. At any point in time the server (arm) is either located at one of these points (performing an I/O operation) or it is in motion between them (seeking). In this model seeks are done to adjacent cylinders only and require $\underline{a}$ time units. Each I/O operation requires a constant, fixed amount of time to complete, corresponding to the reading or writing of an entire track. We shall take this to be T time units. Note that we make no distinction here between reads and writes. The arrival process of requests for the m-th cylinder is a homogeneous Poisson process with rate λ_m. The arrival processes to distinct cylinders are assumed independent of each other and the state of the system (infinite sources and waiting rooms are thus implied). The order of service at each cylinder is FCFS. Transition times between seek termination and beginning of service, as well as between services are assumed to be zero. Under these assumptions the number of requests at each queue and the position of the arm at epochs of service termination form an embedded Markov chain.

D. SUMMARY OF PUBLISHED ANALYSES

D1. Denning, in a paper that is to our knowledge the first description of the SCAN policy [D], calculates an approximation for the expected waiting time of a request. His analysis assumes a steady-state mean backlog of n requests, uniformly distributed across the disk; then he notes that an arrival finds the arm at a distance from its destination, which, when measured in units of cylinders, has the mean value $M/3$. Then the arm has a probability of 1/2 of being in each mode, and all this allows us to conclude that the expected number of cylinders the arm has to transverse before servicing the observed request is $2M/3$, and it serves $2n/3$ requests on the way; he finally obtains (in terms of our model)

$$E(W_{Den}) = 2(Ma + nT)/3 \tag{1}$$

Implicit here is an assumption that $n \ll M$, which allows any event with more than one request at a cylinder to be neglected.

D2. Teorey [T] dispenses with this last assumption, and introduces additional details into the structure of the disk, assuming t tracks (surfaces) at each cylinder and m sectors per track. Requests are constrained, however, to specify exactly one sector. The basic approach of assuming a fixed mean backlog is retained here as well. Proceeding with 'mean value' arguments, he defines n' as the mean number of requests serviced in one sweep of the arm. Since the arrivals are assumed to address each cylinder with equal probability, it is also reasonable to assume that the expected number of requests per cylinder served by the arm is linear in the distance of the cylinder from the beginning of the current sweep. This last assumption allows the following estimate for M_1, the number of occupied cylinders the arm encounters in one sweep:

$$M_1 = M - \sum_{k=1}^{M} \left(1-\frac{k-1}{M-1} \cdot \frac{2}{M}\right)^{n'} \quad . \tag{2}$$

The quantity n' is further related to M_1 through the relationship

$$n' = \lambda T_{SW} \tag{3}$$

where T_{SW} is the time required for one full sweep of the arm; this is given in terms of our model (which obscure to some extent the secondary details of Teorey's model) as

$$T_{SW} = M_1\left(\frac{M}{M_1} a+T\right) + (n'-M_1)T_1 \quad , \tag{4}$$

(T_1 is the service time when no seek is required). Iteration between the relations (2)-(4) yields values for n' and M_1. The mean and variance of the waiting time are then calculated by summing over all combinations of the mutual locations of the arm and an arriving request, and using the calculated values of n' and M_1 to evaluate the work the system will do until that request is served.

D3. We note that in this analysis, although the arguments are wholly based on 'average value' reasoning, the effect of the direction of the sweep (i.e. - there are fewer requests "behind" the arm, than in front of it) is assimilated into the analysis. This approach cannot handle nonuniform addressing patterns and neglects effects of transients in the underlying stochastic processes, which would increase the maximal waiting times and queue lengths (as well as their variances) materially above the values predicted for them by this analysis.

D4. An exact analysis of the SCAN policy is attempted in [CKR], subject to a continuous approximation for the cylinder address space. Unfortunately, although exact results are obtained for the time taken by the disk arm to execute an entire crossing in equilibrium, the subsequent results for conditional waiting times are approximate at best; an error arises which is related to the "paradox of residual life" (proper account is not taken of the fact that random arrivals are more likely to encounter the disk arm executing relatively long crossings). Another mathematical analysis [0] has appeared on this subject, and it too has manifested an error; in this case certain dependent random variables are mistakenly treated as independent. Indeed, the shortcomings of the above results have been one of the principal motivations for the present paper.

E. ANALYSIS OF THE MODEL

E1. We develop now an analysis of the model presented in section C, taking into account its complete stochastic structure. The analysis is essentially based on work by Eisenberg [E], except that the important relation (9) is derived here from probablistic arguments, rather than through analytical requirements. His notation will be employed wherever possible, to facilitate the carrying over of the results we need.

E2. We first introduce the important notion of a "stage". The arm moves in cycles of stages, numbered 1 to 2M-2; the correspondence between the i-th stage and cylinder m_i is given by

$$m_i = \begin{cases} i & 1 \leq i < M \\ 2M-i & M \leq i \leq 2M-2 \end{cases} \tag{1}$$

Further notation:

$\vec{n} = (n_1,\ldots,n_M)$ is a description of the state of the queues at the cylinders; when the position of the arm is also given, the state of the complete system is entirely specified.

$\pi^i(t;\vec{n})$ = number of service terminations at stage i, which occur during the time (0,t) at stage $\vec{n}$*.

$\alpha^i(t;\vec{n})$ = number of stage i beginnings which occur during (0,t) at state $\vec{n}$.

$\beta^i(t;\vec{n})$ = number of stage i completions which occur during (0,t) at state $\vec{n}$.

By summing over all the suitable states n we obtain the total number of stage i beginnings and completions in the period (0,t): $\alpha^i(t)$ and $\beta^i(t)$, respectively. By summing over i as well $\pi(t)$ is correspondingly obtained.

These quantities describe transitions of an irreducible, aperiodic Markov chain. If $\Sigma\,\lambda_m < 1/T$, the chain is also recurrent, and the following limits exist with probability one:

$$\lim_{t\to\infty} [\pi^i(t;\vec{n})/\pi(t)] = \pi^i_{\vec{n}} \quad ; \quad \lim_{t\to\infty} [\alpha^i(t;\vec{n})/\alpha^i(t)] = \alpha^i_{\vec{n}}$$
$$\lim_{t\to\infty} [\beta^i(t;\vec{n})/\beta^i(t)] = \beta^i_{\vec{n}} \quad . \tag{2}$$

*A service or stage completion occurs at state n if this is the state immediately <u>after</u> the completion.

These quantities are the steady state probabilities at the correspondingly defined epochs. We shall employ the related probability generating functions (pgf's), e.g.

$$\pi^i(z) = \sum_{n_1=0}^{\infty} \cdots \sum_{n_M=0}^{\infty} \pi^i_{n_1,\ldots,n_M} z_1^{n_1} \cdots z_M^{n_M} ,$$

with $\alpha^i(z)$ and $\beta^i(z)$ similarly defined.

E3. The probability distribution of the number of arrivals to each cylinder during a time with probability distribution function (pdf) $F(.)$ is given by:

$$p(F;n_1,\ldots n_n) = \int_{t=0}^{\infty} \frac{(\lambda_1 t)^{n_1}}{n_1!} \cdots \frac{(\lambda_M t)^{n_n}}{n_M!} e^{-\lambda t} dF(t);\ \lambda = \sum_{n=1}^{M} \lambda_m \tag{3}$$

If $L(.)$ is the LST corresponding to $F(.)$ then the pgf of $p(..)$ is given by

$$p(F;\vec{z}) = L(\lambda_1-\lambda_1 z_1 \ldots + \lambda_M - \lambda_M z_M) = \tilde{L}(\vec{z}) \tag{4}$$

Note that $\tilde{L}(.)$ has a vector argument.

E4. Using this notation, and further denoting by $\tilde{T}(.)$ and $\tilde{A}(.)$ the transforms that correspond respectively to the service and seek times, we immediately obtain, using the fact that the pgf of a sum of independent variables is the product of their respective pgf's

$$\alpha^i(\vec{z}) = \beta^{i-1}(z)\tilde{A}(\vec{z}) \tag{5}$$

relating the states of the system "across" a seek from stage i-1 to stage i.

E5. To obtain a similar relation "across" the i-th stage we need the distribution of the busy period of the arm at cylinder m_i. The transform of this distribution, denoted $B_{m_i}(.)$ is the solution of the equation

$$B_m(s) = \exp[-T(s+\lambda_m-\lambda_m B_m(s))] \tag{6}$$

Writing

$$\beta^i_{\vec{n}} = \sum_{\vec{k}} \alpha^i_{\vec{k}}\, p(B^{*\,k_i}_{m_i}; \vec{n} - \vec{k}), \tag{7}$$

where $p(B^{*\,k_i}_{m_i};.)$ is the probability distribution of arrivals, as given in (3), during a time which is distributed as the k_i-fold convolution of the busy period of the arm at cylinder m_i. Taking generating functions of both sides and using the fact that at the end of the i-th stage (when $\beta^i_{\vec{n}}$ is evaluated) $n_i = 0$, we obtain the key relation

$$\beta^i(\vec{z}) = \alpha^i(\vec{z}^{(i)}) \tag{8}$$

where the superscript i over z denotes that the m_i-th component there is replaced by $B_{m_i}(\sum_{k \neq m_i} \lambda_k - \lambda_k z_k)$. Combining (5) with (8) we finally obtain

$$\beta^i(\vec{z}) = \beta^{i-1}(\vec{z}^{(i)})\tilde{A}(\vec{z}^{(i)}) \tag{9}$$

which is the basis for the numerical calculations we shall develop. This equation could also be used, as in [E], as the basis of a formal solution for the β functions, but this solution is of limited utility and will not be presented here.

E6. To calculate the waiting time distribution we proceed in a manner very similar to that of Eisenberg in [E]. First we note that since the order of service within each cylinder queue is FCFS, the requests queued at service termination arrived during the waiting and service durations of the request just completed. Hence, at the i-th stage,

Prob(queue m_i holds n_{m_i} customers at the epoch of service termination)

$$= \pi^i_{n_{m_i}} / \pi^i$$

$$= \int \frac{(\lambda_{m_i} t)^{n_{m_i}}}{(n_{m_i})!} e^{-\lambda m_i t}\, d\{ F_W i * F_S(t) \} \tag{10}$$

where $\pi^i_{n_{m_i}} = \Sigma_{n_m;\ m\neq m_i} \pi^i_{\vec{n}}$ is the marginal queue length distribution of queue m_i at stage i service completions, with pgf $\pi^i(z)$, and $\pi^i = \sum_k \pi^i_k = \pi^i(1)$. Calculating the generating functions of both sides we obtain

$$L_{W^i}(s) = \frac{\pi^i(1-s/\lambda_{m_i})}{\pi^i \exp(-Ts)} \quad . \tag{11}$$

The distribution of waiting time at queue m, $F_{W_m}(.)$, is given, by averaging over the stages where $m_i = m$, as

$$F_{W_m}(t) = \frac{\pi^m F_{W^m}(t) + \pi^{2M-m} F_{W^{2M-m}}(t)}{\pi^m + \pi^{2M-m}} \tag{12}$$

E7. A relation is now required between $\beta^i(\vec{z})$, which we can calculate (at least in principle) from (9), and the $\pi^i(.)$ which appear here. This can be taken directly from [E, p.444]

$$\pi^i(z) = \gamma\tilde{T}(\vec{z}) \frac{\vec{\alpha}^i(\vec{z}) - \beta^i(\vec{z})}{z_{m_i} - \tilde{s}(\vec{z})} \tag{13}$$

where $\tilde{T}(\vec{z}) = \exp(-T\sum_m \lambda_m(1-z_m))$, and γ(the limiting ratio of the number of stage completions to the number of services rendered all over) is given by $(1-\Sigma\rho_m)/2a\lambda(M-1)$, ρ_m being the utilization level of cylinder m, $\lambda_m T$. π^i can be expressed, through (13) in terms of first derivatives of β^{i-1} at $\vec{z} = \vec{1}$:

$$\pi^i = \frac{\gamma}{1-\rho_{m_i}} (\beta^{i-1}_{z_{m_i}} + a\lambda_{m_i}) \quad . \tag{14}$$

The calculation of these derivatives is the subject of the next section. Substituting into (11) we obtain (remembering that $\beta^i(z)$ does not depend on z_{m_i})

$$L_{W^i}(s) = \frac{\gamma\lambda_{m_i}}{\pi^i} \frac{1-\alpha^i(1,\ldots,1,1-\frac{s}{\lambda_{m_i}},\ldots,1)}{s-\lambda_{m_i}+\lambda_{m_i}\exp(-Ts)} \tag{15}$$

Differentiating (15) at $s=0$ yields the desired mean value of W^i:

$$E(W^i) = \frac{\beta^{i-1}_{m_i m_i} + 2a\lambda_{m_i}\beta^{i-1}_{m_i} + a^2\lambda^2_{m_i}}{2\lambda_{m_i}(a\lambda_{m_i} + \beta^{i-1}_{m_i})} + \frac{T\rho_{m_i}}{2(1-\rho_{m_i})} \tag{16}$$

where

$$\beta^i_m = \frac{\partial\beta^i(\vec{z})}{\partial z_m}\Big|_{\vec{z}=\vec{1}} \quad , \quad \beta^i_{m,n} = \frac{\partial^2\beta^i(\vec{z})}{\partial z_m \partial z_n}\Big|_{\vec{z}=\vec{1}} \tag{17}$$

E8. The lengths of queues accumulated at the individual cylinders are of interest as well, for practical reasons. The mean value, $E(n_m)$, at request completion epochs (which is the same here as the long-term average) is simply given, using Little's theorem, as $\lambda_m E(W_m)$. To obtain higher moments one needs only to differentiate (13) further, and accumulate contributions, as in (12). The same derivatives of the β functions recur, and it is to their investigation that we now turn our attention.

F. NUMERICAL CALCULATIONS

F1. The expressions we derived for $E(W^i)$ and higher moments include the partial derivatives of the functions $\beta^i(\vec{z})$ at $\vec{z}=\vec{1}$. We show here how these can be calculated. The basis is equation (E9). We shall also have use for the following values and notation:

$$-B'_m(0) = T/(1-\rho_m) \equiv T\gamma_m \tag{1}$$

$$B''_m(0) = T^2\gamma^3_m \tag{2}$$

$$\frac{\partial z^{(i)}_{m_i}}{\partial z_m} = -(1-\delta_{m,m_i})\lambda_m B'_{m_i}[\sum_{j\neq m_i} \lambda_j(1-z_j)] \equiv \zeta_m^{m_i}(\vec{z}) \tag{3}$$

$$\zeta_m^{m_i}(\vec{1}) \equiv \zeta_m^{m_i} = (1-\delta_{m,m_i})\rho_m\gamma_{m_i} \tag{4}$$

We get by straightforward calculation

$$\frac{\partial\tilde{A}(\vec{z}^{(i)})}{\partial z_m} = a(1-\delta_{m,m_i})\tilde{A}(\vec{z}^{(i)})[\lambda_m+\lambda_{m_i}\zeta_m^{m_i}(\vec{z})] \tag{5'}$$

At $\vec{z} = \vec{1}$ the right-hand side becomes $(1-\delta_{m,m_i})a\lambda_m\gamma_{m_i}$.

E2. Proceeding from (E9) we get

$$\frac{d\beta^i(\vec{z})}{dz_m} = \frac{\partial\beta^i(\vec{z})}{\partial z_m} = \beta^i_m(\vec{z}) = (1-\delta_{m,m_i})\{\beta^{i-1}_m(\vec{z}^{(i)})\tilde{A}(\vec{z}^{(i)}) + \beta^{i-1}_{m_i}(\vec{z}^{(i)})\tilde{A}(\vec{z}^{(i)})\zeta_m^{m_i}(\vec{z}) + a\beta^i(\vec{z})[\lambda_m+\lambda_{m_i}\zeta_m^{m_i}(\vec{z})]\} \tag{5}$$

At $\vec{z} = \vec{1}$ these derivatives yield

$$\beta^i_m = (1-\delta_{m,m_i})\{\beta^{i-1}_m+\beta^{i-1}_{m_i}\rho_m\gamma_{m_i}+a\lambda_m\gamma_{m_i}\} \qquad 1\le i\le 2M-2, \quad 1\le m\le M \tag{6}$$

Differentiating $\beta^i_m(\vec{z})$ in (5) by z_n, and evaluating at $\vec{z} = \vec{1}$, we find

$$\beta^{i}_{m,n} = (1-\delta_{m,m_i})(1-\delta_{n,m_i})\{\beta^{i-1}_{m,n}+\beta^{i-1}_{m,m_i}\zeta_n^{m_i}+\beta^{i-1}_{n,m_i}\zeta_m^{m_i}+\beta^{i-1}_{m_i,m_i}\zeta_m^{m_i}\zeta_n^{m_i}$$

$$+\beta^{i-1}_{m}a\lambda_n\gamma_{m_i}+\beta^{i-1}_{m_i}\zeta_m^{m_i}a\lambda_n\gamma_{m_i}+\beta^{i-1}_{m_i}\zeta_m^{m_i}\zeta_n^{m_i}\gamma_{m_i}+\beta^{i}_{n}a\lambda_m\gamma_{m_i}+a\lambda_{m_i}\zeta_m^{m_i}\zeta_n^{m_i}\gamma_{m_i}\} \quad . \tag{7}$$

Higher derivatives are readily formed in this manner.

F3. Equations (6) can be used to calculate all β^{i}_{m}. These equations, while quite cumbersome for symbolic manipulation, are very well suited to computerized numerical solution: (6) is applied 2M-2 times (each time for all values of m), to collect coefficients so as to obtain a set of M equations, linear in (say) β^{1}_{m}. These are straightforward to solve, and re-applying (6) yields us the required first derivatives that we need.

A very similar procedure for equations (7) will determine values for the second order derivatives. We note in passing that although the calculation of the mean waiting time required the values of only a small fraction of these derivatives, the form of the only expression we found that was relatively convenient to solve, requires us to calculate almost all of them in the process.

F4. Consider the amount of calculation required for the described procedure. Each application of (6) uses $0(M^2)$ operations (the number of substitutions per line of the equations increasing from 3 to M), for a total of $0(M^3)$. This is also the order of the complexity of the solution of the resultant set of M-1 equations and the back substitution through (6) - the total is then still $0(M^3)$.

Similarly, each application of (7) requires $0(M^3)$ operations; here the solution of the final set of equations dominates, with $0(M^6)$ operations required. Thus, the numerical evaluation of these equations for realistic devices, where M assumes values in the low hundreds is too expensive for most purposes. One should use it, however, to investigate qualitative features, such as

- Dependence of performance measures on hardware parameters, and on details of the algorithms used for scheduling, as well as for comparison with other scheduling methods, on the same hardware.

- Evaluation of the quality of various approximations to the above analysis, before their application to a full-fledged system.

F5. It is of interest to note that the above described scheme of calculations is very much cheaper than the one suggested in [E], since the repeated (chain) differentiations used there are not required in our method, and the subsequent calculations are fewer in number (e.g., $0(M^4)$ are required there to calculate all the first order derivatives).

G. ELABORATIONS OF THE MODEL

G1. The model, as presented in section C, captures a number of the features and properties of a disk system that are critical to its performance. It does contain however, for the sake of simplicity, a good many assumptions that would seem at once to be both arbitrary and at variance with the real state of affairs in such systems. We discuss here a number of these assumptions, and what their removal or modification entails, mainly in terms of model tractability.

G2. Request service duration - this quantity was assumed constant, and equal for all cylinders simply to keep down the level of detail of the model (and use somewhat less storage during numerical calculations). Since these properties are nowhere used explicitly in the procedures we developed, there is absolutely no effect on the analysis if we assume that the time to service a request is described by any distribution function, which may indeed be cylinder-specific. Let S_m be the variable representing the service duration at cylinder m, with distribution function and its LST $F_{S_m}(.)$ and $\varphi_m(.)$ respectively; the LST of the busy period distribution is then the solution of the equation $B_m(s)=\varphi_m(s+\lambda_m-\lambda_m B_m(s))$. $\varphi_m(.)$ itself should also be substituted in the various equations in sections E and D, instead of $\exp(-Ts)$. No essential change need be made, and the calculations proceed in precisely the same manner.

G3. Meaningful seeks - by this rather fanciful name we refer to the incorporation into the model of the following modification: at stage completion a seek is initiated to the next cylinder in the cycle, as given in (E1), with non-empty queue. We recognize here the fact, that due to acceleration effects the time to traverse k cylinders in a single seek is appreciably less than k times the duration of a single-cylinder seek. This certainly represents better the way a disk facility is managed, but it also introduces a number of complicating factors:

- Instead of a single seek time, we have now a multitude; this can be as high as $M(M-1)$, but it can be reduced, through evident assumptions, that are happily quite borne out in practice, to $M(M-1)/2$ and further to $M-1$.

- The movements of the arm are not prescribed, as before, but rather depend on the state of the system, a feature that has been the undoing of many queueing-theoretical models.

- As a consequence, the key relations of section E do not hold, and a new approach must be found.

Nevertheless, the authors believe that this modification still yields us a tractable situation, and are preparing an analysis of its main features.

G4. Dependent arrivals. The model as described in section C can be rephrased to postulate a single Poisson stream of arrivals, at rate λ, with each request destined to cylinder m with fixed probability $p_m=\lambda_m/\lambda$, independently of the state of the system, and in particular of the history of the arrival process itself. We propose in this paragraph a modification which deviates from this last assumption. In particular, we wish to consider the situation where the destinations of successive arrivals form a first order Markov chain.

Thus, to the description of the state of the system a further index has to be added - the identity of the last cylinder that was addressed by the arrival process. This is a major departure from the model we analysed above, and the methods used there would be ineffective in handling it. Still, inasmuch it represents many common situations better than the simpler version, in particular when one considers systems that employ a large number of disk drives (i.e., there are fewer tasks active at each drive at any time), its analysis would be desirable. The methods used by Coffman and Hofri [CH] or Neuts [N] may be useful here, even if only as a starting point.

References

CH Coffman E.G. Jr., and Hofri, M.: A Class of FIFO Queues arising in Computing Systems. TR #87, Department of Computer Science, Technion Haifa.

CKR Coffman E.G. Jr., Klimko, L.A. and Ryan Barbara: Analysis of Scanning Policies for Reducing Disk Seek Times. SIAM J. Comp. 1 pp.269-279 (1972).

D Denning P.J.: Effects of Scheduling on File Memory Operations. Proc. AFIPS SJCC 1967 31 pp.9-21.

E Eisenberg M.: Queues With Periodic Service and Changeover Time. Opns. Res. 20 pp.440-451 (1972).

F Frank H.: Analysis and Optimization of Disk Storage Devices for Time-Sharing Systems JACM 16 pp.602-620 (1969).

FS Fife D.W., Smith J.L.: Transmission Capacity of Disk Storage Systems With Concurrent Arm Positioning IEEE Trans. Comp. 14 pp.575-582 (1965).

GM Gotlieb C.C., MacEwen: Performance of Moveable-Head Disk Storage Devices JACM 20 pp. 604-623 (1973).

N Neuts M.F. The Single Server Queue With Poisson Input and Semi-Markov Service Times. J. Appl. Prob. 3 pp.202-230 (1966).

O Oney C.W.: Queueing Analysis of the Scan Policy for Moving-Head Disks JACM 22 pp. 397-412 (1975).

S Seaman P.H. et al.: On Teleprocessing System Design Part IV: Analysis of Auxiliary Storage Activity IBM Sys. Jour. 5 pp.158-170 (1966).

T Teorey T.J.: Properties of Disk Scheduling Policies in Multiprogrammed Computer Systems Proc. AFIPS FJCC 41 pp.1-14 (1972).

TP ___, Pinkerton B.T.: A Comparative Analysis of Disk Scheduling Policies CACM 15 pp. 177-184 (1972)

Measuring, Modelling and Evaluating Computer Systems,
H. Beilner and E. Gelenbe, (eds.)
© North-Holland Publishing Company (1977)

MODELLING OF A STORED PROGRAM CONTROLLED TELEPHONE SWITCHING SYSTEM : EVALUATING A REGULATION METHOD FOR TRAFFIC OVERLOADS

L. Romoeuf

Centre National d'Etudes des Télécommunications
Issy les Moulineaux

This paper sets out a study of overloading phenomena on a stored program controlled telephone switching system, through discret events simulation.

After having tested the efficiency of the regulating method adopted, endeavours were made to improve upon the latter.

INTRODUCTION

The purpose of any switching system is the handling of traffic offered through setting-up of a link between the calling subscriber (or trunk) and the called subscriber (or trunk), in a minimum of time.

In the case of SPC systems, the volume of traffic that can be handled is limited by the dimensioning of its hardware and software resources (switching network, terminal circuits, access and auxiliary devices, working and recording memory areas) as well as operating speed of its control units (central processor, telephone peripherals).

Provided that traffic offered remains below a critical threshold (theorically corresponding to the nominal traffic designed into the system), all the calls are handled and their setting-up time is reduced to the minimal value prescribed by the operating speed of control units. If, however, traffic exceeds the critical treshold, waiting times before certain resources are no longer negligible and the system begins to enter an overloading area, where the following phenomena can be observed :

- the grade of service is deteriorating (increasing preselection and selection times, appearance of first call rejections)

- the processing time of a call being handled by the central unit becomes an increasing function of traffic offered (increased path finding time in the switching network, release process of calls rejected due to shortage or resources).

When overloading is growing considerably, an avalanche phenomenon appears and traffic handled collapses suddenly tending to zero limit : all of the processor time is used up by release processes and new accepted calls have no chance to set through.

Those effects due to overloading may be limited through adopting a call resulating strategy based on the following principle :

As soon as the system is in a state of overloading (wich, accordingly must be detected in due time), taking account of new calls is deliberately limited, with a wiew to serve adequately those calls already accepted, the other ones being queued (their processing is postponed until the disappearance of the overload condition) or simply and solely rejected. Of course, the number of calls accepted depends upon the degree of system overloading, wich, accordingly, one must be able to assess.

A fair regulation method for calls must cater for :

. Quelling of avalanche effect, i.e. achievement of a handled traffic graph exibiting a flat level beyond the critical treshold.

. A fair grade of service regarding calls processed by the system.

The study bore on a regulation method applied to a stored program controlled system with space division switching network, being controlled by two processors working together according to the "call load sharing" mode.

Though this is a general investigation, the case of a particular system is instanced : the E11 system, developed for large local exchange [1] , up to 64000 lines, 100 000 busy hour calls.

GENERAL ORGANIZATION OF THE E11 SYSTEM

It includes three main parts : the switching section, the signalling section, the central control (see appendix 1).

The switching section :

It includes the switching network itself, with reed latching crosspoint and map in memory technique, and its associated peripherals : markers and line scanners. The switching network is built up with 3 types of blocks, called switching units : the line switching units (LSU), the intermediate switching units (ISU) and the trunk switching units (TSU). Paths are set or released, in the switching network, via the markers ; a group marker (GM) controls a number of ISU and / or TSU according to the traffic handled by these switching units (maximum 8) ; a line marker (LM) controls a number of LSU depending on the traffic handled by these switching units (maximum 16) ; three orders must be sent by the processor to set or release a path in the network : one per type of switching unit.

With each line marker is associated a line scanner, the function of which is to detect calling lines or lines going out from the "parking" status. For this purpose, under the processor control, each line scanner tests regularly the line circuits, individual per subscriber.

The line scanner stops when a significant line status has been detected (calling line for example) or at the end of the scanning of a group of lines.

The group marker also performs the "false cross and ground" test inside the switching network.

The signalling section :

It includes all the network terminal circuits : trunk circuits and auxiliary devices (trunk senders and receivers, subscriber receivers, tone senders, etc.). It also includes the peripherals associated with these circuits : drivers and scanners, see below.

Relays in network terminal circuits are normally operated or released through slow drivers. A slow driver (SD) controls a number of network terminal circuits (maximum 512) according to the traffic handled by these circuits. Its operation time is 25 ms.

All telephonic events (loop closed or open, multi-frequency code, etc.) are detected by test points implemented in the netword terminal circuits. These test points are tested by an autonomous scanner, under processor control. At each clock interrupt (10 ms), the processor reads the words of the last look memory in which a change has been detected by the scanner. Afterwards, the processor restarts the scanner, which performs again its autonomous work. The capacity of a scanner is 2048 test points.

Relay operation with time constraints (signalling pulses) is performed by a fast driver, a flip-flop associated in this case to each such relay.

In fact, the fast driver is incorporated in the autonomous scanner, the maximum driving capacity being 1024 driving points per so called fast driver autonomous scanner (FDAS). Fast driving is performed by the processor at the beginning of each clock interrupt (10 ms), before the treatment of the last look memory words in which a mismatch has been detected by the scanner.

The central control :

The central control includes two LCT 3200 processors working together according to the "call load sharing" mode, each with :

- one main frame
- a variable number of central memory blocks (each block containing 16 K words, 33 bits, 0.85μs cycle time) : each pair of blocks being connected to the main frame via a memory controller

- various peripherals and associated controllers : teleprinters, displays, disc store, general purpose magnetic tape transports ; one magnetic tape transport is loaded with the master tape for automatic reload of the system in case of software fault.

- direct memory access, which permits direct data transfer between the central memory and some peripherals : mass memory, magnetic tape transport.

The software consiste of some 200 000 instructions, covering multiple functions : call processing, administration (man-machine communications), maintenance, test and diagnosis, installation, table generation, simulation for program debugging.

The meaning of the different sigla used throughout this article is provided in appendix 2.

DESCRIPTION OF THE LOAD REGULATING METHOD USED

Various types of overloading

It must be borne in mind that the condition of overloading is characterized by shortage of resources, and that the origin of overloading may be external (traffic peaks) or internal to the system (outage of units, kipping relaxation).

Overloads will be classified, not according to them origin but according to the type of resources wanting. Accordingly, four types of overload will be considered :

Overloading at the level of the network (f.i. all SR and MFSR being engaged).

Overloading at the level of the netword access devices (too many events to be processed in the line scanning stage, too many orders queuing up at telephone peripherals).

Overloading at the level of the processor (no sufficient processor time available to serve all of the traffic).

Overloading of software resources (all WARA are seized).

Overload detectors

For each type of overloading, there are specific detectors available, that reflect the occupancy rate of the various resources in the system at any instant of time :

At the level of the network :

- number of SR engaged
- number of MFSR engaged

At the level of network access devices :

- number of events detected by line scanning (new local and outgoing calls) and fast scanning (hanging up and new incoming calls)
- length of queues waiting to be served by LM
- length of queues waiting to be served by GM
- length of queues waiting to be served by SD

At the level of processors

- PT used up by the processing ofcalls in 10ms cycles (in fact, time remaining available at level A = lowest priority level dedicated to tasks in relation to management, tests and diagnoses, is measured, this being tantamount).

At the level of software resources :

- number of WARA engaged

Overload indicators. Cyclic positioning program

A cyclic program is activated every 600 ms to scan the whole bank of overloading detectors and position in an appropriate manner overloading indicator flags. Each detector is associated with a pair of pre-set thresholds. Any one indicator is positionned as soon as ONE of its related detectors exceeds the maximum threshold ; it will be reset to zero only when ALL of the associated detectors have returned below the minimum threshold. (in order to avoid "oscillations").

The set of indicators represents the overloading condition of the system, or, which amounts to the same, the relative deterioration of the grade of service. Indeed, those indicators are tested during the various call processing programs, to put off or cancel out certain processings.

The procedure being followed can be summarized as below :

. Appearance of an overload of a given type →
. Surpassing of the maximum threshold authorized by the detector →
. Positioning of the corresponding overload indicator →
. Change in processing (application of regulating means).

If the origin of overloading disappears :

. Return of detector to a value below the minimum threshold →
. Corresponding indicator reset to zero →
. Normal processing of calls.

The number of overload indicators is 5,say S1, S2, S3, FCG and DCX ; the effect of wich upon call processing will be analysed in the following paragraph. The cyclic positioning program also actuates filters F1, F2 that determine the number of calls it is considered possible to handle depending upon the status of the system.

Detectors used, together with the pairs of associated thresholds and corresponding overload indicators, are listed below.

The values of thresholds are provided in terms of occupancy rates of resources used, or average number of tasks queued before each peripheral (sum of tasks relative to number of devices in service).

It is called to mind that there are three pairs of thresholds for WARA, corresponding to increasing levels of overload :

DETECTORS	ASSOCIATED THRESHOLDS	INDICATORS POSITONED
PT	0.8 - 0.9	S1 - FCG - DCX
SR & MFSR	0.9 - 0.95	S2
SD	2 - 3	S1
LM	2 - 3	FCG
GM	2 - 3	FCG - DCX
WARA	0.8 - 0.9	S1
	0.9 - 0.95	S2
	0.95 - 0.97	S3

Effect of indicators upon the processing of calls

. Whatever the system overload status be, it is assumed that incoming calls, calls originating from major lines and precedence calls (special services) that are beyond the preselection stage, are being handled.

. Indicators FCG and DCX are tested by the marker interface program ; once they are positioned, their effect is cancellation of non-indispensable tasks for call processing, namely the FCG test and disconnections in ISU and TSU. In that manner, the load on the markers and CCU transmitting a smaller number of orders to the markers, is decreased.

. Indicators S1, S2, S3 change the value of two filters F1 and F2 that determine the maximum number of non-precedence and non-essential outgoing calls taken into account during the subsequent 600 ms.

Filter F1 is tested during the preselection, after the discriminations of the calling subscriber has been read : only calls originating from essential lines plus a certain number of more calls depending upon the status of the system (no overloading, overloading S1, S2, S3) are processed ; other calls are put off, waiting on their line equipment, and will be re-examined during the next cycle.

Filter F2 is tested, in case of overloading S2 or S3, at the conclusion of the analysis of the first digits : besides precedence calls and those originating from essential lines, only a certain number of calls are handled, depending upon the overload condition, the remaining calls being rejected (release processing).

The values assigned to these filters depend upon the nominal traffic of the exchange under consideration ; they will be specified further down for the configuration looked into.

Lastly, the role of indicator S3 is to stop the actuation of the line scanner ; the assignment of WARA is exclusively reserved for the handling of incoming calls. All outgoing calls are waiting for detection.

THE MODEL AND SIMULATION PROGRAM

The model

The study was not aiming at providing accurate quantitative results on the traffic handling capacity of the system, but to bring to light how the system is inclined to react when faced with overloading. Accordingly, only the cyclic indicators positioning program and operations undertaken regarding the processing of calls in case of overloading, were accurately reproduced.

Generation of calls :

Most of the study used the Poisson model of lost calls, however, making allowance for the limited number of call originating sources. On the subscribers side, the ratio of the number of subscribers engaged to the total number of subscribers permits one to calculate the engaged probability of the called party regarding local calls and incoming calls (all subscribers being assumed having balanced traffic). On the incoming side, the generation of an incoming call when all IJ are engaged, is counted as a rejection (though the exchange does not detect the call, the attempt still took place at the distant exchange). Moreover, a call, waiting in the preselection stage for over 10 seconds, is considered as being rejected.

At the beginning, a model of traffic with repeated attempts was envisaged, but considering the operations cost of the program, it was used in a simplified form, only during the latter stage of the study.

The various parameters of the model of traffic were laid down for the whole study, as below :

- local calls : 10 %
- outgoing calls : 40 % (urban, 7 digits only)
- incoming calls : 50 %
- essential lines : 1 %
- precedence calls : 1 %
- no-answer of the called subscriber : 15 %
- distant called party busy : 15 %
- dialling time : 14 s (end of analysis of 3 initial digits : 6s)
- duration of ringing in case of answer : 10 s
- duration of ringing in case of no-answer : 45 s
- duration of busy tone transmission : 5 s
- duration of conversation : 180 s
- duration of signalling, outgoing calls : 12 s
- duration of signalling, incoming calls : 4 s

Telephone peripherals :

A constant average holding time has been assumed for each telephone peripheral :

- for the mass memory (MM) : 10 ms/32 (number of sectors)
- for slow drivers (SD) : 25 ms
- for the markers : 8 ms

For any action requirement towards a peripheral, the reaction time is computed according to the formula below :

$$T = TS(i) \times [1.5+L(i)/N(i)]$$

where : i = type of peripheral
TS (i)= corresponding average holding time
N (i)= number of peripherals of the i type
L (i)= total number of orders queued before peripherals of the i type at the instant time of the demand.

For line scanning, it was simply assumed that a new call was detected (the case of blocking by indicator S3 excepted), at random between 0 and 320 ms.

Regarding the fast driver autonomous scanner, an incoming call or hanging up is detected between 0 and 90 ms. The FDAS was not simulated ; only the processor time dedicated to its management was put on record.

Processing of calls :

For each type of communication, the processing corresponding to each phase (preselection, selection, end of setting-up and release) are described by a table having n rows (corresponding to the n processing periods) and two columns, the first one indicating the level of processing, the other one the particular task to carry out on said level.

The following levels were adopted : MM, SD, LM, GM, P (enchaining and analysing functions). A queue of waiting tasks corresponds to each one of these levels, but only level P is actually represented by a queue in the model. The other ones were represented by their length and average holding time. Such periods as correspond to the dialling, signalling, ringing, conversation phases, are represented in the tables conformably to a hypothetical level indicating their duration (the only one task to carry out on those levels is simply the transition to the next level).

Central control unit :

In this study, only one processor was assumed to be in service. Indeed, the system must be capable of handling all the traffic under these conditions and overloading at the level of the processor time is much more likely to occur with this mode of operation.

At each 10 ms clock interrupt (basic cycle of the CCU), the processor time PT used up for current calls processing is calculated, making the sum of the durations below :

- 1 ms for actuation of line scanners

- Nx150 mms for the processing of interruptions in telephone peripheral responses (MM, SD, LM, GM),N being the number of interruptions occured during the PRECEDING cycle. In that manner, the operations cost of the simulation program is reduced (the simulated time progressing by 10 ms steps), and may be justified by the fact that under steady state conditions, the load on the CCU changes little between two consecutive cycles (the period - 600 ms - of the indicator positioning cyclic program being long in proportion to the CCU cycle).

- Time dedicated to the management of the FDAS (detection of incoming calls and hanging up, processing of dialling and signalling), is assessed by means of the formula :

$$FDAST \text{ (T for time)} = 1.7 + WARA/200 \text{ (ms)}$$

where WARA is the number of WARA engaged at the instant under consideration. This formula is based upon the results of a previous study bearing on FDAS simulation.

- After that, calls queued at level P are served as long as there is any time available within the current cycle. To simplify, all processings of level P are given a common average value of 400 mms (enchaining at the following level included).

Simulation program

The program is written in SIMSCRIPT language, particulaly attractive for its dynamic storage management and ease of writing regarding events and waiting queues. Still, the management of the file of future events was resumed using a schedule having a pyramidal structure. This permits one to divide by seven the cost in terms of processor time of one run (at the cost, it is true, of an increased store size by about 60 %).

The program comprises 1 200 instructions and 200 data cards. Its exploitation on the CNET ISSY-LES-MOULINEAUX computer of the HB 6080 type, requires a 75 K word-store and one half-hour of processor time for 20 minutes of simulation, 3 of them for load rising time.

It is comprised of 14 subroutines, the major ones being :

- Call generation subroutine
- Overload indicator positioning subroutine (duty cycle 600 ms)
- Clock subroutine (duty cycle 10 ms), processing calls at the P level and computing the PT used up.
- A subroutine translating interruptions in peripheral responses and the conclusion of such stages as dialling, ringing, a.s.o.

STUDY RESULTS

Dimensioning of the system

The study was conducted on one single configuration, and results looked for being mainly of a qualitative order, arrangements were made to obtain a nominal traffic of 25 calls/s, the earliest signs of overloading appearing toward 30 calls/s.

Junctors, auxiliaries and WARA were dimensioned in such a way as to obtain an occupandy rate close to 0.7 at 25 calls/s.

Regarding peripherals of the type such as SD, LM, GM, their number was slightly reduced relatively to a real configuration, in order to be able to observe overshooting of thresholds on their waiting queues. In brief, values adopted for the system dimensioning were :

Subscribers	:	30000	MM	:	1
LJ	:	510	SD	:	10
OJ	:	2220	LM	:	4
IJ	:	2670	GM	:	8
SR	:	430	WARA	:	500
MFSR	:	250			

Values of filters F1 and F2 tested respectively in the preselection stage and at the conclusion of the analysis of the first digits, were laid down as follow :

In the case of no overloading	: F1 = 20	F2 not tested
In the case of overloading S1	: F1 = 8	F2 not tested
In the case of overloading S2	: F1 = 6	F2 = 8
In the case of overloading S3	: F1 = 0	F2 = 6

These values mean the number of non-essential and non-precedence outgoing calls admitted for processing, per 600 ms cycle.

Value F1 = 20 corresponds to a traffic of 33 calls/s and is of use only to limit the effects of a very important but very short peak of traffic. Values 8 and 6 correspond to traffics of 13 and 10 calls/s, respectively, wich values encompass the outgoing portion of the nominal traffic normally capable of being handled.

Présentation of results

The test results are shown on Tables (I to IV) comprising a number of figures (5 or 7) with graphs of the variation of the various parameters that reflect the status of the system depending upon traffic offered (noted : a) ranging from 0 to 60 calls/s.

. Figure 1 : Total loss rate : τ
Efficiency rate : r
Profitability of traffic : ρ, in terms of the ratio of effective traffic to traffic processed, i.e. :

ρ = r.c/h, where
c = duration of conversation
and h = average duration of common user's call.

This figure also shows the values τ_A , r_A, ρ_A corresponding to incoming traffic (dotted lines).

. Figure 2 : Occupancy rates of the following resources : PT, WARA, SD, LM, GM, MM.
. Figure 3 : Traffic handled (noted : e) in terms of calls/s.
. Figure 4 : Mean processing time by CCU of a call HANDLED, in ms.
. Figure 5 : Occupancy rate of junctors and auxiliaries : LJ, OJ, IJ, SR, WARA.

Lastly, a table provides for the various values of traffic offered a, the percentage of calls the duration of which preselection (PSA for subscribers, PSC for circuits) and selection (SL) exceed t seconds.

Various tests conducted

With no overloading control (Table 1)

For comparison purposes, a test was carried out with no overloading control whatsoever, the system accepting all calls whatever their chances of being successful be.

From 35 calls/s onwards, all curves, indeed, reflect avalanche effect. It should be observed that the PT per call handled increases clearly, passing from 27 ms to 55 ms when the traffic offered increases from 25 to 60 calls/s. (with small loading, this time is relatively important, which is accounted for by the fact that even when idle, the occupancy rate of CCU is not zero, because tasks corresponding to the scanning of terminations, still remain). Call rejections are mainly due to the shortage of WARA, and, secondly to a shortage of MFSR, to saturation of IJ, bringing about too long a preselection waiting time (exceeding 10 s).

Figure 1 shows that incomming calls are very slightly priviledged, because their detection is faster than for outgoing calls.

Moreover, the profitability of traffic (curves ρ and ρ_A) drops only beyond 40 calls/s. By contrast, the grade of service is drastically deteriorated beyond 30 calls/s.

<u>With overloading control at the origin</u> (Table 2)

Applying the regulation method described previously test results achieved were those provided by Table 2. A comparison with the preceding test (Table 1) reveals that :

. A drop in traffic handled is initiated from 30 calls/s (fig. 3) instead of 35. In fact, the operation of regulation means begins at 27 calls/s. However, this drop is very small and linear ; increasing PT per call handled (fig. 4) is no longer exponential beyond the critical threshold.

. Figure 1 also reveals that the profitability of traffic decreases very little. Moreover, the efficiency rate r_A of incoming calls, is clearly improved, whereas the global efficiency rate r drops more severely than previously. This means that, no doubt, the method of regulation ensures better processing of incoming traffic in the event of overloading, but at the expense of a considerable deterioration in the processing of outgoing calls. On the other hand, the table providing the grade of service permits one to appreciate the efficiency of the regulation method used relatively to absence of regulation in the following way :

1) In fact, the actual curve of traffic handled exhibits no sudden drop beyond nominal traffic ; accordingly, the avalanche effect characteristic of overloading, has really been reduced considerably, if not eliminated.

2) With equal traffic offered, the volume of incoming traffic handled is not only more important, but the grade of service remains good : even with 60 calls/s, still 58 % of incoming calls (instead of 41 %) are handled, the efficiency being 42 % (against 25 %), and, above all, preselection time exceeds 1 second only for 2 % of the calls (instead of 100 %) and selection time does exceed 2s. for only 3 % of the calls (against 90 %).

3) By contrast, between 30 and 50 calls/s the volume of outgoing traffic handled is less, and the grade of service is even worse.

   . Looking at the graphs in figure 2, one can see, on the one hand, that regulation is actuated from 27 calls/s (drop in occupancy rate of LM and GM due to the positioning of indicators FCG and DCX), and, on the other hand, that the reason of this actuation is the occupancy rate of WARA and of the CCU. Furthermore, it appears that the curves of the occupancy rates of the CCU and MM exhibit a marked "knee" in increase between 27 and 30 calls/s. This phenomenon accounts for the poor performances of the regulation method applied, relatively to outgoing traffic :

. From 27 calls/s, the occupancy rate of WARA begins to exceed at times the upper 0.9 threshold. From that moment, overload indicator S1 is positioned and new outgoing calls are preselection filtered. Those calls which are not accepted, are queued for detection and their WARA is released. Accordingly, these calls appear again a wee bit later (0 to 320 ms), and a phenomenon of renewed preselection processing occurs, causing an overload at the level of the PT and MM (new assignment of WARA, new discrimination of caller, new test of filter F1).

Improving upon the regulating method

First, a new test was made with twice the number of WARA (i.e. 1000), in order to get rid of the first "bottle neck". Curves obtained are altogether similar to those on Table 2 and it is of no use reproducing them here again. Regulation is actuated from 30 calls/s, by the PT detector, however, and a sharp increase in occupancy rates of the CCU and MM are observed again between 30 and 35 calls/s.

Another trial was then conducted, placing the F1 filter test in the preselection stage BEFORE the MM call, in order to diminish the loading of the CCU during this critical acceptance stage of outgoing calls (thus cancelling the processing of a response interruption, assuming, however, that discriminations of subscribers are carried out in the core storage). The knee of sudden increase has disappeared in the MM occupancy rate, but still exists in the CCU occupancy rate (very slightly less sharp), all other curves being identical with those of Table 2.

Therefore, it is obvious that the action undertaken in the preselection stage, in case of overloading (to keep outgoing calls waiting) is not adequate, since it induces additional work on the CCU, and therefore, keeps indicator S1 positioned.

Well now, one can see that once indicators S2, S3, FCG and DCX are positioned, actions undertaken on the processing of calls, did really result in a decrease in the loading of the responsable detectors (rejection of calls by filter F2, whence a reduction in the loading of WARA, SR, MFSR ; suppression of disconnections and FCG test, whence a reduction in the loading of LM and GM).

By contrast, regarding indicator S1, the processing of certain calls is merely delayed, which indeed amounts to recommencing quasi immediately.

Whence the idea to reject unconditionally outgoing calls that do not pass beyond filter F1, in order to relieve actually those detectors responsable of the S1 overloading (WARA, CCU, SD).

The local and outgoing call processing program was therefore modified, by adding a release process (transmission of the busy tone to the calling party) for calls being rejected at the time of the testing of filter F1.

Testing of the new regulating method (Table 3)

This table shows immediately that the curve of traffic handled (fig. 3) exhibits a bent when the number of calls reaches 27 calls/s (actuation of regulation) and remains at a level beyond 35 calls/s. The PT per call handled (fig. 4) remains pratically constant beyond 30 calls/s (26 ms).

. Figure 1 reveals that profitability of traffic stays pratically constant. The efficiency rate for incoming calls (r_A) is the same as with the original method, but the overall rate (r) is clearly higher : in regard to the original method, incoming calls are processed just as well and outgoing calls much better.

Table 3 comprises no data on the grade of service, because the latter stays excellent, even at 60 calls/s (preselection and selection times are always less than 1 s).

. In figure 2, the curve of CCU occupancy rate no longer exhibits any sudden increase and progressively tends to 0.85.
Comparing curves LM and GM with those of Table 2, reveals that putting means of regulation into operation is going on progressively depending upon the loading of the system. The SD occupancy rate keeps increasing beyond 30 calls/s, because of the sending of the busy tone for outgoing calls which did not pass filter F1.

. For comparison purposes, the tabulation below provides the percentage of time during which the various overload indicators were positioned, the traffic offered being 35 calls/s, for both methods :

	ORIGINAL METHOD	NEW METHOD
S1	100 %	68 %
S2	31 %	2 %
S3	16 %	-
FCG,DCX	99 %	1 %

Introduction of a repeated calls model (Table 4)

Consideration having been given to the fact that the calling party did not have his communication and, that for this reason is normally going to try a new call, a repeated calls model was anticipated right going to try a new call, a repeated calls model was anticipated right at the beginning of the study, the model being prompted by theorical studies and traffic observations referred to under [2] and [3] .

Unfortunately, the high operations cost of the simulation program commanded the definition of a simplified model to be used but toward the completion of the study.

The sole cases of renewed calls taken into consideration by the model are :

- receiving of busy tone
- too long a preselection waiting time (over 10 s).

The probability of the calling party making a new attempt is assumed to be 0.5 (independently of the rank of the attempt), within one second after hanging up (which time might appear to be short, but it was chosen in order to be able to observe sufficient a number of renewals of calls during the continuance of simulation).

Test results achieved with the new regulation method are provided on Table 4.
a represents the "fresh" traffic offered (first attempts)
β is the average number of attempts pro first call (β_A for incoming calls)

. First, it appears that curves of traffic handled and PT per call handled (fig. 3 and 4) are apprecially identical with those of the lost call model.
The system bears very well considerable overloading (the total traffic accepted corresponding to 60 first calls/s is 93 calls/s).

. It is worthy of note that there again the grade of service of calls accepted for processing by the system, remains always excellent.

. In figure 1, it appears that the profitability of traffic (ρ and ρ_A) decreases always very little. Of course, the efficiency rate (r and r_A) drops faster than on table 3, the volume of traffic actually offered is no longer "a" but β.a, with β increasing with the efficiency rate r decreasing. The variation of β (β_A for incoming traffic) versus "a" (new calls put in) is represented in figure 6, whereas figure 7 provides the function $\beta = f(r)$, which relation is of the type $\beta = 1/r^{\alpha}$, where $\alpha \# 0.33$, except for high values of r (exceeding 0.7), where $\alpha \# 0.22$, this being possibly due to the small number of repeated calls observed under these conditions.

. Figure 1 also provides the variations of the product $r.\beta$ (and $r_A.\beta_A$) representing the efficiency rate referred to the new calls at the origin, in other words the probability for a given call to be successful, repeated attempts being taken into consideration.
(In fact, the relation $r.\beta = 1-\Pi$, where Π is the rate original calling attempts finally given up, has been checked).

One can notice that curves $r.\beta$ and $r_A.\beta_A$ are identifying with curves r and r_A of Table 3. (lost call model) for $a \geqslant 40$ calls/s, but are lying noticeably above them for $a \leqslant 35$ calls/s. This may be construed in the following way : a new attempt is only "paying" for the subscriber if the overloading is not too heavy (less than 40 % in terms of calls).

Verification of non-oscillation of the regulating system

On all tests carried out, the data below were edited :

- intervals of time between two actuations of regulation (positioning of at least one indicator)

- times during which the regulation was kept going.

It has been checked that these two variables were absolutely at random and non-correlated.

Accordingly it can be stated that the fact of using a pair of thresholds to position and reset to zero the indicators, avoids "oscillations" of the overloading control (periodical positioning and resetting to zero).

CONCLUSION

The aim of a call regulating method for overloaded switching systems is, on the one hand, to keep traffic handled at a level at least equal to that it is capable of handling under normal operating conditions (suppression of avalanche effect), and, on the other hand, to render the system capable of going on with processing most of the traffic considered as having precedence (incoming calls, emergency calls).

If in stored program controlled systems it is easy to implement a program testing overloads that can be detected at the level of the various system ressources, it is still necessary to take adequate measures regarding the deterioration of the processing to which certain calls are to be subjected.

The simulation study described here, bore on a particular switching system taken as an example, but it was conducted in a qualitative manner, in order to reveal the behavioural trend of the system on overloading, and derive an applicable regulating strategy valid for different stored program controlled systems.

Results achieved show that, if it is natural to modulate the number of calls accepted for processing depending upon the seriousness of overloading measured (values of filters F1 and F2 decreasing according to the degree of overloading on S1, S2, S3), and, on the other hand, if the fact of availing oneself of a pair of thresholds per detector, instead of only one, in order to actuate or cancel overloading, results in avoiding oscillations on the control system, still, it is preferable to reject systematically non-accepted calls, rather than letting them in a waiting queue, because doing so ensures a good grade of service for calls processed that do not notice any overloading condition of the system.

APPENDIX I

General organization of the E11 system

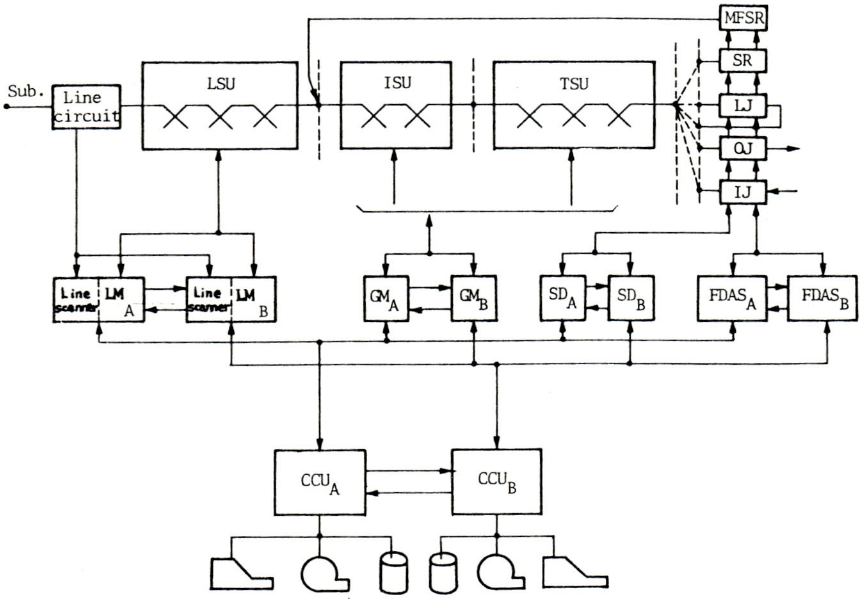

For the meaning of the sigla used, see Appendix II

APPENDIX 2

Meaning of the sigla used :

WARA : Working and recording areas (registers).

FDAS : Fast driver autonomous scanner.

MFSR : Multifrequency code sender and receiver.

ISU : Intermediate switching unit.

TSU : Trunk switching unit.

CCU : Central control unit.

FCG : False cross and ground test.

DCX : Disconnections in the ISU and TSU.

PSA : Subscriber preselection time.

PSC : Circuit preselection time.

SL : Selection time.

LM : Line marker.

GM : Group marker.

SD : Slow driver.

MM : Mass memory

PT : Processor time.

SR : Subscriber receiver (push button or dial pulse).

LJ : Local feed junctor.

OJ : Outgoing junctor.

IJ : Incoming junctor.

TABLE I

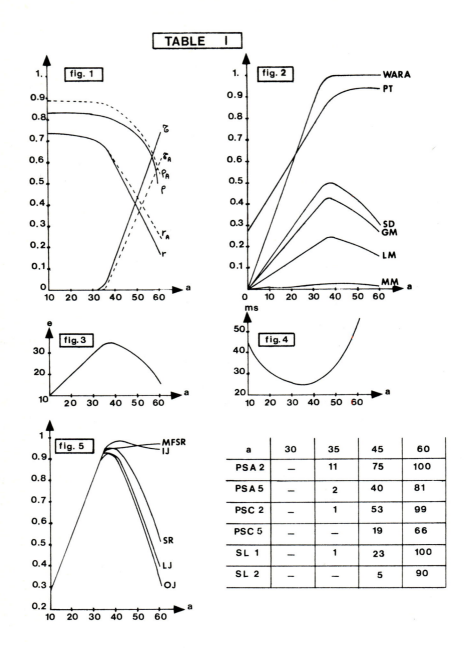

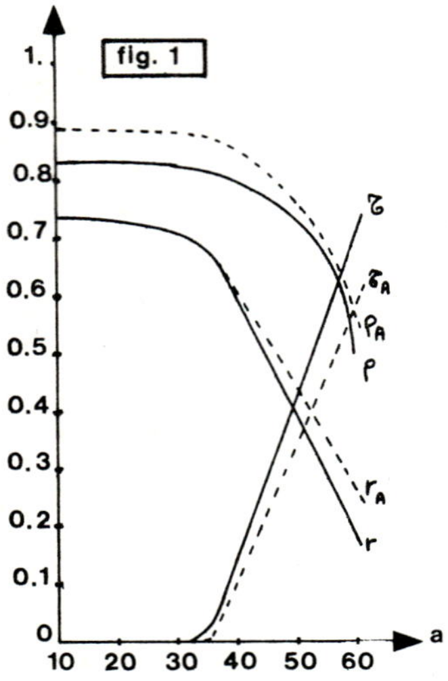

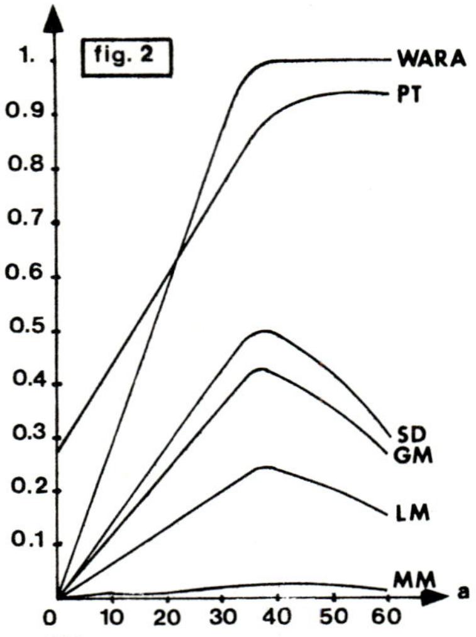

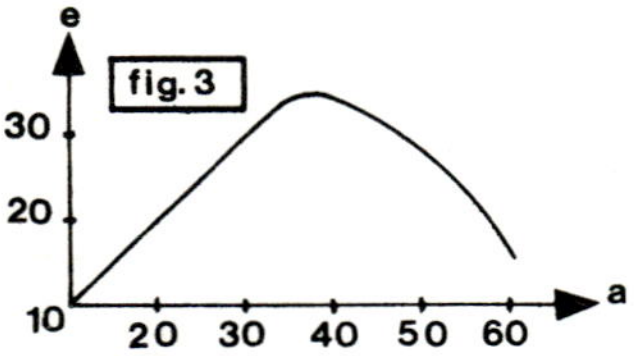

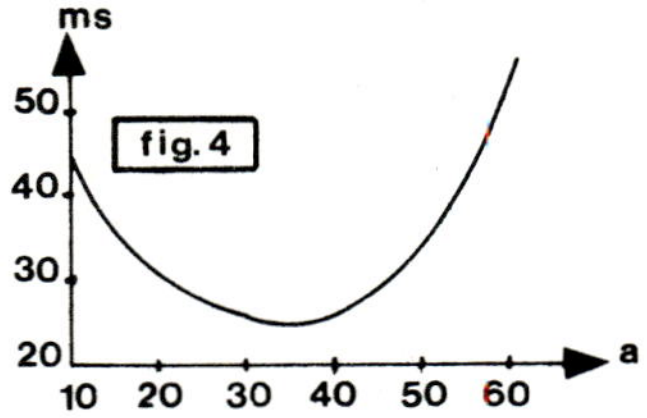

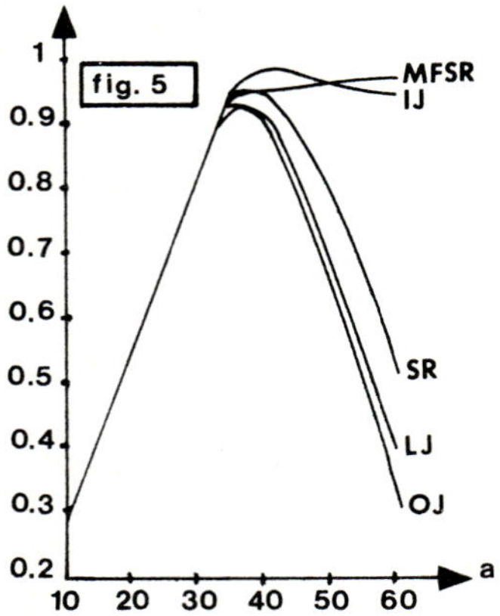

a	30	35	45	60
PSA 2	–	11	75	100
PSA 5	–	2	40	81
PSC 2	–	1	53	99
PSC 5	–	–	19	66
SL 1	–	1	23	100
SL 2	–	–	5	90

TABLE II

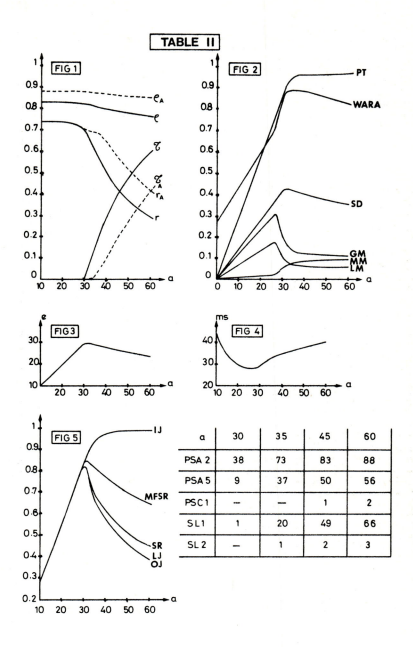

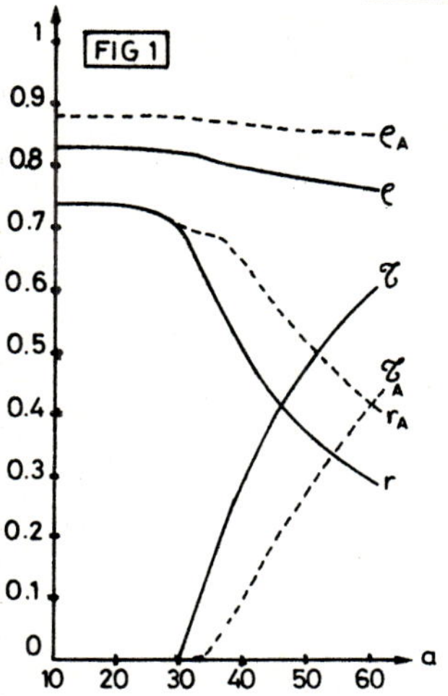

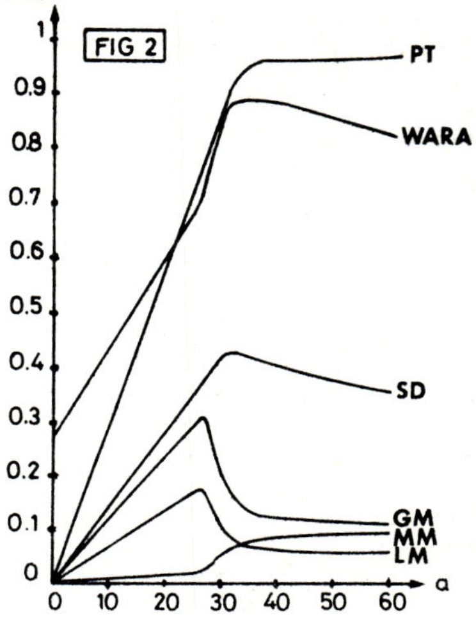

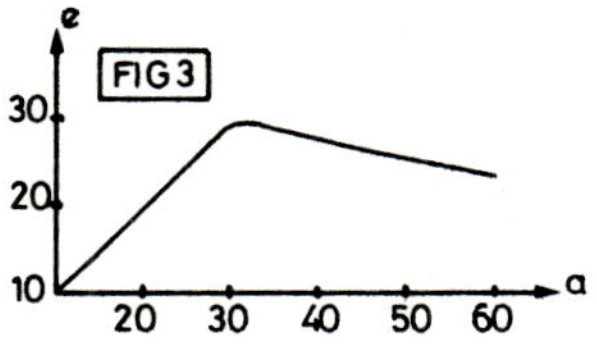

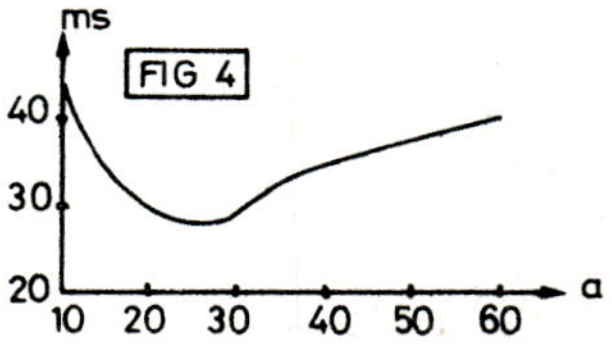

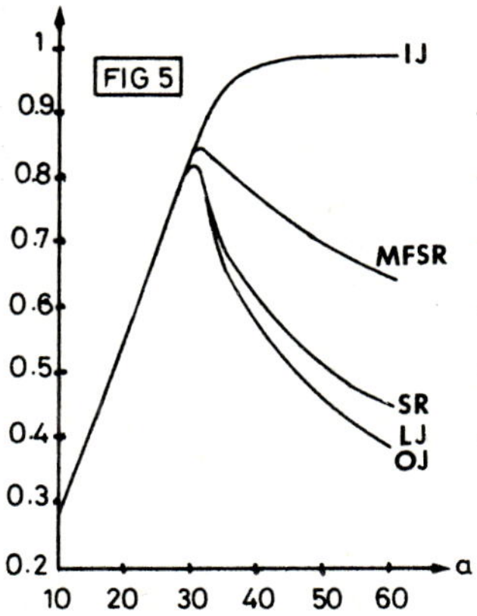

a	30	35	45	60
PSA 2	38	73	83	88
PSA 5	9	37	50	56
PSC 1	—	—	1	2
SL 1	1	20	49	66
SL 2	—	1	2	3

TABLE III

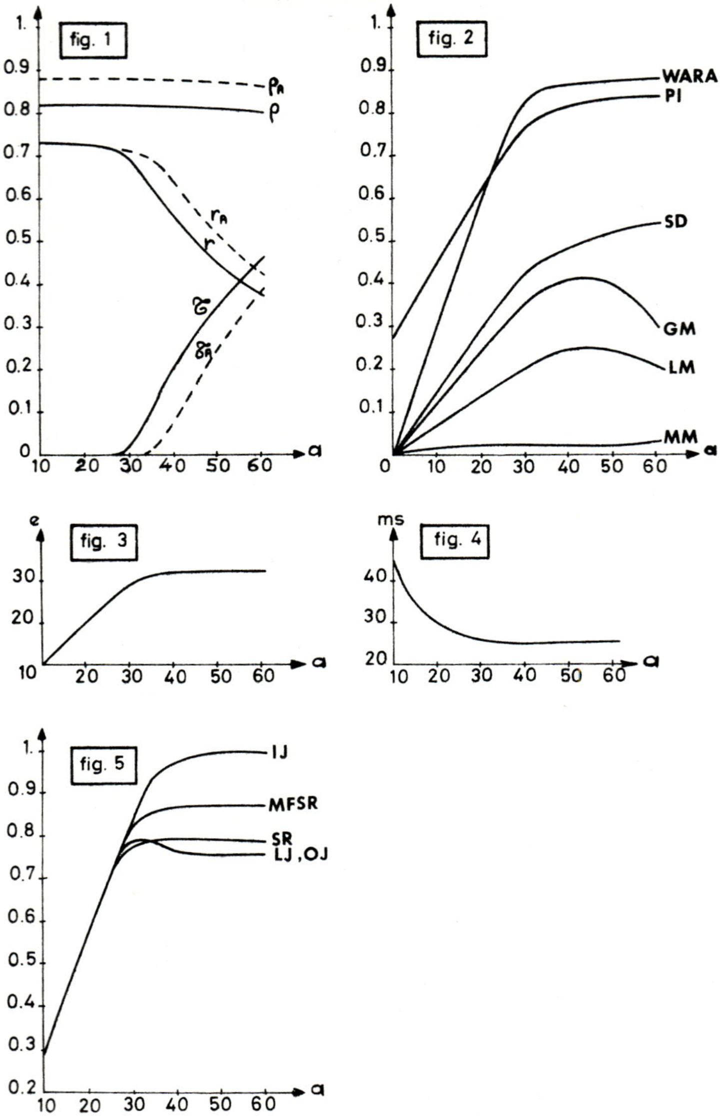
fig. 1
1.
0.9
0.8
0.7
0.6
0.5
0.4
0.3
0.2
0.1
0
10 20 30 40 50 60
a
ρ_A
ρ
r_A
r
fig. 2
WARA
PI
SD
GM
LM
MM
0 10 20 30 40 50 60
fig. 3
e
30
20
10
fig. 4
ms
40
30
20
fig. 5
IJ
MFSR
SR
LJ, OJ

TABLE IV

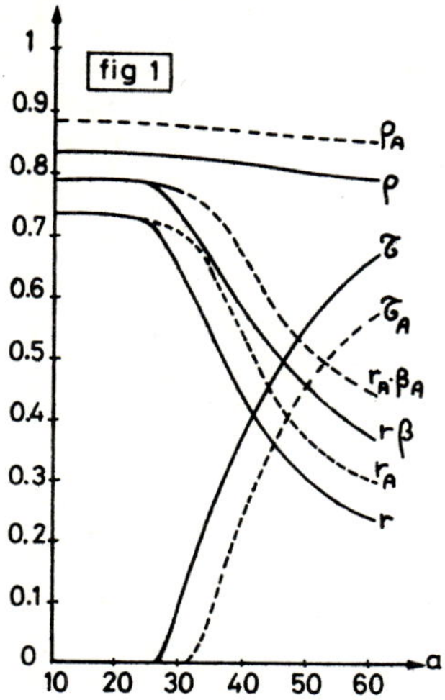
fig 1
1
0.9
0.8
0.7
0.6
0.5
0.4
0.3
0.2
0.1
0
10 20 30 40 50 60
a
ρA
ρ
τ
τA
rA·βA
r·β
rA
r

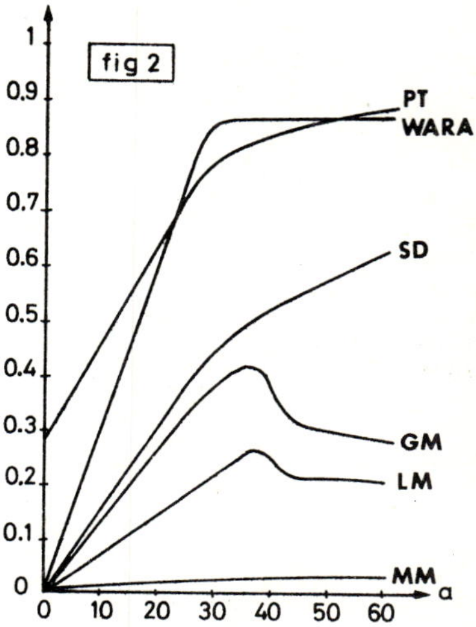
fig 2
1
0.9
0.8
0.7
0.6
0.5
0.4
0.3
0.2
0.1
0
0 10 20 30 40 50 60
a
PT
WARA
SD
GM
LM
MM

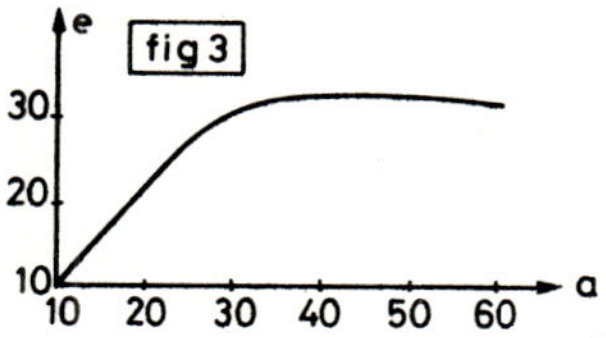
fig 3
e
30
20
10
10 20 30 40 50 60
a

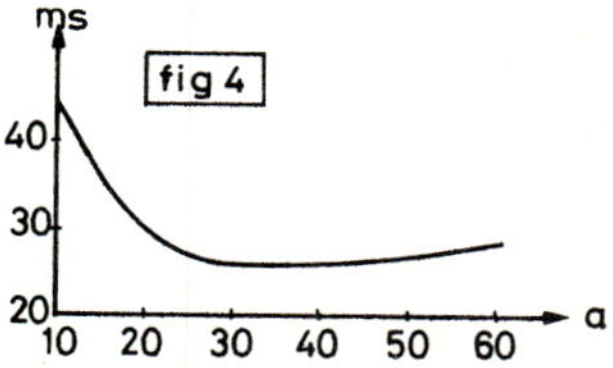
fig 4
ms
40
30
20
10 20 30 40 50 60
a

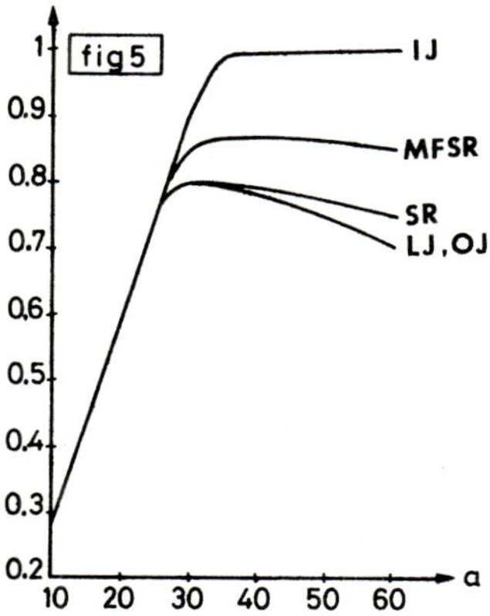
fig5
1
0.9
0.8
0.7
0.6
0.5
0.4
0.3
0.2
10 20 30 40 50 60
a
IJ
MFSR
SR
LJ,OJ

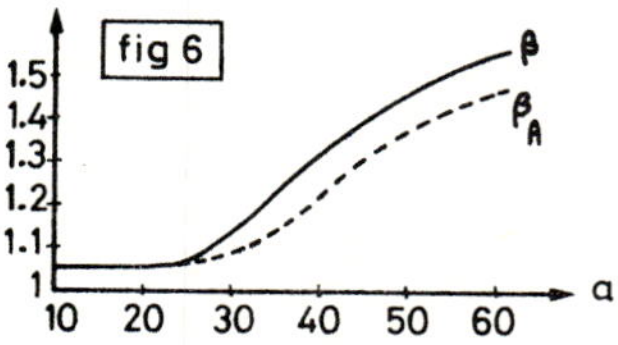
fig 6
1.5
1.4
1.3
1.2
1.1
1
10 20 30 40 50 60
a
β
βA

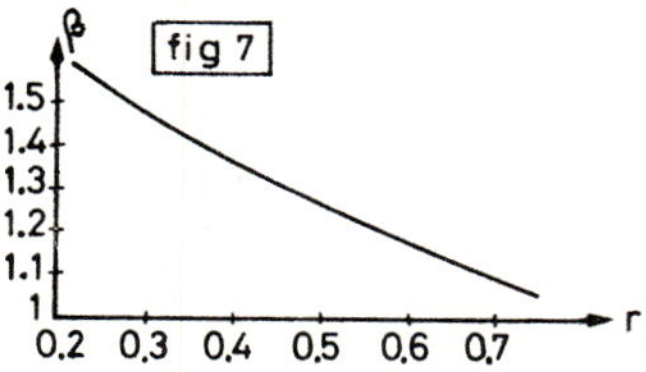
fig 7
β
1.5
1.4
1.3
1.2
1.1
1
0.2 0.3 0.4 0.5 0.6 0.7
r

BIBLIOGRAPHY

[1] : C. ROZMARYN - J. TRELUT - L. VIELLEVOYE : Le systeme de commutation telephonique E11. (E11 telephone switching system). Commutation & Electronique N 47, October 1974.

[2] : P. LE GALL : Sur le taux d'efficacite et la stationnarite du trafic telephonique (On efficiency rate and stationarity of telephone traffic). Commutation & Electronique N 35, October 1971.

[3] : J.P. GUERINEAU - G. PELLIEUX : Nouveaux résultats concernant le comportement de l'abonné du réseau téléphonique de Paris (New results on the behaviour of the subscriber of the Parisian telephone network). Commutation & Electronique N 45, April 1974.

Measuring, Modelling and Evaluating Computer Systems,
H. Beilner and E. Gelenbe, (eds.)
© North-Holland Publishing Company (1977)

STATISTICAL SEQUENTIAL METHODS FOR UTILIZATION IN PERFORMANCE ANALYSIS

M. Arató
Research Institute for Applied
Computer Sciences
Budapest, Hungary

This paper is a survey of certain results concerning point processes and their model approximations in computer systems. We develop a unique method based on known statistical sequential models in order to compute automatic decision rules. Applications of this approach to time-sharing systems and performance analysis are presented. Exact results of Shiryayev and Davis are presented and their use in different approximations are shown.

The independent reference string models are also discussed to show that the separation principle gives computable results in dynamic file assignement and in page replacement too.

1. INTRODUCTION

The purpose of this paper is to present in the manner of statistical sequential decision procedures some of the fundamental results which are directly applicable to the performance analysis of multiprogramming systems. Here we do not use the well known Wald's sequential likelilood ratio conception for distinguishing between two hypothesis, which may be used in many applications of computer systems. Such an example the reader may find in this paper /see fig. 3./ where the overflow and underflow level for the number of allocated pages in a virtual memory system may be found from Wald's rule. For another example we may use the dispatching algorithm in the HASP execution task monitor in IBM OS/360 /see Shohat, Strauss [30] /.

The main goal of this paper is to show that the stopping rule procedures and recursive filtering of stochastic processes may be used in many problems of complex computer performance analyses. If we are interested in a set of service stations interconnected into a network only in "whole" then we can work out decision procedures for such measure of performance effectiveness as degree of multiprogramming, swapping rate, overhead rate, etc. /Some models and measurements the reader may find e.g. in Töke [31] and Asztalos [10]/ Taking into account e.g. the swapping rate we take a complex and stochastic function of the elements in the network which varies stochastically in time. In such a representation it is possible to control this process. The first question which arises is to detect the changes in the behavior of the network system. In this paper, we give the Poisson process description /see Davis [16] /, and the Wiener process case too /see Shiryayev [29] /. The Wiener process representation is used as an approximation applying an appropriate time scale transformation. Here we do not deal with the problem of recursive filtering the reader may find it in the papers of Segall [28], and Arató [7] . The disorder problem is one of the Bayesian sequential procedures which has an elegant solution. Until now this decision procedure was not used in internal work of computer systems. This is one way to analyse a computer system not as a static one. Generally, in sequential procedures we do not assume that the parameters of the system are known or they cannot vary in time. If the parameters of the system vary with time, or they are unknown, a dynamical treatment might give not only a substantial improvement in performance, but there exist also special cases when we have relatively simple solutions /see e.g. Arató, Benczúr, Krámli [8] , Benczúr, Krámli [12] /.

The problem of finding optimal paging algorithm with an independent reference string η_t $(t = 1,2,\ldots)$ is well known /see Aho, Denning, Ullmann [1] , Bélády [13] or Gelenbe [19] /. A simple model of file assignement in computer networks with Markov request string was discussed by Segall [28] . These two models with independent reference strings were discussed on this conference in 1976. The method which we used was the Bayesian and the performance index was the expected number of page faults. We did not assume that the distributions are known /see Arató [5] , Benczúr, Krámli, Pergel [11] /. Later we proved the optimality of the LFU strategy without the Bayesian assumption /Arató, Benczúr, Krámli [8] /. This means that a result similar to Wald's theorem on optimality of the likelihood sequential procedure /where the expectation of sample time is minimal under both hypotheses/ is true. It is known that Wald's theorem on optimality has a more complicated proof than the Bayesian one.

In this paper we present in a unique method the separation principle for independent strings. The separation theorem for linear Gaussian models was proved by Wonham [33] /see also in Lipcer, Shiryayev [25]/. The separation principle means that the estimates of the unknown probability distribution are sufficient statistics for the optimization.

2. THE DISORDER PROBLEM

a/ In complex computer systems we have processors /e.g. central processor units, input-output channels, remote terminals, etc./ which we call service stations, and tasks, processes, messages /called transactions in information management system/, which we call customers. A set of these service stations are interconnected to each other by a topology, and this forms a network. Customers enter the network via sources and are directed to the service stations. A computer system may also be considered from another viewpoint: The processes /or tasks, messages/ could be the service stations which are utilizing a set of resources. The resources are created by the arrival process of customers and may be destroyed by the departure of customers. A resource may be obtained by a process after having been utilized by another process. The precise definition of these models with service stations and $K = \sum_{i=1}^{n} k_i$ number of customers in the whole network the reader may find in the paper of Gelenbe, Muntz [20] . Consider Figure 1. where an n service system is illustrated.

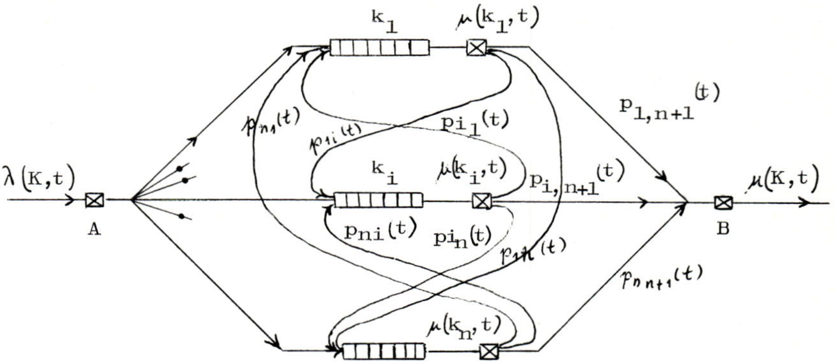

Figure 1.

In many cases in such a system we are interested only in the arrival process of customers at point A and the departure process at point B, or in a complex function of them /e.g. in a performance measure/. We may assume, as a first approximation that the analyzed stochastic processes are Poisson type and the rate $\lambda(K,t)$ /or $\mu(K,t)$ / depends on time and the total number of customers in the system. The parameters $\mu(k_i)$ and $p_{ij}(t)$ mean the departure rate at i-th service station and transition probability from i-th service station to j-th at time t, respectively.

Such point processes were analyzed also by Lewis and Shedler [24] in a model for transactions in a data base system. The case when $\lambda(K,t)$ is a stochastic process is discussed in my paper [7].

Now we assume that the organization of the work of operating system or the data management facility of information management system depends on the parameters λ /or μ /. This is the reason why we want to detect automatically at points A /or B/ any change in rates λ /or μ /. For such a system let us analyse the swapping policy in a virtual storage system /see Chow, Chin [14] /.

In virtual storage operating systems, control of the multiprogramming level is a major area of concern, particularly when some dynamic storage allocation scheme as the working-set strategy is used. However, total storage demand of the working sets changes dynamically with time and sometimes may reach some treshold, thus, causing an "overflow" event. An "underflow" event is caused when allocated storage falls below another treshold. At such events, swapping decisions can be made. If the margin of free storage is small then overflow and underflow events could occur quite frequently. On the other hand, if the margin is large, storage may not be utilized effectively /see Ryan and Coffman [27] /. In MVS, the paging rate is considered only in a swap-out decisions. Performance can be improved if the window size is varied to adapt to the changing needs of storage damand.

The swapping policy studied by Chow and Chiu [14] is of the "look-ahead" type, i.e., predictive values are used to evaluate the criteria for decision.

In practice such predictive values can be obtained from the empirical estimations of a queuing network model /see Fig. 2./.

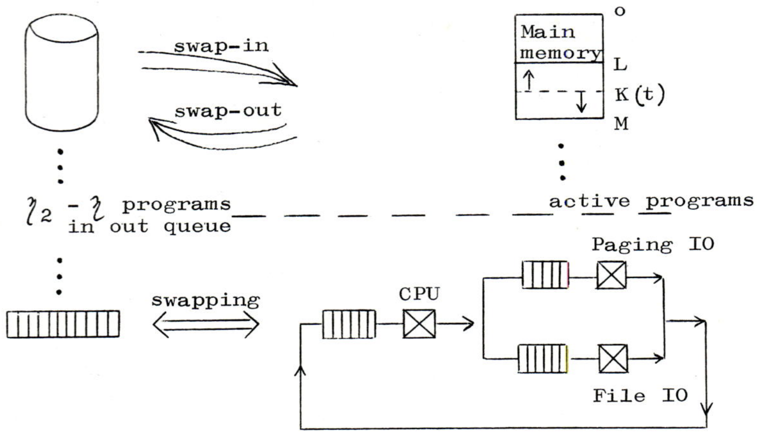

Figure 2.
Swapping and quening model

The following notations are used:

η	degree of multiprogramming, $\eta_1 \leq \eta \leq \eta_2$,
T	working set window size, $T_1 \leq T \leq T_2$,
K(t)	number of allocated pages in main storage at time t,
L	underflow treshold of K(t),
M	overflow treshold of K(t) /capacity/,
U(η, T)	paging device utilization,
V(η, T)	CPU utilization.

The micro states $\{L \leq K(t) \leq M\}$ denote main storage utility which will cause, at the occurrence of overflows or underflows, a transition in macro states $\{(\eta, T, d)\}$, where d indicates the swapping decision.

Table 1

Present state: /η, T, d/. r_1 and r_2 are predetermined tresholds

Event	Criteria	Decision	New state
$K(t) = M$	$U(\eta, T-1) > r_1$	swapout	$(\eta-1, T, 1)$
	$U(\eta, T-1) \leq r_1$	shrink	$(\eta, T-1, 2)$
$K(t) = L$	$U(\eta+1, T) \leq r_2$	swapin	$(\eta+1, T, 3)$
	$U(\eta+1, T) > r_2$	enlarge	$(\eta, T+1, 4)$

If at some time t the number of allocated pages in main storage, $K(t)$ reaches its upper or lower treshold the system may change ist degree of multiprogramming η or the window size T as it is summarized in Table 1.

A typical realization of $K(t)$ is illustrated on Fig. 3., where the <u>macro transitions</u> are detected at times t_1, t_2,...

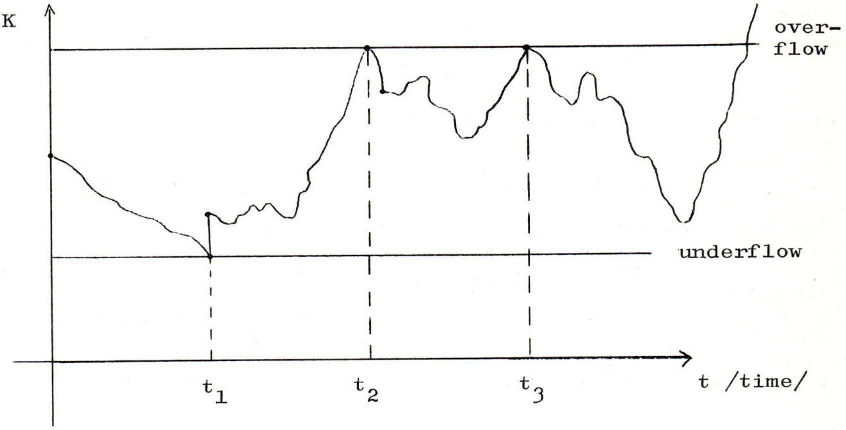

Figure 3.

For measures of performance effectivity we may use such values as overhead rate /the average amount of overhead per unit of time that the CPU is in problem state/, progress rate /proportion of time that the CPU is in the problem state/; the average degree of multiprogramming, the swapping rate, the paging rate, etc.

If we take one of these measures, e.g. the swapping rate, it exhibits significant changes /see Chow, Chiu [14]/. As the time points t_1, t_2, t_3,... forms approximately a Poisson process /see Cramer, Leadbetter [15] or Volkonskij, Rozanov [32]/we may assume that the swapping process forms also a Poisson type one, where the rate may be changed form λ_o to λ_1. The swapping policy /which means Table 1/ will be changed when a change form λ_o to λ_1 will be detected /a disorder occurs/. Analytical and numerical results for swapping rate in a queuing model are discussed in Chow, Chiu's [14] paper, where the detection /disorder/ problem was not treated.

b/ First we formulate the problem and its solution for Poisson process. The number events in the investigated process at A /or at B/ is denoted by N_t. The process N_t is assumed to be a Poisson process whose rate changes from λ_o to λ_1 $(\lambda_1 > \lambda_o > 0/$ at a certain time ξ. ξ is a random variable which is 0 with probability π, and given that $\xi \neq 0$, exponentially distributed with parameter λ, i.e.

/2.1/ $$P\{\xi = 0\} = \pi, \qquad P\{\xi < t \mid \xi > 0\} = 1 - e^{-\lambda t}.$$

We want to tell when ξ occured, from the observations of N_t. Thus the problem is to choose a stopping time τ/a random variable τ which depends only on the past i.e. $\{\tau < t\} \in \sigma\{N_s, s \le t\} = \mathcal{F}_t$, where σ means the σ-algebra of events from the past/ so as to minimize the expected value of some cost function depending on the differences between τ and ξ. Let c, d positive constants and let $I_A(\omega)$ denote the characteristic /or indicator/ function of set A

$$I_A(\omega) = \begin{cases} 1, & \text{if } \omega \in A, \\ 0, & \text{if } \omega \bar{\in} A. \end{cases}$$

We consider the following cost functions

$$s^1_\tau(\omega) = d\cdot(\xi - \tau)\cdot I_{(\tau<\xi)} + c\cdot(\tau - \xi)\cdot I_{(\tau \ge \xi)},$$

/2.2/ $$s^2_\tau(\omega) = I_{(\tau < \xi - \varepsilon)} + c\cdot(\tau - \xi)\, I_{(\tau \ge \xi)},$$

$$s^3_\tau(\omega) = 1 - I_{(\xi - \varepsilon \le \tau \le \xi + \varepsilon)}$$ /"hit or miss" cost/, where $\varepsilon > 0$ constant.

The standard problem is to find the $\mathcal{F}_t$ - stopping time τ^i_o which minimizes $E\, s^i_\tau$, $(i = 1,2,3,$ E means expectation$)$.

To formulate the solution we introduce the process

/2.3/ $$\pi_t = P(t \ge \xi \mid \mathcal{F}_t),$$

i.e. the aposteriori probability of random variable ξ after observing $\{N_s, s \le t\}$.

The evolution of π_t can be written by the following stochastic differential equation /see Davis [16] formula /4.6//.

/2.4/ $$d\pi_t = (\lambda_1 - \lambda_o)(\beta - \pi_t)(1 - \pi_t)dt + g(\pi_{t-})\, dN_t$$

where

/2.5/ $$\beta = \frac{\lambda}{\lambda_1 - \lambda_o},$$

/2.6/ $$g(\pi_{t-}) = \frac{(\lambda_1 - \lambda_o)\pi_t - (1 - \pi_{t-})}{\lambda_o(1-\pi_{t-}) + \lambda_1 \pi_{t-}}$$

The following statement is true.

Theorem. If $\lambda_1 > \lambda_o$ and $k < \beta$, then

/2.7/ $$\tau^* = \inf\{t : \pi_t \geq k\}$$

is optimal, where for s^1: $k = \frac{d}{d+c}$, for s^2: $k = \frac{\lambda'}{\lambda'+c}$, $\lambda' = \lambda e^{-\varepsilon\lambda}$.

The proof may be found in Davis' paper [16].

The cost function s^3 cannot be reduced to the standard form

/2.8/ $$s^k_\tau(\omega) = \int_0^\tau (\pi_s - k)\,ds$$

because

/2.9/ $$E\, s^3_\tau = 1 + E\,(x_{\tau-\varepsilon} - x_{\tau+\varepsilon})$$

and $\tau - \varepsilon$ is not a stopping time in $\mathcal{F}_t$.

It can be shown that τ^* in general is not optimal in case $\lambda_1 > \lambda_o$ and $k > \beta$, or $\lambda_o > \lambda_1$ /see Galchuk, Rozovsky [18] /.

In this case the optimal time τ_o is

/2.10/ $$\tau_o = \inf\{t : \pi_t \geq k_o\}$$

for some $k_o \in [k,1]$. However, no simple way of finding the optimal k_o has yet been found. It involves the conditional distributions of the jump times of N_t, denoted by S_1, S_2, ...

Remark 1. Solution of equation (4) may be given numerically registrating step by step the realization of the process N_t.

Remark 2. In case when N_t is not a Poisson process the optimal stopping rule has not been found. The simple reason is that the observed process is not a Markovian one.

c/ In this part we discuss the diffusion approximation of the above mentioned problem. The Wiener process version of the disorder problem was raised up by Kolmogorov and was studid by Shiryayev. First of all we shall repeat a brief intuitive account and review of a diffusion approximation in the work of a computer system.

Diffusion approximation in the most general case for a single queue, which may be used for queuing networks and open networks, is given in an elagant paper of Gelenbe, Pujolle [21], where a detailed literature is also given. From another viewpoint we give also some exact results for diffusion approximation /see Arató [3], Arató, Knuth, Töke [9], Rét [26] / in utilization problem of CPU, a cyclic queue model and overhead time.

We recall that e.g. in the cyclic queue model $N(t)$, the number in queue at time t will be approximately a Wiener process with $EN(t) = (\lambda - \mu)t$, i.e. the drift is $\lambda - \mu$, and with variance $(\lambda^3 \cdot \sigma_a^2 + \mu^3 \sigma_s^2)t$, where the interarrival /service/ times have mean and variance λ^{-1} (μ^{-1}) and $\sigma_a^2 (\sigma_s^2)$ respectively /see Gelenbe, Pujolle [21]/.

In a similar way /see Arató [3]/ we can prove that the number of swappings in relatively great time intervals T_1, $2T_1$, $3T_1, \ldots$ is nearly normally distributed with parameters

$$E\left(N_{iT_1} - N_{(i-1)T_2}\right) = \lambda T_1,$$

$$D^2\left(N_{iT_1} - N_{(i-1)T_1}\right) = \lambda T_1.$$

This means that taking the process

$$w_{T_1} = N_{T_1},$$

$$w_{T_2} = N_{2T_1} - N_{T_1},$$

$$w_{T_i} = N_{iT_1} - N_{(i-1)\cdot T_1}, \ldots$$

we get in a new time axis a Wiener process with drift λT_1 and wariance λT_1 $(E\, w_{T_i} = \lambda T_1 \cdot i,\ D^2 w_{T_i} = \lambda T_1 \cdot i/.$

Now we can formulate the problem for a continuous time parameter Wiener process, assuming that the number of observation points $i \cdot T_1$ is very great. The problem can be stated roughly as follows. We observe a Wiener process whose drift changes from 0 to r /$r > 0$/ at a certain time ξ. It is a random variable, such that

/2.11/ $$P(\xi = 0) = \pi, \qquad P\{\xi \geq t \mid \xi > 0\} = e^{-\lambda t}, \quad t > 0,$$

where λ $(0 < \lambda < \infty)$ is a known constant and does not depend on π. The observed process ξ_t has the following differential form

/2.12/ $$d_t = r \cdot I_{(t-\xi)} \cdot dt + \sigma\, dw(t),$$

where

$$\sigma > 0, \text{ /does not change/, } I_t = \begin{cases} 1, & t \geq 0, \\ 0, & t < 0. \end{cases}$$

We consider the following cost function

/2.13/ $$s_{\tau}(\omega) = I_{(\tau < \xi)} + c\cdot(\tau - \xi)\cdot I_{(\tau \geq \xi)},\quad c > 0,$$

and let

/2.14/ $$\rho(\pi) = \inf_{\tau}\left\{ P_{\pi}\{\tau < \xi\} + c\, E_{\pi}(\tau - \xi \mid \tau \geq \xi)\cdot P_{\pi}(\tau \geq \xi)\right\}.$$

The stopping time /markov moment/ τ^* is Bayesian if for all $0 \leq \pi \leq 1$:

/2.15/ $$P_{\pi}\{\tau^* < \xi\} + c\cdot E_{\pi}(\tau^* - \xi \mid \tau^* \geq \xi)\, P_{\pi}(\tau^* \geq \xi) = \rho(\pi).$$

Let

$$\pi_t = P_{\pi}\{\xi \leq t \mid \mathcal{F}_t\}$$

the posterior probability distribution of random variable ξ. The evolution of π_t can be written by the following way /see Shiryayev [29] /4.151//:

/2.16/ $$d\pi_t = \lambda(1 - \pi_t)\, dt + \frac{r}{\sigma}\pi_t(1 - \pi_t)\, d\bar{w}(t)$$

where $w(t)$ is a Wiener process, or /Shiryayev [29], /4.160//:

/2.17/ $$d\pi_t = (1 - \pi_t)\left(\lambda - \frac{r^2}{\sigma^2}\pi_t^2\right) dt + \frac{r}{\sigma^2}\pi_t(1-\pi_t)\, d\xi_t.$$

For the Wiener process the following statement is true.

<u>Theorem 2.</u> The Bayesian stopping time τ^* exists and

/2.18/ $$\tau^* = \inf\{t \geq 0 : \pi_t \geq A^*\}.$$

A^* is the solution of the equation:

/2.19/ $$C^{-1} = \int_0^{A^*} e^{-\Lambda[H(A^*) - H(x)]}\cdot \frac{dx}{x(1-x)^2}$$

where

$$C = c\left(\frac{2\sigma^2}{r^2}\right),\quad \Lambda = \lambda\frac{2\sigma^2}{r^2} \text{ and } H(x) = \ln\frac{x}{1-x} - \frac{1}{x}.$$

The proof may be found in Shiryayev's book [29].

<u>Remark 1.</u> As a consequence of theorem 2. we get that among the stopping times τ, for which $P_{\pi}(\tau < \xi) \leq \alpha$, $(0 \leq \alpha < 1)$, the optimal $\tilde{\tau}$, where

/2.20/ $$E_{\pi}(\tilde{\tau} - \xi \mid \tilde{\tau} \geq \xi) \leq E_{\pi}(\tau - \xi \mid \tau \geq \xi),$$

is the following

/2.21/ $$\tilde{\tau} = \inf \{ t \geq o : \pi_t \geq 1 - \alpha \}.$$

Remark 2. The solution /or development/ of equation /17/ may be given only numerically by the registration of the process ξ_t.

3. INDEPENDENT REFERENCE STRING MODELS

a/ There are two main models for a reference /or request/ string $\eta_1, \eta_2, \ldots$. The first one is the independent reference model, when the reference string η_t means a sequence of independent indentically distributed random variables. The second one is the LRU stack model where the distance string D_t $(t = 1,2,\ldots)$, e.g. sequences of stack distances for least recently used /LRU/ replacement, is a sequence of independent, identically distributed random variables. D_t is the total number of distinct references since the last reference to η_t. Lewis and Shedler [23] statistically proved that both of these models are not exactly adequate in paged computer systems. In this part we use the independent reference string model. Let $\eta_1, \eta_2, \ldots, \eta_t, \ldots$ denote the reference string, then by our assumption this sequence of random variables is independent, identically distributed

$$P\{\eta_t = i\} = p_i, \quad i = 1,2,\ldots, n.$$

At first we assume that the probabilities p_i are known and for simplicity $p_1 \geq p_2 \geq \ldots \geq p_n > 0$. $\sum_1^n p_i = 1$.

Let d_t mean the subset of indices /d_t consist of n-m elements/. We assume that decision $d_{t'}$ depends only on the initial decision d_o and the observed reference string $\eta_1, \ldots, \eta_{t'}$, $t' \in [t, N)$. Let us denote by $D_{t,N}$ the set of all possible sequential decision procedures $d_t, \ldots, d_{N-1}$ on a finite time interval $[t,N)$. In our first model, case A, the loss function has the following form:

/3.1/ $$X_t^{d_{t-1}} = \begin{cases} 1, & \text{if } \eta_t \in d_t, \\ 0, & \text{other wise.} \end{cases}$$

In the other case investigated by us, case B, the loss function has the following form:

/3.2/ $$X^{d_t, d_{t-1}} = |d_t \setminus d_{t-1}|,$$

where $|\cdot|$ denotes the number of elements of a finite set. Notice that if $\eta_t \in d_{t-1}$ then $X_t^{d_t, d_{t-1}} \geq 1$.

Our aim is to find the set of sequential decision procedures, $\{d_o, \ldots, d_{N-1}\}$, which minimize the risk function

$$\vartheta(N) = E\left[\sum_{t=1}^{N} X_t^{d_{t-1}}\right],$$

$$\left(\vartheta(N) = E\left[\sum_{t=1}^{N} X_t^{d_t, d_{t-1}}\right]\right),$$

in case A /resp. B/.
Let us denote the conditional expectation under a given realization $y_1,\ldots,y_t$ of $\xi_1,\ldots,\xi_t$ by $E_{\{y_1,\ldots,y_t\}}$ and define the families of conditional risk functions

/3.3/ $$\vartheta\left(y_1,\ldots,y_t, N-t\right) = \min_{\{d_t,\ldots,d_{N-1}\}\in D_{t,N}} E_{\{y_1,\ldots,y_t\}} \sum_{\tau=t+1}^{N} X_\tau^{d_{\tau-1}}$$

and

/3.4/ $$\vartheta\left(y_1,\ldots,y_t, d_t, N-t\right) = \min_{\{d_{t+1},\ldots,d_{N-1}\}\in D_{t+1,N}} E_{\{y_1,\ldots, y_t\}} \sum_{\tau=t+1}^{N} X_\tau^{d_\tau, d_{\tau+1}}$$

in case A and B respectively. Families /3/ and /4/ statisfy the Bellman equations

/3.5/ $$\vartheta\left(y_1,\ldots,y_{t-1}, N-t+1\right) = \min_{d_{t-1}} E_{\{y_1,\ldots y_{t-1}\}}\left[X_t^{d_{t-1}} + \vartheta\left(y_1,\ldots,y_{t-1}, \xi_t, N-t\right)\right],$$

/3.6/ $$\vartheta\left(y_1,\ldots,y_{t-1}, d_{t-1}, N-t+1\right) = \min_{d_t} E_{\{y_1,\ldots,y_{t-1}\}}\left[X_t^{d_t, d_{t-1}} + \vartheta\left(y_1,\ldots,y_{t-1}, \xi_t, d_t, N-t\right)\right].$$

Solving recursively systems of equations /5/ and /6/ we can find the optimal strategies. In case A $\vartheta(y_1,\ldots,y_t, N-1)$ does not depend on d_{t-1} therefore it is sufficient to minimize for every

t the conditional expectation

$$E_{\{y_1,\dots,y_{t-1}\}}\left[X_t^{d_{t-1}}\right].$$

The same statement, with a slight modification, is true in case B.

As

/3.7/ $$\min_{d_{t-1}} E_{\{y_1,\dots,y_{t-1}\}}\left[X_t^{d_{t-1}}\right] = \left(p_n+p_{n-1}+\dots+p_{m+1}\right)$$

and

/3.8/ $$\min_{d_t} E_{\{y_1,\dots,y_{t-1}\}}\left[X_t^{d_t,d_{t-1}}\right] =$$

$$= \left(p_n + p_{n-1} + \dots + p_{m+2} + p_\ell\right),$$

where $1 \le \ell \le m + 1$.

We have thus proved the following result, which generalizes a theorem of A. Lew [27].

Theorem 3. Assume that the reference string ζ_t is an independent sequence with stationary probabilities. Then the policy of taking that index with the least probability of reference is optimal.

b/ The reference string $\zeta_1, \zeta_2, \dots, \zeta_t$ from probabilistic point of view forms a sequence of independent identically distributed random variables; the common probability distribution

$$P_{i,w} = P_w(\zeta_t = i)$$

of the random variables ζ_t depends on a parameter w, value of which is unknown. The dependence on w is given as follows: the range of parameter w is the set W of all permutations of natural numbers $1, \dots, n$; $w(i)$ denotes the one to one mapping of set $\{1,\dots,n\}$ realized by w. There is given a fixed decreasing sequence $p_1 > \dots > p_n > 0$ of probabilities $p_1 + \dots + p_n = 1$ and

$$\{P_{i,w}\} = \{P_w(\zeta_t=i)\} = \{p_{w(i)}\}.$$

Following the Bayesian approach in decision theory we assume that w itself is a random variable. As we have no preliminary information about the distribution $P_w(\zeta_t = i)$ we assume that the prior distribution of parameter w is the uniform one. The optimality of LFU strategy is a consequence of the following lemma /see Benczúr, Krámli, Pergel [11]/.

Lemma 1. If the prior probability distribution of the parameter w is the uniform one and the frequency f_i of page i in the string $\{y_1,\dots,y_{t-1}\}$ is less than that of page j, f_j, then

/3.7/ $$P(\zeta_t = i \mid y_1,\dots,y_{t-1}) < P(\zeta_t = j \mid y_1,\dots,y_{t-1}),$$

i.e. the order of posterior probabilities of indices after observing the string $y_1,\dots,y_{t-1}$ is the same as the order of their frequencies in this string.

Proof. Let i and j two indices such that $f_i < f_j$. If w_1 and w_2 are two permutations with the properties

/i/ $w_1(i) = w_2(j)$,

/ii/ $w_2(i) = w_1(j)$,

/iii/ $w_1(i) < w_1(j) \Leftrightarrow w_2(j) < w_2(i)$,

/iv/ $w_1(k) = w_2(k)$ for $k \neq i, j$,

then, using Bayes' theorem

$$P\{w_1 | y_1,\dots,y_t\} = \frac{\prod_{k=1}^{n} p_{w_1(k)}^{f_k}}{\sum_{w\in W} \prod_{i=1}^{n} p_{w(i)}^{f_i}}$$

and

$$P\{w_2 | y_2,\dots,y_t\} = \frac{\prod_{k=1}^{n} p_{w_2(k)}^{f_k}}{\sum_{w\in W} \prod_{i=1}^{n} p_{w(i)}^{f_i}}$$

we get

$$P\{w_1 | y_1,\dots,y_t\} < P\{w_2 | y_1,\dots,y_t\}.$$

Summing these probabilities we get the required result.

Using Lemma 1 and the uniformity of the prior distribution of parameter $\mathcal{w}$ we get the following statement.

Theorem 4./Separation principle./ The least frequently used strategy minimizes the expected loss $E\left[\sum_{t=1}^{N} X_t^{d_{t-1}}\right]$ in case A, where d_o is arbitrary, and the initial distribution ξ of random variable $\mathcal{w}$ is uniform.

In case B we must argue more carefully. First we prove that the optimal strategies are among the demand paging algorithms, i.e. among the algorithms statisfying the conditions

$$d_t = d_{t-1} \;, \text{ if } \;\zeta_t \,\bar{\in}\, d_{t-1},$$

$$d_{t-1} \setminus d_t = \{\zeta_t\}, \text{ if } \;\zeta_t \in d_{t-1}.$$

The optimality of the LFU strategy in case B follows from Theorem 5.

Theorem 5. If d_t and d_t' are two different decisions for which

$$d_t \setminus d_t' = \{i\},\ d_t' \setminus d_t = \{j\}$$

and the frequency f_i of the page i in the string is less, than the frequency f_j of the page j, then

$$V(y_1,\dots,y_t,\ d_t,\ N-t) < V(y_1,\dots,y_t,\ d_t',\ N-t).$$

The proof can be carried out by induction for $\theta = N-t$. The assertion of Theorem 5 for $\theta = 1$ is an obvious consequence of the observation used in case A /Lemma 1./. The proof of the induction step - the comparison of conditional risk functions

$$V(y_1,\dots,y_t,\ d_t,\ N-t) = E_{\{y_s,\ s\le t\}}\left[\sum_{s=t}^{N} X_s^{d_s,\ d_{s-1}}\right]$$

and

$$V(y_2,\dots,y_t,\ d_t',\ N-t)$$

for $t < N-1$ is not so simple as in case A. Here we use essentially the fact that $V(y_1,\ y_2,\dots,y_t,\ d_t,\ N-t)$ depend only on the frequencies of the pages in the string $\{y_1,\ y_2,\dots,y_t\}$ and on d_t. A detailed proof for page replacement algorithms is given in the paper Benczúr, Krámli, Pergel [11].

c/ The optimality of the LFU strategy without Bayesian assumption we discuss too /see Arató, Benczúr, Krámli [8]/.

Definition 1: A sequence $\{\delta_0,\dots,\delta_{N-1}\}$ of probability distributions on the space Δ of all possible subsets d consisting of /n-m/ elements of the set $\{1,\dots,n\}$ is called randomized sequential decision procedure if and only if for every $0 \le t \le N-1$ the probability distribution δ_t depends only on the prior distribution ξ, and the reference string $\{\eta_1,\dots,\eta_t\}$.

Definition 2: A randomized sequential decision procedure $\{\delta_0,\ \delta_1,\ \dots,\ \delta_{N-1}\}$ is called symmetric if and only if for every moment $0 \le t \le N$ permutation $w \in W$ and realization $\{y_1,\ \dots,\ y_t\}$ the following holds

$$w\left(\delta_t(\xi,\ y_1,\dots,y_t)\right) = \delta\left(\xi,\ w(y_1),\dots,w(y_t)\right).$$

Let us define the "action" $w(\delta)$ of a permutation $w \in W$ on a δ distribution by relation $P_{w(\delta)}(d) = P_\delta(w^{-1}(d))$. The following statement is true.

Lemma 2. For both forms of the loss function /cases A and B/ among the randomized decision procedures the corresponding LFU strategies are optimal, i.e. the procedures $\{\delta_0,\dots,\delta_{N-1}\}$ for which the measure δ_t is concentrated on the subsets d of the set $\{1,2,\dots,n\}$ $(\{1,2,\dots,n\}\setminus\{\eta_t\})$ in case A(B) consisting of the least frequently used indices in the string $\{\eta_1,\dots,\eta_{t-1}\}$.

Notice that in the case of strictly different frequencies δ_t is concentrated on a unique subset d.

Proof. The assertion follows from the fact that in relation (7) stands the strict inequality $<$, if $f_i < f_j$.

We had to extend the sequential decision procedure to the randomized case too if we wanted to preserve the symmetry for the LFU strategies. A nonrandomized LFU strategy cannot be symmetric.

Theorem 6. If the prior distribution ξ is concentrated on a unique permutation $w \in W$, then for both forms of the loss-function among the symmetric randomized sequential decision procedures the LFU strategies are optimal. (The proof may be found in Arató, Benczúr, Krámli [8]).

Remark 1. The theorem states that the LFU strategies are optimal in the non-Bayesian case too.

Remark 2. In a problem of dynamic file assignement let $Y_i(t)$ /$i = 1,2,\dots, n$; $t = 1,2,\dots$/ take the value 1 or 0 according to whether the file is located in memory of i-th computer at time t. Further let $\eta(t) = \{\eta_1(t),\dots, \eta_n(t)\}$ the request string of the file by the n computers. Then

$$X_t^{d_{t-1}} = \sum_{\substack{i,j\\ i\neq j}} \eta_j(t)\; Y_i(t) = \sum_{j\neq d_{t-1}} \eta_j(t)$$

and

$$P\{\eta_j(t) = 1\} = p_j.$$

Remark 3. In demand page replacement algorithms in case A. a page from the second level is delivered to the m + 1 - th place /$m < n$ pages are in the first level/ and after delivering the content of it a page must be removed to the second level. Then, if d_t means the subset of pages being absent of the central memory after moment t,

$$X_t^{d_{t-1}} = \begin{cases} 1, & \text{if } \eta_t \in d_t \\ 0, & \text{otherwise.} \end{cases}$$

In case B each change of a page increases the cost at moment t by 1 and η_t must be stored in the central memory. A page on the first level must be replaced by the requested one.

The loss function has the form

$$X^{d_t, d_{t-1}} = \left| d_t \setminus d_{t-1} \right| ,$$

where $|\cdot|$ denotes the number of elements of a set.

References

[1] AHO A.V., DENNING P.J., ULLMANN J.D. /1971/ Principles of optimal page replacement, Journal A.C.M. 18/1, 80-93.

[2] ARATÓ, M. /1973/ On computing technology for mathematical statistics and stochastic processes and its application for evaluating computer system performance, Proc. Computer Science Conference, Hungary, 231-237.

[3] /1975/ Diffusion approximation for multiprogrammed computer systems, Comp. and Maths. with Appls. 1, 315-326.

[4] /1976/ Számitógépek hierarchikus laptárolási eljárásainak optimalizálásáról, MTA SZTAKI Közlemények v. 16, 7-23, /in Hungarian/.

[5] /1976/ Statistical sequential methods in performance evaluation of computer system, 2nd Internat. workshop on modelling and performance evaluation of computer systems, Stresa-Italy, 1-10.

[6] /1976/ A note on optimal performance of page storage, Acta Cybernetica, Tom 3, fasc. 1, 25-30.

[7] /1977/ Statistical Sequential Decision Methods in Case of Independent Strings, Second Hungarian Computer Sci. Conference Budapest, 33-57.

[8] ARATÓ M., BENCZÚR A., KRÁMLI A. /1977/ On the solution of optimal performance of page storage hierarchies with independent reference string. Banach Center Publications, Vol. 6., Mathematical Statistics, /in print/.

[9] ARATÓ M., KNUTH E., TŐKE P. /1974/ On stochastic control of a multiprogrammed computer based on a probability model, Preprints of the Stochastic Control Symposium /IFAC, Budapest/ 305-313.

[10] ASZTALOS D. /1977/ Performance measurement of MULTIJOB operating System, In this volume

[11] BENCZÚR A., KRÁMLI A., PERGEL J. /1976/ On the Bayesian approach to optimal performance of page storage hierarchies, Acta Cybernetica, v. 3.

[12] BENCZÚR A., KRÁMLI A. /1977/ A probabilistic model for the comparison of different memory handling systems, Second Hungarian Computer Science Conference, Budapest, 178-194.

[13] BÉLÁDY L. /1966/ A study of replacement algorithms for a virtual storage computer, IBM Syst. Journ. 5, 78-101.

[14] CHOW, W.M., CHIU W.W. /1977/ Analysis of swapping policies in virtual storage systems, IEEE Trans. on software Eng. Vol. Se-3, 150-156.

[15] CRAMER H., LEADBETTER M. /1967/ Stationary and related stochastic processes, J. Wiley, London.

[16] DAVIS, M.H.A. /1976/ A Note on the Poisson Disorder Problem Banach Center Publications, Vol. 1, 65-72, Mathematical Control Theory.

[17] DE GROOT, M.H. /1970/ Optimal statistical decisions, Mc Graw-Hill, N.Y.

[18] L.I. GALCHUK, B.L. ROZOVSKY /1971/ The disorder problem for a Poisson process, Theory of Prob. and Appl. 16, 729-734.

[19] GELENBE, E. /1973/ A unified approach to the evaluation of a replacement algorithms, IEEE Trans. Computers, v. C-22, 611-617.

[20] GELENBE, E., MUNTZ R.R. /1976/ Probabilistic Models of Computer Systems-Part I. /Exact Results/, Acta Informatica 7, 35-60.

[21] GELENBE, E., PUJOLLE, G. /1976/ The Behaviour of a Single Queue in General Queuing Network, Acta Informatica 7, 123-126.

[22] LEW, A. /1976/ Optimal Control of demand - paging systems, Information Sciences, 10, 319-330.

[23] LEWIS, P., SHEDLER, G. /1973/ Empirically derived micromodels for sequences of page exceptions, IBM J. Res. Developm. March, 86-100.

[24] /1975/ Statistical analysis of transaction processing in a data base system, Sept. R.J. 1629. IBM Research.

[25] LIPCER, R., SHIRYAYEV, A. /1974/ Statistics of Stochastic Processes, Izd. Nauka Moscow /In Russian/.

[26] RÉT, M. /1977/ On the use of diffusion approximations for the cyclic queue models, MTA SZTAKI Közlemények 18, 99-104.

[27] T.A. RYAN; E.G. COFFMAN /1974/ A problem in multiprogrammed storage allocation, IEEE Trans. Comput. vol. c-23, N°11.

[28] SEGALL, A. /1976/ Dynamic file assignment in a computer network, IEEE Trans. on Automatic Control, Vol. AC-21, N°2, 161-173.

[29] SHIRYAYEV, A. /1969/ Statistical sequential analysis, Izd. Nauka, Moscow /in Russian/.

[30] SHOHAT, Y., STRAUSS, J.C. /1976/ An analytic model of dispatching algorithms. Modelling and Performance Evaluation of Computer Systems, 335-362.

[31] TŐKE, P. /1977/ Issledovanie sloznih algoritmov massovogo obsluzivanija, Second Hungarian Computer Science Conference, Budapest, 871-886.

[32] VOLKONSZKIJ, V.A., ROZANOV, J.A. /1959, 1961/ Some limit theorems for random functions, I and II, Theory of Prob. and Appl. 4, 186-207, and 6, 202-215.

[33] WONHAM, W.M. /1968/ On the separation theorem of stochastic control, SIAM Journ. Control 6, 312-326.

Measuring, Modelling and Evaluating Computer Systems,
H. Beilner and E. Gelenbe, (eds.)
© North-Holland Publishing Company (1977)

A COMPUTER MEASUREMENT AND CONTROL SYSTEM

G. Boulaye, B. Decouty, G. Michel, P. Rolin and C. Wagner

I.R.I.S.A.

Université de Rennes, B.P. 25 A
35031 RENNES CEDEX, FRANCE

ABSTRACT

Existing computer systems measurement tools (Hardware and software monitors) allow static optimisation of these systems. In this paper we define a new system in order to study algorithms for dynamic optimisation of computer systems.

Currently a monitoring sytem is under development which has the following characteristics :

- Measurements are realised by a minicomputer controlled hardware monitor providing raw information through probes. Compared with classical hardware monitors, it has no patch panel. Thus , by eliminating manual intervention, dynamic feedback can be implemented.

- The feedback functions will have two channels to send information : the faster one works with a hard wired event recognition logic and the slower one is software controlled by the minicomputer.

I - INTRODUCTION

Digital systems have become extremely complex and costly while their control systems (operating systems) have been designed with little regard to their optimal use.

To improve performance, two distinct kinds of tools have been developed over the last few years [LUC 71], [EST 72], [DRU 73] :

(1) Measuring methods for improving existing systems and (2) evaluation methods which are concerned more with prediction.

We are primarily interested here of measuring methods. Our aim is to define a system for the study of dynamic optimisation of computer systems.

A study of the problems raised by measurements in digital systems and control possibilities on these systems will enable us to give general specifications for a monitoring system (section 2). In section 3, we list the choices of architecture we have considered, in section 4 we discuss the hardware features and in section 5 we outline the software aspects.

II - PROBLEMS OF MEASUREMENT AND CONTROL IN DIGITAL SYSTEMS.

2.1. Measurement in digital systems

2.1.1. Objectives of measurement

Measurement of digital systems is carried out on large computers systems and is usually concerned with :

- Software tuning : the frequency of the use of system routines determine which routines should be core resident and which could be stored on mass storage ([CAM 68] [CAN 68] [DEN 69]). Measurements on user programs provide information to achieve a higher degree of efficiency in programming ([NEM 71], [COL 76]) and a reduction of the page fault rate [MIL 74].

- Device utilisation : measuring a small channel overlap enables to rearrange devices and data sets to produce better balance between channels, and to forecast the effects of changes in number or in quality of these resources [COC 71].

- Validation of system models : this technique has been especially used for the validation of program behaviour models in their addressing space [BUR 76].

2.1.2. Existing tools

Three categories of tools exist, called monitors ; they are analysed in detail by NUTT in [NUT 75].

2.1.2.1. Hardware monitors

These are machines able to detect, combine, count logicial signals obtained directly from the computer by means of probes. Most manufacturers of computers have developed one for their own specific use : IBM (SMI),Burroughs (SPI), Univac [BOR 71], etc., as have certain research organizations such as IRIA with Harmonie [GAU 73], University of Manchester in their evaluation of the MU5 [HUS 76] and the MIT for the TX-2 [NEM 71].

Monitors of a more general type are sold commercially by two large American companies of which Tesdata is by far the most important. A comparative study can be found in [EDP 74] and [VIL 75]. Their uses are directed essentially toward the optimization of computer centres [VIL 76], [TES 75]. A detailed analysis is provided by ARNDT in [ARN 72] of a study of a real time system for satellite control.

2.1.2.2. Software monitors

Software monitors are programs which are executed on the computer itself which allows the observation of the behaviour of user programs or system programs. This method was used to study the CII SIRIS 8 system [BOI 76].

The possible applications of these two monitors overlap [CAR 71].

2.1.2.3. Hybrid monitors

A hybrid monitor consists of two monitors - a software monitor and a hardware monitor - which, together, can be used to obtain further information on the behaviour of a digital system at the same time, diminishing the interference that notably the software monitor may have on the systems. Generally speaking these hybrid monitors use a minicomputer which overlooks the functioning of both the two components. Experimental systems are described in [ASC 71] : Neurotron Monitor System ; in [RUU 72] : CPM-X ; and in [SEB 74] HEMI.

2.1.2.4. The limitations of these tools

Measurement tools are always limited by their technology.

For hardware monitors, for example, limiting factors are dictated by the specifications of the probes, the length of cables [NOE 74], the physical or contractual inaccessability of the measuring points [SVO 76], the number of probes and preprocessing functions built-in [GAU 74] and so on.

For software monitors, the problems are the level of interference with the system, the difficulties in measurement of time, and the limitations imposed by the machine language (which has no access to the microprogrammed level, nor to certain information on the device controllers).

Hybrid monitors are sometimes limited because of their greater specialization, for example, the HEMI monitor [SEB 74] was conceived solely for the CYBER 70 and 170 series.

2.2. Problems in optimizing systems

The reason for measuring is to obtain feedback on the system observed (except in the case of validation of models).

With existing tools, modifications are left to the operator, and thus are manual. The analysis of the results is often deferred (BATCH Analysis).

Several experiences to control digital systems have been carried out with hybrid monitors. However the automatic triggering of measuring session or the dynamic alteration of certain parameters cannot be envisaged because they always need human intervention with regards to the patch panel [MOR 75].

A study concerning the control of a CII-10070 by a CII-10020 was carried out in Toulouse [BOI 74] with the PASTRE System of dynamic Optimization of the BATCH operating system SIRIS 7.

A certain number of experiments are particularly interesting to do in the field of dynamic optimisation of systems, for example :

- the computation of the level of multiprogramming expressed as a function of the activity of the system [BAD 74] ;

- assignement of resources to sub-systems in terms of their load (e.g. the size of the memory allocated to a time-sharing system in terms of the number of users, or the load-sharing between batch and T.S. sub-systems [LAN 76]) ;

- the size of main memory allocated to user programs in a multiprogrammed system in terms of their behaviour (page fault rate [DEN 75]) which can be optimised by the Denning's "Knee criterion" ;

- the dynamic selection of disc management policies in terms of the corresponding queues ;

- the analysis of bottlenecks in network computers and computer networks.

2.3. Problems raised by existing computer systems

In existing computer systems no measurement or entry points have been included which would allow the modification of certain parameters in the systems. As far as measurement is concerned this means that non-interfering instruments (probes) have to be used and this is very expansive. A certain number of interesting parameters are inacessible due to large scale integration or difficult to reconstitute.

In order to gain access to the desired entry points, quite considerable control system will have to be implemented using the interrupt systems and input-output bus and by the addition of programmed modules. The planning of future systems including measurement points and access to the system parameters would reduce the cost of automatic control systems.

2.4. General specifications for a monitoring system

Here we aim to define a tool which enables one to determine control functions in digital systems.

In the light of the limitations of existing tools, the following principles can be laid down.

- It is possible to reduce technological limitations when envisaging a hybrid type of architecture which is evolutionary and modular. These last two items will enable, after experiments, a definition of all the functions as a whole, which this system has to contain, also taking into account problems raised by real-time operation.

- Control must be dynamic, and this implies total suppression of human intervention at the lowest level (i.e. suppresion of the patch panel).

Associative techniques allow this improvement [HAK 73]. The fact that the equipment is entirely programmable will facilitate the realisation of these experiments. Likewise differed analyses should be reduced to the minimum for the operator (interactive tool).

We have conceived a monitoring system to fulfil these objectives. It must be remembered that this system should be considered as a tool enabling a study of dynamic optimisation algorithms : for instance if one finds that a computer system is in fact well optimised by controlling the degree of multiprogramming, according to the "50 %" criterion [LER 75] or the "L = S" criterion defined by Denning [DEN 76] , it will be less expensive to build the black box (hard, soft or mixed according with real time limitations) which would put into effect this control function, than to keep the complete monitoring system into play to fulfil this function.

III - CAMELEON : A MONITORING SYSTEM

(CAMELEON is the french name for specialised computer for measurement and control of digital systems).

The CAMELEON monitoring system has two complementary features : it is both the basis of a looped control system and a programmable measurement tool.

3.1. The control system

One of the basic characteristics of this system is the possibility for its users to feedback control the behaviour of the observed system. In other words, we hope to be able to dynamically optimise the functionning of an operating system.

It can be considered that several logical levels of feedback exist : the physical organisation of the computer centre, scheduling of the work undertaken, resources allocation, degree of multiprogramming. The monitoring system currently developed has three physical observation levels : the hardware level, the software level, the human level.

3.1.1. The hardware level

The hardware level is the lowest level of observation. The electrical signals from the computer circuitry are sensed by probes whose logical values (for example 0 or 1) can afterwards be combined together.

3.1.2. The software level

The software level uses on one hand the results obtained from the hardware level and on the other hand information on the system being working. This will be sent by means of a special program usually called "software monitor" which runs within the observed system. This program can then easily access to information contained in the computer memory. The software monitor is specific to each computer system.

3.1.3. The human level

The last level is the human level, whose function is to observe the system behaviour in its entirety.

These three levels of observation correspond to three physical feedback paths, such as :

- the observed computer interrupt system
- the use of its peripheral paths which allow a constant dialogue with the machine.
- The possibility for the operator to take priority for the scheduling of work which is being executed.

Furthermore, we have feedback loop between these levels, in order to ensure the knowledge of certain parts of the system behaviour. The three observation and feedback levels are represented by the figure 1.

3.2. A measurement tool

A measurement tool must have the three following characteristics in order to be efficient :

- versatility
- programmability
- speed

3.2.1. Versatility

It is not our wish to design CAMELEON to be a specialised processor. On the contrary we wish our measurement tool to be as flexible as possible, both on the information measurement level and on the level of the feedback aimed for.

This as been solved by opting for the modularity of CAMELEON which makes it an evolutionary tool. This modularity exists in both the number of available probes as well as the type of measurements the monitoring system can carry out.

3.2.2. Programmability

Up until the present time most commercial hardware monitors contains a patch panel into which the desired functions using logical elements such as AND gates, OR gates, flip-flops, etc, are plugged. Consequently all modification of a measurement necessitates the intervention of an operator to re-plug the patch panel. Although this type of combinational unit offers great flexibility for the realisation of complex logical functions, it is, on the other hand, hardly practical and requires a certain minimum level of knowledge of the equipment used.

One gap still needs to be bridged : the complete programming of a measurement. This is what CAMELEON is proposed to achieve. In this way, a user will be able to indicate to the monitor, from a teletype for example, the rate at which he wants the results to be communicated, the events he wants to count, the measurement session start and stop times, etc. So it eliminates all human intervention when a change of measurement is needed because of the current behaviour of the system measured.

3.2.3. Speed

In order to restrict the massive amount of information which before was stored on magnetic tapes, it is necessary to develop the pre-processing of data collected by the probes through successive filters (i.e. combination of signals, count, sequence recognition ...). Another solution consists in an on-line data reduction and analysis, i.e. during the measurement. In this way the sensor points can be checked immediately and development of first results of the measurement can be controlled. Similary the time required for subsequent data processing is reduced.

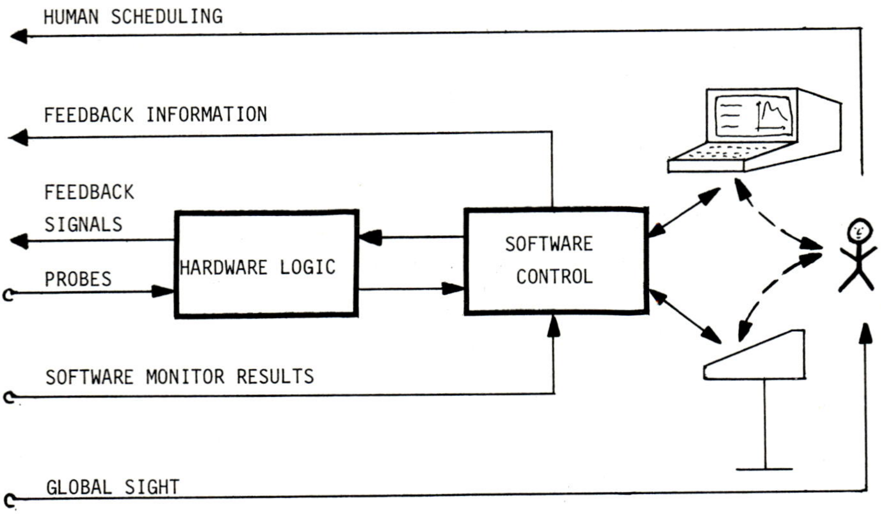

FIGURE 1 - THE OBSERVATION AND FEEDBACK LEVELS

IX - CAMELEON, HARDWARE ARCHITECTURE

The hardware architecture should correspond to the two features examined above :

- the monitoring system modularity
- the presence of several physical observation and feedback levels.

The architecture adopted is shown in fig. 2. One can see two distinct parts which constitutes the CAMELEON monitoring system : the hardware monitor and the monitoring system control unit.

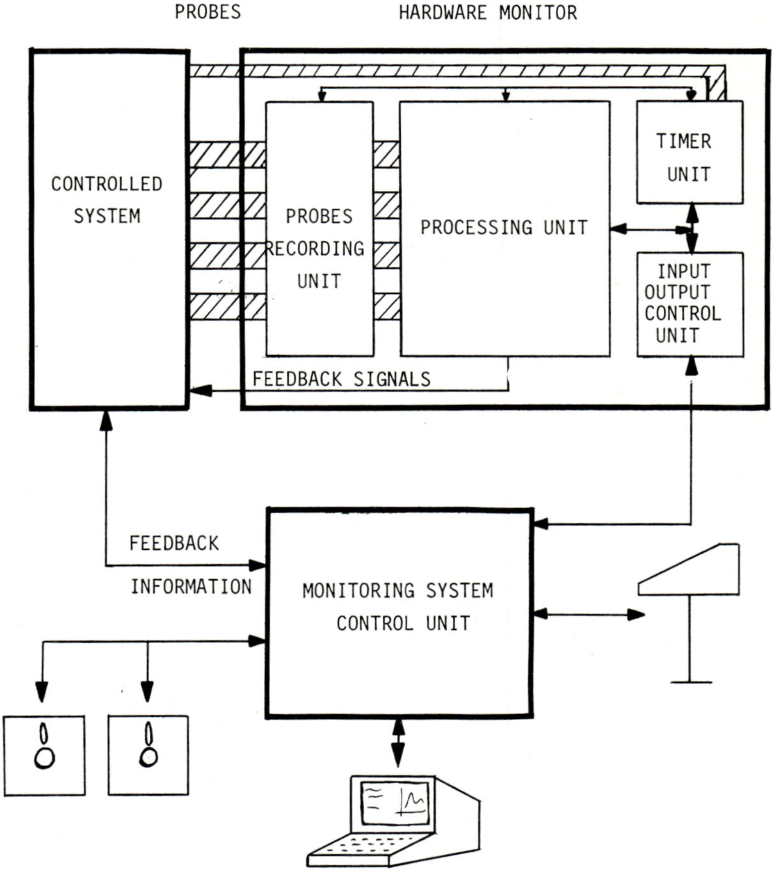

FIGURE 2 - HARDWARE ARCHITECTURE OF CAMELEON

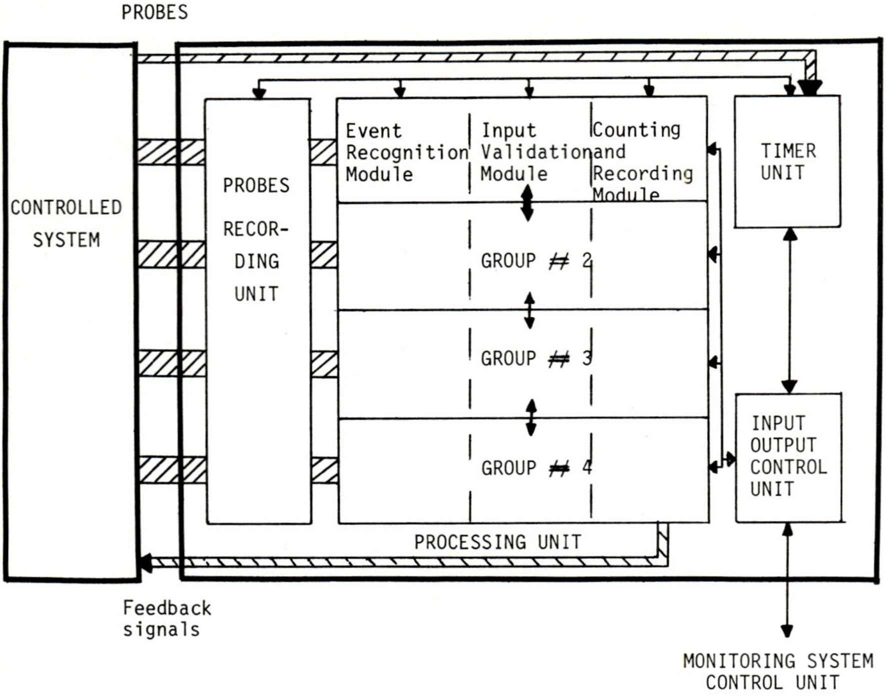

FIGURE 3 - THE HARDWARE MONITOR

4.1. The hardware monitor

The hardware monitor can be divided into four units : the timer unit, the probes recording unit, the processing unit and the Input - Output control unit (fig. 3).

4.1.1. The timer unit

The timer unit function is to distribute the clock pulses required by the processing unit. The clock may be either an external clock or an internal clock the frequency of which is programmed at the beginning of a measurement. Furthermore the timer unit manages the measurement start and stop conditions.

4.1.2. The processing unit

The processing unit is the most important part of the hardware monitor. This feature best demontrates the modularity of the hardware architecture of CAMELEON

It consists of upto four groups of thirty two probes. The composition of each group differs in each case, according to the requirements of each experiment. In each group there are three distinct modules : the event recognition module, the input validation module and the counting and recording module.

4.1.2.1. The event recognition module.

The purpose of the event recognition module is to recognize events requiring combination of system state signals. Such signals are CPU stop, I/Ø Interrupt, problem state, console busy, etc, while events may be any channel busy (channel 1 busy OR channel 2 busy OR ...), CPU channel overlap (CPU active AND any channel busy). In CAMELEON, system state signals, which are picked up by high-impedance probes, are either routed toward an associative memory where the watched events have been stored beforehand, either compared with two values stored in registers, which may contain two addresses enabling you, for instance, to count the number of accesses within that address range.

4.1.2.2. The counting and recording module.

The counting and recording module has been conceived for receiving functions working with the results provided by the event recognition module. Amongst these functions the following may be found : counters, which accumulate the number of occurences of an event or its duration ; histograms, which indicate the distribution of operation codes or memory address ; rapid storage registers, which record a continuous sequence of events and also the future hardware feedback function which constitutes CAMELEON lowest control level.

4.1.2.3. The input validation module

Sometimes, the same data may have different meanings. For example, some minicomputers have a memory bus on which bus one finds either a memory address, or a memory word, depending on status signals. So it is necessary to observe both bus signals and status signals in order to know all the time what is being counted. This is the aim of the input validation module.

4.1.3. The probes recording unit

The probes recording unit consists of a pure electronic interface between the monitoring system and the probes connected to the host computer. This unit also will include, if necessary, a proble-multiplexing device. This device would allow dynamic allocation of a large number of probes to one or many processing groups. This enables two different groups to work on the same data if a single group is not sufficient.

4.1.4. The input-output control unit

The input-output control unit is the interface between the hardware monitor and the minicomputer. It has a special feature in order to check the monitoring system. We have the ability of sending, from the minicomputer, patterns of bits simulating probe signals. By comparing the result with the expected one, we can detect any failure.

4.2. The monitoring system control unit

The control system physical support (figure 4) is a french minicomputer built by the "Télémécanique Electrique", the Solar 16 [TEL 76]. In fact the architecture of this 16 bits minicomputer is designed to be the starting point of multiprocessor systems. The control unit is connected to a teletype, two diskette storage units, a graphic display and, of course, the hardware monitor which behaves as a peripheral device of the Solar. However we enviseage later considering it as a completely separate processor which would have access to all the physical ressources of the minicomputer. The control unit role is developed in the next section.

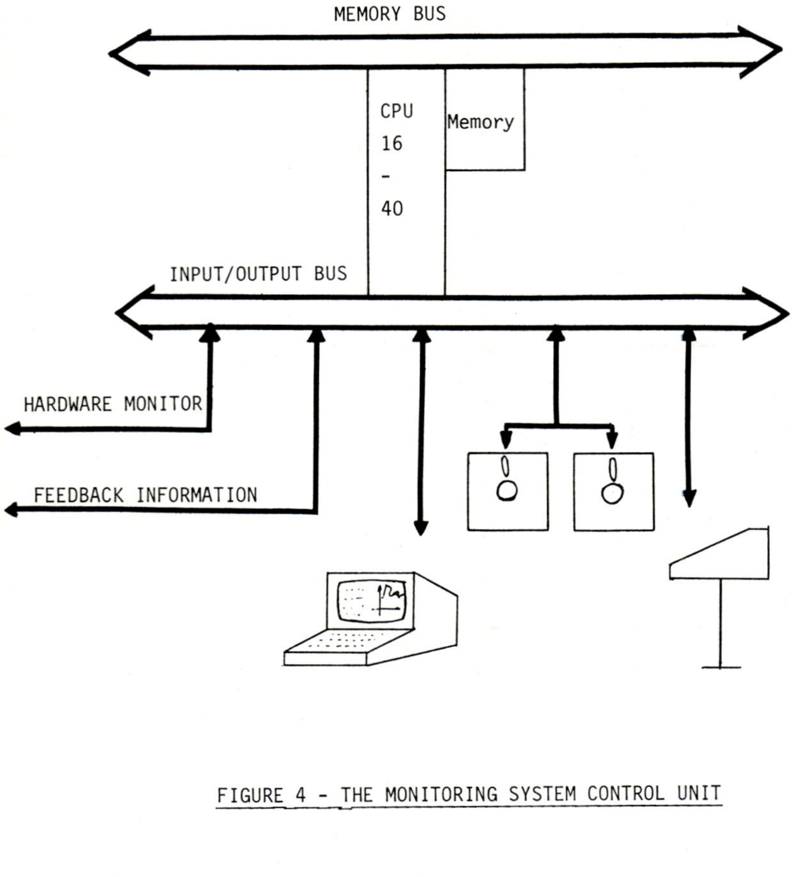

FIGURE 4 - THE MONITORING SYSTEM CONTROL UNIT

V - PRESENTATION OF THE SOFTWARE

5.1. Introduction

All the measurement equipment requires the realisation of data processing software. With CAMELEON we are attempting to accomplish the following goals :

- realisation of a maximul of data processing in real-time
- possibility of feedback by the operator on the experiment

The great inconvenience of first monitors is the further processing of the measurement results. For an extremely short measuring time, large magnetic tapes of data are obtained. These are subsequently processed on the computer under observation. This extremely long operation may provide a large quantity of results, which are occasionally difficult to use and are obtained a long time after what occurred on the machine. The last generation of hardware monitors reduces this problem by including a minicomputer and real time capabilities.

Our aim is therefore to analyse the experiment as it proceeds, thus avoiding a long wait between the actual phenomenon and the results.

Furthermore, as our system has its own computer, it gains portability as the data analysis programs are written for its sole use.

The CRT Display enables the operator to take note of the results at any given moment in the form of Kivigraphs, system profiles,histograms and so on. It allows the operator to choose what he wants to display according to the state of the machine under observation. These results indicate to the operator in which way to best direct the measurement and how to modify the parameters of the observed system or of the measurement in progress.

Between this solution and the traditional one there is as much difference as there is between batch and interactive compilation. As a result of this, time is gained in the analysis of a measurement. This is completely neccessary if we want to implement a quick feedback to the system observed. Our software consists of three main parts (fig. 5) :

- Sampling and storing of the results obtained by the hardware monitor ;
- Analysis of the measurement and display of the results taking into account the decisions made by the operator ;
- Initialisation of the measurement.

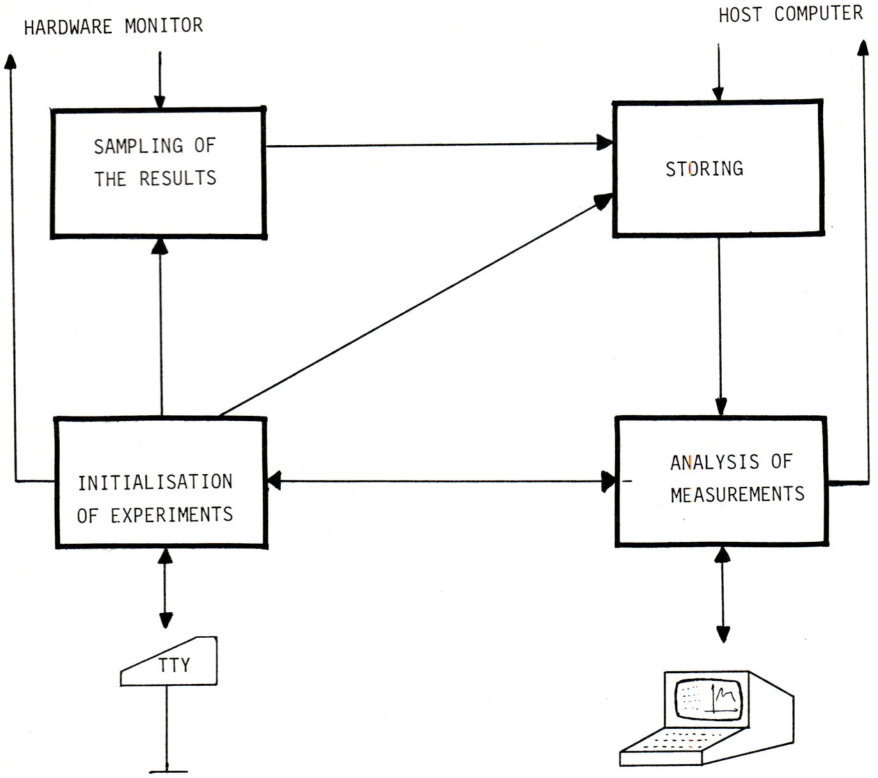

FIGURE 5 - LOGICAL MODULES OF THE MONITORING SYSTEM SOFTWARE

5.2. The sampling module.

This consists of a programmed interface between the measurement equipment and the processing software. This process allows the sampling of results obtained from the hardware monitor either after interruption (e.g. a counter overrunning), or after fixed period of time, decided upon by the programmer. It is possible to know in advance the length of the period of time during which no counter will overrun by means of the clock frequency of the probes recording unit.

In order to optimize the time necessary to get results and the memory size to store these data, the process has always parameters, so that only useful results are selected each time. With each hardware functions (counters, histograms) corresponds a watch dog that the operator may modify during the experiment. That watch dog represents the time between two readings of a same result in the hardware monitor. When the module has collected the results, it then alerts the storage module.

This module is the only element in the system able to collect the results of preprocessing.

5.3. The storage module

Its function is to constitute structured files usable for analysis. In traditional hardware monitor systems, the first task in analysis is to redisbribute experiment files into subfiles which correspond to the particular functions of analysis envisaged. This is task we also assign to it. When the programmer defines his experiment, he defines the analytical functions which he wishes to use and the parameters, i.e. a subsection of the measurements on which these are working. In order to avoid constant access to files, it is better to classify it into subfiles as soon as the measurements are in the main memory. Furthermore certain functions do not necessarily need all the results of the preceding measurements but only those of a subset, e.g. the n last values of a counter. In this case it will be the storage module's task to keep the useful information in the file up to date. This property of the storage module is important for our configuration, indeed we cannot store much information on two floppy discs alone.

A certain amount of processing can be executed on it, if, for example, one needs the total accumulation of a counting stage from the beginning of measurement ...

The module will receive information obtained by a software monitor which will run on the computer under observation.

Thus constituted, the set of files aims to feed the analysis which is carried out in parallel with the measurement.

5.4. Analysis of the measurement.

In order to avoid the rapid contention of the disc and above all to allow the operator to follow his measurement in real time, the analysis functions must be carried out as the experiment progresses.

This analysis corresponds to the definition of the experiment made by the operator at the outset. A certain number of standard functions are required : Kivigraphs, system profile, correlation curves, ... These functions are available in the library and will be called upon when the system is initialized. Other functions may be specific to the experiment and should be defined by the experiment's programmer. One of the functions specific to our hardware is the possibility to dynamically change the experiment. Suppose for example that there is a high rate of activity on one multiplexed channel and a low rate of CPU utilisation. If the probes have previously been connected, one can hope for a finer analysis of what occurs on this channel.

We suppose that this is not possible solely with the help of the results currently sampled. In this case we will start a new experiment planned in advance (experiment file) which will allow us to analyse this phenomenon. Reciprocally it is possible to return to the initial experiment at the end of this phenomenon.

5.5. Display and dialogue with the operator.

With the CRT display, the operator will have the results of the measurement instantaneously and thus with successive requests he will be able to observe the evolution of this phenomenon.

He will be able to modify certain parameters of his measurement from the keyboard, e.g. the sample frequency. He can also decide to change the experiment and to call another measurement session. The flexibility of this interactive tool can be extremely important. However one should take into consideration the cost in computer time of the program governing the display and the keyboard which should not slow down the work of other modules.

VI - CONCLUSION

We have here elaborated the conception of a monitoring system. This system is currently being constructed and the first experiments should start in January 1978.

The paths of evolution for the monitor are the following ones :

- A certain number of experiments will allow us to determine the correct functions to be realised at hardware and programmed levels. The whole can be thought again in a much more condensed way.

- The probes are an extremely expensive part of the system. They are only necessary for studying systems not designed for dynamic optimisation. Digital systems for process control, or future computer systems (perhaps) will include measurement points and entry points and will not need probes.

- Software should evolve towards the development of a measurement and control language.

As concerned with the future uses for the monitor, this tool is designed to determine the control functions for digital systems, which, once determined, it will simply be a matter of building the control system adapted to the system under observation.

REFERENCES

ARN 72 F.R. ARNDT et Capt. G.M. OLIVER, *Hardware Monitoring of Real-Time Computer System Performance*, Computer, vol. 5 n° 4, July/August 1972, pp. 25-29.

ASC 71 R.A. ASCHENBRENNER, L. AMIOT et N.K. NATARAJAN, *The Neurotron Monitor System*, Proc. AFIPS 1971 FJCC, vol. 39, pp. 31-37.

BAD 74 M. BADEL, E. GELENBE, J. LENFANT, L. LEROUDIER, D. POTIER, *Adaptive Optimization of the Performance of a Virtual Memory Computer*, Computer Architecture and Network, 1974.

BOI 74 L. BOI, P. MICHEL, J.P. DRUCBERT, *Emploi d'un petit ordinateur pour l'évaluation et la conduite de systèmes d'exploitation*, Proc. "Mesures et évaluation des systèmes informatiques", colloques IRIA, October 1974, pp. 5-18.

BOI 76 L. BOI, P. CROS, J.P. DRUCBERT, J.Y. ROUSSELOT, P. BOURRET, R. TREPOS, *A performance evaluation of the CII Siris 8 Operating System*, Proc. "IInd international workshop on modelling and performance evaluation of computer system", Stresa (Italy), october 1976, North-Holland pub.

BOR 71 D.T. BORDSEN, *Univac 1108 hardware instrumentation system*, Proc. "ACM (sigops) workshop on system performance evaluation", Harward , april 1971.

BOU 73 G. BOULAYE, G. MICHEL, L. UNGARO, J.L. VINCHON, *An environment for research in computer architecture*, International workshop on computer architecture, Grenoble, 26-28 juin 1973.

BUR 76 P. BURGEVIN, J. LEROUDIER, *Characteristics and models of program behaviour*, Proc. ACM Nat. Conf. 1976.

CAM 68 D.J. CAMPBELL, W.J. HEFFNER, *Measurement and Analysis of Large Operating Systems During System Development*, Proc. AFIPS 1968, vol. 33, part I, pp. 903-914.

CAN 68 H.N. CANTRELL, AL. ELLISON, *Multiprogramming system performance measurement and analysis*, Proc. AFIPS 1968 SJCC, vol. 32, pp. 212-221.

CAR 71 G. CARLSON, *A user's view of hardware performance monitors*, Proc. IFIP Congress, Ljubljana (Yougoslavia), August 1971.

COC 71 J.S. COCKRUM, E.D. CROCKETT, *Interpreting the results of a hardware systems monitor*, Proc. AFIPS 1971 SJCC, vol. 38, pp. 23-38.

COL 76 J.P. COLLINS, *Performance improvement of the CP-V leader through use of the ADAM hardware monitor*, Performance evaluation review, vol. 5 n° 2, april 1976, pp. 63-67.

DEN 69 W.R. DENISTON, *SIPE : A TSS/360 Software measurement technique*, Proc. 24th ACM Nat. Conf. 1969, pp. 229-245.

DEN 75 P.J. DENNING and G.S. GRAHAM, *"Multiprogrammed memory management"* Proc. IEEE, special issue on interactive computer systems. June 1975, pp. 924-939.

DEN 76 P.J. DENNING and K.C. KAHN, *"An L=S criterion for optimal multiprogramming"*, Proc. of the international symposium on computer performance modeling, measurement and evaluation. March 1976. ACM/Sigmetrics.

DRU 73 M.E. DRUMMOND, Jr., *Evaluation and Measurement Techniques for Digital Computer Systems*, 1973, Prentice-Hall-Pub.

EDP 74 *Update on hardware monitors*, EDP Performance Review, vol. 2 n° 10, Oct. 1974.

EST 72 G. ESTRIN, R.R. MUNTZ, R.C. UNZGALIS, *Modeling, Measurement and Computer Power*, Proc. AFIPS 1972 SJCC, vol. 40, pp. 725 738.

GAU 73 B. GAUDEUL, *Le Système Harmonie*, Internal report, IRIA, June 1973.

GAU 74 B. GAUDEUL, *Mesures réalisées à l'aide d'un moniteur de rendement*, Proc. "Mesures et évaluation des systèmes informatiques", colloques IRIA, october 1974, pp. 19-24.

HAK 73 K. HAKOSAKI, M. YAMAMOTO, T. OHNO, M. UMEMURA, *Design and Evaluation System for Computer Architecture*, Proc. AFIPS 1973 NCC, vol. 42, pp. 81-86.

HUS 76 M.A. HUSBAND, R.N. IBBETT, R. PHILLIPS, *The MU5 Computer Monitoring System,* Proc. of European Computing Conference on Computer Performance Evaluation, 1976, pp. 17-28.

LAN 76 C.E. LANDWER, *An Endogenous priority model for load control in combined batch-interactive computer systems,* Proc. of the international symposium on computer performance modeling, measurement and evaluation. March 1976. ACM/Sigmetrics.

LER 75 J. LEROUDIER and D. POTIER, *New results on a model of virtual memory systems performance and evaluation,* Technical report, IRIA-Laboria, June 1975.

LUC 71 H.C. LUCAS, Jr., *Performance evaluation and monitoring,* Computing surveys, vol. 3 n° 3, septembre 1971, pp. 79-90.

MIL 74 W.W. MILLBRANDT, J. RODRIGUEZ-ROSELL, *An Interactive software engineering tool for memory management and user program evaluation,* Proc. AFIPS 1974 NCC, vol. 43, pp. 153-158.

MOR 75 D.E. MORGAN, W. BANKS, D.P. GOODSPEED, R. KOLANKO, *A computer network monitoring system,* IEEE transactions on software engineering, vol. SE-1, n° 3, september 1975, pp. 299-311.

NEM 71 A.G. NEMETH, P.D. ROVNER, *User program measurement in a time-shared environment,* Comm. ACM, vol. 14 n° 10, october 1971, pp. 661-666.

NOE 74 J.D. NOE, *Acquiring and using a hardware monitor,* Datamation, april 1974, pp. 89-95.

NUT 75 G.J. NUTT, *Tutorial : computer system monitors,* Computer, vol. 8 n° 11, november 1975, pp. 51-61.

RUU 72 R.J. RUUD, *The CPM-X- A systems approach to performance measurement,* Proc. AFIPS, 1972 FJCC, vol. 41 part II, pp. 949-957.

SEB 74 P.R. SEBASTIAN, *HEMI, Hybrid Events Monitoring Instrument,* ACM performance evaluation review, vol. 3 n° 4, december 1974.

SVO 76 L. SVOBODOVA , *Computer System Measurability,* Computer vol. 9 n° 6, June 1976, pp. 9-17.

TEL 76 *Télémécanique Electrique*, Division Informatique, série SOLAR 16, manuel de présentation, n° 1/76 MP 8873F, 1976.

TES 75 MS Update, *Tesdata report on computer performance evaluation,* 1975.

VIL 75 L. DE VILMORIN, *Des moniteurs hardware, pourquoi faire ?* 01 Informatique, n° 95, december 1975, pp. 22-27.

VIL 76 L. DE VILMORIN, *Optimiser les systèmes. Une vocation du moniteur Hardware,* 01 Informatique, n° 96, january 1976, pp. 36-40.

Measuring, Modelling and Evaluating Computer Systems,
H. Beilner and E. Gelenbe, (eds.)
© North-Holland Publishing Company (1977)

IMPROVED BOUNDS AND AN APPROXIMATION FOR A DYNAMIC PRIORITY QUEUE.

Bernhard Walke
AEG-TELEFUNKEN, Research Institute,
Elisabethenstraße 3, D-7900 Ulm-Donau,
West Germany

An infinite source model M/G/1 is considered and analyzed for a dynamic (nonpreemptive) priority discipline: Arriving customers at a queue are assigned urgency numbers. The customer with smallest urgency-number-plus-arrival-time is served next. This service discipline has the effect of distinguishing between customers with different priorities while at the same time taking into account the undesirability of having low priority customers wait too long [1,2,3].

The upper and lower bounds on equilibrium mean waiting times of reference [3] are distinctly improved, and an approximation is introduced which yields good agreement with simulation results. From a heavy traffic solution, new insights are gained into typical properties of this dynamic priority discipline. Examples are given to compare results of this discipline with results of the well-known static priority discipline.

1. THE MODEL

In many real-time computer applications service requests must be processed within specified time limits. A strict observation of such limits is impossible if service requests occur at random. In this case a high (given) probability for meeting all deadlines is required. These deadlines result from the sum of arrival times of individual requests and their permissible wait times. Usually this permissible wait time is called relative urgency $\mathbf{V}$.

We consider the model in Fig.1 in which i types of service requests ($1 \le i \le N$) arrive in independent Poisson arrival processes with parameters λ_i. Service times s_i of i-type requests are i.i.d. random variables with general d.f. $F_i(t) = \text{Prob}(s_i \le t)$ and finite second moment. An i-type service request is characterized by a relative urgency ν_i. All the urgencies are related by the condition

$$0 \le \nu_1 < \nu_2 < \ldots \nu_i < \ldots < \nu_N. \tag{1.1}$$

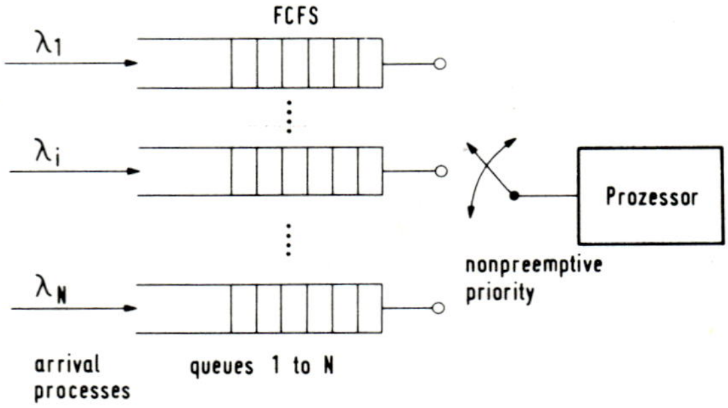

Fig. 1 Model with N queues.

Let the priority $q_i(t)$ of an i-type service request depend on its urgency ν_i, the time of its arrival T_i and its waiting time w_i in the model according to the formula:

$$q_i(t) = \nu_i - t + T_i\,. \tag{1.2}$$

Waiting time w_i at time t is defined as

$$w_i = t - T_i\,. \tag{1.3}$$

From this relationship we have the dynamic priority of i-type requests at time t to be

$$q_i(t) = \nu_i - w_i. \tag{1.4}$$

Waiting-time dependent priorities are called dynamic priorities. Service requests in our model are processed by the server without interruptions. Whenever the server has completed a service request, a new request with highest priority $q_i(t)$ (smallest value of $q_i(t)$) is then serviced. This service discipline is known as nonpreemptive relative-urgency (RU) discipline [1,3].

Fig. 2 shows an example with N=2 types of request with urgencies $\nu_1=2$, $\nu_2=4$ and constant and equal service times $\beta_1 = \beta_2 = 3$. The ordinate shows the actual dynamic priority $q_i(t)$ and the abszissa shows the time t. At the arrival time $t=T_i$ each request has a priority $q_i(0) = \nu_i$ because $w_i=0$. The priority of a waiting request increases linearly (the value of $q_i(t)$ decreases) with its waiting time w_i. Service requests arrive at times t = 1,2,4,5,6,8,12. Their individual priority functions are shown. The server occupation by a service request is shown by means of a hatched bar with intervals denoted by $i(T_i)$, the type i and arrival time T_i of an individual request. In cases of equal priority (e.g. for t=4), the most urgent request is serviced first.

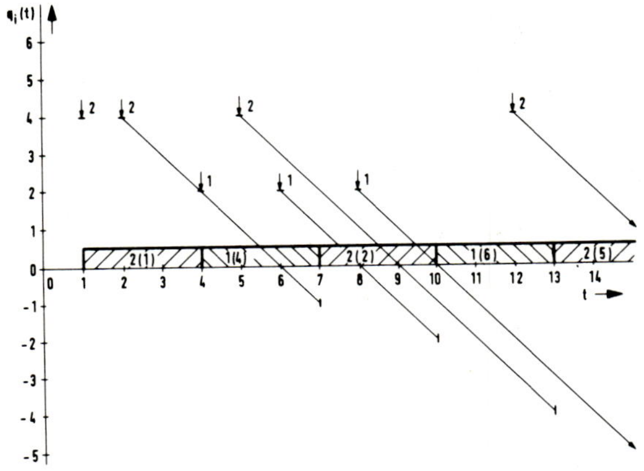

Fig. 2 Example showing the dynamic priority $q_i(t)$ over time t ($N=2$, $\nu_1=2$, $\nu_2=4$, $\beta_1=\beta_2=3$, constant service times). Times of arrival of i-type requests are marked with an indexed arrow↓i. The server occupation by an i-type request, which arrived at time T_i, is shown by the hatched bar with intervals denoted by $i(T_i)$.

An analytic solution for the mean waiting time in the RU discipline is known only for a discrete time model (M1), with service times of all requests following the same geometric d.f. and a Bernoulli input process [1,2]. In addition to this exact solution, upper and lower bounds on the mean waiting time are known for a more general model M/G/1 with a Poisson input process and general service time d.f.'s. But these bounds are unsatisfactory.

Two remarkable properties of the RU discipline should be mentioned: (1) If the variance of all urgencies approaches zero, the FCFS discipline is approximated; (2) if the variance of all urgencies approaches infinity, the HOL (head of the line) discipline [4] is approximated. The HOL discipline usually is also called nonpreemptive static-priority discipline.

In section 2 of this paper an approximate computation of the mean waiting time W_i of i-type requests is introduced, and in section 3 improved bounds for the mean waiting time are derived.

The following abbreviations will be used throughout:

W_i	equilibrium mean waiting time of an i-type request
$\rho_i = \lambda_i/\mu_i$	offered traffic of i-type requests
ν_i	urgency of an i-type request
$\rho_{\le i} = \sum_{j=1}^{i} \rho_i$	offered traffic of all j-type requests together ($1 \le j \le i$); probability for a non-idle server if i=N
$\lambda_{\le N} = \sum_{i=1}^{N} \lambda_i$	total arrival rate
$F_i(t)$	service-time d.f. of an i-type request
$F_{\le N}(t) = \lambda_{\le N}^{-1} \sum_{i=1}^{N} \lambda_i F_i(t)$	weighted service-time d.f.
$\beta_{\le N}^{(r)} = \lambda_{\le N}^{-1} \sum_{i=1}^{N} \lambda_i \beta_i^{(r)}$	r-th moment of $F_{\le N}(t)$
$\beta_{\le N}^{(1)} = \beta_{\le N}$	

$C^2_{\le N} = \beta^{(2)}_{\le N} / \beta^2_{\le N} - 1$	squared coefficient of variance of $F_{\le N}(t)$
$W_o = \lambda_{\le N}\, \beta^{(2)}_{\le N} / 2$	equilibrium mean time to finish a request in service just after arrival of a service request
$W_{FCFS} = W_o/(1 - \rho_{\le N})$	equilibrium mean waiting time in the FCFS discipline
$W_{\le N} = \lambda^{-1}_{\le N} \sum_{i=1}^{N} \lambda_i W_i$	common equilibrium mean waiting time of all service requests

2. APPROXIMATE WAITING-TIME COMPUTATION

We assume that $\rho_{\le N} < 1$ and that equilibrium conditions are satisfied and consider the arrival of a p-type request ($1 \le p \le N$), the tagged request. Upon its arrival, the expected number, $E(n_i)$, of i-type request present in the queue (not being serviced), is [8]

$$E(n_i) = \lambda_i W_i \, . \tag{2.1}$$

Let f_{ip} represent the expected fraction of these i-type requests which are serviced before the tagged request is. The expected number, $E(m_i)$, of i-type requests which arrive during the expected waiting time, W_p, of the tagged request is

$$E(m_i) = \lambda_i W_p . \tag{2.2}$$

Let g_{ip} represent the expected fraction of these i-type requests which are serviced before the tagged request is.

The mean waiting time W_p of the tagged request can be composed of three components: (1) W_o (see abbreviations above) and two products each consisting of the mean number of i-type requests which will be serviced before the tagged request, multiplied by the mean service time β_i of such requests. The first product (2) consists of those requests which are already waiting when the tagged request arrives and the second product (3) of those requests which arrived after the tagged request but are serviced before it. From these observations, we are able to set up a set of N simultaneous equations, one for each value of p, as follows:

$$W_p = W_o + \sum_{i=1}^{N} E(n_i)\, f_{ip}\, \beta_i + \sum_{i=1}^{N} E(m_i)\, g_{ip}\, \beta_i . \qquad (2.3)$$

All i-type requests already waiting when the tagged request, p, arrives and satisfying $i \leq p$ are serviced before it. From this observation it follows that

$$f_{ip} = 1 \qquad \text{for all } i \leq p. \qquad (2.4)$$

All i-type requests which arrive after the tagged request, p, and satisfy $i \geq p$ are serviced after it. From this observation it follows that

$$g_{ip} = 0 \qquad \text{for all } i \geq p. \qquad (2.5)$$

Using this information and solving for W_p in eq.(2.3), we obtain

$$W_p = [W_o + \sum_{i=1}^{N} \rho_i W_i + \sum_{i=p+1}^{N} \rho_i W_i f_{ip}]/(1 - \sum_{i=1}^{p-1} \rho_i g_{ip}). \qquad (2.6)$$

Up to this point the derivation in this section is identical to a derivation published by Kleinrock [9] for another dynamic priority discipline.

<u>Derivation of an expression for $E(n_i)f_{ip}$</u>

Let us assume that the tagged request arrives at time t=0. Its priority upon arrival is $q_p(t) = \nu_p$ (cf. Fig.3). Since w_p is its waiting time, the value of its attained priority at the time it is accepted for service is $q_p(t=w_p) = \nu_p - w_p$, cf. eq.(1.2). The slope of the priority function is constant and does not depend on the type i of a request. From this it follows that all i-type requests, which have arrived before the tagged request and have been waiting for a time w_i, will be serviced before the tagged request, if and only if their priority is

$$q_i(t=0) < \nu_p \quad \text{with} \quad q_i(t=0) = \nu_i - w_i . \qquad (2.7)$$

From this it follows that the arrival time, T_i, of an i-type request (i>p) must satisfy the condition

$$T_i < \nu_p - \nu_i . \qquad (2.8)$$

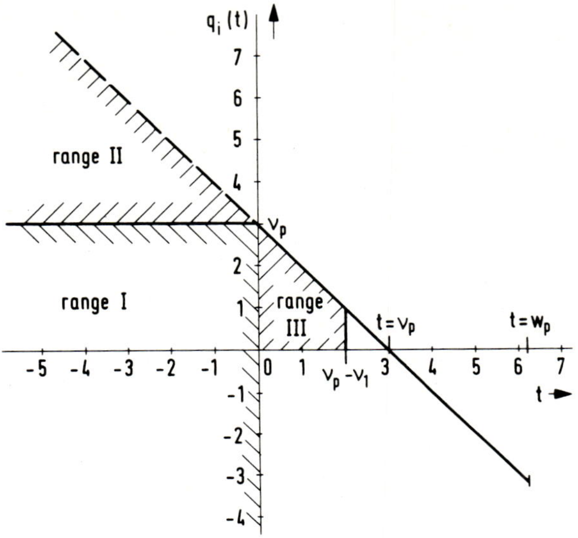

Fig. 3 Priority diagram

Otherwise it will be serviced after the tagged request. The condition in eq.(2.7) can be satisfied by all i-type requests with $i \leq p$ (region I in Fig.3), already considered in eq.(2.4). Other requests which also satisfy this condition are those with urgencies $v_i > v_p$, which satisfy the condition in eq.(2.8) (region II in Fig.3).

The real waiting time $w_i(T_i)$ of less urgent requests (i>p), still waiting at time t=0 and being serviced before the tagged request is

$$|T_i| \leq w_i(T_i) < \infty . \qquad (2.9)$$

The mean number of i-type requests still waiting at time t=0 and being serviced before the tagged request is

$$E(n_i)f_{ip} = \lambda_i \int_{-\infty}^{v_p - v_i} P(t \leq w_i(t) < \infty)\, dt,$$

which is the same as

$$E(n_i)f_{ip} = \lambda_i \int_{\nu_i-\nu_p}^{\infty} P(t \leq w_i(t) < \infty)dt \qquad (2.10)$$

with $i > p$.

In this expression, $\lambda_i dt$ is the mean number of i-type requests that arrived during the time interval$(-t-dt,-t)$ and P() is the probability that a request, which arrived in that interval, spends at least t time units in the queue. The integration limits in eq.(2.10) result from the eqs.(2.8) and (2.9). Eq.(2.10) can be rewritten as

$$E(n_i)f_{ip} = \lambda_i \int_{\nu_i-\nu_p}^{\infty} [1-P(w_i \leq t)]dt - \lambda_i \int_{\nu_i-\nu_p}^{\infty} [1-P(w_i < \infty)]dt$$

$$= \lambda_i \int_{\nu_i-\nu_p}^{\infty} [1-P(w_i \leq t)]dt.$$

Observing that

$$E(w_i) = W_i = \int_{0}^{\infty} [1-P(w_i \leq t)]dt$$

we have

$$E(n_i)f_{ip} = \lambda_i W_i - \lambda_i \int_{0}^{\nu_i-\nu_p} P(w_i > t)dt \qquad (2.11)$$

with $i > p$.

Unfortunately the probability $P(w_i > t)$ is unknown. We now introduce two different approximations for the probability $P(w_i > t)$, and are then able to compute the integral in eq.(2.11).

Approximation 1: The probability of waiting is, presuming non-preemptive prioritites, the same for all types of requests [4] and given by

$$P(w_i > 0) = \rho_{\leq N}.$$

Remember that the offered traffic, $\rho_{\leq N}$, is exactly the probability for the server being non-idle. The assumption that all waiting times, w_i, are greater than the difference $(\nu_i - \nu_p)$ results in

$$P(w_i > [\nu_i - \nu_p]) = \rho_{\leq N} \qquad (2.12)$$

which is called approximation 1 and yields

$$E(n_i)f_{ip} = \lambda_i[W_i - \rho_{\leq N}(\nu_i - \nu_p)]. \qquad (2.13)$$

In this assumption the service discipline for requests, already waiting when the tagged request arrives is FCFS. Approximation 1 may be used to describe the heavy-traffic condition, $\rho_{\leq N} \longrightarrow 1$, of our model. This follows from w_i approaching infinity under this condition.

Approximation 2: Presuming the waiting time of waiting requests being negative exponentially distributed with mean $W_i/\rho_{\leq N}$ results in

$$P(w_i > t) = \rho_{\leq N}\, e^{-\rho_{\leq N} t/W_i}. \qquad (2.14)$$

This waiting time d.f. results from the M/M/1 model using the FCFS discipline. Our model approximates the FCFS model, if the variance of all urgencies approaches zero. The quality of this approximation is discussed in the literature [5] and it has been found to be acceptable.

The factor, $\rho_{\leq N}$, in eq.(2.14) exactly describes the probability $P(w_i > 0)$. Using the approximation 2, eq.(2.11) can be written as

$$E(n_i)f_{ip} = \lambda_i W_i\, e^{\rho_{\leq N}(\nu_p - \nu_i)/W_i}. \qquad (2.15)$$

Derivation of an expression for $E(m_i)g_{ip}$:

Let us assume once more that the tagged request of type p arrives at time t=0. Its priority upon arrival is $q_p(t) = \nu_p$, cf. Fig. 3. In looking for g_{ip}, we must calculate how many i-type requests arrive after t=0, but before $t=w_p$ and attain a priority $q_i(w_p) \leq \nu_p - w_p$.

Such requests will be serviced before the tagged request. Apparently this condition can be satisfied only by those i-type requests ($i < p$) which arrive during the time interval $[t=0,\ t=(\nu_p - \nu_i)]$, cf. region III in Fig. 3. This follows from the assumptions made in the eqs. (1.1) and (1.2). The mean number $E(m_i)g_{ip}$ of i-type requests arriving after the time t=0 but being serviced before the tagged request p is given from

$$E(m_i)g_{ip} = \lambda_i \int_0^{\nu_p - \nu_i} P(w_p > t)\,dt \qquad \text{with } i < p. \tag{2.16}$$

Once again the probability $P(w_p > t)$ is not known, cf. eq.(2.11). Again, we use the same two approximations and obtain for

Approx. 1 with $\qquad P(w_p > [\nu_p - \nu_i]) = \rho_{\leq N} \qquad (2.17)$

which corresponds to eq. (2.12), an expression

$$E(m_i)g_{ip} = \lambda_i(\nu_p - \nu_i)\,\rho_{\leq N} \tag{2.18}$$

Approx. 2, eq.(2.14): $\qquad E(m_i)g_{ip} = \lambda_i W_p(1 - e^{\rho_{\leq N}(\nu_i - \nu_p)/W_p}). \qquad (2.19)$

The mean number, E(n), of requests waiting or being serviced is

$$E(n) = \sum_{i=1}^{N} [E(n_i) + \rho_i].$$

Applying eq.(2.1) we obtain

$$E(n) = \sum_{i=1}^{N} \lambda_i(W_i + \beta_i). \tag{2.20}$$

2.1 Application of the heavy traffic approximation 1

From eqs.(2.6), (2.13), (2.18) we have

$$W_p = (W_o + \sum_{i=1}^{p} \rho_i W_i + \sum_{i=p+1}^{N} \rho_i [W_i - \rho_{\le N}(\nu_i - \nu_p)])/$$

$$[1 - \rho_{\le N} \sum_{i=1}^{p-1} \rho_i (\nu_p - \nu_i)/W_p]$$

$$W_p = W_o + \sum_{i=1}^{N} \rho_i [W_i - \rho_{\le N}(\nu_i - \nu_p)].$$

Using the conservation law [6]

$$\sum_{i=1}^{N} \rho_i W_i = \rho_{\le N} W_o/(1-\rho_{\le N}) \tag{2.21}$$

and setting $W_{FCFS} = W_o/(1-\rho_{\le N})$

we find

$$W_p = W_{FCFS} + \rho_{\le N} \sum_{i=1}^{N} \rho_i (\nu_p - \nu_i) \quad \text{for } \rho_{\le N} \longrightarrow 1. \tag{2.22}$$

From this heavy-traffic solution, two interesting results can be derived:

$$(W_j - W_{j-1})/\rho_{\le N}^2 = \nu_j - \nu_{j-1}, \qquad j > 1,\ \rho_{\le N} \longrightarrow 1, \tag{2.23}$$

and, defining the mean urgency $\bar{\nu}$ by

$$\bar{\nu} = \rho_{\le N}^{-1} \sum_{i=1}^{N} \rho_i \nu_i, \tag{2.24}$$

$$(W_{FCFS} - W_j)/\rho_{\le N}^2 = \bar{\nu} - \nu_j, \quad j \ge 1,\ \rho_{\le N} \longrightarrow 1. \tag{2.25}$$

Both results, eqs. (2.23) and (2.25), are concerned with distance measures between mean waiting times. The close relationship to a similar distance measure is noticeable:
Let $Q_j(f)$ and $Q(f)$ be defined as f-quantiles of the waiting-time d.f. of j-type requests and of requests of a FCFS model,

respectively. Jackson [7] has shown that the waiting-time d.f.'s of j-types requests in the model M1, defined in section 1 above, have two properties:

$$Q(f) - Q_j(f) \longrightarrow \bar{\nu} - \nu_j \text{ for } f \longrightarrow 1, \quad 1 \leq j \leq N \qquad (2.26)$$

and

$$Q_j(f) - Q_{j-1}(f) \longrightarrow \nu_j - \nu_{j-1}, \text{ for } f \longrightarrow 1, \ j > 1. \qquad (2.27)$$

An adequate continuous-time model corresponding to this discrete-time model M1 is a model M/M/1 with RU discipline. The right hand sides of eqs. (2.25) and (2.26) and also eqs. (2.23) and (2.27) are the same. Assuming that Jackson's discrete-time results can be applied to the continuous-time model M/M/1 (which in fact was proposed by Jackson [7] himself), it appears that large mean waiting times and large waiting times of i- and j-type requests in the M/M/1 model differ from each other by the difference of their urgencies $\nu_i - \nu_j$. We might suspect that this should also be true for our model M/G/1. This suspicion is investigated and confirmed in [5].

Eq.(2.12) assumes that all requests arriving before the tagged request of type p are serviced before it, while eq.(2.17) assumes that all i-type requests (i < p) arriving after it, unless its service is started, are also processed before it. In reality not all of these requests are serviced before the tagged request. From this observation one may suspect that, independent of $\rho_{\leq N}$, two relations should hold

$$(W_j - W_{j-1})/\rho^2_{\leq N} \leq \nu_j - \nu_j{-1}, \qquad j > 1 \qquad (2.28)$$

$$(W_{FCFS} - W_j)/\rho^2_{\leq N} \leq \bar{\nu} - \nu_j, \qquad j \geq 1. \qquad (2.29)$$

A proof of these two relations was not found, but for a number of different examples, these relations have been found to be true.

2.2 Application of the approximation 2

The waiting-time d.f. of i-type requests is assumed to follow a degenerated exponential d.f., eq.(2.14), with mean W_i and squared coefficient of variance

$$c^2 = (2 - \rho_{\leq N})/\rho_{\leq N}.$$

The second moment is approximated by

$$W_i^{(2)} = W_i^2(C^2 + 1),$$

which follows directly the assumption in eq.(2.14).
Remember that the upper integration limit in eqs.(2.11) and (2.16) is less than infinity, namely $t = |\nu_i - \nu_p|$. From this it follows that the approximation of the waiting-time d.f. of i-type requests, by the assumption in eq.(2.14), is only of interestfor an interval of the waiting time, w_i, given by $0 \leq w_i \leq |\nu_i - \nu_p|$. It also should be mentioned that the probability $P(w_1 > t)$ is not used in our computation, which means that the waiting-time d.f. of 1-type requests may not be approximated.

From eqs.(2.6), (2.15) and (2.19) we can compute an approximation for W_p which is valid over the whole range of $\rho_{\leq N}$

$$W_p = \frac{W_o + \sum_{i=1}^{p} \rho_i W_i + \sum_{i=p+1}^{N} \rho_i W_i \, e^{\rho_{\leq N}(\nu_p - \nu_i)/W_i}}{1 - \sum_{i=1}^{p-1} \rho_i (1 - e^{\rho_{\leq N}(\nu_i - \nu_p)/W_p})}, \quad \text{for } 0 \leq \rho_{\leq N} < 1$$

and using eq.(2.21) we have

$$W_p[1 - \sum_{i=1}^{p-1} \rho_i (1 - e^{\rho_{\leq N}(\nu_i - \nu_p)/W_p})] =$$

$$W_{FCFS} - \sum_{i=p+1}^{N} \rho_i W_i (1 - e^{\rho_{\leq N}(\nu_p - \nu_i)/W_i}). \qquad (2.30)$$

The mean waiting time, W_p, can be computed by solving a system of N simultaneous transcendent equations which can be solved recursively beginning with p=N. For each value of p the unique zero value, W_p, has to be found by numeric methods.

2.3 Examples and comparisons of approximation and simulation results for W_p.

If the variance of all urgencies approaches infinity, our model approximates the HOL discipline. The mean waiting time of requests with priority i for this static priority discipline is [4]

$$W_{iHOL} = \frac{W_o}{(1-\rho_{\leq i})(1-\rho_{\leq i-1})} . \qquad (2.31)$$

The mean waiting time of our model, with all requests having the same urgency, is the same as results from a FCFS model, W_{FCFS}. Let us consider

Example 1: $N=4$, $\rho_i = \rho_{\leq N}/N$, negative exponential service-time d.f.'s with means $\beta_1=1$, $\beta_2=3$, $\beta_3=5$, $\beta_4=7$, $\beta_{\leq N}=2.4$, $\beta_{\leq N}^{(2)}=19.1$, $C_{\leq N}=1.52$. The urgencies are as given in Fig.5.

It should be mentioned here that the mean waiting times, W_i for this example (with ρ_i being the same for all i) do not denpend on the manner in which the ν_i's are associated with the β_i's. Any other functional dependency (e.g. the same urgencies associated with the inverse order of the β_i's, $\beta_1=7$, $\beta_2=5$, $\beta_3=3$, $\beta_4=1$) yields the same results for the W_i's. Only the common mean waiting time, $W_{\leq N}$, depends on it.

For a static priority model, the mean waiting times, W_i, differ more, the greater the parameter $\rho_{\leq N}$ (cf. Fig.4) is. Even in the case of saturation ($\rho_{\leq N} \geq 1$) the mean waiting times of high priority requests remain small. For a dynamic priority model, it was alread mentioned that the mean waiting times W_i should differ very little from the mean waiting time W_{FCFS} if the variance of the urgency numbers ν_i is small, and should approach the mean waiting times W_{iHOL} if this variance is large. Upper and lower bounds on the times W_i are given by W_{4HOL} and W_{1HOL}.

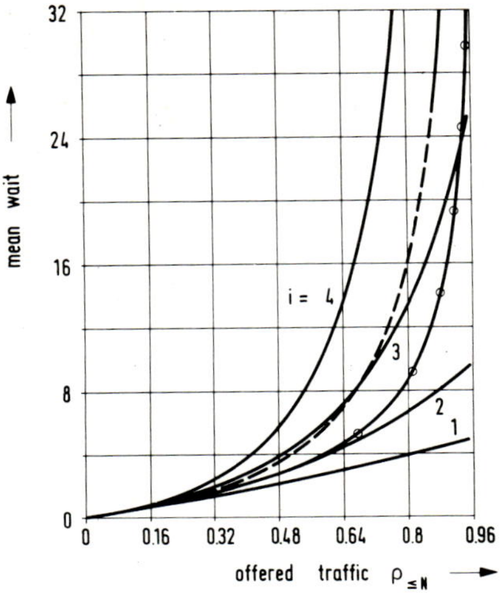

Fig. 4 Mean waiting times over $\rho_{\leq N}$ for example 1. The lines result from a static priority model, the broken line results from the FCFS model. The common mean waiting time $W_{\leq N}$ is shown by the line marked with circles.

2.3.1 Results for the approximation 2

The results in Fig. 5 show the mean waiting time, W_i, as computed from eq.(2.30) for the parameters in example 1. In Fig. 5a only small differences $\nu_i - \nu_{i-1}$ are presupposed; therefore, the mean waiting times, W_i, are close to the curve for W_{FCFS}. In Fig. 5b a greater difference, $\nu_i - \nu_{i-1} = 10$, is assumed which results in a greater deviation of the W_i's from W_{FCFS}. In Fig. 5c a much greater difference, $\nu_i - \nu_{i-1} = 100$, is assumed and from this example the degree of the approximation of the W_{iHOL}-curves can be observed by comparing Fig. 4 to Fig. 5c. The static and dynamic priority models differ in that all mean waiting times of the latter model approach infinity if the offered traffic, $\rho_{\leq N}$, approaches 1 whereas this is not the case for the static priority model.

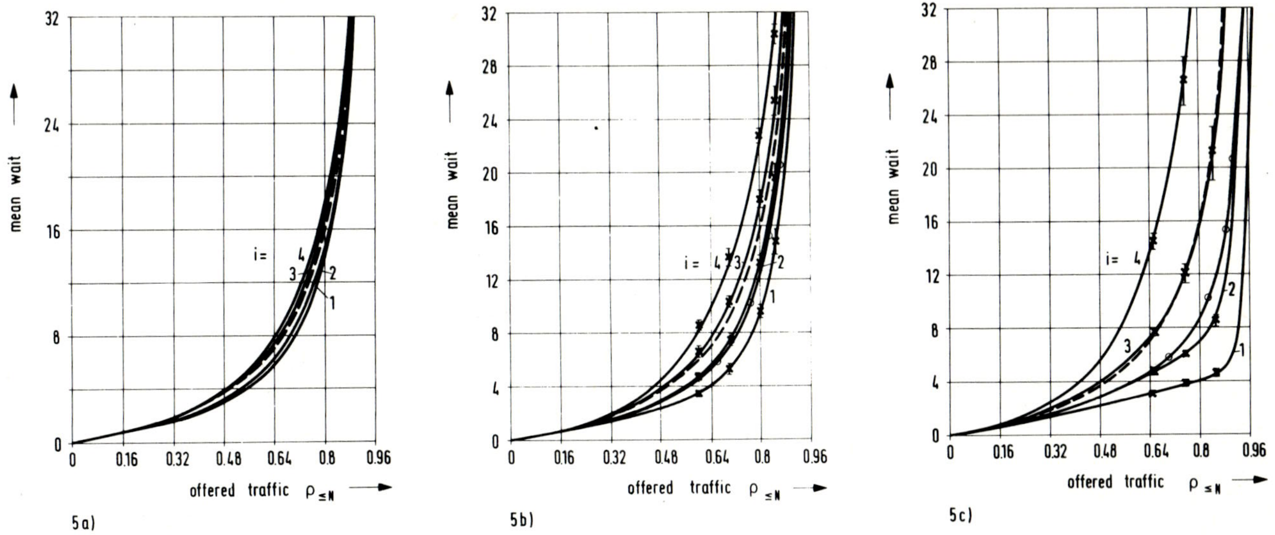

i	1	2	3	4
v_i	3	5	7	11

i	1	2	3	4
v_i	5	15	25	35

i	1	2	3	4
v_i	100	200	300	400

Fig. 5: Approximation 2 of the mean waiting times of example 1. The lines result from the dynamic priority model; the broken lines result from the FCFS model. The common mean waiting time $W_{\leq N}$ is shown by the line marked with circles. Simulation results, marked by x , are shown for a 95 % level of confidence. Three different sets of urgency numbers v_i are assumed for the three different figures a), b) and c).

This example shows that the relation $\nu_i \gg \beta_i$ should be observed (e.g. $\nu_i = 5\,\beta_i$); otherwise, the mean waiting times would differ only very little from the time W_{FCFS}. The common mean waiting time, $W_{\leq N}$, is shown by the curve marked with circles. In example 1 the mean service times, β_i, obey the relation $\beta_i < \beta_{i+1}$. In this case the common mean waiting time is minimized in a static priority model [6] (cf. Fig.4). In a dynamic priority model the curve $W_{\leq N}$ approaches the curve W_{FCFS} closer and closer as the variance of the urgency numbers ν_i becomes smaller and smaller. In this example $W_{\leq N}$ is greater in the dynamic priority model than in the static priority model. If we had chosen the opposite ordering of the β_i's (β_1=1, β_2=3, β_3=5, β_4=7), the dynamic priority model would be superior with respect to a minimal $W_{\leq N}$. Simulation results with a 95 % level of confidence shown in the figures 5b, c confirm our approximation results very well. Other examples show the same tendency (cf.[5]). It should be mentioned that our approximate solution also takes into account that the service-time d.f.'s may have different coefficients of variance (cf. the computation of W_o).

2.3.2 Results for the approximation 1

Approximation 1 yields a heavy traffic solution for the mean waiting time W_i. In just this case, $\rho_{\leq N} \rightarrow 1$, the models with static and dynamic priorities differ greatly, as was shown in section 2.3.1. If we use approximation 1 [eqs. (2.12), (2.17)] with decreasing offered traffic, starting from $\rho_{\leq N} \rightarrow 1$, until the mean waiting time, W_i, becomes smaller than $(\nu_i - \nu_{i-1})$ — a somewhat arbitrary limit — then we obtain for our example 1 the curves shown in Fig. 6a, b at the rigth-hand sides of the hatched areas. A comparison with the results in Fig. 5 reveals that the upturn of the curves to the pole at $\rho_{\leq N} = 1$, which is typical for dynamic priorities, is approximated very well. However the individual curves in Fig. 6 differ too much from each other if $\rho_{\leq N} < 1$; the improved results of approximation 2 in Fig. 5 differ remarkably less from the waiting time W_{FCFS} and from each other.

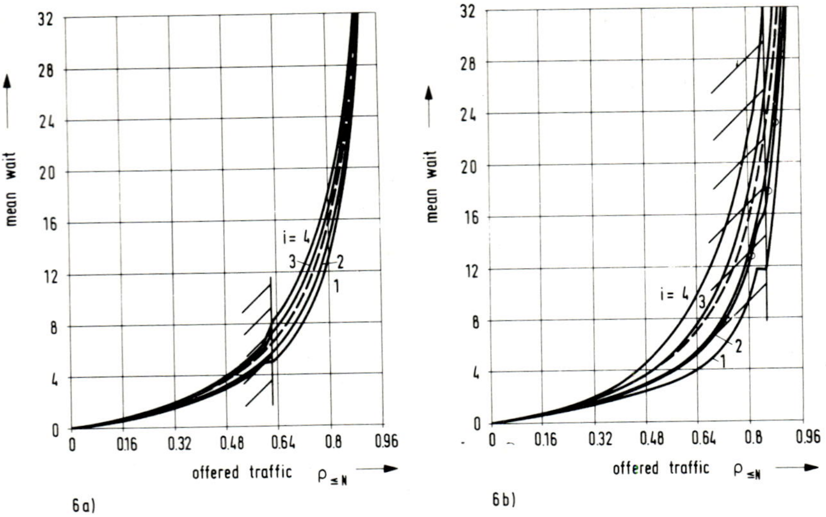

Fig. 6: Mean waiting times of example 1. On the left and right hand side of the limit marked by ⫽ results of the approximation 2 and 1, respectively, are shown. The urgency numbers in Fig. a) and Fig. b) are the same as in the Figs. 5a, 5b.

This comparison shows also that the single curves W_i in Fig. 6 differ more from the curve W_{FCFS}, than they do for the improved approximation 2 in Fig. 5. With regards to the distances $(W_i - W_{FCFS})$, the results of approximation 1 in Fig. 6 can be viewed as bounds: Each curve for W_i is in reality closer to curve W_{FCFS} than that resulting from approximation 1. This statement is already formulated in the relations eqs. (2.28) and (2.29).

3. BOUNDS FOR THE MEAN WAITING TIME

The results of both approximations introduced in section 2 differ more or less from the unknown exact results depending on the parameters of our model. It can be shown by simulation that the approximation results of section 2.3.1 are very good. One example of this was given in Fig. 5.
However, if the exact results are unknown, it is generally advantageous to have close upper and lower bounds. Bounds are known from

a paper by Holtzmann [3]. However, these bounds cannot be called close bounds. These bounds can be improved distinctly as will be shown in section 3.1. First, we will discuss the bounds from literature [3] by means of an example. The abbreviations of section 1 apply here and steady state equilibrium conditions are assumed to hold. From [3] we repeat the results for two upper limits $\bar{W}_p$, $\bar{\bar{W}}_p$ and two lower limits $\underline{W}_p$, $\underline{\underline{W}}_p$ for the mean waiting time W_p of p-type requests in a dynamic priority model:

$$W_p \leq \bar{W}_p = W_{FCFS} - \sum_{i=p+1}^{N} \rho_i \int_0^{\nu_i-\nu_p} g(t)dt + \sum_{i=1}^{p-1} \rho_i \, h(\bar{W}_p, \nu_p-\nu_i), \quad (3.1)$$

$$W_p \geq \underline{W}_p = W_{FCFS} - \sum_{i=p+1}^{N} \rho_i \min\{\bar{W}_i, \nu_i-\nu_p\} + \sum_{i=1}^{p-1} \rho_i \int_0^{\nu_p-\nu_i} g(t)dt, \quad (3.2)$$

$$W_p \geq \underline{\underline{W}}_p = \rho_p^{-1} [\rho_{\leq N} W_{FCFS} - \sum_{i=1, i\neq p}^{N} \rho_i \bar{W}_i], \quad (3.3)$$

$$W_p \leq \bar{\bar{W}}_p = \rho_p^{-1} [\rho_{\leq N} W_{FCFS} - \sum_{i=1, i\neq p}^{N} \rho_i \underline{W}_i] \quad (3.4)$$

with $g(t) = \rho_{\leq N} - \lambda_{\leq N} \int_0^t [1-F_{\leq N}(\tau)]d\tau$

$$h(\bar{W}_p, \nu_p-\nu_i) = \begin{cases} \nu_p-\nu_i, & \text{if } \nu_p-\nu_i \leq \bar{W}_p \\ \bar{W}_p[1+\ln(\nu_p-\nu_i)-\ln\bar{W}_p], & \text{if } \bar{W}_p < \nu_p-\nu_i. \end{cases} \quad (3.5)$$

For our example 1 these equations result in the broken-line curves shown in the figures 7a to 7d. Only the least upper bounds $\bar{W}_p$ or $\bar{\bar{W}}_p$ and the greatest lower bounds $\underline{W}_p$ or $\underline{\underline{W}}_p$ are shown. Some upper bounds are limited by W_{4HOL} and all the lower bounds are limited in a large range of $\rho_{\leq N}$ by W_{1HOL}, both being mean waiting times of a static priority model, cf. eq. (3.31). The difference between upper and lower bounds is too large to be satisfactory.

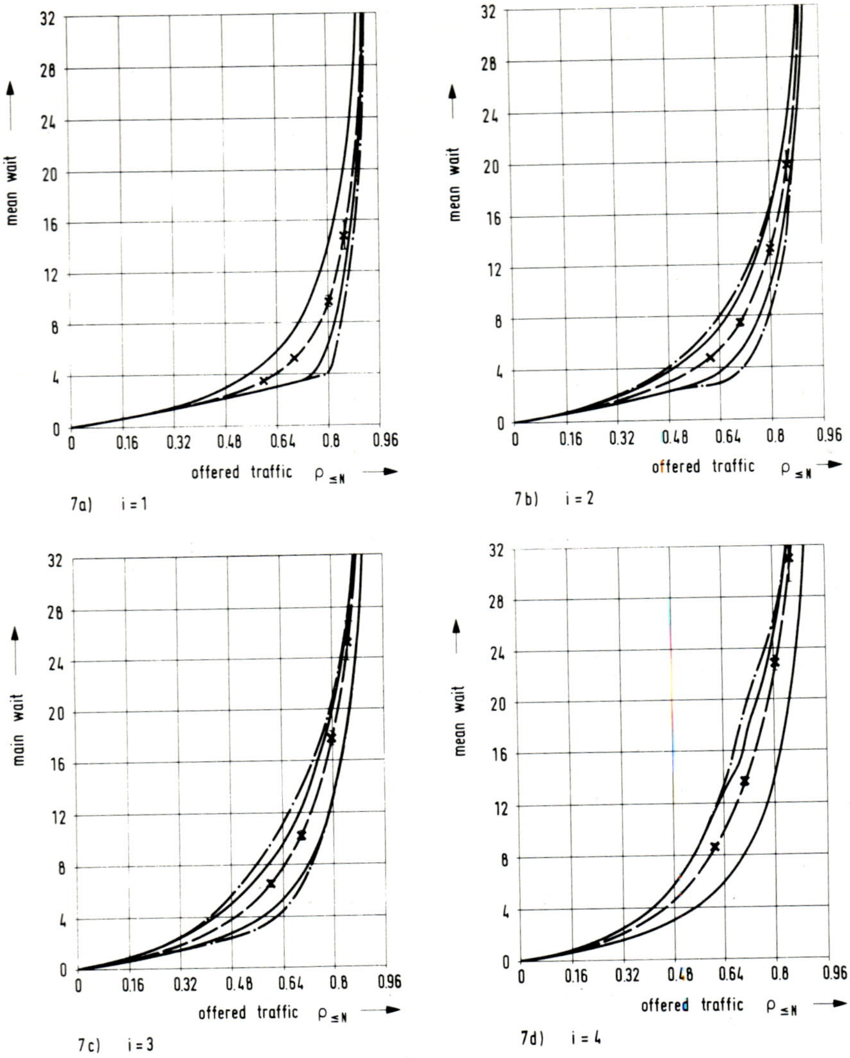

Fig. 7: Holtzmann bounds (centre lines), improved bounds (solid lines) and approximation 2 (broken line) for the mean waiting time W_i of example 1. The $\mathbf{v}_i$'s are as in Fig.5b. Simulation results, marked by x, are shown for a 95 % level of confidence.

3.1 Improved bounds

The upper bound $\bar{W}_p$ is computed by Holtzmann [3] using two relations which can be sharpened. We consider the computation of $E(m_i)g_{ip}$, cf. eq.(2.16), from

$$E(m_i)g_{ip} = \lambda_i \int_0^{\nu_p-\nu_i} P(w_p > t)dt. \qquad (3.6)$$

The probability $P(w_p > t)$ was approximated successfully in section 2, eq.(2.14).
Now we are not looking for an approximation to this probability, but rather for a close upper limit for it. From the considerations which lead to eq. (2.14) it follows that independent of the value of t the following relation must hold:

$$P(w_p > t) \leq \rho_{\leq N}. \qquad (3.7)$$

Instead of this, Holtzmann uses the relation $P(w_p > t) \leq W_p/t$ and derives from this an upper limit

$$P(w_p > t) = \begin{cases} 1 & \text{for } 0 \leq t \leq W_p \\ W_p/t & \phantom{\text{for }} W_p < t. \end{cases} \qquad (3.8)$$

This function, $P(w_p > t)$, is shown over t as a broken line in Fig. 8 for an example with $W_i = 3$, $\rho_{\leq N} = 0.5$. Considering eq.(3.7), we may write down a sharper bound than that given in eq. (3.8):

$$P(w_p > t) = \begin{cases} \rho_{\leq N} & \text{for } 0 \leq t \leq W_p/\rho_{\leq N} \\ W_p/t & \phantom{\text{for }} W_p/\rho_{\leq N} < t. \end{cases} \qquad (3.9)$$

This improved bound is also shown in Fig. 8 as a centre line (-.-.-). Both limits are indentical if the relation $W_p/\rho_{\leq N} < t$ holds; otherwise the new limit is an improvement. It is known that the real waiting time d.f. starts for t=0 at $P(w_p > t) = \rho_{\leq N}$ and that the centre line is an upper limit for $t > 0$. Using the improved limit, eq. (3.8), in computing $E(m_i)g_{ip}$, eq.(3.6), the shaded area in Fig. 8 is partially or completely omitted, depending on W_p. Instead of eq. (3.5) we may now write

$$h(\bar{W}_p, \nu_p-\nu_i) = \begin{cases} \rho_{\leq N}(\nu_p-\nu_i), & \text{if } (\nu_p-\nu_i)\rho_{\leq N} \leq \bar{W}_p \\ \bar{W}_p[1+\ln(\rho_{\leq N}(\nu_p-\nu_i)/\bar{W}_p)], & \text{if } (\nu_p-\nu_i)\rho_{\leq N} > \bar{W}_p. \end{cases} \quad (3.10)$$

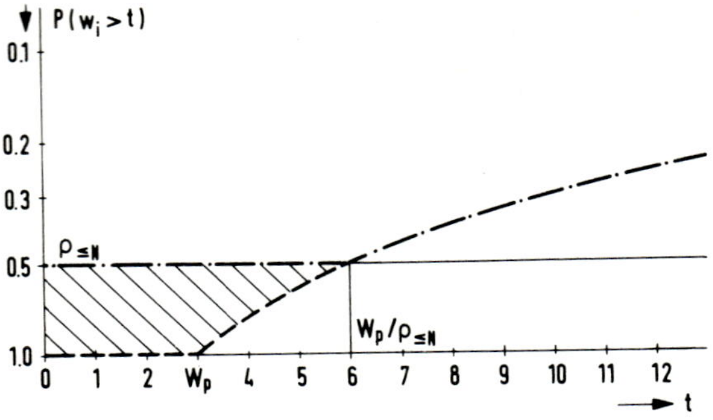

Fig. 8: Comparison of two bounds for the waiting-time d.f. of i-type requests for the parameters $\rho_{\leq N} = 0.5$, $W_i = 3$.

For the numeric calculation of $\bar{W}_p$, it is advantageous to write instead of eqs. (3.1) and (3.10):

$$\bar{W}_p = W_{FCFS} - \sum_{i=p+1}^{N} \rho_i \int_0^{\nu_i-\nu_p} g(t)dt + \bar{W}_p \sum_{i=j}^{p-1} \rho_i[1+\ln \frac{\rho_{\leq N}(\nu_p-\nu_i)}{\bar{W}_p}]$$

$$+ \rho_{\leq N} \sum_{i=1}^{j-1} \rho_i(\nu_p-\nu_i) \quad (3.11)$$

with j such that $\bar{W}_p < \rho_{\leq N}\ (\nu_p-\nu_i)$ for $1 \leq j \leq p-1$.

Again, we have a set of N simultaneous transcendent equations for the unknown variable, W_p. The calculation of W_p can be greatly simplified, with only a small deterioriation in the bound, if eq. (3.7) is used inplace of eq. (3.9).

$$\bar{W}_p{}' = W_{FCFS} - \sum_{i=p+1}^{N} \rho_i \int_0^{\nu_i-\nu_p} g(t)dt + \rho_{\leq N} \sum_{i=1}^{p-1} \rho_i(\nu_p-\nu_i). \quad (3.12)$$

This upper limit $\bar{W}_p'$ can also be used to watch over the computational results of $\bar{W}_p$ from eq.(3.11). The relation $\bar{W}_p' \geq \bar{W}_p$ must hold.

Eq.(3.9) can also be used to improve the result for $E(n_i)f_{ip}$, cf. eq.(2.11). Using eq.(2.11) and eq.(3.9) we have

$$E(n_i)f_{ip} \geq \lambda_i[W_i - \rho_{\leq N}(\nu_i-\nu_p)] \tag{3.13}$$

instead of $$E(n_i)f_{ip} \geq \lambda_i[W_i-(\nu_i-\nu_p)], \tag{3.14}$$

which is used in [3]. Using eq.(3.13), an improved lower bound $\underline{W}_p$ for the mean waiting time W_p results

$$W_p \geq \underline{W}_p = W_{FCFS} - \sum_{i=p+1}^{N} \rho_i \min\{\bar{W}_i, \rho_{\leq N}(\nu_i-\nu_p)\} + \sum_{i=1}^{p-1} \rho_i \int_0^{\nu_p-\nu_i} g(t)dt. \tag{3.15}$$

The bounds $\bar{\bar{W}}_p$ and $\underline{\underline{W}}_p$ still may be computed applying the eqs.(3.3) and (3.4) but substituting $\bar{W}_i$ and $\underline{W}_i$ from the eqs. (3.11) and (3.15). The lines in Fig. 7 show the improved bounds. Apparently, some bounds according to literature [3] are improved distinctly. The bound $\underline{W}_4$ is improved only insignificantly in this example. Generally, for a dynamic priority queue with N different types of requests, all bounds, except the bound $\bar{W}_1$ are improved.

In addition to the old and new bounds and the approximation for W_p from eq. (2.30), simulation results are also shown in Fig. 7 and are marked by an x. It may be observed that the difference between the improved bounds, $\bar{W}_p$ and $\underline{W}_p$, remains unsatisfactorily large and that the simulation results confirm our approximation results for W_p which are always enclosed by these bounds.

Tests with general service-time d.f.'s applied to our model have demonstrated that the difference between the old and improved bounds can be substantially greater than shown in Fig. 7.

3.2 Comparison of improved bounds with particularly narrow bounds computed for a special case

Holtzmann [3] discusses the possibility of improving his own bounds under special circumstances and demonstrates this for a simple Example 2: $N=2$, $\rho_i = \rho_{\leq 2}/2$, negative exponential service-time d.f.'s with parameters $\beta_1 = \beta_2 = 1$, $\beta_{\leq 2} = 1$, $\beta^{(2)}_{\leq 2} = 2$, $C_{\leq 2} = 1$, $\nu_1 = 0$, ν_2 = variabel.

By means of Laplace transforms of waiting times of a static priority model, improved bounds are shown to be computable. The mathematical tools used are highly sophisticated, e.g. the inversion of a transformation required must be performed by an approximation. This technique for computing improved bounds does not seem to be generally applicable.

In Fig. 9, for example 2, the simple Holtzmann bounds, cf. eqs.(3.1) to (3.5), and his special improved bounds, $\overline{\overline{W}}_p$ and $\underline{\underline{W}}_p$, are shown. The unknown mean waiting times are limited to the shaded areas. In addition the general improved bounds, cf. eqs. (3.11) and (3.15), are introduced and shown by a centre line. It can be seen that the new bounds and Holtzmann's special bounds differ only slightly. It is shown that the best possible special bounds known are not substantially better than our improved bounds. The bounds $\overline{W}_1$ and $\underline{W}_2$ remain unchanged.

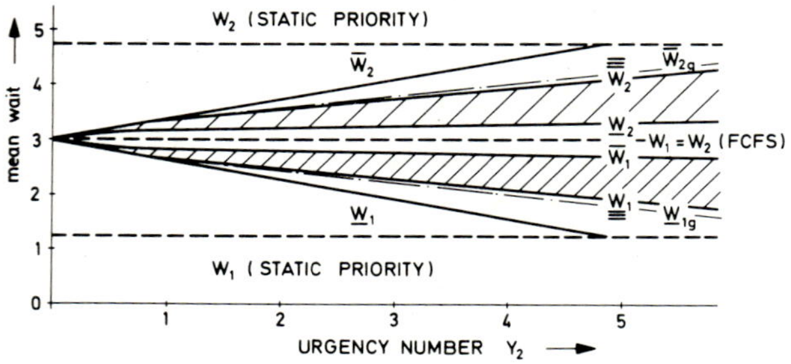

Fig. 9: Simple Holtzmann bounds $\underline{W}_i$ and $\overline{W}_i$, specially improved Holtzmann bounds $\overline{\overline{W}}_2$ and $\underline{\underline{W}}_1$ and generally improved bounds $\overline{W}_{2g}$ and $\underline{W}_{1g}$ (centre line, eqs.(3.11, 3.15) for example 2 and an offered traffic $\rho_{\leq N} = 0.75$.

4. FINAL REMARKS

The model considered in this paper is important for real-time computers in industrial control applications because in such situations scheduling by means of due dates of service requests seems to be much more appropriate than other scheduling algorithms, currently in use. It can be viewed as a disadvantage of our model that only nonpreemptive priorities are permitted. From this results a limitation of the variance of the mean waiting times of different-type requests, possible in this model. This variance can be expected to be somewhat smaller than in the same model using preemptive-resume priorities. Assume that a preemption is permissible only if a waiting service request has and another request being serviced has not reached its dealine. Then the preemptive-priority case can be expected to be solveable approximately in a similar way observing that the probabilities of waiting for service requests with urgencies $v_i > 0$ still remain $\rho_{\leq N}$, independently of the type i. The service time d.f.'s of i-type requests, i>1, must be negative exponential and for i=1 of the general type with means β_i.

Acknowledgements

The simulations mentioned in this paper have been performed by Mr. Dipl.-Ing. W. Rosenbohm. I am indebted to him for contributing to these results.
This work was partly supported by the 2nd EDP Program of the Federal Government of West Germany.

References

[1] J.R. Jackson: Queues with dynamic priority discipline Management Science, Vol.8, No.1, Oct. 1961, pp.18-34.

[2] J.R. Jackson: Some problems in queueing with dynamic priorities. Naval Research Logistics Quarterly, Washington D.C,7, Sept.1960, pp.235-249.

[3] J.M. Holtzmann: Bounds for a dynamic priority queue. Oper. Research (USA)1970, pp.461-468.

[4] A. Cobham: Priority assignment in waiting line problems. Oper. Research (USA), 2, 1954, pp. 70-76.

[5] W. Rosenbohm, B. Walke: Properties of the waiting-time distribution of a dynamic priority queue. To be published.

[6] L. Kleinrock: Queueing Systems, Vol.I: Theory John Wiley & Sons, 1975, New York/London/Sydney/Toronto.

[7] J.R.Jackson: Waiting-Time distributions for queues with dynamic priorities. Naval Research Logistics Quarterly, Washington, D.C,9March 1962, pp.31-36.

[8] J.D.C. Little: A proof for the queueing formula L= λW. Oper. Research, 9 (1961), pp.383-387.

[9] L. Kleinrock: A delay dependent queue discipline. Naval Research Logistics Quarterly, Washingt. D.C., 11, 1964, No.4, pp.329-341.

Measuring, Modelling and Evaluating Computer Systems,
H. Beilner and E. Gelenbe, (eds.)
© North-Holland Publishing Company (1977)

PROJECTOR METHOD AND ITERATIVE METHOD TO SOLVE A PACKET-SWITCHING NETWORK NODE VALIDATION BY SIMULATION

Dr. Monique BECKER* and Professor Robert FORTET
Institut de Programmation and CNRS : Laboratoire associé n° 258
Chaire de Probabilités

Université Paris VI
4, place Jussieu
75230 PARIS CEDEX 05

ABSTRACT :

The analysis of a packet-switching network node is presented. Two ways of analysis are considered : theoretical analysis and simulation. The mathematical model is a constant service time, finite capacity, queues network. It can be calculated when approximations are made by using two methods : the projector method lets us obtain the finite capacity solution from the infinite capacity solution ; an iterative method is also presented. Both of these methods are of general use.

A simulation is also presented which partly validates the approximations of the mathematical model. In fact there is a mutual validation of the theoretical analysis and of the simulation.

The study presented here is an analysis of the node of a packet switching network. We present a simulation and a theoretical analysis. Both of these methods need strong hypotheses and we try to infer a mutual validation of one method by the other. The study was made on a particular example but the methods presented here could be used for a very much modified model.

I DESCRIPTION OF THE NODE : (fig 1)

The packets arrive through n arrival junctions, and s selection connections send them to the convenient departure junctions. One message is a set of a large number of packets. The following analysis will be the probabilistic study of the queues network. Packets will be the customers, and junctions and selection connections will be the servors. The length of the packets being constant the service time will be constant. The service time of selection connections is considered as time unit. The entrance and departure junctions service time are assumed to be an integer number δ. For any of these queues the priority rule is F.C.F.S. The selection connections have capacity 1 and the departure junctions have capacity $r+1$. When a selecting connection cannot send a packet into a departure junction (this one being full) it connects the packet to an intermediate buffer. Each of the selection connections is connected with one intermediate buffer.

* Note : This work was the last chapter of a doctorate thesis, which was passed on June the 25th 1976, in PARIS VI University |2|

The s selection connections treat at most s packets among those which are available in the entrance buffer or in the intermediate buffer. We assumed that the choice is random, but this hypothesis could be easily modified.
We want to choose the sizes of the buffers. The method to choose them is the following. We assume that the capacity of the buffers is infinite. Then we evaluate the probability of each length of the queues. If it appears that it is less than N with probability 0.99, it will be very safe to choose a buffer of size N.

A lot of work has recently been done about computer systems modelling. Let us mention some of what may be useful for us : review papers |6 and 9|, exact results which can be obtained for particular cases |1,5, 8 and 15 |, diffusion approximation methods |7, 10, and 16 | , decomposability method |4|, iterative methods |3 and 12 |, a few papers about finite storage queues |11, 17 and 18| and flow trafic theorems |13 |. But the general solution of one constant service time and finite storage queue is unknown. So we are very far from being able to make the general study of a network of such queues. It is either necessary to make very strong theoretical approximations or to perform and validate simulations.

II HYPOTHESES

Let us sum up the hypotheses we make :
-1- We already mentioned the assumed organisation of the system.
-2- Discretisation : We assume that every event time is an integer number. This hypothesis is not too bad according to the fact that the service times are constant (and we assume them to be integers) and according to the synchronous behaviour of the node.
-3- Entrance process. We assume that :
- the arrival of the messages is a Poisson process, the expected value of the time between two arrivals of messages is d,
- the length of the messages also has an exponential law of rate μ.
- the time between two packets of one message is a constant integer time Δ.

-4- Stationarity : we shall only look for the eventual stationary solution.
The average number of packets arriving into one junction per time unit being :

$$a = \frac{\mu}{nd} \quad ,$$

the admission rate for an entering junction is :

$$a\delta = \frac{\mu\delta}{nd} \ .$$

And we can only expect stationarity if : $a < \delta^{-1}$,
i.o. if:

$$a\delta < 1 \qquad (1)$$

The same condition for one selecting connection is :

$$\frac{\mu}{sd} < 1 \qquad (2)$$

For the application presented here :

$n = 14$, $s = 6$, $\delta = 4$, $\mu = 4000$, $\Delta = 130$

Then(1) and (2) $\Leftrightarrow d > \frac{8000}{7}$

-5- For the mathematical model we make the following approximations :
At any time t, the entering flow into any junction or connection is :
- independent from the entering flow at time t' $(t' \neq t)$.
-independent from the number of packets which are present at time $t-1$.

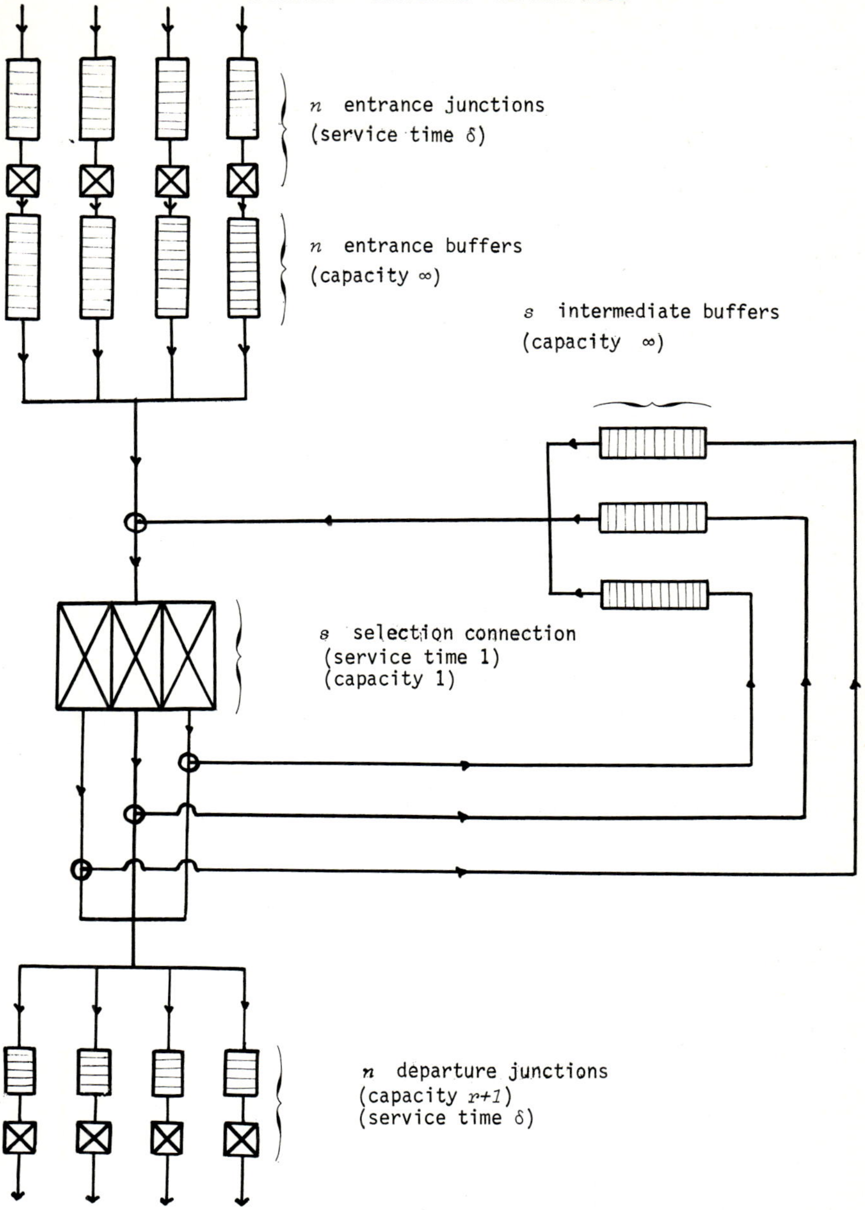

Scheme of the system

Fig. 1

III SET OF EQUATIONS

-1- Notations

- For the Jth departure junction (fig.2), let $S_J(t)$ be the departing flow at time t, i.e. the number of packets departing at time t. Let $N_J(t)$ be the entering flow. Let $Y_J(t)$ be the flow entering into the intermediate buffers and $Z_J(t)$ be the waiting flow at time $t-1$.

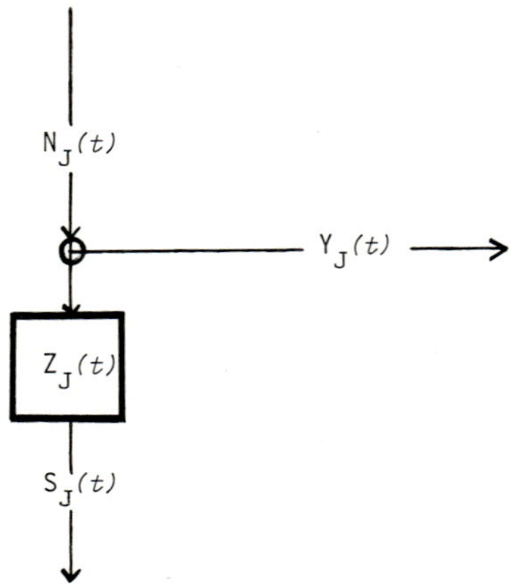

Fig. 2 :
Departure junction

- For the Jth entrance junction the fig.3 shows the analogous notations :

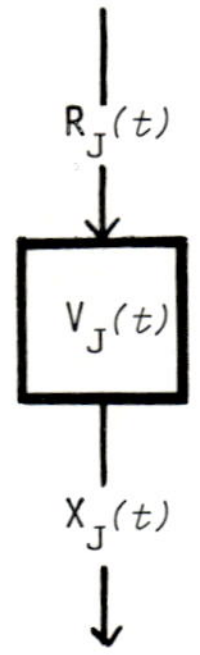

Fig. 3 :
Entrance junction

- For the set of the s selecting connections (fig.4) the arriving flow is composed of arriving flow from the entrance buffers and arriving flow the intermediate buffers. Let $W(t)$ be the waiting flow into the entrance buffers at time $t-1$, and $X(t)$ be the entrance flow into these buffers at time t. For the intermediate buffers let these flows respectively be $M(t)$ and $Y(t)$. Let $N(t)$ be the flow being served at time $t-1$ and departing at time t from the set of s selecting connections, and $L(t)$ be the total waiting flow at time $t-1$.

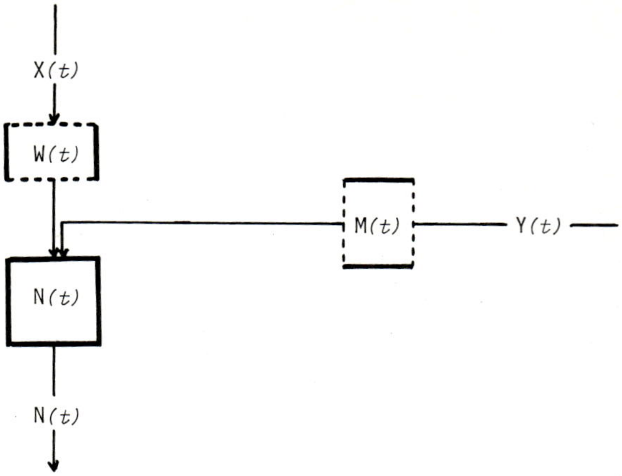

Fig. 4 The set of connection junctions

-2- First thereare some easy equations.

$$X(t) = \sum_J X_J(t) \qquad (3)$$

$$Y(t) = \sum_J Y_J(t) \qquad (4)$$

$$N(t) = \sum_J N_J(t) \qquad (5)$$

$$L(t) = W(t) + M(t) \qquad (6)$$

$$N(t) = \inf (s,\ W(t) + X(t) + M(t) + Y(t)) \qquad (7)$$

$$L(t+1) = \sup (0, L(t) + X(t) + Y(t) - s) \qquad (8)$$

-3- In order to show the complexity of tne set of equations let us give the subset corresponding to one of the departure junctions.

$S_J(t)$ is not a Markov process because it depends of the time interval $D_J(t)$ elapsed since the service of the Jth junction has begun. Because of the approximation II-5-, the couple $(S_J(t), D_J(t))$ is a Markov process solution of the set of equations (9-1), (9-2) and (9-3).

$$\text{if } D_J(t) = \delta - 1 : \left\{ \begin{array}{l} Z_J(t+1) = \inf [r,\ Z_J(t) + N_J(t) - 1] \\ Y_J(t+1) = \sup [0, Z_J(t) + N_J(t) - (r+1)] \\ S_J(t+1) = 1 \\ D_J(t+1) = D_J(t) + 1 \end{array} \right\} \qquad (9\text{-}1)$$

$$\text{if } D_J(t) = \delta \text{ or } 0 : \left\{ \begin{array}{l} Z_J(t+1) = \inf [r+1,\ Z_J(t) + N_J(t)] \\ Y_J(t+1) = \sup [0, Z_J(t) + N_J(t) - (r+1)] \\ S_J(t+1) = 0 \\ \text{if } Z_J(t) = 0, D_J(t+1) = 0 \\ \text{if } Z_J(t) \neq 0, D_J(t+1) = 1 \end{array} \right\} \qquad (9\text{-}2)$$

$$\text{if } D_J(t) \in [1,2\ldots\delta-2] \quad \left\{ \begin{array}{l} Z_J(t+1) = \inf [r+1,\ Z_J(t) + N_J(t)] \\ Y_J(t+1) = \sup [0, Z_J(t) + N_J(t) - (r+1)] \\ S_J(t+1) = 0 \\ D_J(t+1) = D_J(t) + 1 \end{array} \right\} \quad (9\text{-}3)$$

It is usual to calculate first the imbedded Markov chain $Z_J(n)$ which is the number of packets waiting into the Jth junction immediately after the nth departure from this junction. It does not depend on J because of the symmetry. So the imbedded Markov chain is in fact a variable Z_n.

We shall calculate the respective characteristic functions : $A(u)$, $\varphi(u)$, $\alpha(u)$, $\Theta(u)$, $\eta(u)$, $\gamma(u)$, $P(u)$, $\xi(u)$ of the variables : $X(t)$, $L(t)$, $N(t)$, $Y(t)$, $N_J(t)$, $Y_J(t)$, $Z(t)$, Z_n. The respective coefficients of these functions will be :

$$A_0, A_1, \ldots A_n \ldots \varphi_0, \varphi_1 \ldots \varphi_n \ldots, \ldots$$

IV. Projector method

This set of equations has a special structure due to the limited capacity of the waiting rooms. The method proposed here to solve these equations lets us obtain their general solution from the solution of the infinite capacity waiting room case.

-1- Let us **define the projector** Π_r :

For any real variable function $f(u)$ whose series expansion $\sum_{i=0}^{\infty} f_i u^i$ is convergent for $0 \le u \le 1$,

the projector Π_r projects f into the set of the r degree polynomials

$$\boxed{\Pi_r[f] = \sum_{i=0}^{r} f_i\, u^i + u^r \sum_{i=r+1}^{\infty} f_i} \qquad (10)$$

$$\Pi_r(f) = \sum_{0}^{\infty} f_i\, u^i + u^r[f(1) - \sum_{i=0}^{r} f_i]$$

Π_r has some nice and well-known properties, we shall only mention some of them :

(i) Π_r is idempotent :

$$\Pi_r^2 = \Pi_r$$

(Π_r^2 of course means the composition of application Π_r by itself).

(ii) For any polynomial f whose degree is less than or equal to r :

$$\Pi_r[f] = f$$

(iii) Π_r is linear : $\forall\ \lambda$ and $\mu \in R$ and f et g whose series expansion is convergent :

$$\Pi_r\ [\lambda\, f + \mu\, g] = \lambda\, \Pi_r[f] + \mu\, \Pi_r[g]$$

(iv) For any $k \in N, k \ge 0$

$$u^k\, \Pi_r[f] = \Pi_{r+k}[u^k f] \qquad (11)$$

$$\Pi_{r+k}\, \Pi_r = \Pi_r\, \Pi_{r+k} = \Pi_r$$

-2- Let us define the projector $\mathcal{L}_r$:

$$\boxed{\mathcal{L}_r[f] = (1-\Pi_r)[f] = f - \Pi_r[f]} \qquad (12)$$

$$\mathcal{L}_r[f] = -u^r(f_{r+1} + f_{r+2} + \ldots) + u^{r+1}(f_{r+1}) + u^{r+2}(f_{r+2}) + \ldots$$

(i) $\mathcal{L}_r$ is linear.

(ii) $\mathcal{L}_r\,\Pi_r = \Pi_r\,\mathcal{L}_r = 0$

(iii) $\mathcal{L}_r$ is idempotent.

(iv) Let us infer a relation analogous to (11) for the operator $\mathcal{L}$:

$$u^k\,\mathcal{L}_r[f] = u^k f - u^k\,\Pi_r[f]$$

$$= u^k f - \Pi_{r+k}[u^k f]$$

So $$u^k\,\mathcal{L}_r[f] = \mathcal{L}_{r+k}[u^k f]$$

-3- Lemma A Let $g(u)$ be :

$$g(u) = (f_0 + f_1 + \ldots f_r) + u f_{r+1} + \ldots u^k\,f_{r+k} + \ldots.$$

Then $$g(u) = f(1) + u^{-r}\,\mathcal{L}_r[f]$$

-4- Let us define the projector $\mathcal{R}_r$ which is the restriction to the rth degree part of the expansion :

$$\boxed{\mathcal{R}_r[f] = \sum_0^r f_i\,u^i} \qquad (13)$$

-5- Relation between $\mathcal{R}_r$ and Π_r :

$$\Pi_r\,[f] = \mathcal{R}_r\,[f] + u^r\,(f_{r+1}\ldots)$$

$$\Pi_{r+1}\,[f] = \mathcal{R}_r\,[f] + u^{r+1}(f_{r+1} + \ldots)$$

$$\Pi_{r+1}\,[f] - u\,\Pi_r\,[f] = (1-u)\,\mathcal{R}_r\,[f] = \Pi_{r+1}\,[(1-u)f]$$

$$\boxed{\mathcal{R}_r\,[f] = \frac{\Pi_{r+1}\,[(1-u)f]}{1-u}} \qquad (14)$$

-6- Lemma B

$$\Pi_r\,[fg] = \Pi_r\,[f\,\Pi_r\,[g]] = \Pi_r\,[\Pi_r\,[f]\,g] = \Pi_r\,[\Pi_r\,[f]\,\Pi_r\,[g]] = \ldots\ldots$$

-7- Solution of the equation $\Pi_r\,[f] = 0$

$$\Pi_r\,[f] = f_0 + f_1\,u + \ldots f_{r-1}\,u^{r-1} + u^r\,[f_r + f_{r+1} + \ldots] = 0$$

$$f_0 = f_1 = \ldots = f_{r-1} = 0$$

$$f_r + f_{r+1} + \ldots = 0$$

$$\boxed{[\,\Pi_r[f] = 0] \Leftrightarrow [\,f(u) = u^r\,\varphi(u) \text{ with } \varphi(1) = 0]} \qquad (15)$$

It follows that :

$$[\Pi_r [f] = 0] \Rightarrow [\Pi_{r-i} [f] = 0]$$

-8- Solution of the equation : $\Pi_r [fg] = 0$ when $f_0 \neq 0$

(15) gives : $fg = x^r \varphi(x)$

Since $f_0 \neq 0$, we can write $g(x) = x^r \gamma(x)$

So : $[\Pi_r [fg] = 0 \text{ and } f_0 \neq 0] \Rightarrow [g = x^r \gamma(x) \text{ and } f(1)\gamma(1) = 0]$ (16)

V. APPLICATIONS OF THE PROJECTOR METHOD

1. The projector method allowsus to calculate easily the imbedded Markov chain Z_n

The set of equations is (17 - 1) and (17 - 2)

$$Z_n \neq 0 \Rightarrow Z_{n+1} = min(r, Z_n - 1 + N_n^\delta) \qquad (17\text{-}1)$$

where the characteristic function of N_n^δ is

$$\nu(u) = \eta^\delta(u) \qquad (17\text{-}3)$$

and :

$$Z_n = 0 \Rightarrow Z_{n+1} = min(r, M_n^\delta) \qquad (17\text{-}2)$$

where the characteristic function of M_n^δ is :

$$\beta(u) = \eta^\delta(u) \frac{1}{u} \frac{\eta(u) - \eta_0}{1 - \eta_0} \qquad (17\text{-}4)$$

Analysing the transition probabilities and writing :

$$Pr|Z_{n+1} = j| = \sum_i Pr|Z_{n+1} = j / Z_n = i| \, Pr|Z_n = i|$$

it is easy to show that the set of equations (17-1) and (17-2) can be transformed into

$$\left.\begin{aligned} &\forall j,\ 0 \leqslant j \leqslant r-1,\ \xi_j = \xi_0 \mu_j + \sum_{i=0}^{j} \xi_{i+1} \nu_{j-1} \\ &\xi_r = \xi_0 [\mu_r + \mu_{r-1} + \dots] + \xi_1 [\nu_r + \dots] + \dots \xi_r [\nu_1 + \nu_2 + \dots] \end{aligned}\right\} \qquad (18)$$

Let us used the projector Π_r. The set of equations (18) is equivalent to :

$$\boxed{u\,\xi(u) = \Pi_{r+1} [\xi_0 [u\,\beta(u) - \nu(u)] + \nu(u)\,\xi(u)]} \qquad (19)$$

where $\beta(u)$ and $\nu(u)$ are defined by (17-3) and (17-4).

Then $\xi(u)$ is the normalised restriction to degree r of the variable $X(u)$ which is proportional to the solution $x(u)$ of (19) corresponding to infinite capacity :

$$u\,x(u) = x_0 [u\,\beta(u) - \nu(u)] + \nu(u)\,x(u) \qquad (20)$$

From (20) one can get :

$$X(u) = \frac{\nu(u)\ (1-\eta(u))}{\nu(u) - u}$$

Then $\xi(u)$ can be easily calculated :

$$\xi(u) = \frac{\zeta(u)}{\zeta(1)}$$

With :

$$\zeta(u) = \mathcal{R}_r\ [X(u)]$$

and applying (14)

$$\zeta(u) = \frac{\Pi_{r+1}[(1-u)\ X(u)]}{(1-u)}$$

So, as a conclusion, we can say that the calculation of $\xi(u)$ is made very simple by the use of the projectors.

-2- The same method can be applied to calculate the general solution $P(u)$. Analysing the transition probabilities one gets :

$$\boxed{P(u) = (1-u)\,\frac{1-P_0}{\delta}\ \xi(u) + \Pi_{r+1}\ [\eta(u)\ P(u)]} \tag{21}$$

Replacing $\xi(u)$ by its value one gets :

$$P(u) = \frac{1-P_0}{\delta\ \zeta(1)}\ \Pi_{r+1}\ [(1-u)\ \frac{\nu(u)(1-\eta(u))}{\nu(u)-u}] + \Pi_{r+1}[\eta(u)\ P(u)]$$

The degree of $P(u)$ being less than $r+1$:

$$P(u) = \Pi_{r+1}\ [P(u)]$$

Then using the linearity one gets :

$$\Pi_{r+1}\ \{[1-\eta(u)]\ [P(u) - \frac{(1-P_0)}{\delta\ \zeta(1)}\ \frac{(1-u)\ \nu(u)}{(\xi(u)-u)}]\} = 0 \tag{22}$$

(22) can be written :

$$\Pi_{r+1}\ [fg] = 0$$

with

$$f(u) = 1 - \eta(u)$$

$$f_0 = 1 - \eta_0 \neq 0$$

and

$$g(u) = P(u) - \frac{1-P_0}{\delta\ \zeta(1)}\ \frac{(1-u)\ \nu(u)}{(\nu(u) - u)}$$

So from (16), we deduce that the terms of degree 0,1... r are zero and the last one is obtained by normalisation :

$$\boxed{P(u) = P_0\ \mathcal{R}_r\left[\frac{(1-u)\ \nu(u)}{\nu(u)-u}\right] + u^{r+1}\ [1-(P_0+\ldots\ P_r)]} \tag{23}$$

P_0 can be easily calculated by writing that the entrance flow is equal to the departing flow :

$$P_0 = 1 - \delta\ \alpha \tag{24}$$

VI. ITERATIVE METHODS TO GET THE GENERAL SOLUTION :

In order to calculate $\alpha(u)$, $\theta(u)$ and $\varphi(u)$ we have two systems of equations. One of them is deduced from the equations (7) and (8) concerning the selection connections :

$$\begin{cases} \boxed{\alpha(u) = \Pi_s [A(u)\ \theta(u)\ \varphi(u)\ ]} & (25) \\ \varphi(u) = 1+u^{-s}\ \mathcal{L}_s[A(u)\ \theta(u)\ \varphi(u)\ ] & (26) \end{cases}$$

Using (25), (26) can be replaced by :

$$A(u)\ \theta(u)\ \varphi(u) = \alpha(u) + u^s[\varphi(u) - 1] \qquad (27)$$

The other system is the relation between $\theta(u)$ and $\alpha(u)$ concerning what happens into the departure junctions. These equations were precisely written using (9) and (17), and are available on request |2|. We shall only write the relation which is valid when another approximation is made : Let us assume that the degree of $\eta(u)$ is 1. This means that among the less than s packets which are leaving the selection connections and expecting to enter one of the n entrance junctions, there is a probability zero that two or more of them are expecting to enter the same departure junction. This approximation is reasonable as long as :

$$s << n$$

It is then easy to show that :

$$\theta(u) = \sum_{j=0}^{s} \alpha_j\ [1 + \frac{\gamma_1}{\eta_1}(u-1)\ ]^j$$

from which it follows :

$$\theta(u) = \sum_{0}^{s} \alpha_j\ [1+P_{r+1}(u-1)\ ]^j \qquad (28)$$

We need to solve the system of (25), (27) and (28), or eliminating $\theta(u)$ between (27) and (28), we get (29) and the system is reduced to (25) and (29)

$$\boxed{A(u)\ \alpha\ [1+ P_{r+1}(u-1)\ ]\ \varphi(u) = \alpha(u) + u^s\ [\varphi(u)-1\ ]} \qquad (29)$$

We propose an iterative method, in order to calculate $\alpha(u)$. The initial value of $\alpha(u)$ may be the value corresponding to an infinite value of s.

If s tends to the infinite,

$$\varphi^{\infty}(u) = 1$$

$$A(u)\ \alpha^{\infty}\ \{1+ P_{r+1}(u-1)\ \} = \alpha^{\infty}(u) \qquad (30)$$

By equating the coefficients, one can obtain : $\alpha^{\infty}(u)$. For example in the case when :

$$A(u) = e^{n\ a(u-1)} \qquad (31)$$

the solution is :

$$\alpha^{\infty}(u) = e^{n\ \eta_1(u-1)}$$

Then one can alternatively calculate $\varphi^{(i)}(u)$ and $\alpha^{(i)}(u)$ from (25) and (29) :

$$\Pi_s[A\ \Theta^{\infty}] = \alpha^{(1)} = \Pi_s(\alpha^{\infty})$$

$$u_s[1-\varphi^{(1)}] = (1-\Pi_s)[\alpha^{\infty}]$$

$$\alpha^{(1)} = e^{-n\eta_1}\left[1+n\eta_1 u + \dots + \frac{(n\eta_1)^{s-1}u^{s-1}}{(s-1)!} + u^s\left\{\frac{(n\eta_1)^s}{s!} + \dots + \frac{(n\eta_1)^{s+k}}{(s+k)!} + \dots\right\}\right]$$

$$\Theta^{(1)} = \alpha^{(1)}(1 + P_{r+1}(u-1))$$

$$\alpha^{(2)} = \Pi_s[A\ \Theta^{(1)}\ \varphi^{(1)}]$$

$$u^s(1-\varphi^{(2)}) = 1-\Pi_s[A\ \Theta^{(1)}\ \varphi^{(1)}]$$

$$\Theta^{(2)} = \alpha^{(2)}(1 + P_{r+1}(u-1))$$

$$\alpha^{(i)} = \Pi_s[A\ \Theta^{(i-1)}\ \varphi^{(i-1)}]$$

$$u^s[1-\varphi^{(i)}] = 1 - \Pi_s[A\ \Theta^{(i-1)}\ \varphi^{(i-1)}]$$

We ran two iterations for a special case, and got the feeling that the results were reasonably good. Let us present a simplified iterative method which can be used when r is small.

VII. SIMPLIFIED METHOD TO SOLVE THE SYSTEM WHEN r IS SMALL :

As an example let us make the calculation when $r + 1 = 2$.

A direct calculation from the transition probability system, or a derivation of (19) gives :

$$P_1 = (\eta_0^{-\delta}-1)P_0 \qquad (32)$$

$$P_2 = 1 - \eta_0^{-\delta}\ P_0 \qquad (33)$$

Then from $P_0 = 1 - \delta\ a$

by summing these 3 relations one gets :

$$1 - \eta_0 = \frac{a\ \eta_0^{\delta}}{1-\delta\ a} \qquad (34)$$

This equation lets us derive η_0 .

For example a graphical solution can be obtained :

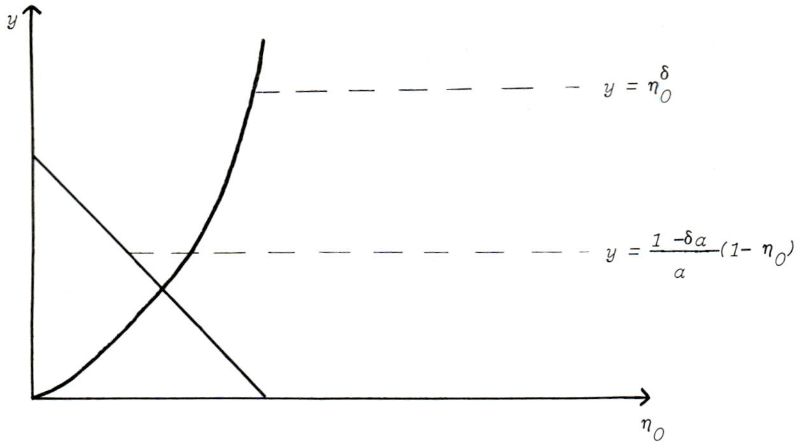

η_0 can also be obtained by using an iterative method with the initial value :

$$\eta_0^{(0)} = 1 - a$$

From η_0 one can derive P_0, P_1, P_2 from (34), (32) and (33), and the expected values :

$$< \eta > = \eta_1 = 1 - \eta_0$$
$$< \alpha > = n\, \eta_1$$
$$< \theta > = n < \gamma > = n(\eta_1 - a)$$

VIII. RESULTS OF SIMULATION

We shall first present here 4 series of results

Simulation A : $d = 2400$, $r + 1 = 2 \Rightarrow a = 0.119$

Simulation B : $d = 1333$, $r + 1 = 2 \Rightarrow a = 0.214$

Simulation C : $d = 1200$, $r + 1 = 2 \Rightarrow a = 0.238$

Simulation D : $d = 2400$, $r + 1 = 3 \Rightarrow a = 0.119$

The simulation was made more valid because of the discretisation hypothesis. Truncation errors were avoided |2|.

-1- Stationarity

Our main difficulty was to prove stationarity. Our problem did not come from what happened into the node, it came from the fact that the entrance flow was not stationary.
The average length of one message being :

$$\mu \Delta = 5.2\ 10^5,$$

we generated messages during an initial 10^6 units time, without simulating the trafic inside the node. We then had got an entrance flow whose law was stationary. Then we ran the whole simulation including the next messages generation and the simulation of the node. But the average time between two beginnings of messages was so long compared with any other time (such as any service time in the node) that in order to get a good average entrance flow (when averaging over the length of the simulation) we had to run much too long simulations |14|.

Example for $d = 2400$, and a confidence of 95%, the confidence interval of the estimation of the expected value of a is :

$100\ \%$ for $T = 10^4$

$31\ \%$ for $T = 10^5$

$10\ \%$ for $T = 10^6$

And these long simulations are very expensive. For example on IBM 370, when asking for a 5 mn job, the length of the simulation (after the initial length of 10^6 time units) is :

Simulation A or D	$T = 10^5$
Simulation B	$T = 7.10^4$
Simulation C	$T = 6.10^4$

So we decided to consider the entrance flow as a non-stationary flow whose expected value is slowly varying.

We mesured the average entrance flow when averaging over the length of the simulation and we chose it as an estimated value of $a : a_{est}$

For small values of T : ($T < 10^5$)

Simulation A and D	$a_{est} = 0.09$
Simulation B	$a_{est} = 0.17$
Simulation C	$a_{est} = 0.195$

Let us give tables of numerical results for these simulations.

T = 800000

SIMULATION A

ENTRANCE BUFFERS AND INTERMEDIATE BUFFERS

PROBABILITY (QUEUE LENGTH = I)

I =	0	1	2	3	4	5	6	7	8	9 OR MORE
FILE 1	0.99948	0.00052	0.0	0.0	0.0	0.0	0.0	0.0	0.0	0.0
FILE 2	0.99968	0.00032	0.0	0.0	0.0	0.0	0.0	0.0	0.0	0.0
FILE 3	0.99955	0.00044	0.0	0.0	0.0	0.0	0.0	0.0	0.0	0.0
FILE 4	0.99924	0.00076	0.0	0.0	0.0	0.0	0.0	0.0	0.0	0.0
FILE 5	0.99966	0.00034	0.0	0.0	0.0	0.0	0.0	0.0	0.0	0.0
FILE 6	0.99907	0.00093	0.0	0.0	0.0	0.0	0.0	0.0	0.0	0.0
FILE 7	0.99940	0.00059	0.0	0.0	0.0	0.0	0.0	0.0	0.0	0.0
FILE 8	0.99937	0.00063	0.0	0.0	0.0	0.0	0.0	0.0	0.0	0.0
FILE 9	0.99950	0.00050	0.0	0.0	0.0	0.0	0.0	0.0	0.0	0.0
FILE 10	0.99928	0.00072	0.0	0.0	0.0	0.0	0.0	0.0	0.0	0.0
FILE 11	0.99920	0.00080	0.0	0.0	0.0	0.0	0.0	0.0	0.0	0.0
FILE 12	0.99912	0.00088	0.0	0.0	0.0	0.0	0.0	0.0	0.0	0.0
FILE 13	0.99906	0.00094	0.0	0.0	0.0	0.0	0.0	0.0	0.0	0.0
FILE 14	0.99939	0.00061	0.0	0.0	0.0	0.0	0.0	0.0	0.0	0.0
FILE 15	0.99788	0.00211	0.00000	0.0	0.0	0.0	0.0	0.0	0.0	0.0
FILE 16	0.99796	0.00203	0.00001	0.0	0.0	0.0	0.0	0.0	0.0	0.0
FILE 17	0.99801	0.00199	0.00000	0.0	0.0	0.0	0.0	0.0	0.0	0.0
FILE 18	0.99801	0.00198	0.00000	0.0	0.0	0.0	0.0	0.0	0.0	0.0
FILE 19	0.99802	0.00198	0.00000	0.0	0.0	0.0	0.0	0.0	0.0	0.0
FILE 20	0.99793	0.00206	0.00001	0.0	0.0	0.0	0.0	0.0	0.0	0.0
ARITH MEAN OF THE 14 FIRST PROBA.	0.99936	0.00064	0.0	0.0	0.0	0.0	0.0	0.0	0.0	0.0
ARITH MEAN OF THE 6 LAST PROBA.	0.99797	0.00203	0.00001	0.0	0.0	0.0	0.0	0.0	0.0	0.0

ARRIVAL PROCESS FOR EACH ENTRANCE BUFFER

PROBA (0 ARRIVAL)	0.89867	0.89289	0.90411	0.85151	0.91932	0.87161	0.92166	
	0.90681	0.84294	0.90221	0.90551	0.91019	0.87427	0.90175	
PROBA (1 ARRIVAL)	0.10133	0.10711	0.09589	0.14849	0.08068	0.12839	0.07834	estimation of α
	0.09319	0.15706	0.09779	0.09449	0.08981	0.12573	0.09825	

SELECTION CONNECTIONS

BUSY RATE FOR EACH CONNECTION : 0.44075 0.44075 0.44022 0.44066 0.43953 0.43976

i :	0	1	2	3	4	5	6
ESTIMATED VALUE OF α_i :	0.06502	0.18184	0.25094	0.22449	0.15263	0.07653	0.04854

DEPARTURE JUNCTIONS	P_0	P_1	P_2
FILE 1	0.52941	0.37027	0.10032
FILE 2	0.50294	0.32802	0.16903
FILE 3	0.48961	0.36964	0.14075
FILE 4	0.65085	0.30433	0.04483
FILE 5	0.59364	0.31877	0.08759
FILE 6	0.56403	0.34333	0.09265
FILE 7	0.57030	0.28006	0.14964
FILE 8	0.45996	0.34088	0.19917
FILE 9	0.49122	0.32580	0.18298
FILE 10	0.53922	0.30878	0.15201
FILE 11	0.56111	0.33303	0.10586
FILE 12	0.52166	0.28491	0.19344
FILE 13	0.50833	0.36087	0.13079
FILE 14	0.50286	0.33524	0.16190
ARITHM. MEAN OF THE 14 PROBA.	0.53465	0.32885	0.13650

T = 70000

SIMULATION B

ENTRANCE BUFFERS AND INTERMEDIATE BUFFERS

PROBABILITY (QUEUE LENGTH = I)

I =	0	1	2	3	4	5	6	7	8	9 OR MORE
FILE 1	0.95090	0.04893	0.00017	0.0	0.0	0.0	0.0	0.0	0.0	0.0
FILE 2	0.93307	0.06646	0.00047	0.0	0.0	0.0	0.0	0.0	0.0	0.0
FILE 3	0.93744	0.06217	0.00039	0.0	0.0	0.0	0.0	0.0	0.0	0.0
FILE 4	0.94580	0.05380	0.00040	0.0	0.0	0.0	0.0	0.0	0.0	0.0
FILE 5	0.95486	0.04497	0.00017	0.0	0.0	0.0.	0.0	0.0	0.0	0.0
FILE 6	0.94654	0.05313	0.00033	0.0	0.0	0.0	0.0	0.0	0.0	0.0
FILE 7	0.94924	0.05056	0.00020	0.0	0.0	0.0	0.0	0.0	0.0	0.0
FILE 8	0.96821	0.03173	0.00006	0.0	0.0	0.0	0.0	0.0	0.0	0.0
FILE 9	0.94390	0.05584	0.00026	0.0	0.0	0.0	0.0	0.0	0.0	0.0
FILE 10	0.94126	0.05837	0.00037	0.0	0.0	0.0	0.0	0.0	0.0	0.0
FILE 11	0.96489	0.03483	0.00029	0.0	0.0	0.0	0.0	0.0	0.0	0.0
FILE 12	0.96011	0.03947	0.00041	0.0	0.0	0.0	0.0	0.0	0.0	0.0
FILE 13	0.94417	0.05538	0.00044	0.0	0.0	0.0	0.0	0.0	0.0	0.0
FILE 14	0.97517	0.02481	0.00001	0.0	0.0	0.0	0.0	0.0	0.0	0.0
FILE 15	0.74046	0.17620	0.05727	0.01839	0.00514	0.00169	0.00064	0.00019	0.00003	0.0
FILE 16	0.72875	0.18313	0.06231	0.01919	0.00561	0.00099	0.00003	0.0	0.0	0.0
FILE 17	0.73079	0.17817	0.06061	0.01979	0.00723	0.00261	0.00067	0.00013	0.0	0.0
FILE 18	0.72739	0.17914	0.06228	0.02166	0.00677	0.00181	0.00069	0.00021	0.00004	0.0
FILE 19	0.73242	0.17823	0.05903	0.02056	0.00677	0.00239	0.00053	0.00009	0.0	0.0
FILE 20	0.73670	0.17843	0.05808	0.01860	0.00604	0.00167	0.00043	0.00004	0.0	0.0
ARITH MEAN OF THE 14 FIRST PROBA.	0.95111	0.04860	0.00028	0.0	0.0	0.0	0.0	0.0	0.0	0.0
ARITH MEAN OF THE 6 LAST PROBA.	0.73275	0.17888	0.05993	0.01969	0.00626	0.00186	0.00050	0.00011	0.00001	0.0

ARRIVAL PROCESS FOR EACH ENTRANCE BUFFER

PROBA (0 ARRIVAL)	0.82693	0.75006	0.76283	0.82136	0.83782	0.80516	0.84409	
	0.88520	0.82226	0.80423	0.86657	0.85067	0.80433	0.89862	
PROBA (1 ARRIVAL)	0.17307	0.24994	0.23717	0.17864	0.16218	0.19484	0.15591	estimation of a
	0.11480	0.17774	0.19577	0.13343	0.14933	0.19567	0.10138	

SELECTION CONNECTIONS

BUSY RATE FOR EACH CONNECTION : 0.91834 0.91713 0.91802 0.91879 0.91673 0.91487

i :	0	1	2	3	4	5	6
ESTIMATED VALUE OF α_i :	0.00019	0.00294	0.01713	0.04429	0.07838	0.12216	0.73492

DEPARTURE JUNCTIONS	P_0	P_1	P_2
FILE 1	0.23904	0.44277	0.31820
FILE 2	0.26147	0.39365	0.34488
FILE 3	0.20858	0.46515	0.32627
FILE 4	0.13877	0.44972	0.41151
FILE 5	0.35544	0.34114	0.30342
FILE 6	0.34897	0.43079	0.22024
FILE 7	0.27855	0.37671	0.34474
FILE 8	0.20890	0.42281	0.36829
FILE 9	0.29411	0.44362	0.26227
FILE 10	0.33570	0.42158	0.24273
FILE 11	0.38417	0.31702	0.29881
FILE 12	0.48549	0.35808	0.15643
FILE 13	0.46205	0.41121	0.12674
FILE 14	0.31841	0.39752	0.28407
AR. MEAN OF THE 14 PROBA.	0.30855	0.40513	0.28633

T = 60000

SIMULATION C

ENTRANCE BUFFERS ANS INTERMEDIATE BUFFERS

PROBABILITY (QUEUE LENGTH = I)

I =	0	1	2	3	4	5	6	7	8	9 OR MORE
FILE 1	0.79799	0.18275	0.01635	0.00267	0.00025	0.0	0.0	0.0	0.0	0.0
FILE 2	0.75710	0.22268	0.01855	0.00153	0.00013	0.0	0.0	0.0	0.0	0.0
FILE 3	0.78335	0.20016	0.01440	0.00195	0.00013	0.0	0.0	0.0	0.0	0.0
FILE 4	0.80449	0.18045	0.01305	0.00175	0.00027	0.0	0.0	0.0	0.0	0.0
FILE 5	0.74985	0.22893	0.01910	0.00203	0.00008	0.0	0.0	0.0	0.0	0.0
FILE 6	0.77037	0.21170	0.01612	0.00165	0.00017	0.0	0.0	0.0	0.0	0.0
FILE 7	0.80157	0.18165	0.01533	0.00142	0.00003	0.0	0.0	0.0	0.0	0.0
FILE 8	0.85542	0.13843	0.00603	0.00012	0.00012	0.0	0.0	0.0	0.0	0.0
FILE 9	0.81214	0.17145	0.01483	0.00138	0.00018	0.00002	0.0	0.0	0.0	0.0
FILE 10	0.74475	0.23278	0.02057	0.00185	0.00005	0.0	0.0	0.0	0.0	0.0
FILE 11	0.84200	0.14743	0.00938	0.00108	0.00010	0.0	0.0	0.0	0.0	0.0
FILE 12	0.78769	0.19603	0.01452	0.00160	0.00017	0.0	0.0	0.0	0.0	0.0
FILE 13	0.79917	0.18736	0.01300	0.00047	0.0	0.0	0.0	0.0	0.0	0.0
FILE 14	0.84479	0.14128	0.01237	0.00140	0.00017	0.0	0.0	0.0	0.0	0.0
FILE 15	0.05495	0.04953	0.04897	0.04398	0.03750	0.03777	0.03757	0.03787	0.03678	0.61609
FILE 16	0.03242	0.02812	0.02470	0.01860	0.01780	0.01593	0.01342	0.01013	0.00943	0.82945
FILE 17	0.06858	0.06008	0.05285	0.04485	0.04045	0.03407	0.03457	0.03350	0.03130	0.59976
FILE 18	0.02347	0.01998	0.01703	0.01453	0.01097	0.01207	0.01210	0.01130	0.01163	0.86702
FILE 19	0.05912	0.05352	0.04340	0.04160	0.04292	0.03795	0.03723	0.03692	0.03478	0.61257
FILE 20	0.03373	0.02710	0.02203	0.01752	0.01495	0.01355	0.01443	0.01403	0.01368	0.82897
AR. MEAN OF THE 14 FIRST PR.	0.79648	0.18736	0.01454	0.00149	0.00012	0.00000	0.0	0.0	0.0	0.0
AR. MEAN OF THE 6 LAST PR.	0.04538	0.03972	0.03483	0.03018	0.02743	0.02522	0.02489	0.02396	0.02292	0.72548

ARRIVAL PROCESS FOR EACH ENTRANCE BUFFER

PROBA (0 ARRIVAL)	0.81382	0.75210	0.79119	0.81249	0.75069	0.77542	0.80820	
	0.85984	0.80550	0.75820	0.85542	0.77444	0.80632	0.86614	
PROBA (1 ARRIVAL)	0.18618	0.24790	0.20881	0.18751	0.24931	0.22458	0.19180	estimation of α
	0.14016	0.19450	0.24180	0.14458	0.22556	0.19368	0.13386	

SELECTION CONNECTIONS

BUSY RATE FOR EACH CONNECTION :	0.99963	0.99942	0.99957	0.99962	0.99952	0.99953	
i :	0	1	2	3	4	5	6
ESTIMATED VALUE OF α_i :	0.00008	0.00007	0.00007	0.00013	0.00018	0.00085	0.99867

DEPARTURE JUNCTIONS

	P_0	P_1	P_2
FILE 1	0.08745	0.50616	0.40639
FILE 2	0.08148	0.49719	0.42133
FILE 3	0.00042	0.27260	0.72699
FILE 4	0.15001	0.51261	0.33738
FILE 5	0.08432	0.49698	0.41871
FILE 6	0.28536	0.49588	0.21876
FILE 7	0.21275	0.50681	0.28045
FILE 8	0.29021	0.48163	0.22816
FILE 9	0.24731	0.52101	0.23168
FILE 10	0.13630	0.52691	0.33679
FILE 11	0.46531	0.40294	0.13175
FILE 12	0.35521	0.46939	0.17540
FILE 13	0.24255	0.48108	0.27638
FILE 14	0.38754	0.43946	0.17300

T = 100000

ENTRANCE BUFFERS AND INTERMEDIATE BUFFERS

SIMULATION D

PROBABILITY (QUEUE LENGTH = I)

I =	0	1	2	3	4	5	6	7	8	9 OR MORE
FILE 1	0.99983	0.00017	0.0	0.0	0.0	0.0	0.0	0.0	0.0	0.0
FILE 2	1.00000	0.0	0.0	0.0	0.0	0.0	0.0	0.0	0.0	0.0
FILE 3	0.99997	0.00003	0.0	0.0	0.0	0.0	0.0	0.0	0.0	0.0
FILE 4	0.99995	0.00005	0.0	0.0	0.0	0.0	0.0	0.0	0.0	0.0
FILE 5	0.99997	0.00003	0.0	0.0	0.0	0.0	0.0	0.0	0.0	0.0
FILE 6	0.99992	0.00008	0.0	0.0	0.0	0.0	0.0	0.0	0.0	0.0
FILE 7	1.00000	0.0	0.0	0.0	0.0	0.0	0.0	0.0	0.0	0.0
FILE 8	0.99989	0.00011	0.0	0.0	0.0	0.0	0.0	0.0	0.0	0.0
FILE 9	0.99998	0.00002	0.0	0.0	0.0	0.0	0.0	0.0	0.0	0.0
FILE 10	0.99987	0.00013	0.0	0.0	0.0	0.0	0.0	0.0	0.0	0.0
FILE 11	0.99995	0.00005	0.0	0.0	0.0	0.0	0.0	0.0	0.0	0.0
FILE 12	0.99993	0.00007	0.0	0.0	0.0	0.0	0.0	0.0	0.0	0.0
FILE 13	1.00000	0.0	0.0	0.0	0.0	0.0	0.0	0.0	0.0	0.0
FILE 14	1.00000	0.0	0.0	0.0	0.0	0.0	0.0	0.0	0.0	0.0
FILE 15	0.99957	0.00043	0.0	0.0	0.0	0.0	0.0	0.0	0.0	0.0
FILE 16	0.99989	0.00011	0.0	0.0	0.0	0.0	0.0	0.0	0.0	0.0
FILE 17	0.99963	0.00037	0.0	0.0	0.0	0.0	0.0	0.0	0.0	0.0
FILE 18	0.99969	0.00031	0.0	0.0	0.0	0.0	0.0	0.0	0.0	0.0
FILE 19	0.99963	0.00037	0.0	0.0	0.0	0.0	0.0	0.0	0.0	0.0
FILE 20	0.99980	0.00020	0.0	0.0	0.0	0.0	0.0	0.0	0.0	0.0
ARITH MEAN OF THE 14 FIRST PROBA.	0.99995	0.00005	0.0	0.0	0.0	0.0	0.0	0.0	0.0	0.0
ARITH MEAN OF THE 6 LAST PROBA.	0.99970	0.00030	0.0	0.0	0.0	0.0	0.0	0.0	0.0	0.0

ARRIVAL PROCESS FOR EACH ENTRANCE BUFFER

PROBA (0 ARRIVAL)	0.89562	0.90613	0.90488	0.85911	0.92132	0.91556	0.93681	
	0.90862	0.85942	0.90578	0.91983	0.88853	0.92975	0.92908	
PROBA (1 ARRIVAL)	0.10438	0.09387	0.09512	0.14089	0.07868	0.08444	0.06319	estimation of α
	0.09138	0.14058	0.09422	0.08017	0.11147	0.07025	0.07092	

SELECTION CONNECTIONS

BUSY RATE FOR EACH CONNECTION : 0.30083 0.30297 0.30095 0.30503 0.30569 0.30103

i :	0	1	2	3	4	5	6
ESTIMATED VALUE OF α_i :	0.15939	0.29450	0.27470	0.15631	0.08005	0.02689	0.00817

DEPARTURE JUNCTIONS

	P_0	P_1	P_2	P_3
FILE 1	0.51680	0.29698	0.13760	0.04862
FILE 2	0.27708	0.33531	0.26231	0.12531
FILE 3	0.56940	0.25797	0.12599	0.04664
FILE 4	0.55268	0.39153	0.05579	0.0
FILE 5	0.64831	0.28409	0.05941	0.00819
FILE 6	0.59633	0.25302	0.10727	0.04338
FILE 7	0.61920	0.18230	0.16126	0.03724
FILE 8	0.50324	0.20525	0.15557	0.13594
FILE 9	0.38889	0.18313	0.21857	0.20942
FILE 10	0.62036	0.26838	0.08960	0.02166
FILE 11	0.61721	0.30604	0.07675	0.0
FILE 12	0.65028	0.16732	0.12567	0.05673
FILE 13	0.45701	0.24098	0.18264	0.11938
FILE 14	0.63368	0.32466	0.04166	0.0
ARITHM. MEAN OF THE 14 PROBA.	0.54646	0.26407	0.12858	0.06089

We may verify then the agreement of the simulation results with the formula (24), which is valid without approximation :

$$P_O = 1 - \delta a \qquad (24)$$

Let $P_{O,est}$ be the estimed values of P_O , and let $P_{O,cal}$ be the value of P_O which can be obtained by calculation from (24).

Simulation A :

$T = 10^4$ $a_{est} = 0.093$ $P_{O,cal} = 0.627$ $P_{O,est} = 0.567$

$T = 10^5$ $a_{est} = 0.0953$ $P_{O,cal} = 0.619$ $P_{O,est} = 0.575$

$T = 10^6$ $a_{est} = 0.1069$ $P_{O,cal} = 0.572$ $P_{O,est} = 0.535$

Simulation D :

$T = 10^4$ $a_{est} = 0.094$ $P_{O,cal} = 0.624$ $P_{O,est} = 0,541$

$T = 10^5$ $a_{est} = 0.094$ $P_{O,cal} = 0.623$ $P_{O,est} = 0.546$

Simulation B :

$T = 10^4$ $a_{est} = 0.172$ $P_{O,cal} = 0.310$ $P_{O,est} = 0.310$

$T = 7.10^4$ $a_{est} = 0.173$ $P_{O,cal} = 0.308$ $P_{O,est} = 0.308$

Simulation C :

$T = 10^4$ $a_{est} = 0.194$ $P_{O,cal} = 0.178$ $P_{O,est} = 0.224$

$T = 6.10^4$ $a_{est} = 0.198$ $P_{O,cal} = 0.208$ $P_{O,est} = 0.216$

Of course the agreement is not very good, when T is small. We explained the cause of this bad agreement. We shall present next a simulation which lets us avoid these problems.

-2- Validation of the hypotheses :

Two main hypotheses have to be verified :

1. the degree of $\eta(u)$ is 1.
2. the processes are renewal processes (II-5)

A direct calculation of the coefficients η_i can let us know whether the coefficients η_i with $i \geqslant 2$ are important.

The results for simulation A were :

$T = 10^4$ $\qquad \eta_0 = 0.88$ $\qquad \eta_1 = 0.15$ $\qquad \eta_2 = 0.02$

$\eta_3 = 0.02$ $\qquad \eta_4 \equiv 0.01$ $\qquad \eta_5 = 0.06$ $\qquad \eta_6 = 0.07$

For $T = 2\ 10^4$ the results happened to be the same.

We can verify whether the system of equations which were derived from these hypotheses is valid.

In that case we got the system :

$$P_0 = 1 - \delta\ a \qquad (24)$$

$$P_1 = P_0(\eta_0^{-\delta} - 1) \qquad (32)$$

$$1 - \eta_0 = \frac{a\ \eta_0^{\delta}}{1 - \delta\ a} \qquad (34)$$

We shall verify the validity of this system by a simulation in 3 steps :

1) direct estimation of a by simulation
2) direct estimation of P_0 and derivation of a from (24)
3) direct estimation of P_0 and P_1, derivation of η_0 from (32), and derivation of a from (34)

Numerical results :

Simulation A $\qquad T = 10^4$

1) $a = 0.0933$
2) $P_0 = 0.567 \Rightarrow a = 0.108$
3) $\eta_0 = 0.900 \Rightarrow a = 0.088$

Simulation A $\qquad T = 10^5$

1) $a = 0.0953$
2) $P_0 = 0.576 \Rightarrow a = 0.106$
3) $\eta_0 = 0.900 \Rightarrow a = 0.088$

Simulation A $\qquad T = 8\ .\ 10^5$

1) $a = 0.1069$
2) $P_0 = 0.535 \Rightarrow a = 0.116$
3) $\eta_0 = 0.887 \Rightarrow a = 0.098$

Simulation B $\qquad T = 10^4$

1) $a = 0.1724$
2) $P_0 = 0.3109 \Rightarrow a = 0.1723$
3) $\eta_0 = 0.812 \Rightarrow a = 0.1344$

Simulation B $\qquad T = 7.\ 10^4$

1) $a = 0.1728$
2) $P_0 = 0.30855 \Rightarrow a = 0.1728$
3) $\eta_0 = 0.811 \Rightarrow a = 0.1348$

Simulation C $\qquad T = 10^4$

1) $a = 0.195$
2) $P_0 = 0.2164 \Rightarrow a = 0.194$
3) $\eta_0 = 0.754 \Rightarrow a = 0.188$

Simulation C $\qquad T = 6.\ 10^4$

1) $a = 0.198$
2) $P_0 = 0.22416 \Rightarrow a = 0.196$
3) $\eta_0 = 0.749 \Rightarrow a = 0.191$

The validity of the hypotheses will be much easier to prove if the entrance process is simplified so that the [illegible] intervals are smaller. So let us give the results of a simplified simulation : simulation E , where the entrance process is assumed to be a Poisson process.

T = 100000 SIMULATION E

ENTRANCE BUFFERS AND INTERMEDIATE BUFFERS

PROBABILITY (QUEUE LENGTH = I)

I	0	1	2	3	4	5	6	7	8	9 OR MORE
FILE 1	0.99793	0.00207	0.0	0.0	0.0	0.0	0.0	0.0	0.0	0.0
FILE 2	0.99786	0.00213	0.00001	0.0	0.0	0.0	0.0	0.0	0.0	0.0
FILE 3	0.99804	0.00196	0.0	0.0	0.0	0.0	0.0	0.0	0.0	0.0
FILE 4	0.99772	0.00228	0.0	0.0	0.0	0.0	0.0	0.0	0.0	0.0
FILE 5	0.99801	0.00199	0.0	0.0	0.0	0.0	0.0	0.0	0.0	0.0
FILE 6	0.99760	0.00240	0.0	0.0	0.0	0.0	0.0	0.0	0.0	0.0
FILE 7	0.99781	0.00219	0.0	0.0	0.0	0.0	0.0	0.0	0.0	0.0
FILE 8	0.99786	0.00214	0.0	0.0	0.0	0.0	0.0	0.0	0.0	0.0
FILE 9	0.99779	0.00221	0.0	0.0	0.0	0.0	0.0	0.0	0.0	0.0
FILE 10	0.99812	0.00188	0.0	0.0	0.0	0.0	0.0	0.0	0.0	0.0
FILE 11	0.99782	0.00218	0.0	0.0	0.0	0.0	0.0	0.0	0.0	0.0
FILE 12	0.99807	0.00193	0.0	0.0	0.0	0.0	0.0	0.0	0.0	0.0
FILE 13	0.99778	0.00222	0.0	0.0	0.0	0.0	0.0	0.0	0.0	0.0
FILE 14	0.99800	0.00200	0.0	0.0	0.0	0.0	0.0	0.0	0.0	0.0
FILE 15	0.98999	0.00965	0.00035	0.00001	0.0	0.0	0.0	0.0	0.0	0.0
FILE 16	0.98982	0.00943	0.00073	0.00002	0.0	0.0	0.0	0.0	0.0	0.0
FILE 17	0.98983	0.00940	0.00072	0.00005	0.0	0.0	0.0	0.0	0.0	0.0
FILE 18	0.99045	0.00881	0.00058	0.00015	0.00001	0.0	0.0	0.0	0.0	0.0
FILE 19	0.98869	0.01020	0.00091	0.00016	0.00004	0.0	0.0	0.0	0.0	0.0
FILE 20	0.98939	0.00990	0.00068	0.00003	0.0	0.0	0.0	0.0	0.0	0.0
ARITH MEAN OF THE 14 FIRST PROBA.	0.99789	0.00211	0.00000	0.0	0.0	0.0	0.0	0.0	0.0	0.0
ARITH MEAN OF THE 6 LAST PROBA.	0.98970	0.00956	0.00066	0.00007	0.00001	0.0	0.0	0.0	0.0	0.0

ARRIVAL PROCESS FOR EACH ENTRANCE BUFFER

PROBA (0 ARRIVAL)	0.88185	0.88299	0.88184	0.88373	0.88300	0.88214	0.88223	
	0.88364	0.88224	0.88332	0.88073	0.88385	0.88321	0.88328	
PROBA (1 ARRIVAL)	0.11815	0.11701	0.11816	0.11627	0.11700	0.11786	0.11777	estimation of a
	0.11636	0.11776	0.11668	0.11927	0.11615	0.11679	0.11672	

<u>SELECTION CONNECTIONS</u>

BUSY RATE FOR EACH CONNECTION :	0.51047	0.51048	0.50794	0.50972	0.50908	0.50576	
i :	0	1	2	3	4	5	6
ESTIMATED VALUE OF α_i :	0.04279	0.13957	0.21733	0.22310	0.17275	0.10784	0.09663

DEPARTURE JUNCTIONS	P_0	P_1	P_2
FILE 1	0.50737	0.33572	0.15691
FILE 2	0.50266	0.34154	0.15580
FILE 3	0.51130	0.33607	0.15263
FILE 4	0.49265	0.34266	0.16470
FILE 5	0.50100	0.33631	0.16269
FILE 6	0.50784	0.33808	0.15408
FILE 7	0.51020	0.33719	0.15261
FILE 8	0.49572	0.33818	0.16611
FILE 9	0.50864	0.33649	0.15487
FILE 10	0.51064	0.33651	0.15285
FILE 11	0.50360	0.33797	0.15843
FILE 12	0.49660	0.33803	0.16537
FILE 13	0.50978	0.33677	0.15345
FILE 14	0.50844	0.33705	0.15451
ARITHM. MEAN OF THE 14 PROBA.	0.50475	0.33775	0.15750

The stationarity is then very good and the agreement between equations (32), (33) (34) and the results of the simulation is excellent, though the simulation is very short :

Theoretical results	Simulation results
$a = 0.1175$	$a = 0.117$
$P_0 = 0.53$	$P_0 = 0.505$
$\eta_0 = 0.87$	$\eta_0 = 0.88$
$P_1 = 0.395$	$P_1 = 0.338$

These results let us assume that the two theoretical hypotheses are valuable. The simulation validates the theory. But les us notice that in some way the theory validatesthe simulation at the same time, since two different methods using two sets of completely different approximations get nearly to the same results, we can expect that the two sets of approximations are reasonably good. In fact there is a mutual validation of the theoretical analysis and of the simulation.

CONCLUSION

Two theoretical methods were presented :
Projector method and iterative method. They let us get the solutions for the example which is presented here.

Projector method will be useful for most of the finite capacity network, since when the capacity is finite one usually gets sets of equations such as (17-1, and 17-2) or (18). Then the solution can be easily derived from an equation such as (19).

Iterative method will be useful for most of the networks, as soon as approximations are possible, so that one may compute the iterations.

When one wants to study a network, two ways of analysis are possible : theoretical method or simulation, and we have the feeling that in any case a mutual validation of those two ways is necessary.

APPENDIX

Proof of Lemma A

Let $g(u)$ be :

$$g(u) = (f_0 + f_1 + \dots f_r) + u f_{r+1} + \dots u^k f_{r+k} + \dots$$

From : $$u^r g(u) = u^r (f_0 + f_1 + \dots f_r) + \sum_{i=r+1}^{\infty} u^i f_i$$

$$u^r g(u) + \Pi_r [f] = \sum_0^{\infty} f_i u^i + u^r f(1)$$

One gets :

$$u^r (g(u) - f(1)) = (1 - \Pi_r) [f]$$

So :

$$g(u) = f(1) + u^{-r} \mathcal{L}_r [f]$$

Proof of Lemma B

Let us prove that :

$$\Pi_r [f g] = \Pi_r [f \Pi_r [g]]$$

$$fg = \sum_{p=0}^{\infty} u^p \sum_{i=0}^{p} (f_i g_{p-i}) \overset{def}{=} \sum_{p=0}^{\infty} (fg)_p u^p$$

$$\Pi_r [fg] = \sum_{p=0}^{r-1} u^p \Big(\sum_{i=0}^{p} f_i g_{p-i} \Big) + u^r \Big(\sum_{p=r}^{\infty} \sum_{i=0}^{p} f_i g_{p-i} \Big)$$

$$= \sum_{p=0}^{r-1} u^p (fg)_p + u^r \alpha$$

with $$\alpha = \sum_{i=0}^{r} f_i \Big(\sum_{p=r}^{\infty} g_{p-i} \Big) + \sum_{i=r+1}^{\infty} f_i \Big(\sum_{p=i}^{\infty} g_{p-i} \Big)$$

$$\alpha = f_0 (g_r + \dots) + f_1 (g_{r-i} + \dots) + \dots + f_{r-1} (g_1 + \dots)$$
$$+ f_r \cdot g(1) \; . \; \dots \; . \; f_{r+k} \cdot g(1) + \dots$$

Let g' be :

$$g' = \Pi_r [g]$$

Then : $$g'_0 = g_0 , \dots g'_{r-1} = g_{r-1} ,$$

$$g'_r = (g_r + \dots), \; g'_{r+i} = 0 \quad \text{for} \quad i \neq 0$$

Let us calculate : $\Pi_r [fg']$. We want to prove that it is equal to $\Pi_r [fg]$

$$\Pi_r [fg'] = \sum_{p=0}^{r-1} u^p (fg)_p + u^r \alpha'$$

$$\alpha' = f_0 \cdot g'_r + f_1 (g_{r-1} + g'_r) + \dots f_r \cdot g(1) + \dots + f_{r+k} \cdot g(1) + \dots$$

$$\alpha' = \alpha$$

References

|1| F. Baskett, M. Chandy, R. Muntz, J. Palacios : Open, closed and mixed network of queues with different classes of customers. J. ACM 22,248-260 (1975).

|2| M. Becker : Validité des simulations de files d'attente. Thèse de doctorat soutenue à l'Université de Paris VI, le 25-6-76. N° Arch. C.N.R.S. : A.0.12.454.

|3| M. Chandy, U. Herzog, L. Woo : Approximate analysis of general queueing networks. IBM Research Report RC 4931, July 1974.

|4| P.J. Courtois : Decomposability. Queueing and Computer systems applications. Academic Press (1976).

|5| D.P. Gaver : Probability models for multiprogramming computer systems. J. ACM 14, 423-438 (1967).

|6| E. Gelenbe, R.R. Muntz : Probabilistic models of computer systems. Part I (Exact results). Acta Informatica 7, 35-60 (1976).

|7| E. Gelenbe and G. Pujolle : The behaviour of a single queue in a general queueing network. Acta Informatica 7, 2, 123-136 (1976).

|8| J.R. Jackson : Jobshop like queueing systems. Management Science, 10-1 (Oct. 1963) p. 131-142.

|9| H. Kobayashi and A.G. Konheim : Queueing models for computer communications system analysis. IBM Research Report RC 5922, Y.H. 1976.

|10| H. Kobayashi : Application of the Diffusion Approximation to Queueing Networks. Part I, J. ACM 21,2 - p. 316-328. 1974.

|11| A.G. Konheim and M. Reiser : A queueing model with finite waiting room and blocking. IBM Research Report RC 5066, Y.H. 1974.

|12| M. Langenbach-Belz : Two stages queueing system with sampled parallel input queues. 7th I.T.C., 1973, p. 434/1.

|13| S.S. Lavenberg : Stability and maximum departure rate of certain open queueing networks having finite capacity constraints. IBM Research RJ 1625 (July 22, 1975).

|14| P. Le Gall : L'ergodisme et la convergence des simulations de phénomènes aléatoires. Ann. des Télécomm. t22 n° 7-8 (Juillet-août 1967) 211-228.

|15| R.R. Muntz : Poisson departure processes and queueing networks. IBM Research Report RC 4145, December 1972.

|16| M. Reiser,H. Kobayashi:Accuracy of the Diffusion Approximation for some Queueing Systems. IBM J. Res. Develop. 18,2 p. 110-124. March 1974.

|17| M. Reiser, H. Kobayashi : Blocking in a queueing network with two exponential servers. IBM Research Report RJ 1360, 1974.

|18| P.J. Schweitzer and A.G. Konheim : Buffer overflow calculations using an infinite capacity model. IBM Research Report RC 5386 (April 28, 1975).

Measuring, Modelling and Evaluating Computer Systems,
H. Beilner and E. Gelenbe, (eds.)
© North-Holland Publishing Company (1977)

ANALYTICAL MODELLING OF THE RELIABILITY OF A FAULT-TOLERANT COMPUTER - COPRA *

F. BROWAEYS
Société d'Applications Générales d'Electricité et de Mécanique
6, Avenue d'Iéna
75783 PARIS CEDEX 16 (FRANCE)

O. MURON
IRIA / LABORIA
Domaine de Voluceau - Rocquencourt
BP5 - 78150 LE CHESNAY (FRANCE) .

To evaluate the reliability of a fault-tolerant computer (COPRA) an analytical method is derived. A probabilistic model is used, based on the analysis of the components failures. One is then led to a set of states. As a direct use of those to evaluate would bring a great complexity the analysis has been split into three steps. First a partition of the system is made, then a detailed modellisation of each part leads to its event trees. They are all incorporated in a model of the whole system.

One is finally able to deal only with a stationary Markov chain with a reasonable number of states. An evaluation is made by an integration program. Numerical results are obtained for COPRA, mainly : the reliability, the safety and the MTBF. It was then possible to choose some of the parameters of the design like the frequencies of the test sequences.

1. INTRODUCTION

Modellisation of the reliability of COPRA is considered. COPRA is a highly reliable reconfigurable multiprocessor designed by SAGEM and EMD for aerospace applications**[3] . Its two goals are safety and disponibility. Safety on one hand implies that no undedected erroneous output should be produced. If at any time a such event happens the calculator will be said to be in the error state (E), the mission will be failed and further evolution will not be considered. Reliability on the other hand means that processing should be continued in case of any component failure. If the computer has to stop by lack of resources (processors or memories) it is said to be in the alarm state (A). The effect of repair will not be considered here, so whenever the system reaches this state no further evolution will be considered.

The method to get the reliability of a complex structure is to divide it into units such that by knowing what units are failed at time t we can tell if the system is working or not at this time. This cannot be the case here because one has to take into account eventual contaminations and because the effect of the failures may depend on the instant they occur.

---

* Calculateur à Organisation Parallèle et à Reconfiguration Automatique

** This work is supported by the DRME (Direction des Recherches et Moyens d'Essais).

Our approach will be the following. We will first do a partitioning of the physical components into homogeneous cells and then starting from a new structure, study with the help of event trees the consequences of failures in each cell. We will be led to define the list of the states of the system and will model its functioning using a continuous time Markov chain [1] . The states E and A as defined ealier will be considered "absorbing" states for the chain. The treatment of such a model is well known ; we will give the numerical reliability evaluation of COPRA ; the method could be transposed to other multiprocessor structures.

2. PARTITIONING OF THE STRUCTURE

We want to group the components into cells such that the failure of any component of a given cell will have the same effect on the computer. Let us take the example of a single processor.

The effect of a particular failure will depend both of the component affected and of the input structure. We are only interested in knowing if the output is right or wrong so with a "pessimistic" approach we will say that a failure of any component of the processor implies instantaneously an erroneous output. This is realistic to assume because if we measure the time in terms of MTBF each function is used very often.

COPRA [3] is made of three kinds of modules : processors, memory blocks and I/O units. They are connected through a matrix network. The units remain in a powered state and all processors are working simultaneously, sharing the computing load. Processors and memory blocks both include an individual detection function. Failure of a unit when detected will be followed by a reconfiguration and the load will then be divided among the remaining units.

The evaluation is made here for the case of a biprocessor with two memory blocks.

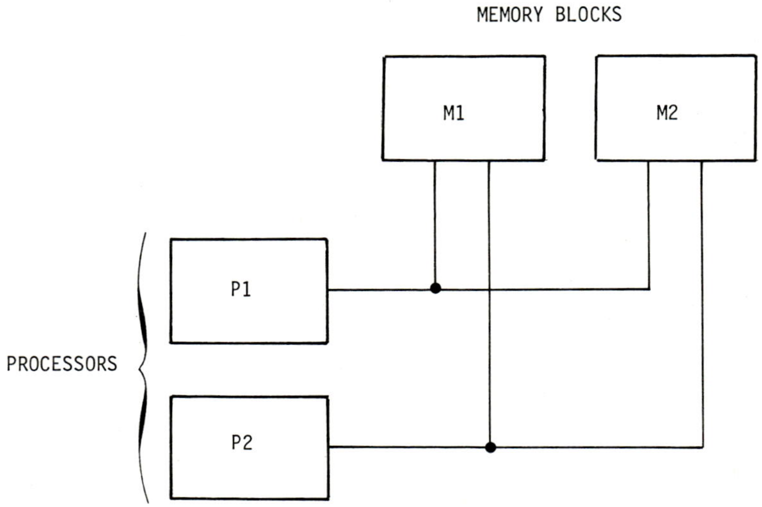

a) Processors

In COPRA the detection at the processor level is made by duplication and comparison. The whole processor is disconnected whenever any of its halves is faulty. This is done by the "disable" function. We will consider three cells for a processor : the functional part (that is the two "half processors"), the detection (comparator) and the disable function.

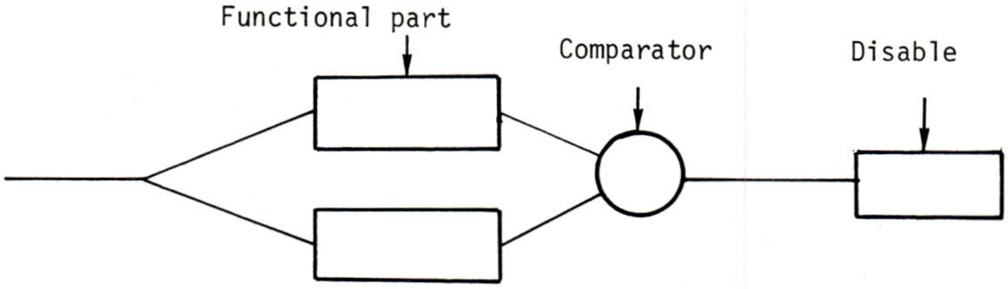

Giving to each cell a failure rate λ we get the following simplified scheme for a processor.

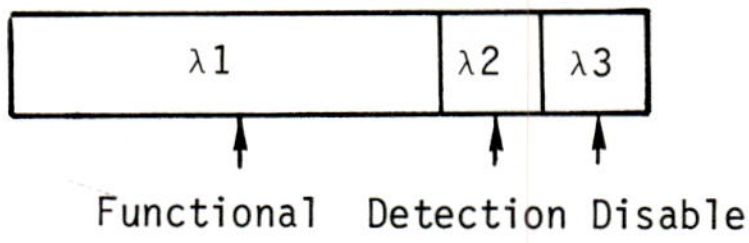

Each cell is considered to be in a serie configuration ; the failure rates are obtained by addition of the failure rates of the components involved.

b) Memory block

Each memory block may be divided into five functional parts. There is first the memorisation itself (μ1) then the transfer part (μ2) and the interface. The interface is split in two : the interface itself (μ5) and its masking (μ4) ; it is conceived in such a way that a simple failure of interface or masking cannot be propagated to the other cells. Checking of the memorisation, finally, is guaranteed by a detection system (μ3).

The schema is therefore the following for a memory block :

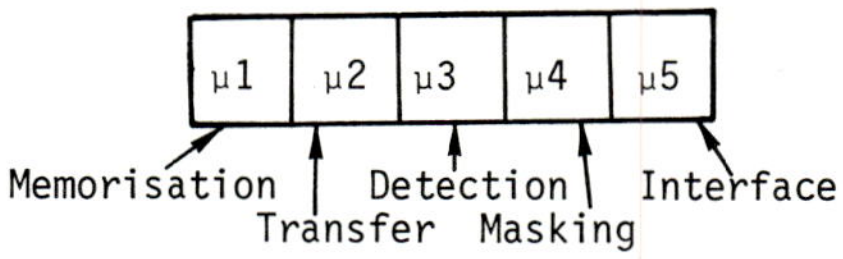

c) Interconnection

The hardware for the interconnection is distributed between processors and memories depending upon the faults they induce on their functioning.

d) I/O units

The study does not include the I/O units because their design, failure rates and failures mode depend on the application.

e) Power supply

The reliability of the redundant power supply was studied separately. It can be considered like being in serie with the other parts of the computer.

3. FUNCTIONING OF THE CELLS

Each cell will now be considered as a serie system. The failure rates of the components are constant. The effect of the transient is not considered because no tractable analytical model was available for them. We study first a processor, then a memory block and finally the global functioning of the system.

a) Processor

As described in 2 the processor consists of a functional part, a comparator and a disable function. Morever there is a periodic test of the comparator. The periodicity of the test is a constant D (to be chosen) and its length is d. Its efficiency is 1-PN2 where PN2 is a small positive number. PN2 decreases as d increases but as testing is a critical period a tradeoff will be found for optimal reliability.

We will call "1" the initial state of the processor, HS the state where it has been disconnected by a reconfiguration, E the state where the processing is erroneous but not detected. There is finally a state that we will call A when a processor initiates a general alarm of the system (even if some resources are still available). The states A, HS and E are absorbing. We shall model the functioning of a processor using a stationary Markov process whose initial state is "1". The transitions and their rates will now be analysed.

Suppose we are in the state "1" and there is a failure in the functional part (this happens with a rate $\lambda 1$) ; as it is the first failure, the comparator is working and initiates a reconfiguration. One should therefore go to the state HS. This is the normal recovery. If however the failure occurs when the comparator is being tested and therefore disactivated, it could cause an error. Being pessimistic one could consider going then in the state E, the conditional probability being d/D.

Another catastrophic event is the case where the recovery process fails. This can happen if another failure appears too soon while one is still recovering from the first. Let PRR be the probability of that event. One gets a bound for PRR using the product Λts where Λ is the total failure rate and ts is the length of the critical part of the recovery process (that is the time when one is sensible to another failure).

Note

To adapt the model to transient failures one should use for PRR a larger value depending on the model used for the shape of the transients.

So far the event tree can be written :

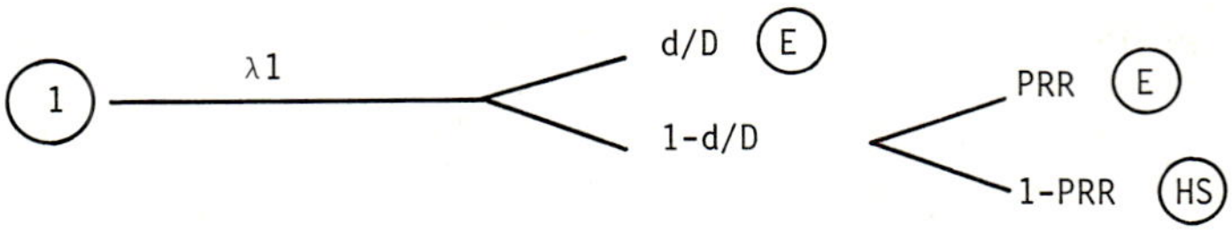

We now suppose the first failure is in the detection cell (the rate is λ2).

It can imply either a false alarm or a non detection of the next failure. We will assume the conditional probability of these two cases is 1/2.

In case of false alarm recovery should be successful except if another failure occurs too soon as it was seen earlier.

The case of non detection should be detected by the periodic test of the comparator and initiate a recovery except in the following cases :

Case 1

If a failure of the functional part occurs before the next test, the error generated may be treated as if it was coming from the other cells connected to it. Being pessimistic one can consider that in this case all resources are consumed and one reaches the state A. By integration over the interval between tests one can evaluate this probability. It is λ1 D/2.

Case 2

If the test does not detect the failure (probability PN2 given by the efficiency of the test) the processor will continue to work with a failed detection system. We will say it is in the state "2".

We finally study the case of a failure of the "disable" cell. They are of two kinds : untimely disconnection or failure to disconnect. A detailed study of the circuits led to an estimation of the conditional probabilities of these two modes : 3/4 for the first, 1/4 for the second. The second case is, as the failures of detection, treated by a periodic test. Its efficiency is 1-PN3 where PN3 is small.

The corresponding part of the event tree is then completely similar to one concerning the detection cell. The state where the processor continues to work with an undetected failure of the "Disable" cell is called "3".

It remains now to study the further transitions from the states "2" and "3" ("A", "HS" and "E" are absorbing).

In state "2" the detection does not work so any failure of the functional part leads to an alarm (as seen earlier). We are not interested in the higher order transitions because a crude majoration shows their influence in the model is negligible.

In a similar manner from state "3" any functional failure leads to E and any failure of detection implies a reconfiguration.

The analysis can be represented by the following event tree.

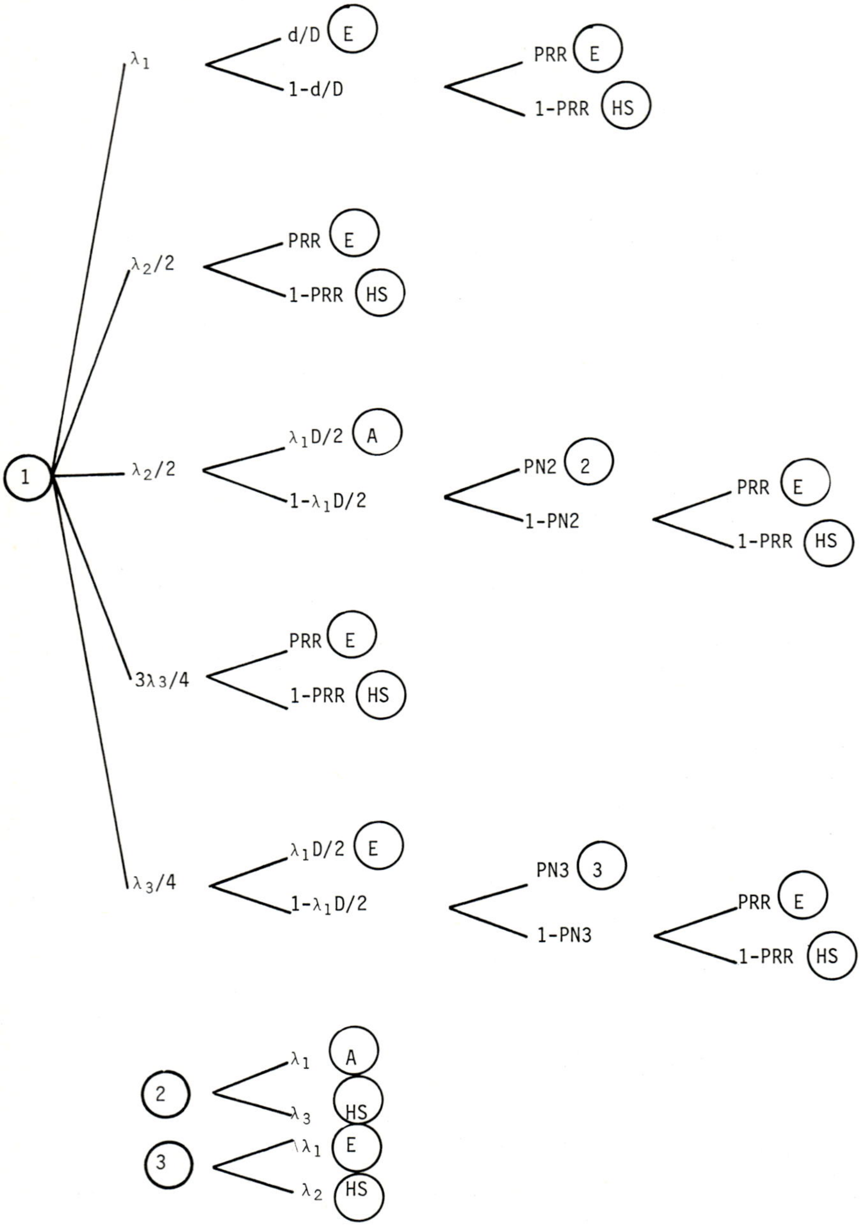

b) Memory block

The initial state is called "1" and the erroneous state E. A failure of a memory block cannot generate an alarm of the system, there is not transition to A.

The analysis is represented by the following event tree. We do not consider the transitions of order greater than two because their effect on the reliability is negligible. In particular the transitions starting from state "2" and "3" are not analysed because no direct transition from them could lead to E.

The possible states are :

1) Initial state
2) Failure of functional part, detected
3) Failure of detection or masking, detected
4) Failure of detection, undetected
5) Failure of transfer, detected
6) Failure of masking, undetected.

The meaning of the parameters used in the event tree are analogous to those used for the processor.

The QNi are probabilities of non detection. QRR is the probability that an initiated reconfiguration is not successfully carried out.

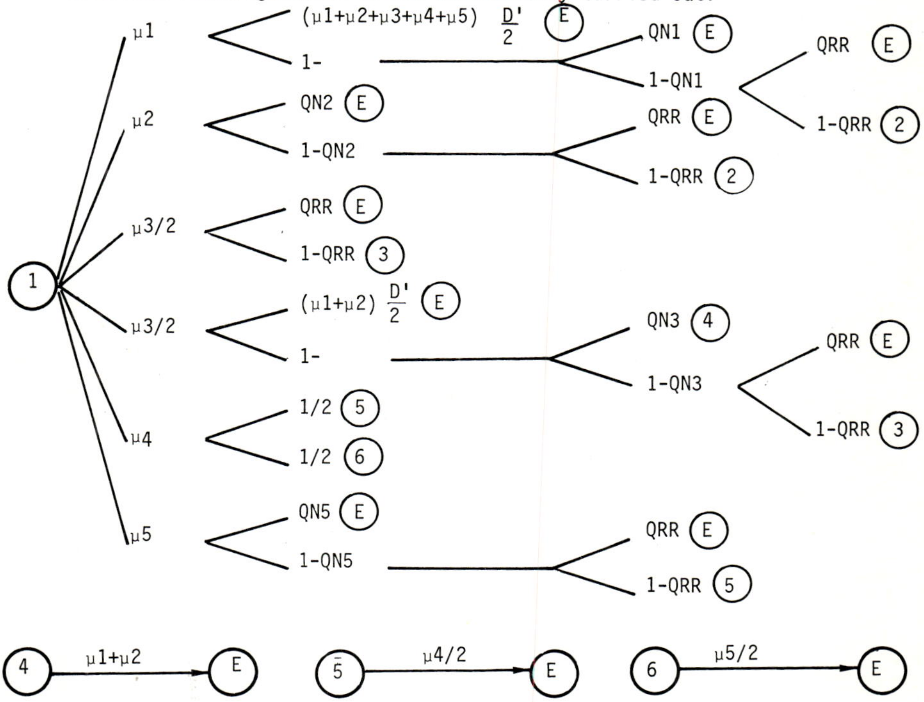

4. GLOBAL FUNCTIONING

The functioning of a processor and a memory block has been modelled in 3 a) and 3 b) by Markov processes. To know the global state of the system one needs only to know whether the cells are working or not, if they initiated an error or an alarm. One will therefore group the states defined previously. A process X (t) will describe the functioning of a processor, a process Y (t) that of a memory block.

Using the previous notations the functioning of a processor is a Markov process where the following transitions are possible :

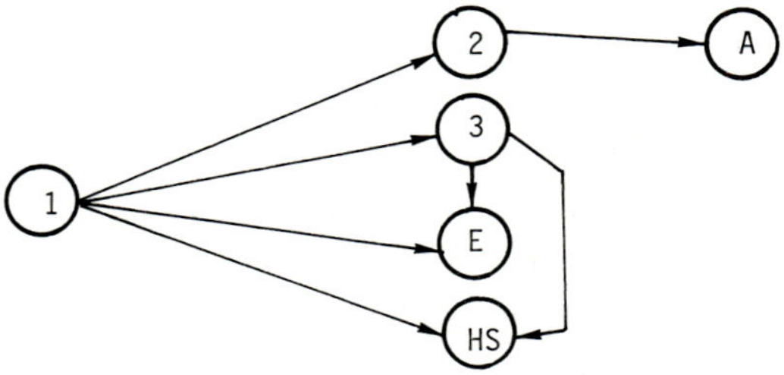

The initial state is "1" ; we want to regroup "1", "2", "3" to get the state F. The resultant distribution of X (t) will then be that of a Markov process with the following time dependent transition rates.

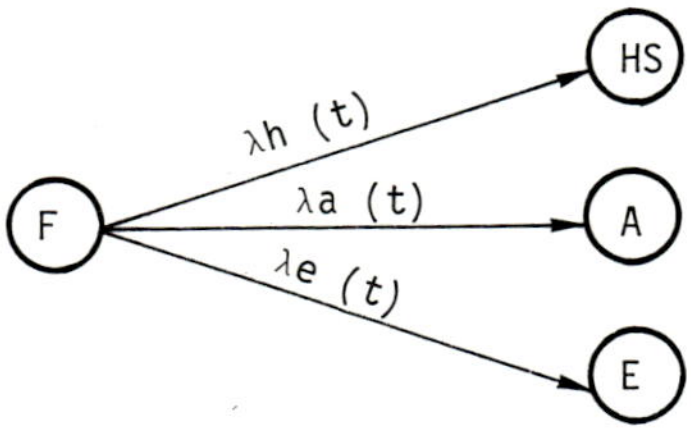

A similar grouping will give the distribution of the process describing a memory block ; but this time there is no transition to A.

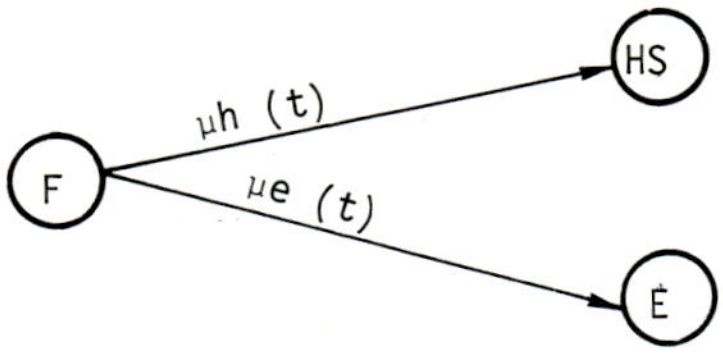

Let us call Z (t) the state of the system at time t. We will consider the case where the initial configuration is of two processors and two memory blocks and where the mission can be carried out as long as at least one processor and one memory block are available. Other cases could be treated with obvious changes in the definition of Z.

We will define six possible values for Z to characterize the level of performance.

STATE	NUMBER OF PROCESSORS	NUMBER OF MEMORY BLOCKS
1	2	2
2	2	1
3	1	2
4	1	1
5	ALARM	
6	ERROR	

The process Z (t) is Markov. We define the transition matrix Λ (t) by :

$$\text{Proba}\left[Z\ (t+dt) = j \mid Z\ (t) = i\right] = \lambda_{ij}(t)dt + o\ (dt) \text{ for } j \neq i$$

$$\text{and } \lambda_{ii}(t) = -\sum_{j\neq i} \lambda ij\ (t)$$

The matrix Λ (t) is written below. The diagonal elements are not written ; they are easily deduced from the others. The dependency on t has been omitted to simplify the notations.

MATRIX OF THE TRANSITION RATES Λ (t)

$$\begin{bmatrix} * & 2\ \mu h & 2\ \lambda h & 0 & 2\ \lambda a & 2\ \lambda e + 2\ \mu e \\ 0 & * & 0 & 2\ \lambda h & 2\ \lambda a + \mu h & 2\ \lambda e + \mu e \\ 0 & 0 & * & 2\ \mu h & \lambda a + \lambda h & \lambda e + \mu e \\ 0 & 0 & 0 & * & \lambda a + \lambda h + \mu h & \lambda e + \mu e \\ 0 & 0 & 0 & 0 & 0 & 0 \\ 0 & 0 & 0 & 0 & 0 & 0 \end{bmatrix}$$

We know that $P\left[Z\ (0) = 1\right] = 1$; if we call

$Pi\ (t) = \text{Proba}\left[Z\ (t) = i\right]$ i = 1.6 and Π (t) the line vector

$$\Pi\ (t) = \left[P1\ (t),\ P2\ (t),\ \ldots,\ P6\ (t)\right]$$

then Π (t) will be the solution of :

$$\frac{d\Pi(t)}{dt} = \Pi\ (t) \times \Lambda\ (t)$$

$$\Pi\ (0) = (1,0\ldots,0)$$

and can therefore easily be computed by an iterative program for different values of t.

The reliability R (t) is the probability that the resources are sufficient to carry out a mission of length t. Therefore :

$$R(t) = 1 - P5(t) - P6(t)$$

The safety S(t) is the probability that there is no non detected erroneous output during a mission of length t ; then :

$$S(t) = 1 - P6(t)$$

The MTBF could also be deduced from the model. However its is not a good measure of reliability, we are mostly interested in the behaviour of R (t) and S (t) in the beginning of the time period.

Note

Another initial value of Π could be chosen if there is some uncertainty on the state of the computer.

5. NUMERICAL RESULTS : INPUT

a) Failure rates

The failure rates for the cells were obtained by adding the individual rates of the components as given by MIL HDBK 217B [4].

The environment chosen here is "Airborne Inhabited"

T = 50°C

In the following evaluation the components are chosen in class B2. The cell "disable" of the processors however has been realised in class A because of its critical influence on the safety.

The following values were obtained for the failure parameters used in the model.

$\lambda 1 = 7.2 \quad 10^{-4}/h$

$\lambda 2 = 2.8 \quad 10^{-6}/h$

$\lambda 3 = .11 \quad 10^{-6}/h$

$\mu 1 = 4.1 \quad 10^{-4}/h$

$\mu 2 = 18. \quad 10^{-6}/h$

$\mu 3 = 5. \quad 10^{-6}/h$

$\mu 4 = 6. \quad 10^{-7}/h$

$\mu 5 = \quad 10^{-5}/h$

b) Parameters of the periodic tests

The periodicity D and D' of the tests have been defined in such a way that the probability of failure of the part being tested between two tests is equal to the probability that the failure occurs during the sensible period of the test. However this choice is not critical it appeared from the numerical results that the values of D and D' could be anything between

.1 and 10 hours without any sizable effect on the overall reliability.

An analogous effect may be noted for the various efficiencies of the tests. The evaluation below is given for :

$PN2 = 10^{-2}$

$PN3 = 10^{-2}$

$QN3 = 10^{-2}$

The influence of these parameters is low because they appear only in the terms involving two transitions.

c) Efficiencies of the detection by hardware

These terms have an effect on the results concerning the safety. They were evaluated under the hypothesis of independent component failures by an analysis of the failure modes. The values below were used in the evaluation :

$QN1 = 10^{-4}$

$QN2 = 10^{-8}$

$QN5 = 10^{-4}$

6. NUMERICAL RESULTS : OUTPUT

The vector Π (t) of probabilities of the various states is computed for various values of t between 0 and 1000 hours (fig.1). R (t) and S (t) are deduced from them as it was explained in 3. Two curves are plotted. One corresponds to short mission durations ($t \leqslant 10$ hours) (fig.2). The other describes the long term evolution ($t \leqslant 1000$ hours) (fig.3). The reliability is compared to that of a non-redundant computer without detection. The failure rate of such a system would be constant :

$$\lambda \simeq \lambda 1/2 + \mu 1 + \mu 2 \simeq 7.9 \quad 10^{-4} \text{ /h.}$$

REFERENCES

1 M. CORAZZA Techniques mathématiques de la fiabilité prévisionnelle CEPADUES - Toulouse 1975

2 BV.GNEDENKO Mathematical methods of reliability theory ACADEMIC PRESS - NEW YORK 1969

3 C. MERAUD, F.BROWAEYS, G. GERMAIN - Automatic Rollback Techniques of the COPRA computer - Proceedings of the international symposium on fault-tolerant computing FTCS6, 1976

4 MIL HDBK 217B Reliability prediction of electronic equipment, United States - Department of Defence.

7. CONCLUSION

As digital system will soon reach field where reliability and safety are the main requirements, good methods to evaluate the reliability of complex system are dramatically needed now. This is the case for instance, for avionic telecommunication systems, nuclear industries, etc...

A good evaluation tool must match the requirements of all the users. Avionic is a good example for it : a new automatic landing system will have to get agreement, by the manufacturer, airlines companies and the certification authorities. Therefore the method to evaluate must be easy and standardised.

After trying without success other ways of evaluating the reliability of the COPRA computer, mainly simulations, the analytical method described here has given us trustable results.

HOURS	NO FAILURE	1 MEMORY FAILURE	1 PROCESSOR FAILURE	1 PROCESSOR +1 MEMORY HAS FAILED	COMPUTER DETECTED FAILURE	UNDETECTED FAILURE
.0	1.	.0	.0	.0	.0	.0
.3	.999E+00	.257E-03	.432E-03	.111E-06	.631E-07	.252E-07
.5	.999E+00	.428E-03	.719E-03	.308E-06	.175E-06	.420E-07
1.0	.998E+00	.854E-03	.144E-02	.123E-05	.701E-06	.840E-07
2.0	.995E+00	.170E-02	.287E-02	.491E-05	.280E-05	.168E-06
3.0	.993E+00	.255E-02	.429E-02	.110E-04	.630E-05	.252E-06
4.0	.991E+00	.340E-02	.572E-02	.196E-04	.112E-04	.336E-06
5.0	.989E+00	.424E-02	.713E-02	.306E-04	.175E-04	.420E-06
6.0	.986E+00	.507E-02	.854E-02	.439E-04	.252E-04	.503E-06
7.0	.984E+00	.591E-02	.994E-02	.597E-04	.342E-04	.587E-06
8.0	.982E+00	.673E-02	.113E-01	.778E-04	.447E-04	.671E-06
9.0	.980E+00	.756E-02	.127E-01	.983E-04	.565E-04	.755E-06
10.0	.977E+00	.838E-02	.141E-01	.121E-03	.697E-04	.838E-06
20.0	.955E+00	.164E-01	.277E-01	.476E-03	.277E-03	.167E-05
30.0	.933E+00	.241E-01	.408E-01	.105E-02	.619E-03	.250E-05
40.0	.912E+00	.315E-01	.533E-01	.184E-02	.109E-02	.333E-05
50.0	.892E+00	.386E-01	.654E-01	.283E-02	.170E-02	.415E-05
60.0	.871E+00	.453E-01	.769E-01	.400E-02	.243E-02	.497E-05
70.0	.852E+00	.518E-01	.880E-01	.535E-02	.328E-02	.579E-05
80.0	.832E+00	.580E-01	.987E-01	.687E-02	.426E-02	.660E-05
90.0	.813E+00	.639E-01	.109E+00	.855E-02	.536E-02	.741E-05
100.0	.795E+00	.695E-01	.119E+00	.104E-01	.657E-02	.821E-05
200.0	.632E+00	.113E+00	.196E+00	.350E-01	.246E-01	.160E-04
300.0	.502E+00	.138E+00	.242E+00	.664E-01	.517E-01	.233E-04
400.0	.399E+00	.149E+00	.266E+00	.995E-01	.858E-01	.302E-04
500.0	.317E+00	.151E+00	.275E+00	.131E+00	.125E+00	.366E-04
600.0	.252E+00	.148E+00	.273E+00	.160E+00	.168E+00	.425E-04
700.0	.200E+00	.140E+00	.263E+00	.184E+00	.213E+00	.480E-04
800.0	.159E+00	.130E+00	.248E+00	.203E+00	.260E+00	.530E-04
900.0	.127E+00	.119E+00	.231E+00	.217E+00	.306E+00	.577E-04
1000.0	.101E+00	.108E+00	.212E+00	.227E+00	.353E+00	.619E-04
1500.0	.319E-01	.575E-01	.124E+00	.224E+00	.563E+00	.779E-04
2000.0	.101E-01	.274E-01	.653E-01	.177E+00	.720E+00	.877E-04
2500.0	.321E-02	.123E-01	.325E-01	.124E+00	.828E+00	.935E-04
3000.0	.102E-02	.533E-02	.156E-01	.817E-01	.896E+00	.969E-04
3500.0	.323E-03	.225E-02	.739E-02	.514E-01	.939E+00	.988E-04
4000.0	.103E-03	.932E-03	.345E-02	.313E-01	.964E+00	.999E-04
4500.0	.326E-04	.382E-03	.160E-02	.187E-01	.979E+00	.101E-03
5000.0	.103E-04	.155E-03	.735E-03	.110E-01	.988E+00	.101E-03

FIGURE 1

PROBABILITY OF THE VARIOUS COMPUTER STATES VERSUS TIME

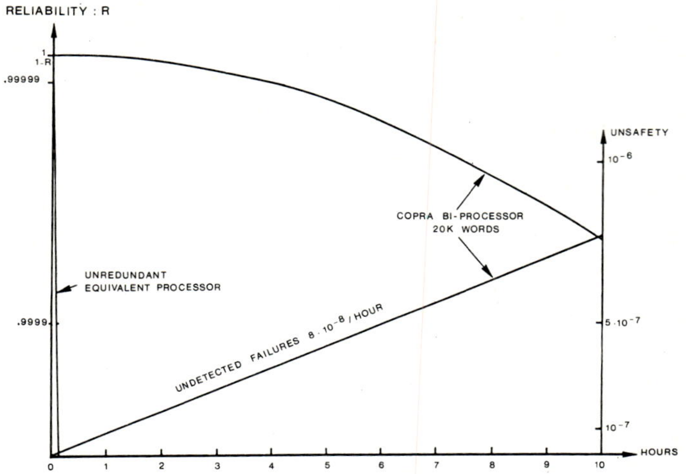

FIGURE 2

SHORT TERM EVALUATION (FOCUS)

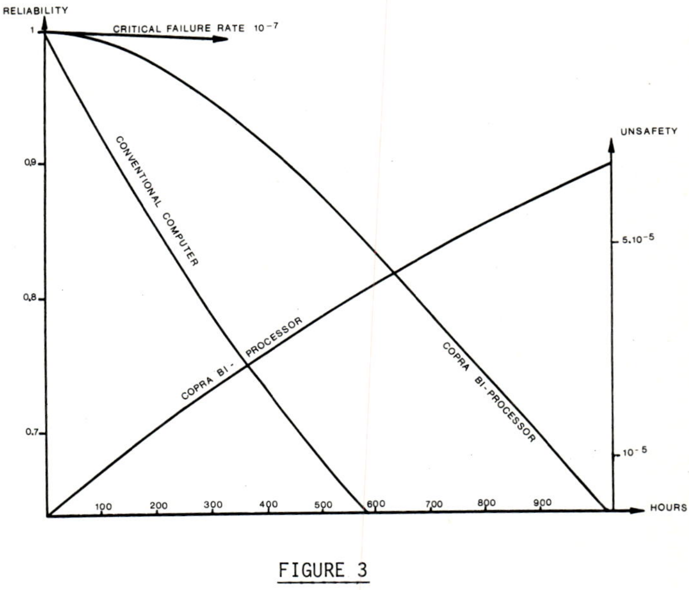

FIGURE 3

LONG TERM EVALUATION

Measuring, Modelling and Evaluating Computer Systems,
H. Beilner and E. Gelenbe, (eds.)
© North-Holland Publishing Company (1977)

PERFORMANCE MODELLING OF DISTRIBUTED SYSTEMS USING PROBABILISTIC COMPUTATION STRUCTURES

Taylor L. Booth
University of Connecticut
Storrs, Connecticut
USA

Colin Whitby-Strevens
University of Warwick
Coventry, West Midlands
England

Analytical techniques have been developed which can be used to assign a performance measure or "cost" to a given realization of a computational task. A computational system is represented as a deterministic computational process which processes information from a probabilistic information source. A computation structure representing both information flow and control flow is used to represent the deterministic computation. Each task in the computation structure can be assigned a cost. The information source is described by a probabilistic language.

A composit system is defined using the individual description of the language and the computation. This system is used to evaluate the expected cost of performing a given computational task using a particular system realization.

This report studies the assignment of resources in a distributed system using an editor as a case-study. Three different operating conditions are considered; mainly inputting, combination of inputting and editing, and mostly editing. Three system configurations are considered; highly centralized, evenly distributed and terminal based. It is shown that the overall system cost is a linear function of a number of system parameters which can easily be measured by an operating system. Examples are used to show how the operating system can adjust its resource allocation to minimize system cost.

INTRODUCTION

Distributed computing systems have introduced another dimension in the design problem. The cost of computer hardware is a relatively small factor in determining overall system cost. Instead transmission costs and response time costs become important considerations in determining the overall quality of system performance in a distributed system. This paper presents an analytical technique

- - - - - - - -

*This work was supported in part by the National Science Foundation under Grant DCR 75-00084 and the Science Research Council under Grants GR/A/0734.8 and GR/A/2747.6.

which can be used to provide an initial evaluation of the expected performance of a distributed system without committing a large amount of time or manpower to a detailed design effort. Using this approach a number of alternative solutions to a design problem can be considered and trade-off studies can be conducted during the initial design stage of a distributed system. These studies can then be used to guide the final designs effort.

The initial design of a simple distributed text editor is used to illustrate the ideas presented. This example also shown how an operating system with the responsibility for the management of resources in a distributed environment could be constructed to vary the organization of the editor as a function of the parameters of the information being processed and the type of task being performed.

PROBABILISTIC COMPUTATION STRUCTURES

From a very general viewpoint a computational system can be represented as shown in Figure 1. The system consists

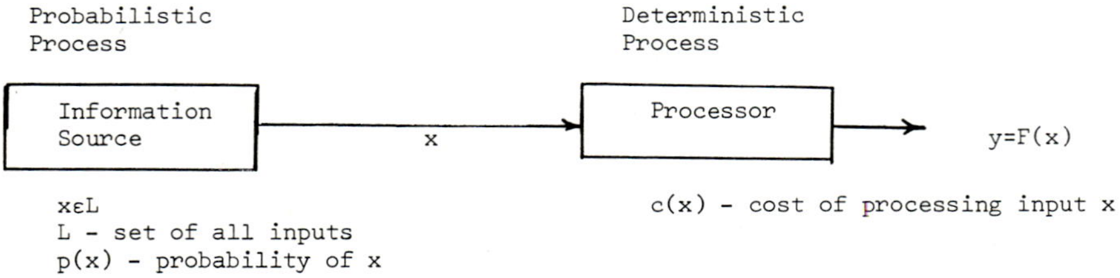

A General Representation of a
Computational System
Figure 1

of two components; an information source which is a probablistic process and a processor which carries out a deterministic computation on each input produced by the source.

The set of all possible inputs which might be generated by the source is contained in a set L. However each of the possible inputs are not of equal importance. The relative importance of an input x is indicated by its probability p(x) where

$$\sum_{x \in L} p(x) = 1$$

For each input x the processor computes an output y = F(x). This involves a *cost* c(x). The cost criterion used will depend upon the particular problem considered. For this paper the cost of interest is the expected processing time and the intercommunication time cost involved in realizing the processor as a distributed system.

The overall performance of a particular system is given by the expected cost defined as

$$\mathcal{C} = \sum_{\forall x \in L} p(x)c(x)$$

This expression illustrates that both the probabilistic properties of the source and the deterministic properties of the process influence the system's performance measure.

To evaluate $\mathcal{C}$ three things are needed. They are:

i) A compact model of the source so that $p(x)$ can be computed

ii) A compact model of the processor to indicate the major steps of the processing in response to the input symbols which make up the input sequence

iii) A model of the internal information-flow and control-flow of the processor.

PROBABILISTIC GRAMMARS

A probabilistic grammar [1,2] can be used to describe probabilistic sources. For this paper it is assumed that the source can be represented by a finite-state probabilistic language L defined by the grammar

$$G = \langle V_T, V_N, R, P, \sigma \rangle$$

where

V_T - finite set of terminal symbols

V_N - finite set of nonterminal symbols

R - finite set of rewrite rules

P - finite set of production probabilities

σ - start symbol

There is a 1-1 correspondence between P and R. The sets R and P have elements of the form

p_u : $A \rightarrow aB$ $\quad A, B \varepsilon V_N \quad a \varepsilon V_T \quad p_u, p_v \varepsilon P$

p_r : $A \rightarrow a$

In a production the term on the left is the premise and the term on the right is the consequence of the production. Suppose that the productions $r_1, r_2, \ldots, r_k$ are all the productions with premise $A \ \varepsilon \ V_N$ and that the associated probabilities are $p_1, p_2, \ldots, p_k$. If for all $A \varepsilon V_N$, $\sum_{i=1}^{k} p_i = 1$ then the grammar is consistent and

$$\sum_{\forall x \varepsilon L} p(x) = 1$$

The techniques which can be used to define the production probabilities are discussed in [2].

It should be noted that a large number of grammars can be used to define the same set L. The probabilities of the strings in L will be strongly influenced, however, by the production rules and their associated probabilities. A typical grammar is illustrated in Section III.

PROCESSOR DESCRIPTION

The processor receives the input sequence one symbol at a time. When it receives a new symbol it carries out one or more processing steps and then waits for the next input. The behaviour of the processor can be described as a state-transition process. The individual nodes of the process correspond the particular tasks that the processor can perform. A path from node i to node j labelled by input symbol

WATERFORD REGIONAL LIBRARY TEC

a means that the current input is an a, the processor processes a according to the task represented by node i and the processor then goes to the task represented by node j to await the next input. This is indicated as

$$q_i \xrightarrow{a} q_j$$

The complexity of the task performed by each node depends upon the process. The cost of performing the task, if a is the current input, is discussed shortly. Figure 4 in Section III illustrates a typical state-transition process.

COMPOSIT PROCESSES

The model of the performance of the complete system must describe both the probabilistic structure of the input and the deterministic structure of the processor. In some cases this can be accomplished by simply applying a transition probability to each transition in the state-transition process [3]. However the structure of the input process also has a very important impact upon system performance. A composit system can be defined [4] which accounts for the properties of the complete system.

Let V_N be the set of nonterminals of the grammar and let Q represent the set of nodes in the state-transition process. The behavior of the composit system is then represented by a composit transition diagram with nodes of the form (q_i,A) or $(q_i,-)$ where $q_i \varepsilon Q$ and $A \varepsilon V_N$. A transition between the node (q_i,A) and (q_j,B) occurs if

$$p_v : A \rightarrow aB \text{ and } q_i \xrightarrow{a} q_j$$

The probability of this transition is p_v and it is assured that a cost $c_{a,\alpha}$ is incurred in making the transition.

There is a transition between (q_i,A) and $(q_j,-)$ if

$$p_w : A \rightarrow b \text{ and } q_i \xrightarrow{b} q_j$$

The probability of the transition is p_v and the cost is $c_{a,\beta}$. Nodes of the form $(q_j,-)$ are terminal nodes. Figure 2 illustrates these two types of transition. Figure 5 shows a complete

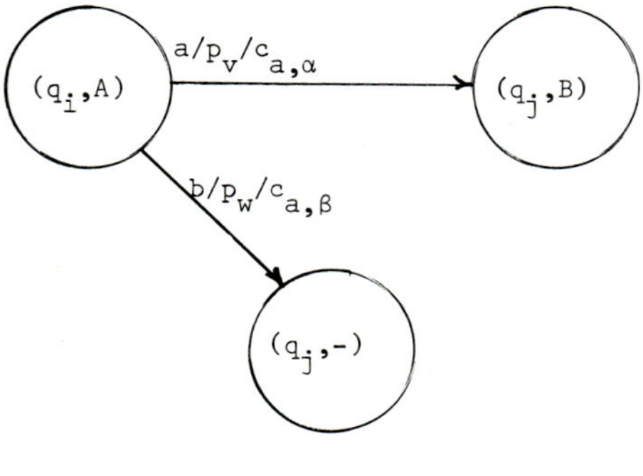

Representation of Composit
System Transitions
Figure 2

composit transition diagram.

THE COST COMPUTATION

The composit diagram can be used to compute the system cost [4]. Let U represent the set of all nodes of the composit system ordered such that nodes $u_1, .., u_n$ represent nonterminal nodes and $u_{n+1}, ..., u_{n+m}$ represent terminal nodes. Assume that the edge leading from u_i to u_j is labelled by the r probability/cost values $p_{i_1}/c_{i_1}, p_{i_2}/c_{i_2}, ..., p_{i_r}/c_{i_r}$

Define the generating function for the i-j transition as

$$g_{ij}(s) = \sum_{k=1}^{r} p_{i_k} s^{c_{i_k}}$$

The system generating function is defined as an nx(n+m) matrix

$$G(x) = [G_T(s), G_W(s)] = [g_{ij}(s)]$$

where $G_T(s)$ is the nxn submatrix associated with the transitions between non-terminal nodes and $G_W(s)$ is the nxm submatrix associated with the transition between nonterminal and terminal nodes.

The system transition probability matrix is

$$M = G(1) = [G_T(1), G_W(1)] = [T, W]$$

The following theorem establishes a formula for system costs

Theorem I The expected cost associated with a composit system is given by

$$= E[I-T]^{-1} \left[\frac{dG_T(s)}{ds} \quad \frac{dG_W(s)}{ds} \right] \Bigg|_{s=1} F_n$$

$$= \Gamma C F_n$$

where E is the initial state probability row vector, $\Gamma = E[I-T]^{-1}$, and F_n is the n-row column vector of all 1's.

Proof: An outline of the proof [4] is given in Appendix A.

The relationship of theorem I shows that the expected cost is a linear combination of the individual costs associated with the tasks which make up the system. An example of how this expression is used is given in Section III.

COMPUTATION STRUCTURES

The costs associated with a computation must be related to the individual tasks involved in the computation. So far the models have been concerned with the gross features of the system. A computation structure [5] can be used to model the details of the algorithm used to perform a given task.

A computation structure is a system

$$\mathcal{C} = \langle A, B, V, C \rangle$$

where

$A = \{\alpha_1,\alpha_2,..\alpha_n\}$ is a set of operations

$B = \{\beta_1,\beta_2,...,\beta_m\}$ is a set of variables

$V = \{v_1,v_2,...v_r\}$ is a set of indicators

C = is a control structure

For each $\beta_i \varepsilon B$ there is a storage unit which can contain values from a domain D_i. Each $v_i \varepsilon V$ represents a truth value (0-FALSE, 1-TRUE). Each operator $\alpha_i \varepsilon A$ has an associated set of inputs

$I_i = \{\beta_{i_1},\beta_{i_2},...,\beta_{i_h}\}$ and an output set

$\mathcal{O}_i = \{\beta_{o_1},\beta_{o_2},...\beta_{o_j}\} \vee \{v_{o_1},v_{o_2},...,v_{o_q}\}$

The operator α_i is a mapping of I_i into $\mathcal{O}_i$.

The control structure C determines the order in which the operators α_i are activated. The sequence of operations are subject to change depending upon the values of the v_{o_i}'s when α_i is activated.

A computation structure is represented by two graphs; an information flow graph which indicates the relationship between each operator and the sets I_i and $\mathcal{O}_i$ and a control flow graph which describes the control structure. These graphs are made up from the symbols shown in Table I.

Figure 6 of Section III illustrates how these symbols can be used to represent a computation. Each operation must be realized by a program segment. One typical cost of interest is the time needed to perform a computation which is, in turn, related to the time required for each operation. Thus the cost associated with each transition in the composit diagram can be related directly to the expected time required to perform each operation in the computation structure. It is up to the system designer to assign these costs in a manner which is representative of the system being investigated.

III SYSTEM DESIGN

To carry out a system design, once a set of performance specifications have been determined requires that the designer considers a number of alternative approaches before selecting the one to be implemented. The analytical methods outlined in Section II provide a way to do this in a systematic manner. The best way to understand these ideas is to carry out a simple design problem.

AN EXAMPLE

The following simple example has been developed to illustrate the design concepts presented in the preceding sections.

A time-shared remote editing facility is to be developed with the general organization shown in Figure 3. It is desired to determine which tasks should be carried out at the remote intelligent terminal and which ones should be carried out at the central facility, so as to minimise the elapsed time taken by the system.

TABLE I

Symbolic Representation of A Computation Structure

Information Flow Symbols

Symbol	Meaning
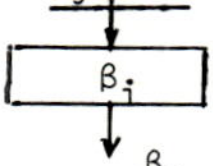	Data element representation
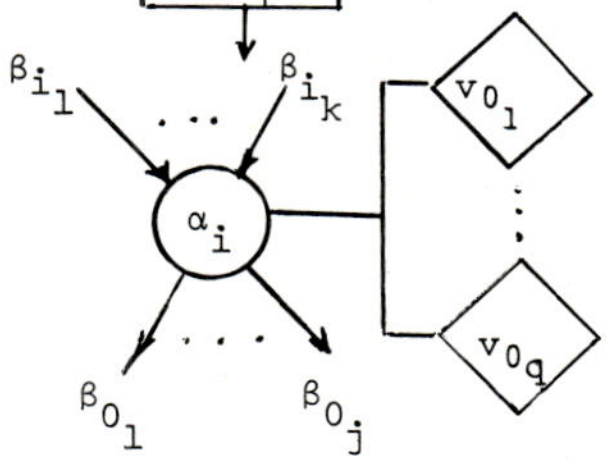	Operator representation

Control Flow

Symbol	Meaning
	Initiate computation by sending out an activate signal
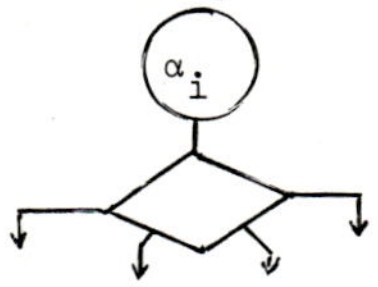	Activate operator α_i when activate signal received. Activate signal leaves on the branch depending upon the values of $\{v_{o_1},..,v_{o_j}\}$.
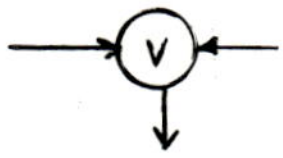	Send out an activate signal whenever one is received.
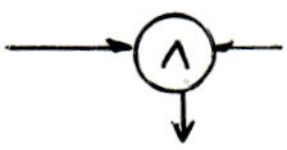	Send out an activate signal only when an activate signal is received on all input lines.
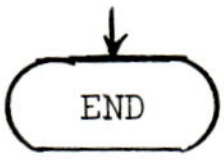	End of computation.

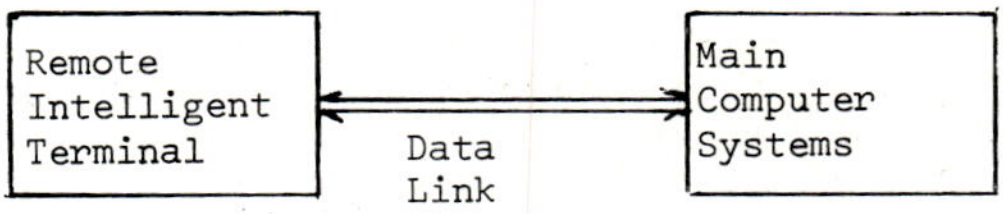

General Organization of System
On Which Editor Is To Be Run
Figure 3

a) Editor Input

The probabilistic grammar, G, is assumed to model a typical session by a user.

$G = <V_T, V_N, R, P, \sigma>$

$V_T = \{i,e,f,v,a,w,z\}$ $\qquad$ $V_N = \{\sigma, A, B, C\}$

R,P

1 : $\sigma \to iA$			
p_1 : $A \to eA$			$p_1+p_2+p_3+p_4+p_5=1$
p_2 : $A \to fA$	r_1: $B \to aC$		$r_1+r_2=1$
p_3 : $A \to vA$	r_2: $B \to zA$		$u_1+u_2=1$
p_4 : $A \to aB$	u_1: $G \to aC$		
p_5 : $A \to w$	u_2: $C \to zA$		

The interpretation of the editing commands which make up V_T are:

i - initiate editing $\qquad$ v - verify a line

e - edit a line $\qquad$ a - add a line

f - edit and verify a line $\qquad$ z - end of line addition segment

w - end of editing

A minimal grammar to represent all editing sequences would not need the nonterminal C. However it is observed that once the user starts to add additional lines to a file it is highly probable that more than one line will be added. This changes the probabilities associated with the a command. Thus the nonterminal C is included to allow for this change in probability.

Additional nonterminals and commands could be added if a greater refinement of the input process description is desired. The grammar, as given, is sufficiently complex for the purpose of this example.

b) Processor Description

At the level being considered the process represented by the editor has a relatively simple form. The transition diagram describing the computational task performed is shown in Figure 4.

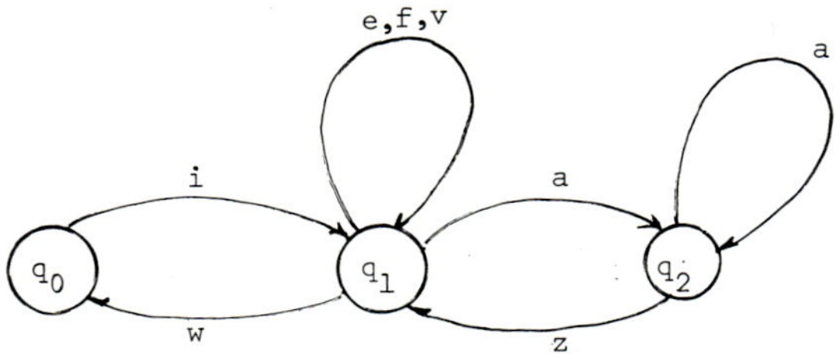

Transition Diagram of Editor
Figure 4

State q_0 is the initial state where the system is waiting to be activated while state q_1, accomplishes all of the standard tasks except that of adding text. The slightly different task of adding one or more lines is accomplsihed by state q_2. A much more complicated process could be specified but the level of complexity represented by this model is sufficient for the current example

c) Composit Process

The composit process represented by the input grammar and the editor process has the form shown in Figure 5.

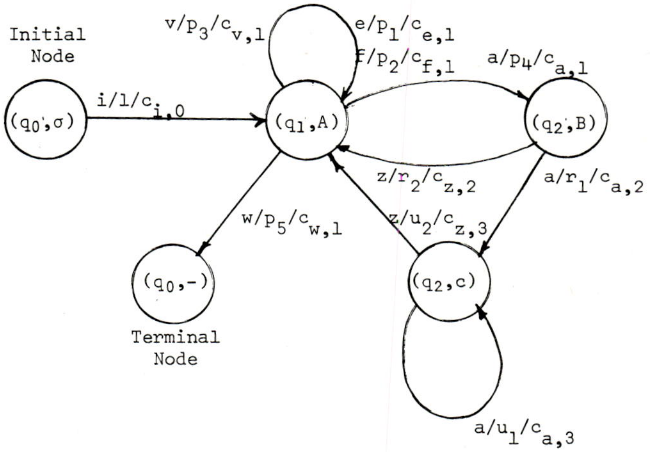

Composit Transition Diagram
For System
Figure 5

Using the information contained in this figure, the following matricies can be determined.

$$T = \begin{bmatrix} 0 & 1 & 0 & 0 \\ 0 & p_1+p_2+p_3 & p_4 & 0 \\ 0 & r_2 & 0 & r_1 \\ 0 & u_2 & 0 & u_1 \end{bmatrix} \qquad W = \begin{bmatrix} 0 \\ p_5 \\ 0 \\ 0 \end{bmatrix}$$

$$C = \begin{bmatrix} \frac{dG_T}{ds} & \frac{dG_W}{ds} \end{bmatrix} = \begin{bmatrix} 0 & c_{i,o} & 0 & 0 & 0 \\ 0 & p\,c_{e,1}+p_2c_{f,1}+p_3c_{v,1} & p_4c_{q,1} & & p_5c_{w,1} \\ 0 & r_2c_{z,2} & 0 & r_1c_{a,2} & 0 \\ 0 & u_2c_{z,3} & 0 & u_1c_{a,3} & 0 \end{bmatrix}$$

letting

$$\Gamma = [1,0,0,0]\,[\,I - T\,]^{-1} \qquad F_5 = \begin{bmatrix} 1 \\ 1 \\ 1 \\ 1 \\ 1 \end{bmatrix}$$

then the cost associated with the system becomes

$$\mathcal{C} = \Gamma C F_5$$

The next task consists of determining values for the C matrix.

d) The Computation Structure

It is assumed that the editor can be represented by the simple computation structure shown in Figure 6. Several refinements could easily be added but this would not add anything to the example.

The main file corresponds to the secondary store where the file to be edited is found when the editor is activated. The file to be edited, possibly

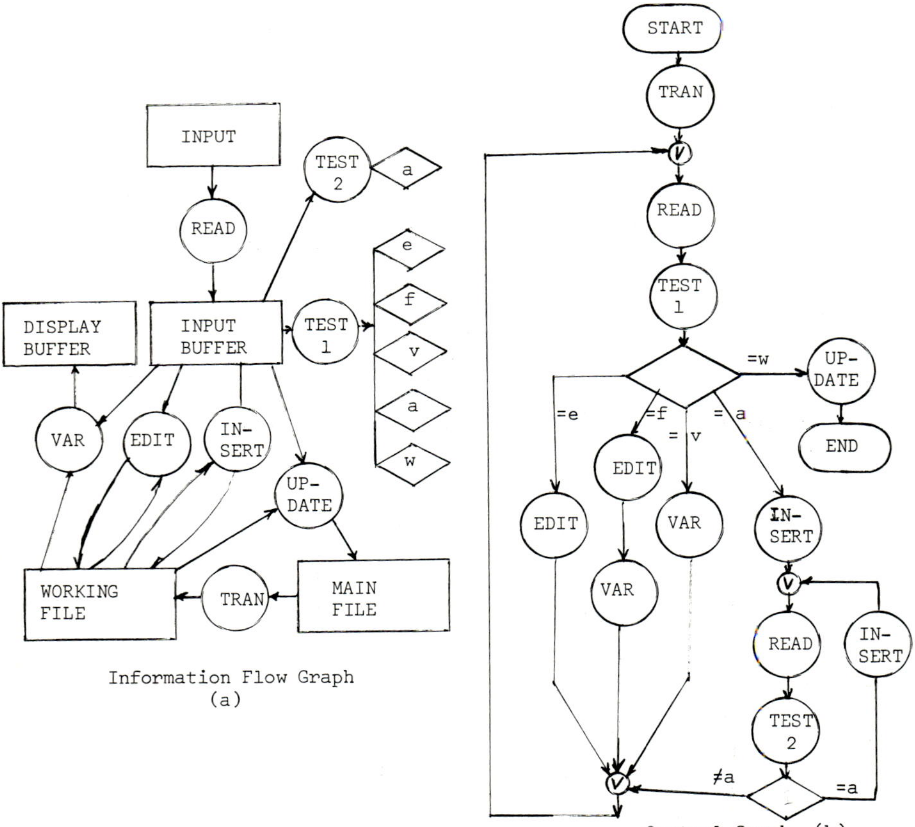

Information Flow Graph (a)

Control Graph (b)

Computation Structure For A Simple Editor
Figure 6

the null file, is transferred to the working file where the editing takes place. After the editing is completed the UPDATE operation returns the edited file to the main file.

At this point the computation structure is still independent of the final realization of the system. This model will now be used to compare the cost of three different realizations of the editor.

Referring back to Figure 3 it is seen that the system consists of two subsystems, an intelligent terminal and a main computer, connected by a data link. Three possible organizations are considered. They are:

Case I

All processing is carried out on the main computer. The terminal simply acts as an I/O device.

Case II

All processing is carried out at the terminal but the working file is retained in the main computer.

Case III

The working file is transferred to the terminal for processing. The main computer only retains the main file.

These three cases provide a broad range of capabilities. When all processing is done on the main computer (Case I) processing is slowed down by the operating system and the fact that other users will wish access to the machine's available resources. When all the processing is done at the terminal (Case III) the processing speeds are faster since the terminal will be dedicated to a single task. However additional storage space must be provided to store the working file. In some cases a considerable amount of time will be needed to transmit the file at the beginning and end of the editing task.

Situated between these two extremes is a system (Case II) which shares the tasks. Most of the processing takes place at the terminal, however the data base being processed remains in the main computer.

3-2 Description of Values Used In Study

The transmission of a command or a line of information is assumed to take place in one packet consisting of 800 bits. The time required to transmit 1 packet is

$$C_{LT} = \frac{800}{\text{(Line transmission rate in bands)}}$$

Three rates are considered

Low - 2,400 baud

Medium - 48,000 baud

High - 1,000,000 baud

The operating system in the main computer must respond to each request after a time depending upon the load of the system. The response cost of the operating system is denoted by C_H and is one of the variable parameters to be investigated.

In Case II the remote terminal need only have access to the working file. This is assumed to take $C_F = .05C_H$ seconds.

The other costs are assigned directly to each operation. Table 2 gives the expression for each of the system costs. Table 3 gives the values assigned to each of the cost and probability terms for the system under investigation.

TABLE 2

Cost Expressions For Editing System

Case I

$$c_{i,0} = N_I C_{TR}$$

$$c_{e,1} = C_R + \alpha(C_{T1}+C_E) + C_{LT} + C_H$$

$$c_{f,1} = C_R + \alpha(C_{T1}+C_E+C_V) + C_{LT} + C_H$$

$$c_{v,1} = C_R + \alpha(C_{T1}+C_V) + C_{LT} + C_H$$

$$c_{a,1} = C_R + \alpha(C_{T1} + C_{I1}) + C_{LT} + C_H$$

$$c_{w,1} = C_R + \alpha(C_{T1}) + C_{LT} + C_H + (N_I+\bar{n})C_{UP}$$

$$c_{a,2} = c_{a,3} = C_R + (C_{T2}+C_{I2}) + C_{LT} + C_H$$

$$c_{z,2} = c_{z,3} = C_R + (C_{T2}) + C_{LT} + C_H$$

Case II

$$c_{i,0} = N_I C_{TR}$$

$$c_{e,1} = C_R + C_{T1} + C_E + 3C_{LT} + 2\,C_F$$

$$c_{f,1} = C_R + C_{T1} + C_E + C_V + 4C_{LT} + 2C_F$$

$$c_{v,1} = C_R + C_{T1} + C_V + 2C_{LT} + C_F$$

$$c_{a,1} = C_R + C_{T1} + C_{I1} + 2C_{LT} + C_F$$

$$c_{w,1} = C_R + C_{T1} + C_{LT} + C_H + (N_I+\bar{n})C_{UP}$$

$$c_{a,2} = c_{a,3} = C_R + C_{T2} + C_{I2} + C_{LT} + C_F$$

$$c_{z,2} = c_{z,3} = C_R + C_{T2} + C_{LT}$$

Case III

$$c_{i,o} = (N_I+2)C_{LT} + C_H + N_I C_{TR}$$

$$c_{e,1} = C_R + C_{T1} + C_E$$

$$c_{f,1} = C_R + C_{T1} + C_E + C_V$$

$$c_{v,1} = C_R + C_{T1} + C_V$$

$$c_{a,1} = C_R + C_{T1} + C_{I1}$$

$$c_{w,1} = C_R + C_{T1} + (N_T+\bar{n}+2)C_{LT} + C_H + (N_I+\bar{n})C_{UP}$$

$$c_{a,2} = c_{a,3} = C_R + C_{T2} + C_{I2}$$

$$c_{z,2} = c_{z,3} = C_R + C_{T2}$$

Symbol

- N_I - initial number of lines
- C_{TR} - cost of transmitting one line from main memory
- C_R - Cost of reading input
- C_{T1} - Cost TEST 1
- C_E - Cost of EDIT
- C_V - Cost of VAR
- C_{LT} - Line transmission cost
- C_H - Operating system delay cost
- C_{I1} - Cost first insert
- C_{I2} - Cost following inserts
- C_F - Cost of accessing file in main computer
- α - Ratio operating speed of remote terminal to main computer
- C_{UP} - Cost of transmitting one line to main memory
- $\bar{n}$ - Expected number of lines added
- C_{T2} - Cost TEST 2

TABLE 3
Assigned Cost Values
Grammar Probabilities and File Size

Term	Inputting	Input and Editing	Editing
1	.001	.1	.1
2	.001	.5	.7
3	.001	.05	.05
4	.467	.34	.14
5	.5	.01	.01
r_1	1	.7	.7
r_2	0	.3	.3
u_1	.995	.9	.6
u_2	.005	.1	.4
N_I	10	100	1000

SYSTEM COST

C_{TR} - .01 sec	C_E - .1 sec
C_{UP} - .01 sec	C_V - .05 sec
C_R - .1 sec	C_{I1} - .3 sec
C_{T1} - .01 sec	C_{I2} - .1 sec
C_{T2} - .005 sec	α - .1
C_H - varied 0 sec. to 2.5 sec.	

Three types of editing conditions are selected.

i) Inputting

The initial file is small and the action consists mostly of adding new lines although some editing is allowed.

ii) Input and Editing

The initial file is of medium size and a mix of editing and inputting is carried out.

iii) Editing

The initial file is large and the main task is editing.

Greater refinements in the cost values could be introduced and a wider range of activities could be studied. However the above assumed conditions and cases are sufficient to illustrate the application of the design technique being presented.

3.3 Results

A program to evaluate was written and the performance of the system was evaluated for the three cases. Figure 7 provides a graphical presentation of the results.

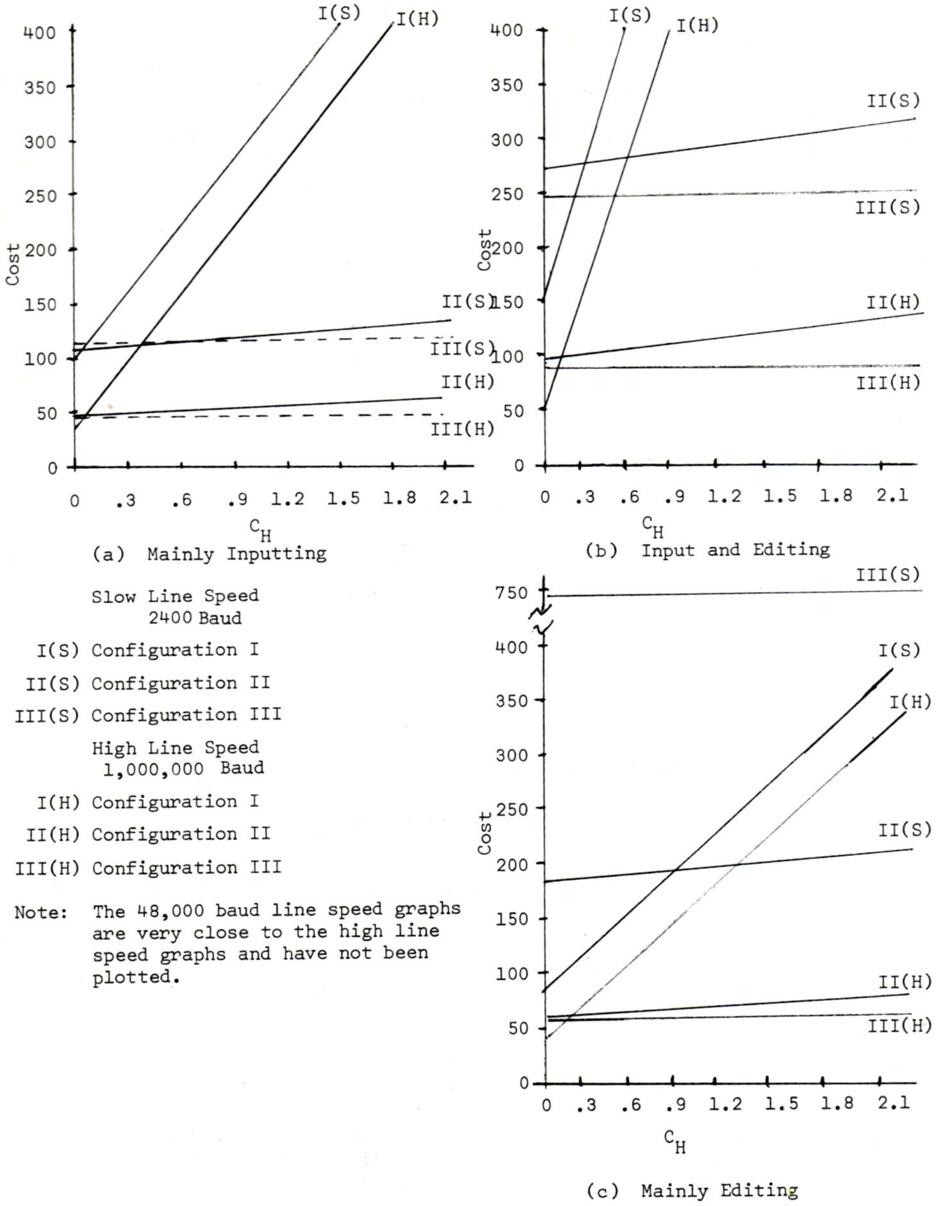

Example of Cost Function For Three Configurations
and Three Operating Conditions

Figure 7

Figure 7a corresponds to the case of mainly inputting. A centralized approach is beneficial only if the average operating system response time is less than 0.1 sec. Otherwise either of the other two approaches is better. In these cases the response of the main machine has relatively little influence on the user. An increase in line speed by a factor of 400 reduces the centralized cost by 12.5% but it reduces the cost of the distributed system by 75%.

Figure 7b corresponds to the mixed inputting and editing case. The cross over point between centralized and distributed computing is 0.2 sec for the slow line speed case and 0.1 seconds for a fast line speed. Of the two distributed approaches, transmitting the whole file of 100 lines to the local machine (Case III) provide, a lower cost than transmitting editing commands back and forth. An improvement in line speed provides the greatest improvement in the distributed case.

Figure 7c corresponds to the editing of a large file (1000 lines). With the slow speed line it becomes prohibitive to transmit the whole file to the remote terminal unless the response of the operating system is greater than 5 seconds. With a slow speed line method 2 (editing only on local machine) is beneficial if the operating system response is greater than 1.2 seconds. At medium speeds (48,000 band) these problems are alleviated and with high speed lines either distributed approach is better when the central machine average response time is more than 0.15 seconds.

IV Results and Conclusions

As shown by the above example the best system configuration depends upon the status of the system when the editor is invoked and the type of task the editor is required to perform. If one configuration must be selected then approach 2, where the working buffer space is permanently "locked down" in the store of the main machine together with a simple access program, is the least sensitive to line speed changes and might be selected.

Consideration should be given to a mode of operation in which the operating system would select the configuration as a function of current system loading, the size of the file to be edited and the line-speed available. All of these parameters are readily available. The type of activity may be deduced either by implication from the size of the file, or by arranging for syntactically different calls to invoke the editor (for example by using INPUT, APPEND or EDIT to indicate the main type of activity expected).

For a general operating system an appropriate cost function must be associated with each identifiable task. When a task is invoked information about the task's parameters which characterize the source requirements must be provided to the operating systems. In a simple system the task would provide a set of fixed parameters to characterize its source requirements and all cost functions are simplified to the point where they are similar in format. Alternatively a specialized "scheduling prelude" may be associated with each task which is used to provide a more precise estimate of resource demands. In either case further research is suggested to provide automatic means of generating the appropriate parameters or functions (e.g. as a byproduct of compilation).

The cost-effectiveness of this approach is demonstrated by observing that in the example of Section III, this function may be expressed in decision-table form requiring the minimum of processor overhead to arrive at a dynamically chosen optimum result.

This paper has shown that it is possible to develop an analytic model which can be used to study the performance of a given software system. A performance measure can be developed for any software package. The measure, which can be developed for any software package. The measure, which can be related to different possible systems configurations, is linearly related to different systems parameters many of which can be easily measured by the operating system. This suggests that in a distributed system the operating system should be designed so that the resource configuration for a particular task is optimized both in terms of the service given to that task and the overall utilization of system resources. Further research to develop more generalized models will be needed to explore these possibilities.

References

|1| T. L. Booth and R. A. Thompson: Applying probability measures to abstract languages, IEEE Trans Comp. Vol. C-22, pp. 442-449, May 1973.

|2| K. S. Fu and T. L. Booth: Grammatical inferance:Introduction and survey Part II, IEEE Trans. Syst. Man, Cybern. Vol. SMC-5 pp. 409-423, July 1975.

|3| T. C. Low: Analysis of an information system model with transfer penalties, IEEE Trans. Comp., Vol C-22, pp. 469-480, May 1973.

|4| T. L. Booth: Design of minimal expected processing time finite-state transducers, 1974 Proc. IFIP North-Holland Publishing Co. 1974.

|5| H. A. Sholl and T. L. Booth: Software performance modeling using computation structures, IEEE Trans. Soft. Engr., Vol. SE-1 No. -4, pp. 414-420, December, 1975.

Appendix A

Proof of Theorem I

Define $H(s) = \sum_{\forall x \varepsilon L} p(x) s^{c(x)}$

and column vector $F = [f_j]$ $\quad f_j = \begin{cases} 0 & \text{node } j \text{ nonterminal} \\ 1 & \text{node } j \text{ terminal} \end{cases}$

$$H(s) = E\,[I + G(s) + G^2(s) + \cdots]F$$

$$= E\,[I - G(s)]^{-1} F$$

$$\mathcal{C} = \left.\frac{dH(s)}{ds}\right|_{s=1} = E[I-G(1)]^{-1} \left.\frac{dG(s)}{ds}\right|_{s=1} [I-G(1)]^{-1} F$$

But $E\,[I-G(1)]^{-1} = \Gamma$ and by direct calculation

$[I-G(1)]^{-1}F = F_n$.

Thus

$$\mathcal{C} = \Gamma\ C\ F_n$$

Measuring, Modelling and Evaluating Computer Systems,
H. Beilner and E. Gelenbe, (eds.)
© North-Holland Publishing Company (1977)

MODELLING OF COMPUTER SYSTEM PERFORMANCE DURING DEVELOPMENT

by K. M. Roehr, IBM Deutschland, Entwicklung und Forschung

Abstract

Computer system modelling is of major importance during all development phases. Gross models will help during the early design phases to arrive at meaningful objectives and to predict performance for achievable system specifications. More detailed models evaluate specific, performance critical design alternatives during the development of subsystem components. When the design has been finalized the results of these subsystem models are used to improve the accuracy of the total system model. After calibration of the system model with data measured on the finished running system it can be used for performance predictions and optimizations for critical customer installations.

To demonstrate the use of models during development three basically different models and their applications will be described.

1. An analytic model of a multiprocessing system structure of processors and main storage modules will be used to optimize the ratio of performance to price.
2. An analytic model of an operating system will be used to evaluate the impact of supervisor design alternatives.
3. A high level overall system model including data base and data communication facilities will be used to predict system performance. Two model implementations, one using analytic the other simulation techniques, will be described together with their relative merits.

1. Introduction

Type of System

A computer system is here considered to consist of all hardware and software necessary to run an application. Our main concern is with the central electronic complex consisting of instruction processing unit, random access main storage, disk and tape file devices, unit record I/O and a set of terminals, in addition to the necessary operating system software to conveniently handle hardware components. Typical user application and data bases are used to exercise the system.

System Characteristics

The performance of a computer system, or its power, represents generally its most salient characteristic to a user. The user is buying a data processing engine and naturally wants to know its horsepower, or its ability to do useful work for him. A sales decision may of course be based on other important features like reliability, availability, serviceability, useability, price, etc. The discussion here will be limited to modelling of computer system performance. For optimization reasons system or subsystem costs will be introduced when needed.

Performance Measures

There is presently no widely accepted measure for global power of performance of computer systems. Traditionally, computer systems have been characterized by listing attributes of subsystems, like cycle time, instruction execution times, memory size and access time, bus width, disk size and access times, software subsystem pathlength and memory space requirements, etc. A widely known classical example of comparing components by listing the various characteristics of every computer was originally published by Adams Associates.

Leo Hellerman (1) has published an interesting approach to find the power of data processing systems by evaluating the power of system components, based on information theoretical ideas. Average CPU processing power was found by using instruction mixes, the most widely known being the so called Gibson Mix.

A more sophisticated method uses a so called "kernel", a complete nucleus problem, like inverting a matrix or evaluating a polynomial, to evaluate relative performance of machines. A more reliable and accurate method of analyzing system performance is to use complete application programs, or abstractions thereof. Such selected programs are often called "benchmarks". As long as the benchmarks are selected to closely represent actual workload characteristics, a good indication of system behaviour can be obtained by actual measurements.

The problems encountered with benchmarking are threefold:

1. It takes usually a large effort to prepare programs and data
2. Actual measurements require well defined hardware system configurations not always readily available.
3. Only a limited set of benchmarks is practically feasible. Predictions for other problems not benchmarked can be risky extrapolations.

The limitation of point 1 can be drastically reduced by synthetic automatic benchmark generation via programming packages specifically designed for this purpose. Point 2 and 3 are effectively attacked by modelling instead of measuring. Any desired system configuration can be readily set up in a model. Due to this ease of generation, any interesting application can be modelled as desired. Extrapolations can remain the exception rather than the rule.

The performance evaluation method described in the following uses benchmarks and models for comparison between systems.

Application Areas

Computer system performance measures and models are most often applied to the finished product to be sold, configured or managed in the field. A salesman has to characterize his product and a user has to compare alternative systems with respect to their ability to sustain a certain application oriented workload.

Once a sales decision was made, the next, somewhat more detailed task is to select the optimum hardware and software configuration to handle the data processing problems most efficiently. A computer center manager finally who has a given set of hardware installed, is interested to dynamically schedule his workload and constantly tune his system to operate at maximum efficiency.

In all these cases complete system performance modelling has been applied successfully in the past. At shipment time the system design status has been sufficiently stabilized to enable the detailed implementation of relatively accurate system models based on actual measurements on the finished system.

Here the application of performance models during the total development cycle, preceeding shipment will be discussed in more detail. This range of time includes the early planning and market analysis phase, and the phases of initial design up to the final implementation and testing for announcement and shipment. At each stage of the development cycle the modelling requirements are somewhat different, depending on the present status of the project.

After a short discussion of the various development phases and their modelling requirements, three basically different models and some of their applications will be described:

1. An analytic model of processors and main storage modules will be used to find the multiprocessing system structure having best price performance.
2. An analytic model of an operating system will be used to evaluate the impact of supervisor design alternatives.
3. A high level overall system model including data base and data communication facilities will be used to predict performance improvements for systems being developed if compared against already existing systems. Two model implementation techniques, will be described together with their relative merits.

2. The Phases of Development

In the following major phases of a data processing system development will be characterized and the use of modelling during these phases will be outlined.

Market Analysis and Planning Phase

During this phase one will ask questions like: what is the market for the new system; how does the potential customer for the new system look like today; what is his present day workload; which hardware system configuration and which software operating system does he have installed today; what are his likely future workload requirements and how should one structure future systems to satisfy his needs; how much more performance can he utilize in a new system; what is the performance/price incentive one has to offer to make the new system sufficiently interesting, etc.

The main performance related work that has to be done during this period is

- to characterize typical potential migrators with respect to workloads and system configurations of today
- to extrapolate from today's users to future users and to identify which new system configurations will accomodate the new, anticipated workloads
- to identify how much more performance the new systems have to deliver at what price.

Characterization of typical present day users is a non-trivial task but certainly can be solved with sufficient patience and inside experience to separate the accidential from the fundamental. The major problem during this work is usually to obtain a consensus on what is considered to by "typical".

Extrapolation from present day workloads into the future and the first pass definition of future system objectives requires a good deal of experience, vision and cognizance of potential new dp technologies and methods on the horizon, if the new system is not merely to become an enlarged copy of the old. The main emphasis at this stage will be placed on characterizing the future workload. First past objectives for a system structure should remain sufficiently general to allow for trade offs between all parts of the system, e. g. between hardware and software.

System modelling at this stage should be used to assure that the proposed new system is potentially able to satisfy the performance objectives expressed in relation to the old system. Before such a relative system comparison can be made one should assure, e. g. by modelling, that both, old and new system configurations have been optimized to give a maximum ratio of performance to price for the selected workloads. If this optimization is not done at the old migrator system, it may be too easy to obtain the desired performance gain by optimally tuning the new system.

Design and Implementation

During this phase the initial system objectives, based on a set of user environments, will be broken up into a number of subsystem objectives, one for each major component of the system. System modelling will help to assure that the conglomerate sum of all component performance objectives is consistent with the overall system performance objectives.

As a next step component development groups will arrive at initial designs guided by preliminary component performance objectives. During this process design alternatives are evaluated by means of models covering smaller portions of the overall system.

Examples of such modelling effort evaluate e. g. scheduler algorithms, disk configurations or multiprocessing CPU arrangements. The outcome of these efforts will be an initial design with associated initial performance specifications for each component.

The initial component performance specifications can now be used for integration into an improved overall system performance model giving a first indication how well system performance objectives can be met.

During the remaining design and implementation process component models will be refined to always reflect the latest status of the design. In case of serious deviations between achievable system characteristics and systems objectives several cycles of redesign and evaluation may become necessary. At the end of this period a viable system has been implemented and for typical environments its major performance characteristics have been obtained by modelling. These characteristics will be used as criteria for passing an overall system performance test.

System Test

This overall system performance test, using typical user workloads, will tell if the system really does satisfy its original objectives and can be offered to the market. During these measurements all components of the system will be monitored with respect to performance related parameter, like response times, thruput, utilization, software pathlengths, etc..

This test will be the first real proof of the quality of previous modelling activities. A good part of the model was naturally based on past systems that have been measured extensively. However, all newly developed system parts have been modelled using best judgement, mostly without any actual proof measurements.

A major purpose of this test, besides system verification, is to generate sufficient measurement data for system and component model validation, respectively calibration. This systems performance measurement and model calibration process is continued for all subsequent system changes and modifications until the systems is ready for shipment. All this time a fully calibrated and validated system model will be available to the field.

Model Usage and Characteristics

In Fig. 1 a pictorial representation of the development process and the models being used during this process is given.

The main development phases of market analysis and planning, design and implementation, and system test have been discussed above. Figure 1 clearly indicates the very basic and central importance which the definition of typical user environments has on all major development activities. These definitions include typical user workloads and system configurations of present and future systems, and are used as base for all performance design activities during the development cycle.

The circle in the center of Fig. 1 indicates that several iteration cycles may be necessary until a satisfactory total system solution was found that satisfies user requirements, can be implemented with present day technology, and meets price performance objectives.

Three basic types of models have been shown in Fig. 1 to support the development process:

THE DEVELOPMENT PROCESS AND ITS MODELS

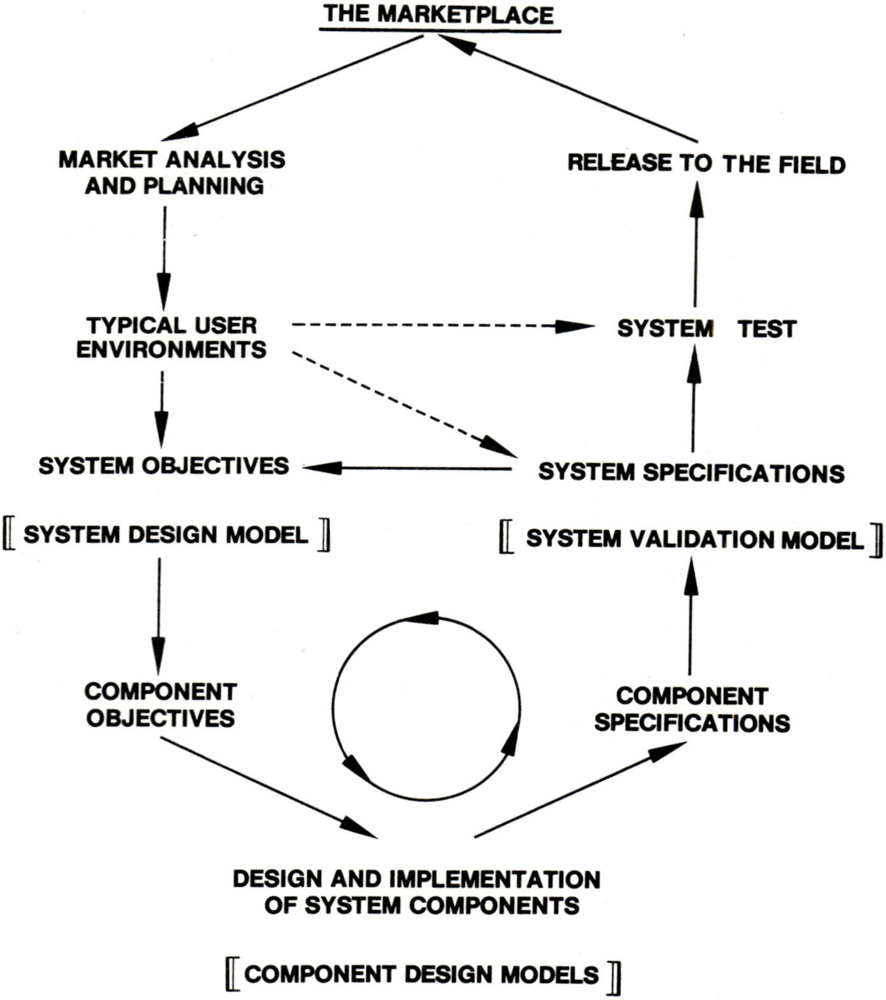

FIG. 1

1. System Design Model
Its primary functions is to support the early systems design process by evaluating a larger number of alternative system proposals to find an optimum overall systems solution. Since it will be used during early stages of the project, it is natural and acceptable that comensurate with the initial uncertainties about system structure and environment. For sensivity analysis and recursive optimization methods many model runs may be required. To conveniently handle these runs short model execution times are mandatory. Such a model will be based on existing system structures. Additional functions of the new system will be added as needed. Analytic modelling techniques seem to be ideally suited for such a first pass high level model. An example of such a model will be described in this paper.

2. System Validation Model
The scope of this model is identical to the system design model. It covers the total data processing system being developed. Its function is to track the design process and to assure that implemented system characteristics match the objectives. The model will be continuously updated and refined as the development cycle proceeds. By nature this model has to be more detailed and accurate than the system design model. To capture the necessary level of detail these models are usually implemented by using simulation languages, e. g. GPSS, CSS or SIMPL1. Care should be exercised to avoid the pitfalls of directly mapping too many design details having no or low impact on overall system performance. Otherwise too much manpower will be needed to update the model and model run time will become exessive. A successful example of such a model will be described in this paper.

3. Component System Design Models
The main function of these models is to support the component design process. They are usually of limited scope, adapted to the particular problem under investigation. Examples of these models are, e. g. a cache simulator, a memory hierarchy optimization procedure, a disk subsystem model, a model to evaluate paging algorithms or scheduling strategies etc.. Their structures may be as different as there are different subsections in complex data processing systems. But, all have the requirement in common to provide answers within a sufficiently short period of time to influence and guide the design process. At this stage it is usually more important to give fast answers rather than to obtain the ultimate in accuracy. In this context ease of model implementation is more important than model run time. Once the model has provided its answers it may never be used again. Both, analytic modelling and the use of interactive, limited scope simulation models may be suitable. Two examples of analytic component support models will be described in this paper.

3. Component Design Models

Model of Memory Contention in Multiprocessing

USAGE: Optimization of Multiprocessing System Structure. Question: given n processors, how many random access main memory modules m are needed to maximize the ratio of system performance to cost.

Major Components:
- n processors
- m memory modules
- m x n switching structure to

connect processors and memory modules (see fig. 2)

Main Inputs:
- storage access timings
- bus transfer time
- processor cycle time
- cache referencing behaviour of application
- DASD storage traffic
- source/sink storage traffic
- cost a per processor
- cost b per memory module
- cost c per switch crosspoint

Main Output: Thruput of Multiprocessing system configuration, compare fig. 3.

Model Structure:
The queueing structure of the model is shown in fig. 2. The storage access to the memory modules are assumed to occur with equal probability. The processor service time represents the average uninterrupted processing time between main memory access requests. For ready analytical solution the service times are assumed to be exponentially distributed. Main emphasis was on obtaining fast answers.

The model was implemented using APL. The main queueing structure was analyzed using Q-NET 4 (Ref. 2,3). A preprocessor was used to generate service times and branching probabilities from input parameters. Model run time for 8 pu´s was typically between 3 and 4 minutes.

Application of Model:
Fig. 3 shows as model output system performance as a function of the number of memory modules m = 1,2,4,8 the number of processors being a parameter. For cost/performance optimization a cost function of cost = 5 n + b m + .08 mn was assumed, where b = 2.5, 5, 7. The ratio of performance to cost was shown in fig. 4 for n = 8 pu`s. For b = 2.5 the optimum 8 processor system will require 5 storage modules.

MEMORY CONTENTION IN MULTIPROCESSING MODEL

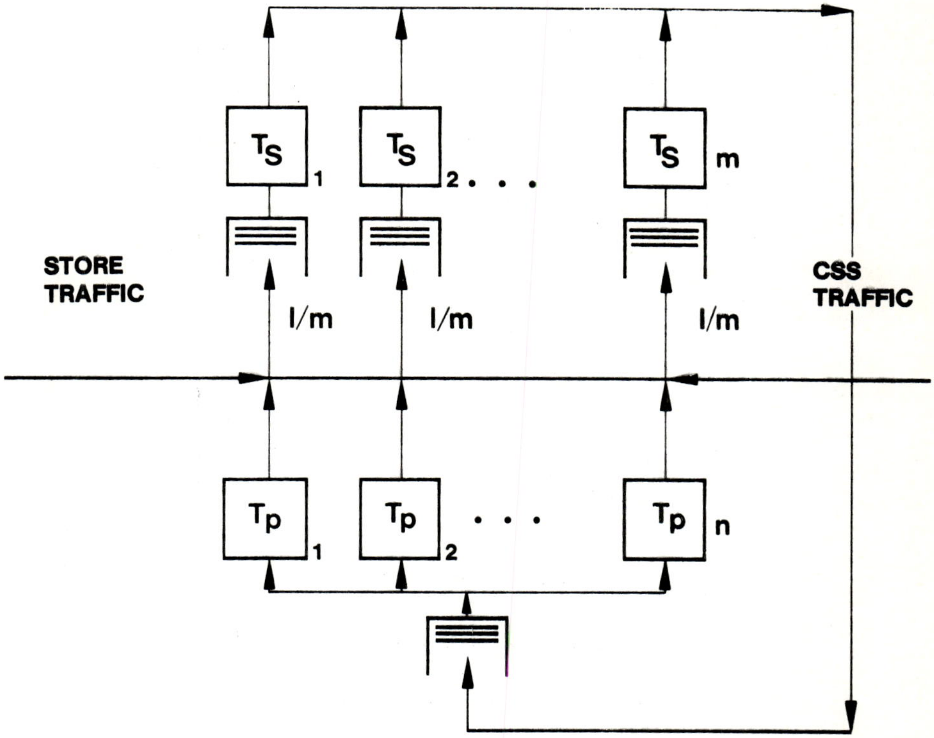

TS = L 3 RD./WR. TIME + ADR./DATA TRANSF. TIME
TP = AV. UNINTERRUPTED PROC. TIME

FIG. 2

PERFORMANCE OF n PROCESSORS AS A FUNCTION OF THE NUMBER OF STORAGE MODULES m

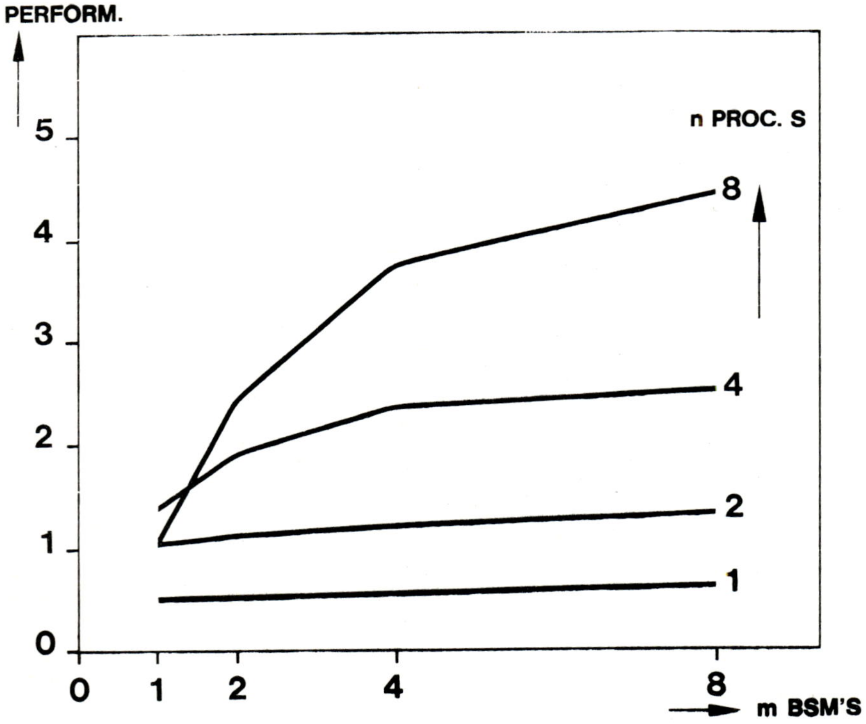

FIG. 3

PERFORMANCE/COST FOR n = 8 PROCESSORS AS A FUNCTION OF THE NUMBER OF STORAGE MODULES m.

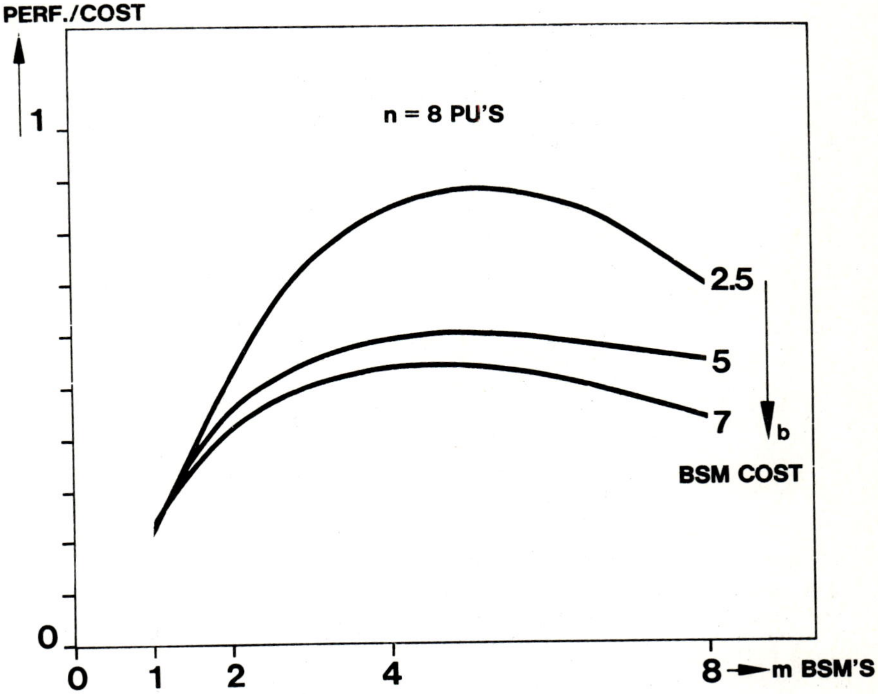

FIG. 4

Model of Operating System

USAGE: Evaluation of design alternatives for operating system, e. g. interruptable versus uninterruptable supervisor code or reentrant versus serially reusable supervisor code.

Major Components:
- I/O interrupt handler
- page manager
- supervisor
- transient areas
- user task phase
- channel device subsystem
- terminal system

Main Inputs:
- supervisor instruction execution rate
- supervisor pathlengths (12)
- page manager gated/reentrant
- supervisor task gated/reentrant
- fraction of pagefaults causing pageout
- fraction of terminals running in single transient area
- number of active partitions with different priorities
- user task times per partition
- time in terminal subsystem
- normal-, fetch-, and page I/O activity per partition
- DASD timings (seek, rotation, sector lead transfer)
- distribution of disk accesses for normal-, fetch-, and page I/O.

Main Outputs:
- CPU utilization total, problem state, supervisor state
- CPU utilization }
- average queue length } per sw and hw component
- average waiting times }
- arrival rates
- occupation time } per DASD
- rotational position sensing probability } device
- I/O response time for normal, fetch and page I/O
- page fault rate
- time in system per job
- number of iterations

Model Structure:
The overall structure of the model is given in fig. 5. The CPU has 4 queues for supervisor services and one queue for service to user programs. This user queue may consist of m subqueues when m partitions are active. The queues are arranged according to priority. I/O interrupts at the left side of fig. 4 have highest priority and the queue for processing transient phases have lowest priority of all supervisor services. If no supervisor work has to be done, dispatchable user tasks are serviced in order of priority.

The model is implemented using queueing analysis methods based on effective decomposition of queueing networks into quasi independent subsystems (compare ref. 4). The main task is the calculation of waiting times of different supervisor services, given priority, interruption and gating structure. This is solved by subdivision of the waiting times into their components like initial waits and subsequent waits.

A detailed description of the model and its implementation can be found in ref. 5. The model has a self-prompting input facility and prints out summaries of inputs and outputs. Typical APL run times are below 1 minute.

Validation of Model:
The model was validated by using special cases leading to known exact analytical solutions, by using the SIMPL-1 simulation language, and by comparison with previous measurement results. The errors introduced by using analytical approximation were found to be below 2 % for the total CPU utilization and around 15 % for total system response time. The total errors including the errors due to the abstraction process were found by comparison with measurements, to be below 5 % for utilizations and up to 20 % for response times. These errors do critically depend on the exact calibration of internal service times, which was not fully possible from the available data.

STRUCTURE OF OPERATING SYSTEM MODEL

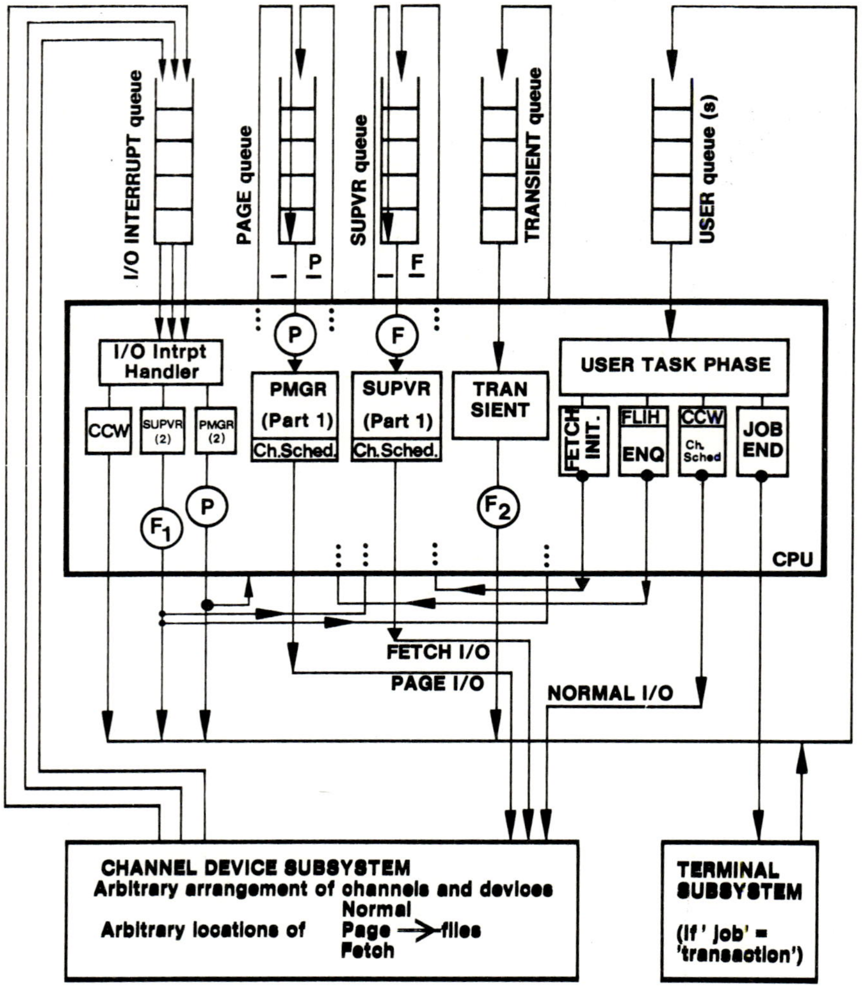

FIG. 5

Application of model:
Fig. 6 shows the results of different design alternatives on system thruput in a TP environment. The cases shown are:

- no paging
- paging and gated page manager
- paging and reentrant page manager
- paging and gated page manager but no headqueue priority for page I/O

The main model parameters were:

- instruction execution rate 100000 instr./sec
- one user partition with up to 30 subtasks
- user task time. 7 sec. per transaction
- time in terminal subsystem 15 sec.
- 6 normal I/O accesses to disk per transaction
- no transient fetch I/O's
- the number of pagefaults per transaction Np is assumed to depend on the number of terminals Nt as

Nt	5	10	15	20	25	30
Np	5	1	2	4	8	16

The system thruput in fig. 6 is shown to grow in the beginning linearly for all cases. In case of no paging it reaches asymptotically an upper limit of about 1.3 runs/sec. In all other cases transaction rates decrease for more than 20 to 25 terminals because of thrashing.

INFLUENCE OF OPERATING SYSTEM DESIGN ALTERNATIVES ON SYSTEM THRUPUT

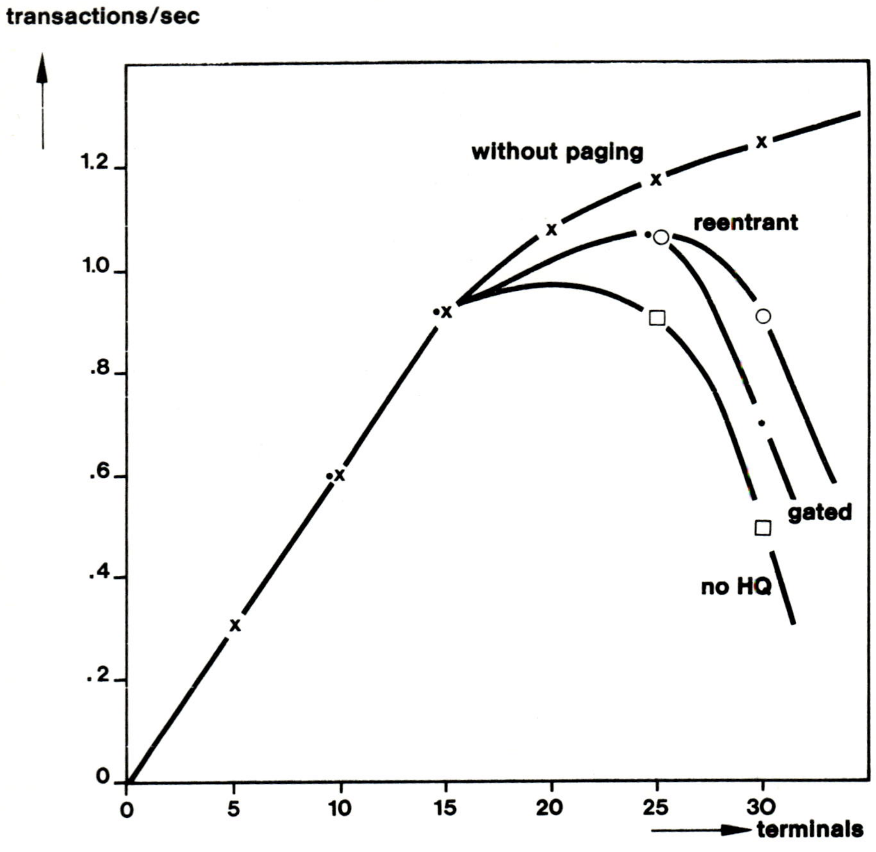

FIG. 6

4. System Design Model

USAGE:
- optimization of total system configurations
- predict input of several component design alternatives on total system performance (sensitivity analysis)
- Find optimum system operating point, e. g. trade-offs between thruput, response time and utilizations.

Major components:
- Control System to handle data base and data communication applications
- operating system
- data base access methods
- teleprocessing access methods
- System 370 processors
- direct access storage devices
- communication controllers
- modems
- lines (1200.. 9600 BD, FDX, HDX, BSC, SDLC)
- terminals

Main Inputs:
- selection of processor model or instruction processing rate
- selection of operating system or specification of 55 different pathlengths
- selection of teleprocessing access method
- definition of disks and allocation of channels
- definition of data files (access method, no. of records, record length...)
- allocation of files to disks
- definition of transactions as a sequence of macros accessing certain files, doing terminal input or problem program processing
- definition of teleprocessing network: number of lines per group, line speed, communication discipline (Start/ Stop, BSC, SDLC), line length, no. of disk controllers, no. of terminals per controller, type of modems, network control parameters
- transaction rates

Main Outputs:
- CPU utilization total and per major software component transaction response times for disks, CPU, host, line and terminal.
- line queueing times and utilizations
- channel rates and utilizations
- disk space usage in cylinders, access rates, utilizations
- file space usage in cylinders, access rates, and access times

Model Structure:
A simplified diagram of the model structure is given in fig. 7. The main queues exist in front of the lines, the CPU and the disk I/O system. The problem of channel queueing and simultaneous usage of disks and channels during data transfer was handled as outlined in ref. 6. The model is implemented by use of analytic queueing techniques. It is

coded in APL, has a selfprompting input facility and typical run times below 1 minute.

The model is primarily intended for handling teleprocessing applications with terminal input/output. The model can also compute system performance for mixed batch/tp environments if the CPU and DASD utilization of the batch workload by itself is known beforehand. The algorithm by which the actual batch CPU utilization UB is found for any required tp CPU utilization UTP is

$$UB = UBO \times \frac{1 - UTP}{UBO + (1-UBO)\ (1-UTP)}$$

Where UBO is the standalone batch CPU utilization for UTP = 0. A number of curves of UB = f (UTP) with UBO as parameter is given in fig. 8.

The problem of finding realistic seek times in a multiprocessing environment, where the disk arm may have been pulled away by another application, is presently handled by using the formula

$$TS = TSR \times (1-p) + TSO \times p$$

where TSR = Random seek time of total active cylinders
TSO = Seek time with zero arm motion
P = probably that arm was not moved between two accesses to the same disk location
and P = $E^{-\lambda t}$
λ being the average disk access rate, and t being the time from previous seek in same transaction.

Validation of Model:
Extensive validation of this model for these different teleprocessing methods show CPU utilizations generally to be within 5 % in absolute value and response time estimates with .5 sec, as long as CPU utilizations stay below 70 %.

STRUCTURE OF SYSTEM MODEL

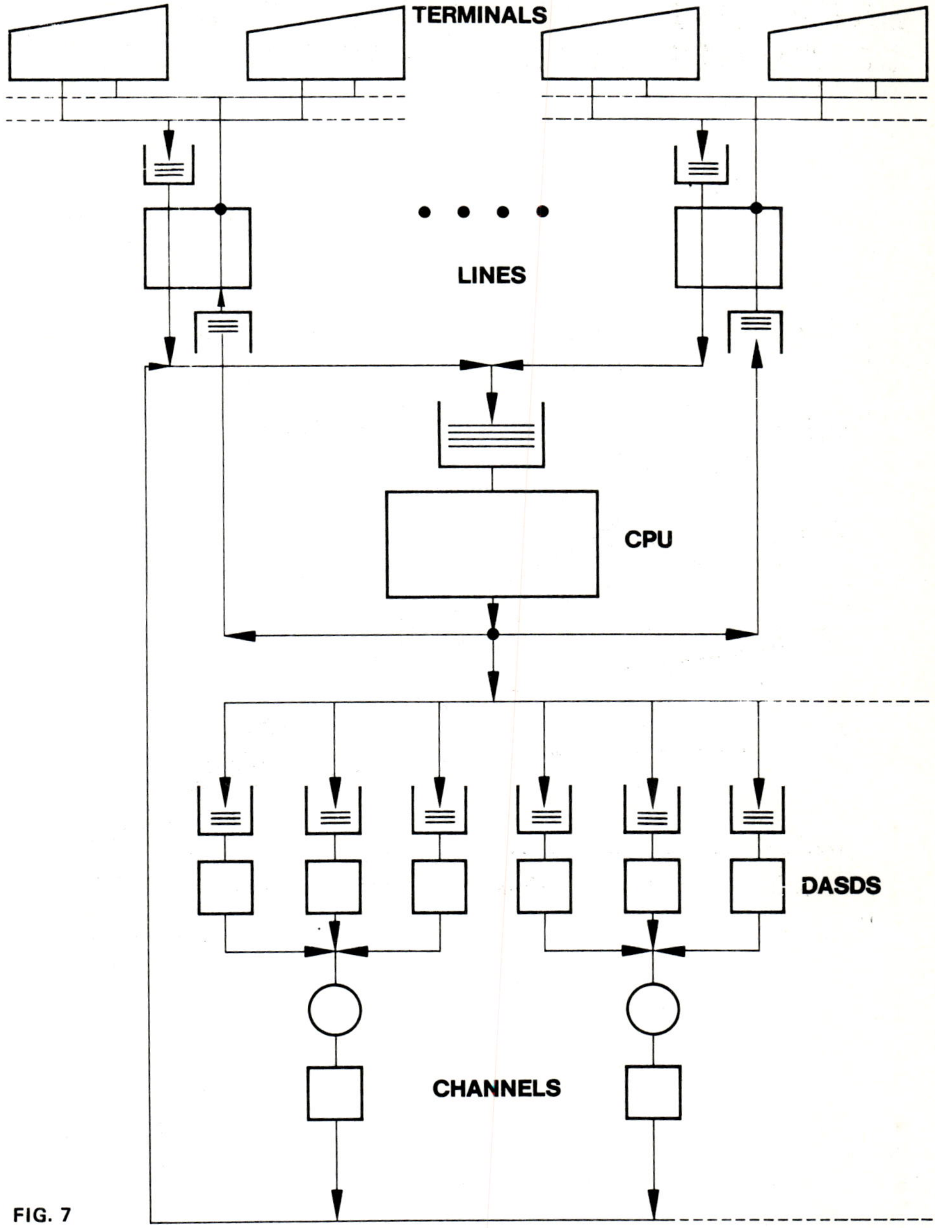

FIG. 7

BATCH CPU UTILIZATION AS A FUNCTION OF CPU UTILIZATION DUE TO TP.

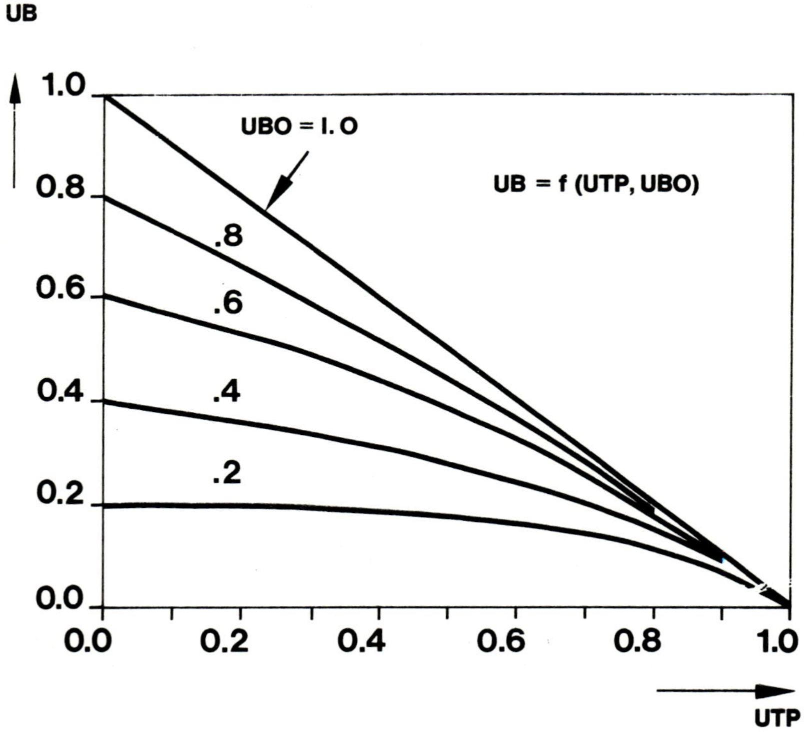

FIG. 8

Application of model:
In fig. 9 the result of a preleminary system evaluation is given in graphical form. The upper part of the figure shows average response time contribution due to DASD accesses, line delay, and CPU processing delay. In the lower part of the figure it is shown how the CPU is utilized by the various software services. The CPU utilization due to batch starts with 20 % for low message rates and approaches zero for high message rates.

If the desired system response time should stay below 3 seconds the analysis shows that message rates up to 1700 transactions per hour can be accomodated. However, the analysis shows also that communication lines and DASD devices are operated well below their rate capacity. Their contribution to total system response time is relatively small and does not grow significantly when message rates increase. For better system price/performance probably a lower speed line should be used and possibly one disk device should be eliminated, if not required by size of data files.

With additional runs on the system design model further optimization of the configuration can be achieved.

PRELIMINARY ANALYSIS OF SYSTEM

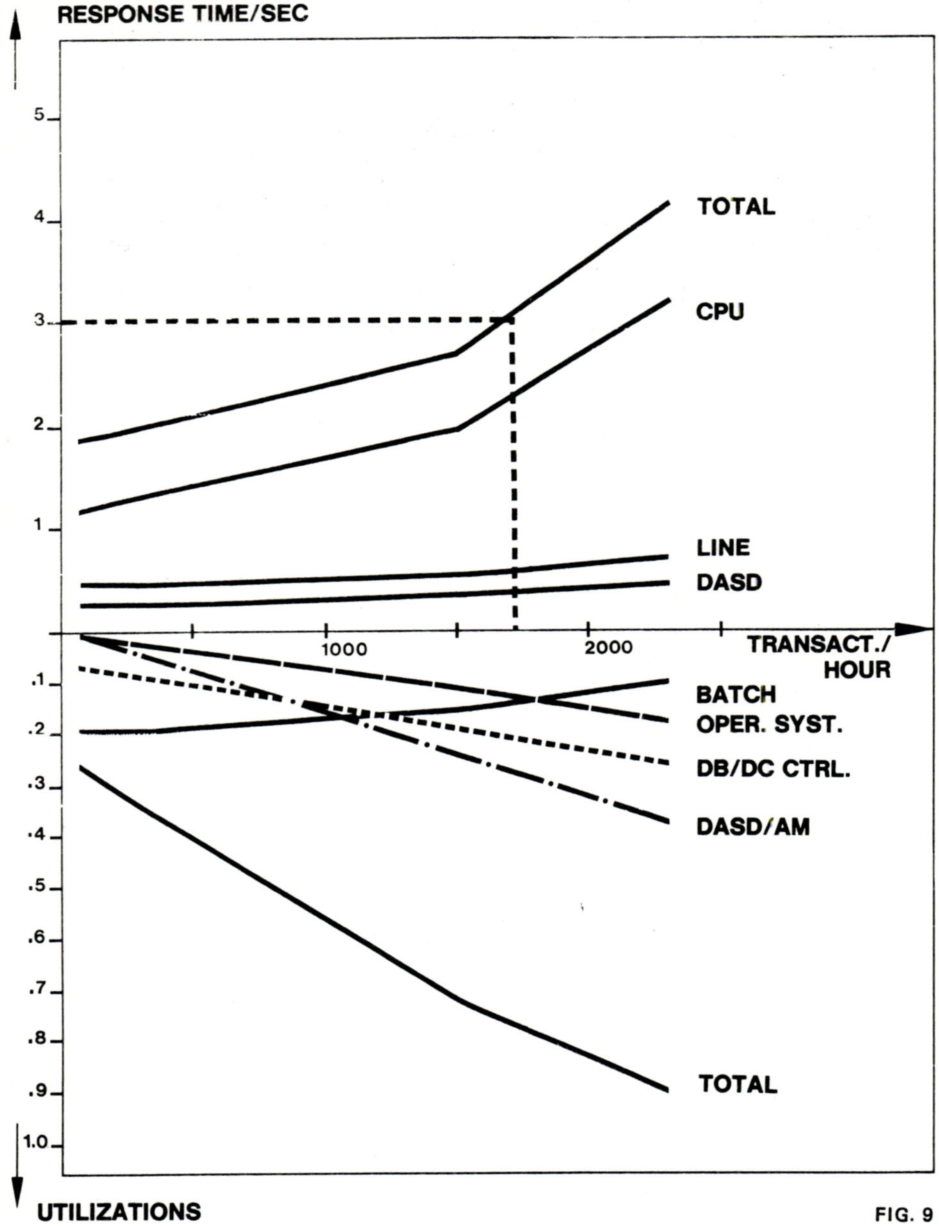

FIG. 9

EXAMPLE OF A DISK AND TERMINAL ACCESS THROUGH SYSTEM VALIDATION MODEL

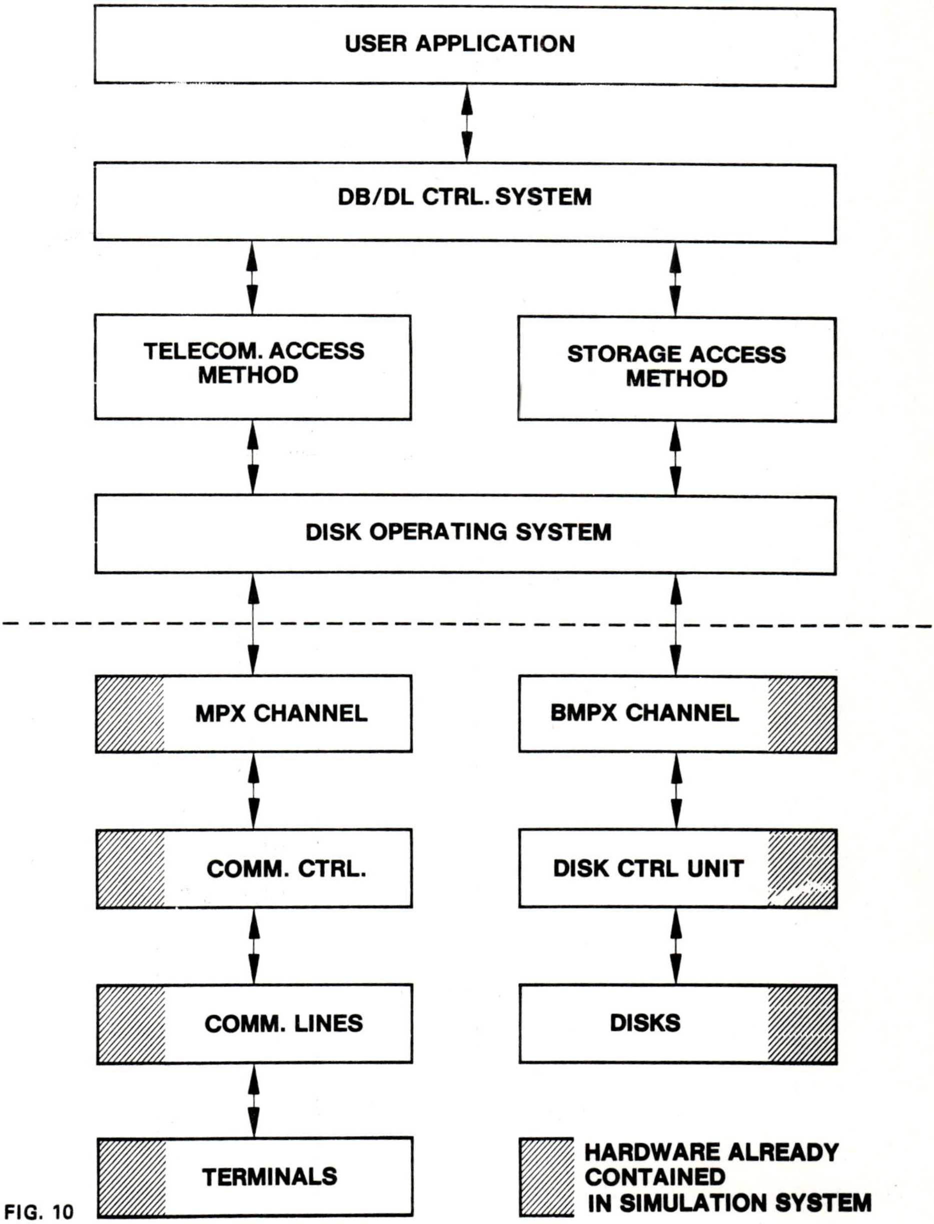

FIG. 10

VSAM DATA BASE ACCESS TIMINGS

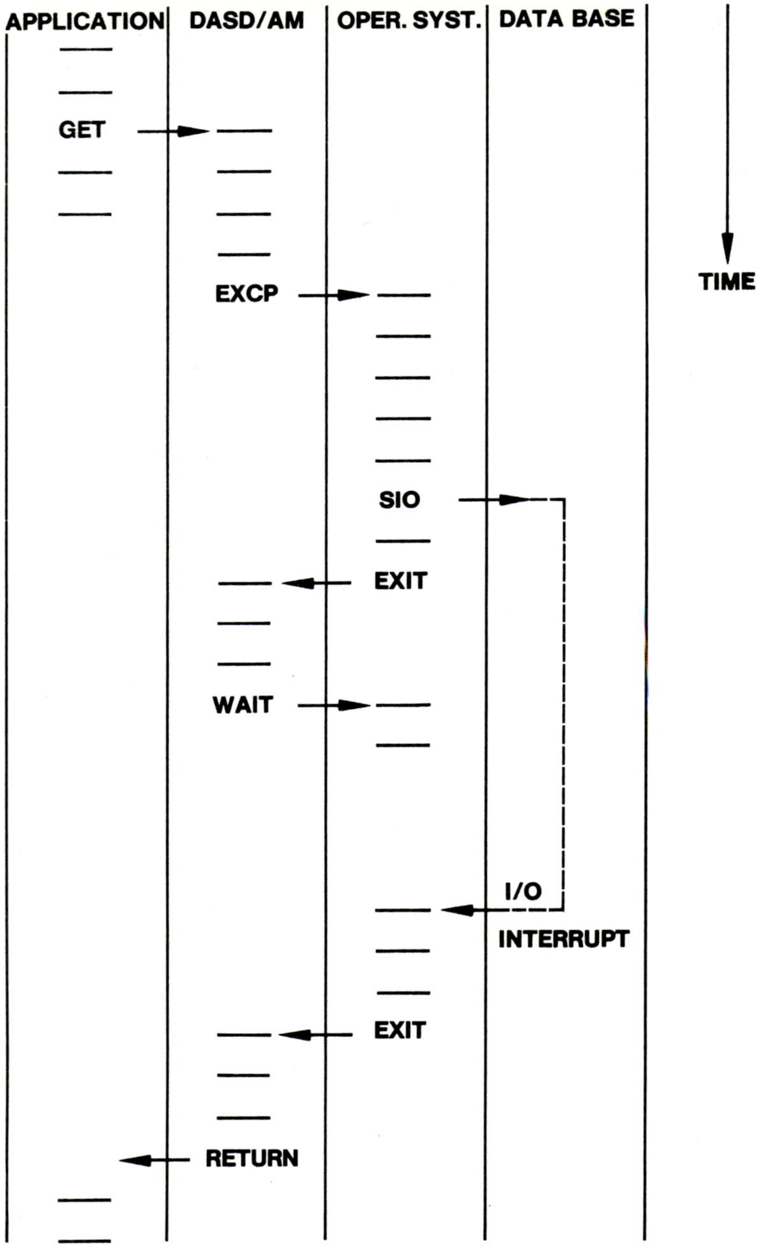

FIG. 11

5. System Validation Model

USAGE:
- system validation for a limited number of well defined environments to assure that objectives are met.
- representation of latest system design status with respect to performance
- calibration of system design model.

Major Components:
- similar to system design model

Main Inputs:
- similar to system design model but in addition
- assignment of batch workload to partitions
- more pathlength information comensurate with the more detailed structure of the model
- exact extends of files
- definition of terminal traffic statistics

Main Outputs:
- similar to system design model but in addition
- queue statistics (maximum, average, standard deviation)
- distribution of system and component response times
- transient behaviour of major system parameters, needed to determine when steady state is reached.

Model Structure:
In contrast to the system design model the system validation model contains more details. The transfer of control from one software or hardware component to the other is modelled for each resource request rather exactly. In fig. 10 the major components and the resource request flow through these components has been shown for a terminal access and a disk access.

Each of these layers, or components, is characterized by a number of timings depending on the type of request. These timings have been obtained from previous measurements or are based as projection for new products. Many of the present day hardware characteristics e. g. for lines, disks, and tapes are already an integral part of the simulation language. As a simple example of the structure of the model a detailed timing diagram for the software portion of a data base access was shown in fig. 11.

EXAMPLE OF A DATA ACCESS RESPONSE TIME DISTRIBUTION

```
5  V S A M -  GET  KSDS,DIR,KEY -  DISK FILE  3

  RANGE     0--------10--------20--------30--------40--------50----- PERCENT
      0     |
   8000     |
  16000     |
  24000     |
  32000     |
  40000     |
  48000     |******
  56000     |**
  64000     |*
  72000     |***************
  80000     |***
  88000     |*************
  96000     |****
 104000     |****
 112000     |**********
 120000     |****
 128000     |*******
 136000     |*****
 144000     |***
 152000     |*****
 160000     |***
 168000     |***
 176000     |**
 184000     |**
 192000     |**
 200000     |*
 208000     |*
 216000     |*
 224000     |*
 232000     |*
 240000     |*
 248000     |*
 256000     |*
 264000     |*
 272000     |*
 280000     |
 288000     |*
 296000     |*
 304000     |*
 312000     |*
 320000     |*
 328000     |
 336000     |
 344000     |
 352000     |
 360000     |
 368000     |
 376000     |
 384000     |
 392000     |
 400000     |
μSEC
```

MEAN ARGUMENT

112375.091

STANDARD DEVIATION

53328.002

FIG. 12

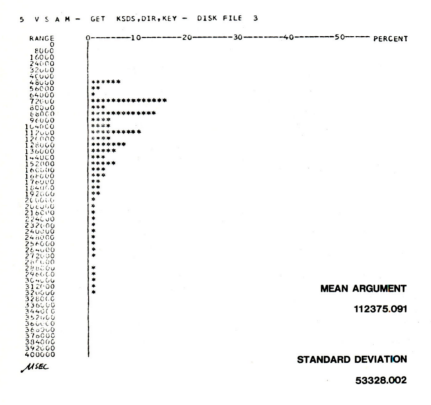

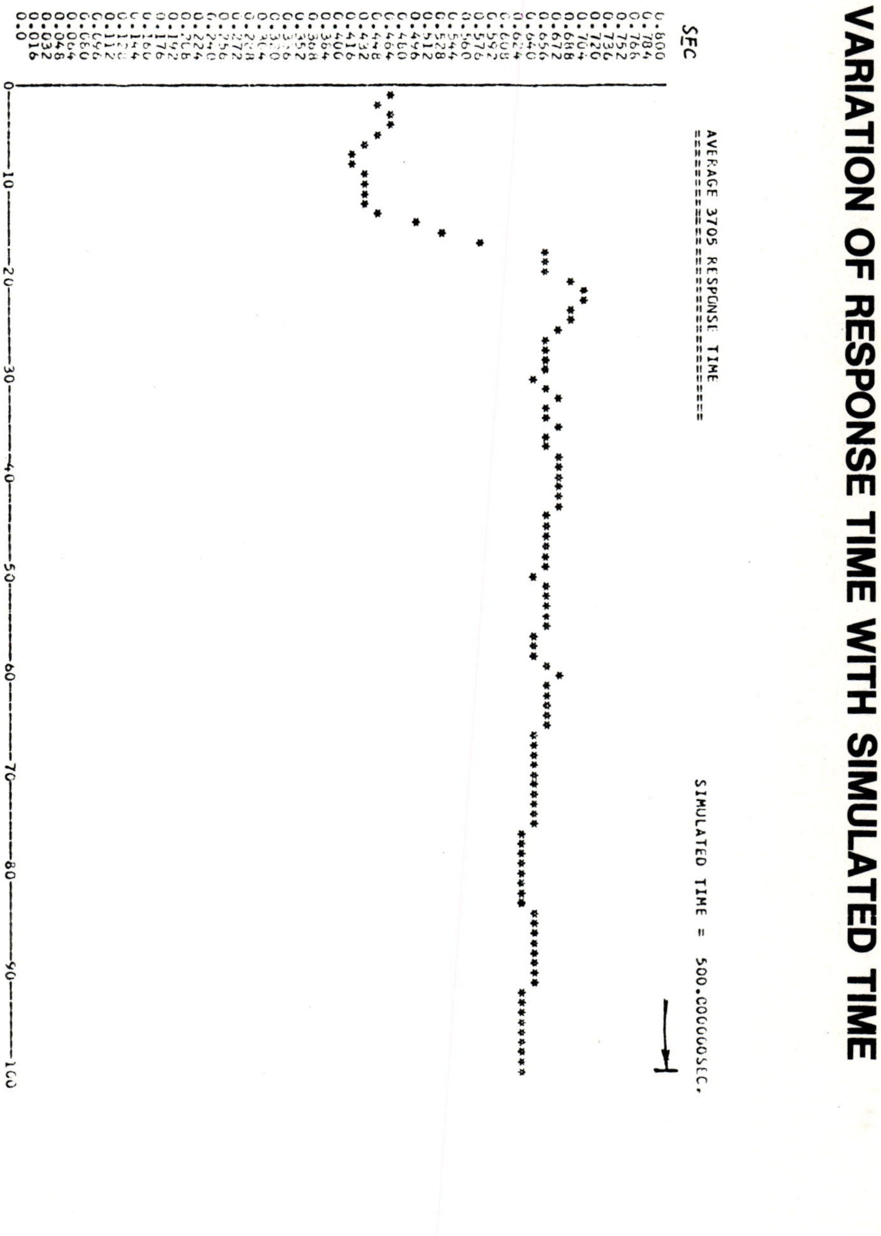
VARIATION OF RESPONSE TIME WITH SIMULATED TIME
SEC
AVERAGE 3705 RESPONSE TIME
SIMULATED TIME = 500.000000SEC.
0.800
0.784
0.768
0.752
0.736
0.720
0.704
0.688
0.672
0.656
0.640
0.624
0.608
0.592
0.576
0.560
0.544
0.528
0.512
0.496
0.480
0.464
0.448
0.432
0.416
0.400
0.384
0.368
0.352
0.336
0.320
0.304
0.288
0.272
0.256
0.240
0.224
0.208
0.192
0.176
0.160
0.144
0.128
0.112
0.096
0.080
0.064
0.048
0.032
0.016
0.0
0
10
20
30
40
50
60
70
80
90
100

FIG. 13

Since the model can handle priorities, it is able to simulate multipartion workloads consisting of batch and teleprocessing applications. In contrast to the analytic system design model it can also handle non-exponential terminal statistics, constant service time, dispatching priorities and actual disk contention between various application programs. However, runtime requirements are at least an order of magnitude higher, which does disqualify it for on-line terminal application in a shared user environment. Simulation of medium size TP systems operating below saturation require typically 10 to 30 min 370/158 CPU time until steady state conditions are reached.

Validation of Model:
A number of measurements were performed to test the validity of the model for data base access methods and teleprocessing access methods. After the specified 3330 disk seek function was replaced by better, actual seek time values, the CPU utilization values were found to be within 2 %, and host system response time values within 5 %. Accuracies in this range can only be obtained with detailed simulation models, with tightly controlled input variables.

Application of Model:
Once an optimum, or nearly optimum system configuration was found by several iterations on the systems design model, the system validation model can be used to obtain a more accurate analysis considering additional detailed information on workload and system.

As an example of the extended output capabilities of the model a copy of a response time distribution output for a VSAM file access was given in fig. 12.

In fig. 13 the variations of average system response time at the 3705 communication controller network output was plotted versus simulated time. At the beginning, before the system is fully loaded, system response times are around .44 seconds until after 500 seconds simulated time the average system response time has stabilized at .624 seconds.

6. Summary

The different phases during the development of a data processing system have been characterized to identify the specific need for distinct type of models during this process. During the early systems planning and initial definition phase a first pass analytic model, here named system design model, was found to be the best answer.

Later, during development and design of individual system components, are intended to answer well defined questions about optimum system structure. As examples for these models a CPU-memory model for multiprocessing and an operating system model were described together with typical applications. Some performance output of these models will provide valuable input to the overall system validation model. The system validation model should be continuously updated to reflect all major performance critical parts of the system as they mature towards finalization. This way it will represent the latest system design status and can be used for calibration of simpler, field usable models having faster turnaround time.

The main message, this paper intends to convey, is that models can be immensely useful during the system development process. Their use can be of invaluable help to understand complex system behaviour, to try out new ideas for alterate system implementations and thus to pave the way for improving the cost effectiveness of future systems to come.

Acknowledgements

All the models mentioned above have been implemented by many persons at various locations of the IBM Corporation. In particular I have to mention K. F. Finkemeyer, as the author of the memory contention model; W. Krämer, who developed the operating system model during a post doctoral followship program; J. van Galen, as the first designer of the CSS system validation model; B. Covert, who developed the initial analytic counter part to this model; P. Seaman, who further developed this initial version into a model that can be conviently used in the field.

References:

(1) L. Hellerman, "A Measure of Computational Work", IEEE Transactions on Computers, C 21,439-446, 1972.

(2) M. Reiser, "QNET 4 User´s Guide", June 24, 1975 IBM Rep. RA 71, No. 23879

(3) M. Reiser, "Interactive Modelling of Computer Systems", "IBM Systems Journal, Vol. 15", Mo. 4, 1976, pp 309-328

(4) J. H. Florkowski, "Extended Analytic Models for Systems Evaluation", August 5, 1974, IBM Report TR 00.2549

(5) W. Krämer, "Modelling and Queueing Analysis of DOS/VS Based Operating Systems", submitted to IBM Systems Journal

(6) P. Seaman, R. A. Lind and T. L. Wilson, "On Teleprocessing System Design, Part IV, An Analysis of Auxiliary-Storage Activity", IBM System Journal, Vol. 5, No. 3, 1966, pp 158-170

Measuring, Modelling and Evaluating Computer Systems,
H. Beilner and E. Gelenbe, (eds.)
© North-Holland Publishing Company (1977)

MODELLING AS A COMMUNICATION DISCIPLINE

C.A. Petri
Gesellschaft für Mathematik und
Datenverarbeitung mbH Bonn
Schloss Birlinghoven
D-5205 St.Augustin 1

The impact of computer technology on society should be seen in the incisive change it effects on the historically grown means and limits of human communication and organization. Hence, it seems necessary to analyse computer activities in terms of communication and organization, rather than in terms of computing, computability, and computing power. In order to do so with formal rigour, but without adulteration of the pragmatic context of practical communication situations, a list of twelve communication disciplines has been proposed. It can be viewed as a list of those functions of a medium for strictly organizable information flow which are amenable to formal treatment.

Synchronization, modelling and valuation are among these disciplines; typical results of the inquiry into these three are exposed by way of examples: the specification of systems by their synchronic structure; the construction of measurement scales; the expression of fairness of resource allotment in terms of synchronic distance.

Modelling as a (communication) discipline is compared with conventional mathematical modelling; it is argued that the existence of computer technology makes a new approach to modelling necessary and, at the same time, feasible. It is further argued that performance evaluation results are meaningful only relative to a given background of valuation, and that a strict discipline of valuation is still lacking or not being observed, while the methods for measurement of isolated features of performance are making good progress.

MODELLING, COMPUTERS AND SOCIETY

Before we start off into three days of highly technical work in a highly specialized area of human effort, it seems appropriate that we first step back a little from our proper objective so that we can view it in perspective.

Even in terms of our own profession, the topic of this symposium is highly specialized; witness the small number of sessions devoted to it at the IFIP 1977 Congress. In my view, this does not necessarily indicate a decreasing importance but rather a growing awareness, among computer professionals, for other urgent concerns touching upon the user, the organization, and society.

My aim here is to point out how these broader concerns might influence the special topic of this symposium; it is certainly not my intention to channel your attention away to other topics. My task is difficult because those broader concerns are not readily expressed in the precise and consistent language of mathematics which is supposedly so well suited to our more technical concerns.

In order to set up a context broad enough to be useful for my purpose, I shall therefore have to touch upon some controversial matters; and I shall have to raise criticism, doubts and questions to which I am not able to give you a convincing answer here and now; partly because time is short, partly because I am not a specialist in the field treated at this symposium. -

Permit me to take a look at the motivations and justifications of your efforts "to make mathematical models of computer systems and to evaluate their performance quantitatively".
In my strictly personal view, there is no doubt that the ultimate driving force behind that effort as a whole is not the intent to make the best possible use of a scarce resource named "computing power", whatever that may be, but rather the competition of manufacturers.

Now this is a perfectly sound and legitimate reason to do such work, and of course it also seems to be profitable to the customer. Would "optimization" (of resource usage) be a better reason? I doubt it. Despite its widespread use, the word seems to be devoid of meaning, since everybody can claim to be optimizing all the time.

The shortest possible form of a meaningful statement in this area is "I decide to give preference to X over Y and act accordingly". A recent computer misadventure which had caused great financial losses to many people was officially explained to the public thus: "The computers in question were not optimally interconnected. The source of the trouble has by now been removed."

I am convinced, however, that the true source of the "trouble" is still present in the first part of that explanation, namely in its language and in the diffuse thinking behind it. Let us keep clear of that language, or a better educated public will accuse us of ignorance, irresponsibility, and even dishonesty.

At first sight, it seems that we are safe against such reproach when we are using the language of mathematics. But at a closer look, our present practices of mathematical modelling and evaluation appear to have several critical imperfections and inherent dangers. Therefore I am afraid that our practices will not remain acceptable for very long; and I shall try to point out some of the dangers and suggest a remedy.

Let me also say that I have no special complaint about the procedures which are the topic of this conference; my critique applies equally to many other areas of modelling and evaluation, so I shall state it in the most general terms.

Mathematical modelling and computer usage are just two types of activity out of a large class of activities that go on within society. We shall first ask how mathematical modelling, as the much older of the two activities under consideration, is (or should be) connected to other activities, mainly to the production of tools. Fig. 1 shows the main direct interconnections; an attempt to show all connections would yield a complete graph, that is, a trivial structure.

Mathematical modelling is seen as part of the area of "symbolic production", as opposed to the production of material tools and goods. The methods derived from modelling influence mainly the ways of (originally informal) thinking and increase the power to guide goal-directed experimentation, the success of which is prerequisite for the development of techniques needed for the production of tools or instruments.
In the computer age, symbolic production (e.g. of software) has greatly increased. And the procedural methods generated by it are no longer mainly fed back to the

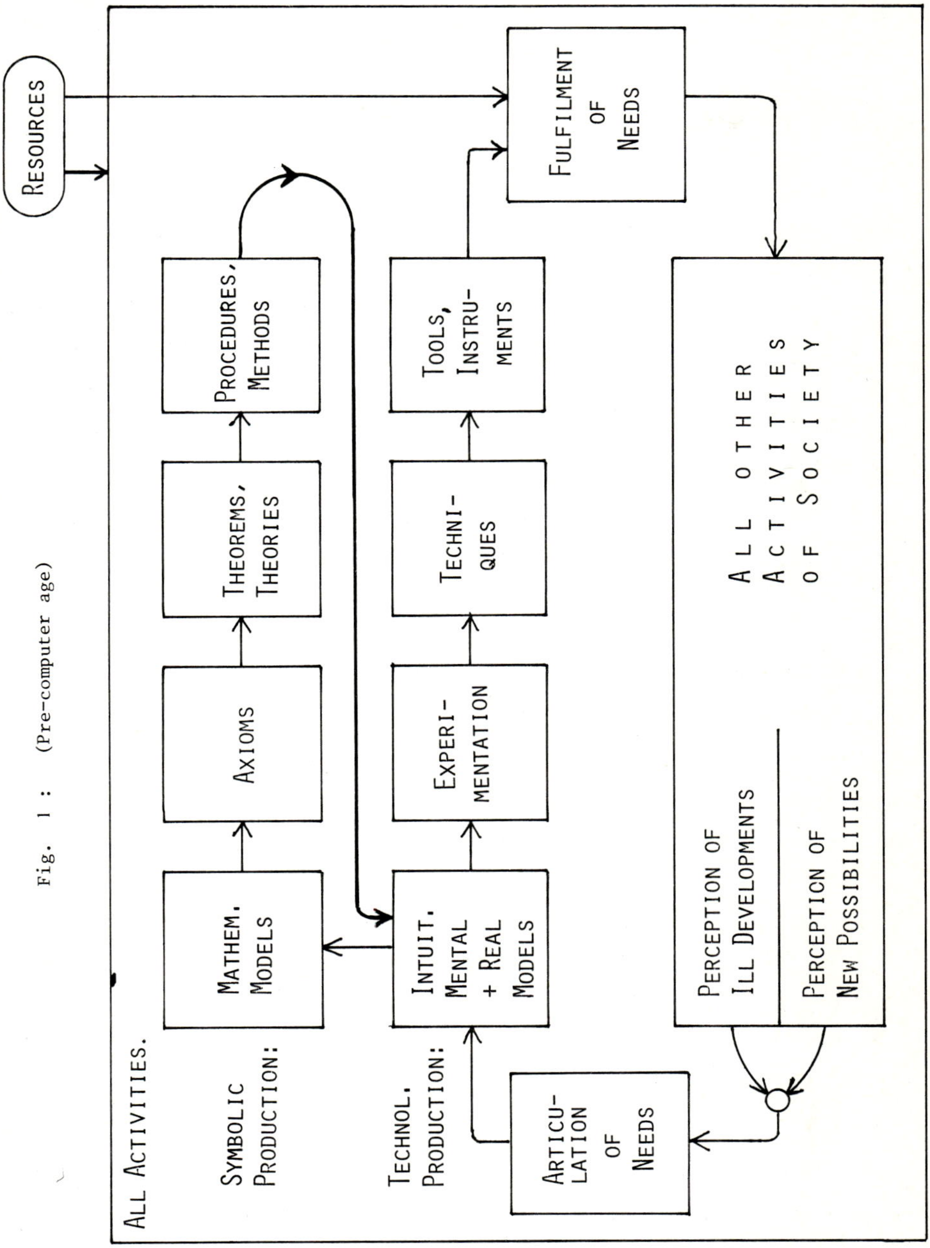

Fig. 1 : (Pre-computer age)

---

human activity of thinking about useful experiments, but are rather fed directly into the activity of using computers (Fig. 2) :

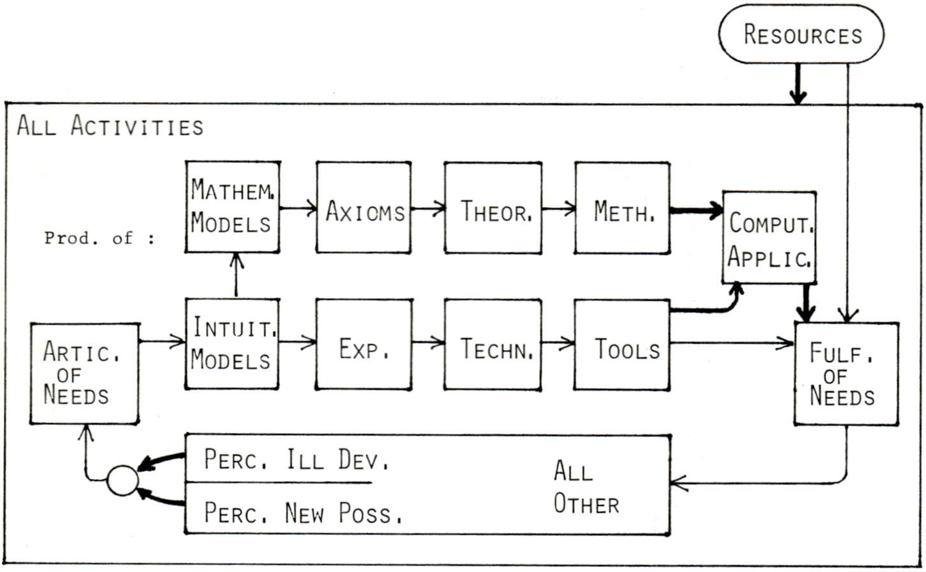

Fig. 2 (Present)

As a consequence, the final products of symbolic activities are allowed to become much more complex and "powerful" than when they had to be used directly by humans only. And as a further consequence, the slightest mistake in the long course of symbolic production may multiply by millionfold repetition through the use of computers before being detected, since it is no longer filtered through control by common sense and experimentation (except through the very coarse filters of program testing and program "correctness proofs" which are themselves subject to possible mistakes and can by their nature detect only certain types of errors). In view of this, we are tempted to characterize the computer as an Error Amplifier.

THE NEED FOR A STRICT DISCIPLINE OF MODELLING

Note that the gravest errors arise at the initial stages of the chain of symbolic production; they have the most serious consequences and cannot be detected, with very few exceptions, within the area of formal symbolic production; that is, not until it is too late.
Something has to be done about this: the connections between symbolic and technological activities must be changed to establish a new control loop.

Since we are neither able nor inclined to change the interconnections between the box labelled "computer application" and the other activities, we may consider the following proposal (Fig. 3) :
The diagram in Fig. 3 re-establishes the connections A and D which were distinctly existent at the historical origin of "symbolic production" in our sense, i.e. 2500 years or more ago. The arrow B is inverted, to show that modelling as an activity of merely abstracting and formalizing the historically grown informal prejudices is to be substituted by an activity which we might call "disciplined modelling" and which draws on quite different sources. The E arrow is doubled to indicate the necessary close interaction between disciplined modelling and the

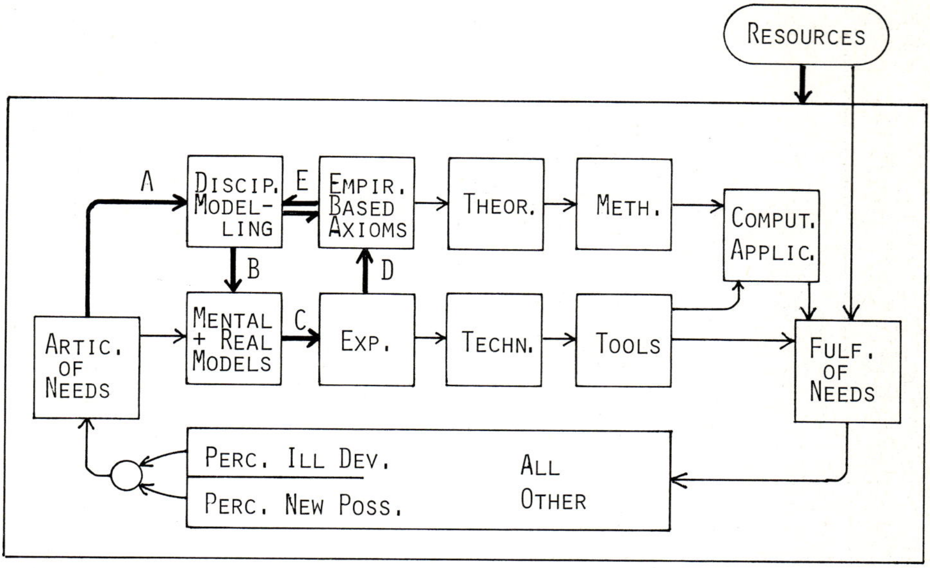

Fig. 3 (Proposed)

responsible production of empiry-based axiom systems: it is required that, ideally, each axiom (-system) is accompanied by a definite justification in the form of an experimental strategy by which its validity in the context of a given application can be tested in the strictest terms.

Also, the double E arrow implies the proposal to bring three very different meanings of the word "model" in science ("model of an airplane"; "model of an axiom system"; "model farm") as close together as possible - after they have drifted so dangerously far apart, through the self-imposed splendid isolation ("autonomy") of symbolic production. -

BCDE is the resulting control cycle, a cycle which is kept alive by A .

Before going on to small examples of the proposed way of axiomatic procedure and disciplined modelling, we shall take a look at the question of how modelling is embedded in other practical concerns of computer applications.

COMMUNICATION DISCIPLINES AND BASIC FUNCTIONS OF COMPUTERIZED MEDIA

In the preceding sections we have spoken of the computer as a physical tool, with the special property that a wide range of symbolic products can be incorporated in it.
But in public opinion as well as in the minds of computer professionals we can discern a number of entirely different roles attributed to the computer concerning its relevance to mankind. As far as I could observe, most people have changed their views several times in succession as their experience grew, and they have certainly begun to reject some gross over- and underestimations of the relevance of having computers.

Since a large amount of effort has been invested in projects based on such judgements which are no longer tenable, I would like to think that the sequence of opinions converges towards a stable and fruitful assessment of the role of computers |1| (Fig. 4) :

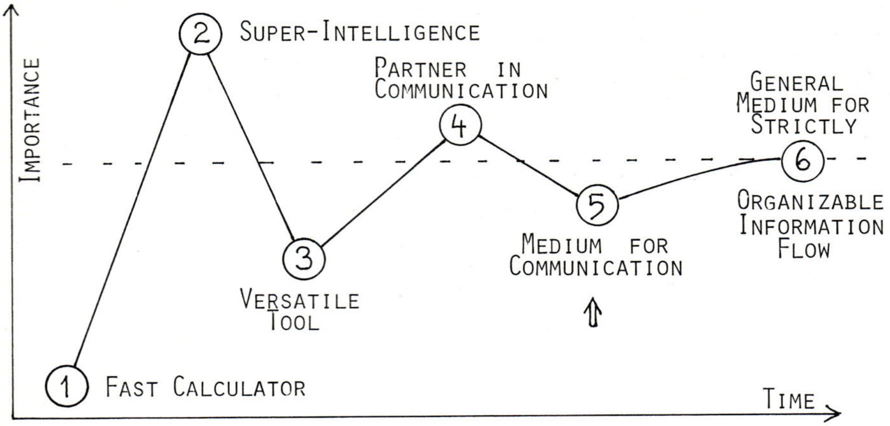

Fig. 4 : The role of the computer

For the following considerations, we shall regard computer systems as a medium for communication, i.e. we shall assume viewpoint (5) . We do so because it is on the safe (lower) side of the supposed level of convergence ("feasibility line"); because the mental obstacles to reach this viewpoint are the highest in the present situation; and because only minor difficulties of merely technical nature have to be overcome to reach stage (6) from there |2| .

When we try to analyse computer activities in terms of communication, we are first led to the naive approach (Fig. 5): to enumerate the functions of classical communication media, to observe that computers can indeed fulfil all of them, and then to ask what computers can do in addition to those classical functions.

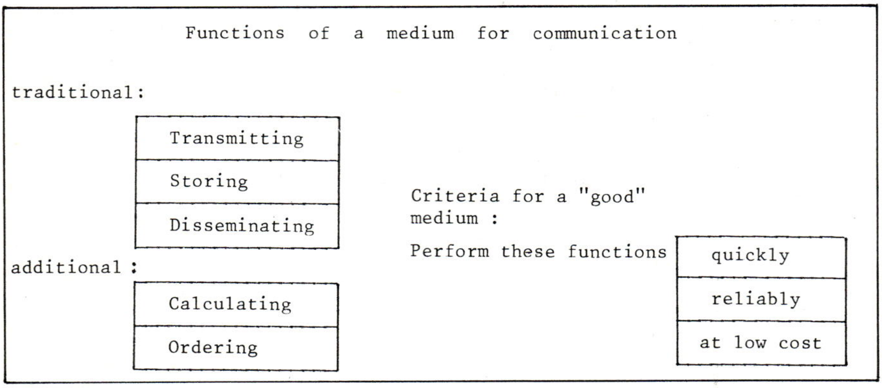

Fig. 5 : First approach

Experience has shown that this analysis, plausible as it seems, does not lead to new constructions, mathematical tools, or deeper insights than those we have already gained long ago.

Therefore, as a second approach a large set of malfunctions on all levels of computer usage was analysed, with the intention to trace each malfunction back to definite violations of a small set of basic principles; a set of rules or conventions to be observed if miscommunication is to be avoided.
The areas in which such principles must exist - implicitly or explicitly - are shown in Fig. 6 (and explained in |2|) :

Functions of a medium for communication
("Communication disciplines")

Synchronization	Identification
Addressing	Naming
Copying	Cancelling
Composition	Modelling
Authorization	Valuation
Delegation	Reorganization

Criterion for a "good" medium :
Perform these functions.

Fig. 6 : Second approach

The list given in Fig. 6 is complete only in the sense that each malfunction which has been analysed so far could be interpreted as non-observance of one or more - as yet incompletely formalized - rules in the areas named. The degree of formalization is indeed very inhomogenous over the twelve areas; while a fairly well-developped and firmly founded axiomatic theory of synchronization exists, nothing remotely comparable is known about the discipline of authorization (the use of passwords scratches only the surface of this discipline).

The theory of synchronization, within which rules for a discipline of synchronization (i.e. co-operation in terms of time) can be formulated, is an outcome of a strict discipline of modelling, as outlined in the preceding sections. Likewise, in order to make progress in the other areas, I plead for a more disciplined modelling based on a broader palette of needs, and for a disciplined and explicit valuation, or exposition of value structures, which must come before any attempt at evaluation.
Let me apply this general idea to the topic of this symposium.

A high overall throughput rate is not the only thing of value in a computer installation. Optimizing throughput may very well be an obstacle to data security, or to error detection. It is most certainly an obstacle to a user who has to meet deadlines. As users come of age, and depend more and more on computers for more and more serious matters, they will need a qualified guarantee of accessibility.

The probabilistic approach prevalent today in performance modelling is absolutely and finally excluding any form of respectable guarantees for meeting deadlines. We are getting close to the point where all deadlines are imposed upon people and no deadlines at all upon machines.

If we reach this point, I should not hesitate to call it an absurd and unacceptable situation. Stronger words would be in order on the consequences of the all-out probabilistic approach in other areas of technology, and in economics. Kolmogoroff cautioned explicitly against rash application of his axiomatic theory of probability, and advocated a combinatorial concept of information (and therefore a combinatorial approach to situations of partial knowledge, i.e. to practically all situations).

Some considerate dentists provide a door in their waiting-room which opens directly into the street, for those patients who want to leave without embarrassment before proper treatment. Mathematics provides probability. -

There are deeper issues than users' deadlines touched by probabilistic modelling, and there are more serious diseases than a toothache. In any case, most patients will return. -

The topic of valuation includes, of course, the subject matter treated by the theories of utility in economics; theories which have concentrated on the attempt to measure utility, rather than on exploring the structure of "value spaces". By the standards of disciplined mathematical modelling, not very much can be regarded as certain in this area, and some widely accepted assumptions are demonstrably unjustified. (An example will be given in the following section.)

To have a "discipline of valuation" does not at all mean that all participants in a communication process do or should have an identical interest profile. On the contrary, it is the difference in interest profiles which keeps communication going and gives substance to it. It may be argued that no two individuals can have the same interest profile. On the other hand, total disjointness of interests makes communication impossible. The subjective valuation of an individual is relative to a set of possibilities structured by assumed mutual exclusion; it is subject to quick changes, not fully communicable and not fully explorable by other individuals, etc.

By collecting a list of similar statements, a conceptual basis for a mathematical theory of valuation might conceivably be found: a first step towards formal pragmatics.

Computer scientists tend to regard such considerations as belonging to the realm of philosophy, and the hope for reliable and useful results in this area as very remote.

I must contradict this view. First, results of such a theory - though admittedly modest - have been successfully applied long ago; further results could be applied right away. Second, because of the increasing awareness and importance to treat computer systems as a communication medium, the activity of programming is to be regarded as an activity of partial delegation of tasks to non-personal agencies. This makes obvious the necessity to take those precautions in programming which are usual in delegation between persons - and some more precautions in addition. Whether or not we are conscious of it, matters of valuation are inevitably involved in acts of delegation, and very tangible dangers arise when this involvement is not made explicit.

One readily understandable conclusion is this: the pride which is usually taken in complete delegation (total automation, algorithmization) is in general quite out of place. If e.g. a programmer (or microprogrammer, or computer architect) thinks he has delegated responsibility along with his algorithm, he is mistaken. And so is his employer.

Instead of making this string of non-technical exhortations any longer, let me return to simple technical examples of mathematical modelling. The first of these is about the construction of scales for measurement in general; it applies as well to the measurement of time and length as to the "more complicated" (less well-defined) measurement of performance or utility.

TWO EXAMPLES OF A STRICT MODELLING DISCIPLINE

"It is a deeply rooted popular idea that mathematics is but another name for measurement", N. Wiener stated in 1919 |3|. In the computer age, that idea appears to be more popular than ever, since the quantity of measurement results ("data") which we handle has increased so enormously.

In spite of Carnap's convincing demonstration that (at least) four stages of structuring our observations and concepts must be gone through before we are able to make measurements in the usual sense, and that in many areas we have to content ourselves with much less than the final (?) stage of a real-valued metric scale, the unrestrained use of such scales is our practice almost without exception.

Remember now that a computer is an error amplifier, an amplifier also of mistakes made before the advent of computers. On the other hand, measurement in terms of real numbers is a most successful basis of all exact sciences, and of some more. It is so firmly established and entrenched that it is hard to believe that, in the very idea of such measurement, several non-trivial neglects of "the discipline of mathematical modelling" should have remained without repair for so long. Yet it is so :

At least three assumptions about measurement have to be refuted by the standards of disciplined modelling : one about the aim of measurement, one about the nature of metrical indifference, and one about the representation of continuity.

If the correction of these mistakes were not of considerable practical consequence for the treatment (and concept!) of measurement data, nobody would have to worry.

It is the merit of Pfanzagl |4| to have made all assumptions about measurement explicit in a concise axiomatic form together with rules for their application; many of the axioms are already contained in Principia Mathematica.

Pfanzagl states: "The general aim of measurement consists in the assignment of real numbers to every element of a given set M in such a way that the strongest possible conclusion can be drawn from the relations between the assigned numbers to corresponding relations between the related elements of the set M ".

Aside from the impossibility to lay on the table the infinite "one out of $\mathbb{R}$ " - amount of information in any case, we also want our conclusions to be not only as strong as possible, but also correct. E.g. if the set M is ordered, our conclusions about remaining disorder must also be correct. It is not certain that this will be possible with real numbers; we shall be more careful and substitute "elements of a suitably chosen structure" for "real numbers" in the above statement.

We speak of one-dimensional scales only. Consider a set M of phenomena (time intervals; utilities; etc) in which a relation $<_M$ of total or partial order is assumed; i.e. $<_M$ is antireflexive and transitive. Let $<$ without index denote the observed order relation. We define the observed disorder thus :

$$(1) \qquad a \sim b \quad :\Longleftrightarrow \quad \neg\, (a < b \;\vee\; b < a)$$

$a \sim b$ obtains when a and b cannot be arranged in an order by single acts of comparison. If such comparisons are to be consistent, $\sim$ clearly has to be reflexive and symmetric :

(2) $a \sim a$ and $a \sim b \rightarrow b \sim a$

The naive and idealistic assumption that the "indifference" relation $\sim$ is <u>transitive</u>, and therefore an equivalence relation, has been repeatedly attacked, especially by Armstrong |8| (1950); and Luce in his fundamental paper |5| invokes even "a basic philosophical objection to the assumption that $\sim$ is transitive".

Since everybody who has carried out comparisons can reject this assumption anyway on personal experience, it seems strange that the matter has not been settled; as early as 1919, N. Wiener in |3| p.184 has proposed a way out by defining what he calls "genuine equality" $\approx$:

(3) $a \approx b \;:\Longleftrightarrow\; \bigwedge c : a \sim c \leftrightarrow b \sim c$

It is easily proved that $\approx$ is an equivalence relation; note, however, that it can be established only by comparing a and b with <u>all</u> elements c of M . We have

(4) $a = b \rightarrow a \approx b$ and $a \approx b \rightarrow a \sim b$

(If $<$ were a <u>total</u> order, it would be characterized by $a = b \Leftrightarrow a \sim b$).

Wiener used this to construct an "inferred order" relation $<_w$ stronger than $<$ by defining

(5) $a <_w b \; : \; a < b \vee \bigvee c : (a \sim c \wedge c < b) \vee (a < c \wedge c \sim b)$

so that for all $a, b \in M$:

(6) $a \approx b \Longleftrightarrow \neg (a <_w b \vee b <_w a)$ in analogy to (1)

In naming $\approx$ "genuine equality", Wiener seemed to hope that his $<_w$ is isomorphic to $<_M$, or that a distinction between them is not overly genuine (we cannot know this for certain; Wiener's own standard comment on expressions like "genuine equality" was "That is not mathematics").
The property (6) alone does not guarantee that $<_w$ defined by (5) is an order relation at all; if we want to establish the necessary property for all observations of a, b, ... that

(7) Exactly one of $a \approx b$, $a <_w b$, $b <_w a$ holds

we have to assume that, in addition to (6) :

(8) $\neg (a <_w b \wedge b <_w a)$ holds for all $a, b \in M$.

The example 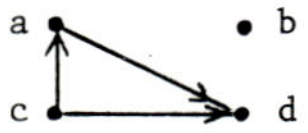

(where arrows denote $<$) proves that

assumption (8) is not a theorem. To justify (8), a very plausible sounding axiom is introduced :

(9) "... an unnoticable difference is always <u>to be treated</u> as less than a noticable one" (Wiener |3| p.185)

(9)' "... an indifference interval never spans a preference interval" (Luce |5| p.181)

Luce is careful enough to qualify (9)' by the preface that "we should like to" (construct an order such that (9)' holds).
Indeed we have a strong preference for simple mathematical models. But models which are slightly less simple than the simplest ones can also be treated with ease; eventually, the preference for simplicity has to yield to the necessity of precise modelling of experience.

Consider now that $\approx$ is an equivalence relation, and that under assumption (8) resp. (9) the $\approx$-equivalence classes are totally ordered by $<_w$. If differences $a < b$ can be observed at all, $<_w$ is not empty, and we have more than one $\approx$-equivalence class. Then it follows that, if the elements of M really possess a real-valued attribute, every difference $<_M$ however small can be detected by observations of $<$ however crude.

This consequence of (9) seems much less plausible than (9), and indeed an outcome of wishful thinking, as indicated by Luce.
For either $\approx$ reflects equality of values in M : then our conclusion is obvious. Or else there exists an interval A of length $L > 0$ which is a $\approx$-equivalence class; then within this interval, a difference of say L/2 is unnoticable ($\sim$) and even undetectable ($\approx$), while around each end of the interval, differences of L/2000 are detectable by (5) and (6) . This is not in contradiction with the wording of (9), but not in keeping with the spirit of (9).

Anyway, the construction (5) of $<_w$ is in general meaningless if $<_M$ is not assumed to be a total order. E.g. the objective (Lorentz-invariant) temporal order of events has been explicitly declared by physicists - well before 1919 - to be a partial order (in which (8) is false and $<_w$ is not an order relation at all).

For disciplined modelling, it seems appropriate to propose such properties of the observed relation $<$ which can be disproved by experimental strategies in the area under consideration; then to discard assumed properties which are rejected by this test; then to collect experimental results, and then cautiously infer statements about the structure of M .

In this procedure, the axiom of density

(10) $$a < b \longrightarrow \bigvee c : a < c < b$$

has to be discarded, for I can give you a piece of string which you cannot cut in two pieces 10^{1000} times in succession, what (10) would imply you could. (10) has to be substituted by weaker axioms |6|; likewise, the assumption that $\sim$ is transitive has to be replaced, for the measurement of "continuous" quantities like length, by the "coherence" axiom

(11) $$\sim^* = \not\sim^*$$

where $\not\sim$ is the negation of $\sim$, and $\sim^*$ denotes the transitive closure of $\sim$.
The main implication of (11) is that every b can be reached from every a in a finite number of unnoticable steps. The absence of jumps and of gaps in our scales for measurement (Dedekind continuity) can be reformulated in such a way that coherent combinatorial models exist; i.e. (11) holds, and also

(12) $$< \; = \bigcup_{n>0} \lessdot^n$$

where $\lessdot$ is the "immediate lower neighbour"-relation :

(13) $$a \lessdot b \;:\Longleftrightarrow\; a < b \wedge \neg \bigvee c : a < c < b$$

We shall not pursue the matter further here; the simplest scale satisfying (11), (12) and having "K-density" |6| is, with arrows denoting the $\lessdot$ relation:

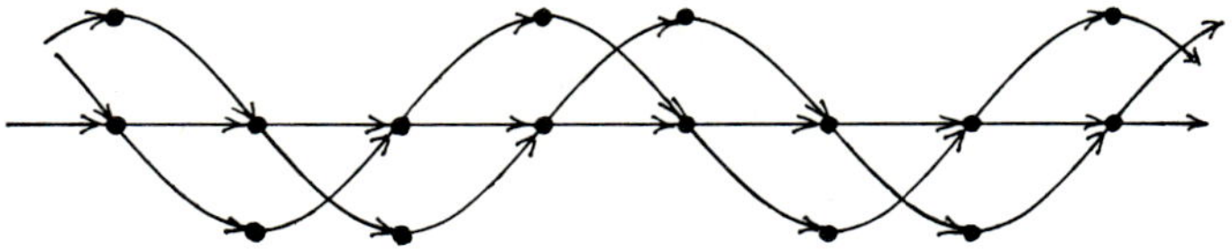

Fig. 7

The physicist will be reminded of the quantum-mechanical (p,q)-history of an oscillator and the natural "time-scale" generated by it; the responsible scale reader (data collector) will detect to his relief that he is not forced to express his findings by selecting one out of a set of mutually exclusive assertions, numbered e.g. 0, 1, 2, 3 ..., but is free to assert "1.5" when in doubt whether 1 or 2 obtains.
Note that it is not correct to assume that "$1 < 1.5$" is implied by the scale structure. Rather, in this context, $1 \sim 1.5 \sim 2$, while certainly $1 < 2$.
For the measurement of spatial distances, this is illustrated by the measuring rod shown in Fig.8, where length intervals correspond one-to-one to the points of Fig. 7 which are not on the middle line :

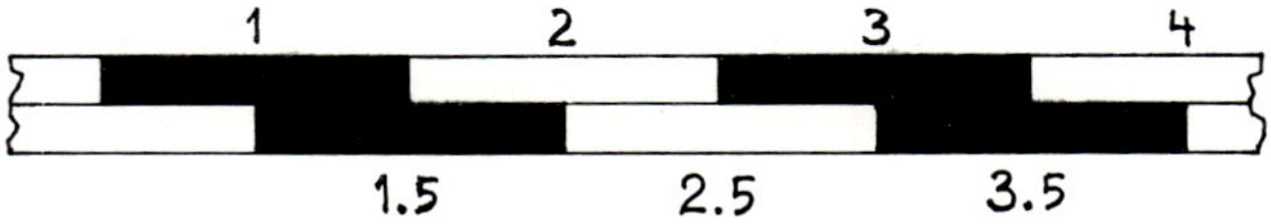

Fig. 8

It does not matter whether an interval is regarded as open or closed to the right or left, because in case of doubt with respect to the upper classical scale, the observer is free to express his assertion in terms of the lower scale, and vice versa.-

As a final example of modelling, we consider a formalization of "fairness" in resource distribution. Again, we will confine ourselves to the smallest possible structure which exhibits the relevant features.

Imagine two parties A and B who have a single indivisible resource R at their disposal; each of A and B occasionally need R for exclusive use in some phase of their activity. It is possible that on some occasions both A and B need R , but they cannot predict these occasions, which make an arbitration necessary.
It is obvious that A and B cannot both insist on getting R on such occasions; they cannot hope to come to a symmetrical contract which guarantees instant availability of R since they cannot precisely predict their needs. Yet, A and B want a contract which guarantees the fulfilment of their overall needs; they will regard the contract as fair, or fully acceptable to both (all) parties concerned, if the arbitration mechanism is specified to the extent that the guarantees can be deduced within the contract, and if any breach of contract becomes immediately apparent in a definite way.

Fig. 9 describes the situation of A (left cycles) and B (right cycles) by means of a place-transition-net; the activity RR restores the resource R to availability after each usage. For details and proofs, see Lautenbach's paper |7| . The dotted lines show the relations to be negotiated in order to complete the schema to yield a contract proposal.

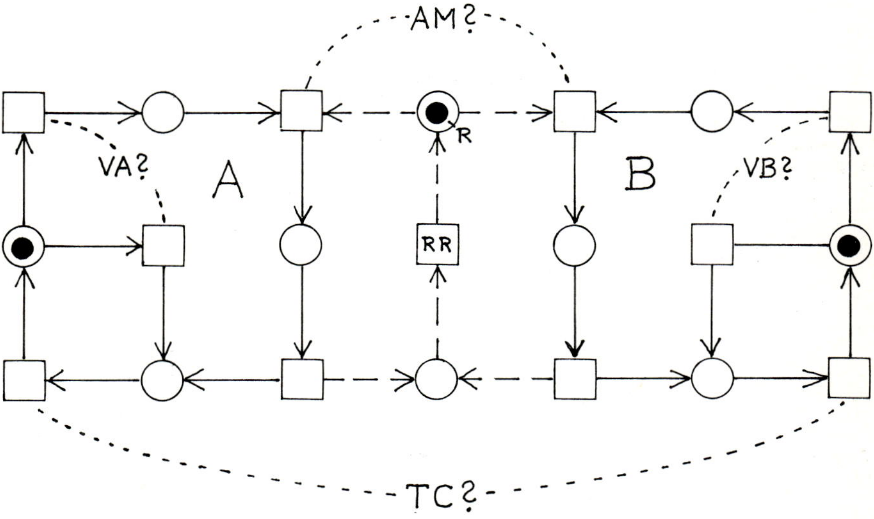

Fig. 9

In Fig. 9, AM denotes the arbitration mechanism; more exactly, the specification of its effect on the distribution of R . TC denotes the basis for time comparison between A and B ; VA and VB denote the valuation of the usage of R as declared by A resp. by B .

The principal result of |7| is that arbitration, valuation and time-convention can all be expressed by the same mathematical construct : the <u>weighted synchronic distance</u> between two transitions (events) $\boxed{a}$ and $\boxed{b}$.
Each square symbol in Fig. 9 represents such a transition. We select two of them and connect them by an additional place thus :

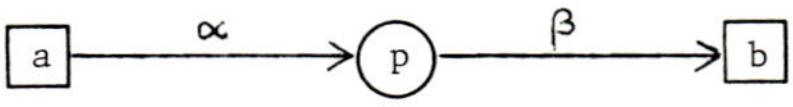

and require that each occurrence of event $\boxed{a}$ deposits α tokens in ⓟ , and that each occurrence of $\boxed{b}$ removes β tokens from ⓟ . Let ⓟ originally (e.g. in the contract proposal) contain a sufficient number p_o of tokens.
Let Π denote the class of finite (connected) processes permitted under the contract; the number of tokens on ⓟ may increase or decrease during each process $\pi \in \Pi$. The difference between the maximum possible number and the minimum possible number of tokens on ⓟ may be finite; if it is, this difference is obviously the minimal needed capacity of ⓟ for tokens; we call it $\sigma_{\alpha,\beta}$ (a,b) .
We may define

$$(14) \qquad \sigma_{\alpha,\beta}(a,b) := \underset{\pi\in\Pi}{\mathrm{Max}} \left(\left| \alpha \cdot \mathrm{Occ}(a,\pi) - \beta \cdot \mathrm{Occ}(b,\pi) \right| \right)$$

where Occ (a,π) is the number of occurrences of $\boxed{a}$-events in the process π .

Now all the missing links AM, TC, VA, VB can be represented each by a bridging place, and specified by stating weights α, β ; the place capacity σ ; and initial token number p_o .

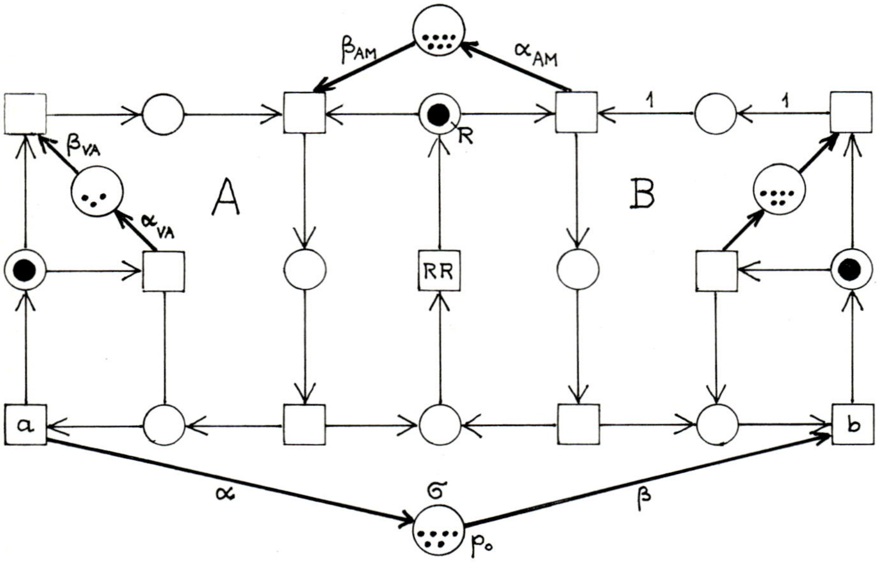

Fig. 10

The feasible arbitration mechanisms can be computed from TC, VA, VB ; no such mechanism exists for extreme valuations VA or VB ; clearly, an additional resource is required in such a case. If the contract is to be closed for a certain maximal number of uses of R only, this can be expressed by the same mathematical device (σ, α, β, p_o) . If we do so, the number of feasible AM can be increased, etc.

In conclusion, let me call your attention to the following facts about the arbitration mechanism AM :

For "fairness" of resource distribution, neither $\alpha = \beta$ nor $2\,p_o = \sigma$ are necessary or sufficient at AM , in contrast to intuitive assumptions. Relative frequencies for resource usage by A and B can be deduced from α and β , but the probability of conflict resolution in favor of A cannot be deduced from α and β . A probabilistic AM cannot support guarantees; and if we attempt to specify an AM to reflect precisely what is meant by equal probability for A and B to get the resource R , and start with some number $\alpha = \beta$, we end up with $\sigma = \infty$, and, to be fair, $p_o = \infty$. This means the assumed AM cannot have any effect on A and B at all.
A feasible and effective arbitration mechanism is neither deterministic nor probabilistic in the classical sense. Yet it can be regarded as well-defined.

References

|1| H.J. Genrich : Belästigung der Menschen durch Computer, GMD-SPIEGEL 5/75. GMD St. Augustin, Dec. 1975

|2| C.A. Petri : Kommunikationsdisziplinen, Internal Report GMD-ISF-76-01. GMD St. Augustin, Mar. 1976
Communication Disciplines, in: Computing System Design, Proceedings of the Joint IBM University of Newcastle upon Tyne Seminar. Ed. by B. Shaw. University of Newcastle upon Tyne, 1976

|3| N. Wiener : A New Theory of Measurement: A Study in the Logic of Mathematics, Proceedings of the London Mathematical Society, Vol. 19, 1919, p. 181-205, London 1921

|4| J. Pfanzagl : Die axiomatischen Grundlagen einer allgemeinen Theorie des Messens, Physica Verlag Würzburg 1959

|5| R.D. Luce : Semiorders and a Theory of Utility Discrimination, Econometrica 24 (1956) p. 178 ff. 1956

|6| C.A. Petri : Nicht-sequentielle Prozesse, in: Parallelismus in der Informatik Tagungsbericht IMMD Universität Erlangen-Nürnberg, Bd. 9, Nr. 8, Erlangen Dec. 1976
Nonsequential Processes, Translated by P. Krause and J. Low, Internal Report GMD-ISF-77-05, GMD St. Augustin, Jun. 1977

|7| K. Lautenbach : Ein kombinatorischer Ansatz zur Beschreibung und Erreichung von Fairness in Scheduling-Problemen, to appear in: Applied Computer Science, Hanser-Verlag München 1977

|8| W.E. Armstrong : A Note on the Theory of Consumers' Behaviour, Oxford Economic papers 2 (1950) p. 119-122, Oxford 1950

Measuring, Modelling and Evaluating Computer Systems,
H. Beilner and E. Gelenbe, (eds.)
© North-Holland Publishing Company (1977)

STUDY BY MATHEMATICAL MODELIZATION OF THE BEHAVIOR OF A CONVERSATIONAL SYSTEM

C. Vasseur, A. Guillon
G.I.X.I. ingenierie informatique s.a.
Orsay, France

The purpose of this paper is to present an actual case study which is as close as possible to the most frequent concerns: that of a TSO conversational system on IBM 360/370.

Although this study deals with an IBM product, the approach we present is applicable to similar products of other computer manufacturers. This paper will be divided into the following main section:

1 - Presentation (comprehension, synthesis)

2 - Design and analysis of the model

3 - Measurements

4 - Validation

5 - Utilization

6 - Derivation of the mathematical expression representing the model

1 - PRESENTATION OF THE PROBLEM

The person responsible for an installation including an IBM computer functioning under OS/MVT is concerned with the capacities of the computer's time sharing TSO. His objective questions are the following:

. Is the present response time acceptable?

. Can I plan an increase in the load of this service without making any change in the system.

. If there are any changes to be made, what is the order of priority of the changes to be performed.

2 - THE ANALYSIS AND DESIGN PHASE

One temptation that must be resisted is to dash forth with one's chronometer and start measuring this way and that.

On the contrary, we are entering a first phase which must only be a phase of reflection which is divided into three stages. First, it will be necessary to have attained a more thorough understanding of the problem. In a second stage, a synthetic representation of the phenomenon will have to be found, which, finally, will allow to design the model describing the problem under study.

2.1. Understanding the problem

The evaluator's first action will be to become acquainted with the functioning of the TSO system with a frame of thought different from that of the system engineer. The latter works with logic. We for our part, must work with physics and, in this sense, having seen the system function, we would like to understand which are the elements having a perceptible impact on the time factor. By perceptible impact, we simpl mean that the total duration (service plus conflicts) consumed in this element represents a perceptible portion of the lifetime of the phenomenon under study (say approximately 1%).

2.1.1. The TSO system

The TSO system behaves within the machine as a unique job, having the highest priority. One can furthermore consider that it is not perturbed in the central unit by the other jobs implanted within the same computer.

It manages a certain number of consoles, each one working independently and sending transactions out towards the computer whose contents, until proof of the contrary, are not considered relevant. All we are concerned with are the elements where these transactions can consume or waste time. Two of these elements are obvious : time wastage in input-output and in the CPU produced by the transaction job itself. But beforehand, the transaction must be taken into account by the system and the corresponding time is not necessarily negligible; our attention is thus drawn to the initialization processes of a transaction. The TSO system contains a fixed number of "regions". Each region contains the entirety of those elements necessary to <u>one</u> user : tabels, job zones, ect... When a transaction arrives, there are two different possibilities, according to whether at least one of the regions contains the elements of a completed transaction, or whether all are active. In the first case, the region is swapped out onto a disk or drum, and is totally replaced by the totality of the data necessary to the new transaction. When all the regions contain transactions that are active within the computer, a newly arrived transaction will wait during at most, a "quantum" of time defined as parameter in the system. This quantum represents the maximum quantity of CPU time that a transaction can consume before being swapped out and replaced by a new transaction.

2.1.2. Surrounding system

The elements set forth above do not necessarily include all the points at which an appreciable amount of time can be spent. There is also the serialization primitives system, the macros ENQ and DEQ which are abundantly used by the TSO functions.

Other serialization procedures exist, mainly with respect to the utilization of reusable but non reentrant modules.

All these operations must therefore be kept under observation.

2.2. Synthesis

Having analyzed the problem and determined the principal elements responsible for time wastage, although the list cannot be exhaustive and perfect at the first try, the moment has arrived to form an overall view of this problem.

In order to do so, we shall use a top down method. This consists, in the first place, of taking into account the circulation of the processes in their most general and global aspect ; then in refining, step by step, each part of whatever element we encounter.

More precisely, the most general process will be circulating among a few very global points or services. But as soon as these principal elements have been thoroughly determined, it becomes necessary to examine each one of them in more detail, as if one were observing a phenomenon through a lens changing the magnification, in order to study the essential parts. Under this magnification one might note a circulation of processes identical to those discovered at the level above ; these in turn, might have generated other subprocesses, and there might then be circulation of an entirely different population which would have to be studied.

Having concluded the analysis at a given level, must one stop, or increase once again the magnification? The answer depends on the question originally posed. If, as in our case, a study of the response time of a given system is being carried out, as soon as one reaches magnitudes which could reasonably appear as profile or configuration parameters, there is no need to go beyond that point. If, on the contrary, the study is being carried out by a constructor who is interested in the architecture of a new machine, it will be necessary to continue to the study of the queues in the hardware. In short, one must stop as soon as possible, that is, at the moment one manipulates elements which may play the role of basic paramaters.

Whith this in mind, we decompose system operation into the following operations :

2.2.1. The terminal cycle

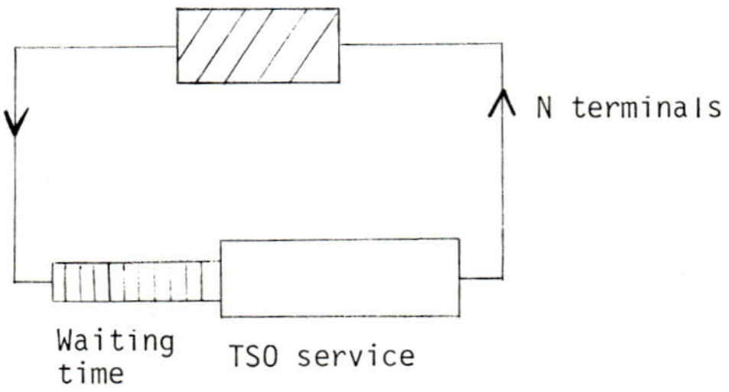

The most global aspect shows us N terminals representing all of the open sessions at a given time. Each is inactive with respect to the system during a certain lapse of time which we shall call the think time. This consists of the print-out time of the preceding response, of the actual thinking time of the user and of the time during which the new command is typed.

In short, the time included between the moment the system begins sending its response and the moment the user initiates his request for the execution of the new command (generally, the interrupt resulting from the carriage return).

However, between this instant and the initiation of the response, the terminal user will either be active within the system, or waiting before being connected with the system. This latter waiting period will be obtained from the mathematical model. There still remains the activity of the terminal user in the system for which we must increase our magnification in order to analyze it in greater detail.

2.2.2. The activity within the system

This activity regroups all the elements that we detected in the first part, and in particular :

. swapping time
. logical serialization (ENQ, DEQ) time
. CPU time
. input-output time

The question which then comes to mind for the evaluator is whether his analysis is completed.

We note that time wastage per command in the central unit is raw data which can be determined. However, the three other elements contain variable effects which are none other than the conflicts resulting either from the set of TSO activities, or from the entirety of the activities within the machine. We must, therefore, proceed with a new magnification of our objective.

2.2.3. Input - Output

If the input-output is carried out on drums, the determination of the activity rate of this unit, as well as the characteristics (average, standard deviation) of the gross input-output time, will suffice to estimate the duration of the queueing delays taking into account the number of independent requests that can be issued by the computer.

Let us now consider the case of a disk (IBM 3330 in our present case). In general, these units do not contain a unique path per disk pack;on the contrary, the same path serves several disk packs (up to 8 if there is only one control unit).

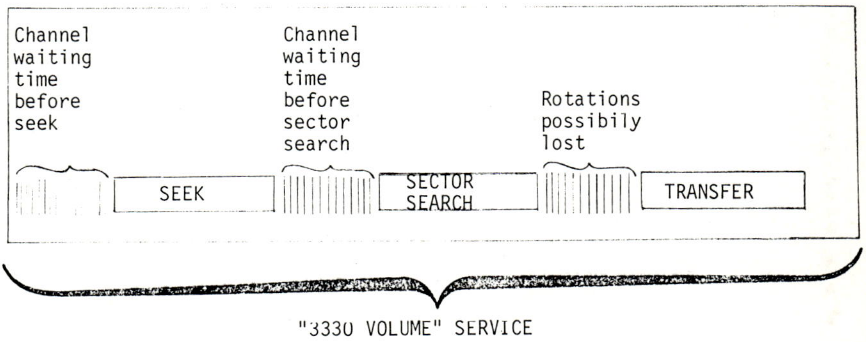

Another and last magnification of our objective will allow us to evaluate the conflict on the path which serves the disk pack in question, knowing the path's occupancy rate, the characteristics of the time during which it is totally occupied by one disk pack, and the number of disk packs which frequent it.

2.2.4. Serializations

A measurement of the length of the serialization queues informs us that the average time thus consumed, even during peak hours, constitutes a negligible quantity. We shall therefore disregard this item for the time being.

2.3. Design of the model*

At this point, there remains to express in terms of queueing models the analysis that has just been made. One need only consult one's arsenal of available techniques and determine at each stage that which is best adapted, applying at each level the model which seems the most judicious.

2.3.1. The terminal cycle

One notes that the closed model with finite population is more particularly adapted to this aspect of the system.

The parameters remain to be determined. The average running time results from the calculations which appear in further sections hereof. The think time at the terminal must be measured. The population n is easily obtained : knowing that N terminal are active and that there are r regions :

$$n = \frac{N}{r}$$

2.3.2. Running time of a command

It is the sum of the durations of each element indicated in subparagraph 2.2.2. For the CPU, just one measurement will suffice. For the input-output, we must proced to the next stage.

---

* In fact, a few simplifications are made with respect to the actual configuration.

2.3.3. Input-Output

2.3.3.1. Drums

Two types of requests are directed to the drum. One of them is non other than the swapping input-output ; the other includes a certain number of system requests. Each of the two types uses distinct units and paths.

The population requiring swapping consists only of the TSO regions. As its number is very small, we prefer to use the finite population model in order to determine the possible conflicts.

For the second type, as the population of requests may be larger, one may choose the M/G/1 model, which will allow to take into account the variation coefficient of I/O time which is substantially less than 1. This aspect of more or less intuitive approximation is characteristic of what makes the evaluator's work so similar in method to that of the physicist.

2.3.3.2. Disk

We are led to distinguish between input-output on a permanent file and input-output on a temporary file. The difference resides essentially in that, as the seek process is much more frequent for the latter than for the former, input-output time on a temporary file is 50% longer.

Actually, there is no need to conceive different models for each type: the same model may be constructed for both types, the paramaters only differing.

Before input-output can be initiated, the volume must be free. This gives rise to a first conflict resulting in a first queue, before a service which consists of the totality of the input-output. The question is whether to use a finite population model or not. The population of the requests is, at first glance, limited by the number of jobs executed simultaneously within the machine. In fact, each job can produce several input-outputs(generally 2), since IBM access methods foresee several buffers. The number of requests must, therefore, be able to exceed approximatively ten, in order that, taking into account the relatively low utilization rate of the volume (less than 10%), infinite population constitutes a realistic hypothesis.

One may then use the M/G/1 model. For the M/M/1 queue, the average number of waiting customers is $\frac{\rho}{1-\rho}$ and the probalitity that there are n or more is ρ^n. It is then easily shown that if there cannot be more than N individuals within the system, there will be an error of $\rho^N/1-\rho \simeq \rho^N$; for ρ very small and for N = 10 this error would be negligible.

There remains then to be determined the input-output time proper, channel conflict included. A first delay may take place before input-output can be initiated : the channel must be free. And to this end, the transmission in process, if any, originating from another volume, must be completed. But this duration is insignificant for normal I/O's on 3330 (a transmission time of a few ms, multiplied by the channel rate... the result remains beneath the ms). A delay of the same sort takes place at the end of I/O to notify the computer. This delay will also be disregarded.

Finally, one other delay, which, this time, may be substantial concerns the transfer initialization operation. For it to be carried out, the channel must be free at the moment the beginning of the record passes under the head. The calculation can be easily accomplished.

Adding this delay to the durations of the different physical operations (seek, rotation time, transmission and, if necessary, erasing the remainder of the track for the sequential operations) determines input-output time as it is seen from the volume.

3 - THE MEASUREMENT PHASE

In observing the development of these operations, we find that the whole of the model has been designed, formulae included, although we have not even begun to examine the problem of measurements. Here we perceive how efficient this procedure is, in that it results in the two following benefits. On the one hand, no extraneous measurement will be attempted whose usage is not explicitly required by the model so conceived. On the other hand, no data will be overlooked.

It should furthermore be noted that we are immediately able to execute a logical classification of the paramaters in the model, with the result that, when it becomes necessary to change those parameters that will be entered into previsional hypotheses, this can be easily accomplished.

3.1. Determination of the necessary measurements

The next step consists therefore in elaborating a plan that will cover the numerical determination of each of the parameters necessary to complete this study. These parameters are the constants related to the installation and to the hardware (number of TSO regions, number of volumes of each type, both total and per path, physical characteristics of the volumes). Other parameters concern the profile of the load outside of the TSO system (all the parameters concerning non TSO I/O's).

There finally remain the parameters proper to the TSO system :

N = number of active terminals

T = think time at the terminal

s_u = run time of a command at the CPU

ε_e = number of swaps per command

θ_e = gross swapping time

ε_i = number of type i I/O's per TSO command

In order to obtain all this information and for reasons connected to homogeneity and global cost considerations, it was necessary to write a measurement package to be inserted into a TSO module. This program allows to count the I/O's by type, but also to detect time wastage in the central unit and to note the swapping decisions.

In this manner, all elements proper to TSO are determined (or can be recalculated) on the basis of data originating from the same measuring instrument.

3.2. The measurement operation

At this point, a measurement operation is planned. The tools of this operation include not only the aforesaid software which has just been constructed, but also those which usually determine the profile of the global load. Thus the values obtained will belong to a same experiment and will constitute coherent sets of measurements.

Moreover, we are attempting to obtain several sets of measurements, which will be very useful at the validation stage to confront the model to sets of data covering a certain spectrum.

4 - VALIDATION

4.1. Reliability

Before entering the validation stage, one must take the precaution of checking the reliability of the model, that is, its sensitivity to hypotheses. We shall just give a few examples.

Infinite population models are dangerous at a high rate of service utilization. However, we have only chosen such a model for the canal services (for drums) or for the volume services; their occupancy rate remains at most in the vicinity of 20%.

Another hypothesis we have set forth that is contrary to reality is that of the independence of arrivals and services : obviously "volume" service time on a disk depends on the arrival rate of the requests, and an increase of this rate produces a larger number of seeks. However, precise measurements have shown that the average utilization time, θ, of the disks which are most sensitive to this phenomenon (the temporary files) can be described in ms by the following formula :

$$\theta = 30 + 30\ \rho_V$$

where ρ_V is the volume occupancy rate. For an occupancy rate of 10% which exceeds that of the case under consideration here, the above formula gives θ equal to 33 ms, while with θ equal to 30 ms, the occupancy rate would be null. By resolving the model with these two extreme values, we obtain extremely close results. We conclude therefore that the system remains only slightly sensitive to this assumption.

A number of other assumptions must be verified in the same manner with respect to their influence on the model. For instance, we always assume that the arrival process is poisson, we know that its importance is, in a first approximation related, to its variation coefficient. It is therefore necessary to make sure that we are within the zones where this coefficient is close to 1.

4.2. Validation

Validation consists of comparing the results of the model with reality, by means of "redundant" paramaters.

The objects of this study being simply the "response time" element, an element of equivalent sensitivity is sufficient for our purposes.

Such an element was determined at the outset by the measurement software we had constructed. It represents the time during which a region remains within the core after the processing of the transaction is completed. Let us indeed recall that, as the completion of a processing, the corresponding region is swapped out onto a disk, to be replaced by the region corresponding to the first waiting transaction ; however, swapping is not immediately executed when no transaction is waiting. Swapping will only take place, if it does, at the moment a new request arrives.

Thus, during a certain time, the region of the transaction may remain in the memory even though it has completed its job. But the average duration of this event can be calculated on the basis of the exponential service and think time hypotheses.

We have thus obtained for two different profiles following values:

	measured value	calculated value
. First profile	387 ms	385 ms
. Second profile	655 ms	661 ms

One notes the very good approximation obtained by the calculated value.

5 - UTILIZATION

The first utilization is, of course, to furnish the answer to the initially posed questions. Nevertheless, the answer furnished will never be a simplistic one, no matter how elementary the question may be. In reality, a whole set of answers is provided, constituting a grid within which the responsible person can locate the information necessary for reaching his decisions.

This set of answers is extended by a whole set of extrapolations that can be effected fairly spontaneously. Let us indeed consider pur TSO case. Once a certain number of representative profiles have been determined and validated, the value of the response time at different hours of the day can be calculated.

But obviously, the question which immediately arises is that of the possible improvements and optimizations brought about by the decrease in waiting time.

			CPU		DRUMS		PERMANENT FILES		TEMPORARY FILES	
Peak load	Response time	Waiting time at region	Rate	Waiting time	Running time	Waiting time	Running time	Waiting time	Running time	Waiting time
Present load N = 12	2.46	0.37	5%	0.004	0.37	0.05	0.31	0.04	0.80	0.23
X 1.5 N = 18	3.10	0.82	7.5%	0.004	0.37	0.06	0.31	0.05	0.80	0.38
X 2 N = 24	4.15	1.65	10%	0.004	0.37	0.08	0.31	0.06	0.80	0.59

(with 3340 disk and 3 regions)

By reading this table, one immediately knows where to apply one's efforts :

. increasing the number of regions,

. more rapid disks.

Influence of the number of regions	1 region	2 regions	3 regions	4 regions	5 regions
N = 12	4.78	2.99	2.63		
N = 18	11.25	4.33	3.40		
N = 24				4.01	3.43

Influence of the disks	2 regions	3 regions	4 regions	6 regions
N = 24 - with 3330		4.7	4.01	3.43
N = 24 - with 3340	6.05	4.15	3.54	3.08

Conclusion

Now that we have such a tool at our disposal, it is quite apparent that the decision problem is greatly facilitated in view of the numerical values that we are capable of providing from now on, for all the cases of interest to us.

6 - FORMULA OF THE MODEL

6.1. Legend

* in front of a parameter : datum of the model

(I) in front of * = installation parameter

(E) in front of * = load parameter

others = parameters proper to TSO

6.2. Console cycle

* N = total number of active consoles

(I) *r = number of TSO regions

*T = think time at the console

s_o = running time of the transaction

ρ_c = activity rate of a TSO region

a = waiting time before entering the region

R = response time

$$n = \frac{N}{r}$$

$$z_c = \frac{T}{s_o} \qquad \rho_c = \frac{z_c^n / n!}{\sum_{o}^{n} z_c^i / i!}$$

$$a = s_o \left(\frac{n}{\rho_c} - z_c - 1 \right)$$

$$R = a + s_o = s_o \left(\frac{n}{\rho_c} - z_c \right)$$

6.3. Running time of a command

θ_i = type i input-output time

$*\varepsilon_i$ = number of type i input-output per command

$*s_u$ = gross running time per command in the central unit

s_e = swapping time

a_u = waiting time before entering the central unit

$$z_u = \frac{s_e + \sum_i \varepsilon_i \theta_i}{s_u}$$

$$\rho_u = 1 - \frac{z_u^r / r!}{\sum_1^r z^k/k!}$$

$$a_u = s_u \left(\frac{z}{\rho_u} - 1 - z_u\right)$$

$$s_o = (s_u + a_u) + s_e = \sum_i \varepsilon_i \theta_i$$

6.4. Input-output

6.4.1. Swapping

$*\theta_e$ = gross input-output time

ρ_e = activity rate of the volume onto which this swapping is being effected

$*\varepsilon_e$ = number of swappings per command

α = number of commands per second

if $r = 1$ $s_e = \varepsilon_e \theta_e$

if $r \neq 1$ $\alpha = \frac{N}{T + R}$

$\rho_e = \varepsilon_e \theta_e \alpha$ and $\rho_e = 1 - \frac{X^{r/r!}}{\sum_0^r X\ i/i!}$ whence s_e

$$s_e = \theta_e \varepsilon_e \left(\frac{r}{\rho_e} - X\right)$$

6.4.2. Other drum input-output

m = number of regions generating I/O's onto a drum

$*\varepsilon_1$ = number of I/O's generated by TSO commands

(E) $*\theta_1$ = average gross I/O time

(E) $*C_1$ = variation coefficient of the above

ρ_1 = volume activity rate

(E) * ρ'_1 = activity rate resulting from non TSO I/O's

$$\rho_1 = \rho'_1 + \varepsilon_1 \theta_1 \alpha$$

$$\theta_1 = \theta'_1 \left(\frac{\rho_1}{1-_1} \times \frac{1 + C_1^2}{2} + 1\right)$$

6.4.3. Input-output on temporary files (index 2) or permanent files (index 3)

(E) * ε'_2 or ε'_3 = number of type 2 or 3 TSO I/O's (per second)

* ε_2 or ε_3 = number of I/O's generated by TSO command

θ'_2 or θ'_3 = I/O time seen from the volume

(E) * θ''_2 or θ''_3 = gross I/O time

(E) * tr = data transmission time

(E) * p_2 = probability that an I/O is a sequential operation (p_3 is negligible and taken equal to 0)

(I) * m_2 or m_3 = number of volumes corresponding to type 2 or 3

(I) * m'_2 or m'_3 = number of volume per path

(I) * t = track rotation time

ρ_V = occupancy rate of the path onto which a volume is placed

(E) * ρ'_V = path occupancy rate by non TSO I/O's

The number of input-output per volume is :

$$\alpha_i = \frac{\varepsilon'_i + \varepsilon_i \alpha}{m_i} \quad \text{whence the occupancy rate} \quad \rho_i = \frac{\varepsilon'_i + \varepsilon_i \alpha}{m_i} \theta_i$$

$$\theta_i = \theta'_i \left(\frac{\rho_i}{1 - \rho_i} \times \frac{1 + C^2_i}{2} + 1\right)$$

Volume contention

If ρ_v is the path occupancy rate, there exists a probability of ρ_v that one rotation will be lost, of ρ_v^2 that a second rotation will be lost .....

$$s = t\,(\rho_v + \rho_v^2 + \ldots\rho_v^n + \ldots) = \frac{t\rho_v}{1 - \rho_v}$$

Erasure of the remainder of the track $\rightarrow \rho_2 \times \frac{t}{2}$

whence $\theta'_i = \theta''_i + \dfrac{t\rho_v}{1 - \rho_v} + \rho_2 \dfrac{t}{2}$

$$\rho_v = \rho'_v + \sum_i m'_i \frac{\varepsilon i\alpha}{im_i} \left(tr + \rho_i \frac{t}{r}\right)$$

E R R A T A

A USER-ORIENTED APPROACH TO THE DESIGN OF DISTRIBUTED INFORMATION SYSTEMS

Giacomo Bucci

Istituto di Elettronica and CIOC
Università di Bologna, Bologna, Italy

Donald N. Streeter

IBM Thomas J. Watson Research Center
Yorktown Heights, New York, 10598, U.S.A.

p.35, line 9: It should be noted (not It shoulded be noted)

p.37, line 8: working on them (not working of them)

p.44, first line: $P/\mu o$ = 100000 instr/cycle (not $P/\mu o$ = 10000 instr/cycle)

p.47, first line: the centralized solution (not the centralizes so-ution)

p.48, quotation on horizontal axis must be shifted one position left, that is, it must look like this:

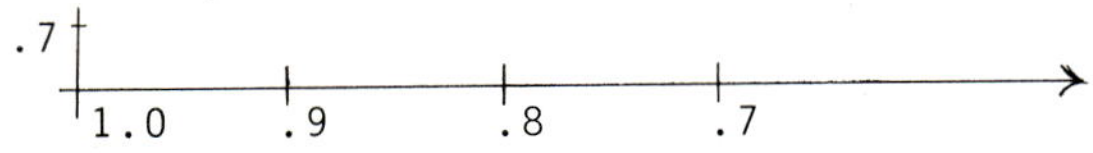

p.50, top of Fig. 18(6): $\frac{C_d}{C_c+\delta} = 1.0$ not $\frac{C_d}{C+\delta} = 10$

p.51, top line, equation should read:

$$\text{REL.COST}\left(\frac{\text{HIERARCHIC}}{\text{CENTRALIZED}}\right) = \frac{C_d}{C_c+\delta} + (1-p)$$

p.52, line 13: Next, assuming the (not Newt, assuming the).

USE OF PETRI NETS FOR PERFORMANCE EVALUATION

Joseph Sifakis

Institut de Mathématiques Appliquées, Informatique
Grenoble, France

p.80, line 4: $J_o^t Q(\tau_o) \geq J_o^t ZC^+ I = J_o^t ZC^- I$ (Vc)

p.85, in example 2: $D = \begin{bmatrix} 1 & 1 & 1 & 1 & 0 & 0 \\ 0 & 0 & 0 & 0 & 1 & 1 \end{bmatrix}$

AN EVALUATION NET MODEL FOR THE PERFORMANCE EVALUATION OF A COMPUTER NETWORK

R. Winter
Philips GmbH Forschungslaboratorium Hamburg
2000 Hamburg 54, Germany

p.112, line 16: The following results are missing: Utilization of the CPU: 83% including 75% of SSM activity.

TASK SCHEDULING IN SYSTEMS WITH NONPREEMPTIBLE RESOURCES

W. Cellary
Institute of Control Engineering
Technical University of Poznan
Poznan, Poland

p.120, line 17: pointer definition should read:

$$I_q = \begin{cases} \min\limits_{q_k=0} \{k\}, & \text{if there exists } q_k=0, \\ t+1, & \text{otherwise.} \end{cases}$$

p.123, line 28: pointer definition should read:

$$I_s = \begin{cases} \min\limits_{s_k=0} \{k\}, & \text{if there exists } s_k=0, \\ t+1, & \text{otherwise.} \end{cases}$$

IMPLEMENTATION OF ALGORITHMS FOR PERFORMANCE ANALYSIS OF A CLASS OF MULTIPROGRAMMED COMPUTERS

Mauro Brizzi, Davide Grillo
Fondazione Ugo Bordoni
Roma, Italy

p.132, line 6: "service station - job class" (not "service center - job class") p.136, line 7: $$\ldots \sum_{r \in R(i,e)} \ldots \quad (\text{not } \ldots \sum_{r \in R(i,r)} \ldots)$$

p.138, line 6: "service station - job class" (not "node-job class")

p.141, line 19: Section 8 (not Section 7)

p.144, line 8: Considering(7-4) (not Considering(6-4)

p.146, line 2: exhau- (not axhau-)

p.148, insertion between line 12 and 13
In the present version of the package, row-wise production of G(.) coefficients is adopted whenever folded use of core is allowed.

A COMPUTER MEASUREMENT AND CONTROL SYSTEM

G. Boulaye, B. Decouty, G. Michel, P. Rolin and C. Wagner
I.R.I.S.A.
Université de Rennes, B.P. 25 A
35031 Rennes Cedex, France

p. VI (contents), line 15: Read G. BOULAYE, B. DECOUTY, G. MICHEL, P. ROLIN, C. WAGNER (G.MICHEL omitted).

p.306 § 2.1.1, line 1: ... on large computer systems ... (not computer<u>s</u> systems)

p.313 § 4.1.3, line 3: .... if necessary, a probe-multiplexing device ... (not a pro<u>ble</u> ...)

PROJECTOR METHOD AND ITERATIVE
METHOD TO SOLVE A PACKET-SWITCHING NETWORK NODE
VALIDATION BY SIMULATION

Monique Becker and Robert Fortet
Université Paris VI
4, place Jussieu
75230 Paris cedex 05

p.354, 5 corrections for equation(18):

$$\xi_j = \xi_o \beta_j + \sum_{i=o}^{j} \xi_{i+1} \nu_{j-i}$$

$$\xi_r = \xi_o [\beta_r + \beta_{r+1} + \ldots] + \xi_1 [\nu_r + \ldots] + \ldots \xi_r [\nu_1 + \nu_r + \ldots] \quad (18)$$

So that the 3 μ have to be replaced by 3 β

ν_{j-1} has to be replaced by ν_{j-i}

μ_{r-1} has to be replaced by β_{r+1}